Basic Skills Workbook

FOR THE
GED® Test, TASC™, and HiSET®

Second Edition

Mark Koch

Catherine Bristow

BARRON'S

About the Authors

Mark Koch lives and works in Henrico County, Virginia with his wife Tera and son Calvin. He has experience teaching in a maximum security prison, public high schools, and on the university level. He enjoys traveling and hiking in the Rocky Mountains during the summer.

Catherine Bristow lives and works in Philadelphia, where she has been active in adult education for over twenty years. She is the author of *My Strange and Terrible Malady* (AAPC), a book for teens with Asperger Syndrome. Currently she teaches at the Philadelphia Housing Authority Pre-Apprenticeship Program.

© Copyright 2015 by Barron's Educational Series, Inc.
Previous edition © copyright 2012 under the title *Pre-GED* by Barron's Educational Series, Inc.

All inquiries should be addressed to:
Barron's Educational Series, Inc.
250 Wireless Boulevard
Hauppauge, New York 11788
www.barronseduc.com

Library of Congress Catalog Card Number: 2015955336

ISBN: 978-1-4380-0624-6

PRINTED IN THE UNITED STATES OF AMERICA
9 8 7 6 5 4 3 2 1

Contents

UNIT 4: SOCIAL STUDIES

Introduction

TO THE INSTRUCTOR

After the GED test reformatted in 2014, seismic shifts appeared across the High School Equivalency (HSE) landscape. The phrase "high school equivalency" itself is indicative of how far things have moved: no longer do students in all 50 states "earn a GED." And though the academic shorthand of "getting a GED" was well established nationally, in actuality students were earning an HSE credential issued by their state. Since 2014 some states have approved different tests, specifically the TASC and the HiSET, for students to earn an HSE credential. Some states have dropped the GED test entirely in favor of either the TASC or the HiSET, while still other states offer a choice among the three tests.

What has not changed, however, is the nature of the students taking these tests. Though all want to earn the credential, not all students are ready for high school level material in every content area. The purpose of this book is to help differentiate your instruction, and to aid in meeting students at their individual levels. The readings and exercises found here are designed for students assessed below the high school level, and care has been given to balance the readings to that degree.

The GED, TASC, and HiSET may differ in delivery method, such as computer or paper based. Likewise, there are differences in test structure. For example, the GED asks students to write an essay in social studies, but the TASC features questions on poetry that the GED eschews. The major differences between these exams in content and configuration are noted in the table of contents so you can tailor your instruction to the needs of students in your state.

Where all three tests come together is in their alignment to the Common Core State Standards. Accordingly, these standards form the baseline of instruction in this text. Additionally, as the complexity and emphasis of academic thinking has moved from Bloom's Taxonomy to Webb's Depth of Knowledge, you will find that this book also aligns with this shift. Though you will see familiar Bloom's verbs like contrast, describe, and paraphrase, you will also see students develop arguments and create meaning from visual information. The bridge to these higher level interpretive skills in the Depth of Knowledge is unstable for many students, so this book provides the foundation and vocabulary necessary for students who may be encountering these aptitudes for the first time.

Since these learners frequently possess vast "potholes" of knowledge, accurately assessing the needs of your students and skillfully targeting remediation is critical. To that end, the pretests and posttests located at the beginning and end of each unit will help to narrow precisely what content and skills to prioritize.

Each unit contains in depth lessons on the broad content areas found on the tests. In addition to providing a groundwork of critical thinking skills, these lessons will boost student background knowledge of key concepts. A variety of activities is employed to avoid the tedium of solely answering multiple-choice questions. Still, a wealth of diverse critical thinking questions in the multiple-choice format can be easily found in separate sections within each unit. This book will allow you to quickly and easily assess areas where you need help, target instruction, and remediate in the most efficient and effective way for you and your students.

TO THE LEARNER

Congratulations on your decision to become a better student! This book will help you develop the skills necessary to pass any high school equivalency test, such as the GED, TASC, or HiSET. Not sure which test to take? Contact your local school district or adult education office. Different states offer different tests, and you may even have a choice among the three.

The first thing to know about these tests is that they are not strictly memory tests. This means that you will not be asked to recall exact facts on each question. For example, a test is not likely to ask you to name the second President of the United States (John Adams). Instead, a test is more likely to have you read a few paragraphs about John Adams, and then answer critical thinking questions about what you just read.

So, what are critical thinking questions? These are questions that ask you to process information and apply what you have just learned. Have you ever needed to "read between the lines" or predict an outcome to something? These skills, and many others, are the types of abilities needed on the high school equivalency tests. This book will help you develop strategies to understand what the question is asking, as well as how to answer it correctly.

That said, critical thinking questions are certainly easier to answer when you know a little about the subject. This is called background knowledge, and this book will help you build that in the five content areas found on the tests. In addition, this book will help you to understand the many types of visual information, like maps, graphs, and even cartoons that you will find on the test.

Please note that even though each high school equivalency test (GED, TASC, HiSET) is based on the same standards, each test is a little different. For example, on the GED testers are asked to write an essay in the social studies exam. However, the TASC and HiSET social studies exams do not include an essay. Therefore, this book includes some chapters that apply only to certain tests. These sections are noted in the table of contents and at the start of those specialized chapters.

HOW THIS BOOK IS ORGANIZED

The high school equivalency tests cover five sections: Writing, Math, Science, Social Studies, and Reading. The GED combines reading and writing into one test called language arts. This book is organized to cover each content area. Before and after each unit you will also find a test. These tests will help you to focus on what you need to know, and help you measure what you have learned when you finish.

Unit 1: Writing

Writing is communication. We all have something to say, and writing well helps us to say it as effectively as possible. Whatever path you take in your future life, you will be called upon to write many messages. Well-written resumes and cover letters communicate what a valuable employee you would be. Well-written reports and emails send the message that you know your job and can be relied on.

Throughout this unit you will have the opportunity to practice skills as soon as you learn them. Practices may be multiple-choice questions, write-in answers, or essays. Use these exercises to master saying what you want to say, clearly and efficiently.

The unit is divided into lessons focusing on

- Sentence Structure—to master mechanics
- Paragraph Organization—to build correctly structured paragraphs from correct sentences
- Arguments—analysis to understand and respond in writing to other articles on a variety of subjects

Unit 2: Mathematics

The world of math is a lot like a ladder: it is easy to climb up one rung at a time, but it is difficult to jump straight to the top. And like a ladder, each step builds on the previous one. The point of this unit, then, is to give you a solid foundation in math one step at a time. With a good understanding of the basics, you will be much more successful on all types of math questions.

This unit is divided into eight topics. Each chapter contains in depth examples and instructions on specific math concepts. Additionally, this unit features

- A chapter on specific strategies for solving word problems
- End-of-chapter questions that feature word problems in the multiple-choice format
- A chapter devoted to how to use the same calculator you will be allowed to use on the GED, HiSET, or TASC
- A chapter focusing on how to read graphic materials, like charts and graphs, that appear throughout the math test

Unit 3: Science

This unit will help to give you a solid foundation in the three primary content areas of the science test: life science, earth and space science, and physical science. The lessons here are designed to introduce you to the vocabulary of the world of science, as well as some basic scientific concepts. Additionally, each chapter contains

- Dozens of targeted critical thinking skill questions in the multiple-choice format
- Specific lessons on graphic materials like Venn diagrams and data tables

Unit 4: Social Studies

This unit will help to give you a solid foundation in five main content areas of the social studies test: United States history, government, world history, geography, and economics. Like the science unit, the goal of the social studies unit is to familiarize you with the common vocabulary used in each content area. Furthermore, each lesson will brief you on important concepts and topics. Also, each chapter contains

- Dozens of targeted critical thinking skill questions in the multiple-choice format
- Specific lessons on graphic materials like Venn diagrams and data tables, political cartoons, and maps
- An entire chapter dedicated to the unique writing task on the GED social studies test

Unit 5: Reading

The lessons in this unit will help you to comprehend, analyze, and respond to reading passages on all types of subjects.

The unit is divided into

- Reading Skills—These skills, once mastered, will help you on every section of your test.
- Nonfiction
- Fiction
- Poetry (HiSET and TASC Only)
- Drama (HiSET and TASC Only)
- Comparing Texts

As in the other units, you will have ample opportunity to practice every skill you learn.

GETTING STARTED

To get started, take a pretest at the beginning of one of the units. After you've checked your answers, use the chart at the end of the test to find your strengths and weaknesses. Then, after completing the lessons recommended by the pretest, take the posttest to chart your improvement. The posttest will also identify areas that you may need to study more.

If you score well on a pretest, then you probably have a good foundation in that subject. However, you should still try the end-of-chapter questions for each topic. These questions will appear in the multiple-choice format and will address the critical thinking skills that are so important on the test.

UNIT 1
Writing

Writing Pretest

The writing pretest has 25 questions. The questions follow the chapters in the writing unit. The writing unit is divided into chapters on sentence structure, paragraph organization, and argument analysis. You can use this test to get a sense of which areas you need to study. Make sure you have at least 60 minutes of quiet time available to complete the test (this includes time for you to complete the writing sample). Read each question carefully and do your best. However, do not guess on these questions. If you don't know the answer to a question, simply skip it and go on to the next one. The purpose of this test is to find out what areas you need to work on, and random guessing might throw you off course.

Some questions on this test will ask you about grammar and punctuation. Others will test your ability to analyze evidence or understand an author's argument. The writing prompt asks you to read two arguments and then produce your own response.

After you have finished, check your answers on pages 9–10, and complete the pretest evaluation chart on page 8 by circling the number of each question you answered correctly. This way you can easily see your strengths and weaknesses as well as where information on each question you missed is located in the book.

If you score very well on the pretest, it is a great sign that you have a solid foundation in the different skills needed for writing. Still, make sure to check out the end-of-chapter questions for each topic. You'll want to double check that your skills are sharp.

For questions 1 through 5, fill the blank with the correct form of the verb provided.

1. When we _____ checkers, my brother always wins. (play)

2. Last night I _____ a terrible story on the news. (hear)

3. The sun _____ in the east. (rise)

4. When the water boils, the teakettle _____. (whistle)

5. Tomorrow, I _____ the garden. (weed)

Out of the following four sentences, two are correct and two are incorrect. Mark the correct sentences C and the incorrect I.

____ 6. He say that all the time.

____ 7. When I give the signal, you start the car.

____ 8. I wanted some masking tape, but they were all out.

____ 9. You look out the window, you'll see someone riding a horse.

10. Which of the following facts could NOT support the following topic sentence:

I don't enjoy playing popular vocabulary board games.

(A) I always end up with four I's and nowhere to play them.
(B) I can never make the word "pizza" because there is only one Z.
(C) I've never heard of some of these words. What's a "Qi"?
(D) It's better for my back than jumping rope.

Read the following paragraph and answer questions 11 through 14.

(1)Mr. Dunfee couldn't stand people who gushed over scenery. (2) Look at that group over there. (3) Oohing and ahhing over the mountains and sunset. (4) They made such a fuss you'd think they'd lived underground all their lives and had only just been released this minute. (5) Mr. Dunfee had no use for mountains, or winding rivers, or fields of flowers, or any of it. (6) He had been raised in a town that was not particularly known for being ugly. (7) It should have been. (8) As a boy, Mr. Dunfee grew up in a muddy gray building surrounded by other muddy gray objects. (9) The only river in town was brown and had a nasty smell. (10) Trees grew just big enough to crack the sidewalks and then died. (11) Grass was always yellow and straw-like. (12) It had been an <u>ugly town, as far</u> as Mr. Dunfee was concerned that fact hadn't hurt him one bit.

11. What is the most likely meaning of the word **gushed**?
   (A) praised enthusiastically
   (B) laughed at
   (C) hated
   (D) ridiculed

12. What is given as the main reason Mr. Dunfee does not appreciate scenery?
   (A) The other people around him are distracting him.
   (B) He grew up in ugly surroundings.
   (C) He used to live underground.
   (D) He thinks the group next to him is silly.

13. Which of the following sentences is incomplete?
   (A) Sentence 3
   (B) Sentence 7
   (C) Sentence 9
   (D) Sentence 11

14. What is the best way to correct the underlined portion of sentence 12?
   (A) It is correct as it is.
   (B) ugly town as far
   (C) ugly town, though as far
   (D) ugly town so as far

On the lines provided below, provide three supporting details for the following topic sentence:

Artie did not like visiting his in-laws.

15. _____

   _____

16. _____

   _____

17. _____

   _____

18. Now, write an appropriate topic sentence for the following three supporting details.

   - Having a designated driver means everyone can relax and have a good time without worrying about safety.
   - A group can rotate the duty among themselves so no one gets stuck with it all the time.
   - A designated driver can help the group save money on cab fares and parking fees.

   _____

   _____

19. Which of the following sentences is a restatement of the proverb "Many hands make light work"?
   (A) Too many people working on a project can be confusing.
   (B) Many people working together can finish a job quickly.
   (C) Too many cooks spoil the broth.
   (D) Many people working together will have disagreements.

20. You are writing a paper on the federal budget. Which of the following is the best source for valid information about government spending?
   (A) A political campaign ad
   (B) A television comedian's routine on federal spending
   (C) An informational publication from the Treasury Department
   (D) A friend who "heard something somewhere"

21. Read the following short paragraph.

   You should shop at Bell's Crossing Market. We are the best! We are much better than all the rest of the stores in this neighborhood. There's no comparison. Sure our prices are a little higher, but it's worth it. Don't even consider going to any of those other markets. You'd be sorry. Take our word for it, you'll be so much happier shopping here. We are the best in the business!

   ### WRITING PROMPT

   The above paragraph encourages the reader to shop at Bell's Crossing Market. State whether you think the paragraph is or is not well supported. Give one or two examples to support your opinion.

22. Read the following paragraph. Answer the question that follows. Respond to the prompt on a separate piece of paper.

The subject of ethics has been described as the struggle between what is good and what is right. On an elemental level, if a child is hungry, he thinks it is good if he can eat a piece of cake. But what if there are three other hungry children at the table? What if there is only one piece of cake? Is it split evenly? Does it go to the hungriest? To the best-behaved? A professor once described a moral dilemma to his class. He said, "Three people are drowning—your mother, your wife (husband), and your child. You can only save one. Who do you save?" The class argued for hours.

According to the paragraph, which of the following is NOT an ethics problem (conflict between the good and the right)?
(A) A man who badly needs money finds a lost wallet with $100.00 in it.
(B) A woman discovers she was not charged for one of the items in her shopping cart.
(C) An aunt wants to buy an expensive birthday present for a favorite niece.
(D) A man needs a certain printer, but can't afford it. He switches its price tag with that of a cheaper model.

WRITING PROMPT

The paragraph above gives examples of moral dilemmas. Write a response to the question posed by the professor in regard to the second dilemma. Give your reasons for what actions you would take.

Circle the correct form of the verb in the sentences below.

23. The young man (ran/runned) in the marathon.

24. Cindy (was sorry/were sorry) for how she spoke.

25. I (will be going/ be going) to talk to Human Resources.

PRETEST EVALUATION CHART

After checking your answers on the following pages, circle the numbers of the questions you got correct in column B. Record the total number of correct questions for each skill in Column C. Column D gives you the number of questions you need to answer correctly to indicate that you have a good understanding of the skill. If you got fewer correct answers than shown in Column D, study the pages shown in Column E. Using this analysis will allow you to focus on your challenges and use your study time more effectively.

A		B	C	D	E
Skill Area		Questions	Number of Correct Answers	Number Correct to Show a Good Understanding	Pages to Study
Sentence Structure	Subjects and Predicates	13	___/1	1	11–15
	Compound Sentences	8, 9, 14	___/3	2	16–20
	Complex Sentences	7	___/1	1	20–25
	Verb Forms and Tenses	1, 2, 3, 4, 5	___/5	3	25–29
	Subject–Verb Agreement	6, 23, 24, 25	___/4	3	29–33
Paragraph Organization	Paragraph Structure				43–45
	Topic Sentences	18	___/11	1	45–47
	Development and Details	10, 11, 12	___/3	2	48–51
	Repetition and Restatement	19	___/1	1	52–54
Argument Analysis	Determining What Positions are Presented				61–62
	Analyzing Evidence	21	___/1	1	63–68
	Creating an Argument	22	___/1	1	69–71
	Providing/ Citing Evidence	15, 16, 17, 20	___/4	3	72–74
TOTAL			___/25	19	

If you answered enough of the questions in Column D for a skill, you know enough about that skill already. You may want to do the Review at the end of these skill areas as a check.

To use your study time wisely, improve your skills in the other areas by studying the pages noted in Column E.

PRETEST ANSWER EXPLANATIONS

1. play
2. heard
3. rises
4. whistles
5. will weed (am going to weed)
6. I
7. C
8. C
9. I
10. **(D)** It's better for my back than jumping rope. Since this is a benefit of playing the vocabulary game and all the other choices are things the writer dislikes, this choice cannot support the topic sentence.
11. **(A)** praised enthusiastically. The group likes beautiful scenery, but all the other choices are negative responses.
12. **(B)** He grew up in ugly surroundings. (A) and (D) are true, but they are the results of his dislike, not the causes. (C) is untrue.
13. **(A)** Sentence 3 is missing a subject and part of its verb.
14. **(C)** ugly town, though as far. (A) Sentence 12 is a comma splice. (B) This choice makes the sentence a run-on rather than a comma splice. Neither is correct. (D) This conjunction does not fit the meaning of the sentence.

15–17. Answers will vary, but some examples follow:

They served such small portions of food that he was always hungry.

They kept the house much colder than he liked it.

His father-in-law insisted on hosting family karaoke nights.

18. The topic sentence should be some variation of: Having a designated driver is a benefit to a social group.
19. **(B)** Many people working together can finish a job quickly. (A), (C), and (D) have the opposite meaning.
20. **(C)** An informational publication from the Treasury Department. The Treasury Department is a reliable source, and its employees know about the subject you are researching. (A) The object of a political ad is to influence people's votes, not provide neutral information. (B) A comedian's purpose is to entertain, and he or she is probably not an expert in finance. (D) If the source cannot be traced, the information is hearsay. It might be true, but there is no way to tell.
21. The paragraph is not well supported. Its sentences are either repetition (We are much better…We are the best…) or commands (Don't even consider going to any of those other markets). There are no specific examples of higher quality or lower prices.
22. **(C)** *An aunt wants to buy an expensive birthday present for a favorite niece.* There is no ethical dilemma in wanting to buy a family member a present and doing so. All of the other choices involve decisions on the part of people to choose either what is right or what is good for them.

Writing Prompt

Answers will vary. Students should state the nature of the problem; what they decided to do; and why they took those actions.

23. ran

24. was sorry

25. will be going

To say that writing is important is an understatement. It is so important that it defines the moment that history began. Have you ever heard someone speak of "prehistoric times"? Prehistory is that time before written records existed.

Just what is so important about putting marks on clay, or papyrus, or paper, or a computer? Writing is, quite simply, the collective memory of our species. It allows the past to speak to us and us to speak to future generations.

That's quite a legacy to consider when you are making out your "to-do" list!

On a personal level, writing enables you to communicate effectively when you are not face-to-face with someone. Imagine personally making a positive impression on someone—a coworker, a boss, or a prospective employer or college. What could be worse than destroying that impression by following up with a letter or memo full of spelling, punctuation, and grammar mistakes?

The best way to improve your writing is to write! However, if you wait until you "feel" like writing, you may wait forever. There is a saying, "motivation follows action." Just start writing. Don't worry if it isn't perfect or pretty. You will have the opportunity to fix it later, even if it is only minutes later. That is what writers call editing, and all writers do it. Nobody gets it perfect the first time he puts fingers to keyboard!

This unit covers three areas:

SENTENCE STRUCTURE: Sentence skills are the nuts and bolts of composition. Learn the rules and write correct sentences. This gives you a solid foundation to build on.

PARAGRAPH ORGANIZATION: This chapter provides fundamentals of effective paragraph writing and organization.

ARGUMENT ANALYSIS: This section helps you look at other writers' work critically. You will learn to compare and contrast arguments and evidence. You will also understand how to craft an effective response to readings and writing prompts.

Sentence Structure

LESSON 1: SUBJECTS AND PREDICATES

Every complete sentence needs at least one **subject** and one **predicate**.

Subjects

A subject is usually a noun or pronoun: the person, place, thing, or idea that is acting (or being acted on) in the sentence.

EXAMPLES

Keturah smiled.

Happiness is precious.

The **country** sounds quiet at night.

A subject may have more than one word. In the sentence, "The mayor and his staff gave a news conference," **the mayor and his staff** is a **compound** subject—it has more than one element.

EXAMPLES

Bagels and cream cheese go well together.

The **sofa and piano** would not fit in the same room.

My **aunt and my cousin** came to visit.

Subjects may also include **modifiers**, or descriptive words. In the sentence, "The lonely little puppy howled all night," **lonely** and **little** are modifiers.

EXAMPLES

The **sleepy baby** could not keep her eyes open.

A **cold, rainy night** spoiled our camping weekend.

The **ringing phone** interrupted our conversation.

Practice Exercise 1

Circle the subject in each sentence below (include modifiers and both elements of compound subjects):

1. Husbands and wives don't always agree on everything.

2. Many hands make light work.

3. The small, shabby restaurant was actually very popular.

4. Eleanor's new phone was broken by the fall.

5. Honesty is the best policy.

6. The new kitchen will be beautiful.

7. We love the new fall TV shows.

8. My best friend will be away on vacation in June.

9. Too much sugar is not good for you.

10. The Great Wall of China is a magnificent sight.

Predicates

A **predicate** is a word, phrase, or several phrases that shows what action the subject is taking—or what action is being taken on the subject. The specific action word in the predicate is called the **verb.** A predicate may include other elements, but it must always have a verb. Example of predicate with verb only: John **eats.**

Like subjects, verbs in predicates can be compound; there may be more than one of them in a sentence.

EXAMPLES

John **eats** and **reads** in the kitchen.
Elsinore **eats** in the kitchen and **reads** in the living room.
The cat **stretched** and **yawned.**

Practice Exercise 2

Circle the verb (action word) part of the predicate in the sentences below.

1. A train whistled in the distance.

2. I tripped and fell on the pile of laundry in the hall.

3. Sam runs 5 miles every day.

4. Freedom is never free.

5. We swam in the morning and rode bikes in the afternoon.

6. The kids don't like macaroni and cheese.

7. Two wrongs don't make a right.

8. I didn't say that.

9. She finally turned her phone off.

10. Elections will be in November.

What are these other elements that can exist as part of a predicate? Two of the most common are **objects** and **prepositional phrases**.

A **direct object** is usually a noun, like the subject. It is the person, place, thing, or idea that the verb acts on.

EXAMPLES

John eats **arugula**.
Trees shadowed **the house**.
My cat hates **its carrier**.

A **prepositional phrase** can function in place of or with an object. Common prepositions, which start phrases, are in, on, above, around, over, under, and many more.

Fun fact: A preposition describes almost any place a cat can sit in relation to a chair!

EXAMPLES

The cat sits **under the chair**.
John eats **in the kitchen**.
The copy machine is **behind the door**.

Practice Exercise 3

Circle the entire predicate of each sentence below, including any objects or prepositional phrases.

1. John eats arugula in the kitchen.

2. I like parakeets.

3. Daffodils bloom in April.

4. The cat put its mouse on the chair.

5. Love is blind.

6. The mail will get here at 5:00.

7. My uncle left his keys in the car.

8. The woman in front of me got out of her car.

9. She wanted to ask directions.

10. You can't push that car by yourself.

We learned at the beginning of the lesson that every sentence needs at least one subject and one predicate. A sentence must also be **a complete thought**.

Checking to make sure a sentence is complete can be tricky. A sentence may have a subject and predicate and still not be complete! A good way to test for completeness is the "open-and-shut-door test."

Imagine you are in a room and someone opens the door and says, "Come on, we're going to go to . . ." and then shuts the door and leaves. Would you know what that person meant to communicate?

Why not?

The sentence has a subject (we) and a predicate (going to go to) but it does not complete its thought.

Practice Exercise 4

*Label one in each pair of sentences below with **C** for complete or **I** for incomplete.*

____ 1. A. Tickets for tonight's movie will.

____   B. Tickets for tonight's movie will be discounted.

____ 2. A. This sentence is.

____   B. This sentence is complete.

____ 3. A. Send that package to the mailroom.

____   B. Send that package to.

____ 4. A. Follow me to the back yard.

____   B. To the back yard.

____ 5. A. I am going to.

____   B. I am going to apply for that job.

A sentence that is missing something (subject, predicate, or complete thought) is a **fragment**.

Practice Exercise 5

*Identify complete sentences **(C)** and fragments **(F)**. In identifying fragments, you need not specify what exactly is missing. If anything is missing, label the phrase with an F.*

What is the difference between hydrating and moisturizing? _____ The answer is simple. _____ Although many cosmetic companies would like us to believe it is complicated. _____ To hydrate means to add water. _____ To moisturize means practically the same thing, but can also mean using creams, oil, and other products to soften as well as. _____ Spend millions of advertising dollars to tout their "secret formulas," "advanced technology," and "revolutionary discoveries." _____ However, the savvy consumer should realize (before spending precious income) that keeping skin moist and supple always comes down to simple oil and water. _____

LESSON 2: COMPOUND SENTENCES

A simple sentence needs a subject, predicate, and a complete thought. But a paragraph, essay, or book full of nothing but simple sentences would be dull! Combining simple sentences into **compound** and **complex sentences** gives writing variety and style.

A compound sentence links two complete, simple sentences (or **independent clauses**) into one. There are several correct ways to do this (and several incorrect ways to avoid!).

Rule: Link with a comma and a conjunction.

A conjunction word (*and, or, but, for, yet, so, nor*) is one of the most common linking devices.

CONJUNCTIONS

and   or   but   for   yet   so   nor

The two simple sentences below:

> The batter hit a home run.
> The crowd went wild.

can be linked with the conjunction *and*.

EXAMPLE

The batter hit a home run, **and** the crowd went wild.

Conjunctions should be chosen carefully so as to express exactly what the writer means. *But* and *yet*, for instance, signal that the second clause in some way disagrees with the first.

EXAMPLES

My sister never studies for tests, **yet** she always passes.
It was cold outside, **but** I didn't want to wear my coat.

Rule: Link with a semicolon.

A semicolon (;) may also link two independent clauses into a compound sentence.
I am not what you'd call a friendly person.
I hate when strangers strike up conversations.

EXAMPLE

I am not what you'd call a friendly person; I hate when strangers strike up conversations.

Rule: A conjunctive adverb may be used after a semicolon.

EXAMPLES OF CONJUNCTIVE ADVERBS

| additionally | consequently | finally | moreover |
| similarly | subsequently | then | therefore |

EXAMPLE

We waited for hours in the heat; **finally**, the doors opened.

If a conjunctive adverb is used with a semicolon, a comma must come after the conjunctive adverb.

Practice Exercise 1

For each number, rewrite simple sentences A and B as one compound sentence, using any of the methods described above.

1. A. The clap of thunder scared the frogs in the pond.
   B. They all jumped into the water.

   _____

   _____

2. A. The power failure was a major one.
   B. All the lights on the avenue were dark.

   _____

   _____

3. A. I didn't want to see the movie.
   B. I agreed to go anyway.

   _____

   _____

Halt! Caution!

There are several methods of combining sentences that, while common, are incorrect. One of these is the **comma splice**. A comma splice attempts to combine two independent clauses using just a comma with no conjunction. However, a comma alone is not enough to connect two simple sentences.

The Rocky Mountains are beautiful, I took a lot of pictures.

 The Rocky Mountains are beautiful, and I took a lot of pictures.

The Rocky Mountains are beautiful; I took a lot of pictures.

The Rocky Mountains are beautiful; therefore, I took a lot of pictures.

Another common mistake beginning writers make is to combine simple sentences with nothing at all—no comma, no semicolon, and no conjunction! This creates a **run-on sentence**.

Pink is my mother's favorite color she does not like orange.

Like the comma splice, the run-on sentence is the

To find where to punctuate a run-on, try reading it quietly to yourself. Notice where your voice drops or wants to take a pause. That is normally where you will want to place your comma and conjunction or semicolon. Another way to locate the punctuation break is to find the subject and verb in the first clause and the subject and verb in the second. The punctuation should be placed between them.

> ## PUNCTUATION BREAK
>
> Wolves *are* wild animals   they *do not make* good pets.
> subj. verb   ↑ subj.   verb

Practice Exercise 2

Four of the following sentences are run-ons or comma splices. One is a correct compound sentence. Fix the incorrect sentences and label the compound sentence CS.

1. Balloons are at every child's party, they often scare young children.

    _____

    _____

2. Forget about today, for tomorrow is another day.

_____

_____

3. My friend cannot sew she fixes her ripped clothes with tape.

_____

_____

4. It is almost the end of the school year, my teacher is so happy.

_____

_____

5. Lionel's wheelchair broke his friends rushed to help him.

_____

_____

Practice Exercise 3

Read the following sentences. Label the simple sentences (SS), fragments (F), compound sentences (CS), run-ons (RO), and comma splices (CSP).

____ 1. Children love stories.

____ 2. About other children.

____ 3. They also like fantasy they like adventure stories.

____ 4. Even children too young to read.

____ 5. They will ask parents to read the same book over and over, they never get bored.

____ 6. Parents may tire of the same book, but the experience is important to the child.

____ 7. TV does not provide the same enrichment.

Practice Exercise 4

Read the following paragraph and answer the questions below.

Family Dynamics in the 21st Century

(1) Forty-five years ago in American society, many young adults automatically planned to leave their parents' homes. (2) As soon as they were able. (3) Single young people were supposed to aspire to their own <u>apartment, they might bring</u> in a roommate if they couldn't swing it financially. (4) Nowadays young people—"Millenials"—are discovering the advantages of staying under Mom and Dad's roof. (5) Living at home gives job seekers fresh out of school breathing room, so they can consider job offers under less economic pressure. (6) Young adults can save money—not spend it all on rent and utilities. (7) Older parents benefit too. (8) They have a chance to get to know their children as adult individuals. (9) Plus there is always someone young and strong around to lift up the end of that sofa!

1. Which of the following sentences is a fragment (not complete)?
   (A) Sentence 2
   (B) Sentence 5
   (C) Sentence 7
   (D) Sentence 8

2. What is the best way to rewrite the underlined portion of Sentence 3?
   (A) It is fine the way it is.
   (B) apartment, or they might
   (C) apartment. Or they might
   (D) apartment? Or they might

LESSON 3: COMPLEX SENTENCES

Like compound sentences, complex sentences offer another way to add variety to your writing. The relationship between clauses in a complex sentence is different than in a compound sentence. A compound sentence's clauses have equal weight—they are equally important to the meaning. A good model would be a balanced scale.

A complex sentence, though, is like a scale that is heavier on one side or the other.

It was rainy.

I didn't take an umbrella.

> **EXAMPLE**
>
> Although it was rainy, I didn't take an umbrella.

Rule: A complex sentence has one independent clause (strong) and one dependent clause (weak).

Notice a word has been added! *Although* is an example of a **dependent word.** A dependent word signals the beginning of the dependent clause.

> **EXAMPLES OF DEPENDENT WORDS**
>
> after   because   before   even though
>
> if   now that   since   though
>
> until   whenever   where   while

> **EXAMPLES**
>
> **Because** the meeting was boring, my coworker spent most of the time doodling.
>
> My coworker spent most of the time doodling **because** the meeting was boring.

When the dependent clause comes first, a comma separates the clauses. When the independent clause comes first, no comma is needed.

Practice Exercise 1A

Combine the simple sentences below using the dependent word provided. Place the dependent clause first. Remember to use a comma!

Example: Before you open that oven, get your oven mitts.

1. A. I can't listen to music.
   B. I do my homework.

   (when) _____

   _____

2. A. It's been very quiet here.
   B. The neighbors moved away.

   (since) _____

   _____

3. A. The river flooded.
   B. Some people had to leave their houses.

   (after) _____

   _____

4. A. My mother had five children.
   B. She had little time to herself.

   (because) _____

   _____

Practice Exercise 1B

Combine the simple sentences below using the dependent word provided. Place the independent clause first. Remember NOT to use a comma!

Example: Let's put on some soft music while we're eating.

5. A. The crowd booed.
   B. The candidate came onstage.

   (when) _____

   _____

6. A. We were in bed for the night.
   B. There was a loud knock on the door.

   (after) _____

   _____

7. A. They have a new baby.
   B. They don't go out much at night.

   (now that) _____

   _____

8. A. I see him.
   B. Jamal is in a hurry.

   (whenever) _____

   _____

Rule: Use the right dependent word when crafting a complex sentence.

What is the right word? It is the word that communicates the relationship between the two clauses that you intend. For example, *because*, *since*, and *in order that* indicate that one clause **causes** the other.

EXAMPLES

I have lost weight since I stopped eating candy.

In order to build the hospital, the old buildings were demolished.

Dependent words like *although*, *even though*, and *unless* signal a change in meaning or direction.

EXAMPLES

Although it was already 10:00, the manager refused to open the store.

That store will not take returns unless you have a receipt.

After, *before*, and *while* express a relationship in time.

EXAMPLES

We had a delicious pecan pie after we finished dinner.

Before you leave the room, turn out the light.

Practice Exercise 2

Circle the dependent word that best completes the sentence.

1. We can go to the playground _____ you finish your homework.
   (after, ever since)

2. You must put your books under the desk _____ the test is over.
   (until, although)

3. Jules is probably sick _____ she didn't get enough sleep.
   (unless, because)

4. _____ I go, I see advertisements for that new movie.
   (Everywhere, Until)

Complex, compound, and simple sentences are all punctuated differently. Keep this in mind, especially if you are editing your own work and changing sentences from one type to another. For instance, if you put a dependent word in front of a simple sentence and make no other changes, you will have created a fragment.

EXAMPLE

I was unbelievably surprised.
Though I was unbelievably surprised. (fragment)

If you put a dependent word in front or in the middle of a compound sentence and do not remove the conjunction, your meaning will be unclear.

EXAMPLE

I practiced for the interview, but it went badly.
Even though I practiced for the interview, but it went badly.

Practice Exercise 3

Label the sentences below Simple (S), Complex (Cx), or Compound (C). One of the sentences is incorrect. Label it (I).

____ 1. I need absolute quiet when I am sleeping.

____ 2. Because the auditorium was not dark, but I tripped on the stage steps.

____ 3. Friends help their friends.

____ 4. Let's not argue; that won't solve anything.

Practice Exercise 4

Read the following paragraph and answer the questions below.

(1) Although Devonia was having a bad day, but she didn't realize it until almost lunchtime. (2) She woke up an hour late. (3) Because the cat accidentally turned off the alarm. (4) She spilled coffee on her new blouse. (5) And she missed her bus looking for a clean one. (6) At work, Devonia had to cover for her sick coworker. (7) She also had an important report due. (8) When lunchtime came, she realized she had left her lunch bag on the kitchen table. (9) Devonia started to get a headache from not eating. (10) She knew then that the day was not going to get better. (11) She would have gone home <u>then, but she</u> couldn't find her bus pass.

1. What is the best way to rewrite sentence (1)?
    (A) It is correct as it is.
    (B) Remove the comma
    (C) Remove the word "Although"
    (D) Change "was" to "is"

2. What is the best way to combine sentences (2) and (3)?
   (A) They should remain separate.
   (B) She woke up an hour late because the cat accidentally turned off the alarm.
   (C) She woke up an hour late, because the cat accidentally turned off the alarm.
   (D) She woke up an hour late; because the cat accidentally turned off the alarm.

3. What is the best way to combine sentences (4) and (5)?
   (A) They should remain separate.
   (B) She spilled coffee on her new blouse and she missed her bus looking for a clean one.
   (C) She spilled coffee on her new blouse, she missed her bus looking for a clean one.
   (D) She spilled coffee on her new blouse, and she missed her bus looking for a clean one.

4. What is the best way to rewrite the underlined portion of sentence (11).
   (A) It is correct as it is.
   (B) then but she
   (C) then she
   (D) then, she

LESSON 4: VERB FORMS AND TENSES

Verb Forms

All verbs (except *to be*) have five **forms**. A form is a category of appearance. No verb ever uses any form other than one of its basic five.

EXAMPLE

	Form	Usage
Base:	Laugh	Used with to (to laugh), in some present tenses (I laugh), as a command (Laugh!), and in future tenses (she will laugh, we are going to laugh)
s form	Laughs	Used in 3rd person singular present (he laughs, she laughs)
ing form	Laughing	Used with *is*, *are*, *was*, and *were* as helping verbs (Priya is laughing, Raj and Priya were laughing)
Past form	Laughed	Used for the simple past (I laughed, you laughed, he laughed, we laughed, they laughed)
Past participle	Laughed	Used in perfect tenses (we have laughed, you had laughed, he has laughed, they had laughed)

You may notice that the past form and past participle form are the same. <u>Laugh</u> is a regular verb—it doesn't change its root (base form). An irregular verb, one that changes its base form—like the verb *to do*, for example—could have different past and past participle forms. Such an irregular verb would look like this:

	Go	Usage	Run	Usage
Base form	go	I go.	run	I run.
s form	goes	It goes.	runs	She runs.
ing form	going	We are going.	running	He is running.
Past form	went	You went.	ran	You ran.
Past participle	gone	They have gone.	run	They had run.

One way to check that verbs in your writing are correct is to make sure they match the right verb form. "Goed" and "runned," for instance, do not match any of the forms. Therefore, they cannot be used.

Practice Exercise 1

Here are the forms of the two verbs bring and to be.

Bring: bring, brings, bringing, brought, brought
To be: be, am, are, is, being, was, were, been

Does the following sentence use these verbs correctly? Explain your answer below.

The little boy <u>was</u> happy all the way home, because he <u>had brung</u> his mother some flowers.

_____

_____

_____

Verb Tenses

The original Latin root of the word **tense** meant time. That is exactly what a verb tense shows: the time an action takes place. In comparison to some other languages, English has an almost bewildering variety of tenses.

However difficult they may be to memorize and keep straight, all these tenses give our language richness and an ability to express our exact meaning.

All verb tenses fall into one of three categories: past, present, or future. We will review those most commonly used.

SIMPLE PRESENT

Simple present is used for actions that are always true, or that occur repeatedly over a period of time.

> **EXAMPLES**
>
> The Earth **revolves** around the Sun.
> Every day I **buy** my lunch at the corner store.

SIMPLE PAST

Simple past is used for actions that begin and end at one point in time in the past.

> **EXAMPLES**
>
> The vase **fell** to the floor and **shattered**.
> The operation **was** a success.
> Stores **closed** during the blizzard.

FUTURE TENSE

English speakers and writers have a choice of two future tenses. Although there can be slight differences in the ways they are used, in general they are **equivalent** (equal).

> **EXAMPLES**
>
> John **is going to marry** Marcia.
> I **am going to return** this book.

Note: the helping verb (*to be*) must always be conjugated in the future tense. There is no such construction as, "I be going to return this book."

> **EXAMPLES**
>
> Jane **will try** to stop the wedding.
> The library **will not close** early tomorrow.

Practice Exercise 2

Write the appropriate tense of the verb that appears under the line. Use time keywords (yesterday, tomorrow) to help you decide.

Yesterday _____ such a beautiful day that we _____ to go on a picnic. Every
        to be   to decide

year we _____ to picnic as soon as the weather _____ warm. We _____ to
        to like   to get   to drive

a park that we had never been to before. Wouldn't you know it! As soon as we got to the

park, it _____ to rain. Next time, we _____ the weather forecast.
      to start   to check

PRESENT CONTINUOUS

Present Continuous describes something that is happening **right now**. It is formed with *to be* and *-ing*.

EXAMPLES

Right now, Giorgio **is taking** a test.
Right now, you **are studying** for the test.
Right now, the Moon **is rising** above the horizon.

There are also several **Perfect** verb tenses in English. These tenses are usually conjugated with some form of the verb *to have*. One example of a present tense commonly used is the **Present Perfect**.

PRESENT PERFECT (FORMED WITH *HAVE* OR *HAS* AND THE PAST PARTICIPLE)

The Present Perfect tense tells us that an action started in the past and is continuing now.

EXAMPLES

Olive **has gone** to the State Fair.
We **have turned on** the air conditioning.
The cows **have wandered** out of their field again.

PAST PERFECT (FORMED WITH *HAD* AND THE PAST PARTICIPLE)

The Past Perfect tense describes an action that finished before another past action began.

EXAMPLES

Mom **had** just **left** when we **noticed** she forgot her phone.
The game **had** already **started** before we **found** the stadium.
The photographer **had left** long before the reception **ended**.

Practice Exercise 3

Rewrite the following sentence in the indicated tense. Use time keywords (yesterday, tomorrow) to help you.

The lion runs through the tall grass.

1. Present Continuous

   Right now, _____

   _____

2. Simple Past

   Last night, _____

   _____

3. Past Perfect

   _____

   _____, before the hunter saw him.

4. Future

   In a minute, _____

   _____when he sees the gazelle.

LESSON 5: SUBJECT-VERB AGREEMENT

Subject–verb agreement means that a **singular** subject must have a singular subject. A **plural** subject must have a plural verb. Singular means one, and plural means more than one.

Singular subjects ⟶ I, he, the car, my friend, New York, soccer
Plural subject ⟶ We, they, the cars, my friends, cities, teams

Rule: Subjects and verbs must always match in number (singular or plural).

Understanding **pronouns** helps us to understand subject–verb agreement. A pronoun is a word that replaces a noun. Some examples of pronouns are *I, you, he, she, it, we, you* (plural), and *they*. Pronouns are used to avoid too much repetition of nouns.

Chester reached for his keys. It was 5:00 and he was ready to go home. He was looking forward to dinner and watching his favorite TV show. Suddenly, his boss appeared in front of him. "Can you work late tonight?" Chester's boss asked him.

Imagine if we did not have the pronouns *he, his,* or *him*:

Chester reached for Chester's keys. It was 5:00 and Chester was ready to go home. Chester was looking forward to dinner and watching Chester's favorite TV show. Suddenly, Chester's boss appeared in front of Chester. "Can Chester work late tonight?" Chester's boss asked Chester.

Pronouns are used when we **conjugate** a verb. Conjugating a verb means looking at its use with different pronouns (**persons**).

The following verb is conjugated in present tense.

I	run
You	run
He, She, It	runs

We	run
You	run
They	run

Notice that one of the verbs above is different?

THE BIG "S" DIFFERENCE

Rule: Present tense verbs take -s and -es endings for third person singular subjects.

This includes:

The pronouns *he*, *she*, and *it*.
Any nouns that can be replaced by *he*, *she*, or *it*.

Some examples include:

The Statue of Liberty **stands** in the harbor.
The bureau **creaks** when its drawers open.
Aunt Jessie **collects** teapots.
That swimmer always **finishes** second.
The man next door **mows** his grass every weekend.
A leaf **blows** in the wind.

Practice Exercise 1

Fill the space after the subject with the correct form of the verb from the choices in parentheses.

1. Birds _____. (sing, sings)

2. This train _____ to Washington. (travel, travels)

3. Daffodils _____ in the spring. (bloom, blooms)

4. The mall _____ at 9:30. (close, closes)

5. Her diploma _____ on the wall. (hang, hangs)

This *s* rule is only for present tense verbs. For past and future tenses, see Lesson 4: Verb Forms and Tenses.

There are some situations where you may not be sure if the *s* rule applies: the word **group**, for example. A group is made of many things or people, which makes it seem like a plural subject. However, those many things or people make up **one** group; therefore, we say

The group **is** meeting from 7:00 to 8:30.

Some **indefinite pronouns** also cause confusion. An indefinite pronoun replaces a noun, but not one distinct noun. Examples of indefinite pronouns are *all*, *any*, *everyone*, *everything*, *everybody*, *few*, *nobody*, *someone*, and *something*.

Rule: Indefinite pronouns that begin with *any-*, *every-*, *no-*, or *some-* take singular verbs.

EXAMPLES

Everybody goes to Rocky's.
Nobody is home.

Rule: Some indefinite pronouns take plural verbs.

EXAMPLES

Both are correct.
Few are chosen.

Rule: A few indefinite pronouns may even be singular or plural!

EXAMPLES

All is forgiven.   **Some are** in the living room.
All are welcome.   **Some is** left over from dinner.

Practice Exercise 2

Choose the form of the verb that correctly completes each sentence.

1. Someone _____ his or her car next to the fire hydrant every day.
   (park/parks)

2. Everyone _____ to go on vacation with us.
   (want/wants)

3. Both _____ to me.
   (belong/belongs)

4. Nobody _____ liver but you.
   (like/likes)

5. Few _____ that fast.
   (read/reads)

Another situation where agreement may be confusing is when too many words come between the subject and verb. These words might be a phrase describing the subject or a related thought in parentheses. It is necessary to locate the actual subject so that the verb may correctly agree.

<table>
<tr><td colspan="3" align="center">**EXAMPLES**</td></tr>
<tr><td colspan="3">The **boy** who has just come home from playing with his friends **looks** hungrily at</td></tr>
<tr><td>Subject</td><td>Descriptive phrase</td><td>verb</td></tr>
<tr><td colspan="3">the cookies in the refrigerator.</td></tr>
<tr><td colspan="3">**I** (and this is hard for me to say—I have given a lot of thought to it) **do not want** to</td></tr>
<tr><td>Subject</td><td>Parenthetical phrase</td><td>verb</td></tr>
<tr><td colspan="3">run for the office of Councilwoman.</td></tr>
</table>

The verb "looks" must agree with "boy"—the subject who is doing the looking! Likewise, "do not want" must agree with "I," no matter how far apart they are.

Rule: The verb always agrees with the subject, no matter how many words are between them.

Practice Exercise 3

Read the following paragraph and answer the questions below.

(1) <u>Whenever I goes</u> to my old childhood home, I get a weird sense of being 5 years old again. (2) My mother, who cannot throw anything away, <u>keep</u> everything I have ever used. (3) This includes the blanket my parents brought me home from the hospital in. (4) <u>Everyone always marvels</u> at how spotless my mother's house is. (5) <u>They does not see</u> the mountains of memorabilia from my childhood piled high in the attic.

1. What correction should be made to the underlined portion of sentence 1?
   (A) No correction
   (B) When I goes
   (C) Whenever I go
   (D) Whenever I went

2. What correction should be made to the underlined portion of sentence 2?
   (A) No correction
   (B) keeps
   (C) keeping
   (D) will keeping

3. What correction should be made to the underlined portion of sentence 4?
   (A) No correction
   (B) Everyone always marvel
   (C) Every one always marvels
   (D) Everyone always marveling

4. What correction should be made to the underlined portion of sentence 5?
   (A) No correction
   (B) They does not seeing
   (C) They sees not
   (D) They do not see

For questions 1 and 2, read the paragraph below.

Every day, I wake up at 6:30. I usually have cereal and toast for breakfast. At 7:45 I leave to catch my bus. The bus ride takes about 20 minutes, which gets me to work a little early. That gives me time to stop at the little store in the lobby to get my coffee, some juice, and fruit for a morning snack. When I get upstairs to my company, I still have time to say hello to my coworkers and settle myself in before starting work. I follow this schedule so that I don't have to rush in the morning.

1. Assuming this paragraph was written yesterday, change all appropriate verbs to past tense (there will be some you do not need to change).

    Yesterday, _____

    _____

    _____

    _____

    _____

2. Assuming this paragraph will be written tomorrow, change all appropriate verbs to future tense (there will be some you do not need to change).

    Tomorrow, _____

    _____

    _____

    _____

    _____

For questions 3–5, fill the blank with the correct verb. Choose from the list below the blank.

3. Every week, my best friend _____ in the church choir.
                              (sing/sings)

4. Right now, my sister _____.
                    (vacuuming, is vacuuming)

5. Last year we _____ to Disneyworld.
              (gone, went)

6. What is needed to make the following fragment a complete sentence?

Just gave up and bought a new one.

   (A) Nothing is missing
   (B) It needs a subject
   (C) It needs a verb
   (D) It needs a predicate

Using one of the methods described in Lessons 2 and 3, combine the simple sentences in questions 7–11 into compound or complex sentences.

7. I don't really like exercise. I have joined a gym.

   _____

   _____

8. Stone Harbor is their favorite beach. They go there as often as they can.

   _____

   _____

9. She stayed up all night on her phone. She has a headache this morning.

   _____

   _____

10. The Johnsons moved. They realized they forgot to label their boxes.

   _____

   _____

11. I need two AA batteries. We're out of batteries.

   _____

   _____

Read the following paragraph and answer questions 12–15.

(1) There are two kinds of people in the <u>world; people</u> who like it cold and people who like it hot. (2) Folks will argue to the death about why their particular temperature preference makes more sense. (3) "You can always put on more clothes," <u>insists</u> those who like to freeze, "but when it's hot, there are only so many clothes you can take off." (4) "No," answer the heatwave lovers. (5) <u>"Cold weather is depressing. (6) Can't relax."</u> (7) Somebody should invent a device that <u>lets</u> people create their own mini-environments. (8) That person would make a fortune!

12. How would you rewrite the underlined portion of sentence 1?
    (A) It is fine the way it is.
    (B) world; and people
    (C) world. People
    (D) world: people

13. How would you rewrite the underlined portion of sentence 3?
    (A) It is fine the way it is.
    (B) are insisting
    (C) insisting
    (D) insist

14. What would be the best combination of sentences 5 and 6?
    (A) "Cold weather is depressing. Really can't relax."
    (B) "Cold weather is depressing, and nobody can relax."
    (C) "Cold weather is depressing, nobody can relax."
    (D) "Cold weather is depressing, but nobody can relax."

15. How would you rewrite the underlined portion of sentence 7?
    (A) It is fine the way it is.
    (B) let's
    (C) had let
    (D) have let

16. On the lines below, list three things you did in the past that you continue to do today. (Example: I have lived in the same apartment for three years.) Use the present perfect.

    A. _____

    B. _____

    C. _____

17. On the lines below, list three things you are doing right now. (Example: I am listening to the teacher.) Use the present continuous.

A. _____

B. _____

C. _____

18. Your neighbor's daughter, Noelle, is in Mrs. Heigle's 5th grade class. The class was given the following assignment: write a letter to an adult you know. Your neighbor's daughter wrote you the letter below.

Dear Neighbor,

In our 5th grade class we are learning about how knowledge is passed down from generation to generation, and what an important resource our elders are. Please help me by giving me the benefit of your experience.

What is the single best piece of advice you have ever received?

What was the best lesson you ever learned from a mistake?

What would you go back and tell your younger self if you could?

Thank you very much for helping me with my assignment!

Your friend,
Noelle Ajavon

Use a separate piece of paper to write an answer to Noelle. Check it thoroughly for grammar, spelling, and punctuation errors.

CHAPTER 1 ANSWER EXPLANATIONS

Lesson 1: Subjects and Predicates

PRACTICE EXERCISE 1 (PAGE 12)

1. Husbands and wives
2. Many hands
3. The small, shabby restaurant
4. Eleanor's new phone
5. Honesty
6. The new kitchen
7. We
8. My best friend
9. Too much sugar
10. The Great Wall of China

PRACTICE EXERCISE 2 (PAGE 13)

1. whistled
2. tripped/fell
3. runs
4. is
5. swam/rode
6. don't like
7. don't make
8. didn't say
9. turned off
10. will be

PRACTICE EXERCISE 3 (PAGE 14)

1. eats arugula in the kitchen
2. like parakeets
3. bloom in April
4. put its mouse on the chair
5. is blind
6. will get here at 5:00
7. left his keys in the car
8. got out of her car
9. wanted to ask directions
10. can't push that car by yourself

PRACTICE EXERCISE 4 (PAGE 15)

1. A. I
   B. C
2. A. I
   B. C

3. A. C
   B. I
4. A. C
   B. I
5. A. I
   B. C

PRACTICE EXERCISE 5 (PAGE 15)

C; C; F; C; F; F; C

Lesson 2: Compound Sentences

PRACTICE EXERCISE 1 (PAGE 17)

The following are samples of how A and B can be linked. Other solutions are possible.
1. The clap of thunder scared the frogs in the pond, and they all jumped into the water.
2. The power failure was a major one; all the lights on the avenue were dark.
3. I didn't want to see the movie, but I agreed to go anyway.

PRACTICE EXERCISE 2 (PAGE 18)

Alternate solutions are possible.
1. Balloons are at every child's party, but they often scare young children.
2. CS
3. My friend cannot sew, so she fixes her ripped clothes with tape.
4. It is almost the end of the school year, and my teacher is so happy.
5. Lionel's wheelchair broke. His friends rushed to help him.

PRACTICE EXERCISE 3 (PAGE 19)

1. SS
2. F
3. RO
4. F
5. CSP
6. CS
7. SS

PRACTICE EXERCISE 4 (PAGE 20)

1. **(A)** Sentence 2 has no subject or verb.
2. **(B)** Sentence 3 is a comma splice. Only choice (B) fixes it correctly with a comma combined with the conjunction *or*.

Lesson 3: Complex Sentences

PRACTICE EXERCISE 1A (PAGE 21)

1. When I do my homework, I can't listen to music.
2. Since the neighbors moved away, it's been very quiet here.
3. After the river flooded, some people had to leave their houses.
4. Because my mother had five children, she had little time to her.

5. The crowd booed when the candidate came on stage.
6. There was a loud knock on the door after we were in bed for the night.
7. They don't go out much at night now that they have a new baby.
8. Jamal is in a hurry whenever I see him.

PRACTICE EXERCISE 2 (PAGE 23)

1. after
2. until
3. because
4. Everywhere

PRACTICE EXERCISE 3 (PAGE 24)

1. Cx
2. I
3. S
4. C

PRACTICE EXERCISE 4 (PAGE 24)

1. **(C)** Removing the word "Although" changes sentence 1 into a correct compound sentence.
2. **(B)** She woke up an hour late because the cat accidentally turned off the alarm. The two sentences become a correct complex sentence with the period removed and a lowercase "b" on because. None of the other choices are punctuated correctly. If left alone (A), sentence 3 is a fragment.
3. **(D)** She spilled coffee on her new blouse, and she missed her bus looking for a clean one. When combining two complete sentences, a comma should always precede the conjunction ("and"). (C) is a comma splice. The sentences should not be left alone because sentence 5 begins with a conjunction.
4. **(A)** The sentence is correct as it is.

Lesson 4: Verb Forms and Tenses

PRACTICE EXERCISE 1 (PAGE 26)

The verb "was" is correct, but "brung" is not one of the forms of *bring*. The correct form is "brought."

PRACTICE EXERCISE 2 (PAGE 28)

Was; decided; like; gets; drove; started; will check

PRACTICE EXERCISE 3 (PAGE 29)

1. the lion is running through the tall grass.
2. the lion ran through the tall grass.
3. The lion had run through the tall grass
4. the lion will run (is going to run)

Lesson 5: Subject–Verb Agreement

PRACTICE EXERCISE 1 (PAGE 30)

1. sing
2. travels
3. bloom
4. closes
5. hangs

PRACTICE EXERCISE 2 (PAGE 32)

1. parks
2. wants
3. belong
4. likes
5. read

PRACTICE EXERCISE 3 (PAGE 33)

1. **(C)** Whenever I go. (A) and (B) "goes" is not correct with "I." (D) "Went" is not correct because the writer is describing something she does on a regular basis.
2. **(B)** The sentence is in the present tense, which means *s* is used with nouns that can be replaced by the pronoun "she."
3. **(A)** The sentence is correct as it is.
4. **(D)** The pronoun "they" never takes a verb with an *s* ending.

End-of-Chapter Questions (Page 34)

1. Yesterday, I woke up at 6:30. I had cereal and toast for breakfast. At 7:45 I left to catch my bus. The bus ride took about 20 minutes, which got me to work a little early. That gave me time to stop at the little store in the lobby to get my coffee, some juice, and fruit for a morning snack. When I got upstairs to my company, I still had time to say hello to my coworkers and settle myself in before starting work. I followed this schedule so that I didn't have to rush yesterday morning.
2. Tomorrow, I will wake up at 6:30. I will have cereal and toast for breakfast. At 7:45 I will leave to catch my bus. The bus ride will take about 20 minutes, which will get me to work a little early. That will give me time to stop at the little store in the lobby to get my coffee, some juice, and fruit for a morning snack. When I get upstairs to my company, I will still have time to say hello to my coworkers and settle myself in before starting work. I am going to follow this schedule so that I won't have to rush tomorrow morning. ("am going to" may be used as an alternate future tense)
3. sings
4. is vacuuming
5. went
6. **(B)** It needs a subject. (**Who** just gave up?)

Answers may vary for questions (7–11). The following answers are samples.

7. Although I don't really enjoy exercise, I have joined a gym.
8. Stone Harbor is their favorite beach; they go there as often as they can.
9. She stayed up all night on her phone, so she has a headache this morning.

10. After the Johnsons moved, they realized they forgot to label their boxes.

11. I need two AA batteries, but we're out of batteries.

12. **(D)** A colon correctly separates the independent clause from the dependent clause list of types of people.

13. **(D)** The sentence is in present tense; "those" is plural and should not have an *s* ending.

14. **(B)** Cold weather is depressing, and nobody can relax. This is a correct compound sentence. (A) contains a fragment. (C) is a comma splice. (D) contains a conjunction that does not make sense in that context.

15. **(A)** Sentence 7 is correct as it is.

16. Answers will vary.

17. Answers will vary.

18. Answers may be in letter form with salutation (Dear Noelle,) and closing (Sincerely, Name) or they may be in paragraph form. Whichever form the student chooses, there should be a topic sentence that is the answer to one of the questions (The best piece of advice I ever received was to . . .). There should also be at least three examples to support the topic sentence.

Paragraph Organization

LESSON 1: PARAGRAPH STRUCTURE

The key to good academic and business writing is not word count, as so many students seem to think, but organization. Perhaps the misunderstanding comes from assignments in school in which the word count was **mandated**, or required. Obsessions with word counts more often lead to student panic than they do to excellent writing.

Organize

A paragraph is a group of sentences. How many sentences? A good rule of thumb is four to six, but many paragraphs are longer, and some are only one sentence. A paragraph may stand alone or be grouped with other paragraphs in an essay, report, or book. There are two rules to consider when deciding where a paragraph should end (and, if necessary, where the next one should begin).

1. A paragraph covers only one subject, or one aspect of a subject.
2. When beginning a new subject, begin a new paragraph.

EXAMPLE

The following is a stand-alone paragraph.

Most pet owners know not to feed birdseed to a guinea pig or fish food to a rabbit. Surprisingly few are aware of the very different nutritional needs of dogs and cats. While we think of dogs as carnivores, in reality they can tolerate a variety of foods. As long as owners stay away from known hazards, such as splintering bones and chocolate, their canine friends will be happy. There are even dogs that enjoy snacking on green beans! Cats need little else but meat, poultry, or fish—they are true carnivores. Pet food companies take these differences into account when making up their formulas. Most dogs can eat cat food without ill effects. Cats, though, cannot exist for any period of time on dog food without developing nutritional deficiencies. For a healthy pet, feed the right food—not the next best thing.

When writing a piece that includes several paragraphs, there must be some way for the reader to know when one paragraph is finished and the next one begins. The most common way to indicate a new paragraph is the indentation. When you have finished one paragraph, hit enter and drop down to the next line. Then tab over once and begin your new paragraph. See the example below.

Someone who wants to cut down on his or her caffeine intake, for health or other reasons, would do well to research some of America's most popular beverages. Although caffeine can be absorbed from medicine or food, much of our consumption of it comes from coffee, tea, soda, and energy drinks.

Soda, often cast as a heavy-caffeine bad guy, actually offers many choices (like some root beers and decaffeinated colas) that contain no caffeine at all. Eight ounces of cola has around 25 mg (milligrams)—not bad on the caffeine scale, although the high sugar content still makes this a questionable choice health-wise.

Tea offers many decaffeinated varieties. However, 8 ounces of regular tea can have anywhere from 5 to about 70 mg of caffeine. When home-brewing tea, of course, the amount will depend somewhat on how long the tea bag or leaves are steeped.

Coffee also contains different amounts of caffeine, according to how strongly it is brewed. In general, 8 ounces contains more caffeine (30–200 mg) than the same amount of tea. The exception is espresso, which can contain a whopping 600 mg in 8 ounces. (Fortunately, most people stop at one or two ounces!) Coffee also comes decaffeinated.

Finally, most energy drinks pack from 70 to under 100 mg caffeine for 8 ounces (the exceptions are products that are intended to be consumed in smaller quantities).

By knowing more about what we put in our bodies when we satisfy our thirst, we are on our way to making better-informed health decisions.

Practice Exercise 1

Read the following passage and answer questions 1 and 2.

(1) I was driving south on Ravensford Ave. (2) I was in the left lane. (3) I had been stopped at a red light, and traffic had just started moving again. (4) We could not have been going more than five or ten miles an hour. (5) I looked up into my rearview mirror and saw a silver SUV speeding towards me. (6) He was probably going about 15 to 20 miles an hour. (7) I thought to myself, "He's not stopping." (8) He hit my rear bumper and pushed me into the intersection. (9) Luckily there was no one right in front of me, so he did not make me hit anyone. (10) Afterwards, two police officers showed up. (11) They asked me to pull to the side of the road. (12) I gave them my information. (13) Officer Brent said that as I was not hurt and my vehicle was drivable I could continue on to work. (14) She advised me to seek medical attention if I started to feel pain during the day.

The passage above needs to be divided into three paragraphs.

1. Which sentence should begin the second paragraph?

   _____

2. Why? _____

   _____

3. Which sentence should begin the third paragraph?

_____

4. Why? _____

_____

WRITING PROMPT

Describe a process—how to park a car, how to change a light bulb, or how to plan a party—that takes several steps. Every time you begin to describe a new step, remember to start a new paragraph!

LESSON 2: TOPIC SENTENCES

Every paragraph is about something. It has a **topic** or subject. If there were no subject, there would be nothing to write about! It is important that you, the writer, communicate your topic to your reader and not leave him or her to guess at it. What is the most effective way to do that? Plan to include a **topic sentence,** a sentence that directly states your subject, in every paragraph.

Including a topic sentence not only helps your reader, it helps you, the writer! In order to state your topic you must define it and understand it. Understanding and conveying your topic clearly is part of the business of organization.

A topic sentence should not just state the topic—it should also state the writer's attitude about that topic.

EXAMPLES OF TOPIC SENTENCES

Bad—This paragraph will be about Mount Rushmore.
This sentence is just an announcement. It does not give any indication what aspect of Mount Rushmore the author will discuss.

Better—Mount Rushmore is a national monument in South Dakota.
While not extremely informative, this sentence does at least let the reader know that the mountain will be discussed in relation to its sculpture and historical importance.

Best—Mount Rushmore, a national monument in South Dakota, should never have been built because the land was seized from the Lakota tribe.
This sentence gives your readers the most complete idea of what you, the writer, intend to say in your paragraph.

Practice Exercise 1

Rate the following topic sentences as acceptable (A) or unacceptable (U).

_____ 1.   I want to talk about gun control.

_____ 2.   If you want to be a parent, you better have a good sense of humor.

_____ 3.   Paper books are better than Kindles.

_____ 4.   Ringling Brothers has a circus museum in Florida.

_____ 5.   For a fun-filled afternoon, visit Ringling Brothers Circus Museum in Florida.

_____ 6.   This paragraph is about my favorite dessert.

Where should the topic sentence be placed? There is no hard-and-fast rule, but at or near the beginning of the paragraph is a common spot. Topic sentences may be placed at the end of a paragraph as well. The middle is not a popular location, as it breaks up a writer's supporting details and can be awkward.

Kara was required to write an essay about an aspect of city life that is changing. This is her first paragraph:

> ***Over the last few years, my city has become much more bicycle-friendly***. It used to be a hair-raising experience to try to ride a bike on a busy street; now over 70% of all streets have bike lanes. Traffic policemen make sure to enforce respect for these lanes, so very few motorists disobey the markings. The city has also implemented bike-share programs. Citizens who don't own bikes can now take one for a spin and simply return it at their destination!

Kara has made the first sentence in her paragraph her topic sentence. She has also stuck to one subject within her paragraph.

Practice Exercise 2

Now look at Kara's second paragraph and answer the questions below it.

Bicycle riders in my city have responded to their new opportunities by becoming much more safety-conscious themselves. Before the changes, those riders brave enough to dare the streets seemed to feel that entitled them to make their own rules. Motorcycle riders kind of do this too. Riders without helmets were a common sight. When lights turned green, drivers had to check for that stray bike illegally whizzing through the intersection—or risk tragedy. Riders often thought nothing of riding on sidewalks or against traffic. After the changes, helmets are much more in evidence. Bikers use the correct lanes, signal, and obey traffic laws. It is a better situation for everybody.

1. In which sentence does Kara express her topic and attitude?

_____

_____

2. Which sentence in the above paragraph is off the topic?

_____

_____

Practice Exercise 3

Below is the final paragraph of Kara's assignment.

(1) People spend more time out in the open air, not cooped up in their houses or cars. (2) Bicycling is good aerobic exercise. (3) It stimulates circulation and is good for the heart. (4) Biking helps a person exercise his or her leg muscles. (5) It improves balance and helps to reduce stress. (6) Riding a bike is also cheaper than spending money on gas and parking. (7) By relying on their cars less, bikers are also helping to improve the city's air quality. (8) Who wouldn't want all these benefits?

1. Kara forgot to write her topic sentence! Which of the following would be the most appropriate topic sentence for this paragraph?
   (A) Spending time on a bike offers many health benefits.
   (B) I have a bike.
   (C) This paragraph is about bicycles.
   (D) Spending time on a bike offers many economic advantages.

2. Where would the best place be for the topic sentence?
   (A) Any place is fine.
   (B) Before the first sentence
   (C) Between sentences 2 and 3
   (D) Between sentences 3 and 4

3. Which sentence should be removed from the paragraph?
   (A) Sentence 2
   (B) Sentence 4
   (C) Sentence 6
   (D) Sentence 7

WRITING PROMPT

Choose one of the topic sentences below and write a paragraph of 4–8 sentences.

1. My favorite genre of movie is _____.
2. The state I would most like to visit is _____.
3. My favorite person in the world is _____.
4. The biggest mistake I ever made was _____.

LESSON 3: DEVELOPMENT AND DETAILS

In the previous lesson, we learned that a paragraph needs a topic sentence. No less important are the supporting details with which you develop your topic. Think of a grocery list.

The topic sentence of your grocery list might be: I really need these things from the store. That's fine, but if you were to hand that list to someone to do your shopping and there were no foods listed (i.e., no supporting details), she couldn't very well know what to bring you from the store!

Supporting details prove your point. The more detailed and memorable they are, the more your reader will remember your words.

It's important to remember four things when you are choosing the facts, examples, and details that will support your main point. Your supporting details must

1. Be accurate (true)
2. Stick to the subject
3. Not contradict your attitude or point of view
4. Be specific

Accuracy

You cannot include statements that are based on rumor or hearsay or that can be proved wrong with simple research. All your evidence must be information that you know to be true from experience or that has been proven true by a reliable authority.

Practice Exercise 1

Consider the following short paragraph.

Although not a usual situation, close relatives have a few times succeeded each other in the office of President of the United States. John Adams was the father of John Quincy Adams; George Bush was the father of George W. Bush; William Henry Harrison was the grandfather of Benjamin Harrison; Thomas Jefferson was an uncle of James Buchanan's; and James Madison and Zachary Taylor were cousins, as were Theodore and Franklin Roosevelt.

1. One of the facts above is false. Using an Internet search or a reference book (such as a history text or encyclopedia), confirm which set of presidents are not really related.

_____

Unity

Your support must not stray from the subject of the topic sentence. Imagine our shopping list again. What if you listed details, but they had nothing to do with groceries?

☑ **An evening gown**
☑ **Aluminum siding**
☑ **Skis**
☑ **Tires for the car**

Your poor friend would not find this any more helpful.

Practice Exercise 2

Match the topic sentence on the left with the best support on the right.

_____ 1. Many things that we fear are actually unlikely to happen to us.

(A) I can't accept a job offer if the office is above the 3rd floor.

_____ 2. The Grand Canyon is a magnificent sight.

(B) He once worked three jobs just to support us.

_____ 3. Phobias can be crippling.

(C) Only 5 people died from shark attacks last year.

_____ 4. My father is a remarkable man.

(D) It is a mile deep and the colors are gorgeous.

Consistency

In addition to staying on subject, remember that your details must support the point you want to make. If you want to write a paragraph about the benefits of a vegetarian diet, it defeats your purpose to note that vegetarians risk not getting enough vitamin B12. That fact would fit better into a paragraph about the **risks** of a vegetarian diet.

Practice Exercise 3

Read the following paragraph and answer the questions that follow.

(1) Most students would benefit from taking a year's break from study between high school and college. (2) For one thing, a break would give students a chance to calmly plan when, and where they wish to attend college, rather than force them to make all these decisions while dealing with the pressures of their senior years. (3) Another advantage is that a year working, volunteering, or traveling would give young people a chance to question if college is actually right for them. (4) There are, after all, many other possible paths to success. (5) The odds of winning any State Lottery are almost impossibly low. (6) Most colleges are very competitive, and the sooner a student applies, the better. (7) If a student does not apply right out of high school, he or she will be shut out of financial aid forever. (8) Finally, a year away can help a student think more about exactly what to study when he or she does start a college career.

1. Which sentence is off topic?
   (A) Sentence 2
   (B) Sentence 5
   (C) Sentence 6
   (D) Sentence 8

2. Which two sentences do not support the author's main point?
   (A) Sentences 2 and 4
   (B) Sentences 4 and 5
   (C) Sentences 6 and 7
   (D) Sentences 7 and 8

Get Specific

Focus on adding interesting, specific details to your supporting evidence. Adding adjectives (descriptive words) helps a reader visualize the sights or feel the sensations you are discussing.

EXAMPLE

The coat was in the trash.

More Descriptive: The old coat was in today's trash.

Even More Descriptive: The cracked leather coat was flung in the trash like an old friend who had ceased to be fun.

However, while you want to capture your reader with vivid descriptions, you do not want to distract her with unnecessary information.

Too Descriptive: The old, cracked, faded leather coat was cruelly left to its fate at the hands of indifferent trash men in blue overalls, who dragged it to their truck as one would drag a screaming, terrified prisoner to his early and painful death on a remote island prison in the cold sea.

Practice Exercise 4

Consider the sentence: The boy stood on the deck overlooking the water. Author A adds the following modifiers (descriptive adjectives and phrases):

The sobbing boy stood shivering in the rain on the deck overlooking the cold gray water.

Author B uses different modifiers:

The happy boy stood basking in the sun on the deck overlooking the turquoise-blue water.

Now use your own descriptive words to create a third situation from the same basic sentence.

_____

_____

_____

Another way to support your main point is to eliminate adjectives and replace them with facts that communicate the same point more effectively.

EXAMPLE

Dana was pretty.   Dana had won every beauty contest she ever entered.

The test was hard.   The test had 50 questions. None were multiple choice, and five were essay questions.

Practice Exercise 5

Rewrite the sentences below. Use modifiers to add detail or replace adjectives with facts.

1. The car was expensive.

   _____

2. Music was coming from next door.

   _____

3. The instructions for the DVD player were confusing.

   _____

Who? What? When? Where? How? Why?

When it comes to your own writing, asking yourself these questions can generate details you may not have considered before. Try applying this technique when you work on the writing prompt below. Some sample questions to ask yourself:

WHO should I write about? My child or myself?

WHAT are the most important benefits extracurricular activities give to kids?

WHY do extracurricular activities have to go? Are there other options?

HOW can we come up with solutions to this problem?

WRITING PROMPT

These days, many school systems are feeling the squeeze of budget cuts. Budget cuts often mean fewer resources for teachers and students. They can also lead to more children in the classroom, cuts in support staff, and cancellation of extracurricular activities like school newspapers and arts clubs.

Do you have children in school? Perhaps your own school days are not very far behind you. Write a paragraph describing the most important change you would make in either your child's school or your own former school.

LESSON 4: REPETITION AND RESTATEMENT

Restatement

In a longer piece of writing—an essay or a report—it is often necessary to restate information. Restatement means saying the same thing in different words. In an essay, for example, the thesis statement, or main idea, is often restated in the conclusion for emphasis and clarity.

EXAMPLE

Thesis statement—With a little practice and attention to detail, basic cooking skills can be easily mastered.

Concluding restatement—Anyone who is willing to put in the time and work can expect to start turning out breakfasts, lunches, and dinners in no time.

The main points of the thesis may also appear as topic sentences in each paragraph.

EXAMPLE

Thesis statement—Certain steps toward a successful evening out with a friend or partner are to be on time, be pleasant and polite, and be sure you have chosen an activity you will both enjoy.

Topic sentence of second paragraph—Showing up at your companion's house on time starts the night out on the right foot.

Repetition

Restatement is not generally necessary in a paragraph. Too much repetition overwhelms a short piece, confusing and boring the reader. It also takes up space that could be better used describing supporting details.

Practice Exercise 1

Compare how the following two paragraphs develop the same topic sentence.

Paragraph A

Bright blue coloration in processed foods is a fairly new phenomenon. Every time I turn around, I see another turquoise-colored drink or piece of candy for sale. You never used to see all this blue food. I remember before there was any blue candy or blue drinks. Years ago, you never ate anything blue. There just wasn't any blue food. There's blue coloring in just about everything these days, but that didn't used to be the case. Where did all this blue food come from all of a sudden? It seems like it's everywhere today. I mean it's just everywhere you look.

Paragraph B

Blue coloration in processed foods is a fairly new phenomenon; it dates back only to the last decade or two of the 20th century. Before that, blue coloration was reserved largely for cleaning products and other nonedible products. For example, several popular window-cleaning products were a distinctively bright blue. Many parents instinctively reacted negatively to turquoise-colored candy and drinks, as they were accustomed to these blue-tinged toxic substances. Even today blue coloring is not widely used, except in highly processed snack foods; for most people, chowing down on a blue pork chop or blue chicken is an unappetizing thought. No one wants to eat blue spaghetti.

1. Which paragraph overuses restatement/repetition?

   _____

2. Which paragraph offers a variety of supporting details?

   _____

3. List two supporting details from the paragraph you chose in question 2.

   A. _____

   _____

   B. _____

   _____

Practice Exercise 2

Each of the statements below is followed by one restatement and one supporting detail. Label the restatement (R) and the supporting detail (SD).

1. HVAC offers promising employment for someone interested in a skilled labor job.

   _____ A. Someone who likes to work with his hands should look into a heating and cooling technician's job.

   _____ B. HVAC technicians can earn up to $20.00 per hour.

2. Every workplace should have a first aid kit in an accessible place.

   _____ A. A first aid kit should be hanging where everyone in the office can reach it.

   _____ B. Prompt attention to minor injuries can keep them from becoming worse.

3. Following the latest clothing fashions runs into too much money.

    _____ A. Buying designer purses to go with each outfit could cost several thousand dollars.

    _____ B. Being a devotee of fashion can get too expensive.

4. Ellen really should not marry that man.

    _____ A. If Ellen marries him, it will be a bad situation.

    _____ B. They argue all the time and can never seem to agree.

5. Winter is my favorite time of year.

    _____ A. I enjoy participating in winter sports.

    _____ B. I love winter!

Read the paragraph below and follow the directions in the writing prompt.

Anais had been feeling depressed all day. When she woke up, she was depressed. When she got to work, she was depressed. Lunch did not make her feel any better. Talking to her friends at work did not make her feel any better. She was still depressed when she got home. She felt that she could not remember having been this depressed for a long time. She had been depressed before, but it had been a long time ago. She was depressed all day. Dinner did not make her feel any better. She was still depressed. Anais spent the whole day feeling depressed.

WRITING PROMPT

The paragraph above is filled with unnecessary repetition. Rewrite the paragraph keeping only the first sentence as your topic sentence. In place of the deleted repetitious sentences, create some detailed, specific reasons for Anais's mood. Use techniques discussed in Lesson 3 under Get Specific! (Hint: Use question words to get started.)

Read the following short essay and answer the questions that follow.

Paragraph 1

(1) Carpooling is supposed to be the environmental solution to saving gas, money, and effort. (2) However, I am here to tell you that it isn't the rosy picture painted in all those cheerful online articles. (3) "Save money! (4) Save the planet! (5) Make friends!" they all promise. (6) Bushwah! (7) Carpooling is a never-ending source of annoyance, inconvenience, and expense. (8) It saves nothing and helps nobody.

Paragraph 2

(9) In the first place, socializing with people at 7:15 a.m. means nobody is at his best. (10) One person wants to talk about global warming, while the other wants to listen to the oldies quiz on the radio. (11) One person wants to hum, but his partner in the back seat wants to sleep. (12) Nobody at all wants to hear Marge crack her gum.

Paragraph 3

(13) Going home is even worse. (14) Everyone wants to make "just a quick stop" somewhere. (15) Can we stop at the pharmacy? (16) Can we stop at the dry cleaner? (17) Oh look, there's a sale on kumquats! (18) Can we stop?

Paragraph 4

(19) By the time you've made all these stops, you're home an hour later than if you'd just driven alone. (20) If you thought you'd save money, take another think. (21) No one ever wants to chip in gas money when it's your turn to drive. (22) Driving here, there, and everywhere to pick up and drop off people adds expensive wear and tear to your car. (23) Don't forget all the mess from five people consuming nuts, candy, coffee, energy drinks, doughnuts, and who knows what else; you'll need your car's interior steam-cleaned practically every other week.

Paragraph 5

(24) I love the environment as much as the next guy, but I love my sanity more. (25) If driving my car every day creates too many pollutants, then I'll just walk. (26) It's only 15 miles.

1. Which sentence states the thesis for this essay?
    (A) Sentence 1
    (B) Sentence 2
    (C) Sentence 7
    (D) Sentence 8

2. What is the best change to make to Sentence 19?
   (A) Move it to the end of the first paragraph.
   (B) Move it to the end of the third paragraph.
   (C) Move it to the end of the essay.
   (D) Leave it where it is.

3. Which is the best paragraph for the following supporting detail?

   Some jolly soul always wants to stop somewhere "to have a few laughs together" when everyone else just wants to go home and collapse on the sofa.

   (A) Paragraph 1
   (B) Paragraph 2
   (C) Paragraph 3
   (D) Paragraph 4

4. Which of the following is a correct restatement of Sentence 2?
   (A) Carpooling is not as fun or beneficial as it appears in the media.
   (B) Articles about carpooling usually have lots of illustrations.
   (C) Most articles about carpooling paint a pretty accurate picture.
   (D) Articles online tend to try to discourage people from carpooling.

WRITING PROMPT

The essay above gives examples of why one person hates carpooling. In a short 5 paragraph essay of your own, take the opposite position. Give examples of all the benefits of organizing or joining a carpool.

Read the following paragraph and answer the questions that follow.

Paragraph 1

Eva knows that every generation finds its own horrible, evil, time-wasting temptations to fear on behalf of its youth. Right now that thing is video games. Video games create pale, flabby, unfocused youth with the attention spans of gnats and never-satisfied lusts for violence. Shaking her head, Eva reads these predictions and more like them to her son. Her son, who grew up on video games, laughs. He then heads out to the gym, where he works out after an eight hour day teaching Web Design. Eva herself was lectured, in the long-ago seventies, for watching too much television. Her own mother held to the belief that watching from less than ten feet away would render Eva blind and sterile. Eva enjoys sometimes catching up on the old shows when her three kids are out and she takes a break from her job as a Commercial Artist. Eva's grandmother received stern lectures about going to the moving pictures. Did she know what sitting in the dark with strangers could lead to? What kind of women were these actresses who dressed up and kissed men who were not their husbands? Did Eva's grandmother never fear being abducted during these shocking performances? Eva's grandmother grew up to run a farm and a dairy business single-handed. But she still occasionally spoke sentimentally of Charlie Chaplin. This chain of blaming is nothing new: no doubt it could be followed back to the Middle Ages when mothers feared for the safety of daughters who listened to too many troubadour songs.

5. What is the main idea of the passage?
   (A) Young people should not play video games.
   (B) Being suspicious of a new entertainment's effects is traditional, but often unfounded.
   (C) Many new forms of technology can be dangerous.
   (D) Being suspicious of a new entertainment's effects is perfectly logical and should be encouraged.

6. Which of the following details supports the main idea?
   (A) Video games create pale, flabby, unfocused youth.
   (B) Daughters who listened to troubadours in the Middle Ages got in trouble.
   (C) People were often abducted from movie theaters in the 1920's.
   (D) Eva's grandmother ran a farm and dairy business by herself.

Using the above paragraph as a model, write three supporting details for the following topic sentence. You may agree or disagree with the statement.

Many people feel that children should not have to do chores to earn an allowance.

7. _____

_____

8. _____

_____

9. _____

_____

WRITING PROMPT

Is there an aspect of today's society that you feel harms one or more groups? State what the problem is and who it harms. Give examples. If possible, add one or two sentences at the end of the paragraph that suggest a solution.

CHAPTER 2 ANSWER EXPLANATIONS

Lesson 1: Paragraph Structure

PRACTICE EXERCISE 1 (PAGE 44)

1. The second paragraph should begin at sentence 5.
2. Sentence 5 is a new paragraph because it begins a new thought. The first four sentences describe the situation before the accident; sentence 5 begins to describe the accident itself.
3. The third paragraph should begin at sentence 10.
4. Sentence 10 is a new paragraph because it begins a new thought. Sentences 5–9 describe the accident; sentence 10 begins to describe the aftermath.

WRITING PROMPT

When describing the steps of the process in the writing prompt, make sure to follow time order.

Lesson 2: Topic Sentences

PRACTICE EXERCISE 1 (PAGE 46)

1. U	3. A	5. A
2. A	4. U	6. U

PRACTICE EXERCISE 2 (PAGE 46)

1. Kara's subject (bike riders) and attitude (more safety conscious) are expressed in the first sentence.
2. The sentence "Motorcycle riders kind of do this too" has nothing to do with the subject of bicycles.

PRACTICE EXERCISE 3 (PAGE 47)

1. **(A)** All of the examples center on improving health. (B) and (C) are announcements of the subject with no attitude. (D) is about money, which is not addressed in most of the paragraph.
2. **(B)** Before the first sentence. Although a topic sentence may appear elsewhere in a paragraph, the most logical place for it is usually at the beginning.
3. **(C)** Sentence 6 is about money. All the other examples are about health improvements.

WRITING PROMPT

You should complete one sentence and add 5–7 sentences of detailed examples.

Lesson 3: Development and Details

PRACTICE EXERCISE 1 (PAGE 48)

1. Thomas Jefferson was not an uncle of James Buchanan's. This is false.

PRACTICE EXERCISE 2 (PAGE 49)

1. C   **2.** D   **3.** A   **4.** B

PRACTICE EXERCISE 3 (PAGE 49)

1. **(B)** Sentence 5 is off topic. The State Lottery has nothing to do with education.
2. **(C)** Sentences 6 and 7. These sentences present reasons for going to college right after high school, which is the opposite of what the author recommends.

PRACTICE EXERCISE 4 (PAGE 50)

The student's descriptive words should create a different mood than that of the two examples. "The frightened boy stood shaking in the wind on the rotting deck over the deep water" for instance.

PRACTICE EXERCISE 5 (PAGE 51)

1–3. These sentences offer an opportunity to experiment with modifiers and metaphors. Get creative and have fun. Answers might be

The gleaming car was as expensive as if it were covered in gold leaf.

The instructions for the DVD player were ungrammatical and accompanied by tiny, smudged diagrams.

WRITING PROMPT

Write a paragraph of around 6–8 sentences. Remember to include a topic sentence and supporting details. An example might be

One of the most important things a school can offer is a good physical education department. In my child's school, I would like to see less emphasis on team and varsity sports and a stronger emphasis on intramural sports for all. Unfortunately, team and varsity sports often get the lion's share of attention because they attract alumni dollars. However, all children need a sound understanding of how physical activity enhances their health. While children with no initial interest in sports may not be attracted to football or basketball, they might enjoy yoga, archery, or ballroom dancing!

Lesson 4: Restatement and Repetition

PRACTICE EXERCISE 1 (PAGE 52)

1. Paragraph 1
2. Paragraph 2
3. Blue coloring used to be used mostly for nonfoods.
   Parents had trouble getting used to blue food.
   Most foods with blue coloring are processed snack foods.
   Many foods would still be unappetizing if colored blue.

PRACTICE EXERCISE 2 (PAGE 53)

1.	**A.** R	**3.**	**A.** SD	**5.**	**A.** SD
	B. SD		**B.** R		**B.** R
2.	**A.** R	**4.**	**A.** R
	B. SD		**B.** SD

WRITING PROMPT

Answers will vary. However, a sample paragraph is presented below.

Anais had been feeling depressed all day. To begin with, she had had trouble sleeping last night, and she had a headache. She was out of aspirin, though, and so she thought, "Guess I'll just have to suffer through." She had weighed herself this morning, and noticed she had gained a pound. Even though everyone she asked said she looked fine, she didn't believe them. "They're just being nice," she thought. She found out in the morning that a report she thought she had submitted was lost, and so she would have to do it again. At lunch she realized the leftovers she had brought were spoiled, and she had no money to buy something else. As soon as she got home from work, she realized she had left some papers she needed at the office. She spent the rest of the night looking through bills that had come in the mail.

End-of-Chapter Questions (Page 55)

1. **(C)** Sentence 7. This sentence states the topic, attitude, and gives a list of three aspects the author intends to talk about.

2. **(B)** Move it to the end of the third paragraph. Since this sentence talks about inconvenience on the way home, it should go in the third paragraph.

3. **(C)** Paragraph 3. This sentence also concerns inconvenience on the way home.

4. **(A)** Carpooling is not as much fun or as beneficial as it appears in the media. (B) is irrelevant. (C) and (D) contradict the main point of the essay.

WRITING PROMPT

A sample of the way the thesis should begin is, "A carpool can benefit its members by . . ." Examples of support might be those things that the essay insists don't happen. Give examples of a carpool that DOES save money, save time, and provide companionship.

5. **(B)** Being suspicious of a new entertainment's effects is traditional but often unfounded. The paragraph provides several examples of generations who enjoyed entertainment in their youth but became productive members of society.

6. **(D)** Eva's grandmother ran a farm and dairy business by herself. Eva's grandmother is one of the examples of people who became productive in spite of enjoying popular entertainment in their youth. (A), (B), and (C) are not supported by any of the evidence in the essay.

7–9. Samples of support agreeing with the topic sentence might be

A. It makes helping around the house seem like something unpleasant.

B. Children fall into the habit of bargaining a price for everything they do.

Samples of support for an opposing topic sentence

A. It teaches children responsibility.

B. It give them pride in their own accomplishment.

Argument Analysis

LESSON 1: DETERMINING WHAT POSITIONS ARE PRESENTED

"What is your position?" The answer to that question may seem obvious. You are probably positioned in a chair, perhaps at home or in school. The word *position*, however, can describe more than just where something is located.

Some test questions may ask you about the position a particular reading sample takes. In this way, the question "what is the author's position?" actually means "what point is the author trying to prove?" Sometimes this will be obvious, as the reading will clearly take a side on an issue. Another term for this is an **argument**, but not the shouting kind. An argument is an idea that an author is trying to convince you is correct.

The sentence that clearly states the author's position or argument is the **thesis statement.** This basically is the main idea of what you are reading, and all of the other sentences will serve to support that position. Finding the thesis statement and identifying an author's position is an important skill on the test. The essay questions on the tests will ask you to read about different positions on a topic and then develop an argument of your own.

Practice Exercise 1

1. What is the position of the paragraph below?

   Jurassic World is the greatest movie of all time. My little brother has seen it six times. The main character is played by Chris Pratt, and he is definitely the funniest actor in the history of the world. The website movieguy.com gave it ten thumbs up. If I could watch just one movie for the rest of my life, *Jurassic World* would be it. I'm sure it made millions of dollars.

   Answer: *Jurassic World* is the greatest movie of all time.

In this case, the thesis statement was the first sentence in the paragraph, although it does not always need to be located there. However, it does make sense for it to come first to give the reader the main idea, and then all of the sentences after the thesis provide evidence for the author's argument.

2. Underline the sentence that states the author's position in the paragraph below.

After winning three Academy Awards in 1973, including best picture, *The Godfather* is still considered to be the best film of all time. Professor John Bartlet of the Columbia University film school called it "a masterpiece." Many of the stars in the movie, such as Al Pacino, have gone on to win awards throughout their careers. The movie was so good that the sequel, *The Godfather Part Two*, also won the award for best picture.

3. Underline the sentence that states the author's position in the paragraph below.

A recent survey of people standing at the Main Street bus stop showed that 75% of people say spring is their favorite season. The most common reason given by people in the survey is that spring is not too cold. Additionally, spring is widely considered to be the best time to visit national parks due to the increase in blooming flowers. Though the fall has its own colors as the leaves change, these leaves must be raked up. My uncle hurt his back last year raking leaves, so it's probably the most dangerous yard work you can do. This added work in the season hurts fall's popularity. Though some people like the fall, spring is the best time of the year.

4. Underline the sentence that states the author's position in the paragraph below.

Fall is the most popular season in the nation. In a telephone survey conducted by *Current Events* magazine, over 100,000 people listed fall as their favorite season. This total beat the second most popular season, spring, by over 20,000 votes. Another reason for fall's popularity is Halloween. This American holiday occurs at the end of October and is a favorite of both kids and adults. Finally, as the newspaper the *New York Tribune* points out, "people from coast to coast love fall because of the changing color of the leaves."

5. Underline the sentence that states the author's position in the paragraph below.

Bicycling is the best mode of transportation, especially when compared to cars. First of all there is the cost. An average car costs thousands of dollars, not to mention the ever rising price of gas. A sturdy bike, however, will never need gas and can be purchased new for just a couple of hundred dollars. Furthermore, as the February 1926 issue of *Life Magazine* points out, "most people prefer bike riding as their favorite way to get around town." Besides, everybody knows that riding in cars every day is bad luck. And unlike cars, which can only travel on roads, bikes can be ridden safely through a park, across the lawn, and even down a mountain!

6. Underline the sentence that states the author's position in the paragraph below.

The automobile has changed the world, and it is by far the best mode of transportation. According to the 2010 US Census, over 70% of Americans own a car. With millions of cars on the road each day, this number shows the usefulness and popularity of cars. The automobile has changed the world, and it is by far the best mode of transportation. Bikes may be fun to ride in good weather, but who would want to ride to work on a rainy day? Now imagine walking home from the store in the hot sun with your arms filled with grocery bags. With a car one can just put the bags in the trunk and then speed home. No doubt about it, cars are the best.

LESSON 2: IS IT VALID? ANALYZING EVIDENCE

What is the best movie of all time?

That is a difficult question to answer. Different people will have different answers, or positions, to a question like that. And while you may be knowledgeable enough about movies to know if someone's answer makes sense, on the test you will have to read about unfamiliar topics.

So how do you know if someone's argument makes sense if you don't know much about the topic? By looking at the evidence, or the reasons they give to back up their answer. Let's take a look at the following two paragraphs about the best movie of all time.

Best movie Paragraph 1

Jurassic World is the greatest movie of all time. My little brother has seen it six times. The main character is played by Chris Pratt, and he is definitely the funniest actor in the history of the world. The website movieguy.com gave it ten thumbs up. If I could watch just one movie for the rest of my life, *Jurassic World* would be it. I'm sure it made millions of dollars.

What is the author arguing? That *Jurassic World* is the greatest movie of all time.

Now let's list the evidence the author uses to support his argument.

1. His little brother has seen it six times.
2. He thinks one of the actors is very funny.
3. A website gave it ten thumbs up.
4. The author would watch it again and again for the rest of life.
5. The author thinks the movie made lots of money.

Best Movie Paragraph 2

After winning three Academy Awards in 1973, including best picture, *The Godfather* is still considered to be the best film of all time. Professor John Bartlet of the Columbia University film school called it "a masterpiece." Many of the stars in the movie, such as Al Pacino, have gone on to win awards throughout their careers. The movie was so good that the sequel, *The Godfather Part Two*, also won the award for best picture.

What is the author's argument? *The Godfather* is the best film of all time.

List of evidence the author uses to support his position:

1. It won the award for best picture.
2. A university professor called it a masterpiece.
3. Al Pacino and other actors went on to win awards.
4. The sequel also won best picture.

So which paragraph gave the better argument? Let's look at the evidence. Analyzing the evidence will help you determine which position is better supported.

The first paragraph had five pieces of evidence compared to the second paragraph only having four. So does that mean that *Jurassic World* is better than *The Godfather*? Probably not. His little brother liked *Jurassic World* enough to see it multiple times, but he may only be seven years old. *The Godfather*, on the other hand, won an award for best picture. This tells you that many people liked the move and not just someone's little brother.

Looking at the evidence in this way means determining if it is **valid**. In other words, is it convincing? Is it from a source you can trust? Does it help to prove the author's argument?

How to Analyze Evidence

A key part of analyzing a paragraph (or longer passage) is looking carefully and critically at the statements the author uses to support his or her point. It is useful to remember the old saying that just because something is printed (or on the Internet) that doesn't make it true! Who decides whether a supporting fact or example is true, convincing, or valid? You, the reader, do. That is what makes your critical reading skills so important.

Every time an author offers support, you, the reader, should have the opportunity to learn where his or her facts originated (came from). Here are some things to keep an eye out for when analyzing evidence.

1. EXPERT OPINION

An expert in any field should be cited by name and/or credentials (example: Dr. Shawn Guess, leading endocrinologist at Our Savior General Hospital).

2. HEARSAY

In general, any information presented with the words "Everyone knows that . . ." or "People usually say . . ." or "It's general knowledge that . . ." (or any similar phrase) is considered hearsay. Be careful: Hearsay may sound convincing, but there is no way to know if it is true. Therefore, it is not good evidence to use in supporting an argument. For example, consider the phrase "everybody knows all tall people play basketball." It sounds true, but is that actually accurate?

3. PRIMARY SOURCE

Primary source information comes from someone who has direct experience with a topic. For example, an astronaut talking about his work in space is a primary source. Someone's diary recording an event as they saw it happen would be a primary source. This type of eyewitness testimony is strong evidence to use in support of a position.

4. WEBSITES

We need to look at websites carefully because anyone can make a website, and there is no way to know if what you are reading is true. However, websites from educational sources (.edu) or government sources (.gov) are typically trustworthy.

5. TIMELINESS

Some evidence may sound good, but it may be too out of date to be effective. For example, the average price of a new house in 1940 was about $4,000. Would that information help someone arguing that today's home prices are cheap?

6. CREDIBLE NEWS ORGANIZATIONS

A recognizable news source like a local newspaper can be trusted over an advertisement like a billboard. Likewise, respected news websites like the cbsnews.com is better evidence than an unknown blogger or YouTube video.

7. IRRELEVANT INFORMATION.

Be on the lookout for evidence that isn't directly related to the author's argument. For example, say someone's reason for choosing their best movie of all time was the fact that they saw it with their best friend. That may be true, but it doesn't really tell you about the quality of the movie.

Remember—you be the judge!

Practice Exercise 1

For each paragraph below identify the argument and then list three pieces of evidence.

1. A recent survey of people standing at the Main Street bus stop showed that 75% of people say spring is their favorite season. The most common reason given by people in the survey is that spring is not too cold. Additionally, spring is widely considered to be the best time to visit national parks due to the increase in blooming flowers. Though the fall has its own colors as the leaves change, these leaves must be raked up. My uncle hurt his back last year raking leaves, so it's probably the most dangerous yard work you can do. This added work in the season hurts fall's popularity. Though some people like the fall, spring is the best time of the year.

   Author's position: _____

   Evidence: 1. _____

   2. _____

   3. _____

   What evidence do you consider to be valid and why?

   _____

   _____

   _____

   _____

   What evidence do you consider invalid and why?

   _____

   _____

   _____

   _____

2. Fall is the most popular season in the nation. In a telephone survey conducted by *Current Events* magazine, over 100,000 people listed fall as their favorite season. This total beat the second most popular season, spring, by over 20,000 votes. Another reason for fall's popularity is Halloween. This American holiday occurs at the end of October and is a favorite of both kids and adults. Finally, as the newspaper the *New York Tribune* points out, "people from coast to coast love fall because of the changing color of the leaves."

Author's position: _____

Evidence:　1. _____

　　　　　　　2. _____

　　　　　　　3. _____

What evidence do you consider to be valid and why?

_____

_____

_____

_____

What evidence do you consider invalid and why?

_____

_____

_____

_____

Practice Exercise 2

1. Bikes are the best mode of transportation, especially when compared to cars. First of all there is the cost. An average car costs thousands of dollars, not to mention the ever rising price of gas. A sturdy bike, however, will never need gas and can be purchased new for just a couple of hundred dollars. Furthermore, as the February 1926 issue of *Life Magazine* points out, "most people prefer bike riding as their favorite way to get around town." Besides, everybody knows that riding in cars every day is bad luck. And unlike cars, which can only travel on roads, bikes can be ridden safely through a park, across the lawn, and even down a mountain!

Author's position: _____

Evidence: 1. _____

2. _____

3. _____

What evidence do you consider to be valid and why?

_____

_____

_____

_____

What evidence do you consider weak and why?

_____

_____

_____

_____

2. The automobile has changed the world, and it is by far the best mode of transportation. According to the 2010 US Census, over 70% of Americans own a car. With millions of cars on the road each day, this number shows the usefulness and popularity of cars. The automobile has changed the world, and it is by far the best mode of transportation. Bikes may be fun to ride in good weather, but who would want to ride to work on a rainy day? Now imagine walking home from the store in the hot sun with your arms filled with grocery bags. With a car one can just put the bags in the trunk and then speed home. No doubt about it, cars are the best.

Author's position: _____

Evidence: 1. _____

2. _____

3. _____

What evidence do you consider to be valid and why?

_____

_____

_____

_____

What evidence do you consider weak and why?

_____

_____

_____

_____

LESSON 3: CREATING AN ARGUMENT BASED ON TEXTS

To get started, make sure you have completed the exercises in lesson two on analyzing evidence. This will help you to complete the exercises in the lesson.

Practice Exercise 1

For each set of paragraphs determine which paragraph is better supported by its evidence. Use the evidence you gathered in Lesson 2, and remember to determine if it is valid.

1. Which position is better supported and why? Cite three specific reasons from the paragaphs.

   ### *Jurassic World* Is the Best!

   Jurassic World is the greatest movie of all time. My little brother has seen it six times. The main character is played by Chris Pratt, and he is definitely the funniest actor in the history of the world. The website movieguy.com gave it ten thumbs up. If I could watch just one movie for the rest of my life, *Jurassic World* would be it. I'm sure it made millions of dollars.

   —Khalil Alam, Crestview Elementary News

   ### *The Godfather*: A Timeless Classic

   After winning three Academy Awards in 1973, including best picture, *The Godfather* is still considered to be the best film of all time. Professor John Bartlet of the Columbia University film school called it "a masterpiece." Many of the stars in the movie, such as Al Pacino, have gone on to win awards throughout their careers. The movie was so good that the sequel, *The Godfather Part Two*, also won the award for best picture.

   —Janice Westham, favoritemovies.com

2. Which position is better supported and why? Cite three specific reasons from the paragraphs.

   ### The Best Time of Year Is Spring Time

   A recent survey of people standing at the Main Street bus stop showed that 75% of people say spring is their favorite season. The most common reason given by people in the survey is that spring is not too cold. Additionally, everybody knows spring is widely considered to be the best time to visit national parks due to the increase in blooming flowers. Though the fall has its own colors as the leaves change, these leaves must be raked up. My uncle hurt his back last year raking leaves, so it's probably the most dangerous yard work you can do. This added work in the season hurts fall's popularity. Though some people like the fall, spring is the best time of the year.

   —Alex Castro

   ### Why America Loves the Fall

   Fall is the most popular season in the nation. In a telephone survey conducted by *Current Events* magazine, over 100,000 people listed fall as their favorite season. This total beat the second most popular season, spring, by over 20,000 votes. Another reason for fall's popularity is Halloween. This American holiday occurs at the end of October and is a favorite of both kids and adults. Finally, as the newspaper the *New York Tribune* points out, "people from coast to coast love fall because of the changing color of the leaves."

—Gia Hancock

3. Which position is better supported and why? Cite three specific reasons from the paragraphs.

Bikes are the Best Choice

Bikes are the best mode of transportation, especially when compared to cars. First of all there is the cost. An average car costs thousands of dollars, not to mention the ever rising price of gas. A sturdy bike, however, will never need gas and can be purchased new for just a couple of hundred dollars. Furthermore, as the February 1926 issue of *Life Magazine* points out, "most people prefer bike riding as their favorite way to get around town." Besides, everybody knows that riding in cars every day is bad luck. And unlike cars, which can only travel on roads, bikes can be ridden safely through a park, across the lawn, and even down a mountain!

—*Modern Cyclist Magazine*, June 2015

Cars Make Life Easier

The automobile has changed the world, and it is by far the best mode of transportation. According to the 2010 US Census, over 70% of Americans own a car. With millions of cars on the road each day, this number shows the usefulness and popularity of cars. The automobile has changed the world, and it is by far the best mode of transportation. Bikes may be fun to ride in good weather, but who would want to ride to work on a rainy day? Now imagine walking home from the store in the hot sun with your arms filled with grocery bags. With a car one can just put the bags in the trunk and then speed home. No doubt about it, cars are the best.

—*American Car Monthly*, August 2014

Now that you have cleared up which paragraph is better supported, it is time to write your own thesis statement. This will be a topic sentence that clearly defines which paragraph is better supported.

SAMPLE WRITING PROMPT

Both paragraphs identify reasons for different movies to be considered the best of all time.

In your response, analyze both articles to determine which position is better supported. Use specific evidence from both articles in your response.

TIPS FOR WRITING A THESIS STATEMENT

1. Don't give your opinion on the topic. The prompt does not ask for your opinion on your favorite movie. It asks which side is better supported. As a general rule, the word "I" should not appear in your response.
2. Choose a side. You need to create an argument, and your position cannot be that both paragraphs are both supported equally well. You need to be decisive: pick one and go with it.
3. Be specific. Name the article that is better supported by its title or author.

Sample Thesis Statements

The paragraph titled "*The Godfather: A Timeless Classic*" is better supported than "*Jurassic World* Is the Best!"

Although the article titled "*The Godfather: A Timeless Classic*" raises good points, "*Jurassic World* Is the Best!" by Khalil Alam is better supported.

The evidence used in the paragraph by Janice Westham in "*The Godfather: A Timeless Classic*" is stronger than the evidence in "*Jurassic World* Is the Best!"

Practice Exercise 2

1. Write a thesis statement describing which article is better supported, "The Best Time of Year Is Spring Time" or "Why America Loves the Fall."

_____

_____

_____

_____

2. Write a thesis statement describing which article is better supported, "Bikes Are the Best Choice" or "Cars Make Life Easier."

_____

_____

_____

_____

LESSON 4: PROVIDING EVIDENCE BY PARAPHRASING

Making a statement is the first step in creating your written response. Now the responsibility lies with you to support—prove, back up—what you say. If you've completed Lessons 2 and 3, then you have already chosen 3 pieces of evidence to back up your arguments. But how will you present the evidence in your words to show that you understand its strengths and weaknesses?

One of the best ways to show that you understand an author's ideas is to *rephrase them in your own words.* This is also called **paraphrasing** or **restating.** This can be tricky to do: you need to use examples from the readings, but you don't want to just copy the evidence word for word in your response

---

EXAMPLES

Direct quote: "The high temperatures last week were between 95 and 99 degrees. 8 people were sent to the hospital with heat exhaustion."

Paraphrase: With temperatures nearing 100 degrees last week, several people were hospitalized with heat exhaustion.

Quotes:

1. "After winning three Academy Awards in 1973, including best picture"
2. "Professor John Bartlet of the Columbia University film school called it 'a masterpiece.'"
3. "My little brother has seen it six times."

When using evidence in your writing, whether as a paraphrase or a direct quote, it is important to cite where the information came from. This can be as simple as naming the title of the article, the author, or the source it came from like a newspaper or website.

Paraphrases:

1. As the website favoritemovies.com points out, *The Godfather* won several awards, with the most prestigious being a trophy for best picture in 1973.
2. The paragraph by Janice Westham notes that an expert from a university called *The Godfather* a masterpiece
3. The *Jurassic World* article is mainly just the author's opinion, and facts like his little brother seeing it six times are irrelevant.

Practice Exercise 1

Paraphrase the following passages by putting them into your own words.

1. Dogs make good pets. They can run fast, and they like to play fetch. Dogs can also help you feel safe because they bark when strangers approach the house.

   _____

   _____

   _____

   _____

2. Cats make good pets. They are quiet and do not require constant attention like other pets. Additionally, they cost less to feed than dogs that can be many times their size.

   _____

   _____

   _____

   _____

3. Fish make great pets. Fish never need to be walked outside, and that can be important when the weather is wet or cold. You can also easily own many fish at the same time and keep them in the same tank.

   _____

   _____

   _____

   _____

Practice Exercise 2

Paraphrase the specific evidence you collected from the two sets of paragraphs on fall vs. spring and bikes vs. cars in the previous lessons.

1. **Fall vs. Spring**

   Thesis Statement: _____

   Evidence/Quotes:

   1. _____

   2. _____

   3. _____

   Paraphrases:

   1. _____

   2. _____

   3. _____

2. **Bikes vs. Cars**

   Thesis Statement: _____

   Evidence/Quotes:

   1. _____

   2. _____

   3. _____

   Paraphrases:

   1. _____

   2. _____

   3. _____

LESSON 5: HOW EVIDENCE SUPPORTS THE ARGUMENT

> **ATTENTION: You need to complete Lessons 1–4 in this chapter before working on this lesson.**

In the previous lessons you learned to identify an author's position, analyze the evidence, and then create an argument of your own based on strength of the evidence. We also worked on citing the evidence correctly by paraphrasing in your own words.

Effective writing, though, means more than just making a list of evidence. A skilled writer will make a "bridge" that connects the evidence to why it is important. In other words, after you use one of the points of evidence you selected from the text, take a minute to explain why it is important.

Thesis: The paragraph *"The Godfather: A Timeless Classic"* by Janice Westham is better supported than the paragraph titled *Jurassic World Is the Best!*.

Quotes:

1. "After winning three Academy Awards in 1973, including best picture"
2. "Professor John Bartlet of the Columbia University film school called it 'a masterpiece.'"
3. "My little brother has seen it six times."

Paraphrases:

1. As the website favoritemovies.com points out, *The Godfather* won several awards, with the most prestigious being a trophy for best picture in 1973.
2. The paragraph by Janice Westham notes that an expert from a university called *The Godfather* a masterpiece.
3. The *Jurassic World* article is mainly just the author's opinion, and facts like his little brother seeing it six times are irrelevant.

Bridge explaining why each point is important.

1. Winning nationally recognized awards shows that many others agree that *The Godfather* is a great film.
2. The opinion of a professor is expert testimony that further shows how great *The Godfather* is.
3. The evidence used in the *Jurassic World* paragraph is invalid and does not really support the position that it is the best.

Practice Exercise 1

Create "bridge" sentences that explain why your evidence is important. Remember, each point you make must support your thesis.

1. **Fall vs. Spring**

   Thesis Statement: _____

   Evidence/Quotes:

   1. _____

   2. _____

   3. _____

   Paraphrases:

   1. _____

   2. _____

   3. _____

   Bridge Sentences:

   1. _____

   2. _____

   3. _____

2. **Bikes vs. Cars**

   Thesis Statement: _____

   Evidence/Quotes:

   1. _____

   2. _____

   3. _____

   Paraphrases:

   1. _____

   2. _____

   3. _____

   Bridge Sentences:

   1. _____

   2. _____

   3. _____

LESSON 6: SAMPLE PARAGRAPHS

Writing an evidence-based argumentative essay is a bit like putting together a puzzle. All of the pieces you need are in the readings, but how do they fit together? To help you better visualize the process, here are some paragraphs based on the readings covered in this chapter. These aren't the only possible answers to these questions. They are just one possibility using the evidence.

Practice Exercise 1

Underline the thesis statement in each paragraph. Each paragraph uses three pieces of evidence. Write the numbers 1, 2, or 3 above each sentence that provides specific evidence. Each paragraph also has three "bridge" sentences that explain why the evidence is important. Write A, B, or C above these sentences.

The paragraph "*The Godfather*: A Timeless Classic" by Janice Westham is better supported than the paragraph titled "*Jurassic World* Is the Best!" As the website favoritemovies.com points out, *The Godfather* won several awards, with the most prestigious being a trophy for best picture in 1973. Winning nationally recognized awards shows that many others agree that *The Godfather* is a great film. Next, Westham notes that an expert from a university called *The Godfather* a masterpiece; the opinion of a professor is expert testimony that further shows the greatness of *The Godfather*. Finally, The *Jurassic World* article is mainly just the author's opinion, and facts like his little brother seeing it six times are irrelevant. The evidence used in the *Jurassic World* paragraph is invalid and does not really support the position that it is the best. Therefore, Westham's position is superior to Alam's.

The paragraph "Why America Loves the Fall" is the better supported argument. A large survey conducted by *Current Events* demonstrated that more people prefer the fall than the spring. This shows that when you survey more than just a bus stop, as Mr. Castro did in his article, you get much different results. Second, Ms. Hancock cites the *New York Tribune* in recognizing people's love for the changing colors of fall leaves. A respected source like the *Tribune* can be trusted over statements like "everybody knows" in the opposing article. Last, Mr. Castro's argument uses irrelevant information like the fact that his uncle hurt his back doing yard work. Such statements have nothing to do with his position! In conclusion, "Why America Loves the Fall" presents the more convincing argument.

The position in "Cars Make Life Easier" is much better supported than "Bikes Are the Best Choice." To begin, the article in *American Car Monthly* uses government data to prove that over 70% of Americans are car owners. Because that number is so high, it clearly demonstrates that the nation has already decided that cars are superior to bikes. Additionally, the article in *Modern Cyclist* uses evidence from 1926. Evidence that old cannot be reliable and does not help their argument. Finally, the bike article claims that "everyone knows that riding in cars every day is bad luck." This is unprovable hearsay! Because the evidence in support of bikes is so weak, "Cars Make Life Easier" is the better supported position.

Use the following template to help you answer the writing prompts.

Analyzing Argument Essay Template

1. Thesis (which side you are choosing):

    _____

    _____

2. Evidence A:

    _____

    _____

3. Bridge (why that evidence is important):

    _____

    _____

4. Evidence B:

    _____

    _____

5. Bridge (why that evidence is important):

    _____

    _____

6. Evidence C:

    _____

    _____

7. Bridge (why that evidence is important):

    _____

    _____

UNIT 1: WRITING

1. Use the readings on the greatest movie of all time to answer the following writing prompt:

> Both paragraphs identify reasons for different movies to be considered the best of all time.
>
> In your response, analyze both articles to determine which position is better supported. Use specific evidence from both articles in your response.

2. Use the readings on which season is better, fall or spring, to answer the following writing prompt:

> Both paragraphs identify reasons for a different season to be considered the best.
>
> In your response, analyze both articles to determine which position is better supported. Use specific evidence from both articles in your response.

3. Use the readings describing two forms of transportation, cars and bikes, to answer the following writing prompt:

> These two paragraphs compare two distinct modes of transportation, cars and bikes.
>
> In your response, analyze both articles to determine which position is better supported. Use specific evidence from both articles in your response.

> The paragraphs below present different viewpoints on smart phones.
>
> In your response, analyze both articles to determine which position is better supported. Use specific evidence from both articles in your response.

Smart Phones Are Actually Making Us Dumb

If these phones are so smart, why do their users do such dumb things? It seems like every time I leave the house I see someone in a minor car accident—undoubtedly another victim of texting and driving. People don't have the ability to actually enjoy life any more unless they can instantly upload a picture to social media. And how many times have you been in a restaurant only to see two people staring at their phones instead of talking to each other? They should be called dumb phones, because that's what they are doing to society. And everyone knows they are too expensive. Smart phones are a waste of time and money.

—Jerry Oldman, Letter to the Editor, *Springfield Times*, 6/20/15

Building a Better Tomorrow, One Smart Phone at a Time

Smart phones have made the world a better place. The Springfield Police Department crime statistics for 2014 indicate that over two dozen criminals were convicted thanks to the video evidence recorded on smart phones. Plus, they just make life easier. Who hasn't looked up directions, or a new restaurant while driving around town? And as the Internet Research Foundation stated in their annual report, over 75% of Americans are connected through social media. Our society loves to share our thoughts and experiences, and smart phones are the most convenient way to do so.

—Tina Ager, Letter to the Editor, *Springfield Times*, 7/4/15

CHAPTER 3 ANSWER EXPLANATIONS

Lesson 1: Determining What Positions Are Presented

PRACTICE EXERCISE 1 (PAGE 61)

1. *Jurassic World* is the greatest movie of all time.
2. After winning three Academy Awards in 1973, including best picture, *The Godfather* is still considered to be the best film of all time.
3. Though some people like the fall, spring is the best time of the year.
4. Fall is the most popular season in the nation.
5. Bicycling is the best mode of transportation, especially when compared to cars.
6. The automobile has changed the world, and it is by far the best mode of transportation.

Lesson 2: Is it Valid? Analyzing Evidence

PRACTICE EXERCISE 1 (PAGE 65)

1. **Author's position:** Spring is the best season.
   Evidence:

   1. Survey showing 75% say spring is their favorite
   2. Not too cold
   3. Best time for flowers
   4. Uncle hurt back raking leaves

   What evidence do you consider to be valid and why?
   The survey could be valid, but we don't know how many people were in the survey.
   What evidence do you consider invalid and why?
   The fact the uncle hurt his back is not valid evidence for why spring is better.

2. **Author's position:** Fall is the most popular season.
   Evidence:

   1. Magazine survey
   2. Popular holiday
   3. *New York Tribune*

   What evidence do you consider to be valid and why?
   All of the above evidence is valid. The survey had over 100,000 participants, which makes it more credible than the bus stop survey. Citing a major newspaper is usually solid evidence to use.
   What evidence do you consider invalid and why?
   None.

PRACTICE EXERCISE 2 (PAGE 67)

1. **Author's position:** Bikes are the best mode of transportation
   Evidence:

   1. Cheaper
   2. 1926 *Life Magazine* quote
   3. Cars are bad luck
   4. Bikes can be ridden almost anywhere

   What evidence do you consider to be valid and why?
   The cost is a significant factor.
   What evidence do you consider invalid and why?
   The magazine quote is almost 100 years old and therefore out of date. Likewise, the saying "everybody knows" is hearsay.

2. **Author's position:** Cars are the best mode of transportation.
   Evidence:

   1. Census data
   2. Cars are better in bad weather
   3. Can carry more in car

   What evidence do you consider to be valid and why?
   All of the evidence is valid, particularly the government census data.
   What evidence do you consider invalid and why?
   None.

Lesson 3: Creating an Argument Based on Texts

PRACTICE EXERCISE 1 (PAGE 69)

1. *The Godfather:* A Timeless Classic
   "After winning three Academy Awards in 1973, including best picture"—a nationally recognized award
   "Professor John Bartlet of the Columbia University film school called it "a masterpiece." —expert testimony
   "My little brother has seen it six times."—irrelevant information

2. "Why America Loves the Fall"
   Magazine survey with over 100,000 participants is more credible than a bus stop survey.
   A favorite holiday is in the fall, and that would increase the season's popularity.
   A newspaper quote adds credibility.
   The other article on spring includes irrelevant information.

3. "Cars Make Life Easier"
   Facts from the U.S. census can be trusted.
   Cars work better than bikes on rainy days, and can carry more.
   The bike article cites info from 1926, which is way out of date and includes hearsay.

PRACTICE EXERCISE 2 (PAGE 71)

1. Possible thesis statements include:

    The paragraph titled "Why America Loves the Fall" is better supported than "The Best Time of Year Is Spring Time."

    Although the article titled "The Best Time of Year Is Spring Time" raises good points, "Why America Loves the Fall" is better supported.

    The evidence used in the paragraph by Gia Hancock in "Why America Loves the Fall" is stronger than the evidence in "The Best Time of Year Is Spring Time."

2. Possible thesis statements include:

    The paragraph titled "Cars Make Life Easier" is better supported than "Bikes Are the Best Choice."

    Although the article titled "Bikes Are the Best Choice" raises good points, "Cars Make Life Easier" is better supported.

    The evidence used in the paragraph by the *American Car Monthly* in "Cars Make Life Easier" is stronger than the evidence in "Bikes Are the Best Choice."

Lesson 4: Providing Evidence by Paraphrasing

PRACTICE EXERCISE 1 (PAGE 73)

Answers will vary, but cannot include a direct quotation from the original passage. All responses must be in the student's own words.

1. Dog are great pets because their loud barking can scare off intruders, and because they are fast runners that love to play games.

2. Cats make for easy, low-maintenance pets that are inexpensive to feed in comparison to many dogs.

3. A fish owner can stock a variety of species in the same tank and never need to worry about walking his pet in poor weather conditions.

PRACTICE EXERCISE 2 (PAGE 74)

Answers will vary, but cannot include a direct quotation from the original passage. All responses must be in the student's own words.

Lesson 5: How Evidence Supports Argument

PRACTICE EXERCISE 1 (PAGE 76)

Answers will vary depending on the evidence chosen, and why the student believes it is important.

Lesson 6: Sample Paragraphs

PRACTICE EXERCISE 1 (PAGE 78)

The paragraph "*The Godfather:* A Timeless Classic" by Janice Westham is better supported than the paragraph titled "*Jurassic World* Is the Best!" **1.** As the website favoritemovies.com points out, *The Godfather* won several awards, with the most prestigious being a trophy for best picture in 1973. **A.** Winning nationally recognized awards shows that many others agree that *The Godfather* is a great film. **2.** Next, Westham notes that an expert from a university called *The Godfather* a masterpiece; **B.** the opinion of a professor is expert testimony that further shows the greatness of *The Godfather*. **C.** Finally, The *Jurassic World* article is mainly just the author's opinion, **3.** and facts like his little brother seeing it six times are irrelevant. The evidence used in the *Jurassic World* paragraph is invalid and does not really support the position that it is the best. Therefore, Westham's position is superior to Alam's.

The paragraph "Why America Loves the Fall" is the better supported argument. **1.** A large survey conducted by *Current Events* demonstrated that more people prefer the fall than the spring. **A.** This shows that when you survey more than just a bus stop, as Mr. Castro did in his article, you get much different results. **2.** Second, Ms. Hancock cites the *New York Tribune* in recognizing people's love for the changing colors of fall leaves. **B.** A respected source like the *Tribune* can be trusted over statements like "everybody knows" in the opposing article. **3.** Last, Mr. Castro's argument uses irrelevant information like the fact that his uncle hurt his back doing yard work. **C.** Such statements have nothing to do with his position! In conclusion, "Why America Loves the Fall" presents the more convincing argument.

The position in "Cars Make Life Easier" is much better supported than "Bikes Are the Best Choice." **1.** To begin, the article in *American Car Monthly* uses government data to prove that over 70% of Americans are car owners. **A.** Because that number is so high, it clearly demonstrates that the nation has already decided that cars are superior to bikes. **2.** Additionally, the article in *Modern Cyclist* uses evidence from 1926. **B.** Evidence that old cannot be reliable and does not help their argument. **3.** Finally, the bike article claims that "everyone knows that riding in cars every day is bad luck." **C.** This is unprovable hearsay! Because the evidence in support of bikes is so weak, "Cars Make Life Easier" is the better supported position.

End-of-Chapter Questions (Page 79)

Examples of responses that include a thesis, specific evidence, and bridge statements include:

1. The paragraph "*The Godfather:* A Timeless Classic" by Janice Westham is better supported than the paragraph titled "*Jurassic World* Is the Best!" As the website favoritemovies.com points out, *The Godfather* won several awards, with the most prestigious being a trophy for best picture in 1973. Winning nationally recognized awards shows that many others agree that *The Godfather* is a great film. Next, Westham notes that an expert from a university called *The Godfather* a masterpiece; the opinion of a professor is expert testimony that further shows the greatness of *The Godfather*. Finally, The *Jurassic World* article is mainly just the author's opinion, and facts like his little brother seeing it six times are irrelevant. The evidence used in the *Jurassic World* paragraph is invalid and does not really support the position that it is the best. Therefore, Westham's position is superior to Alam's.

2. The paragraph "Why America Loves the Fall" is the better supported argument. A large survey conducted by *Current Events* demonstrated that more people prefer the fall than the spring. This shows that when you survey more than just a bus stop, as Mr. Castro did in his article, you get much different results. Second, Ms. Hancock cites the *New York Tribune* in recognizing people's love for the changing colors of fall leaves. A respected source like the *Tribune* can be trusted over statements like "everybody knows" in the opposing article. Last, Mr. Castro's argument uses irrelevant information like the fact that his uncle hurt his back doing yard work. Such statements have nothing to do with his position! In conclusion, "Why America Loves the Fall" presents the more convincing argument.

3. The position in "Cars Make Life Easier" is much better supported than "Bikes Are the Best Choice." To begin, the article in *American Car Monthly* uses government data to prove that over 70% of Americans are car owners. Because that number is so high, it clearly demonstrates that the nation has already decided that cars are superior to bikes. Additionally, the article in *Modern Cyclist* uses evidence from 1926. Evidence that old cannot be reliable and does not help their argument. Finally, the bike article claims that "everyone knows that riding in cars every day is bad luck." This is unprovable hearsay! Because the evidence in support of bikes is so weak, "Cars Make Life Easier" is the better supported position.

4. The letter to the editor by Tina Ager uses better evidence than the letter by Jerry Oldman. "Building a Better Tomorrow, One Smart Phone at a Time" uses crime statistics to show that smart phones can make people safer. Since these numbers come from a government source, they add reliability to her argument. Next, Ms. Ager cites a report stating that 75% of Americans use social media. This high number lends support to the idea that people enjoy the convenience of smart phones. Mr. Oldman's letter, however, is all opinion and provides no valid facts.

Writing Posttest

The writing posttest has 50 questions. After you review the material in this unit, you can use the test to get a sense of what areas you still need to study. Make sure you have at least 90 minutes of quiet time available to complete the test. Read each question carefully and do your best. As with the pretest, it is better if you do not guess on these questions. If you don't know the answer to a question, simply skip it and go on to the next one. The purpose of this test is to find out what areas you still need to work on and random guessing might throw you off course.

Once you have finished, check your answers on pages 101–103 and complete the posttest evaluation chart on page 100 by circling the number of each question you answered correctly. This way you can easily see your strengths and weaknesses as well as where information on each question you missed is located in the book.

If you score very well on the posttest, it is a great sign that you have a solid foundation in the different skills needed for writing. You are ready to begin studying higher-level material in this subject.

Read the following 2 paragraphs and answer questions 1–4.

Paragraph A

(1) Philadelphia is a city of murals. (2) An unobtrusive work quietly set back from Broad St. honors Horace Pippen (1888–1946), an African-American artist. (3) Painted flowers bloom on the brick walls of a public housing development. (4) Philadelphia also has exciting nightclub choices. (5) The profile of an Asian woman, surrounded by colorful Chinese imagery, graces one of the buildings of the city's Chinatown district. (6) Such offerings brighten the lives of countless city residents. (7) Going about their daily business. (8) These murals prove that art can be a part of everyday life and need not be confined to silent museums.

Paragraph B

(1) The Philadelphia Mural Arts Program (founded in 1984) seeks to connect young people to art and local artists. (2) The program hires many local artists. (3) To work with youth. (4) Under a professional artist's direction, young people help design and create a work that will be displayed permanently on one of the city's streets. (5) The program was conceived as an alternative creative outlet to <u>graffiti, graffiti</u> was becoming more and more of a problem. (6) The professional painters help teenagers to find a way to express themselves other than spraying graffiti. (7) It's a program for youth.

1. Which paragraph has a problem with repetition?
   (A) Paragraph A
   (B) Paragraph B
   (C) both
   (D) neither

2. Which two sentences above are fragments (not complete)?
   (A) sentence 7 in Paragraph A and Sentence 2 in Paragraph B
   (B) sentences 2 and 3 in Paragraph B
   (C) sentence 7 in Paragraph A and sentence 3 in Paragraph B
   (D) sentences 3 and 4 in Paragraph B

3. Which sentence in Paragraph A is off topic and should be removed?
   (A) sentence 3
   (B) sentence 4
   (C) sentence 5
   (D) sentence 6

4. How should the underlined portion of sentence 5 in Paragraph B be rewritten?
   (A) No rewriting is necessary. The sentence is correct as it is.
   (B) graffiti since graffiti
   (C) graffiti, since graffiti
   (D) graffiti, although graffiti

For questions 5–8, choose the correct form of the verbs to enter in the space.

5. Yesterday, Dionne _____ to her aunt's house.
   - (A) go
   - (B) went
   - (C) goes
   - (D) gone

6. Your hair _____ great.
   - (A) look
   - (B) looking
   - (C) looks
   - (D) are looking

7. The first woman in space _____ Valentina Tereshkova in 1963.
   - (A) was
   - (B) been
   - (C) be
   - (D) were

8. I _____ that movie we saw last night.
   - (A) hated
   - (B) been hating
   - (C) been hated
   - (D) hates

Read the following paragraph and answer questions 9–11.

(1) We are probably all familiar with the usual fried foods. (2) Chicken, French fries, fish, and onion rings. (3) But have you ever heard of fried butter? (4) What about fried ice cream? (5) People who love to create have come up with deep-fried combinations that most of us never dreamt of. (6) For example, fried pickles, a southern delicacy, have recently become popular in other areas of the country as well. (7) Fried butter is gooey and delicious, and fried cookies will satisfy any sweet tooth. (8) Perhaps the most unusual recipe is for fried Coke, invented by Abel Gonzales of Texas. (9) Where can you find this concoction and other deep-fried delicacies? (10) You cannot do better than to head for the nearest State Fair. (11) Happy eating!

9. What is the topic sentence of the above paragraph?
   - (A) sentence 1
   - (B) sentence 5
   - (C) sentence 10
   - (D) sentence 11

10. Which of the following would be the best topic sentence for a paragraph opposing the piece above?
    (A) A regular diet of fried and fatty foods can lead to serious health problems.
    (B) The State Fair is a great place for family fun.
    (C) Fried cookies do not have as much fat as a fried candy bar.
    (D) Oranges would not taste good fried.

11. What is the error in sentence 2?
    (A) There is nothing wrong with it; it is correct.
    (B) It is a fragment. There is no subject or verb.
    (C) "Onion" is misspelled.
    (D) It is a comma splice.

12. In a science paragraph on electric light, Lydia used the following four sentences as support. Which two sentences contain the least amount of detail?

    A. Thomas Edison began researching how to improve the lightbulb in 1878.
    B. Some light bulbs last longer than others.
    C. The government prohibits putting CFL bulbs in the trash because of dangerous materials they contain.
    D. Fluorescent lights are annoying.

    (A) A and B
    (B) B and D
    (C) A and C
    (C) B and C

13. Consider the following three support sentences.

    A. Bats fly at night by using echolocation, a sort of biological radar.
    B. Contrary to their "vampire" reputations, many bats live mostly on fruit.
    C. In spite of their small size and sometimes cute appearance, bats are wild and do not make good pets.

    What is the best topic sentence for these three details?
    (A) Bats are fascinating, surprising creatures.
    (B) Bats are always dangerous to humans.
    (C) Bats are a good surprise birthday gift.
    (D) Bats are disgusting.

Read the following paragraphs and answer questions 14–17.

Paragraph A

Going to the dentist is a nightmare. I get so nervous I often can't sleep for days before. Thus I am already jittery and overtired before I even walk into the dental office. The fact that I usually have to wait doesn't help. It gives me time to imagine all sorts of horrors. As soon as I lay back in the dentist's chair he shines that bright light in my eyes. He scrapes, pokes, and stretches my mouth until everything is sore. I then get to sit under a heavy apron while the dental hygienist goes out of the room to avoid the lethal doses of radiation she is aiming at me. If I have a cavity, then I hear the happy news that I will need to come back to face THE DRILL. Finally, the hygienist comes back to scold me because I do not floss three times a day. I hate the dentist.

Paragraph B

Dr. Jones is the best dentist I have ever visited. His staff is efficient and pleasant. They make sure to send me reminder notices and call me the day before my appointment. There is never a long wait. Dr. Jones takes the time to talk to me and ask questions about any problems I might be having. He is a nice man who jokes a lot, but he is also very good at his job. When he examines my teeth and gums, he is gentle. My mouth is never sore afterwards. He and his hygienist always explain what they are about to do, so there are no unpleasant surprises! When the hygienist does my X-ray, she reminds me that the radiation will not hurt me. If the dentist finds I will need a tooth drilled, I am not upset. Even when he has to give me a shot to fill a cavity, he numbs the spot first. Finally, the hygienist reminds me (nicely) to floss and asks if I have any questions. I love my dentist!

14. Organizing a paragraph in time order is called **chronological** order. Which of the above paragraphs is organized in chronological order?
    (A) Paragraph A
    (B) Paragraph B
    (C) both
    (D) neither

15. Which of the sentences below can be used as support for this topic sentence?

    That website posts nothing but lies.

    (A) They correctly predicted the winner of last month's election.
    (B) They exposed an embezzler who was later convicted.
    (C) They predicted the end of the world last July.
    (D) They suggested drinking 6 glasses of water a day.

16. Which of the sentences below would be off topic in a paragraph on global warming?
    (A) Arctic ice floes are shrinking.
    (B) Rising carbon levels are affecting the ozone level.
    (C) The Polar Bear has an insulating layer of fat to adapt to its environment.
    (D) Rising global temperatures will change coastlines.

17. Which of the following modifications to the sentence below would create a sentence structure error?

I want to buy a new phone, but I can't afford it.

(A) Leave the sentence as it is.
(B) Take out the comma.
(C) Change the comma to a period and remove the word "but."
(D) Rewrite the sentence as "I can't afford to buy a new phone."

18. A compound sentence consists of
(A) two dependent clauses
(B) two independent clauses
(C) one independent and one dependent clause
(D) one independent clause

Read the following paragraph and answer question 19.

People identify themselves by where they live and where their ancestors lived in the past. This means that one person may answer to multiple identifiers. Betty Flynn can be a Bostonian, a Bay Stater, a New Englander, a Northerner, and an American. That's without even considering her ancestry. Betty considers herself Irish-American, Italian-American, and German-American. Henry Wong lives in Houston. That means he is a Houstonian and also a Texan. But Henry was born in San Francisco, so he also identifies as a native Californian. His family came to the U.S. over 150 years ago, but they refer to themselves as Chinese-American. New York is full of New Yorkers, and the Midwest is full of Midwesterners. Place matters to people.

19. Which of the following sentences would not support the above paragraph's position?
(A) People from Trenton, NJ call themselves Trentonians.
(B) Puerto Ricans are American citizens.
(C) People from Connecticut are called Nutmeggers.
(D) People whose ancestors lived in North America call themselves Native Americans.

For questions 20–23, match the subject on the left with the correct predicate on the right.

____ 20. Martha   (A) went to his friend's softball game.

____ 21. We   (B) goes to her choir practice every Thursday.

____ 22. I   (C) are almost finished our lunch.

____ 23. Jonathan   (D) am thinking of a number between 1 and 10.

Read the following paragraph and answer questions 24–26.

(1) Children have a creative sense of color. (2) My daughter loves to draw and paint, she will keep herself amused all day. (3) "Look!" she says to me. (4) I look. (5) I see purple horses. (6) Naturally, they have purple and gold tails. (7) There are green people driving in orange cars. (8) A pink sun shines over everything. (9) She likes to play with her musical toys too. (10) Sometimes I wish I could see the world the way she does.

24. Which of the following is the topic sentence for the paragraph?
    (A) sentence 1
    (B) sentence 3
    (C) sentence 7
    (D) sentence 10

25. Which sentence is off topic?
    (A) sentence 1
    (B) sentence 3
    (C) sentence 7
    (D) sentence 9

26. Sentence 2 is a comma splice. Which of the following is the best way to fix it?
    (A) Change the comma into a period.
    (B) Put the coordinating conjunction "but" after the comma.
    (C) Put the coordinating conjunction "and" after the comma.
    (D) Put another comma after the word "draw."

27. Which of the following sentences is a restatement of the following sentence?

    All work and no play makes Jack a dull boy.

    (A) Hard work will get you where you want to go.
    (B) Work and recreation should be balanced.
    (C) People who don't work are lazy.
    (D) People who work hard are usually interesting.

28. Which of the following dependent words best completes this sentence:

    _____ we go to the ice cream parlor, I always get mint chocolate chip.

    (A) Because
    (B) Whenever
    (C) Although
    (D) Even though

29. Which of the choices is the best way to correct the following sentence:

    I was awarded a scholarship, so I will be able to afford college!

    (A) It is correct as it is.
    (B) Change "so" to "but."
    (C) Remove "so."
    (D) Change "will be able" to "will not be able."

For questions 30–32, choose the correct verb form and tense that agrees with the subject.

30. Money_____a blessing if used wisely.
    (A) am
    (B) is
    (C) are
    (D) were

31. Our class _____ on a trip every year.
    (A) goes
    (B) go
    (C) am going
    (D) have gone

32. My favorite singer_____in town last summer.
    (A) were
    (B) been
    (C) was
    (D) will be

For 33–37, pick the subject that agrees with the verb in the sentence.

33. _____ really like that pizza place.
    (A) Terry
    (B) She
    (C) We
    (D) Susan

34. _____ needs a truck to get that home.
    (A) Johnson
    (B) We
    (C) You
    (D) Terry and Susan

35. _____ was the tallest girl in the class.
    (A) You
    (B) Barry and Gordon
    (C) Marianne
    (D) They

36. _____ are planning on ordering takeout tonight.
    (A) He
    (B) My Dad
    (C) I
    (D) They

37. _____ prefer to swim in a heated pool.
    (A) I
    (B) He
    (C) She
    (D) Lydia

Use the passages below to answer questions 38–50.

Learn to Love School Uniforms

School uniforms should be mandatory across the United States. Students are in school to learn, and removing the distraction of what others are wearing would keep the focus on school work. A review of school data from 2012 shows that children that year performed better in districts requiring uniforms. School uniforms help to make schools safer. "When all of the students are dressed the same, it is easy to see when someone does not belong there," says state police chief Laura Brown. Requiring school uniforms also helps to reduce peer pressure and save families money. When everyone has on the same clothing, the desire and cost to keep up with the latest fashions in school are erased.

—Janice Rodgers, *www.educationtoday.org*

Uniforms Are a Bad Idea

School uniforms are un-American! The Bill of Rights guarantees freedom of speech, and that should cover what you wear no matter what. Plus, the 1940 issue of *Student Life* magazine talks all about how much students hate them. In that issue, twenty students are interviewed and all of them are against wearing uniforms at school. School uniforms just look dumb, and everybody knows that. Uniforms are a bad idea and should not be used in schools.

—*Theawesomestudent.blog.com*

38. What is the position of the paragraph titled "Learn to Love School Uniforms?" Write down the entire sentence that gives the author's thesis statement.

39. What is the position of the paragraph titled "Uniforms Are a Bad Idea?" Write down the entire sentence that gives the author's thesis statement.

40. What are two pieces of evidence used by the author of "Learn to Love School Uniforms"?

    1. _____

    2. _____

41. What are two pieces of evidence used by the author of "Uniforms Are a Bad Idea?"

    1. _____

    2. _____

42. What makes the quote by the state police chief valid to use as evidence?
    (A) It is irrelevant.
    (B) It is expert testimony.
    (C) It comes from a trusted website.
    (D) It was obtained with a warrant.

43. Why can the issue of *Student Life* magazine be considered invalid in supporting "Uniforms Are a Bad Idea?"
    (A) It is hearsay.
    (B) It comes from a trusted government source
    (C) The information is too out of date to be useful
    (D) It was obtained without a warrant

44. Which sentence is an example of hearsay?
    (A) School uniforms just look dumb, and everybody knows that.
    (B) Plus, the 1940 issue of *Student Life* magazine talks all about how much students hate them.
    (C) A review of school data from 2012 shows that children that year performed better in districts requiring uniforms.
    (D) None of the above

45. Which statement is an acceptable paraphrase of "Airplanes travel over 500 miles per hour, and approximately eight million people fly every day."
    (A) Flying on an airplane is safer now than at any time in history.
    (B) Airplanes are the best form of transportation.
    (C) More people should take public transportation.
    (D) Millions of people ride on an airplane annually, and these planes speed through the air at hundreds of miles per hour.

46. Paraphrase the following sentences in your own words:

"School uniforms are un-American! The Bill of Rights guarantees freedom of speech, and that should cover what you wear no matter what."

_____

_____

_____

_____

47. Paraphrase the following sentences in your own words:

"Requiring school uniforms also helps to reduce peer pressure and save families money. When everyone has on the same clothing, the desire and cost to keep up with the latest fashions in school are erased."

_____

_____

_____

_____

Use the following writing prompt to answer questions 48–50.

> The paragraphs on page 95 present different positions on the issue of uniforms in schools.
>
> In your response, analyze both articles to determine which position is better supported. Use specific evidence from both articles in your response.

48. What is your position? Write your thesis statement below.

_____

_____

_____

_____

49. Fill in the Argument Analysis Essay Template

1. Thesis (which side you are choosing):

_____

_____

2. Evidence A:

_____

_____

3. Bridge (why that evidence is important):

_____

_____

4. Evidence B:

_____

_____

5. Bridge (why that evidence is important):

_____

_____

6. Evidence C:

_____

_____

7. Bridge (why that evidence is important):

_____

_____

50. Compose your response:

_____

_____

_____

_____

_____

_____

_____

_____

_____

_____

POSTTEST EVALUATION CHART

After checking your answers on the following pages, circle the number of the questions you got correct in Column B. Record the total number of correct questions for each skill in Column C. Column D gives you the number of correct questions you need to answer correctly to indicate that you have a good understanding of the skill. If you got fewer correct answers than shown in Column D, go back and review the pages shown in Column E. Using this analysis will allow you to focus on your challenges and use your study time more effectively.

A		B	C	D	E
Skill Area		Questions	Number of Correct Answers	Number Correct to Show a Good Understanding	Pages to Study
Sentence Structure	Subjects and Predicates	2, 11, 20, 21, 22, 23	____/6	4	11–15
	Compound Sentences	17, 18, 19, 29	____/4	3	16–20
	Complex Sentences	4, 26, 28	____/3	2	20–25
	Verb Forms and Tenses	5, 6, 7, 8, 30, 31, 32	____/7	5	25–29
	Subject–Verb Agreement	31, 32, 33, 34, 35	____/5	3	29–33
Paragraph Organization	Paragraph Structure	3, 14, 25	____/3	2	43–45
	Topic Sentences	9, 10, 13, 24	____/4	3	45–47
	Development and Details	12, 15, 16	____/3	2	48–51
	Repetition and Restatement	1, 27	____/2	2	52–54
Argument Analysis	Determine What Positions Are Presented	38, 39	____/2	2	61–62
	Analyzing Evidence	40–45	____/6	5	63–68
	Creating an Argument	48–50	____/3	2	69–71
	Providing/Citing Evidence	46, 47			72–74
TOTAL			____/50		

If you have correctly answered more than the number of questions in the Column D TOTAL, you are ready for Higher-Level Writing!

POSTTEST ANSWER EXPLANATIONS

1. **(B)** *Paragraph B.* For example, sentence 7 repeats sentence 3.
2. **(C)** *Sentence 7 in Paragraph A and Sentence 3 in Paragraph B.* Both sentences are missing a subject.
3. **(B)** *Sentence 4*
4. **(B)** *graffiti since graffiti.* (C) When the dependent clause comes second, no comma is needed. (D) The word "although" confuses the sense of the whole sentence.
5. **(B)** *went*
6. **(C)** *looks*
7. **(A)** *was*
8. **(A)** *hated*
9. **(B)** *Sentence 5* expresses the main idea.
10. **(A)** *A regular diet of fried and fatty foods can lead to serious health problems.* This sentence emphasizes the problems of fried foods rather than their fun and deliciousness.
11. **(B)** *It is a fragment. There is no subject or verb.*
12. **(B)** *B and D* (A) contains details of names and dates. (C) contains details of reasoning. (B) and (D) have neither.
13. **(A)** *Bats are fascinating, surprising creatures.* This fits the supporting details. (B) and (C) are untrue. (D) is a matter of taste.
14. **(C)** *Both.* Both paragraphs describe one visit from beginning to end.
15. **(C)** *They predicted the end of the world last July.* This is the only choice that is demonstrably a lie.
16. **(C)** *The Polar Bear has an insulating layer of fat to adapt to its environment.* This is not a response to global warming, but an adaptation to existing conditions.
17. **(B)** *Take out the comma.* (A) The sentence is correct. (C) and (D) change the existing sentence to another, equally correct sentence.
18. **(B)** *Two independent clauses.* See the definition of a compound sentence in Chapter 1, Lesson 2.
19. **(B)** *Puerto Ricans are American citizens.* This choice concerns the rights and responsibilities of Puerto Ricans, not what they call themselves.
20. **(B)**
21. **(C)**
22. **(D)**
23. **(A)**
24. **(A)** *Sentence 1.* This sentence expresses the main idea and attitude. The others provide specific details.
25. **(D)** *Sentence 9.* The paragraph is about art and color, not music.
26. **(A)** *Change the comma into a period.* This creates two separate correct sentences.
27. **(B)** *Work and recreation should be balanced.* (A), (C) and (D) stress the advantages of hard work. The sentence stresses the advantages of having leisure time.
28. **(B)** *Whenever.*
29. **(A)** *It is correct as it is.* (B) This option changes the meaning but does not correct anything. (C) makes the sentence a comma splice. (D) makes the meaning nonsensical.
30. **(B)** *is*
31. **(A)** *goes*
32. **(C)** *was*

33. **(C)** *We*

34. **(A)** *Johnson*

35. **(C)** *Marianne*

36. **(D)** *They*

37. **(A)** *I*

38. School uniforms should be mandatory across the United States.

39. Uniforms are a bad idea and should not be used in schools.

40. Possible answers include

    1. Uniforms eliminate distractions

    2. school data from 2012

    3. Quote from police chief on safety

    4. uniforms are cheaper and reduce peer pressure

41. Possible answers include

    1. Clothes could be protected as free speech

    2. *Student Life* magazine article

    3. Uniforms look bad

42. **(B)** The police chief would be considered an expert on safety, so it is not irrelevant.

43. **(C)** The issue of *Student Life* is from 1940, and that is far too long ago to be relevant to a modern issue.

44. **(A)** Hearsay evidence sounds convincing by making it seem like popular knowledge or common sense. However, hearsay cannot be proved. The words "everybody knows" signals that it is hearsay.

45. **(D)** A paraphrase accurately restates the information without quoting it directly. The other answers do not restate the information, but instead change the meaning of the sentence.

46. An acceptable answer will restate the sentences without quoting directly. Example: People should be able to wear whatever they want in school because the Bill of Rights gives freedom of speech. Clothes should be considered as speech, and anything else is the opposite of American values.

47. An acceptable answer will restate the sentences without quoting directly. Example: Students often feel the need to stay in style by buying trendy clothing, but this can be very expensive. Families would pay less for school clothes if uniforms were standard.

48. Answers will very, but must clearly state which article is better supported. Example: The paragraph titled "Learn to Love School Uniforms" by Janice Rodgers is the best supported article.

    Although "Learn to Love School Uniforms" makes good points, the paragraph titled "Uniforms Are a Bad Idea" is better supported.

49. Answers will vary depending on the thesis and evidence used. Here is one possible answer:

    Fill in the Analyzing Argument Essay Template

    Thesis (which side you are choosing): The paragraph titled "Learn to Love School Uniforms" by Janice Rodgers is the best supported article.

    1. Evidence A: School data shows that children perform better in districts with uniforms

    2. Bridge (why that evidence is important): Clothes can have an effect on learning, it's not just style.

    3. Evidence B: Quote from police chief

4. Bridge (why that evidence is important): This is expert testimony from someone who knows firsthand about school safety.

5. Evidence C: School uniforms look dumb, everybody knows that—irrelevant

6. Bridge (why that evidence is important): Hearsay weakens the argument of the opposing side.

50. Essays will vary by student. This is just one example:

The paragraph titled "Learn to Love School Uniforms" by Janice Rodgers is the best supported article. Ms. Rodgers uses school data to prove that uniforms improve student performance. This is significant because it shows that uniforms are not just a fashion choice, but can have a positive impact on learning. Next, the article quotes a police chief who states that uniforms make schools safer. This is expert testimony from someone who knows firsthand about school safety. Finally, the opposing article resorts to hearsay claiming that "uniforms just look dumb, and everybody knows that." Weak evidence like that does not support the argument. Therefore, "Learn to Love School Uniforms" is the best supported paragraph.

UNIT 1: WRITING

UNIT 2

Mathematics

Mathematics Pretest

The math pretest has 27 questions. It is organized by groups of questions that follow the chapters in the math unit. You can use this test to get a sense of which areas you need to study.

Make sure you have at least 30 minutes of quiet time available to complete the test. Read each question carefully and do your best. However, *do not guess on these questions*. If you don't know how to work a problem, simply skip it and go on to the next one. The purpose of this test is to find out what areas you need to work on, and random guessing might throw you off course.

Once you have finished, check your answers on pages 116–117. Then, complete the pretest evaluation chart on page 114 by circling the number of each question you missed. This way you can easily see your strengths and weaknesses as well as where information on each question you missed is located in the book.

If you score very well on the pretest, that is a great sign that you have a solid math foundation. Still, make sure to check out the end-of-chapter questions for each topic. These pages will include more problems for you to practice. You'll want to make sure your skills are sharp before moving on to the next section.

Do not use a calculator for questions 1 through 20.

Whole Numbers

1. $4\overline{)368}$

2. Rewrite the number 45,379 by switching the tens digit with the thousands digit to create a new number.

3. This question has three parts.
   Round the number 4,829

   (A) To the nearest ten: _____

   (B) To the nearest hundred: _____

   (C) To the nearest thousand: _____

Understanding Word Problems

4. Gino makes $9 an hour at his job. He always works 40 hours a week. Today he is working 6 hours, and tomorrow he is working for 10 hours. How many hours does he have left to work this week?

5. Sweaters that normally cost $50 are on sale for $10 off. At the same store, a pair of shorts costs $15 and socks are $5. How much will you spend if you buy two pairs of socks, one pair of shorts, and two sweaters?

Decimals

6. Rewrite the following number 4.0739 by switching the tenths digit with the thousandths digit to create a new number.

7. This question has three parts.
   Round the number .6291

   (A) To the nearest tenth: _____

   (B) To the nearest hundredth: _____

   (C) To the nearest thousandth: _____

8.   .42
     $\underline{\times\ .15}$

9. Estimate to find the answer. If you spend $115 on bills, $565 on rent, and $250 on food, approximately how much did you spend?
   (A) $730
   (B) $800
   (C) $830
   (D) $1,000

Fractions

10. Put the following fractions in order from highest to lowest:

$$\frac{1}{5},\ \frac{1}{10},\ \frac{2}{5},\ \frac{1}{2},\ \frac{4}{5},\ \frac{9}{10}$$

___, ___, ___, ___, ___, ___,

11. Convert the following mixed number to an improper fraction: $3\frac{3}{4}$

12. $\frac{3}{4} + \frac{1}{2} =$

13. Reduce the following fractions to lowest terms:

$\frac{4}{8} = $ ___ $\frac{4}{16} = $ ___ $\frac{3}{9} = $ ___

Ratios and Proportions

14. Last month it rained 16 out of 30 days. Write a ratio comparing rainy days to non-rainy days.

15. Solve the following proportion:

$$\frac{7}{2} + \frac{?}{6} =$$

16. Jan's map shows that the scale is one inch equals 50 miles. If Capital City is seven inches away on the map, how far away is Capital City in real life?

17. A recipe calls for two lemons and three cups of sugar for every dozen cookies. If we increase the recipe to use six lemons, how many cups of sugar will we need?

Percentages

18. Rewrite the fraction $\frac{1}{4}$ to decimal and percent.

19. What is 10% of 90?

20. A group of coworkers went out for lunch to celebrate a birthday party. If the bill before the tip was $80, how much will the final bill be after a 15% tip is added?

You may use a calculator for questions 21 through 27.

21. A recipe calls for $1\frac{1}{3}$ cups of flour to make a cake.

    If you are going to make four cakes, how many cups of flour will you need?

Use the chart below to answer question 22.

Survey of 500 People

Unemployed
10%

Employed
Full Time
52%

Employed
Part Time
38%

22. According to the survey, how many people are employed full time? _____

Use the chart below to answer question 23.

Morning and Afternoon Customer Totals by Store

Store Name	A.M.	P.M.
Super Mart	230	300
Good Buys	150	210
Right Price	0	350
Shop Saver	275	220

23. How many more customers went to Shop Saver in the morning than to Good Buys in the afternoon? _____

24. Plot the point (–2,3) on the diagram below.

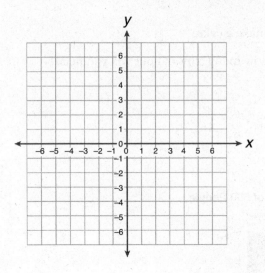

Use the graph below to answer question 25.

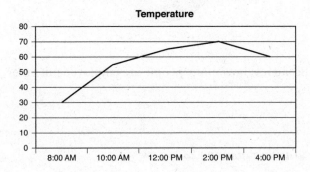

25. Between what two hours did the greatest increase in temperature occur?

  (A) 8:00–10:00

  (B) 10:00–12:00

  (C) 12:00–2:00

  (D) 2:00–4:00

Use the information below to answer questions 26 and 27.

Elliott owns a restaurant, and he wrote down every time someone ordered a large anchovy pizza last week.

> Monday: 5
> Tuesday: 2
> Wednesday: 5
> Thursday: 4
> Friday: 4

26. What is the average number of large anchovy pizzas ordered each day?
    (A) 2
    (B) 3
    (C) 4
    (D) 5

27. Use the anchovy pizza data for the week to create a dot plot. Place an X over each number as many times as you need.

```
   ────────────────────────────────
    1      2      3      4      5
```

PRETEST EVALUATION CHART

After checking your answers on the following pages, circle the numbers of the questions you got correct in Column B. Record the total number of correct questions for each skill in Column C. Column D gives you the number of correct questions you need to answer correctly to indicate you have a good understanding of the skill. If you got fewer correct answers than shown in Column D, study the pages shown in Column E. Using this analysis will allow you to focus on your challenges and use your study time more effectively.

A Skill Area		B Questions	C Number of Correct Answers	D Number Correct to Show a Good Understanding	E Pages to Study
Whole Numbers	Division	1			131-134
	Place Value	2			119-121
	Rounding	3			135-139
	Total		____ /3	3	
Understand Word Problems	Unnecessary Information	4			150-151
	Multistep	5			153-155
	Total		____ /2	2	
Decimals	Place Value	6			163-165
	Rounding	7			166-168
	Multiplication	8			171-173
	Estimation	9			166-168
	Total		____ /4	4	
Fractions	Ordering	10			192
	Improper	11			194-197
	Addition	12			198-202
	Reducing	13			189-191
	Total		____ /4	3	
Ratios and Proportions	Write a Ratio	14			219
	Solve Proportion	15			223-224
	Map Scale	16			221
	Word Problem	17			224-231
	Total		____ /4	3	

A		B	C	D	E
Skill Area		Questions	Number of Correct Answers	Number Correct to Show a Good Understanding	Pages to Study
Percentages	Percent Conversion	18			248–252
	Find %	19			256–261
	% Word Problem	20			262–264
	Total		___ /3	3	
Calculator Use Fractions	Fraction multiplication	21	___ /1	1	279–280
Graphic Materials	Pie Chart	22			307–311
	Table	23			304–306
	Coordinate Plane	24			314–317
	Line Graph	25			297–304
	Dot Plot	26			312–313
	Total		___ /6	5	
Mean, Median, Mode	Average	27	___ /1	1	285–287
	Total		___ /1	1	
TOTAL			___ /27	24	

If you answered enough of the questions in Column D for a skill, you know enough about that skill already. You may want to do the Review at the end of these skill areas as a check.

To use your study time wisely, improve your skills in the other areas by studying the pages noted in Column E.

UNIT 2: MATHEMATICS

PRETEST ANSWER EXPLANATIONS

1. 92

2. 47,359

3. (A) Ten: 4,830
(B) Hundred: 4,800
(C) Thousand: 5,000

4. 40 − 16 = 24 hours left to work.

5. **$105.** Two pairs of socks cost $10, one pair of shorts cost $15, and two sweaters cost $80.

6. 4.3709

7. (A) Tenth: .6
(B) Hundredth: .63
(C) Thousandth: .629

8. .063

9. **(D)** 100 + 600 + 300

10. $\dfrac{9}{10}, \dfrac{4}{5}, \dfrac{1}{2}, \dfrac{2}{5}, \dfrac{1}{10}$

11. 4 × 3 = 12. 12 + 3 = 15. This will be the top number (numerator)

$\dfrac{15}{4}$ The bottom number (denominator)

12. $\dfrac{3}{4} + \dfrac{1}{2} = \dfrac{6}{8} + \dfrac{4}{8}$

$\dfrac{6}{8} + \dfrac{4}{8} = \dfrac{10}{8}$ or $1\dfrac{2}{8}$, or $1\dfrac{1}{4}$

13. $\dfrac{4}{8} \div \dfrac{4}{4} = \dfrac{1}{2}$ $\dfrac{4}{16} \div \dfrac{4}{4} = \dfrac{1}{4}$ $\dfrac{3}{9} \div \dfrac{3}{3} = \dfrac{1}{3}$

14. 16:14 or 8:7

15. 7 × 6 = 42
42 ÷ 2 = 21

16. $\dfrac{1}{50} = \dfrac{7}{?}$
50 × 7 = 350
350 ÷ 1 = 350 miles

17. $\dfrac{2}{3} = \dfrac{6}{?}$
6 × 3 = 18
18 ÷ 2 = 9 cups of sugar

18. $\dfrac{1}{4}$ = .25 = 25%

19. $90 \times .10 = 9$

20. $80 \times .15 = 12$
$80 + 12 = 92$

21. $5\dfrac{1}{3}$

22. **(260)** 52% of 500 is 260.
$500 \times .52 = 260$

23. **(65)** $275 - 210 = 65$

24.

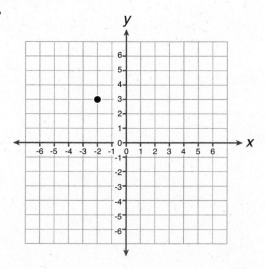

25. **(A)** To find the greatest increase, look for the steepest line on the graph.

26. **(C)** To find the average, first add up all of the numbers. $5 + 2 + 5 + 4 + 4 = 20$.
Then divide by how many numbers you added. $20 \div 5 = 4$.

27.

			X	X
	X		X	X
1	2	3	4	5

Whole Numbers

LESSON 1: PLACE VALUE

Imagine somebody dropped a box of toothpicks on the floor, and it is your job to pick them up and count them. You pick them up one at a time, and eventually you count 74. Wouldn't it have been easier if they were held together in groups of ten by rubber bands? Then you could quickly count seven groups of ten, plus four extra ones, for a total of 74. This is what place value does: it tells us the value of each number. 74 ones is the same thing as 7 tens and 4 ones.

Place Value Chart

Billions	Hundred-millions	Ten-millions	Millions	Hundred-thousands	Ten-thousands	Thousands	Hundreds	Tens	Ones
								7	4

We use place value every day. If your paycheck was $200, would you rather have 200 one dollar bills, ten twenty dollar bills, or two one hundred dollar bills? Because of place value, they all equal the same thing; what matters is the place and order of the digits. *Your job is to make sure you know all of the place values on the above chart.*

Practice Exercises—Place Value

Write the place value of each underlined digit. The first two have been completed for you.

1. 3<u>7</u>   3 tens
2. 45<u>1</u>   1 ones
3. <u>1</u>,387   _____
4. 47,<u>9</u>58   _____
5. <u>7</u>4,958   _____
6. <u>3</u>,987,412   _____

7. 31,1<u>2</u>4   _____
8. 1<u>2</u>4,784,761   _____
9. 432,511,00<u>6</u>   _____
10. <u>6</u>11,354,870   _____
11. 47,<u>0</u>91   _____
12. <u>1</u>,234,567,890   _____

TIP

When you write large numbers, place a comma after every 3 digits. Start counting right to left. For example:
1,483
251,483
9,251,483

When you think of numbers, you are probably thinking of **whole numbers**. Whole numbers are digits like 7 or 112. They are called whole numbers because they don't contain decimals or fractions. When we read whole numbers out loud, we start from the left.

Write out each number in words. The first one has been completed for you.

1. 84,354   Eighty four thousand three hundred fifty four
2. 954   _____
3. 6,212   _____
4. 45,078   _____
5. 1,000,783   _____
6. 245,698,232   _____
7. 5,634,512,734   _____

Write out each number using digits. The first one has been completed for you.

1. Four hundred thousand, nine hundred ninety nine   400,999
2. Seven hundred twelve   _____
3. Thirty seven thousand, six hundred twenty eight   _____
4. Ten million, three hundred forty six thousand, one hundred sixteen   _____
5. Seventy seven million, one hundred thousand, three hundred eleven   _____

Identify the correct digit. The first one has been completed for you.

1. What is the tens digit in the number 312?   One
2. What is the ten thousands digit in 536,918?   _____
3. What is the millions digit in 24,357,547?   _____
4. What is the hundred thousands digit in 5,897,035?   _____
5. What is the hundreds digit in 457,892?   _____

What new number is created when you switch place values? The first one has been completed for you.

1. 3,974   Switch the tens digit and the thousands digit.   7,934

2. 12,576   Switch the ones digit and the ten thousands digit.   _____

3. 452,756   Switch the thousands digit and the hundred thousands digit. _____

4. 3,798,015   Switch the ten thousands digit with the millions digit. _____

5. 56,983,512 Switch the hundreds digit with the ten millions digit. _____

LESSON 2: ADDING AND SUBTRACTING

Adding and subtracting are two basic math operations that we all use regularly. However, since a calculator is not allowed on some math tests, we are going to review the basics. The section will also provide you with different techniques to help you "see" math problems better. There is often more than one way to work a problem. Getting better at "seeing" math will help you with general number sense, and on the test as well.

Using a Number Line

When we add we are combining numbers to create a new total. Let's use the number line below to visualize addition.

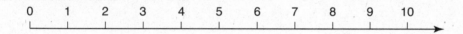

If we start with two apples and then add five more, we are moving five spaces to the right on the number line.

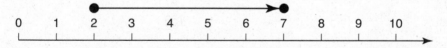

On the number line below, draw what 5 + 2 looks like.

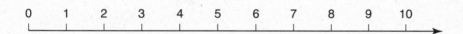

Did you notice how on the two number lines above, 2 + 5 and 5 + 2 give the same answer? With addition, the order of the numbers does not matter. Using number lines is a great way to learn addition, but it's not practical with large numbers.

Rules for Addition

1. Always line the numbers up to the right. Make sure to line up the place values so that ones are above ones, tens are above tens, etc.

214 + 53 should be written

$$
\begin{array}{r}
214 \\
+53 \\
\end{array}
$$

2. Start adding each column from the right.

$$
\begin{array}{r}
214 \\
+53 \\
\hline
267 \\
\end{array}
$$

3. Remember to CARRY if one column adds up to 10 or more.

$$
\begin{array}{r}
14 \\
+8 \\
\hline
\end{array}
$$

(1) → Carried Digit

$$
\begin{array}{r}
14 \\
+8 \\
\hline
2 \\
\end{array}
$$

(1)
$$
\begin{array}{r}
14 \\
+8 \\
\hline
22 \\
\end{array}
$$

> Since 4 + 8 = 12, we can't fit it in our answer. Only digits 1–9 will fit.
>
> Anything larger, write down the ones digit and "carry" the tens digit above the tens column.
>
> Do the same to carry the tens column to the hundreds, etc.

Practice Exercises—Rules for Addition

Complete the following without a calculator.

1.
$$
\begin{array}{r}
12 \\
+9 \\
\hline
\end{array}
$$

3.
$$
\begin{array}{r}
47 \\
+55 \\
\hline
\end{array}
$$

2.
$$
\begin{array}{r}
593 \\
+61 \\
\hline
\end{array}
$$

4.
$$
\begin{array}{r}
180 \\
+197 \\
\hline
\end{array}
$$

Rewrite the following problems vertically then solve.

5. 39 + 118

7. 123 + 456 + 789

6. 945 + 55

8. 8 + 12 + 200

9. On Monday, Janice made 37 sandwiches at her job. On Wednesday, she made 41 sandwiches, and on Friday, she made 60. How many total sandwiches did she made that week?

10. Eric scored 15 points in game one. In the second game he played really well and scored five more points than he did in game one. How many points did he score in the two games?

Grouping in Addition

TIP

When grouping, look for pairs of numbers that add up to 10, 20, 30, etc. Sums that end in zero are easier to use!

Because the order in which we add numbers doesn't matter, sometimes it can be easier to regroup the numbers in a problem. For example, which would be easier to solve:

A. 17 + 26 + 3 + 10 + 4
B. 20 + 30 + 10

Both of these problems equal the same amount, but B is much easier to solve. Here's how it works.

17 + 26 is difficult to do in your head. 17 + 3 is much easier.

$\widehat{17}$ + 26 + $\widehat{3}$ + 10 + 4   17 + 3 = 20

Next, look to see if there's a number that would combine easily with 26.

17 + $\widehat{26}$ + 3 + 10 + $\widehat{4}$ 26 + 4 = 30

So, after regrouping the problem we are left with 20 + 30 + 10.

Practice Exercises—Grouping in Addition

Circle numbers that could be regrouped to make an easier addition problem.

1. 9 + 15 + 1

2. 13 + 18 + 7

3. 21 + 5 + 18 + 15

4. 94 + 11 + 6 + 29

5. 108 + 12 + 77 + 3

6. 7 + 16 + 14 + 33

7. 12 + 23 + 34 + 46 + 57 + 68

Rewrite the above problems after grouping numbers, then solve. The first one has been done for you.

1. 10 + 15 = 25 _____

2. _____

3. _____

4. _____

5. _____

6. _____

7. _____

Subtraction

Subtracting is the opposite of adding. When we subtract we move to the left on the number line. For example, 8 – 5 looks like:

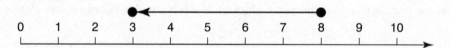

On the number line below, draw what 6 – 2 looks like.

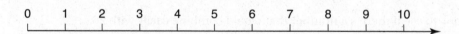

On the number line below, now draw what 2 – 6 looks like.

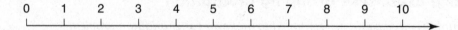

Notice how that doesn't work? That's because unlike addition, *the order of numbers in subtraction is important.* You will not get the correct answer if you do not subtract in the correct order.

Rules for Subtraction

1. Always line the numbers up to the right. Make sure to line up the place values so that ones are above ones, tens are above tens, etc.

$$\begin{array}{r} 548 \\ -\,37 \end{array}$$
548 – 37 should be written

2. Start subtracting each column from the right.

$$\begin{array}{r} 548 \\ -\,37 \\ \hline 511 \end{array}$$

3. If the bottom number is larger from the top, then you must "borrow" from the column to the left.

$$\begin{array}{r} 23 \\ -\,17 \end{array}$$

Since 7 is larger than 3, we must borrow from the column on the left.

A.
$$\begin{array}{r} {}^{1}2\!\!\!/3 \\ -17 \end{array}$$

B.
$$\begin{array}{r} {}^{1}2\overset{1}{\!\!\!/}3 \\ -17 \end{array}$$
Since 13 is larger than 7, we can subtract

$$\begin{array}{r} {}^{1}2\overset{1}{\!\!\!/}3 \\ -17 \\ \hline 06 \end{array}$$
Since 13 is larger than 7, we can subtract

> **When borrowing:**
>
> A. **Cross out the number in the tens column. Write one less than that number above the tens.**
> B. **Add a one in front of the ones column.**
> C. **Do the same to borrow from the hundreds column, etc.**

Practice Exercises—Subtraction

Complete the following without a calculator.

1.	2.	3.	4.	5.
78	398	9,418	301	65
– 23	– 361	– 5,326	– 212	– 47

Rewrite the problems vertically, then solve.

6. 2,048 – 1,123

7. 546 – 213

8. 798 – 699

9. 46 – 9

10. 825 – 336

11. Gary started the day with $1,200. After work he stopped by the store and bought $50 of groceries. On his way home he paid his rent of $600. Finally, Gary paid his phone bill of $75 for the month. How much money does Gary have at the end of the day?

12. Rodrigo is stocking shelves at his job. At the beginning of his shift there are 200 loaves of bread on the shelves. By lunch the store had sold 89 loaves of bread. By the time the store closes, another 52 loaves of bread were sold.

    How many loaves are left on the shelves? _____

    How many loaves will Rodrigo have to restock to have 200 loaves on the shelves again? _____

LESSON 3: MULTIPLYING AND DIVIDING

Multiplication

Multiplying is a short cut for addition. Let's say you need to count out $100. You could individually count one dollar bills, but you would need to do that one hundred times. Or, you could use five $20 bills. Which would be easier? It is much easier (and faster) to do 5×20 than it is to count to 100 by ones.

Here is another example. Let's say milk is on sale for $3 a gallon. Use the chart below to figure out how much you will spend.

Number of gallons	Money spent
1	$3
2	$6
4	
8	
10	

If you know your multiplication facts, you probably filled in the above chart very quickly. If you aren't so sure, you probably used scratch paper to add up 3 + 3 + 3 + 3 as many times as you needed to fill in the chart. However, since HSEs are timed tests, you will want to use multiplication to save time.

Now let's say that on your job your boss tells you to make two stacks of boxes with four boxes each. That would probably look something like this:

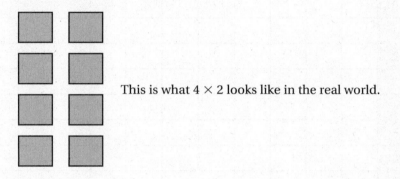

This is what 4×2 looks like in the real world.

Now let's say your boss changed his mind. Now he wants four stacks of boxes with two each. What would that look like? Draw it in the space below.

This is what 2×4 looks like in the real world.

Notice how there are eight boxes in each group? That's because *the order of numbers does not matter in multiplication.* You still have to put the boxes in the order your boss says, but in the world of math it doesn't matter because you will always get the same answer!

It has probably been a while since you've sat down and thought about the multiplication tables, so let's take a couple of minutes and see how much you remember. Don't cheat! You need to get a picture of what you need to work on.

Practice Exercises—Multiplication Table

Without a calculator, fill in the chart below. Only fill in the facts that you know; it is OK to leave some blank.

×	0	1	2	3	4	5	6	7	8	9	10
0											
1											
2											
3											
4											
5											
6											
7											
8											
9											
10											

KEEP IN MIND

1. It may seem like a lot to remember. But since 2 × 4 is the same as 4 × 2, you are really only learning half of the table. Once you know one, you know the other!
2. Anything times zero is zero. Anything times one is the same number.

HOW TO LEARN THE MULTIPLICATION TABLES

Did you have some blank spaces in the chart above? A lot of blank spaces? It's OK. What you want to do is make flash cards of the facts you don't know or weren't sure of. For example, on a note card write 7 × 8 on one side and then the answer, 56, on the back of the card. Do this for every blank fact on the chart. If you don't have note cards you can make some out of paper at home.

Now, plan on reviewing a set of those, like the 7s, during commercial breaks while you watch TV, on the bus, or whenever you have a couple of minutes to yourself. You don't need to find 30 minutes every day to work on this. But, if you can work on it for a few minutes a day, you'll be surprised how quickly it comes to you.

Also, don't feel like you can't pass your HSE test if you don't have every multiplication fact memorized. Doing so, though, will make things much easier for you. You want to be able to get the easier questions correct so that so you can spend more time on the more difficult questions.

Multiplying with Multiple Digits

1. Always line the numbers up to the right. Make sure to line up the place values so that ones are above ones, tens are above tens, etc.

12×8 should be written

$$\begin{array}{r} 12 \\ \times\ 8 \\ \hline \end{array}$$

2. Start from the right. Multiply the numbers in the top row by the eight. Like in addition, "carry" if an answer is greater than 10.

$$\begin{array}{r} 1\ \\ 12 \\ \times\ 8 \\ \hline 6 \end{array}$$ Since $2 \times 8 = 16$, write down the 6 and carry the 1.

$$\begin{array}{r} 1\ \\ 12 \\ \times\ 8 \\ \hline 96 \end{array}$$ $8 \times 1 = 8$, then add the 1 that was carried.

Example with three digits:

$$\begin{array}{r} 246 \\ \times\ 3 \\ \hline 8 \end{array}$$ $6 \times 3 = 18$, carry the 1.

$$\begin{array}{r} 1\,1\ \\ 246 \\ \times\ 3 \\ \hline 38 \end{array}$$ $3 \times 4 = 12$, add the 1 and it's 13. Write down the 3, carry the 1.

$$\begin{array}{r} 246 \\ \times\ 3 \\ \hline 738 \end{array}$$ 3×2 is 6, then add the 1 that was carried.

3. When multiplying two multiple digit numbers, like 21×14, repeat steps one and two. REMEMBER: When you multiply the tens column, you must put a zero in the ones column!

$$\begin{array}{r} 21 \\ \times\ 14 \\ \hline 84 \end{array}$$ $4 \times 1 = 4$, and $4 \times 2 = 8$

$$\begin{array}{r} 21 \\ \times\ 14 \\ \hline 84 \\ 0 \end{array}$$ Now, we will multiply the top row by one. But first, you must put a zero in the ones column under the 4.

$$\begin{array}{r} 21 \\ \times\ 14 \\ \hline 84 \\ 210 \end{array}$$ Now, multiply the top row. $1 \times 1 = 1$, and $1 \times 2 = 2$. Write those answers next to the zero.

$$\begin{array}{r} 21 \\ \times\ 14 \\ \hline 84 \\ 210 \\ \hline 294 \end{array}$$ Now add the 84 and the 210 for your final answer.

294 is the final answer.

Practice Exercises—Multiplying with Multiple Digits

Complete the following without a calculator.

1.   17
     $\times\,3$
	3. 598
	     $\times\,2$
		5. 91
		     $\times\,60$
			7. 900
			     $\times\,36$

9.   343
    $\times\,25$

2.   136
    $\times\,5$

4.   44
    $\times\,23$

6.   398
    $\times\,21$

8.   611
    $\times\,10$

10.   100
     $\times\,45$

Rewrite the following problems vertically then solve.

11. 12×9

14. 571×12

12. 202×6

15. 387×41

13. 35×34

16. During a typical day, Beverly works 8 hours. This week, her paycheck will include all of the hours she works during a 2-week period. If Beverly worked 9 days in this period, how many hours did she work?

17. Using the information from above, determine how much Beverly will be paid if she earns $9 an hour?

18. Each egg carton holds one dozen eggs. If you buy twelve cartons of eggs, how many total eggs will you have?

19. Jaquan recently bought a car that gets 35 miles per gallon of gasoline. If Jaquan fills his tank with 15 gallons of gas, how many miles can he drive?

20. Every night, Ray's ice cream stand sells 250 ice cream cones. If Ray keeps his stand open for 90 days in the summer, how many ice cream cones will he sell?

Division

When was the last time you sat down and did some long division? There will be questions on your test that ask you to divide without a calculator, so make sure you refresh your memory on the steps of long division.

Dividing is the opposite of multiplying. In the last lesson we began by creating two stacks of four boxes, for a total of eight boxes. With division, we start with the eight boxes, and divide them into two stacks. How many boxes are in each stack?

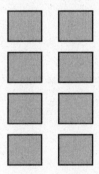

Clearly, there are four boxes in each stack, so eight divided by two is four. In the space below, draw what 12 boxes divided into four stacks would look like.

Rules of Long Division

Since multiplication and division are so closely related, you will find that doing long division is a lot easier if you know your multiplication tables. There are just four steps you need to know to work any division problem. To remember them, memorize this phrase: _Dirty Mice Smell Bad._ Sound funny? Good. Look at the first letters of each word and it will help you remember that the four steps are _division, multiplication, subtraction,_ and _bring down._

Start with this: 72 divided by 4. We could write it like this 72 ÷ 4, or like 4)‾72‾. That last one looks backwards, but writing it this way makes solving it easier.

STEP 1 **Divide** (_Dirty_)   4)72

How many times does 4 go into 7? It doesn't divide evenly, but 4 can go into seven once without going over. Write a 1 above the 7.

STEP 2 **Multiply** (_Mice_)

$$\begin{array}{r} 1 \\ 4\overline{)72} \\ 4 \end{array}$$

Now multiply the one and the four. Write the answer below the 7.

STEP 3 **Subtract** (_Smell_)

$$\begin{array}{r} 1 \\ 4\overline{)72} \\ -4 \end{array}$$

Now subtract the 4 from the 7. Write the answer below the 4.

STEP 4 **Bring Down** (_Bad_)

$$\begin{array}{r} 1 \\ 4\overline{)72} \\ -4\downarrow \\ \hline 32 \end{array}$$

Now bring down the next number, and start the process again with Step 1.

How many times does 4 go into 32? Eight. Write that number at the top.

$$\begin{array}{r} 18 \\ 4\overline{)72} \\ -4 \\ \hline 32 \end{array}$$

Now multiply 8 and 4, then subtract the answer.

$$\begin{array}{r} 18 \\ 4\overline{)72} \\ -4 \\ \hline 32 \\ -32 \end{array}$$

There are no other numbers to bring down so we are done! Since 32 minus 32 is zero, there is no remainder.

Division Example with Two Digits: Zeros

$$\begin{array}{r} 13 \\ 12\overline{)156} \\ -12 \\ \hline 36 \\ -36 \\ \hline 0 \end{array}$$

Use the same steps when dividing by a two-digit number.

$$\begin{array}{r} 60 \\ 6\overline{)360} \\ \underline{-36} \updownarrow \\ 00 \\ \underline{-00} \\ 0 \end{array}$$

Remember to always bring down the next digit, even if it is a zero.

Also, always check to make sure your answer is reasonable.

Since $36 \div 6 = 6$, $360 \div 6$ can't also be 6.

DID YOU KNOW?

Division problems are also written using the fraction bar.

For example, $10 \div 5 = 2$ can also be written as $\dfrac{10}{5} = 2$, or $24 \div 6$ is the same thing as $\dfrac{24}{6}$ and $\dfrac{35}{7}$ is the same thing as $35 \div 7$.

Practice Exercises—Long Division

Complete the following without a calculator.

1. $3\overline{)87}$
2. $8\overline{)168}$
3. $4\overline{)176}$
4. $7\overline{)4,907}$
5. $9\overline{)450}$
6. $15\overline{)630}$
7. $20\overline{)8,040}$
8. $2\overline{)796}$
9. $12\overline{)492}$
10. $12\overline{)4,920}$

Rewrite the following problems as long division problems, then solve.

11. $560 \div 8$

12. $164 \div 4$

13. $\dfrac{75}{7}$

14. $\dfrac{990}{30}$

15. $12,372 \div 12$

16. Last summer, Frank drove from New York to California. The distance was 2,400 miles. If Frank drove the same amount each day, and it took him 8 days to get to California, how many miles did he drive per day?
(THINK: Is your answer reasonable?)

17. After washing her clothes, Stephanie put all of her shirts into three drawers in her dresser equally. If she has 21 shirts, how many shirts did she put in each drawer?

18. Zach works at the bank as a teller. Every day he must count all of the money in his drawer. If Zach has $4,000 in twenty dollar bills, how many twenty dollar bills does he have?

19. For a party at school, gift bags are given to all of the children. Each bag gets five pieces of candy. If there are 275 pieces of candy, how many gift bags can be made?

20. Julio's MP3 player holds 5,400 minutes of music. How many hours of music will fit on his MP3 player?

LESSON 4: ESTIMATION AND ROUNDING

Estimating

Most of the time in math we are looking for an exact answer. Some questions on your HSE test, however, will ask you to estimate. When we estimate, we are looking for an approximate number. For example, let's say you have $9.87 in your pocket. If someone asked you how much money you had, you could estimate and say "about ten dollars."

Estimating is an important skill to use on the test. Take a look at the question below, but don't figure out the answer exactly.

> If Jerry works 6.25 hours a day, and he works 6 days a week, how many hours does he work in a week?
> (A) 10
> (B) 37.5
> (C) 87.5
> (D) 375

This question asks you for an exact answer, but we are going to figure it out through estimation. Take a look at the answer choices. Which ones don't seem reasonable?

(A) is too low. If Jerry works 6 days at 6 hours per shift, he will obviously work more than 10 hours. (B) Seems reasonable, so let's hold on to it and read the other answers. (C) 87.5 is a lot of hours to work in a week. 40 hours is typically considered full time, so Jerry would need to work a lot more than 6.25 hours a day for that to be correct. (D) is also way too high. Jerry would have to work 24 hours a day for over two weeks to even get close to 375 hours.

Therefore, the best answer is (B). Estimation is a great tool to help you quickly eliminate unreasonable answers. Estimation is also a great way to check your work to see if your answer is reasonable.

Rounding

The key to estimating is rounding off numbers. When we round numbers we either raise them or lower them to the nearest 10, 100, 1,000, etc., because they are easier to use. For example, what is 87 – 18? That question is difficult to do in your head, but what about 90 – 20? Now figure out the exact answers to these two problems.

$$87 - 18 =$$
$$90 - 20 =$$

Notice how the answers are only one apart? That is why estimating is so useful. It's not exact, but it gives us a reasonably close answer.

KEY WORDS FOR ESTIMATING

About

Almost

Approximately

Nearly

Roughly

UNIT 2: MATHEMATICS

HOW TO ROUND NUMBERS

1. IDENTIFY THE PLACE VALUE YOU ARE ROUNDING, AND UNDERLINE THAT DIGIT.

Round 87 to the nearest ten.

8̲7

2. LOOK AT THE DIGIT TO THE RIGHT OF THE UNDERLINED DIGIT. If that number is 5 or higher, the underlined digit goes up one. If the digit to the right is four or lower, the underlined digit stays the same.

Round 87 to the nearest 10.

8̲7   The digit to the right is a 7. Since that is higher than 7, the underlined digit will go up one.

3. CHANGE ALL OF THE DIGITS TO THE RIGHT OF THE UNDERLINED DIGIT TO ZEROS.

Round 87 to the nearest 10.

90

Here's another way to think of it. Is 87 closer to 80 or 90? Take a look on the number line.

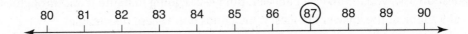

87 is clearly closer to 90 than to 80.

EXAMPLE 1

Round 439 to the nearest hundred.

4̲39   4 is the hundreds digit

4̲39   3 is the digit immediately to the right.

400   Since 3 is lower than 5, the rounded digit stays the same. All the numbers to the right are replaced with zeros.

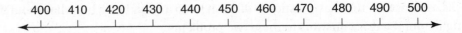

Where would 439 fall on the number line? Would it be closer to 400 or 500?

EXAMPLE 2

Round 876 to the nearest thousand.

_ 876   Here, there is no thousands digit. But is 876 closer to 1,000 or 0? We can't round it to 900 because that would to the nearest hundred and not the nearest thousand.

_ 876   If we look immediately to the right of the thousands place, we see an eight.

1,000   The thousands place then goes up from having nothing there to a one. All other digits to the right are zeros.

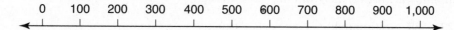

| 0 | 100 | 200 | 300 | 400 | 500 | 600 | 700 | 800 | 900 | 1,000 |

Where would 876 fall on the number line? Would it be closer to zero or 1,000?

Practice Exercises—Rounding

Round to the nearest ten.

1. 18 _____

2. 99 _____

3. 1,021 _____

4. 3 _____

5. 85 _____

6. 34,278 _____

7. 34 _____

8. 282 _____

9. 7,999 _____

10. 500 _____

Round to the nearest hundred.

11. 740 _____

12. 1,949 _____

13. 1,950 _____

14. 3,274,588 _____

15. 45 _____

16. 41,001 _____

17. 687 _____

18. 9,240 _____

19. 71 _____

20. 367 _____

Round to the nearest thousand.

21. 7,467 _____

22. 34,789 _____

23. 501 _____

24. 5,051 _____

25. 1,094 _____

26. 12,978,432 _____

27. 3,740 _____

28. 1,000,000 _____

29. 39,500 _____

30. 145,623 _____

First estimate the answer, then find the exact answer.

31. 423 + 568   estimated: _____   exact: _____

32. 952 − 477   estimated: _____   exact: _____

33. 78 × 8   estimated: _____   exact: _____

Estimate the answers to the following questions.

34. On Wednesday, Jim spent $44 at the grocery store. That night he spent $61 at the mall. If he spends another $77 on his electric bill, approximately how much did he spend this week?

35. Lavon has saved $10,324 to buy a car. Yesterday she found a nice used car that she really likes. If the car costs $7,899, about how much money would she have left over?

36. Peter averages 18 sales a day at his job. If he keeps up this pace, approximately how many total sales will he have in seven days?

37. Last year, 375,265 people lived in Springfield County. If another 4,838 people move to Springfield this year, roughly how many people will live in Springfield?

38. Ellen drives 34 miles each day to her job and back home. If she works 5 days a week, approximately how many miles will she drive?

39. Greg writes checks for $670, $438, and $509. If he originally had $1,835 in his bank account, how much does he have after the checks clear?

END-OF-CHAPTER QUESTIONS

Identify the place value of each underlined digit. The first one has been completed for you.

1. 45   Four tens
2. 678
3. 19,105
4. 7,564,514

Write out each number in words. The first one has been completed for you.

5. 7,021   Seven thousand twenty one
6. 599
7. 237,807
8. 3,843,680

Write out each number using digits. The first one has been completed for you.

9. One million three hundred twelve thousand nine hundred eight   1,312,908

10. Fifty six thousand four hundred thirty one _____

11. Two hundred ninety four thousand six hundred eighteen _____

12. Three thousand _____

13. Seven million seven hundred seventy seven thousand seven hundred seventy seven

_____

What new number is created when you switch place values? The first one has been completed for you.

14. 51,906   Switch the thousands digit and the ones digit.   <u>56,901</u>

15. 952   Switch the hundreds digit and the tens digit.   _____

16. 4,728,521   Switch the millions digit and the hundred thousands digit.   _____

17. 842,359   Switch the ten thousands digit with the hundreds digit.   _____

Complete the following without a calculator.

18.
$$\begin{array}{r} 34 \\ +\ 7 \\ \hline \end{array}$$

19.
$$\begin{array}{r} 578 \\ +\ 33 \\ \hline \end{array}$$

20.
$$\begin{array}{r} 405 \\ +\ 696 \\ \hline \end{array}$$

21. $523 + 69$

22. $145 + 278 + 10$

23.
$$\begin{array}{r} 64 \\ -\ 7 \\ \hline \end{array}$$

24.
$$\begin{array}{r} 237 \\ -\ 28 \\ \hline \end{array}$$

25.
$$\begin{array}{r} 797 \\ -\ 488 \\ \hline \end{array}$$

26. $765 - 374$

27. $812 - 713$

28.
$$\begin{array}{r} 15 \\ \times\ 5 \\ \hline \end{array}$$

29.
$$\begin{array}{r} 87 \\ \times\ 11 \\ \hline \end{array}$$

30.
$$\begin{array}{r} 100 \\ \times\ 37 \\ \hline \end{array}$$

31. 45×90

32. 20×25

33. $5\overline{)375}$

34. $8\overline{)496}$

35. $12\overline{)228}$

36. $84 \div 4$

37. $\dfrac{749}{7}$

38. Round 54,928   to the nearest ten _____

to the nearest hundred _____

to the nearest thousand _____

39. Round 781,981   to the nearest ten _____

to the nearest hundred _____

to the nearest thousand _____

to the nearest ten thousand _____

to the nearest hundred thousand _____

40. 713 + 279   estimated: _____   exact: _____

41. 482 − 216   estimated: _____   exact: _____

42. 28 × 9   estimated: _____   exact: _____

43. Each bag of potato chips contains 216 calories. If there are 11 bags of chips in a box, approximately how many calories of chips are in the box?

CHAPTER 4 ANSWER EXPLANATIONS

Lesson 1: Place Value

WRITE THE PLACE VALUE OF EACH UNDERLINED DIGIT (PAGE 120)

1. 3 tens
2. 1 ones
3. 1 thousands
4. 9 hundreds
5. 7 ten thousands
6. 3 millions
7. 2 tens
8. 2 ten millions
9. 6 ones
10. 6 hundred millions
11. 0 hundreds
12. 1 billions

WRITE OUT EACH NUMBER IN WORDS (PAGE 120)

1. Eighty four thousand, three hundred fifty four
2. Nine hundred four
3. Six thousand, two hundred twelve
4. Forty five thousand, seventy eight
5. One million, seven hundred eighty three
6. Two hundred forty five million, six hundred ninety eight thousand, two hundred thirty two
7. Five billion, six hundred thirty four million, five hundred twelve thousand, seven hundred thirty four

WRITE OUT EACH NUMBER USING DIGITS (PAGE 120)

1. 400,999
2. 712
3. 37,628
4. 10, 346,116
5. 77,100,311

IDENTIFY THE CORRECT DIGIT (PAGE 120)

1. One
2. Three
3. Four
4. Eight
5. Eight

WHAT NEW NUMBER IS CREATED WHEN YOU SWITCH PLACE VALUES? (PAGE 121)

1. 7,934
2. 62,571
3. 254,756
4. 9,738,015
5. 56,983,512

Lesson 2: Adding and Subtracting

PRACTICE EXERCISES—RULES FOR ADDITION (PAGE 122)

1. 21
2. 654
3. 102
4. 377
5. 157
6. 1,000
7. 1,368
8. 220
9. 37 + 41 + 60 = 138
10. 15 + 20 = 35

PRACTICE EXERCISES—GROUPING IN ADDITION (PAGE 123)

1. ⑨+ 15 +①
2. ⑬+ 18 +⑦
3. 21 +⑤+ 18 +⑮
4. ⑭+⑪+⑥+㉙
5. ⑩⑧+⑫+⑰+③
6. ⑦+⑯+⑭+㉝
7. ⑫+㉓+㉞+㊻+㊼+㊽

PRACTICE EXERCISES—REWRITE THE ABOVE PROBLEMS AFTER GROUPING NUMBERS, THEN SOLVE (PAGE 124)

1. 10 + 15 = 25
2. 20 + 18 = 38
3. 20 + 21 + 18 = 59
4. 100 + 40 = 140
5. 120 + 80 = 200
6. 30 + 40 = 70
7. 80 + 80 + 80 = 240

PRACTICE EXERCISES—SUBTRACTION (PAGE 125)

1. 55
2. 37
3. 4,092
4. 89
5. 18
6. 925
7. 333
8. 99
9. 37
10. 489
11. 1,200 – 50 – 600 – 75 = 475
12. 200 – 89 – 52 = 59 loaves left

    200 – 59 = 141 loaves have to be restocked to reach 200

Lesson 3: Multiplying and Dividing (Page 126)

Number of gallons	Money spent
1	$3
2	6
4	12
8	24
10	30

PRACTICE EXERCISES—MULTIPLICATION TABLE (PAGE 128)

×	1	2	3	4	5	6	7	8	9	10
1	1	2	3	4	5	6	7	8	9	10
2	2	4	6	8	10	12	14	16	18	20
3	3	6	9	12	15	18	21	24	27	30
4	4	8	12	16	20	24	28	32	36	40
5	5	10	15	20	25	30	35	40	45	50
6	6	12	18	24	30	36	42	48	54	60
7	7	14	21	28	35	42	49	56	63	70
8	8	16	24	32	40	48	56	64	72	80
9	9	18	27	36	45	54	63	72	81	90
10	10	20	30	40	50	60	70	80	90	100

PRACTICE EXERCISES—MULTIPLYING WITH MULTIPLE DIGITS (PAGE 130)

1. 51
2. 680
3. 1,196
4. 1,012
5. 5,460
6. 8,358
7. 32,400
8. 6,110
9. 8,575
10. 4,500
11. 108
12. 1,212
13. 1,190
14. 6,852
15. 15,867
16. $9 \times 8 = 72$
17. $72 \times 9 = 648$
18. $12 \times 12 = 144$
19. $35 \times 15 = 525$
20. $250 \times 90 = 22,500$

PRACTICE EXERCISES—LONG DIVISION (PAGE 133)

1.	29	**11.**	70
2.	21	**12.**	41
3.	44	**13.**	15
4.	701	**14.**	33
5.	50	**15.**	1,031
6.	42	**16.**	$2,400 \div 8 = 300$
7.	402	**17.**	$21 \div 3 = 7$
8.	398	**18.**	$4,000 \div 20 = 200$
9.	41	**19.**	$275 \div 5 = 55$
10.	410	**20.**	$5,400 \div 60 = 90$

Lesson 4: Estimating and Rounding

PRACTICE EXERCISES—ROUNDING (PAGE 137)

1.	20	**22.**	35,000
2.	100	**23.**	1,000
3.	1,020	**24.**	5,100
4.	0	**25.**	1,100
5.	90	**26.**	12,978,400
6.	34,280	**27.**	4,000
7.	30	**28.**	1,000,000
8.	280	**29.**	39,500
9.	8,000	**30.**	146,000
10.	500	**31.**	Estimate: $400 + 600 = 1,000$
11.	700		Exact: 991
12.	1,900	**32.**	Estimate: $1,000 - 500 = 500$
13.	2,000		Exact: 475
14.	3,274,600	**33.**	Estimate: $80 \times 8 = 640$
15.	0		Exact: 624
16.	41,000	**34.**	$40 + 60 + 80 = 180$
17.	700	**35.**	$10,000 - 8,000 = 2,000$
18.	9,200	**36.**	$20 \times 7 = 140$
19.	100	**37.**	$375,000 + 5,000 = 380,000$
20.	400	**38.**	$30 \times 5 = 150$
21.	7,000	**39.**	$2,000 - 700 - 400 - 500 = 400$

End-of-Chapter Questions (Page 139)

1. Four tens
2. Eight ones
3. Nine thousands
4. Seven millions
5. Seven thousand twenty one
6. Five hundred ninety nine
7. Two hundred thirty seven thousand, eight hundred seven
8. Three million eight hundred forty three thousand, six hundred eighty
9. 1,312,908
10. 56,431
11. 294,618
12. 3,000
13. 7,777,777
14. 56,901
15. 592
16. 7,428,521
17. 832,459
18. 41
19. 611
20. 1,101
21. 592
22. 433
23. 57
24. 209
25. 309
26. 391
27. 99
28. 75
29. 957
30. 3,700
31. 4,050
32. 500
33. 75
34. 62
35. 19
36. 21
37. 107
38. Ten: 54,930
    Hundred: 54,900
    Thousand: 55,000
39. Ten: 781,980
    Hundred: 782,000
    Thousand: 782,000
    Ten thousand: 780,000
    Hundred thousand: 800,000
40. Estimated: $700 + 300 = 1,000$
    Exact: 992
41. Estimated: $500 - 200 = 300$
    Exact: 266
42. Estimated: $30 \times 10 = 300$
    Exact: 252
43. $200 \times 10 = 2,000$

Word Problems 5

Many of the questions you will encounter on your HSE math test will be word problems. Chances are, your blood pressure just shot up after reading that. But don't worry, we are going to use a step-by-step process to solve every word problem.

Word problems are important because that is how we use math in real life. You will probably never walk down the street, see a sign that says "what is 8×16," and then solve it. At some point, though, you will probably need to figure out how much you made after a day of work. A simple word problem then would be, "If you make $16 dollars an hour, how much will you earn after an eight-hour shift?" So keep that in mind as we go forward. Word problems aren't designed to be unsolvable riddles but are instead just little stories about everyday life.

> 1. You are hoping to earn $200 this weekend because you are taking 3 days off next week. If you earn $16 an hour at your job, how much will you make after an 8-hour shift?
> 2. How much will you make after an 8-hour shift?
> 3. Necessary: $16 an hour, 8 hours per shift.
>   Unnecessary: $200, 3 days off
> 4. Multiply.

STEPS FOR SOLVING WORD PROBLEMS

STEP 1 **Read the entire question.** That sounds simple enough, but a common mistake is to begin trying to work the problem right away. If it is a long question, or if it seems complicated, read it twice.

STEP 2 **Figure out what the question is actually asking.** Each question may be several sentences in length, so make sure you understand what the actual question is asking. It is critical to do this before you start working the problem.

STEP 3 **Find the necessary information and eliminate the unnecessary information.** Now that you know what the question is, you will go back through the question and find what you need to solve the problem. Don't assume you will use every number in the problem. There will be extra information in some questions that you don't need.

STEP 4 **Choose the operation or formula.** Once you have the information you need, decide how you will solve the problem. For example, if you want to know how much money you will make at work, would you divide or multiply?

STEP 5 **Does the answer make sense?** Always check to see if your answer is reasonable. In our example, if you divided $16 by 8 you would get $2. That's not much money for an eight-hour shift! Multiplying gives you $128, and that makes much more sense for a hard day at work.

LESSON 1: KEY WORDS
Understanding the Question Using Key Words

Knowing the vocabulary of math makes answering word problems much easier. Take a look at these commonly used words. Each one indicates which mathematical operation you will use in the problem.

Addition	Subtraction	Multiplication	Division
Sum	Difference	Product	Quotient
Altogether	Fewer	Total	Each
Both	How much more	Factor of	Equally
In all	Left	Every	Per
Total	Less	At this rate	Sharing
Increased by	Minus	In all	Splitting
Combined	Remains	Total	
Together		Doubled	
		Tripled	

Practice Exercises—Key Words

For the following questions, circle the key word and then write which operation you would use to solve the problem. The first one is completed for you.

1. Calvin's uncle is 37, and Calvin is 15. What is the (difference) in their ages?

   <u>Subtraction</u>

2. Alesha serves nine customers an hour. At this rate, how many customers would she serve during a 3-hour lunch rush?

   _____

3. What is the sum of 348 and 912?

   _____

4. What is the product of 348 and 912?

   _____

5. What is the quotient of 900 and 45?

   _____

6. Tom's goal is to save $5,000 dollars for a down payment on a new car. If he has $3,512 in the bank after 6 months, how much more does he need to save?

_____

7. On Thursday, 145 people went to the new superhero movie. Over the weekend, that amount tripled. How many people went to the movies over the weekend?

_____

8. The auto repair shop normally works on 12 cars a day. Tomorrow, that total will be increased by four. How many cars will the shop work on tomorrow?

_____

9. 70 people work in an office building. On Tuesday, 20 people were out sick. How many workers remained at the office building?

_____

10. In the auditorium, there are 20 rows of chairs. Each row has 25 chairs. How many chairs are there in all?

_____

11. You have a bag with 24 pieces of candy. If you give each of your three cousins an equal amount, how many pieces of candy will each cousin receive?

_____

12. In the winter, approximately 100 people visit the beach. In the summer, this number increases by a factor of six. How many people visit the beach in the summer?

_____

LESSON 2: ELIMINATING UNNECESSARY INFORMATION

TIP

Once you have determined what the question is asking, ask yourself "what information will I need to find the answer?"

Some questions on the test will provide you with more information than you need to solve the problem. That is why it is critical *to read the question thoroughly, and make sure you understand what it is asking.* Otherwise, you may get distracted and wind up answering the wrong question. Whatever you do, don't just assume all of the numbers given in a problem will be used to find the answer. Sometimes you will need to pick and choose.

Practice Exercises—Eliminating Unnecessary Information

For each problem below, write down what the question is actually asking. Then, circle the information you will need to answer the question. Finally, cross out any unnecessary information that will not help you answer the problem. The first one has been completed for you.

1. ~~This weekend you are planning on driving to New York, which is approximately 300 miles away. If traffic is good you should make it there in about 6 hours.~~ You are planning on filling up your car with gas before you go, and gas currently costs (\$3.35) a gallon. ~~If traffic is bad, however, it might take you 8 hours to get to there. You are planning at leaving at 9 A.M.~~ How many gallons of gas will you buy if your tank holds (14 gallons?)

   How many gallons of gas will you buy if your tank holds 14 gallons?

2. You need to bake 36 cookies for a school party. The recipe says the oven should be preheated to 350 degrees for 30 minutes. You will need two eggs for each dozen cookies, and three cups of sugar. How many eggs will you need to make 36 cookies?

   _____

3. With average temperatures in the 80s, July is the busiest month at the park. Every bus going to the park can hold 25 people. If 110 people are at the bus stop, how many buses will be needed to get everyone to the park? Temperatures usually peak in the 90s during August.

   _____

4. A sweater that normally costs \$39 is on sale for \$29. Gavin typically spends around \$50 on holiday gifts, but another store at the mall has jeans specially priced for \$59. How much will Gavin save from the normal price if he buys two sweaters on sale?

   _____

5. On Tuesday at 1 P.M., 25 people get on the bus. At 1:30, ten people get off the bus. The bus route takes a total of 3 hours for a round trip. At 2:00, five people board the bus. At 3:00, eight people get off the bus and six more get on. If more people ride the bus on Tuesday than Wednesday, how many people are on the bus after the 3:00 stop?

   _____

6. The manager of Ray's pizza is figuring out the monthly budget. Ray's usually sells twice as many pizzas as Pizza King. Pizza King sells approximately 200 pizzas a weekend. Ray's spends 50 cents per pizza box, and one dollar on cheese per pizza. If Ray's uses 150 pizza boxes tonight, how much will they spend on pizza boxes?

_____

7. On Saturday morning, it rained 1 inch, and that night it rained another inch. Sunday morning, 2 more inches of rain fell, but then it stopped raining that evening. If it didn't rain at all on Monday, what is the total amount of rain that fell during the mornings of the 3-day period?

_____

8. Half of the people who enter Dan's Hardware store make a purchase. Of those people making a purchase, 75% purchase a tool. During the Winter, sales fall by 10%, but the average shopper spends 22% more. If 200 people enter the store on Friday, how many people make a purchase?

_____

LESSON 3: IS THE ANSWER REASONABLE?

The math test is mainly multiple choice. While this may seem easier because the answer has to be one of the choices listed, you still must be careful. Some of the incorrect answer choices will be numbers that seem correct if you don't check to see if your answer is reasonable.

Try the sample question below. Before you compute your final answer, estimate what should be an appropriate answer.

> You are hoping to earn $200 this weekend because you are taking 3 days off next week. If you earn $16 an hour at your job, how much will you make after an 8-hour shift?
> (A) $2
> (B) $8
> (C) $24
> (D) $128
> (E) $216

Just by looking at the answer choices, we can eliminate answers (A), (B), and (C). After all, who would work an 8-hour shift to earn under $24? Those are not reasonable answers. Also note how some answers can be found by choosing the wrong operation:

- $16 \div 8 = 2$. If you don't understand the actual question and just divide the two necessary numbers in the problem, you will get 2, but that is incorrect.
- $16 - 8 = 8$. Performing the wrong operation may show up as this answer choice, but it is incorrect.
- $16 + 8 = 24$. Again, this answer can be found using the numbers in the problem, but it is a distractor and incorrect.
- $200 + 16 = 216$. This is another answer that can be created by using unnecessary information in the problem.

The correct answer is (D). Eight hours of work at 16 dollars an hour is computed $8 \times 16 = 128$.

TIP

Always make sure you understand the question, and then estimate what a reasonable answer might be.

UNIT 2: MATHEMATICS

Always check
to see if your
answer is
reasonable. Don't
just choose an
answer because
you were able
to randomly
produce an
answer on the
calculator.

Practice Exercises—Is the Answer Reasonable?

For the following questions, estimate in your head what should be a reasonable answer. Then cross out unreasonable answers.

1. Brittany is saving up to buy a new computer that costs $1,200. If she has already saved $400, how much more money does she need to buy the computer?
   (A) $3
   (B) $800
   (C) $1,600
   (D) $4,800

2. Alex lives 15 miles from his job. Every Monday through Friday, he drives to work and back. On weekends, he drives an additional 60 miles taking his son to football practice. Approximately how many miles does Alex drive each day to and from work?
   (A) 4 miles
   (B) 20 miles
   (C) 150 miles
   (D) 750 miles

3. Dave has been working out to lose weight. He started the year at 250 pounds, but he has been working out three times a week for the last few months. Dave also tries to eat salads and healthy foods at least ten times a week. If Dave loses 50 pounds by the end of the year, how much will he weigh?
   (A) 5 pounds
   (B) 25 pounds
   (C) 200 pounds
   (D) 300 pounds

4. Shay is planning a trip to visit her family over the holidays. Her mother lives 200 miles away. If it takes her 4 hours to get to her mother's house, how fast did she drive?
   (A) .02 miles per hour
   (B) 50 miles per hour
   (C) 204 miles per hour
   (D) 800 miles per hour

5. In her garden, Candice is planting vegetables. If she digs four rows with eight plants each, how many plants will she have?
   (A) .5
   (B) 4
   (C) 12
   (D) 32

6. For Halloween, Al is giving candy to the neighborhood children. He has 90 pieces to give away, and 30 children stop by his house. If he gives each child an equal amount of candy, how many pieces of candy does each child receive?

(A) .33

(B) 3

(C) 60

(D) 270

7. Each MP3 download costs $1.00. This weekend, a website is offering every download at 15% off. If 10,000 songs are downloaded over the weekend, how much money will the website earn?

(A) $1.15

(B) 8,500

(C) 10,000

(D) 15,000

8. This summer it rained every third day. Allison kept track of the weather all summer and counted every day that it rained. If she kept a record of 90 days, how many of those days did it rain?

(A) 3

(B) 30

(C) 60

(D) 87

LESSON 4: MULTISTEP PROBLEMS

Many problems on the math test will have more than one step. This means that you will have to make more than one calculation to get the correct answer. Here's an example:

On her way home from work, Cassie stops by the grocery store. She buys three apples at $.60 each and two loaves of bread that each cost $2.50. How much does Cassie spend at the store?

To solve this question, let's work through our problem-solving steps.

- **WHAT IS THE QUESTION ASKING?** What is the total amount of money spent?
- **WHAT INFORMATION DO WE NEED?** How much each item costs, and how many of each item was purchased.
- **CHOOSE THE OPERATION AND MAKE A PLAN**—To solve this, we can't just add everything up, or multiply everything together. We have to think about it, and break it down into steps. To get the correct answer, we need separate totals for the apples and the bread. Then we can add them together for the final answer.

    Let's start with the apples first. Three apples at $.60 each would cost $1.80. You can find that by either adding .60 + .60 + .60, or by multiplying 3 × .60.

    Next find the total cost of the bread. Two loaves at $2.50 each is $5.00. You can find that answer by adding 2.50 + 2.50, or by multiplying 2 × 2.50.

    Added together, our final answer is $6.80.

Practice Exercises—Multistep Problems

For the following questions identify what calculation you perform in each step and then solve. The first one has been completed for you.

1. Paul buys five bags of chips for $1.25 each. At the cash register, he hands the cashier a $20 bill. How much change should he receive?

   (STEP 1) Total money spent. 5 × $1.25 = $6.25

   (STEP 2) Subtract money spent from $20. $20 − $6.25 = $13.75

2. Ernesto wrote three checks this month for $40, $25, and $55. He also deposited $50 into his checking account. If he started the month with $500 in the account, how much does he have now?

   (STEP 1)

   (STEP 2)

   (STEP 3)

3. Darius is going to buy a new air conditioner for his house. If he makes a $500 down payment and 24 monthly payments of $100, how much will the air conditioner cost?

   (STEP 1)

   (STEP 2)

4. Three friends go out to dinner for a birthday party. One orders a steak for $15, another the chicken for $12, and the other has a salad for $9. If they split the bill evenly, how much will each one owe?

   (STEP 1)

   (STEP 2)

5. Ramon buys three pairs of socks that each cost $5. If he also uses a coupon for $2 off his purchase, how much change will he receive if he pays with $20?

   (STEP 1)

   (STEP 2)

   (STEP 3)

6. At the movie theater, children's tickets cost $6, and adults' tickets cost $9. If three children and two adults go to the movies, how much will the tickets cost?

   (STEP 1)

   (STEP 2)

   (STEP 3)

Use the graph to answer questions 7 and 8.

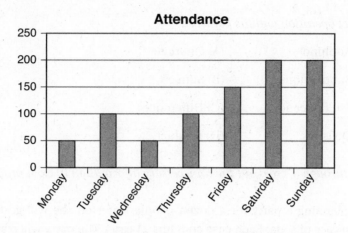

Attendance

7. How many more people attended the park on Saturday and Sunday than on Monday and Tuesday?

STEP 1

STEP 2

STEP 3

8. How many fewer people attended the park on Wednesday and Thursday than attended on Friday and Saturday?

STEP 1

STEP 2

STEP 3

Match the correct operation with its key word.

_____ 1. Addition   (A) Quotient

_____ 2. Subtraction   (B) Sum

_____ 3. Multiplication   (C) Difference

_____ 4. Division   (D) Product

For questions 5 through 8, cross out the unnecessary information in each problem, then solve.

5. Thanh is planning a party for a dozen people. Later on she will go to the store and purchase a case of soda. Each case contains 24 cans. The party will start 6 P.M. and last approximately 3 hours. If the sodas cost $12, how much does one can cost?

6. Leon types approximately 50 words a minute. He normally works 8 hours a day, 5 days a week. At this pace, how many words can he type in 10 minutes?

7. Jack purchased his car for $15,000. He made a down payment of $5,000. He chose this car because it gets good gas mileage, approximately 40 miles per gallon. The gas tank can hold 15 gallons. He is planning on making car payments of $200 a month. After the down payment, how many months of payments will he make to pay off the car?

8. Jack purchased his car for $15,000. He made a down payment of $5,000. He chose this car because it gets good gas mileage, approximately 40 miles per gallon. The gas tank can hold 15 gallons. He is planning on making car payments of $200 a month. How many miles can he drive on a full tank?

UNIT 2: MATHEMATICS

For questions 9 through 11, check to make sure your answer is reasonable.

9. Tony is making a book shelf. Each shelf can hold 24 books. If Tony has 96 books, how many shelves will he need?

   (A) .25
   (B) 4
   (C) 6
   (D) 72

10. Donna made a deposit for $1,000, and another one for $500. If she later writes checks for $200, $300, and $500, how much money would be left in her account?

    (A) $25
    (B) $500
    (C) $1,500
    (D) $2,500

11. Jim bought a set of four plates for $60. How much did he pay per plate?

    (A) $4
    (B) $15
    (C) $56
    (D) $240

For the following questions, identify what calculation you perform in each step and then solve.

Use the table below to answer questions 12–15.

Pizzas	Price	Number of Slices	Price Per Extra Topping
Small	$8.99	6	$1.00
Medium	$12.99	8	$1.50
Large	$16.99	12	$2.00

12. What is the total cost of purchasing two small pizzas and two medium pizzas?

    (STEP 1)

    (STEP 2)

    (STEP 3)

13. How much would you save if you purchased two large pizzas instead of three medium pizzas?

STEP 1

STEP 2

STEP 3

14. What is the total cost of buying a small pizza with two extra toppings and buying a large pizza with three extra toppings?

STEP 1

STEP 2

STEP 3

15. How much cheaper is a medium pizza per slice than a small pizza per slice? (THINK: How can you find out how much one slice costs?)

STEP 1

STEP 2

STEP 3

CHAPTER 5 ANSWER EXPLANATIONS

Lesson 1: Key Words (Page 148)

1. Calvin's uncle is 37, and Calvin is 15. What is the (difference) in their ages?
Subtraction

2. Alesha serves nine customers an hour. (At this rate) how many customers would she serve during a 3-hour lunch rush?
Multiply

3. What is the (sum) of 348 and 912?
Add

4. What is the (product) of 348 and 912?
Multiply

5. What is the (quotient) of 900 and 45?
Divide

6. Tom's goal is to save $5,000 dollars for a down payment on a new car. If he has $3,512 in the bank after 6 months, how (much more) does he need to save?
Subtraction

7. On Thursday, 145 people went to the new superhero movie. Over the weekend that amount (tripled.) How many people went to the movies over the weekend?
Multiply

8. The auto repair shop normally works on 12 cars a day. Tomorrow that total will be (increased) by four. How many cars will the shop work on tomorrow?
Add

9. 70 people work in an office building. On Tuesday, 20 people were out sick. How many workers (remained) at the office building?
Subtract

10. In the auditorium, there are 20 rows of chairs. Each row has 25 chairs. How many chairs are there (in all)?
Multiply

11. You have a bag with 24 pieces of candy. If you give each of your three cousins an (equal) amount, how many pieces of candy will each cousin receive?
Divide

12. In the Winter, approximately 100 people visit the beach. In the summer, this number (increases) by a (factor) of six. How many people visit the beach in the summer?
Multiply

Lesson 2: Eliminate Unecessary Information (Page 150)

1. ~~This weekend you are planning on driving to New York, which is approximately 300 miles away. If traffic is good you should make it there in about 6 hours.~~ You are planning on filling up your car with gas before you go, and gas currently costs $3.35 a gallon. ~~If traffic is bad, however, it might take you 8 hours to get to there. You are planning at leaving at 9 A.M.~~ How many gallons of gas will you buy if your tank holds 14 gallons?
How many gallons of gas will you buy if your tank holds 14 gallons?

2. You need to bake 36 cookies for a school party. ~~The recipe says the oven should be pre-heated to 350 degrees for 30 minutes.~~ You will need (two eggs for each dozen cookies) ~~and three cups of sugar.~~ **How many eggs will you need to make 36 cookies?**

3. ~~With average temperatures in the 80s, July is the busiest month at the park.~~ Every bus going to the park can hold (25 people.) If (110 people) are at the bus stop, **how many buses will be needed to get everyone to the park?** ~~Temperatures usually peak in the 90s during August.~~

4. A sweater that normally costs ($39) is on sale for ($29.) ~~Gavin typically spends around $50 on holiday gifts, but another store at the mall has jeans specially priced for $59.~~ **How much will Gavin save from the normal price if he buys (two) sweaters on sale?**

5. On Tuesday at 1 P.M., (25 people) get on the bus. At 1:30, (ten people) get off the bus. ~~The bus route takes a total of 3 hours for a round trip.~~ At 2:00, five people board the bus. At 3:00, (eight people) get off the bus and (six more) get on. ~~If more people ride the bus on Tuesday than Wednesday,~~ **how many people are on the bus after the 3:00 stop?**

6. ~~The Manager of Ray's pizza is figuring out the monthly budget. Ray's usually sells twice as many pizzas as Pizza King. Pizza King sells approximately 200 pizzas a weekend.~~ Ray's spends (50 cents) per pizza box, ~~and one dollar on cheese per pizza.~~ If Ray's uses (150 pizza) boxes tonight, **how much will they spend on pizza boxes?**

7. On Saturday morning it rained (one inch,) ~~and that night it rained another inch.~~ Sunday morning (two more) inches of rain fell, but then it stopped raining that evening. If it didn't rain at all on Monday, **what is the total amount of rain that fell during the mornings of the 3-day period?**

8. (Half of) the people who enter Dan's Hardware store make a purchase. ~~Of those people making a purchase, 75% purchase a tool. During the Winter, sales fall by 10%, but the average shopper spends 22% more.~~ If (200 people) enter the store on Friday, **how many people make a purchase?**

Lesson 3: Is the Answer Reasonable? (Page 152)

1. **(B)** (A) is too low for a computer, and (C) and (D) are more expensive than the computer originally cost.
2. **(C)** (A) and (B) are unreasonable because that is less than the 30 miles he drives to and from work each day. (D) is too high.
3. **(C)** (A) and (B) are unreasonable because adults cannot weigh that little. (D) is unreasonable because that is more than he weighed to begin with.
4. **(B)** (A) is unreasonable because that is too slow to drive, and (C) and (D) are way too fast.
5. **(D)** All of the other answers are too unreasonably small for four rows of eight plants.
6. **(B)** (A) is unreasonable because you can't really give a fraction of a candy bar, and (C) and (D) are way too much to give to each child.
7. **(B)** (A) is unreasonable because that is not anywhere close to what 10,000 downloads would cost. (C) is unreasonable because that's what it would cost if each download

were a dollar, but these downloads are on sale so it must be cheaper than that. (D) is too much if each download is less than a dollar.

8. **(B)** (A) is unreasonable because if it rained every third day all summer that would be more than 3 days total. (C) and (D) are unreasonable because those are both more than half of 90, and we know it rained less than every other day.

Lesson 4: Multistep Problems (Page 154)

1. **STEP 1** Total money spent. $5 \times \$1.25 = \$6.25$
   STEP 2 Subtract money spent from $20. $\$20 - \$6.25 = \$13.75$

2. **STEP 1** Add the checks together: $\$40 + \$25 + \$55 = \$120$
   STEP 2 Subtract checks from $500 = \$380$
   STEP 3 Add $50 deposit = \$430$

3. **STEP 1** Compute monthly payments: $24 \times \$100 = \$2,400$
   STEP 2 Add down payment: $\$500 + \$2,400 = \$2,900$

4. **STEP 1** Total each dinner: $\$15 + \$12 + \$9 = \$36$
   STEP 2 Divide total by 3: $\$36 \div 3 = \$12$

5. **STEP 1** Total socks: $3 \times \$5 = \$15$
   STEP 2 Subtract coupon: $\$15 - \$2 = \$13$
   STEP 3 Subtract new total from $20: $\$20 - \$13 = \$7$

6. **STEP 1** Total children's tickets: $3 \times \$6 = \$18$
   STEP 2 Total adult's tickets: $2 \times \$9 = \$18$
   STEP 3 Add both totals: $\$18 + \$18 = \$36$

7. **STEP 1** Total Saturday and Sunday: $200 + 200 = 400$
   STEP 2 Total Monday and Tuesday: $50 + 100 = 150$
   STEP 3 Subtract to find the difference: $400 - 150 = 250$

8. **STEP 1** Total Wednesday and Thursday: $50 + 100 = 150$
   STEP 2 Total Friday and Saturday: $150 + 200 = 350$
   STEP 3 Subtract to find the difference: $350 - 150 = 200$

End-of-Chapter Questions (Page 156)

1. **B**
2. **C**
3. **D**
4. **A**
5. ~~Thanh is planning a party for a dozen people.~~ Later on she will go to the store and purchase a case of soda. Each case contains 24 cans. ~~The party will start 6 P.M. and last approximately 3 hours.~~ If the sodas cost $12, how much does one can cost?
   $\$12 \div 24 = 50¢$
6. Leon types approximately 50 words a minute. ~~He normally works 8 hours a day, 5 days a week.~~ At his pace, how many words can he type in 10 minutes?
   $50 \times 10 = 100$

7. Jack purchased his car for $15,000. He made a down payment of $5,000. ~~He chose this car because it gets good gas mileage, approximately 40 miles per gallon. The gas tank can hold 15 gallons.~~ He is planning on making car payments of $200 a month. After the down payment, how many months of payments will he make to pay off the car?

15,000 – 5,000 down payment = 10,000

10,000 ÷ 200 = 50 months

8. ~~Jack purchased his car for $15,000. He made a down payment of $5,000.~~ He chose this car because it gets good gas mileage, approximately 40 miles per gallon. The gas tank can hold 15 gallons. ~~He is planning on making car payments of $200 a month.~~ How many miles can he drive on a full tank?

40 × 15 = 600 miles

9. (C) (A) is unreasonable because you can't have .25 of a book shelf, and (D) is unreasonable because you wouldn't need 72 bookshelves for 96 books.

10. (B) (A) is too low, and (C) and (D) are too high.

11. (B) (A) is too low per plate, and (C) and (D) are too high since he bought four plates.

12. (STEP 1) Total small pizzas: $17.98

(STEP 2) Total medium pizzas: $25.98

(STEP 3) Add both totals together: $43.96

13. (STEP 1) Total large pizzas: $33.98

(STEP 2) Total medium pizzas: $38.97

(STEP 3) Subtract to find difference: $4.99

14. (STEP 1) Cost of small with two toppings: $10.99

(STEP 2) Cost of large with three toppings: $22.99

(STEP 3) Add totals together: $33.98

15. (STEP 1) Cost per slice medium pizza: $12.99 ÷ 8 = $1.62

(STEP 2) Cost per slice small pizza: $8.99 ÷ 6 = $1.50

(STEP 3) Subtract to find difference: $1.62 – $1.50 = 12¢

Decimals

6

LESSON 1: DECIMAL PLACE VALUE

Decimals are used to count numbers that don't fall precisely on a whole number like 1, 2, or 3. We see this most commonly with money. For example, let's say you had five quarters in your pocket. How could you write that numerically? $1.25. You have between one and two dollars, and you can express the exact amount using a decimal point. The period used between the one and the two is the decimal point. Just like with whole numbers, place value is very important with decimals.

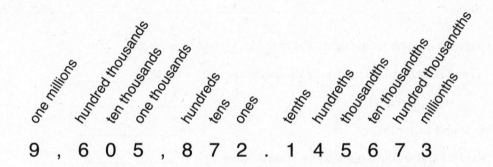

Three things to know about decimals:

■ They begin to the right of the decimal point.

■ They all end in "th."

■ The first place to the right is the tenths place, not the ones place.

UNIT 2: MATHEMATICS

Practice Exercise—Decimal Place Value

Write the place value of each underlined digit. The first two have been completed for you.

TIP

Use "and" when writing a decimal point. For example 2.3 is written two and three tenths.

1. .9̲2   Nine tenths

2. .7̲82   Eight hundredths

3. 12.17̲6   _____

4. .70̲8   _____

5. .552̲1   _____

6. 76.15378̲4   _____

7. .149̲1   _____

8. .85208̲7   _____

9. 123.321̲0   _____

Write out each number in words. The first one has been completed for you.

1. 237.498   Two hundred thirty seven and four hundred ninety eight thousandths

2. .9   _____

3. .406   _____

4. 34.34   _____

5. 91.005   _____

6. .2345   _____

Write out each number using digits. The first one has been completed for you.

1. Six and nine hundred thirty one thousandths   6.931

2. Forty six hundredths   _____

3. Nine and six tenths   _____

4. Sixty six and six hundred sixty six thousandths   _____

5. Three hundred twelve thousandths   _____

What new number is created when you switch place values? The first one has been completed for you.

1. .2356 Switch the tenths digit and the thousandths digit   .5326

2. 1.6549 Switch the hundredths digit and the ten thousandths digit.   _____

3. 43.790 Switch the ones digit and the hundredths digit.   _____

4. 627.890 Switch the hundredths digit with the hundreds digit.   _____

5. 10,495.2167 Switch the thousands digit with the thousandths digit.   _____

LESSON 2: COMPARING DECIMALS

Which is worth more, nine cents or twenty cents? That's easy when it's written like that, but it can be easy to overlook in decimal form. After all, at first glance .09 seems larger than .2 because nine is larger than two.

> ### HOW TO COMPARE DECIMALS
>
> 1. Line up each number at the decimal point.
> 2. Start with the first number to the right of the decimal (tenths place).
> 3. If one is larger than the other, that is the larger number.
> 4. If the numbers are the same, repeat the process with the second number to the right (hundredths place).
> 5. Keep going until one number is larger, or you run out of decimal places.

Let's try comparing these four numbers: .2489, .1999, .2490, .25

STEP 1 Line them at the decimal point:

.2489
.1999
.2490
.25
↓

STEP 2 Start with the tenths place:

.2489
.1999
.2490
.25

STEP 3 One number is lower than the rest, so we know that is the lowest number.

STEP 4 The other three all have two tenths so we need to move over and compare the next number.

↓
.2489
.2490
.25

Since five is larger than four, we know that .25 is larger than all of the other numbers.

STEP 5 Now compare the thousands place of the last two numbers

↓
.2489
.2490

The list from lowest to highest is .1999 .2489 .25 .2890

Practice Exercise—Comparing Decimals

Circle which number is higher. The first one has been done for you.

1. (.54) or .49

2. .09 or .11

3. .325 or .40

4. .91 or .90999

5. .763 or .6109

6. .50505 or .50555

7. .24009 or .24010

8. .11113 or .111121

9. 1.1 or 1.011

10. 2.01 or 1.987

LESSON 3: ESTIMATION AND ROUNDING WITH DECIMALS

If you have ever shopped for groceries, chances are you have experience in rounding decimals. For example, if you bought a gallon of milk for $3.89, a pound of turkey for $6.99, and a loaf of bread for $2.09, about how much money would you need? We could take the time to write it down and figure it out to the penny. Or, we could just say the milk is $4, the turkey is $7, and the bread is $2. Which price list would be easier to total?

In that example we rounded off our decimals to the nearest dollar. Just as with whole numbers, the key to rounding decimals is understanding their place value. Likewise, the rules for rounding decimals are the same as with whole numbers.

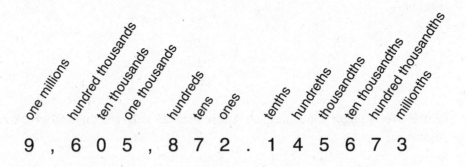

How to Round Numbers

STEP 1 **Identify the place value you are rounding, and underline that digit.**

Round .67 to the nearest tenth.

.6̲7

STEP 2 **Look at the digit to the right of the underlined digit.** If that number is 5 or higher, the underlined digit goes up one. If the digit to the right is four or lower, the underlined digit stays the same.

Round .67 to the nearest tenth.

.6̲7   The digit to the right is a 7. Since that is higher than 5, the underlined digit will go up one.

STEP 3 **Drop all of the digits to the right of the underlined digit.**

Round .67 to the nearest 10.

.7

Here's another way to think of it. Is .67 closer to .60 or .70? Take a look at the number line.

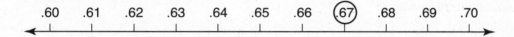

.67 is clearly closer to .7 than to .6.

> When rounding decimals, you always stop at the place being rounded. For example, if you need to round to the hundredths, do not put a zero in the thousandths.
>
> .789 to the nearest hundredth is .79, not .790
> .24 to the nearest tenth is .2, not .20.

EXAMPLE 1

Round .439 to the nearest hundredth.

.43̲2   3 is the hundredths digit.

.43̲2   2 is the digit immediately to the right.

.43   Since 2 is lower than 5, the rounded digit stays the same. All the numbers to the right are dropped.

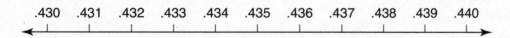

Where would .432 fall on the number line? Would it be closer to .43 or .44?

UNIT 2: MATHEMATICS

EXAMPLE 2

Round .95 to the nearest tenth.

.95   Nine is the tenths digit.

.95   If we look immediately to the right of the tenths place, we see a five.

1.0   The tenths place then goes up one from 9 to 10. This means we need to put a one in the ones place. Put a zero in the tenths place because we are rounding to the nearest tenth.

```
   .90   .91   .92   .93   .94   .95   .96   .97   .98   .99   1.0
◄───┼─────┼─────┼─────┼─────┼─────┼─────┼─────┼─────┼─────┼─────┼───►
```

.95 is in the middle of the number line, but the rule is that numbers 5 or higher round up. For example, 95 cents rounds up to one dollar and not down to 90 cents.

Practice Exercies—Rounding

Round to the nearest tenth.

1. .44 _____   6. 1.23 _____

2. .45 _____   7. 32.09 _____

3. .81 _____   8. .10005 _____

4. .09 _____   9. .06000 _____

5. .64 _____   10. 19.99 _____

Round to the nearest hundredth.

1. .454 _____   6. 3.678 _____

2. .506 _____   7. 87.263 _____

3. .393 _____   8. .67902 _____

4. .289 _____   9. 8.75000 _____

5. .788 _____   10. 5.999 _____

Estimate to find the answer.

1. This week you worked 7.75 hours on Monday, 8.2 hours on Tuesday, 6.00 hours on Wednesday, and 5.5 hours on Thursday. Approximately how many hours did you work this week?

2. Candy bars are on sale 3 for $1.99. If you buy nine candy bars, about how much money will you spend?

LESSON 4: OPERATIONS WITH DECIMALS

Fortunately, there are no special tricks involved in doing simple calculations with decimals. If you can add, subtract, multiply, and divide whole numbers, then you already know how to do the same with decimals! The only thing we must watch out for is where the decimal point goes in our answer.

Adding and Subtracting Decimals

STEP 1 Line up the numbers by their decimal points.

$$2.4 + 5.17 \qquad\qquad 6.38 - 4.5$$

$$
\begin{array}{r}
5.17 \\
+\,2.4 \\
\hline
\end{array}
\qquad\qquad
\begin{array}{r}
6.38 \\
-\,4.5 \\
\hline
\end{array}
$$

STEP 2 Fill in empty decimal places with a zero.

$$
\begin{array}{r}
5.17 \\
+\,2.40 \\
\hline
\end{array}
\qquad\qquad
\begin{array}{r}
6.38 \\
-\,4.50 \\
\hline
\end{array}
$$

STEP 3 Add or subtract, and borrow or carry digits as necessary. Bring the decimal point straight down into your answer.

$$
\begin{array}{r}
5.17 \\
+\,2.40 \\
\hline
7.57 \\
\end{array}
\qquad\qquad
\begin{array}{r}
^{5}\!6.38 \\
-\,4.50 \\
\hline
1.88 \\
\end{array}
$$

Practice Exercises—Adding and Subtracting with Decimals

Make sure the decimal point goes in the correct place.

1. $\begin{array}{r} 2.45 \\ +\,5.11 \\ \hline \end{array}$
2. $\begin{array}{r} .35 \\ +\,2.69 \\ \hline \end{array}$
3. $\begin{array}{r} 45.725 \\ +\,149.31 \\ \hline \end{array}$
4. $\begin{array}{r} 879.0 \\ -\,276.8 \\ \hline \end{array}$
5. $\begin{array}{r} 12.24 \\ -\,7.33 \\ \hline \end{array}$

6. $78.999 - 45.83$ _____

7. $245.867 + 371.6$ _____

8. $34.08 - 21.327$ _____

9. $381.16 + 275.84$ _____

10. $67.367 - 45.418$ _____

11. Ana waited on three tables during the lunch rush. Each table gave her the following in tips: $7.45, $6.30, and $5.10. How much did she earn in tips over lunch?

12. Russel started the day with $500 in his bank account. If he writes a check for $210.50, how much will be left in his account?

13. Jolisa tries to exercise every day. On Monday she runs 3.25 miles. On Tuesday she runs 2.5 miles, and on Wednesday she runs 2.8 miles. How many miles did she run this week?

14. Use the information in question 13 to answer the following: If Jolisa sets a goal to run 10 miles a week, how many miles will she have to run on Thursday to make her goal?

15. Last night Sharife went to the store. He spent $2.99 on chips and $1.19 on a soda. If he paid with a $10 bill, how much change should he receive?

Multiplying Decimals

STEP 1 Line up the numbers to the right. Do not line them up at the decimal point.

$$4.25 \times 6.1$$

Should be written:
$$\begin{array}{r} 4.25 \\ \times\ 6.1 \end{array}$$

STEP 2 Multiply using the same method as whole numbers.

$$\begin{array}{r} 4.25 \\ \times\ 6.1 \\ \hline 425 \\ 25500 \\ \hline 25925 \end{array}$$

STEP 3 **Do not just move the decimal point down like in addition or subtraction.** Count how many spaces each decimal point is from the right.

$$\begin{array}{r} 4.25 \\ \times\ 6.1 \\ \hline 425 \\ 25500 \\ \hline 25925 \end{array}$$

This decimal point is two places over.
This decimal point is one place over.

STEP 4 **Put the decimal point in your answer. Start at the right and move it over the same number of places you counted in step 3.**

$$\begin{array}{r} 4.25 \\ \times\ 6.1 \\ \hline 425 \\ 25500 \\ \hline 25.925 \end{array}$$

This decimal point is two places over.
This decimal point is one place over.

Since the decimal points moved a total of three places from the right in our problem, we move the decimal point over three places in our answer.

Practice Exercises—Multiplying Decimals

The following problems have been solved for you, but the answer is missing a decimal point. Count the decimal places and put the decimal point in the correct place. The first one has been completed for you.

1.   12.6   One decimal place from right
      × 6.2   One decimal place from right } Two total places
     78.12   Decimal place two from right

2.   8.1
       × 6
      486

4.   17
    × 35.75
     60775

3.   23.54
    × 5.90
  1388660

5.   .123
    × .456
   056088

Solve the following questions. Make sure the decimal point goes in the right place.

6.   5.8
    × 2

8.   6.90
    × 5.34

7.   14.2
    × 7.3

9.   3.75
    × 2.25

10. 6×2.5

11. 5.6×2.3

12. 8.11×2.67

13. 56.10×10

14. Robert is going to a cookout later on tonight. If he stops at a store that is selling hamburgers for $4.89 a pound, how much will he spend if he buys 4 pounds?

15. Jezelle can round the track one time in 45.6 seconds. If she does five laps around the track, how long was she running?

16. Ken works 5 days a week. If he works for 7.5 hours each day, how many hours does he work in a week?

Dividing Decimals

There are two basic parts to every division problem. The dividend and the divisor. Knowing this vocabulary will help you with the steps in dividing decimals.

The dividend is the number being divided, and the divisor is the number you are dividing by.

$$16 \div 4$$

Dividend   Divisor

$$4\overline{)16}$$

Divisor   Dividend

If there is no decimal in the divisor, just divide as normal. Move the decimal point straight up into your answer.

$$
\begin{array}{r}
5\ 75 \\
2\overline{)11.50} \\
-10 \\
\hline
1\ 5 \\
-1\ 4 \\
\hline
10 \\
-10 \\
\hline
0
\end{array}
$$

$$
\begin{array}{r}
5.75 \\
2\overline{)11.50} \\
-10 \\
\hline
1\ 5 \\
-1\ 4 \\
\hline
10 \\
-10 \\
\hline
0
\end{array}
$$

Simply move the decimal point straight up.

STEP 2 If there is a decimal in the divisor, move it over all the way to the right.

$$5.5\overline{)16.50} \text{ becomes } 55\overline{)16.5}$$

STEP 3 Now move the decimal in the dividend over to the right.

$$55\overline{)16.5} \text{ becomes } 55\overline{)165.0}$$

STEP 4 Once the decimals are moved over in both parts of the problem you can divide normally. Simply move the decimal straight up for your answer.

$$
\begin{array}{r}
3.0 \\
55\overline{)165.0} \\
-165 \\
\hline
00 \\
-00 \\
\hline
0
\end{array}
$$

Practice Exercises—Dividing Decimals

Solve the following questions. Make sure the decimal point goes in the right place.

1. $5\overline{)22.5}$

2. $7\overline{)45.5}$

3. $8\overline{)65.000}$

4. $4\overline{)37.00}$

5. $2.5\overline{)5.0}$

6. $4.4\overline{)79.2}$

7. $8.6\overline{)240.8}$

8. $1.8\overline{)36.0}$

9. Alex rode his bike 42.3 miles this week. If he rode his bike 3 days this week, how many miles did he ride per day?

10. Two friends go out to dinner. The bill comes to $37.50. If they split the bill evenly, how much will each pay?

11. Al made $100.80 mowing lawns this week. If he mowed four lawns, how much did he make per lawn?

12. Sidney is pouring lemonade into glasses for her family. If each glass holds 6.5 ounces of lemonade, how many glasses will she pour if she starts with 32.5 ounces of lemonade in the pitcher?

LESSON 5: DECIMAL WORD PROBLEMS

1. Luke's soccer team jogs every practice to stay in shape. On Monday, the team ran 1.56 miles, on Tuesday they ran 1.21 miles, and on Wednesday they ran 1.74 miles. What is the total number of miles the team ran in a week?

2. Every frame that Deana makes uses 2.3 feet of wood. If Deana uses 13.8 feet of wood, how many frames did she make?

3. Paul has a great recipe for chocolate cake. Each cake uses 2.5 cups of flour. If he makes 15 cakes, how much flour will he need?

4. Jarrell keeps all of his change in a jar in his room. Last night he counted it all and discovered he had $35.60. If he uses 75 cents every day on the way to work to pay a toll, how much will he have left in his change jar if he works 4 days this week?

5. Jarrell sorted all of his change into piles of similar coins. He counted 37 dimes, and $16.50 in quarters. How many quarters does he have?
   (A) 16.5
   (B) 66
   (C) 165
   (D) 610.5

6. Everyone in Sue's family measured their height last night in meters. Sue was 1.4 meters tall, her brother was 1.75 meters tall, her mom was 1.35 meters tall, and her father was 1.98 meters tall. What is the sum of all of their heights?
   (A) 4.5
   (B) 6.48
   (C) 6.55
   (D) 7.00

7. Trey earns $11.50 an hour painting. Sometimes he works on the weekends as well as during the week. If he works 40 hours this week, how much money will he earn?
   (A) $3.47
   (B) $28.50
   (C) $51.50
   (D) $460

8. Susan uses ribbon every time she wraps gifts. Today she used 1.05 feet on one present, and 2.35 on a larger present. If a spool of ribbon contains 5 feet of ribbon, how much ribbon does she have left?
   (A) 1.6
   (B) 3.4
   (C) 8.4
   (D) 10.8

9. Paul uses 3.81 gallons of gas driving to and from work. If he works 5 days a week, how much gas does he use driving?
   (A) 7.62
   (B) 11.43
   (C) 15.24
   (D) 19.05

10. Silas deposits $300 in his bank account on Wednesday. On Thursday he writes a check for $13.35. If he deposits a check for $45.80 on Friday, how much money will he have in his account?
    (A) $240.85
    (B) $313.35
    (C) $332.45
    (D) $359.30

Use the menu below to answer questions 11 through 14.

Item	Price
Hamburger	$3.75
Fries	$2.50
Chicken Sandwich	$3.50
Soft Drink	$1.05
Milk Shake	$1.95

11. If Jerry buys a burger, fries, and a soft drink for lunch, how much change will he get if he pays with a $20 bill?

12. On Monday, the lunch special is a chicken sandwich, fries, and soft drink for $6. How much cheaper is the special than if you bought those items at the regular price?

13. Samantha has $50 to spend on a company party. How many burgers can she buy with that amount?

14. How much would five shakes, three burgers, and four orders of fries cost?

END-OF-CHAPTER QUESTIONS

Identify the place value of each digit. The first one has been completed for you.

1. .40<u>5</u>   Five thousandths

2. .<u>1</u>98   _____

3. .9<u>0</u>6   _____

4. 12.3<u>67</u>   _____

Write out each number in words. The first one has been completed for you.

5. .321   Three hundred twenty one thousandths

6. .55   _____

7. 0.8   _____

8. 9.915   _____

Write out each number in digits. The first one has been completed for you.

9. Sixty hundred twelve thousandths   .612 _____

10. Ninety two hundredths _____

11. Three tenths _____

12. Seven and twenty one hundredths _____

13. five hundred fifty five thousandths _____

What new number is created when you switch place values? The first one has been completed for you.

14. .5604 Switch the ten thousandths digit with the tenths digit.   .4605

15. .79270 Switch the hundredths digit with the thousandths digit.   _____

16. .495256 Switch the thousandths digit with the ten thousandths digit.   _____

17. 41.638 Switch the tens digit with the tenths digit.   _____

Circle which number is higher. The first one has been completed for you.

1. (.49) or .055

2. .9 or .890

3. .1211 or .1221

4. 5.1 or 4.9

5. .0056 or .0156

Round the following numbers to the place shown.

1. .8265   to the nearest tenth   _____

                 to the nearest hundredth   _____

                 to the nearest thousandth   _____

2. .7946   to the nearest tenth   _____

                 to the nearest hundredth   _____

                 to the nearest thousandth   _____

3. 5.0545   to the nearest tenth   _____

                 to the nearest hundredth   _____

                 to the nearest thousandth   _____

Complete the following without a calculator.

1. 3.78
    + 2.11

2. 5.12
    + .38

3. 9.07
    + 1.85

4. 4.6 + 7.1

5. 2.03 + 5.8

6. 8.32
    − 6.21

7. 6.724
    − 3.811

8. 1.81
    − 0.92

9. 6.54 − 2.73

10. 6.01 − 2.98

11. 5.6
    × .2

12. 2.3
    × 1.75

13. 3.11
    × 3.12

14. 4.1 × 10.2

15. .5 × 40

16. .5)‾1.5‾

17. .2)‾28.2‾

18. .6)‾36.6‾

19. 20.5 ÷ 5

20. $\frac{4}{2}$

21. Al spent $12.69 on nails, $100.45 on lumber, and $37.12 on paint. What is the total amount of money Al spent fixing his deck?

22. Jill earns $9.50 an hour at her job. If she works 40 hours this week, how much will she earn?

23. Tim has 50 pounds of concrete mix in his truck. At the first job he uses 12.5 pounds, and later that afternoon he uses 20.25 pounds. How many pounds of concrete mix does he have left?

24. Grace has 73.5 cups of sugar in her cabinet. If a recipe calls for 3.5 cups of sugar for every cake, how many cakes can she make?

CHAPTER 6 ANSWER EXPLANATIONS

Lesson 1: Decimals Place Value

WRITE THE PLACE VALUE OF EACH UNDERLINED DIGIT (PAGE 164)

1. Nine tenths
2. Eight hundredths
3. One tenth
4. Eight thousandths
5. One ten thousandths
6. Eight hundred thousandths
7. Nine thousandths
8. Seven millionths
9. Zero ten thousandths

WRITE OUT EACH NUMBER IN WORDS (PAGE 164)

1. Two hundred thirty seven and four hundred ninety eight thousandths
2. Nine tenths
3. Four hundred six thousandths
4. Thirty four and thirty four hundreths
5. Ninety one and five thousandths
6. Two thousand three hundred forty five ten thousandths

WRITE OUT EACH NUMBER USING DIGITS (PAGE 164)

1. 6.931
2. .46
3. 9.6
4. 6.666
5. .312

WHAT NEW NUMBER IS CREATED WHEN YOU SWITCH PLACE VALUES? (PAGE 164)

1. .5326
2. 1.6945
3. 49.730
4. 927.860
5. 16495.2107

Lesson 2: Comparing Decimals

COMPARING DECIMALS (PAGE 166)

1. .54
2. .11
3. .40
4. .91
5. .763
6. .50555
7. .24010
8. .11113
9. 1.1
10. 2.01

Lesson 3: Estimation and Rounding with Decimals

ROUND TO THE NEAREST TENTH (PAGE 168)

1. .4
2. .5
3. .8
4. .1
5. .6
6. 1.2
7. 32.1
8. .1
9. .1
10. 20.0

UNIT 2: MATHEMATICS

ROUND TO THE NEAREST HUNDREDTH (PAGE 168)

1. .45
2. .51
3. .39
4. .29
5. .79
6. 3.68
7. 87.26
8. .68
9. 8.75
10. 6.00

ESTIMATE TO FIND THE ANSWER (PAGE 168)

1. $8 + 8 + 6 + 6 = 28$
2. $3 \times 2 = 6$

Lesson 4: Operations with Decimals

ADDING AND SUBTRACTING WITH DECIMALS (PAGE 169)

1. 7.56
2. 3.04
3. 195.035
4. 602.2
5. 4.91
6. 33.169
7. 617.467
8. 12.753
9. 657
10. 21.949
11. $18.85
12. $289.50
13. 8.55
14. $1.45
15. $5.82

MULTIPLYING DECIMALS (PAGE 172)

1. 78.12
2. 48.6
3. 138.8660
4. 607.75
5. .056088
6. 11.6
7. 103.66
8. 36.846
9. 8.4375
10. 15
11. 12.88
12. 21.6537
13. 561
14. 19.56
15. 228 seconds or 3.8 minutes
16. 37.5

DIVIDING DECIMALS (PAGE 175)

1. 4.5
2. 6.5
3. 8.125
4. 9.25
5. 2
6. 18
7. 28
8. 20
9. 14.1
10. $18.75
11. $25.20
12. 5

Lesson 5: Decimal Word Problems (Page 176)

1. $1.56 + 1.21 + 1.74 = 4.51$
2. $13.8 \div 2.3 = 6$
3. $15 \times 2.5 = 37.5$
4. $.75 \times 4 = \$3.00$
   $35.60 - 3.00 = \$32.60$
5. $16.50 \div .25 = 66$
6. **(B)** $1.4 + 1.75 + 1.35 + 1.98 = 6.48$
7. **(D)** $40 \times 11.5 = \$460$
8. **(A)** $1.05 + 2.35 = 3.40$
   $5 - 3.4 = 1.6$
9. **(D)** $3.81 \times 5 = 19.05$
10. **(C)** $300 - 13.35 = \$286.65$
    $286.65 + 45.8 = \$332.45$

11. $3.75 + 2.5 + 1.05 = \$7.30$
    $20 - 7.30 = \$12.70$
12. $3.5 + 2.5 + 1.05 = \$7.05$
    $7.05 - 6.00 = \$1.05$
13. $50 \div 3.75 = 13.33.$
    She can buy 13 burgers.
14. $5 \times 1.95 = \$9.75$
    $3 \times 3.75 = \$11.25$
    $4 \times 2.50 = \$10.00$
    Total: $31.00

End-of-Chapter Questions (Page 178)

1. Five thousandths
2. One tenth
3. Zero hundredths
4. Six hundredths
5. Three hundred twenty one thousandths
6. Fifty five hundredths
7. Eight tenths
8. Nine and nine hundred fifteen thousandths

9. .612
10. .92
11. .3
12. 7.21
13. .555
14. .4605
15. .72970
16. .492556
17. 61.438

CIRCLE WHICH NUMBER IS HIGHER (PAGE 179)

1. .49
2. .9
3. .1221
4. 5.1
5. .0156

ROUND THE FOLLOWING NUMBERS TO THE PLACE SHOWN (PAGE 179)

1. Tenth: .8
   Hundredth: .83
   Thousandth: .827

2. Tenth: .8
   Hundredth: .79
   Thousandth: .795

3. Tenth: 5.1
   Hundredth: 5.05
   Thousandth: 5.055

COMPLETE THE FOLLOWING WITHOUT A CALCULATOR (PAGE 180)

1. 5.89
2. 5.5
3. 10.92
4. 11.7
5. 7.83
6. 2.11
7. 2.913
8. .89
9. 3.81
10. 3.03
11. 1.12
12. 4.025

13. 9.7032
14. 41.82
15. 20
16. 3
17. 141
18. 61
19. 4.1
20. 2
21. 12.69 + 100.45 + 37.12 = $150.26
22. 9.50 × 40 = $380
23. 50 − 12.5 − 20.25 = 17.25
24. 73.5 ÷ 3.5 = 21

Fractions

LESSON 1: WHAT ARE FRACTIONS?

If you ask the next ten adults that you meet if they are good with fractions, don't be surprised if nine of them say they just can't do it. But don't worry. You are about to become a person who is good with fractions.

Fractions. The very word can make a grown-up feel scared. However, as you are about to see, there is nothing to fear. You've already been using fractions your entire life. If you've ever had a coin in your pocket, guess what? You were using fractions.

So, what is a fraction? A fraction is just a number that is not a whole number like 1, 2, 3, etc. In that way, it is exactly like a decimal. Take a look:

How could you write twenty-five cents as a decimal?   .25

What's another way to write that same amount of money as a quarter?

$\frac{1}{4}$ Because you have one quarter, and it takes four to make a dollar.

You already knew that a quarter was .25, and you probably already knew that you could write that as a fraction $\frac{1}{4}$. Fractions are just another way to write a part of a whole number. They are also a great way to show that you are dividing up a number or an object into equal pieces.

Fraction Basics

Every fraction has two parts: the top number (numerator), and the bottom number (denominator).

- Top number, aka numerator, is the number of shaded pieces.
- Bottom number, aka denominator, is the total number of pieces in the pie.

$$\frac{1}{4}$$

1   Numerator, number of shaded pieces

4   Denominator, number of total pieces in pie

Practice Exercises—Fraction Basics

Write a fraction for each drawing.

1.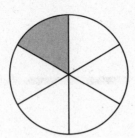

2.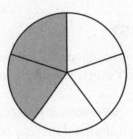

3.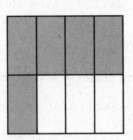

4.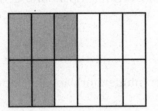

Shade the correct number of slices for each fraction.

5. $\frac{3}{4}$

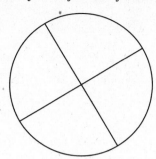

6. $\frac{6}{7}$

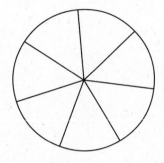

7. $\frac{3}{8}$

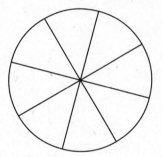

UNIT 2: MATHEMATICS

Draw your own diagram to show the following fractions.

8. $\dfrac{9}{10}$

9. $\dfrac{1}{5}$

10. $\dfrac{2}{4}$

11. $\dfrac{3}{6}$

Using a Ruler

Rulers are an everyday tool used for measurement. Many rulers use fractions to mark the spaces between the whole numbers. The ruler below is marked every half inch.

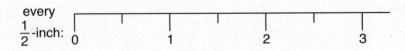

This ruler is marked every quarter, or $\dfrac{1}{4}$ inch.

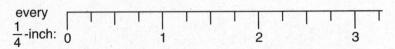

Mark where $\frac{1}{4}$ and $\frac{3}{4}$ of an inch would be on the ruler below.

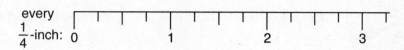

every
$\frac{1}{4}$-inch:

Some rulers, including those you may see on your HSE test, are marked every $\frac{1}{8}$ of inch.

Practice Exercises—Using a Ruler

On the ruler below, mark where $\frac{1}{8}$, $\frac{4}{8}$, and $\frac{7}{8}$ are located on the ruler.

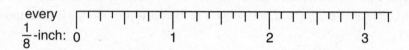

every
$\frac{1}{8}$-inch:

Now, mark where 1 and $\frac{1}{8}$ inch is on the ruler. After that, mark $2\frac{3}{8}$ inches.

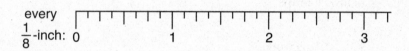

every
$\frac{1}{8}$-inch:

LESSON 2: REDUCING AND COMPARING FRACTIONS
Reducing Fractions

Let's say you and a friend buy a pizza. You open the box and there are six slices. You eat half of the pizza, and your friend eats three slices. Who ate more?

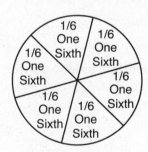

This is how the pizza was sliced into six pieces.

Each slice is worth $\frac{1}{6}$.

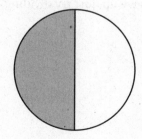

This is how much you ate. One half, or $\frac{1}{2}$.

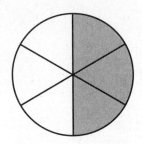

This is how much your friend ate, $\frac{3}{6}$ slices, or the other half.

Therefore, we can see that $\frac{1}{2}$ is the same thing as $\frac{3}{6}$. These are equivalent fractions. This means that even though they use different numbers, they mean the same amount. For example, let's say the pizza had eight total slices. If you still eat half, how many slices would your friend get now?

How can you tell if fractions are equivalent? You must simplify them into lowest terms. All of the fraction answers on your HSE test will be in lowest terms, so this is an important skill to have.

STEPS TO REDUCE A FRACTION

STEP 1 Find a number that divides into the top and bottom of the fraction evenly.

Simplify $\frac{6}{9}$ to lowest terms

$$\frac{6 \div 3}{9 \div 3} = \frac{2}{3}$$ This works.

$$\frac{6 \div 2}{9 \div 3}$$ This does not work. Even though 2 goes into 6 evenly, you must divide the top and bottom by the same number.

STEP 2 Sometimes you will need to divide more than once to get to lowest terms.

Simply $\frac{4}{16}$

$$\frac{4 \div 2}{16 \div 2} = \frac{2}{8}$$ This fraction has been reduced, but it is not yet at its lowest term.

$$\frac{2 \div 2}{8 \div 2} = \frac{1}{4}$$

Reducing fractions takes a little trial and error. Sometimes you find a number that divides into the numerator but not the denominator. Don't give up, just try dividing by another number until you get it!

Practice Exercises—Reducing Fractions

Reduce the following fractions to lowest terms. The first one has been completed for you.

1. $\dfrac{6 \div 6}{9 \div 6} = \dfrac{2}{3}$

2. $\dfrac{12}{15}$

3. $\dfrac{6}{10}$

4. $\dfrac{4}{10}$

5. $\dfrac{20}{30}$

6. $\dfrac{2}{8}$

7. $\dfrac{5}{10}$

8. $\dfrac{8}{20}$

9. $\dfrac{5}{15}$

10. $\dfrac{4}{6}$

11. $\dfrac{6}{14}$

12. $\dfrac{18}{20}$

13. $\dfrac{2}{18}$

14. $\dfrac{9}{12}$

15. $\dfrac{4}{32}$

16. $\dfrac{5}{20}$

17. $\dfrac{20}{24}$

Comparing Fractions

Part of being good with fractions is having a sense of which number is larger than another. In fact, you may encounter test questions that ask you to do just that. For example, we know that $\dfrac{3}{4}$ is larger than $\dfrac{1}{4}$.

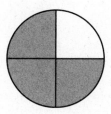 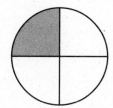

Notice the symbol in the middle. > means "greater than," as in $\dfrac{3}{4}$ is greater than $\dfrac{1}{4}$. This means that it is a larger number.

> **>**
> Greater than

> **<**
> Less than

You can use these symbols to show that a number is larger or smaller than another. For example:

$5 < 10$

Five is less than 10

$\dfrac{1}{2} > \dfrac{1}{4}$

One half is greater than one quarter

$\dfrac{3}{4} < 1$

Three quarters is less than one.

TIP

Think of the greater than sign as an open alligator's mouth: No matter which way it is facing, it wants to eat the largest number.

Which fraction is greater, $\frac{1}{8}$ or $\frac{1}{12}$?

It may seem like $\frac{1}{12}$ is larger, but try to visualize what these fractions look like.

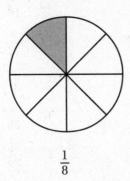

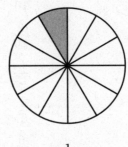

$\frac{1}{8}$ $\frac{1}{12}$

TIP

Just because a fraction uses a larger number does not necessarily mean it is the larger fraction. Stop and visualize what the fraction looks like.

When you look at them side by side, it is easy to see that $\frac{1}{8}$ is bigger than $\frac{1}{10}$.

Think of it like a pizza. If you split a pizza between eight friends, your slice would be slightly larger than if you split it with twelve friends.

Practice Exercise—Ordering Fractions

Order the following fractions from smallest to largest.

1. $\frac{1}{5}, \frac{1}{9}, \frac{1}{2}, \frac{1}{8}, \frac{1}{4}$ $\frac{\square}{\square}, \frac{\square}{\square}, \frac{\square}{\square}, \frac{\square}{\square}, \frac{\square}{\square}$

2. $\frac{1}{6}, \frac{1}{15}, \frac{1}{13}, \frac{1}{3}, \frac{1}{10}$ $\frac{\square}{\square}, \frac{\square}{\square}, \frac{\square}{\square}, \frac{\square}{\square}, \frac{\square}{\square}$

3. $\frac{1}{2}, \frac{1}{4}, \frac{1}{6}, \frac{1}{3}, \frac{1}{8}$ $\frac{\square}{\square}, \frac{\square}{\square}, \frac{\square}{\square}, \frac{\square}{\square}, \frac{\square}{\square}$

Write three fractions larger than $\frac{1}{10}$.

$\frac{\square}{\square}, \frac{\square}{\square}, \frac{\square}{\square}$

Comparing fractions is easy when the top number (numerator) is one. But what about fractions like $\frac{2}{3}$ and $\frac{3}{5}$? Then how do you know which is larger?

Steps for Comparing Fractions

STEP 1 Cross-multiply diagonally starting at the top left.

Which is bigger?

$$\frac{2}{3} \qquad \text{or} \qquad \frac{3}{5}$$

$\frac{2}{3} \searrow \frac{3}{5}$ $2 \times 5 = 10$ Use this answer to judge the left fraction. ($\frac{2}{5}$)

STEP 2 Cross-multiply the other direction starting at the top right.

$\frac{2}{3} \swarrow \frac{3}{5}$ $3 \times 3 = 9$ Use this answer to judge the right fraction. ($\frac{3}{5}$)

STEP 3 Compare the two answers. The highest number is the largest fraction. REMEMBER: Start at the top left for the left fraction; start at the top right for the right fraction.

$10 > 9$. Therefore, $\frac{2}{3}$ is greater than $\frac{3}{5}$.

Here's another example:

Which is larger?

$\frac{4}{7}$ or $\frac{5}{9}$

$\frac{4}{7} \searrow \frac{5}{9}$ Multiply $4 \times 9 = 36$.

$\frac{4}{7} \swarrow \frac{5}{9}$ Multiply $5 \times 7 = 35$.

Compare the two answers. $36 > 35$. Therefore, $\frac{4}{7}$ is larger than $\frac{5}{9}$.

Practice Exercises—Comparing Fractions

Use the greater than (>) or less than (<) symbols to show which fraction is larger. The first one has been completed for you.

1. $\frac{7}{10}$ ⤫ $\frac{3}{4}$ $4 \times 7 = 28$
    $3 \times 10 = 30$ <

7. $\frac{2}{6}$ ☐ $\frac{2}{5}$

2. $\frac{8}{9}$ ☐ $\frac{4}{5}$

8. $\frac{3}{4}$ ☐ $\frac{5}{6}$

3. $\frac{3}{7}$ ☐ $\frac{2}{6}$

9. $\frac{3}{8}$ ☐ $\frac{2}{7}$

4. $\frac{1}{3}$ ☐ $\frac{6}{10}$

10. $\frac{4}{5}$ ☐ $\frac{4}{6}$

5. $\frac{6}{9}$ ☐ $\frac{9}{10}$

11. $\frac{2}{7}$ ☐ $\frac{1}{3}$

6. $\frac{8}{8}$ ☐ $\frac{6}{7}$

12. $\frac{7}{8}$ ☐ $\frac{3}{4}$

LESSON 3: IMPROPER FRACTIONS AND MIXED NUMBERS

So far, we have looked at fractions that are less than one, such as, $\frac{3}{4}$ of a cake, $\frac{1}{2}$ of a dollar, or $\frac{1}{4}$ of a pie. But fractions can also be used for numbers greater than one. For example, let's say you have two pizzas, and each pizza has four slices. If you eat three pieces, how many pieces do you have left?

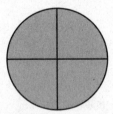 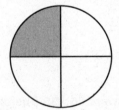

Clearly there are five pieces left. Or, another way to look at it is that there is one whole pizza and one slice left. Both are correct, there are two different ways to write fractions greater than one.

Improper Fractions

In an improper fraction, the top number (numerator) is greater than the bottom number (denominator). So, for our pizza example above, you could write an improper fraction as 5/4. There are five slices left (numerator), and there are four slices per pizza (denominator).

Mixed Numbers

A mixed number uses a whole number and a fraction. So, for our pizza example above, you could write a mixed number as $1\frac{1}{4}$. There is one whole pizza (whole number), and one slice (numerator) out of four slices per pizza (denominator) left.

Practice Exercises—Improper Fractions and Mixed Numbers

Write an improper fraction and mixed number for each diagram. The first one has been completed for you.

		Improper Fraction	Mixed Number
1.		$\frac{11}{4}$	$2\frac{3}{4}$
2.		$\frac{\square}{\square}$	$\square\frac{\square}{\square}$
3.		$\frac{\square}{\square}$	$\square\frac{\square}{\square}$
4.		$\frac{\square}{\square}$	$\square\frac{\square}{\square}$
5.		$\frac{\square}{\square}$	$\square\frac{\square}{\square}$

Changing an Improper Fraction to a Mixed Number

STEP 1 Divide the top number (numerator) by the bottom number (denominator). The answer is the whole number of your mixed number.

Write $\frac{7}{4}$ as a mixed number.

$$\begin{array}{r} 1 \\ 4\overline{)7} \\ \underline{-4} \\ 3 \end{array}$$

One is the whole number.

STEP 2 If there is a remainder, use it as the numerator in your mixed number. The denominator always stays the same.

$$\begin{array}{r} 1 \\ 4\overline{)7} \\ \underline{-4} \\ 3 \end{array}$$

Three is the remainder.

$\frac{7}{4}$ written as a mixed number is $1\frac{3}{4}$

Another example:

Write $\frac{15}{6}$ as a mixed number.

$$\begin{array}{r} 2 \\ 6\overline{)15} \\ \underline{-12} \\ 3 \end{array}$$

$\frac{15}{6}$ written as a mixed number $2\frac{3}{6}$. In lowest terms, it is $2\frac{1}{2}$.

Practice Exercises—Changing Improper Fractions to Mixed Numbers

Change the following improper fractions to mixed numbers.

1. $\frac{9}{5} = \square\frac{\square}{\square}$

2. $\frac{9}{2} = \square\frac{\square}{\square}$

3. $\frac{15}{4} = \square\frac{\square}{\square}$

4. $\frac{20}{3} = \square\frac{\square}{\square}$

5. $\frac{7}{2} = \square\frac{\square}{\square}$

6. $\frac{11}{3} = \square\frac{\square}{\square}$

7. $\frac{15}{7} = \square\frac{\square}{\square}$

8. $\frac{11}{5} = \square\frac{\square}{\square}$

9. $\frac{41}{10} = \square\frac{\square}{\square}$

10. $\frac{16}{9} = \square\frac{\square}{\square}$

Changing Mixed Numbers to Improper Fractions

Change $2\frac{3}{4}$ to an improper fraction.

STEP 1 Multiply the bottom number (denominator) and the whole number.

$$2 \diagdown \frac{3}{4}$$

$$2 \times 4 = 8$$

STEP 2 Add the answer from Step 1 to the top number (numerator). Write that answer in the numerator spot.

$$2 \, \frac{\textcircled{3}}{4}$$

$$8 + 3 = 11$$

$$\frac{11}{4}$$

The denominator always stays the same.

Another example:

Change $5\frac{1}{3}$ to an improper fraction.

$$5 \, \frac{1}{3}$$

$3 \times 5 = 16$ (Step 1)

$16 + 1 = 17$ (Step 2)

$\frac{17}{3}$ is the answer.

Practice Exercises—Changing Mixed Numbers to Improper Fractions

Change the following mixed numbers to improper fractions.

1. $2\frac{1}{2} = \dfrac{\square}{\square}$

2. $4\frac{2}{3} = \dfrac{\square}{\square}$

3. $1\frac{5}{6} = \dfrac{\square}{\square}$

4. $6\frac{4}{9} = \dfrac{\square}{\square}$

5. $3\frac{4}{5} = \dfrac{\square}{\square}$

6. $8\frac{2}{3} = \dfrac{\square}{\square}$

7. $6\frac{1}{4} = \dfrac{\square}{\square}$

8. $4\frac{2}{7} = \dfrac{\square}{\square}$

9. $3\frac{3}{4} = \dfrac{\square}{\square}$

10. $5\frac{1}{6} = \dfrac{\square}{\square}$

LESSON 4: OPERATIONS WITH FRACTIONS

The good news is that the test will not ask you to do a lot of adding, subtracting, multiplying, or dividing with fractions. Furthermore, you are allowed to use a calculator on the test, and there is a fraction key on the official calculator. You will learn how to use the calculator in later lessons.

So please don't think that if you are rusty on fractions you cannot pass the math test. That said, it would still be a good idea to refresh your memory on how to do some basic math with fractions.

Adding and Subtracting Like Fractions

Fractions that have the same bottom numbers (denominators) are called like fractions. These are the easiest fractions to add and subtract.

$\frac{1}{4}$ and $\frac{3}{4}$ are like fractions.

$\frac{1}{2}$ and $\frac{3}{4}$ are not like fractions.

STEP 1 Add or subtract the top numbers (numerators).

Example One $\quad \frac{1}{8} + \frac{3}{8} \quad$ Example Two $\quad \frac{7}{8} - \frac{1}{8}$

$1 + 3 = 4 \qquad\qquad\qquad 7 - 1 = 6$

STEP 2 Put that answer in the numerator. The denominator stays the same.

$\frac{4}{8} \qquad\qquad\qquad\qquad \frac{6}{8}$

STEP 3 Always reduce to lowest terms if possible.

$\frac{4 \div 4 = 1}{8 \div 4 = 4} \qquad\qquad\qquad \frac{6 \div 2 = 3}{8 \div 2 = 4}$

Fractions that have the same numerators and denominators always equal one.

For example, $\frac{3}{3} = 1 \qquad \frac{5}{5} = 1 \qquad \frac{12}{12} = 1$

Practice Exercises—Adding and Subtracting Like Numbers

Complete the following exercises.

1. $\dfrac{2}{5} + \dfrac{2}{5}$

2. $\dfrac{3}{7} + \dfrac{4}{7}$

3. $\dfrac{4}{9} + \dfrac{2}{9}$

4. $\dfrac{5}{6} - \dfrac{2}{6}$

5. $\dfrac{6}{8} - \dfrac{5}{8}$

6. $\dfrac{5}{9} + \dfrac{5}{9}$

7. $\dfrac{4}{7} - \dfrac{3}{7}$

8. $\dfrac{15}{20} - \dfrac{5}{20}$

9. $\dfrac{1}{6} + \dfrac{2}{6}$

10. $\dfrac{6}{9} - \dfrac{3}{9}$

Subtracting a Fraction from the Number One

Let's say you opened a one pound box of pasta. If you cook $\dfrac{1}{3}$ of pound, how much do you have left?

To answer this, you will need to change the whole number to a like fraction.

$$1 - \dfrac{1}{3}$$

STEP 1 Change the whole number to a like fraction. Use the same denominator.

$$\textcircled{\dfrac{}{3}} - \textcircled{\dfrac{1}{3}}$$

STEP 2 Any number with the same numerator and denominator equals one. Therefore, make the numerator the same as the denominator then subtract.

$$\dfrac{3}{3} - \dfrac{1}{3} = \dfrac{2}{3}$$

Subtracting Fractions from Whole Numbers Other than One

Let's say we use $\dfrac{3}{4}$ of a gallon of paint from a 5-gallon can. How much paint do we have left?

To do this, we will need to borrow.

$$\begin{array}{r} 5 \\ - \dfrac{3}{4} \\ \hline \end{array}$$

STEP 1 Borrow one from the whole number column and turn it into a fraction. Use the same denominator as the fraction in the problem to create a like fraction. This is like changing a five dollar bill for four one dollar bills and four quarters.

$$\begin{array}{r} 5 \\ - \dfrac{3}{4} \\ \hline \end{array} \qquad\qquad \begin{array}{r} 4\dfrac{4}{4} \\ - \dfrac{3}{4} \\ \hline \end{array}$$

Subtract.

$$4\frac{4}{4}$$
$$-\frac{3}{4}$$
$$4\frac{1}{4}$$

Practice Exercises—Subtracting Fractions from Whole Numbers

Complete the following exercises. Borrow to form a like fraction to subtract.

1. $\begin{array}{r} 1 \\ -\frac{2}{3} \\ \hline \end{array}$

2. $\begin{array}{r} 1 \\ -\frac{3}{5} \\ \hline \end{array}$

3. $\begin{array}{r} 1 \\ -\frac{1}{2} \\ \hline \end{array}$

4. $\begin{array}{r} 1 \\ -\frac{4}{5} \\ \hline \end{array}$

5. $\begin{array}{r} 1 \\ -\frac{7}{8} \\ \hline \end{array}$

6. $\begin{array}{r} 3 \\ -\frac{3}{4} \\ \hline \end{array}$

7. $\begin{array}{r} 4 \\ -\frac{1}{4} \\ \hline \end{array}$

8. $\begin{array}{r} 5 \\ -\frac{1}{3} \\ \hline \end{array}$

9. $\begin{array}{r} 6 \\ -\frac{2}{7} \\ \hline \end{array}$

10. $\begin{array}{r} 7 \\ -\frac{5}{6} \\ \hline \end{array}$

Subtracting Mixed Numbers

Emily has $2\frac{3}{8}$ feet of yarn. If she uses $1\frac{1}{8}$, how much does she have left?

STEP 1 Subtract the fractions first.

$$2\frac{3}{8}$$
$$-1\frac{1}{8}$$
$$\frac{2}{8}$$

Subtract the whole numbers. Reduce to lowest terms if necessary.

$$2\frac{3}{8}$$

$$-1\frac{1}{8}$$

$$1\frac{2}{8} = 1\frac{1}{4}$$

Practice Exercises—Subtracting Mixed Numbers

Complete the following exercises.

1. $3\frac{4}{5}$ 2. $4\frac{3}{4}$ 3. $5\frac{2}{3}$ 4. $6\frac{5}{7}$ 5. $7\frac{5}{6}$

    $-1\frac{2}{5}$ $-2\frac{1}{4}$ $-1\frac{1}{3}$ $-6\frac{2}{7}$ $-4\frac{5}{6}$

Adding and Subtracting Fractions with Unlike Denominators

This gets a little more tricky. We know that when the bottom numbers (denominators) of fractions are the same, we can simply add up the numerators. However, when the denominators are not the same, we need to do a little math first to make them the same.

STEP 1 Multiply the denominators to find a common denominator.

$\frac{1}{4} + \frac{2}{5}$ These fractions cannot be added because they have different denominators.

$\frac{1}{4} \longleftrightarrow \frac{2}{5}$ Multiply the denominators to find a common denominator.
$4 \times 5 = 20$, so 20 will be the common denominator.

STEP 2 Cross-multiply to find the numerators.

$\frac{1}{4} \times \frac{2}{5}$ $1 \times 5 = 5$. 5 will be the numerator on the left.
$2 \times 4 = 8$. 8 will be the numerator on the right.

STEP 3 Rewrite the problem with the new numbers and solve.

$$\frac{1}{4} + \frac{2}{5} = \frac{5}{20} + \frac{8}{20}$$

$$\frac{5}{20} + \frac{8}{20} = \frac{13}{20}$$

Another example:

$$\frac{3}{4} - \frac{1}{2}$$

$$\frac{3}{4} \longleftrightarrow \frac{1}{2}$$ $4 \times 2 = 8$. 8 will be the common denominator.

$$\frac{3}{4} \diagdown\diagup \frac{1}{2}$$ $3 \times 2 = 6$. 6 will be the numerator on the left.
                      $4 \times 1 = 4$. 4 will be the numerator on the right.

$$\frac{6}{6} - \frac{4}{8} = \frac{2}{8}$$ Reduce answer to lowest terms whenever possible.

$$\frac{2}{8} = \frac{1}{4}$$

Practice Exercises—Adding and Subtracting Fractions with Unlike Denominators

Complete the following exercises.

1. $\dfrac{3}{4} + \dfrac{1}{2}$ 5. $\dfrac{2}{3} + \dfrac{3}{5}$ 9. $\dfrac{1}{3} - \dfrac{1}{4}$

2. $\dfrac{2}{5} + \dfrac{2}{5}$ 6. $\dfrac{3}{4} - \dfrac{1}{2}$ 10. $\dfrac{2}{3} - \dfrac{1}{5}$

3. $\dfrac{1}{4} + \dfrac{1}{2}$ 7. $\dfrac{2}{5} - \dfrac{1}{4}$

4. $\dfrac{1}{3} + \dfrac{1}{4}$ 8. $\dfrac{3}{4} - \dfrac{1}{3}$

Multiplying Fractions

Many people find that multiplying is the easiest task to perform with fractions. To multiply fractions there are just three simple steps:

STEP 1 Multiply the numerators.

$$\frac{1}{3} \times \frac{3}{4}$$

$$\frac{1}{3} \times \frac{3}{4} = \frac{3}{}$$

STEP 2 Multiply the denominators.

$$\frac{1}{3} \times \frac{3}{4} = \frac{3}{12}$$

STEP 3 Reduce the answer to lowest terms as necessary.

$$\frac{3}{12} \div \frac{3}{3} = \frac{1}{4}$$

Another example:

$$\frac{2}{3} \times \frac{3}{7}$$

$$\frac{2}{3} \times \frac{3}{7} = \frac{6}{21}$$

$$\frac{6}{21} = \frac{2}{7}$$

Practice Exercises—Multiplying Fractions

Complete the following exercises.

1. $\frac{3}{4} \times \frac{2}{3}$

2. $\frac{1}{6} \times \frac{5}{7}$

3. $\frac{4}{9} \times \frac{2}{5}$

4. $\frac{3}{6} \times \frac{3}{6}$

5. $\frac{4}{5} \times \frac{1}{2}$

6. $\frac{4}{5} \times \frac{2}{5}$

7. $\frac{6}{1} \times \frac{6}{7}$

8. $\frac{4}{8} \times \frac{6}{5}$

9. $\frac{6}{4} \times \frac{5}{1}$

10. $\frac{3}{5} \times \frac{1}{3}$

Dividing with Fractions

Dividing with fractions is very similar to multiplying. In fact, the only difference is that you need to find the **inverse** of the number you are dividing by. This just means that you need to find the opposite of that number, so you need to turn that fraction upside down.

For example, the inverse of $\frac{1}{5}$ is $\frac{5}{1}$.

The inverse of $\frac{2}{3}$ is $\frac{3}{2}$.

STEP 1 Find the inverse of the number you are dividing by.

$$\frac{2}{3} \div \frac{1}{6}$$

$$\frac{2}{3} \div \frac{6}{1}$$

STEP 2 Once inverted, multiply the fractions.

$$\frac{2}{3} \times \frac{6}{1} = \frac{12}{3}$$

STEP 3 Reduce to simplest terms as necessary.

$$12 \div 3 = \underline{4}$$
$$3 \div 3 = 1$$

Another example:

$$\frac{4}{5} \div \frac{2}{3}$$

$$\frac{4}{5} \times \frac{3}{2} = \frac{12}{10}$$

$$\frac{12}{10} = \frac{6}{5} \text{ or } 1\frac{1}{5}$$

Practice Exercises—Dividng with Fractions

Complete the following exercises.

1. $\frac{2}{5} \div \frac{4}{7}$

2. $\frac{1}{3} \div \frac{2}{7}$

3. $\frac{4}{6} \div \frac{3}{5}$

4. $\frac{7}{6} \div \frac{1}{6}$

5. $\frac{3}{5} \div \frac{1}{4}$

6. $\frac{5}{3} \div \frac{2}{4}$

7. $\frac{6}{6} \div \frac{1}{7}$

8. $\frac{2}{3} \div \frac{4}{5}$

9. $\frac{9}{4} \div \frac{1}{5}$

10. $\frac{3}{5} \div \frac{1}{5}$

LESSON 5: FRACTION WORD PROBLEMS

1. Paul has a goal to jog 10 miles this weekend. If he runs $3\frac{3}{4}$ miles on Saturday, how many miles does he need to run on Sunday to meet his goal?

2. A recipe for a cake calls for $\frac{2}{3}$ of a cup of flour. If you plan on making four cakes, how many cups of flour will you need?

3. You have a shoe box that measures $\frac{4}{5}$ of a foot long, and you are going to put some old books into the shoe box. If each book measures $\frac{1}{10}$ of a foot wide, how many books can you put into the shoe box?

4. 100 people went to the movie theater on Saturday afternoon. If $\frac{3}{4}$ of those people were children, how many children were in the theater?

5. Ken worked $7\frac{1}{2}$ hours on Friday, $6\frac{1}{4}$ hours on Saturday, and $8\frac{1}{4}$ hours on Sunday. How many total hours did he work?

6. Alice makes one chair every $3\frac{1}{2}$ hours at work. If she works 21 hours this week, how many chairs will she make at work?

(A) 6

(B) $17\frac{1}{2}$

(C) $24\frac{1}{2}$

(D) $73\frac{1}{2}$

7. Jarrel is weighing packages at the post office. One package weighs $\frac{3}{8}$ of a pound, and the other package weighs $\frac{5}{8}$ of a pound. What is the total weight of both packages?

(A) $\frac{2}{8}$

(B) $\frac{8}{16}$

(C) 1

(D) $\frac{15}{8}$

8. Calvin started with $\frac{3}{4}$ of a pound of turkey. If he makes a sandwich using $\frac{3}{8}$ of a pound of turkey, how much turkey does he have left?

(A) $\frac{9}{32}$

(B) $\frac{6}{12}$

(C) $\frac{3}{8}$

(D) $\frac{6}{4}$

9. Jen needs to cut a board into $\frac{1}{5}$ foot sections. If the board is 2 feet long, how many sections will she have?

(THINK: 2 can be written as a fraction $\frac{2}{1}$.)

(A) $\frac{2}{5}$

(B) $\frac{3}{5}$

(C) 10

(D) 15

10. Each bolt in Kevin's toolbox is $\frac{7}{8}$ of an inch long. If he lays nine bolts end to end, how long will the line of bolts be?

(A) $\frac{2}{8}$

(B) 2

(C) $7\frac{7}{8}$

(D) 63

11. Sam rides his bike to school every day. He rides $4\frac{1}{2}$ miles to school, but today he took a longer route home. If his route home was $\frac{1}{8}$ of a mile longer, how many total miles did Sam ride today?

(A) $4\frac{3}{8}$

(B) $4\frac{5}{8}$

(C) 9

(D) $9\frac{1}{8}$

12. Sidney has a long piece of licorice that measures $2\frac{2}{3}$ feet long. If she splits it in half with her sister, how long will each piece be?

(A) 1

(B) $1\frac{1}{3}$

(C) 2

(D) $5\frac{1}{3}$

13. Tim gets $7\frac{3}{4}$ hours of sleep a night. How many hours will he sleep over a week?

(A) $38\frac{3}{4}$

(B) 40

(C) 49

(D) $54\frac{1}{4}$

14. A restaurant served 200 people on a busy Saturday night. $\frac{2}{5}$ of the people there ordered the dinner special. How many people *didn't* order the special?

(THINK: First figure out what fraction *didn't* order the special.)

(A) 25

(B) 40

(C) 80

(D) 120

END-OF-CHAPTER QUESTIONS

Write a fraction for each drawing.

1.

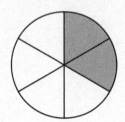

2. $\frac{\square}{\square}$

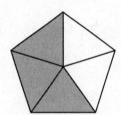

Shade each of the following fractions correctly.

3. $\frac{2}{7}$

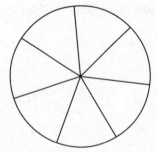

4. $\frac{1}{2}$

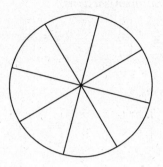

5. Label the following points on the ruler: $\frac{1}{8}$, $\frac{3}{8}$, $\frac{1}{2}$, $\frac{7}{8}$.

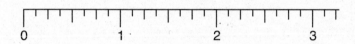

Write an improper fraction and mixed number for each diagram.

	Improper Fraction	**Mixed Number**

6.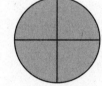

7.

Change the following improper fractions to mixed numbers.

8. $\frac{5}{4}$ = ☐ $\frac{☐}{☐}$ $\frac{8}{3}$ = ☐ $\frac{☐}{☐}$ $\frac{15}{10}$ = ☐ $\frac{☐}{☐}$ $\frac{11}{6}$ = ☐ $\frac{☐}{☐}$

Change the following mixed numbers to improper fractions.

9. $3\frac{1}{2} = \frac{\square}{\square}$ $\qquad$ $1\frac{5}{6} = \frac{\square}{\square}$ $\qquad$ $4\frac{2}{5} = \frac{\square}{\square}$ $\qquad$ $2\frac{2}{3} = \frac{\square}{\square}$

Reduce the following fractions to lowest terms.

10. $\frac{5}{10} = \frac{\square}{\square}$ $\qquad$ $\frac{9}{12} = \frac{\square}{\square}$ $\qquad$ $\frac{6}{9} = \frac{\square}{\square}$ $\qquad$ $\frac{2}{8} = \frac{\square}{\square}$

Order the following fractions from smallest to largest.

11. $\frac{1}{5}, \frac{1}{4}, \frac{1}{6}, \frac{1}{2}, \frac{1}{7}$ $\qquad\qquad$ $\frac{\square}{\square}, \frac{\square}{\square}, \frac{\square}{\square}, \frac{\square}{\square}, \frac{\square}{\square}$

Use the greater than or less than symbols to show which fraction is larger.

12. $\frac{2}{3}$ $\square$ $\frac{3}{4}$

13. $\frac{1}{2}$ $\square$ $\frac{4}{5}$

14. $\frac{2}{5}$ $\square$ $\frac{1}{2}$

15. $\frac{3}{4}$ $\square$ $\frac{3}{5}$

Complete the following exercises.

16. $\frac{1}{5} + \frac{2}{5}$ $\qquad\qquad$ 19. $\frac{5}{6} - \frac{1}{3}$ $\qquad\qquad$ 22. $\begin{array}{r} 4 \\ -\frac{1}{4} \\ \hline \end{array}$

17. $\frac{5}{7} - \frac{4}{7}$ $\qquad\qquad$ 20. $\frac{6}{8} - \frac{1}{4}$ $\qquad\qquad$ 23. $3\frac{5}{6} - 1\frac{1}{6}$

18. $\frac{1}{2} + \frac{1}{4}$ $\qquad\qquad$ 21. $\begin{array}{r} 3 \\ -\frac{3}{4} \\ \hline \end{array}$ $\qquad\qquad$ 24. $5\frac{1}{5} - 2\frac{1}{5}$

25. $\dfrac{2}{4} \times \dfrac{3}{5}$

27. $\dfrac{4}{5} \div \dfrac{1}{5}$

29. $\dfrac{3}{5} \div \dfrac{1}{10}$

26. $\dfrac{3}{1} \times \dfrac{2}{3}$

28. $\dfrac{5}{2} \div \dfrac{1}{2}$

30. Josh works $5\dfrac{1}{3}$ hours per shift. He works 5 days this week, how many total hours will he work?

31. Tina has a 5-foot long board. If she cuts $1\dfrac{3}{4}$ feet of the end of the board, how long will the board be now?

32. Paula is stocking a shelf with boxes at work. If the shelf measures 15 feet long, how many boxes can she put on the shelf if each box measures $1\dfrac{1}{4}$ feet wide?

33. If Deandria measures one string to be $4\dfrac{1}{2}$ inches long, and another string to be $4\dfrac{3}{4}$ inches long, how long are both strings together?

CHAPTER 7 ANSWER EXPLANATIONS

Lesson 1: What Are Fractions?

PRACTICE EXERCISES—FRACTION BASICS (PAGE 186)

1. $\frac{1}{6}$

2. $\frac{2}{5}$

3. $\frac{5}{8}$

4. $\frac{5}{12}$

5. $\frac{3}{4}$

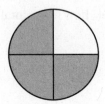

6. $\frac{6}{7}$

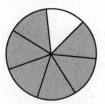

7. $\frac{3}{8}$

8. $\frac{9}{10}$

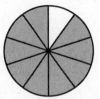

UNIT 2: MATHEMATICS

9. $\frac{1}{5}$

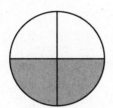

10. $\frac{2}{4}$

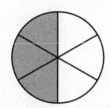

11. $\frac{3}{6}$

PRACTICE EXERCISES—USING A RULER (PAGE 189)

Mark where $\frac{1}{4}$ and $\frac{3}{4}$ of an inch would be on the ruler below.

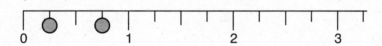

On the ruler below, mark where $\frac{1}{8}$, $\frac{4}{8}$, and $\frac{7}{8}$ are located on the ruler.

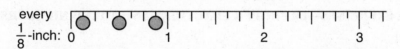

Now, mark where 1 and $\frac{1}{8}$ inch is on the ruler. After that, mark $2\frac{3}{8}$ inches.

UNIT 2: MATHEMATICS

Lesson 2: Reducing Fractions and Comparing Fractions

PRACTICE EXERCISES—REDUCING FRACTIONS (PAGE 191)

1. $\frac{2}{3}$ 6. $\frac{1}{4}$ 11. $\frac{3}{7}$ 16. $\frac{1}{4}$

2. $\frac{4}{5}$ 7. $\frac{1}{2}$ 12. $\frac{9}{10}$ 17. $\frac{5}{6}$

3. $\frac{3}{5}$ 8. $\frac{2}{5}$ 13. $\frac{1}{9}$

4. $\frac{2}{5}$ 9. $\frac{1}{3}$ 14. $\frac{3}{4}$

5. $\frac{2}{3}$ 10. $\frac{2}{3}$ 15. $\frac{1}{8}$

PRACTICE EXERCISES—ORDERING FRACTIONS (PAGE 192)

1. $\frac{1}{9}, \frac{1}{8}, \frac{1}{5}, \frac{1}{4}, \frac{1}{2}$

2. $\frac{1}{15}, \frac{1}{13}, \frac{1}{10}, \frac{1}{6}, \frac{1}{3}$

3. $\frac{1}{8}, \frac{1}{6}, \frac{1}{4}, \frac{1}{3}, \frac{1}{2}$

PRACTICE EXERCISES—COMPARING FRACTIONS (PAGE 194)

1. $\frac{3}{4}$ 4. $\frac{6}{10}$ 7. $\frac{2}{5}$ 10. $\frac{4}{5}$

2. $\frac{8}{9}$ 5. $\frac{9}{10}$ 8. $\frac{5}{6}$ 11. $\frac{1}{3}$

3. $\frac{3}{7}$ 6. $\frac{8}{8}$ 9. $\frac{3}{8}$ 12. $\frac{7}{8}$

Lesson 3: Improper Fractions and Mixed Numbers

PRACTICE EXERCISES—IMPROPER FRACTIONS AND MIXED NUMBERS (PAGE 195)

1. $\frac{11}{4}, 2\frac{3}{4}$

2. $\frac{13}{10}, 1\frac{3}{10}$

3. $\frac{9}{5}, 1\frac{4}{5}$

4. $\frac{19}{8}, 2\frac{3}{8}$

5. $\frac{20}{6}, 3\frac{2}{6}$

PRACTICE EXERCISES—CHANGING IMPROPER FRACTIONS TO MIXED NUMBERS (PAGE 196)

1. $1\frac{4}{5}$
2. $4\frac{1}{2}$
3. $3\frac{3}{4}$
4. $6\frac{2}{3}$
5. $3\frac{1}{2}$
6. $3\frac{2}{3}$
7. $2\frac{1}{7}$
8. $2\frac{1}{5}$
9. $4\frac{1}{10}$
10. $1\frac{7}{9}$

PRACTICE EXERCISES—CHANGING MIXED NUMBERS TO IMPROPER FRACTIONS (PAGE 197)

1. $\frac{5}{2}$
2. $\frac{14}{3}$
3. $\frac{11}{6}$
4. $\frac{58}{9}$
5. $\frac{19}{5}$
6. $\frac{26}{3}$
7. $\frac{25}{4}$
8. $\frac{30}{7}$
9. $\frac{15}{4}$
10. $\frac{31}{6}$

Lesson 4: Operations with Fractions

PRACTICE EXERCISES—ADDING AND SUBTRACTING LIKE NUMBERS (PAGE 199)

1. $\frac{4}{5}$
2. $\frac{7}{7} = 1$
3. $\frac{6}{9} = \frac{2}{3}$
4. $\frac{3}{6} = \frac{1}{2}$
5. $\frac{1}{8}$
6. $\frac{10}{9}$
7. $\frac{1}{7}$
8. $\frac{10}{20} = \frac{1}{2}$
9. $\frac{3}{6} = \frac{1}{2}$
10. $\frac{3}{9} = \frac{1}{3}$

PRACTICE EXERCISES—SUBTRACTING FRACTIONS FROM WHOLE NUMBERS (PAGE 200)

1. $\frac{1}{3}$
2. $\frac{2}{5}$
3. $\frac{1}{2}$
4. $\frac{1}{5}$
5. $\frac{1}{8}$
6. $2\frac{1}{4}$
7. $3\frac{3}{4}$
8. $4\frac{2}{3}$
9. $5\frac{5}{7}$
10. $6\frac{1}{6}$

PRACTICE EXERCISES—SUBTRACTING MIXED NUMBERS (PAGE 201)

1. $2\frac{2}{5}$
2. $2\frac{2}{4} = 2\frac{1}{2}$
3. $4\frac{1}{3}$
4. $\frac{3}{7}$
5. 3

PRACTICE EXERCISES—ADDING AND SUBTRACTING FRACTIONS WITH UNLIKE DENOMINATORS (PAGE 202)

1. $1\frac{1}{4}$
2. $\frac{4}{5}$
3. $\frac{3}{4}$
4. $\frac{7}{12}$
5. $1\frac{4}{15}$
6. $\frac{1}{4}$
7. $\frac{3}{20}$
8. $\frac{5}{12}$
9. $\frac{1}{12}$
10. $\frac{7}{15}$

PRACTICE EXERCISES—MULTIPLYING FRACTIONS (PAGE 203)

1. $\frac{6}{12} = \frac{1}{2}$
2. $\frac{5}{42}$
3. $\frac{8}{45}$
4. $\frac{9}{36} = \frac{1}{4}$
5. $\frac{4}{10} = \frac{2}{5}$
6. $\frac{8}{25}$
7. $\frac{36}{7}$
8. $\frac{24}{40} = \frac{3}{5}$
9. $\frac{30}{4} = \frac{15}{2}$
10. $\frac{3}{15} = \frac{1}{5}$

1. $\dfrac{14}{20} = \dfrac{7}{10}$ 　　3. $\dfrac{20}{18} = \dfrac{10}{9}$ 　　5. $\dfrac{12}{5}$ 　　7. $\dfrac{42}{6} = 7$ 　　9. $\dfrac{45}{4}$

2. $\dfrac{7}{6}$ 　　4. $\dfrac{42}{6} = 7$ 　　6. $\dfrac{20}{6} = \dfrac{10}{3}$ 　　8. $\dfrac{10}{12} = \dfrac{5}{6}$ 　　10. $\dfrac{15}{5} = 3$

Lesson 5: Fraction Word Problems (Page 205)

1. $10 - 3\dfrac{3}{4} = 6\dfrac{1}{4}$

2. $4 \times \dfrac{2}{3} = \dfrac{8}{3}$, or $2\dfrac{2}{3}$ cups

3. $\dfrac{4}{5} \div \dfrac{1}{10} = 8$

4. $100 \times \dfrac{3}{4} = 75$

5. $7\dfrac{1}{2} + 6\dfrac{1}{4} + 8\dfrac{1}{4} = 22$

6. **(A)** $21 \div 3\dfrac{1}{2} = 6$

7. **(C)** $\dfrac{3}{8} + \dfrac{5}{8} = \dfrac{8}{8}$ or 1

8. **(C)** $\dfrac{3}{4} - \dfrac{3}{8} = \dfrac{3}{8}$

9. **(C)** $2 \div \dfrac{1}{5} = 10$

10. **(C)** $9 \times \dfrac{7}{8} = 7\dfrac{7}{8}$

11. **(D)** $4\dfrac{1}{2} + 4\dfrac{1}{2} + \dfrac{1}{8} = 9\dfrac{1}{8}$

12. **(B)** $2\dfrac{2}{3} \div 2 = 1\dfrac{1}{3}$

13. **(D)** $7 \times 7\dfrac{3}{4} = 54\dfrac{1}{4}$

14. **(D)** $200 \times \dfrac{3}{5} = 120$

End-of-Chapter Questions (Page 208)

1. $\dfrac{2}{6} = \dfrac{1}{3}$

2. $\dfrac{3}{5}$

3. $\dfrac{2}{7}$

4. $\dfrac{1}{2}$

5. $\frac{1}{8}$, $\frac{3}{8}$, $\frac{1}{2}$, $\frac{7}{8}$

6. $\frac{5}{4}$, $1\frac{1}{4}$

7. $\frac{13}{10}$, $1\frac{3}{10}$

8. $1\frac{1}{4}$, $2\frac{2}{3}$, $1\frac{1}{2}$, $1\frac{5}{6}$

9. $\frac{7}{2}$, $\frac{11}{6}$, $\frac{22}{5}$, $\frac{8}{3}$

10. $\frac{1}{2}$, $\frac{3}{4}$, $\frac{2}{3}$, $\frac{1}{4}$

11. $\frac{1}{7}$, $\frac{1}{6}$, $\frac{1}{5}$, $\frac{1}{4}$, $\frac{1}{2}$

12. $\frac{2}{3} < \frac{3}{4}$

13. $\frac{1}{2} < \frac{4}{5}$

14. $\frac{2}{5} < \frac{1}{2}$

15. $\frac{3}{4} > \frac{3}{5}$

16. $\frac{3}{5}$

17. $\frac{1}{7}$

18. $\frac{3}{4}$

19. $\frac{1}{2}$

20. $\frac{1}{2}$

21. $2\frac{1}{4}$

22. $3\frac{3}{4}$

23. $2\frac{4}{6} = 2\frac{2}{3}$

24. 3

25. $\frac{6}{20} = \frac{3}{10}$

26. $\frac{6}{3} = 2$

27. $\frac{20}{5} = 4$

28. $\frac{10}{2} = 5$

29. $\frac{30}{5} = 6$

30. $5 \times 5\frac{1}{3} = 26\frac{2}{3}$

31. $5 - 1\frac{3}{4} = 3\frac{1}{4}$

32. $15 \div 1\frac{1}{4} = 12$

on the shelf

33. $4\frac{1}{2} + 4\frac{3}{4} = 9\frac{1}{4}$

Proportions and Ratios

8

LESSON 1: WHAT ARE RATIOS?

A ratio is a way to compare two numbers. For example, we could write a ratio to compare the number of apples to oranges. Using the picture below, we can clearly see there are three apples and one orange. Therefore, the ratio of apples to oranges is 3 to 1.

Ratios can also be written like this 3:1. The symbol between the digits means that it is a ratio, and that the two items are being compared. Ratios also can be written as a fraction, such as $\frac{3}{1}$.

All three expressions, 3 to 1, 3:1, and $\frac{3}{1}$ mean the same thing. All are ratios.

The most important thing to remember about ratios is that the order the numbers appear in is essential. From the picture, we know that the ratio of apples to oranges is 3:1. Writing the numbers out of order, like 1 to 3, means that there is only one apple and three oranges. This means that it is critical to read your ratios carefully to make sure the quantities are compared correctly.

Practice Exercise—Writing Ratios

Fill in the chart below, rewriting each ratio two different ways. The first one is completed for you.

5 to 7	5:7	$\frac{5}{7}$
3 to 4		
	6:1	
		$\frac{1}{8}$
2 to 5		
	8:3	

Another rule with ratios is that they must always be written in lowest terms. For example, in a parking lot there are eight cars and four trucks. What is the ratio of cars to trucks?

$$\frac{8}{4} \div \frac{4}{4} = \frac{2}{1} \text{ or } 2 \text{ to } 1 \text{ or } 2:1$$

Write each statement as a ratio.

1. Five boys to three girls.

2. Seven elephants to nine tigers.

3. 100 forks to three spoons.

4. One pound to eight dollars.

Write each statement as a ratio, and check the order of each quantity.

1. Six chairs and eleven stools.

2. Eleven stools and six chairs.

3. Three socks and nine shoes.
   (Remember to reduce.)

4. Nine socks and three shoes.
   (Remember to reduce.)

Use the statement below to answer the following questions. Remember to reduce all ratios if possible.

The Cardinals played 50 games. They won 30 games and they lost 20.

5. What is the ratio of games won to games lost?

6. What is the ratio of games lost to games won?

7. What is the ratio of games won to games played?
   (THINK: what is being compared?)

8. What is the ratio of games played to games lost?

Rates

Ratios that compare different quantities, like money and time, are known as rates. Rates are calculated exactly like ratios, but the answers can be read with the word *per*.

- Find the rate of pay for $108 in 9 hours.

    To find the answer, write the expression as a ratio.

    $\dfrac{108 \text{ dollars}}{9 \text{ hours}}$ then reduce it to lowest terms $\dfrac{12 \text{ dollars}}{1 \text{ hour}}$

    The rate of pay is 12 dollars *per* hour.

- Sam works 40 hours in 5 days. What rate does he work per day?

    $\dfrac{40 \text{ hours}}{5 \text{ days}} = \dfrac{8 \text{ hours}}{1 \text{ day}} = 8 \text{ hours per day.}$

Practice Exercise—Calculate Rates

1. Find the rate for traveling 600 miles in 15 hours.

2. Find the rate for earning $75 in 10 hours.

3. Find the rate if you read 50 pages in 2 hours.

4. Find the rate if three peppers cost $6.30.

5. Find the rate if 6 pounds of beans cost $3.00.

LESSON 2: WHAT ARE PROPORTIONS?

Proportions are equations that compare two equal ratios. That definition may sound confusing, but you probably use proportions every day without realizing it. Let's say you were making a dozen cookies, and the recipe called for two cups of sugar. If you later decided you wanted two dozen cookies, how many cups of sugar would you need?

You would need four cups of sugar, because the ingredients increase proportionally with the amount of cookies made. Here are some other real life uses of proportions:

- Figuring out your paycheck based on how many hours you will work in a week.
- Determining the prices in stores, like if apples are three for a dollar, how much will five cost?
- If your car gets 30 miles per gallon, how far can you drive on a full tank?
- The actual distance between two cities if they are 5 inches apart on a map.

These are just a few examples of how solving proportions can benefit your daily life. Proportions are also a major skill on the test. You can use proportions to solve percentage questions, algebra problems, and even geometry, so it is critical you know how they work. Take a look at the sample proportion below.

$\frac{1}{2} = \frac{2}{4}$ Notice how the proportion is really just two equivalent fractions separated by an equal sign. Keep in mind that ratios can be written as fractions, and what you have is just a way to compare two ratios.

$\frac{15}{5} = \frac{3}{1}$ *How can you tell if the numbers are proportional?* Numbers are proportional if they increase or decrease at the same rate. Doubling the number of cookies only works if we precisely double the cups of sugar. A way to check this is to cross-multiply diagonally.

$\frac{15}{5} \diagdown\kern-0.9em\diagup \frac{3}{1}$ **15 × 1 = 15 and 5 × 3 = 15.** Multiplying diagonally gives the same answer, so the numbers are proportional.

$\frac{2}{5} = \frac{6}{8}$ Are these numbers proportional? Cross-multiply diagonally to find out. If the answers are the same, then they are proportional.

$\frac{2}{5} \diagdown\kern-0.9em\diagup \frac{6}{8}$ **2 × 8 = 16 and 5 × 6 = 30.** Since cross-multiplying gave different answers, the numbers are <u>not</u> proportional. You may also notice that these are <u>not</u> equivalent fractions, because $\frac{6}{8}$ does not reduce to $\frac{2}{5}$.

Practice Exercise—Identifying Proportions

Check to see if each equation is a proportion.

Hint: Cross-multiply diagonally. If the answers are the same, then the equation is a proportion.

1. $\frac{3}{12} = \frac{1}{4}$ 2. $\frac{2}{6} = \frac{1}{4}$ 3. $\frac{1}{3} = \frac{7}{21}$ 4. $\frac{36}{4} = \frac{9}{4}$ 5. $\frac{5}{2} = \frac{10}{3}$

To better understand the nature of proportions, fill out the following charts.

Two cups of sugar for 12 cookies

Cups of Sugar	2	4	6		8	
Cookies	12	24		48		72

You can see that there is a pattern to how the cups of sugar increase along with the cookies. This is a proportional relationship.

Fill out the chart for the proportion of $1 buys two candy bars.

Dollars	1	2				
Candy Bars	2	4				

Solving Proportions

Proportions can be solved by creating charts, but you may not always have time to make one. Likewise, sometimes the numbers may be too large for you to easily put into a chart. For these reasons, it is critical to know another way to solve proportions.

In this example, our recipe for baking cookies calls for two cups of sugar per dozen cookies. *How many cups of sugar would we need to make 30 cookies?* Questions like these can be answered by using a proportion. Fortunately, there are only two steps to remember to solve any proportion.

HOW TO SOLVE PROPORTIONS

1. Cross-multiply diagonally
2. Divide that answer by the other number in the proportion

The proportion for our sugar would look like this:

$$\frac{2 \text{ cups}}{12 \text{ cookies}} = \frac{?}{30 \text{ cookies}}$$

To solve it, begin with Step 1, *cross-multiply diagonally.*

$$\frac{2 \text{ cups}}{12 \text{ cookies}} \quad \frac{?}{30 \text{ cookies}}$$

$$2 \times 30 = 60$$

Next, follow Step 2, and *divide that answer by the other number in the proportion.* In this case, 12.

$$60 \div 12 = 5$$

That's it! The answer is 5. You would need five cups of sugar to make 30 cookies. We can check this answer by filling in 5 for the question mark in our proportion, then checking through cross-multiplication to see if it is proportional.

$$\frac{2 \text{ cups}}{12 \text{ cookies}} \quad \frac{5 \text{ cups}}{30 \text{ cookies}}$$

$$2 \times 30 = 60 \text{ and } 12 \times 5 = 60$$

The answers are the same, so the proportion is correct!

Practice Exercise—Solving Proportions

Solve for the missing term in each proportion.

Remember: Cross multiply, then divide. The first one is completed for you.

1. $\frac{3}{12} = \frac{?}{4}$

    $3 \times 4 = 12$

    $12 \div 12 = 1$

    The answer is 1.

2. $\dfrac{?}{5} = \dfrac{10}{25}$ 6. $\dfrac{5}{3} = \dfrac{10}{?}$ 10. $\dfrac{?}{2} = \dfrac{24}{1}$ 14. $\dfrac{2.5}{?} = \dfrac{5}{4}$

3. $\dfrac{2}{?} = \dfrac{12}{18}$ 7. $\dfrac{36}{?} = \dfrac{3}{2}$ 11. $\dfrac{?}{5} = \dfrac{10}{25}$ 15. $\dfrac{5}{9} = \dfrac{?}{81}$

4. $\dfrac{3}{4} = \dfrac{12}{?}$ 8. $\dfrac{?}{9} = \dfrac{40}{45}$ 12. $\dfrac{24}{18} = \dfrac{4}{?}$ 16. $\dfrac{3}{6.5} = \dfrac{?}{26}$

5. $\dfrac{?}{42} = \dfrac{5}{6}$ 9. $\dfrac{30}{35} = \dfrac{?}{7}$ 13. $\dfrac{120}{70} = \dfrac{?}{7}$

LESSON 3: PROPORTION AND RATIO WORD PROBLEMS

The trick with proportion word problems is that you will have to write your own proportions. The test questions will typically not supply you with them already written like in the questions above. To write a proportion, begin by writing a ratio comparing the two items in the question.

In this case, we know the recipe needs two cups of sugar for 12 cookies. How many cookies can you make with seven cups of sugar?

$$\dfrac{2 \text{ cups}}{12 \text{ cookies}}$$

Then write an equal sign = to separate that ratio from the other side of the proportion.

$$\dfrac{2 \text{ cups}}{12 \text{ cookies}} =$$

Next, write a fraction using the other term in the problem.

$$\dfrac{2 \text{ cups}}{12 \text{ cookies}} = \dfrac{7 \text{ cups}}{? \text{ cookies}}$$

$$12 \times 7 = 84 \text{ and } 84 \div 2 = 48$$

You can make 48 cookies.

Proportion questions will always give you three of the four numbers you need to make a proportion. Your job is to put them into the right place. Notice how the **cups** are on top of both sides of the proportion, and the **cookies** are both on the bottom. With proportions, you need to keep your quantities separated to the top and bottom to get the correct answer.

Steve drove 130 miles in 2 hours. If he continues driving at the same speed, how far will he drive in 5 hours?

To begin this problem, write a fraction about what is being compared. This fraction will always compare two different things, in this case it's 130 miles and 2 hours.

$$\dfrac{130 \text{ miles}}{2 \text{ hours}} =$$

Now ask yourself, what other information is in the problem? The only other number we haven't used is 5 hours. Will this go on the top or the bottom of the right side of our proportion?

$$\frac{130 \text{ miles}}{2 \text{ hours}} = \frac{?}{5 \text{ hours}}$$ The 5 hours goes on the bottom right of the proportion because the hours are already on the bottom left.

To solve this proportion, simply cross-multiply and divide. $130 \times 5 = 650$. $650 \div 2 = 325$. Steve will drive 325 miles in 5 hours.

Practice Exercises—Ratio and Proportion Word Problems

Complete the proportion in each word problem, then solve.

(**THINK:** Should this number go on the top or bottom?)

1. The currency exchange rate is $1 for 7 pesos. If Hal goes to the bank with $25, how many pesos will he receive in return?

    $$\frac{1 \text{ dollar}}{7 \text{ pesos}} = \frac{?}{?}$$

2. A new car gets 35 miles per gallon. How far can it travel on 15 gallons?

    $$\frac{35 \text{ miles}}{1 \text{ gallon}} =$$

3. Julio earns $9.50 an hour at his new job. If he works 35 hours a week, how much money will he earn?

    $$\frac{\$9.50}{1 \text{ hour}} =$$

4. Last week, there were three rainy days and four sunny days. If this pattern continues for the rest of the month, how many sunny days will there be if there are 12 rainy days?

    $$\frac{3 \text{ rainy days}}{4 \text{ sunny days}} =$$

In the following word problems, you will need to read the question carefully to set up your proportion, then cross-multiply and divide to solve.

5. A basketball player makes three baskets out of every five that he shoots. If he takes 25 shots in a game, how many will he make?

6. When Betty arrives at her friend's birthday party, the ratio of boys to girls is 6:4. If this pattern continues, how many girls will be at the party if there are 24 boys?

   (**THINK:** A ratio can be written like a fraction. This will help you solve the left side of your proportion.)

7. LaTonya is at the store and sees that her favorite chips are on sale, three bags for $5. How much will she spend if she buys seven bags?

Use the following statement to answer questions 8 and 9.

   On a recent test, Omar answered three out of every four questions correctly.

8. How many did he get right if there were 60 questions on the test?

9. Write a proportion to figure out how many questions he got wrong on the test.

   (**THINK:** If he got three of four correct, what is the ratio of wrong answers to questions?)

10. The printer in the office can print nine pages a minute. John needs to print 16 pages. What is the ratio of pages to minutes produced by the printer?
    (A) 1 to 9
    (B) 9:1
    (C) 1:9
    (D) 9 to 16
    (E) 16:9

11. Juan opens his dresser drawer and notices that he has six red socks and 12 black socks. What is the ratio of black to red socks?

(A) $\dfrac{2}{12}$

(B) 6:12

(C) 1 to 2

(D) 12:1

(E) 2:1

12. Steve drove to visit his four brothers in Boston last weekend, and the trip took him 3 hours. If the distance between the two cities is 180 miles, which expression gives his rate in miles per hour?

(A) $\dfrac{180}{4}$

(B) $\dfrac{1}{60}$

(C) $\dfrac{60}{1}$

(D) $\dfrac{4}{180}$

(E) $\dfrac{45}{1}$

13. Jackie is traveling to France and needs to exchange her dollars for euros. Currently the exchange rate is 2 euros for each dollar. What is the ratio of dollars to euros?

14. On a busy Friday night, Kim delivered 36 pizzas. Nine of his customers paid with coupons, and 20 paid in cash. If he worked for 6 hours, what is the rate of pizzas delivered per hour?

(A) $\dfrac{6}{1}$

(B) $\dfrac{36}{20}$

(C) $\dfrac{9}{5}$

(D) $\dfrac{6}{20}$

(E) $\dfrac{9}{36}$

15. Al recently went shopping for new cars. After doing some research online, he decided on a model that can drive 420 miles on a single tank of gas. If the tank holds 12 gallons, how many miles per gallon does the car get?

(A) 408

(B) 432

(C) 5,040

(D) 35

(E) 20

16. Shavazz works at a popular restaurant, and most of his paycheck comes from tips. Last weekend he made $240 in 16 hours of work. How many dollars did he make per hour?

(A) 256

(B) 15

(C) 7.50

(D) 224

(E) 3,840

17. After dinner, Anthony decided to take his dog for a walk. He normally walks his dog 5 days a week. If Anthony walks 3 miles in an hour, how far could he walk in 2.5 hours?

(A) 6 miles

(B) 1.2 miles

(C) 7.5 miles

(D) 5.5 miles

(E) 75 miles

18. Central High School is taking a field trip to the history museum. On the trip, there will be two teachers for every 30 students. If 150 students go on the field trip, how many teachers will there be?

(A) 450

(B) 120

(C) 180

(D) 60

(E) 10

19. A 1-pound bag of potatoes costs $2.50. How much money would three bags of potatoes cost?

(A) $7.50

(B) $12.50

(C) $10.50

(D) $2

(E) $.50

Questions 20 and 21 refer to the following chart and information.

Shanna works a full-time job, and keeps a busy social life. Still, she likes to unwind after a long day and watch TV. The chart below shows how many hours she works, and how many hours she watches TV a day.

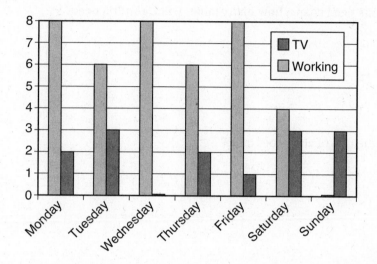

20. What is the ratio of hours worked to hours spent watching TV on Tuesday?
    (A) 8:2
    (B) 1:4
    (C) 1:2
    (D) 4:1
    (E) 2:1

21. What is the ratio of hours worked to hours spent watching TV for the entire week?
    (A) 40 to 20
    (B) 20 to 40
    (C) 54 to 40
    (D) 20 to 27
    (E) 20 to 7

22. The local library just purchased a new book shelf. If the librarian can put 27 books on each shelf, how many books can he put on nine shelves?
    (A) 243
    (B) 9
    (C) 36
    (D) 24.3
    (E) 270

Questions 23 and 24 refer to the following information.

DeAndria has been planning her wedding for 3 months. She is planning on a lot of guests and is working on the seating arrangement for her guests. She is planning on using six chairs for every two tables.

23. If 78 guests need chairs, how many tables will DeAndria need?
    (A) 39
    (B) 13
    (C) 468
    (D) 12
    (E) 26

24. What is the rate of chairs per table?
    (A) $\dfrac{12}{1}$

    (B) $\dfrac{12}{2}$

    (C) $\dfrac{1}{3}$

    (D) $\dfrac{3}{1}$

    (E) $\dfrac{13}{1}$

25. Armando is making a fruit salad for his family of four. Normally he uses two bananas, but now his neighbors are coming over for dinner. How many bananas will Armando need if he has 14 people over for dinner?
    (A) 7
    (B) 8
    (C) 28
    (D) 3.5
    (E) 12

26. Lee Ann has a family photo that measures 5 inches wide by 10 inches high. What will be the height of the photo if it is enlarged to 11 inches wide?
    (A) 15
    (B) 6
    (C) 55
    (D) 50
    (E) 22

Questions 27 through 29 refer to the following information.

Map scales can be used to calculate distance. On this map, the scale is located on the bottom left, and shows that 1 inch equals 100 miles. This can be written as rate, $\dfrac{1 \text{ inch}}{100 \text{ miles}}$.

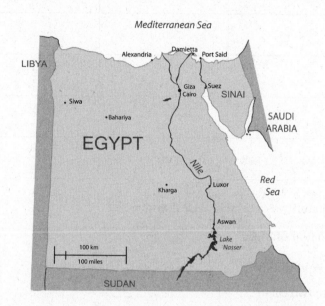

27. The distance between Siwa and Bahariya on the map is 2 inches. How many miles is that?
    (A) 50 miles
    (B) 200 miles
    (C) 500 miles
    (D) 10 miles
    (E) 150 miles

28. The distance between Giza and Luxor is approximately 3 inches on the map. How many miles is the actual distance?
    (A) 600 miles
    (B) 33.3 miles
    (C) 200 miles
    (D) 300 miles
    (E) 60 miles

29. The distance between Kharga and Luxor on the map is approximately 2 inches. If Sam drives 50 miles per hour, how long will it take him to drive from Kharga to Luxor? (THINK: How many miles is the actual distance? How long will it take him to drive that at this speed?)
    (A) 200 hours
    (B)   2 hours
    (C)   50 hours
    (D) 25 hours
    (E)   4 hours

1. Complete the chart to write each ratio two different ways.

2:3		
	5 to 1	
		$\frac{3}{2}$
4:7		
	4 to 9	

2. Write each quantity as a ratio in lowest terms.

   Six lemons to four oranges   _____

   Three pears to nine apples   _____

   Seven dogs to two cats   _____

   12 men to six women   _____

   Eight pigs to two horses   _____

   16 pies to 12 cakes   _____

3. Read the statement below to answer the following questions. Pay attention to the order of each quantity.

   Lucia recently went to the bookstore and purchased three books and four magazines.

   What is the ratio of books to magazines?

   _____

   What is the ratio of magazines to books?

   _____

   What is the ratio of books to total items purchased?

   _____

   What is the ratio of magazines to total items purchased?

   _____

4. During a recent storm, Mr. Davis measured a total rainfall of 4 inches. If it rained for 8 hours, write the rate of rainfall per hour.

   _____

5. Sandy uses a machine at work that creates boxes. She works 8-hour shifts, and can make 240 boxes in that time. Write the rate of boxes per hour.

Use the following information to complete the chart below.

Kayla is a saleswoman, and she earns $20 for every three sales she makes.

Sales	3	6		12		18		24
Money	$20		$60		$100		$140	

A. Check to see if the following equations are proportional.

1. $\dfrac{4}{5} = \dfrac{16}{20}$

2. $\dfrac{25}{5} = \dfrac{5}{1}$

3. $\dfrac{3}{16} = \dfrac{2}{4}$

4. $\dfrac{9}{2} = \dfrac{27}{6}$

B. Solve each proportion.

1. $\dfrac{7}{2} = \dfrac{?}{6}$

2. $\dfrac{3}{8} = \dfrac{9}{?}$

3. $\dfrac{?}{1} = \dfrac{20}{5}$

4. $\dfrac{11}{?} = \dfrac{22}{8}$

5. $\dfrac{?}{20} = \dfrac{6}{40}$

6. $\dfrac{1}{?} = \dfrac{6}{36}$

7. $\dfrac{15}{8} = \dfrac{60}{?}$

8. $\dfrac{24}{2} = \dfrac{96}{?}$

C. Use proportions to solve the following problems.

1. Bruce jogs 2 miles in 30 minutes. If he continues at the same pace, how far will he jog after 90 minutes?
   (A) 15 miles
   (B) 6 miles
   (C) 60 miles
   (D) 32 miles
   (E) 28 miles

2. Cans of tomato soup are on sale three for 5 dollars. If Alice buys ten cans of soup, how much money will she spend?
   (A) $16.67
   (B) $30.00
   (C) $6.00
   (D) $15.00
   (E) $8.00

3. A picture that originally measured 3 inches wide by 4 inches tall is enlarged to fit into a frame that is 18 inches wide. How tall is the picture frame?
   (A) 12 inches
   (B) 14 inches
   (C) 13.5 inches
   (D) 24 inches
   (E) 21 inches

4. David is planning a trip to Brazil and needs to exchange his dollars for Brazilian reals. If the exchange rate is 1.6 reals for $1, how many reals will David get for $250?
   (A) 156.25
   (B) 75.00
   (C) 160
   (D) 80
   (E) 400

Use the chart to answer questions 5 and 6.

Jamal is the manager of a large department store. The chart below lists his part-time and full-time employees each day of the week.

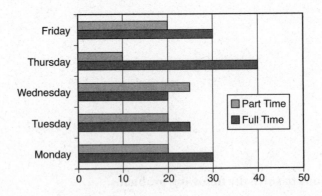

5. What is the ratio of full-time to part-time employees on Thursday?
   (A) 2:3
   (B) 1:4
   (C) 5:4
   (D) 3:2
   (E) 4:1

6. On which 2 days are the ratios of part time to full time employees the same?
   (A) Friday and Thursday
   (B) Tuesday and Wednesday
   (C) Friday and Monday
   (D) Tuesday and Monday
   (E) Wednesday and Friday

Use the map to answer questions 7 and 8.

7. The map scale is 1 inch = 600 miles. The distance on the map between Alice Springs and Adelaide is 2 inches. How many miles is the actual distance?
   (A) 50 miles
   (B) 200 miles
   (C) 300 miles
   (D) 1,200 miles
   (E) 1,800 miles

8. The actual distance between Perth and Brisbane is approximately 2,400 miles. How many inches on the map would these two cities be apart?
   (A) 4 inches
   (B) 8 inches
   (C) 40 inches
   (D) 60 inches
   (E) 80 inches

CHAPTER 8 ANSWER EXPLANATIONS

Lesson 1: What Are Ratios?

PRACTICE EXERCISE—WRITING RATIOS (PAGE 219)

5 to 7	5:7	$\frac{5}{7}$
3 to 4	3:4	$\frac{3}{4}$
6 to 1	6:1	$\frac{6}{1}$
1 to 8	1:8	$\frac{1}{8}$
2 to 5	2:5	$\frac{2}{5}$
8 to 3	8:3	$\frac{8}{3}$

WRITE EACH STATEMENT AS A RATIO (PAGE 220)

1. Five boys to three girls.

   5:3, 5 to 3, $\frac{5}{3}$

2. Seven elephants to nine tigers.

   7:9, 7 to 9, $\frac{7}{9}$

3. One hundred forks to three spoons.

   100:3, 100 to 3, $\frac{100}{3}$

4. 1 pound to eight dollars.

   1:8, 1 to 8, $\frac{1}{8}$

WRITE EACH STATEMENT AS A RATIO, AND CHECK THE ORDER OF EACH QUANTITY (PAGE 220)

1. Six chairs and eleven stools.
   6:11
2. Eleven stools and six chairs.
   11:6
3. Three socks and nine shoes.
   (Remember to reduce)
   3:9, reduced = 1:3
4. Nine socks and three shoes.
   (Remember to reduce)
   9:3, reduced = 3:1

The Cardinals played 50 games. They won 30 games and they lost 20.

5. What is the ratio of games won to games lost?

30:20, reduced = 3:2

6. What is the ratio of games lost to games won?

20:30, reduced = 2:3

7. What is the ratio of games won to games played?

(THINK: what is being compared?)

30:50, reduced = 3:5

8. What is the ratio of games played to games lost?

50:20, reduced = 5:2

PRACTICE EXERCISE—CALCULATE RATES (PAGE 221)

1. Find the rate for traveling 600 miles in 15 hours.

$$\frac{600 \text{ miles}}{15 \text{ hours}} = \frac{40 \text{ miles}}{1 \text{ hour}} = 40 \text{ miles per hour}$$

2. Find the rate for earning $75 in 10 hours.

$$\frac{75 \text{ dollars}}{10 \text{ hours}} = \frac{\$7.50}{1 \text{ hour}} = \$7.50 \text{ per hour}$$

3. Find the rate if you read 50 pages in 2 hours.

$$\frac{50 \text{ pages}}{2 \text{ hours}} = \frac{25 \text{ pages}}{1 \text{ hour}} = 25 \text{ pages per hour}$$

4. Find the rate if three peppers cost $6.30.

$$\frac{3 \text{ peppers}}{\$6.30} = \frac{1 \text{ pepper}}{\$2.10} = \$2.10 \text{ per pepper}$$

5. Find the rate if six pounds of beans cost $3.00.

$$\frac{6 \text{ pounds}}{\$3.00} = \frac{2 \text{ pounds}}{1 \text{ dollar}} = 2 \text{ pounds per dollar}$$

Lesson 2: What Are Proportions?

PRACTICE EXERCISE—IDENTIFYING PROPORTIONS (PAGE 222)

1. $\frac{3}{12} = \frac{1}{4}$

$4 \times 3 = 12$

$12 \times 1 = 12$

Proportional

2. $\frac{2}{6} = \frac{1}{4}$

$4 \times 2 = 8$

$6 \times 1 = 6$

Not proportional

3. $\frac{1}{3} = \frac{7}{21}$

$1 \times 21 = 21$

$3 \times 7 = 21$

Proportional

4. $\frac{36}{4} = \frac{9}{4}$

$36 \times 4 = 144$

$9 \times 4 = 36$

Not proportional

5. $\frac{5}{2} = \frac{10}{3}$

$5 \times 3 = 15$

$2 \times 10 = 20$

Not proportional

Cups of Sugar	2	4	6	8	10	12
Cookies	12	24	36	48	60	72

Answers may vary depending on how many dollars the student inputs. Below is an example for increasing the proportion $1 at a time.

Dollars	1	2	3	4	5	6
Candy Bars	2	4	6	8	10	12

PRACTICE EXERCISE—SOLVING PROPORTIONS (PAGE 223)

1. $\dfrac{3}{12} = \dfrac{?}{4}$

    $3 \times 4 = 12$

    $12 \div 12 = 1$

    The answer is 1.

2. $\dfrac{?}{5} = \dfrac{10}{25}$

    $5 \times 10 = 50$

    $50 \div 25 = 2$

    The answer is 2.

3. $\dfrac{2}{?} = \dfrac{12}{18}$

    $2 \times 18 = 36$

    $36 \div 12 = 3$

    The answer is 3.

4. $\dfrac{3}{4} = \dfrac{12}{?}$

    $4 \times 12 = 48$

    $48 \div 3 = 16$

    The answer is 16.

5. $\dfrac{?}{42} = \dfrac{5}{6}$

    $42 \times 5 = 210$

    $210 \div 6 = 35$

    The answer is 35.

6. $\dfrac{5}{3} = \dfrac{10}{?}$

    $3 \times 10 = 30$

    $30 \div 5 = 6$

    The answer is 6.

7. $\dfrac{36}{?} = \dfrac{3}{2}$

    $36 \times 2 = 72$

    $72 \div 3 = 24$

    The answer is 24.

8. $\dfrac{?}{9} = \dfrac{40}{45}$

    $40 \times 9 = 360$

    $360 \div 45 = 8$

    The answer is 8.

9. $\dfrac{30}{35} = \dfrac{?}{7}$

    $30 \times 7 = 210$

    $210 \div 35 = 6$

    The answer is 6.

10. $\dfrac{?}{2} = \dfrac{24}{1}$

    $2 \times 24 = 48$

    $48 \div 1 = 48$

    The answer is 48.

11. $\dfrac{?}{5} = \dfrac{10}{25}$

    $5 \times 10 = 50$

    $50 \div 25 = 2$

    The answer is 2.

12. $\dfrac{24}{18} = \dfrac{4}{?}$

    $18 \times 4 = 72$

    $72 \div 24 = 3$

    The answer is 3.

13. $\dfrac{120}{70} = \dfrac{?}{7}$

    $7 \times 120 = 840$

    $840 \div 70 = 12$

    The answer is 12.

14. $\dfrac{2.5}{?} = \dfrac{5}{4}$

    $4 \times 2.5 = 10$

    $10 \div 5 = 2$

    The answer is 2.

15. $\dfrac{5}{9} = \dfrac{?}{81}$

$81 \times 5 = 405$

$405 \div 9 = 45$

The answer is 45.

16. $\dfrac{3}{6.5} = \dfrac{?}{26}$

$26 \times 3 = 78$

$78 \div 6.5 = 12$

The answer is 12.

Lesson 3: Proportion and Ratio Word Problems

PRACTICE EXERCISE—RATIO AND PROPORTION WORD PROBLEMS (PAGE 225)

(**THINK:** Should this number go on the top or bottom?)

1. The currency exchange rate is $1 for 7 pesos. If Hal goes to the bank with $25, how many pesos will he receive in return?

$\dfrac{1 \text{ dollar}}{7 \text{ pesos}} = \dfrac{25 \text{ dollars}}{?}$

$7 \times 25 = 175$

$175 \div 1 = 175$

The answer is 175 dollars.

2. A new car gets 35 miles per gallon. How far can it travel on 15 gallons?

$\dfrac{35 \text{ miles}}{1 \text{ gallon}} = \dfrac{?}{15 \text{ gallons}}$

$35 \times 15 = 525$

$525 \div 1 = 525$

The answer is 525 miles.

3. Julio earns $9.50 an hour at his new job. If he works 35 hours a week, how much money will he earn?

$\dfrac{\$9.50}{1 \text{ hour}} = \dfrac{?}{35 \text{ hours}}$

$9.50 \times 35 = 332.50$

$332.50 \div 1 = 332.50$

The answer is 332.50 dollars.

4. Last week there were three rainy days and four sunny days. If this pattern continues for the rest of the month, how many sunny days will there be if there are 12 rainy days?

$\dfrac{3 \text{ rainy days}}{4 \text{ sunny days}} = \dfrac{12 \text{ rainy days}}{?}$

$4 \times 12 = 48$

$48 \div 3 = 16$

The answer is 16 sunny days.

5. A basketball player makes three baskets out of every five that he shoots. If he takes 25 shots in a game, how many will he make?

$\dfrac{3 \text{ made baskets}}{5 \text{ shots}} = \dfrac{?}{25 \text{ shots}}$

$25 \times 3 = 75$

$75 \div 5 = 15$

The answer is 15 shots.

6. When Betty arrives at her friend's birthday party, the ratio of boys to girls is 6:4. If this pattern continues, how many girls will be at the party if there are 24 boys.

(THINK: A ratio can be written like a fraction. This will help you solve the left side of your proportion.)

$$\frac{6 \text{ boys}}{4 \text{ girls}} = \frac{24 \text{ boys}}{?}$$

$4 \times 24 = 96$

$96 \div 6 = 16$

The answer is 16 girls.

7. LaTonya is at the store and sees that her favorite chips are on sale, three bags for $5. How much will she spend if she buys seven bags?

$$\frac{3 \text{ bags}}{5 \text{ dollars}} = \frac{7 \text{ bags}}{?}$$

$5 \times 7 = 35$

$35 \div 3 = 11.66$

The answer is $11.66.

Use the following statement to answer questions 5 and 6.

On a recent test, Omar answered three out of every four questions correctly.

8. How many did he get right if there were 60 questions on the test?

$$\frac{3 \text{ correct}}{4 \text{ answered}} = \frac{?}{60 \text{ answered}}$$

$3 \times 60 = 180$

$180 \div 4 = 45$

The answer is 45 correct.

9. Write a proportion to figure out how many questions he got wrong on the test.

(THINK: If he got three of four correct, what is the ratio of wrong answers to questions?)

$$\frac{1 \text{ wrong}}{4 \text{ answered}} = \frac{?}{60 \text{ answered}}$$

$1 \times 60 = 60$

$60 \div 4 = 15$

The answer is 15 wrong answers.

10. **(B)** Nine pages to 1 minute. The fact that John needs to print 16 pages is unnecessary information to the ratio.

11. **(E)** 12 black socks to six red socks. When reduced, the answer is 2:1.

12. **(C)** $\frac{180 \text{ miles}}{3 \text{ hours}}$. When reduced, the answer is $\frac{60}{1}$. The four brothers is unnecessary information.

13. $\frac{1}{2}$

14. **(A)** $\frac{36 \text{ pizzas}}{6 \text{ hours}}$. When reduced, the answer is $\frac{6}{1}$. The number of customers paying with cash or coupons is unnecessary information.

15. **(D)** $\dfrac{420 \text{ miles}}{12 \text{ gallons}}$. When reduced, the answer is $\dfrac{35 \text{ miles}}{1 \text{ gallons}}$.

16. **(B)** $\dfrac{240 \text{ dollars}}{16 \text{ hours}}$. When reduced, the answer is $\dfrac{15 \text{ dollars}}{1 \text{ hour}}$.

17. **(C)** $\dfrac{3 \text{ miles}}{1 \text{ hour}} = \dfrac{?}{2.5 \text{ hours}}$.

$3 \times 2.5 = 7.5$

$7.5 \div 1 = 7.5$

The answer is 7.5 hours.

18. **(E)** $\dfrac{2 \text{ teachers}}{30 \text{ students}} = \dfrac{?}{150 \text{ students}}$

$2 \times 150 = 300$

$300 \div 30 = 10$

The answer is ten teachers.

19. **(A)** $\dfrac{1 \text{ bag}}{\$2.50} = \dfrac{3 \text{ bags}}{?}$

$3 \times 2.5 = 7.5$

$7.5 \div 1 = 7.5$

The answer is $7.50.

20. **(E)** 6 hours worked to 3 hours watching TV. When reduced, 2:1.

21. **(E)** 40 hours worked all week to 14 hours watching TV all week. When reduced, 20:7.

22. **(A)** $\dfrac{27 \text{ books}}{1 \text{ shelf}} = \dfrac{?}{9 \text{ shelves}}$

$9 \times 27 = 243$

$243 \div 1 = 243$

The answer is 243 books.

23. **(E)** $\dfrac{6 \text{ chairs}}{2 \text{ tables}} = \dfrac{78 \text{ chairs}}{?}$

$2 \times 78 = 7.5$

$156 \div 6 = 26$

The answer is 26 tables.

24. **(D)** $\dfrac{6 \text{ chairs}}{2 \text{ tables}}$ When reduced, $\dfrac{3}{1}$.

25. **(A)** $\dfrac{2 \text{ bananas}}{4 \text{ people}} = \dfrac{?}{14 \text{ people}}$

$2 \times 14 = 28$

$28 \div 4 = 7$

The answer is 7 bananas.

26. **(E)** $\dfrac{5 \text{ wide}}{10 \text{ high}} = \dfrac{11 \text{ wide}}{?}$

$10 \times 11 = 110$

$110 \div 5 = 22$

The answer is 22 inches high.

27. (B) $\dfrac{1 \text{ inch}}{100 \text{ miles}} = \dfrac{2 \text{ inches}}{?}$

$100 \times 2 = 200$

$200 \div 1 = 200$

The answer is 200 miles.

28. (D) $\dfrac{1 \text{ inch}}{100 \text{ miles}} = \dfrac{3 \text{ inches}}{?}$

$100 \times 3 = 200$

$300 \div 1 = 300$

The answer is 300 miles.

29. (E) This problem has two steps. First, figure out the distance from Kharga to Luxor.

$\dfrac{1 \text{ inch}}{100 \text{ miles}} = \dfrac{2 \text{ inches}}{?}$

$100 \times 2 = 200$

$200 \div 1 = 200$

The answer is 200 miles.

Then, take that answer and divide by the speed Sam drives. $200 \div 50 = 4$.

The final answer is 4 hours.

End-of-Chapter Questions (page 232)

1. Complete the chart to write each ratio two different ways.

2:3	2 to 3	$\dfrac{2}{3}$
5:1	5 to 1	$\dfrac{5}{1}$
3:2	3 to 2	$\dfrac{3}{2}$
4:7	4 to 7	$\dfrac{4}{7}$
4:9	4 to 9	$\dfrac{4}{9}$

2. 3:2, 3 to 2, $\dfrac{3}{2}$ 1:3, 1 to 3, $\dfrac{1}{3}$ 7:2, 7 to 2, $\dfrac{7}{2}$

2:1, 2 to 1, $\dfrac{2}{1}$ 4:1, 4 to 1, $\dfrac{4}{1}$ 4:3, 4 to 3, $\dfrac{4}{3}$

3. What is the ratio of books to magazines?

3:4

What is the ratio of magazines to books?

4:3

What is the ratio of books to total items purchased?

3:7

What is the ratio of magazines to total items purchased?

4:7

4. $\dfrac{4 \text{ inches}}{8 \text{ hours}} = \dfrac{1 \text{ inch}}{2 \text{ hours}} = 1$ inch per 2 hours

5. $\dfrac{240 \text{ boxes}}{8 \text{ hours}} = \dfrac{30 \text{ boxes}}{1 \text{ hour}} = 30$ boxes per hour

Sales	3	6	9	12	15	18	21	24
Money	$20	$40	$60	$80	$100	$120	$140	$160

A. Check to see if the following equations are proportional.

1. $\dfrac{4}{5} = \dfrac{16}{20}$

$20 \times 4 = 80$

$5 \times 16 = 80$

Proportional

2. $\dfrac{25}{5} = \dfrac{5}{1}$

$25 \times 1 = 25$

$5 \times 5 = 25$

Proportional

3. $\dfrac{3}{16} = \dfrac{2}{4}$

$3 \times 4 = 12$

$16 \times 2 = 32$

Not proportional

4. $\dfrac{9}{2} = \dfrac{27}{6}$

$9 \times 6 = 54$

$2 \times 27 = 54$

Proportional

B. Solve each proportion.

1. $\dfrac{7}{2} = \dfrac{?}{6}$

$7 \times 6 = 42$

$42 \div 2 = 21$

2. $\dfrac{3}{8} = \dfrac{9}{?}$

$8 \times 9 = 72$

$72 \div 3 = 24$

3. $\dfrac{?}{1} = \dfrac{20}{5}$

$1 \times 20 = 20$

$20 \div 5 = 4$

4. $\dfrac{11}{?} = \dfrac{22}{8}$

$11 \times 8 = 88$

$88 \div 22 = 4$

5. $\dfrac{?}{20} = \dfrac{6}{40}$

$20 \times 6 = 120$

$120 \div 40 = 3$

6. $\dfrac{1}{?} = \dfrac{6}{36}$

$1 \times 36 = 36$

$36 \div 6 = 6$

7. $\dfrac{15}{8} = \dfrac{60}{?}$

$8 \times 60 = 480$

$480 \div 15 = 32$

8. $\dfrac{24}{2} = \dfrac{96}{?}$

$2 \times 96 = 192$

$192 \div 24 = 8$

C. Use proportions to solve the following problems.

1. **(B)** $\dfrac{2 \text{ miles}}{30 \text{ minutes}} = \dfrac{?}{90 \text{ minutes}}$

   $2 \times 90 = 180$

   $180 \div 30 = 6$

   The answer is 6 miles.

2. **(A)** $\dfrac{3 \text{ cans}}{5 \text{ dollars}} = \dfrac{10 \text{ cans}}{?}$

   $10 \times 5 = 50$

   $50 \div 3 = 16.666$

   The answer is $16.67.

3. **(D)** $\dfrac{3'' \text{ wide}}{4'' \text{ tall}} = \dfrac{18'' \text{ wide}}{?}$

   $18 \times 4 = 72$

   $72 \div 3 = 24$

   The answer is 24 inches high.

4. **(E)** $\dfrac{1.6 \text{ reals}}{1 \text{ dollar}} = \dfrac{?}{250 \text{ dollars}}$

   $250 \times 1.6 = 400$

   $400 \div 1 = \$400$

   The answer is 400 Reals.

5. **(E)** 40 full time to 10 part time. When reduced, 4:1.

6. **(C)** The ratios of part time to full time workers on Monday is 2:3. This is the same as Friday.

7. **(D)** $\dfrac{1 \text{ inch}}{600 \text{ miles}} = \dfrac{2 \text{ inches}}{?}$

   $600 \times 2 = 1,200$

   $1,200 \div 1 = 1,200$

   The answer is 1,200 miles.

8. **(A)** $\dfrac{1 \text{ inch}}{600 \text{ miles}} = \dfrac{?}{2400 \text{ miles}}$

   $1 \times 2,400 = 2,400$

   $2,400 \div 600 = 4$

   The answer is 4 inches.

UNIT 2: MATHEMATICS

Percents

LESSON 1: WHAT ARE PERCENTS?

A percent is a lot like a decimal or fraction. Just like those things, percentages can be used to show a part of a number. Percentages play an important part on HSE tests, and in real life as well. For example, you have probably seen an ad like this before:

This Weekend Only: All Electronics 20% off!

Here we can plainly see that a sale is taking place, so all electronic items will be marked down to a cheaper price. How much will you save? This is what your knowledge of percentages will be able to tell you.

- Percent literally means "out of 100."
- Per *cent*, just like a dollar has one hundred cents.
- % is the percent symbol. Ten percent can be written 10%.

Visualizing Percents

What is 15% of a dollar?

Since percent means per 100, visualize a dollar broken into 100 equal parts. This is easy to do because 100 pennies makes a dollar.

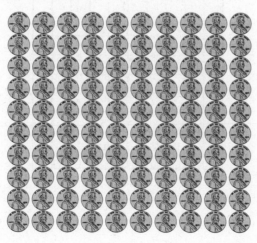

We need 15%, so we will be taking 15 out of those 100 pennies.

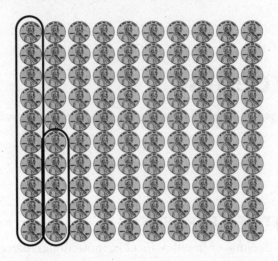

That's it! That's all a percentage is, a part of a whole.

Here are a few more examples.

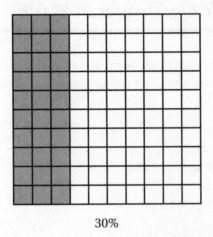

30%

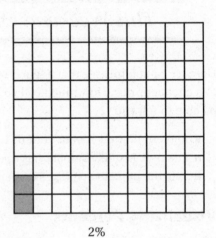

2%

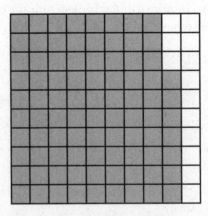

87%

Practice Exercises—Visualizing Percents

Shade the correct percent for each figure.

1. 25%

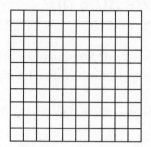

2. 33%

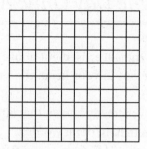

3. 50%

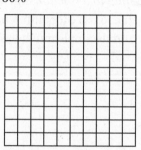

4. 75%

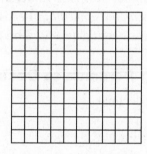

5. 110%

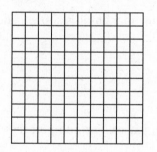 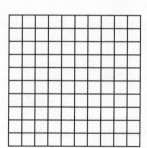

(**THINK:** How many total boxes do you need to shade?)

Use the following information to answer questions 6 through 8.

Like inches and feet, you can use centimeters to measure a distance smaller than a meter. 100 centimeters equals 1 meter.

6. James measured his shoe at exactly 25 centimeters. What percent of a meter is his shoe?

7. How long in centimeters is 45% of a meter?

8. Samantha's desk measures exactly 1 meter across. Next year, the school is purchasing new desks that will be slightly larger. If the new desks are 12% larger, how many centimeters across will they be?

LESSON 2: COMPARING FRACTIONS, DECIMALS, AND PERCENTS

One Day Only: All $1 pencils are 50% off!

Take a look at the advertisement above. How much will a pencil cost? You might be able to figure that one out in your head: the pencil would cost 50 cents. But ask yourself, how did you know that?

You may have already known that 50% equals one half, so all you needed to do was divide that $1 price in half. In other words:

50% off equals ½ off, which is $**.50** from a dollar.

Take another look at what is underlined above. *A percent is equal to a fraction and a decimal. They all mean the same thing.* Recognizing this, and being able to use them interchangeably, will make answering questions on percentages, fractions, and decimals much easier.

Converting Percents to Decimals

Write 35% as a decimal.

STEP 1 Remove the percent sign.

$$35$$

STEP 2 Move the decimal point two places to the left. If no decimal point is shown, start to the right of the last digit.

$$35\% = .35$$

$$72\% = .72$$

Be careful to always move the decimal point over <u>two</u> places. For numbers less than 10%, you will need to fill in a zero.

> **EXAMPLE**
>
> 5% is not .5, but .05
>
> 8% is not .8, but .08.

Also, watch out for percents over 99%. You still just need to move the decimal point <u>two</u> places to the left, but it is easy to make a careless mistake.

> **EXAMPLE**
>
> 115% is not .115, but 1.15
>
> 460% is not .460, but 4.60

Practice Exercises—Converting Percents to Decimals

Convert the following percents to decimals.

1. 55%
2. 21%
3. 91%
4. 17%
5. 80%

6. 147%
7. 250%
8. 5%
9. 10%
10. 100%

Converting Decimals to Percents

This process is the same as percents to decimals, only in reverse.

Write .75 as a percent.

(STEP 1) Add a percent sign to the right of the number.

(STEP 2) Move the decimal point two to the right.

$$.75 = 75\%$$

That's all there is to it. Just be careful to always move it over twice, and watch out for numbers less then ten. There you will need to add a zero. For example,

> **EXAMPLE**
>
> .9 is not 9%, but 90%
>
> .6 is not 6%, but 60%

Keep an eye out for decimals 1.0 or higher. You still need to move <u>two</u> places to the right. No more, no less. For example:

> **EXAMPLE**
>
> 2.45 is not 2.45%, but 245%
>
> 6.539 is not 6539%, but 653.9%

Practice Exercises—Converting Decimals to Percents

Convert each decimal to a percent.

1. .23
2. .44
3. .78
4. .91
5. .40

6. .04
7. .4
8. 1.50
9. 1.05
10. .6

Converting Fractions to Decimals and Percents

This is a simple process if you have a calculator. All you need to do is divide the top number.

EXAMPLE

$\frac{3}{4}$ means 3 ÷ 4, or .75

$\frac{5}{8}$ means 5 ÷ 8, or .625

However, you will only have a calculator for half of the test. One shortcut that will come in handy is to memorize a list of the most commonly used fractions. Sound impossible? Don't be surprised to find out you already know most of them. You just need to think about money.

EXAMPLE

How much is a quarter worth?	$\frac{1}{4}$ = .25
How much are two quarters worth?	$\frac{2}{4} = \frac{1}{2}$ = .50
How much are three quarters worth?	$\frac{3}{4}$ = .75

Now, let's think about dimes. It takes ten dimes to make $1.00, and one dime is worth $.10.

EXAMPLE

How much is one dime worth?	$\frac{1}{10}$ = .10
Convert 2/10 to a decimal	$\frac{2}{10} = \frac{1}{5}$ = .20
What is 3/10 as a decimal?	$\frac{3}{10}$ = .30

Notice a pattern? Just like with dimes and money, every $\frac{1}{10}$ goes up by .10. Also notice how $\frac{2}{10}$ and $\frac{1}{5}$ are the same thing when reduced to simplest terms.

Practice Exercises—Converting Fractions to Decimals

Complete the chart converting fractions to decimals.

Fraction	Decimal
$\frac{1}{10}$	
$\frac{2}{10}$ -OR- $\frac{1}{5}$	
$\frac{1}{4}$	
$\frac{1}{3}$	.333
$\frac{4}{10}$ -OR- $\frac{2}{5}$	
$\frac{1}{2}$ -OR- $\frac{5}{10}$	
$\frac{6}{10}$ -OR- $\frac{3}{5}$	
$\frac{2}{3}$	.666
$\frac{7}{10}$	
$\frac{3}{4}$	
$\frac{8}{10}$ -OR- $\frac{4}{5}$	
$\frac{9}{10}$	
$\frac{10}{10}$	

THE TWO MOST COMMONLY MISSED FRACTIONS

$$\frac{1}{3} = .333 \qquad \frac{2}{3} = .666$$

Unlike quarters and tenths, we do not use coins for one-third or two-thirds. Therefore, these often do not make sense to people. Just commit them to memory because you will see them again.

Now let's try putting it all together. You'll want to do your best to memorize the following chart because these are the most commonly used fractions, decimals, and percents.

Practice Exercises—Converting Fractions to Decimals and Percents

Fill in the missing information on the chart below. If you get stuck, remember how coins and money can help with fractions.

Fraction	Decimal	Percent
$\frac{1}{10}$		
	.20	
		25%
$\frac{1}{3}$		
	.4	
		50%
$\frac{6}{10}$ -OR- $\frac{3}{5}$		
	.666	
		70%
$\frac{3}{4}$		
	.8	
		90%
$\frac{1}{1}$		

Practice Exercises—Fractions, Decimals, and Percents

Write a fraction, decimal, and percent for each diagram. The first one has been completed for you.

1. $\frac{1}{10}$, _.10_ , _10_ %

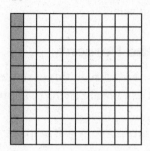

2. $\frac{\Box}{\Box}$, _____ , _____ %

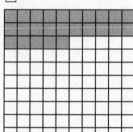

3. $\frac{\Box}{\Box}$, _____ , _____ %

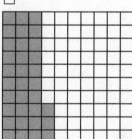

4. $\frac{\Box}{\Box}$, _____ , _____ %

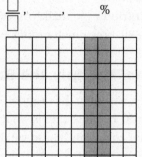

5. $\frac{\Box}{\Box}$, _____ , _____ %

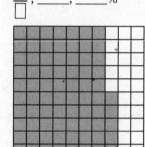

6. $\frac{\Box}{\Box}$, _____ , _____ %

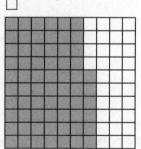

7. Phil spends 33% of his money on rent each month and $\frac{1}{4}$ on food. What fraction of his money does he spend on rent?

8. Danny drank $\frac{2}{5}$ of a liter of soda after work. Write the amount of soda he drank as a decimal.

LESSON 3: USING PERCENTAGES

There are a couple of ways to solve percent questions. Whichever works better for you (and that you can remember!) is fine. To start, let's take a look at a common situation using percentages in real life.

"On a recent trip to the mall, you see a sweater that is on sale for 20% off. If the sweater originally cost $30, how much money will you save buying it on sale?"

Method One: Multiply the Base Number by the Percent

By base number, we mean the original, or whole number we started with. In this example, the base number is 30, because that is what the sweater originally cost. We are trying to figure out what *part* of that cost is on sale so we don't have to pay for it.

This may seem confusing now, but being familiar with this terminology will help you with other percentage problems down the road.

STEP 1 Convert the percent to a decimal.

$$20\% = .20$$

STEP 2 Multiply the base number by the decimal.

$$30 \times .20 = 6.00$$

STEP 3 Double check that the decimal point is in the right place.

It can be very easy to multiply 60 and 20 together to get 600. However, there is no way that a $30 sweater can be $600 off, so always double check your work. The correct answer is that you would save $6.00.

> **EXAMPLE**
>
> Find 45% of 50.
>
> 45% = .45
>
> 50 × .45 = 22.5

Practice Exercises—Multiplying by the Decimal

Find the percent of each number by multiplying by the decimal. The first one has been completed for you.

1. What is 15% of 90?

    $$\begin{array}{r} 90 \\ \times\ .15 \\ \hline 450 \\ 900 \\ \hline 13.50 \end{array}$$

2. What is 50% of 60?

3. What is 90% of 100?

4. What is 25% of 80?

5. What is 12% of 50?

6. What is 75% of 400?

7. 35% of 900 is what number?

8. 110% of 50 is what number?

9. What is 200% of 80?

10. A local restaurant has a policy of including an 18% gratuity (tip) for parties of six or more. If a family of eight goes to the restaurant and spends $100 before the gratuity is included, how much of a tip will be added?

11. The local sales tax in Spring County is 5%. If Leon buys $35 worth of food at the store, how much will he pay in tax?

Method Two: Find the Percent Using a Proportion

In addition to multiplying by the decimal, you can also use a proportion to solve every percentage question. Some people find this way easier, while others prefer the first method. Make sure you are familiar with this proportion because it can be a big help later on with more complicated percent questions. We'll start by using the same example as in Method One.

"On a recent trip to the mall, you see a sweater that is on sale for 20% off. If the sweater originally cost $30, how much money will you save buying it on sale?"

For every percent question, we will use the same proportion:

$$\frac{?}{\text{BASE}} = \frac{\%}{100}$$

(STEP 1) Write down the basic percent proportion.

$$\frac{?}{\text{BASE}} = \frac{\%}{100}$$

(STEP 2) Fill in the percent given in the problem in the upper right of the proportion. IMPORTANT: Do not convert the percent to a decimal!

$$\frac{?}{\text{BASE}} = \frac{20}{100}$$

STEP 3 Write the base number in the bottom left of the proportion.

$$\frac{?}{30} = \frac{20}{100}$$

STEP 4 Solve the proportion by cross-multiplying and dividing.

$$\frac{?}{30} \diagup \frac{20}{100}$$

$$20 \times 30 = 600$$
$$600 \div 100 = 6$$
$$\$6.00 \text{ is the answer.}$$

EXAMPLE

Find 45% of 50.

$$\frac{?}{\text{BASE}} = \frac{\%}{100}$$

$$\frac{?}{50} = \frac{45}{100}$$

$$50 \times 45 = 2,250$$
$$2,250 \div 100 = 22.5$$

Practice Exercises—Find the Percent Using a Proportion

Find the percent of each number using a proportion. The first one has been completed for you.

1. What is 20% of 80?

$$\frac{?}{80} \diagup \frac{20}{100}$$

$$80 \times 20 = 1,600$$
$$1,600 \div 100 = 16$$

2. What is 35% of 70?

_____ = _____

3. What is 10% of 350?

_____ = _____

4. What is 80% of 10?

_____ = _____

5. What is 110% of 50?

_____ = _____

6. What is 50% of 400?

_____ = _____

7. 15% of 70 is what number?

8. 200% of 300 is what number?

9. 75% of 100 is what number?

10. Smith Corporation has 400 employees. If 55% of those employees take public transportation to work, how many people take public transportation to Smith Corp.?

11. Jenna's income tax rate is 15%. If she earns 30,000 dollars this year, how much will she pay in taxes?

LESSON 4: TIPS AND TRICKS WITH PERCENTS

We all know someone who is "good" at math. These people are no smarter than the rest of us; they just know a few tricks that make solving complicated problems easier. Fortunately, with a little work you too can be one of those people who are "good" at percentages.

This lesson will show you how to find 10%, 20%, 25%, 33%, and 50%, of any number in the world while doing very little math. In fact, though you may not realize it, you already know how to find most of these commonly used percents.

How to Find 10% of Any Number

Let's start with this: find 10% of 80.

Method 1	Method 2
80	$\dfrac{?}{80} = \dfrac{10}{100}$
$\times\ .10$	
00	
800	$80 \times 10 = 800$
8.00	$800 \div 100 = 8$

So, 10% of 80 is 8.

What do you notice about the number you started with, 80, and the answer, 8?

The only difference is that we dropped a zero off of 80 and wound up with 8. Or, another way to look at it is we moved the decimal point over one spot to the left. *Remember:* If no decimal point is given, you can just assume the decimal point is at the end on the right.

TO FIND 10% OF ANY NUMBER

Simply move the decimal point one spot to the left.

10% of 50	50.0	5.0
10% of 750	750.0	75.0
10% of 34.7	34.7	3.47

That's it! You don't need a calculator or scratch paper, all you need to do is move a decimal point.

Practice Exercises—Finding 10% of a Number

Find 10% of each of the following numbers by moving the decimal point.

1. 50
2. 76.2
3. 675
4. 8.10
5. 327

6. 10
7. 100
8. 900.0
9. 44.4
10. 2

How to Find 20% of Any Number

To do this, you'll need to know how to find 10% of any number, so make sure you are comfortable with the steps above.

So what is the difference between 10% and 20%? Well, what is the difference between $10 and $20? $20 is exactly double $10, and 20% is exactly double 10%.

TO FIND 20% OF ANY NUMBER

Find 10%, and then double it.

What is 20% of 80?

$$10\% \text{ of } 80 = 8 \quad \text{now double that.}$$
$$\underline{\times\, 2} \qquad \underline{\times\, 2}$$
$$20\% \text{ of } 80 = 16$$

UNIT 2: MATHEMATICS

Find 20% of 75.

    10% of 75 = 7.5   7.5   or, you could do 7.5 + 7.5 = 15

                                       × 2

                                       15

    20% of 75 = 15

Find 20% of 2.5.

    10% of 2.5 = .25   .25   or .25 + .25 =.50

                                   × 2

                                   .50

Practice Exercises—Finding 20% of a Number

Find 20% of each of the following numbers by moving the decimal point and then doubling.

1. 20
2. 50
3. 15
4. 100
5. 7.0

6. 1,000
7. 9
8. 25
9. 30
10. 60

How to Find 25% of Any Number

For this one, you need to remember that all percents can be written as a decimal, and therefore a fraction.

What is 25% as a fraction? 25% is the same thing as one quarter, or $\frac{1}{4}$.

So let's think about what $\frac{1}{4}$ really means: Take the whole number, and divide it into four pieces.

TO FIND 25% OR $\frac{1}{4}$ OF ANY NUMBER

Divide by 4.

25% of 60	60 ÷ 4 = 15	15 is 25% of 60
Find 25% of 120	120 ÷ 4 = 30	30 is 25% of 120
What is 25% of 96?	96 ÷ 4 = 24	24 is 25% of 96

Practice Exercises—Finding 25% of a Number

Find 25% or $\frac{1}{4}$ of each number by dividing by 4.

1. 80
2. 600
3. 16
4. 76
5. 40

6. 2
7. 120
8. 64
9. 44
10. 100

How to Find 33% of Any Number

For this one, you need to remember that all percents can be written as a decimal, and therefore a fraction.

What is 33% as a fraction? 33% is the same thing as one third, or $\frac{1}{3}$.

So let's think about what $\frac{1}{3}$ really means: Take the whole number, and divide it into three pieces.

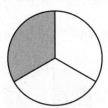

TO FIND 33% OR $\frac{1}{3}$ OF ANY NUMBER

Divide by 3.

33% of 60	60 ÷ 3 = 20	20 is 33% of 60
Find 33% of 120	120 ÷ 3 = 40	40 is 33% of 120
What is 33% of 81?	81 ÷ 3 = 27	27 is 33% of 81

Practice Exercises—Finding 33% of a Number

Find 33% or $\frac{1}{3}$ of each of the following numbers by dividing by three.

1. 66
2. 45
3. 75
4. 93
5. 300

6. 900
7. 15
8. 333
9. 21
10. 54

How to Find 50% of Any Number

This is the easiest one of all. Remember that 50% is one half, or $\frac{1}{2}$. Here all we need to do is split our number into two.

TO FIND 50% OR $\frac{1}{2}$ OF ANY NUMBER

Divide by 2.

50% of 90	90 ÷ 2 = 45	50% of 90 is 45
What is 50% of 30?	30 ÷ 2 = 15	50% of 30 is 15
Find 50% of 620	620 ÷ 2 = 310	50% of 620 is 310

Practice Exercises—Finding 50% of a Number

Find 50% of each number by dividing it by two.

1. 50
2. 40
3. 66
4. 250
5. 84

6. 78
7. 110
8. 6
9. 12
10. 1,000

LESSON 5: WORD PROBLEMS WITH PERCENTS

1. The bill for dinner at a local restaurant totals $40. If you leave a 15% tip, how much money is the tip?

2. Ellen seldom misses a day of work. In the last 200 days on the job, she was sick and missed work 4% of the time. How many days was Ellen out sick?

3. If sales tax is 5%, how much tax will you pay on a new TV that cost $500?

4. Blue jeans are on sale 25% off. If the regular price is $40, how much will you save during the sale?

Multiple-Step Word Problems with Percents

Many times you will have to perform more than one calculation per problem. **The key is to read the problem carefully to make sure you answer the right question.**

Try this:

5. The bill for dinner at a local restaurant totals $40. If you leave a 15% tip, how much money will you spend altogether?

   This is basically the same information you had in question 1 above, but now the actual question has changed. What is different?

   This question wants to know the total money you will spend. In other words, add the tip to the bill.

   15% of 40 = $6.

   $40 for dinner plus the $6 tip = $46.

   So be on the lookout; to answer the following questions, you will need to do more than just find the percent.

6. Alexis found a pair of shoes for 20% off. If they originally cost $60, how much will they cost after the discount?

7. Brittany earns $10 an hour at her job. If she gets a 10% raise at the end of the year, how much will she earn per hour?

8. Ann buys a loaf of bread for $3, a jar of peanut butter for $2.50, and a jar of jelly for $2.50. If tax is 5%, what is the total amount of money she will spend?

9. A local restaurant is offering a special promotion where if you buy one burger, you get the second one half off. If a burger costs $6, how much would two cost with the promotion?

10. The movie theater sells two types of tickets, children and adult. This weekend 45% of the tickets sold were children's tickets. If 200 total people were at the theater, how many adult tickets were sold?
    (A) 90
    (B) 100
    (C) 110
    (D) 155

11. Steve's office recently went out to lunch together. The bill was $50. If they leave a 15% tip, what is the total amount of money the office spent at lunch?
    (A) $7.50
    (B) $35
    (C) $50.15
    (D) $57.50

12. This year it rained 20% of the days in September. If there are 30 days in September, how many days had no rain?
    (A) 6
    (B) 12
    (C) 24
    (D) 28

13. Compare the final prices to decide which is the better deal. At Al's Appliances, a $500 TV is on sale for 40% off. Across town at Bob's TVs, the same TV is on sale for $400 and 25% off. Which is the better deal?
    (A) Al's Appliances
    (B) Bob's TVs
    (C) They are the same price

14. On Saturday 500 people came to the city park. On Sunday 20% more people came to the park than on Saturday. How many people came to the park on Sunday?
    (A) 400
    (B) 500
    (C) 520
    (D) 600

15. This season, Ronnie made 80% of his free throws playing basketball. If he shot 50 free throws, how many did he miss?
    (A) 10
    (B) 30
    (C) 40
    (D) 70

16. A store coupon gives 15% off every purchase over $100. If you buy $120 worth of merchandise at the store, how much will you pay with the coupon?
    (A) $18
    (B) $102
    (C) $105
    (D) $138

END-OF-CHAPTER QUESTIONS

Shade the correct percent for each figure.

1. 50%

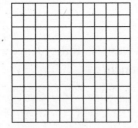

3. 33%

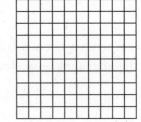

2. 25%

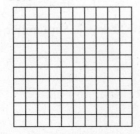

4. Fill in the missing information on the chart below.

Fraction	Decimal	Percent
$\frac{1}{10}$		
	.20	
		25%
$\frac{1}{3}$		
		50%
$\frac{6}{10}$ or $\frac{3}{5}$		
		70%
$\frac{3}{4}$		
	.8	
		90%
$\frac{1}{1}$		

Find the percent of each number by multiplying by the decimal. The first one has been completed for you.

5. What is 15% of 90?

$$\begin{array}{r} 90 \\ \times\ .15 \\ \hline 450 \\ 900 \\ \hline 13.50 \end{array}$$

6. What is 40% of 30?

7. What is 80% of 100?

8. What is 25% of 180?

9. What is 10% of 65?

10. What is 35% of 40?

Find the percent for each number using a proportion. The first one has been completed for you.

11. What is 20% of 80?

$$\frac{?}{80} \nearrow \frac{20}{100}$$

$$80 \times 20 = 1,600$$

$$1,600 \div 100 = 16$$

12. What is 15% of 60?

____ = ____

13. What is 20% of 250

____ = ____

14. What is 10% of 100?

15. What is 110% of 70?

16. What is 25% of 16?

Find 10% of each of the following numbers by moving the decimal point.

17. 67

18. 289

19. 5

20. 32.4

21. 901

Find 20% *of each of the following numbers by moving the decimal point and then doubling.*

22. 10

23. 40

24. 25

25. 100

26. 8.0

Find 25% *or* $\frac{1}{4}$ *of each number by dividing by* 4.

27. 60

28. 100

29. 28

30. 80

31. 60

Find 33% *or* $\frac{1}{3}$ *of each of the following numbers by dividing by three.*

32. 99

33. 45

34. 15

35. 126

36. 300

Find 50% *of each number by dividing it by two.*

37. 400

38. 56

39. 18

40. 410

41. 100

Solve the following questions.

42. A new phone you like costs $200. This weekend you see that the phone is on sale for 10% off. How much will you save by buying the phone on sale?

43. A local restaurant includes an 18% tip for parties of six or more. You and ten friends are celebrating a birthday at the restaurant. If the bill is $100 before the tip, how much of a tip will be added?

44. Forty percent of the employees at the factory work part time. If there are 250 total employees at the factory, how many people work part time?
   (A) 10
   (B) 100
   (C) 150
   (D) 210

45. Eric got a 90% score on his math test. If there were 40 questions, how many did he get correct?
   (A) 4
   (B) 9
   (C) 36
   (D) 44

46. If sales tax is 5%, how much is the total cost of a refrigerator that sells for $600?

47. $\frac{1}{4}$ of the customers at a local restaurant order dessert. If the restaurant serves 200 customers today, how many people don't order dessert?

Use the table below to answer questions 48 and 49. All three stores are having a sale this weekend on the same model of TV.

Al's	Bob's	Chris's
$400, 20% off	$500, 40% off	$440, 25% off

48. After comparing the prices between Al's and Bob's, which store has the better deal?
   (A) Al's
   (B) Bob's
   (C) They are the same price

49. Which of the three stores has the best deal?
   (A) Al's
   (B) Bob's
   (C) Chris's
   (D) They are all the same price.

CHAPTER 9 ANSWER EXPLANATIONS

Lesson 1: What Are Percents?

PRACTICE EXERCISES—VISUALIZING PERCENTS (PAGE 247)

1. 25%

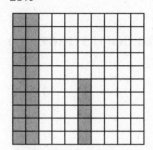

3. 50%

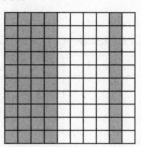

2. 33%

4. 75%

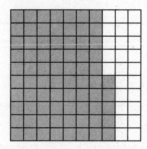

5. 110%

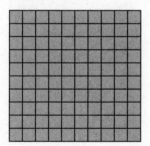

6. 25%

7. 45 centimeters

8. 112 centimeters

Lesson 2: Comparing Decimals, Fractions, and Percents

PRACTICE EXERCISES—CONVERTING PERCENTS TO DECIMALS (PAGE 249)

1. .55

2. .21

3. .91

4. .17

5. .80

6. 1.47

7. 2.5

8. .05

9. .10

10. 1.00

PRACTICE EXERCISES—CONVERTING DECIMALS TO PERCENTS (PAGE 249)

1.	23%	**6.**	4%
2.	44%	**7.**	40%
3.	78%	**8.**	150%
4.	91%	**9.**	105%
5.	40%	**10.**	60%

PRACTICE EXERCISES—CONVERTING FRACTIONS TO DECIMALS (PAGE 251)

Fraction	Decimal
$\frac{1}{10}$	.10
$\frac{2}{10}$ -OR- $\frac{1}{5}$	.20
$\frac{1}{4}$	.25
$\frac{1}{3}$	.333
$\frac{4}{10}$ -OR- $\frac{2}{5}$	.40
$\frac{1}{2}$ -OR- $\frac{5}{10}$	.50
$\frac{6}{10}$ -OR- $\frac{3}{5}$	.60
$\frac{2}{3}$	.666
$\frac{7}{10}$	.70
$\frac{3}{4}$	.75
$\frac{8}{10}$ -OR- $\frac{4}{5}$	.80
$\frac{9}{10}$	.90
$\frac{10}{10}$	1.00

PRACTICE EXERCISES—CONVERTING FRACTIONS TO DECIMALS AND PERCENTS (PAGE 252)

Fraction	Decimal	Percent
$\frac{1}{10}$	.10	10%
$\frac{2}{10}$ -OR- $\frac{1}{5}$	.20	20%
$\frac{1}{4}$	.25	25%
$\frac{1}{3}$	.33	33%
$\frac{4}{10}$ -OR- $\frac{2}{5}$	.4	40%
$\frac{1}{2}$	.50	50%
$\frac{6}{10}$ -OR- $\frac{3}{5}$	.60	60%
$\frac{2}{3}$	.666	66%
$\frac{7}{10}$	.70	70%
$\frac{3}{4}$	.75	75%
$\frac{8}{10}$ -OR- $\frac{4}{5}$	.8	80%
$\frac{9}{10}$	.90	90%
$\frac{1}{1}$	1.00	100%

PRACTICE EXERCISES—WRITE FRACTIONS, DECIMALS, AND PERCENTS (PAGE 253)

1. $\frac{1}{10}$, .10, 10%

2. $\frac{1}{4}$, .25, 25%

3. $\frac{1}{3}$, .33, 33%

4. $\frac{1}{5}$, .20, 20%

5. $\frac{3}{4}$, .75, 75%

6. $\frac{2}{3}$, .66, 66%

7. $\frac{1}{3}$

8. .40

Lesson 3: Using Percentages

PRACTICE EXERCISES—MULTIPLY BY THE DECIMAL (PAGE 254)

1. $90 \times .15 = 13.50$

2. $60 \times .50 = 30$

3. $100 \times .90 = 90$

4. $80 \times .25 = 20$

5. $50 \times .12 = 6$

6. $400 \times .75 = 300$

7. $900 \times .35 = 315$

8. $50 \times 1.10 = 55$

9. $80 \times 2.00 = 160$

10. $100 \times .18 = \$18$

11. $35 \times .05 = \$1.75$

PRACTICE EXERCISES—FIND THE PERCENT USING A PROPORTION (PAGE 256)

1. $80 \times 20 = 1,600$
$1,600 \div 100 = 16$

2. $70 \times 35 = 2,450$
$2,450 \div 100 = 24.5$

3. $350 \times 10 = 3,500$
$3,500 \div 100 = 35$

4. $10 \times 80 = 800$
$800 \div 100 = 8$

5. $50 \times 110 = 5,500$
$5,500 \div 100 = 55$

6. $400 \times 50 = 20,000$
$20,000 \div 100 = 200$

7. $70 \times 15 = 10,500$
$10,500 \div 100 = 10.5$

8. $200 \times 300 = 60,000$
$60,000 \div 100 = 600$

9. $100 \times 75 = 7,500$
$7,500 \div 100 = 75$

10. $400 \times 55 = 22,000$
$22,000 \div 100 = 220$

11. $30,000 \times 15 = 450,000$
$450,000 \div 100 = \$4,500$

Lesson 4: Tips and Tricks with Percents

PRACTICE EXERCISES—FINDING 10% OF A NUMBER (PAGE 258)

1. 5

2. 7.62

3. 67.5

4. .81

5. 32.7

6. 1

7. 10

8. 90

9. 4.44

10. .2

PRACTICE EXERCISES—FINDING 20% OF A NUMBER (PAGE 259)

1. 4

2. 10

3. 3

4. 20

5. 1.4

6. 200

7. 1.8

8. 5

9. 6

10. 12

PRACTICE EXERCISES—FINDING 25% OF A NUMBER (PAGE 260)

1. 20
2. 150
3. 4
4. 19
5. 10

6. .5
7. 30
8. 16
9. 11
10. 25

PRACTICE EXERCISES—FINDING 33% OF A NUMBER (PAGE 261)

1. 22
2. 15
3. 25
4. 31
5. 100

6. 300
7. 5
8. 111
9. 7
10. 18

PRACTICE EXERCISES—FINDING 50% OF A NUMBER (PAGE 261)

1. 25
2. 20
3. 33
4. 125
5. 42

6. 39
7. 55
8. 3
9. 6
10. 500

Lesson 5: Word Problems with Percents (Page 262)

1. $6
2. 8 days
3. $25
4. $10
5. $46
6. **$48**   20% of 60 = $12, $60 – 12 = $48
7. **$11**   10% of 10 = $1, $10 + 1 = $11
8. **$8.40**   5% of 8 = .40, $8 + .40 = $8.40
9. **$9**   50% of 6 = 3, two burgers cost $12. $12 – 3 = $9
10. **(C)** 55% of tickets were adult. 55% of 200 = 110
11. **(D)** 15% of 50 = $7.50, $50 + 7.50 = $57.50
12. **(C)** 20% of 30 = 6, 30 – 6 = 24
13. **(C)** 40% of 500 = $200, $500 – 200 = $300, 25% of $400 = $100, $400 – 100 = $300
14. **(D)** 20% of 500 = 100, 500 + 100 = 600
15. **(A)** 80% of 50 = 40, 50 – 40 = 10
16. **(B)** 15% of $120 = 18, $120 – 18 = $102

End-of-Chapter Questions (Page 264)

1. 50%

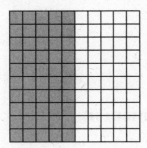

3. 33%

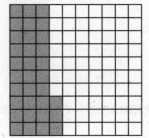

2. 25%

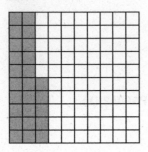

4.

Fraction	Decimal	Percent
$\frac{1}{10}$	.10	10%
$\frac{2}{10}$ -OR- $\frac{1}{5}$	.20	20%
$\frac{1}{4}$	.25	25%
$\frac{1}{3}$	.33	33%
$\frac{1}{2}$	.50	50%
$\frac{6}{10}$ -OR- $\frac{2}{3}$	.6	60%
$\frac{7}{10}$	.70	70%
$\frac{3}{4}$	.75	75%
$\frac{8}{10}$ -OR- $\frac{4}{5}$	.80	80%

Fraction	Decimal	Percent
$\frac{9}{10}$	.90	90%
$\frac{1}{1}$	1.00	100%

5. $90 \times .15 = 13.50$

6. $30 \times .40 = 12$

7. $100 \times .80 = 80$

8. $180 \times .25 = 45$

9. $65 \times .10 = 6.5$

10. $40 \times .35 = 14$

11. $80 \times 20 = 1,600$

$1,600 \div 100 = 16$

12. $60 \times 15 = 900$

$900 \div 100 = 9$

13. $250 \times 20 = 5,000$

$5,000 \div 100 = 50$

14. $100 \times 10 = 1,000$

$1,000 \div 100 = 10$

15. $70 \times 110 = 7,700$

$7,700 \div 100 = 77$

16. $16 \times 25 = 400$

$400 \div 100 = 4$

17. 6.7

18. 28.9

19. .5

20. 3.24

21. 90.1

22. 2

23. 8

24. 5

25. 20

26. 1.6

27. 15

28. 25

29. 7

30. 20

31. 15

32. 33

33. 15

34. 5

35. 42

36. 100

37. 200

38. 28

39. 9

40. 205

41. 50

42. 10% of 200 = $20

43. 18% of 100 = $18

44. **(B)** 40% of 250 = 100

45. **(C)** 90% of 40 = 36

46. 5% of 600 = 30

$600 + 30 = \$630$

47. $\frac{1}{4} = 25\%$, 25% of 200 = 50,

$200 - 50 = 150$

48. **(B)** 40% of 500 = 200, 500 − 200 = 300, that is the lowest price

49. **(B)**

Calculator Use

LESSON 1: THE FRACTION KEY

The key circled above allows you to enter fractions into the calculator.

HOW TO USE THE FRACTION KEY

To write $\frac{3}{4}$ in the calculator, first press the $\boxed{\frac{n}{d}}$ key.

The screen will look like $\frac{\square}{\square}$.

Push the $\boxed{3}$ button, and the number 3 will appear in the top box.

Next, push the $\boxed{\text{down arrow}}$ on the 4-way directional pad.

Now press the number $\boxed{3}$. The screen will look like $\frac{3}{4}>$

NOTE: After entering your fraction, you must press the right arrow on the 4-way directional pad. Otherwise, numbers will continue to appear on the bottom half of the fraction.

Practice Exercises—Entering Fractions

Practice entering the following fractions into the calculator.

1. $\frac{4}{5}$ 2. $\frac{5}{6}$ 3. $\frac{57}{69}$ 4. $\frac{3}{11}$

HOW TO USE THE FRACTION KEY

To write $2\frac{3}{4}$ in the calculator, first press the $\boxed{\text{2nd}}$ function key.

The screen will look like $\square\frac{\square}{\square}$.

Push the $\boxed{2}$ button, and the number 2 will appear in the left box.

Next, push the $\boxed{\text{right arrow}}$ on the 4-way directional pad.

Now press the number $\boxed{3}$, then the down arrow.

Now press the number $\boxed{4}$. The screen will look like $2\frac{3}{4}>$

NOTE: After entering your fraction, you must press the right arrow on the 4-way directional pad. Otherwise, numbers will continue to appear on the bottom half of the fraction.

Practice entering the following fractions into the calculator.

1. $5\frac{1}{2}$
2. $4\frac{3}{4}$
3. $500\frac{1}{10}$
4. $62\frac{8}{9}$

Operations with Fractions and the Calculator

> Use the $\boxed{\frac{n}{d}}$ key to enter the fractions.
>
> Use the $\boxed{+}$, $\boxed{-}$, $\boxed{X}$, or $\boxed{\div}$ keys as needed.

For example, to compute $1\frac{4}{5} + \frac{2}{10}$

Press the $\boxed{\text{2nd}}$ function key; then press the $\boxed{\frac{n}{d}}$ key. Press $\boxed{1}$, and then use the directional arrow to the right.

Next, press $\boxed{4}$ and then use the $\boxed{\text{down directional arrow}}$. Press $\boxed{5}$, and then use the directional arrow to the right to complete the fraction.

Press the $\boxed{+}$, and then use the $\boxed{\frac{n}{d}}$ key to complete the next fraction.

Finally, press $\boxed{\text{enter}}$ to add the numbers.

If you have entered everything correctly, then the screen should read $\frac{19}{20}$

IMPORTANT CALCULATOR TIPS!

1. *To change a fraction to a decimal,* use the answer toggle key. This key has arrows pointing $\boxed{< >}$ and is located above $\boxed{\text{enter}}$.

   For example, enter $\frac{19}{20}$, press $\boxed{< >}$, and then press $\boxed{\text{enter}}$.

   The fraction is converted to .95.

2. *To reduce any fraction to lowest terms,* use $\boxed{\text{enter}}$.

   For example, enter $\frac{25}{525}$ and then press $\boxed{\text{enter}}$.

   The fraction is reduced to $\frac{1}{21}$.

Practice Exercises—Operations with Fractions and the Calculator

Solve the following questions using the calculator.

1. $\dfrac{3}{4}+\dfrac{1}{2}$

2. $\dfrac{5}{6}+\dfrac{2}{3}$

3. $2\dfrac{1}{2}+1\dfrac{4}{5}$

4. $\dfrac{1}{10}+\dfrac{1}{5}$

5. $\dfrac{7}{8}-\dfrac{3}{8}$

6. $2\dfrac{1}{3}-\dfrac{4}{3}$

7. $1\dfrac{3}{4}-1\dfrac{3}{5}$

8. $8\dfrac{8}{10}-7\dfrac{8}{10}$

9. $3\times\dfrac{1}{2}$

10. $2\dfrac{1}{2}\times2$

11. $3\dfrac{2}{3}\times\dfrac{1}{3}$

12. $2\dfrac{4}{5}\times1\dfrac{1}{4}$

13. $6\div\dfrac{1}{2}$

14. $8\div\dfrac{1}{4}$

15. $4\dfrac{1}{2}\div\dfrac{3}{4}$

16. $7\dfrac{1}{3}\div\dfrac{1}{3}$

LESSON 2: THE PERCENT KEY

This book shows you two ways to calculate percentages without a calculator. With both of those methods, multiplying by the decimal or using a proportion, a calculator can make your life easier. But did you know there is also a special key just for percentages on the calculator?

Look carefully at the key above the number 8. Written above the $($ key is the % symbol. This means that it is the secondary, or alternate, function of the $($ key. We can activate it if we press the 2nd function key first. The shift key is located near the top left. Notice how the 2nd button is a different shade? Pressing this key will allow you to use any of the secondary functions of the calculator.

Here's an example: Find 15% of 80.

STEP 1 Enter the percentage. In this case 15.

STEP 2 Press 2nd. This turns on the % key above the $($ sign.

STEP 3 Press X to multiply.

STEP 4 Enter the other number. In this case 80.

The screen should read 15% * 80

STEP 5 Press enter.

The answer is 12.

TO FIND A PERCENT ON THE CALCULATOR

What is 30% of 50?

REMEMBER: Just multiply the two numbers together, but use the 2nd
key to enter the percent.

50 × 30 *Note: Do not change the percent to a decimal.*

Add the percent sign by hitting 2nd and then =.

50 × 30% = 15

Use the % key to answer the following questions.

1. 25% of 60   3. 10% of 48   5. 110% of 90   7. 50% of 46

2. 35% of 200   4. 60% of 180   6. 5% of 50   8. 75% of 300

Using the Calculator for Multiple-Step Problem Percent Problems

The lesson on word problems with percents featured questions that ask you to do more than
just find a simple percent. For example:

The bill for dinner was $40. If you leave a 15% tip, what is the new total?

Answering this question requires two steps. First, we must figure out the amount of the
tip. To do this, we need to calculate 15% of 40. To do this using the percent key, you would
do the following:

STEP 1 Press 4 0 × 1 5.

STEP 2 Press SHIFT.

STEP 3 Press % enter.

If you did this correctly, the screen should read "6."

That is the amount of the tip, but the question asked what the new total would be. To find
that, we must add the tip to the original bill.

STEP 4 Press +.

The screen should read "ans+" This means your previous answer, in this case 6, will be added
to what you type next.

STEP 5 Press 4 0 enter.

The answer is 46. That is the cost of the $40 bill plus the $6 tip.

Example:

A $50 pair of jeans is on sale for 40% off. How much will the jeans cost after the discount?

STEP 1 Press [5] [0] [×] [4] [0].

STEP 2 Press [2nd]

STEP 3 Press [%] [enter]   The screen should read "20."

STEP 4 Press [−] to subtract that discount from the original price.

The screen should say "ans−."

Input the original price; then press [enter].

The final price is $30 because that is $50 minus the $20 discount.

Use the [%] key and then the [+] or [−] key to solve these two-step percentage problems.

1. A new washing machine costs $400. If the sales tax of 6% is applied at the cash register, what is the final price?

2. 30 people work in Jeff's office. Lately a lot of people have been catching a cold. If 20% of his coworkers are out sick tomorrow, how many will be at work tomorrow?

3. Clara earns $1,800 a month. If 35% of her salary goes to taxes and insurance, how much money will she take home a month?

4. 7 friends went out to lunch at Sal's. If the bill was $56 before the tip, what will the final bill be after an 18% tip is added?

5. A mattress set that normally costs $500 is on sale for 25% off. How much will the set cost after the discount?

6. The monthly sales at Alpha Corporation total $600,000. If sales increase by 12% next month, how much money will Alpha Corporation bring in next month?

CHAPTER 10 ANSWER EXPLANATIONS

Lesson 1: The Fraction Key

PRACTICE EXERCISES—OPERATIONS WITH FRACTIONS AND THE CALCULATOR (PAGE 280)

1. $1\frac{1}{4}$ **5.** $\frac{1}{2}$ **9.** $1\frac{1}{2}$ **13.** 12

2. $1\frac{1}{2}$ **6.** 1   **10.** 5   **14.** 32

3. $4\frac{3}{10}$ **7.** $\frac{3}{20}$ **11.** $1\frac{2}{9}$ **15.** 6

4. $\frac{3}{10}$ **8.** $1\frac{1}{10}$ **12.** $3\frac{1}{2}$ **16.** 22

Lesson 2: The Percent Key

PRACTICE EXERCISES—USING THE PERCENT KEY (PAGE 282)

1. 15   **3.** 4.8   **5.** 99   **7.** 23
2. 70   **4.** 108   **6.** 2.5   **8.** 225

PRACTICE EXERCISES—USING THE CALCULATOR FOR MULTIPLE-STEP PERCENT PROBLEMS (PAGE 283)

1. $424   **3.** $1,170   **5.** $375
2. 24 people   **4.** $66.08   **6.** $672,000

Standard Deviation

11

LESSON 1: MEAN

Have you ever tried to follow a conversation when everyone is speaking at the same time? That can be difficult to do. Likewise, it can be difficult to figure out what a set of numbers can tell us when they all appear at once.

Take a look at the following sales numbers for a local restaurant, Pete's Pizza.

Monday	400
Tuesday	550
Wednesday	600
Thursday	425
Friday	550

Pete knows he needs to make $500 a day to stay in business. Will Pete's Pizza stay open? It can be hard to tell when some days he sells much more than $500, and other days he sells much less.

What Pete needs to find is his **average**, or **mean**, sales for the week.

HOW TO FIND THE AVERAGE OR MEAN

STEP 1 Add up all of the numbers.

STEP 2 Divide that answer by how many numbers you added.

So, Pete must first add up the sales for each day.

$$400 + 550 + 600 + 425 + 550 = 2,525$$

Then, Pete will take that answer and divide it by how many numbers he added. Since he totaled five days of sales, he will divide by five.

$$2,525 \div 5 = 505$$

So, Pete averaged $505 in sales for the week.

Here is another example as a word problem.

Davon's parents said they would take him to his favorite restaurant if his average grade in math class is a 90 or higher. So far, Davon has scored 80, 100, 95, 85, and a 65. Will Davon get to go to his favorite restaurant.

THINK: What key word in the problem tells me what to do? Average.

$$80 + 100 + 95 + 85 + 85 = 445$$

$$445 \div 5 = 89$$

So, since Davon averaged an 89, he was one point short of his goal!

Practice Exercises—Mean

1. What is the average of the following numbers: 1, 2, 3, 4, 5?

2. Find the mean of these numbers: 5, 3, 1, 4, 2.

Use the table below to answer questions 3 and 4.

Temperatures

Monday	Tuesday	Wednesday	Thursday	Friday	Saturday	Sunday
70	75	55	60	50	80	100

3. What was the mean temperature for the entire week?

4. What was the average temperature for the weekend (Saturday and Sunday)?

Use the table below to answer questions 5 and 6.

Game 1	100	225	300	200
Game 2	150	175	200	200
Game 3	200	140	100	200
	Al	Bill	Chris	Dan

5. Four friends went bowling. What was the average score of each person?

   Al:

   Bill:

   Chris:

   Dan:

6. Al and Bill are on a team. Chris and Dan are on the other team. Which team had the highest score, and by how many points?

Shoe Size and Age

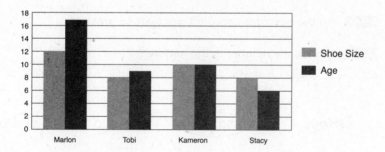

Using the chart above, answer questions 7 and 8.

7. What is the mean shoe size for the group?

8. Marlon and Kameron are boys. Tobi and Stacy are girls. What is the difference of the average ages of boys and girls?

   (**THINK:** What is the question asking? What information do I need to solve the problem?)

LESSON 2: MEDIAN

Finding the mean for a set of numbers can be very useful. However, it can also be misleading. For example, look at the following salary information for the houses along Main Street below.

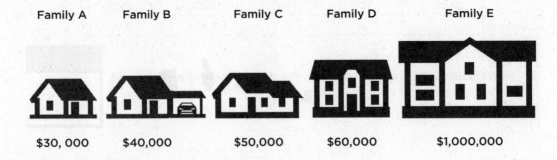

Family A	Family B	Family C	Family D	Family E
$30, 000	$40,000	$50,000	$60,000	$1,000,000

What is the average income for the five families on the street?

$$30,000 + 40,000 + 50,000 + 60,000 + 1,000,000 = 1,180,000$$

$$1,180,000 \div 5 = 236,000$$

So the average salary for Main Street is $236,000. But does that really describe any of the families on Main Street? Not really, most of the families earn far less than $236,000, and one wealthy family earns over four times that amount!

The **median** would help us to better describe a typical income on Main Street.

HOW TO FIND THE MEDIAN

STEP 1 Put the numbers in order from least to greatest.

STEP 2 Choose the number in the middle.

~~$30,000~~ ~~$40,000~~ $50,000 ~~$60,000~~ ~~$1,000,000~~

The median income for the houses on the street is $50,000. That is much closer to what a typical family on the street earns and is much closer than the average amount. A number that is out of place with the others is called an **outlier**. What is the outlier in this group?

Here is another example, find the median of the following set of numbers:

5, 2, 9, 10, 1

Order the numbers from least to greatest: 1, 2, 5, 9, 10

1, 2, 5, 9, 10

Think of the median like the median of a highway. It is in the middle!

Sometimes you will not be able to narrow down the median to just one number. This happens when there are an even number of numbers in the set.

MEDIAN WHERE THERE IS MORE THAN ONE MIDDLE NUMBER

STEP 1 Put the numbers in order from least to greatest.

STEP 2 Add the two middle numbers together.

STEP 3 Divide that answer by two.

For example, let's find the median of the following set:

20, 30, 40, 10

First we'll put them in order: 10, 20, 30, 40

However, we have two digits in the middle 10, 20, 30, 40

Add them together: 20 + 30 = 50

Divide by two: 50 ÷2 = 25.

The median is 25.

Practice Exercises—Median

1. What is the median of the following numbers: 100, 600, 300, 800, 200.

2. Find the median: 2, 4, 6, 8.

Use the table below to answer the next question.

Number of Customers per Day

Monday	Tuesday	Wednesday	Thursday	Friday	Saturday	Sunday
20	30	20	50	60	55	40

3. What is the median number of customers for the week?

4. Everyone in the Johnson family measured their heights. Tim was 48 inches, John was 60 inches, Claire was 46 inches, and Norah was 58 inches. What is the median height of the Johnson family?

Use the following information for questions 5 through 7.

Five-year-old Sofia had a birthday party. She invited four friends whose ages were 5, 4, 6, and 5. She also invited her 100-year-old grandmother.

5. What was the median age of the guests at the party?

6. What was the average age of the party?

7. Which measurement, median or mean, gave the most accurate age for the party?

Use the table below to answer questions 8 and 9.

Daily Customers by Meal

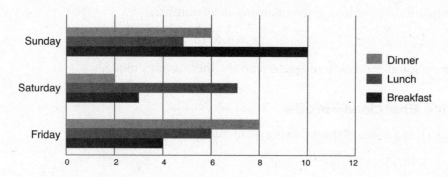

8. What was the median number of customers for dinner?

9. What was the median number of total customers for all of the meals combined, Friday through Sunday?

LESSON 3: MODE

The **mode** is the number that appears the most often.

> ### HOW TO FIND THE MODE
> Choose the number that appears the most often.

For example, let's find the mode of the following set of numbers:

2, 4, 8, 10, 4

Since the number 4 appears more than any other number, 4 is the mode. That's all there is to it! You do not need to add or subtract anything.

> Some sets of numbers may have more than one mode.

For example, let's take a look at the following set of numbers:

4, 9, 50, 50, 9

Here two numbers appear the most. 50, and 9. Therefore, the mode is 50 and 9.

For example, let's take a look at the following set of numbers:

2, 4, 6, 8, 10

Since all the numbers appear the same amount, there is not a mode.

Practice Exercises—Mode

1. What is the mode of the following set of numbers?

    5, 10, 150, 15, 5, 50

2. What is the mode of the following set of numbers?

    20, 200, 200, 55, 75, 20

3. What is the mode of the following set of numbers?

    10, 20, 30, 15, 25, 35

Number of Pages Read by Day

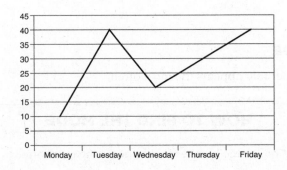

4. Jay loves to read. He reads a few pages each night before bed. Using the graph above, what is the mode value?

END-OF-CHAPTER QUESTIONS

Fill in the chart below to answer the following questions.

Bowling Scores

	Alexander	Maria	Nick	Average per Game
Game One	100	150	200	150
Game Two	205	175	100	160
Game Three	110	125	75	70
Average per person	138.3	150	125	

1. What player had the highest average?
   (A) Alexander
   (B) Maria
   (C) Nick
   (D) Alexander and Nick

2. What is the mode of the numbers shown?
   (A) 100
   (B) 175
   (C) 200
   (D) 205

3. What was the median of Maria's scores?
   (A) 125
   (B) 150
   (C) 175
   (D) There is no median.

4. What was the average score of all players for game three?
   (A) 70
   (B) 100
   (C) 150
   (D) 200

5. Which player had the lowest average?
   (A) Alexander
   (B) Maria
   (C) Nick
   (D) Alexander and Maria

6. Which player had a median score of 100?
   (A) Alexander
   (B) Maria
   (C) Nick
   (D) None of the above

7. What is the mode of Nick's scores?
   (A) 75
   (B) 100
   (C) 200
   (D) There is no mode.

8. Which player's median score was the same as his or her average score?
   (A) Alexander
   (B) Maria
   (C) Nick
   (D) None of the above

9. What is the *difference* between Nick's mean score and his median score?

   (**THINK:** How do you find the difference between two numbers?)

   (A) 25
   (B) 75
   (C) 100
   (D) 125

10. The bowling alley had a special for the players. Anyone who averaged over 100 over three games would receive a prize. The prize is 10 cents off at the snack bar for every point over 100. How much of a discount would Maria receive at the snack bar?

    (**THINK:** What is the question asking? What information do you need to solve it?)

    (A) $.50
    (B) $5.00
    (C) $50.00
    (D) $150.00

CHAPTER 11 ANSWER EXPLANATIONS

Lesson 1: Mean

PRACTICE EXERCISES—MEAN (PAGE 286)

1. 3. The sum of the numbers is 15. 15 divided by 5 is 3.
2. 5. The sum of the numbers is 15. 15 divided by 5 is 3.
3. 70. The sum of the numbers is 490. 490 divided by 7 is 70.
4. 90. The sum of the numbers is 180. 180 divided by 2 is 90.
5. Al: 150. The sum of the numbers is 450. 450 divided by 3 is 150.
   Bill: 150. The sum of the numbers is 540. 540 divided by 3 is 180.
   Chris: 150. The sum of the numbers is 600. 600 divided by 3 is 200.
   Dan: 150. The sum of the numbers is 600. 600 divided by 3 is 200.
6. Chris and Dan had the highest score. Together they scored 1,200 points. Al and Bill scored 990 points, so Chris and Dan won by a total of 210 points.
7. 9.5 The sum of the numbers is 38. 38 divided by 4 is 9.5.
8. 6. First find the average age of Marlon and Kameron. The graph shows that they are 17 and 9, for a total of 26. Divided by two, their average age is 13.5. Now do the same for Tobi and Stacy ages 9 and 6 for a total of 15. Divided by two, their average age is 7.5. To find the difference subtract 13.5 and 7.5.

Lesson 2: Median

PRACTICE EXERCISES—MEDIAN (PAGE 290)

1. Placed in order from least to greatest, the median number is 300.
2. Since there is not one number in the middle, we must add up the two middle numbers and divide by two. 4 + 6 = 10. 10 ÷ 2 = 5.
3. Placed in order from least to greatest, the median number is 40.
4. Since there is not one number in the middle, we must add up the two middle numbers and divide by two. 48 + 58 = 106. 106 ÷ 2 = 53.
5. Placed in order from least to greatest, the median number is 5.
6. 24. The sum of the ages is 120. 120 divided by 5 is 24.
7. The median. Most of the people at the party were close to 5 years in age, so that is more accurate than the average. The grandmother's age raised the average to 24, but no one at the party was close to that age. All of the kids were much younger, and the grandmother was much older.
8. 6. Placed in order from least to greatest, the median number for dinner is 6.
9. 6. Placed in order from least to greatest, the median number for all meals is 6.

Lesson 3: Mode

PRACTICE EXERCISES—MODE (PAGE 292)

1. The number that appears the most is 5.
2. The numbers that appear the most are 20 and 200. Both appear twice, so they are both counted as modes.
3. Since all of the numbers appear the same amount of times, there is no mode.
4. 40. Tuesday and Friday are both 40.

End-of-Chapter Questions (Page 293)

1. **(B)** Maria averaged 150.

2. **(A)** 100 appears the most on the chart.

3. **(B)** Placed in order from least to greatest, 150 is the median number.

4. **(A)** The sum of the scores for game three is 210. 210 divided by 3 is 70.

5. **(C)** Nick had the lowest average, a 125.

6. **(C)** Nick.

7. **(D)** All of Nick's scores appear only once so there is no mode.

8. **(B)** Both Maria's average and median were 150.

9. **(A)** Nick's mean was 125 and his median was 100. Subtract the two to find the difference.

10. **(C)** First, compute Maria's average, and it is 150. Then figure out how many points she scored over 100. She scored 50 points over 100. Then multiply 50 times .10, and the answer is 5.00. Answer D is incorrect because it multiplies all of her points times .10, but she only gets the prize for points over 100.

Graphic Material

12

LESSON 1: READING GRAPHS IN MATH

Line Graphs

Graphs play an important role on the test. Line graphs can be used to show how something changes over time. On the test you will need to be able to look up information on a graph and perform calculations based on that information. You will also need to be able to describe the overall trend of a graph. Both of these skills are easy to do when you know the basics of reading graphs.

To get started, there are three things you must do with every line or bar graph.

1. **FIND THE TITLE OF THE GRAPH.** This is typically in larger letters above or below the graph.

2. **READ THE LABELS ON THE SIDES OF THE GRAPH.** When people are confused by line graphs, it is usually because they skipped this step. Using these labels will help us to easily find specific information.

3. **LOOK AT THE OVERALL TREND OF THE GRAPH.** This means to judge if the line is generally going up, down, or staying the same.

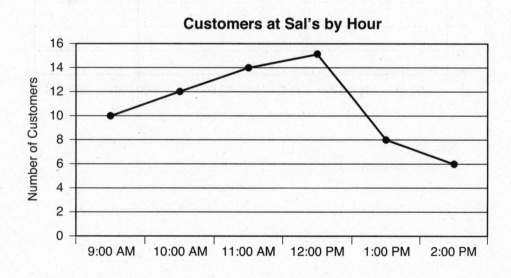

Practice Exercises

We can see that the title of the above graph is "Customers at Sal's by Hour."

1. What information is found on the vertical axis?
    (THINK: The vertical line going up and down.)

    _____

2. What information is found on the horizontal axis?
    (THINK: The horizontal is going sideways.)

    _____

3. What is the overall trend of the graph?
    (THINK: Is the line going up or down, and what does that mean for Sal's restaurant?)

    _____

    Now that you know your way around this graph, let's use these skills to find some specific information.

    Let's say you were asked to find out how many customers were in Sal's Restaurant at 1:00 P.M. On this graph, we know that times are on the horizontal axis, so let's start there. Once you find 1:00 P.M., go straight up until you hit the line of the graph.

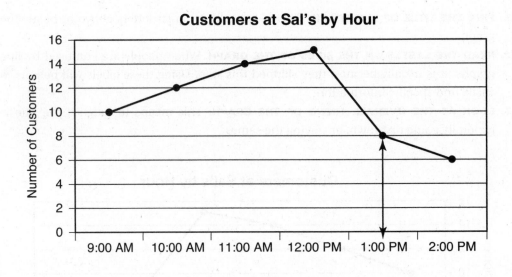

Once you hit that line, move straight over to the vertical axis on the left.

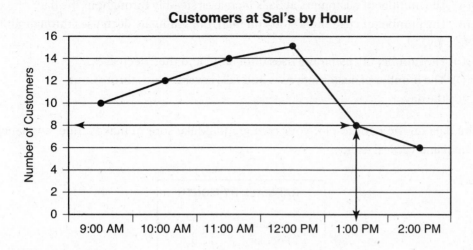

Customers at Sal's by Hour

That's it! According to the graph there were eight customers at Sal's at 1:00 P.M. Using these techniques will help you with every line graph you see.

Now let's try one going the other way. At what time were 14 customers at Sal's?

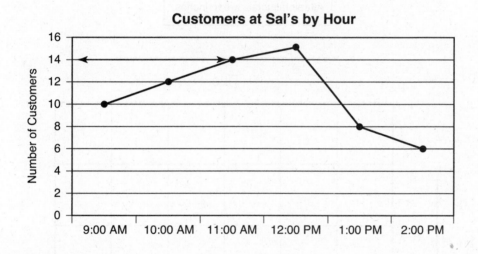

Customers at Sal's by Hour

Trace the line from the number 14 on the vertical axis until it hits the line. Now draw your own line straight down to the horizontal axis.

Your line should point to 11:00 A.M. This means there were 14 customers at 11:00 A.M.

4. At what time were the most customers in Sal's? _____

5. At what time were the fewest customers in Sal's? _____

6. At what time were 15 customers in Sal's? _____

   (**THINK:** About where would 15 fall on the vertical axis?)

7.   Which statement best describes the overall trend of the graph?
      (A) The number of customers at Sal's increases steadily throughout the day.
      (B) The number of customers starts off high, but gradually decreases throughout the day.
      (C) The number of customers rises until noon and then decreases.
      (D) The number of customers rises and falls several times throughout the day.

Use the data on the right to plot your own graph. Make sure to make a title, and label the horizontal and vertical axes.

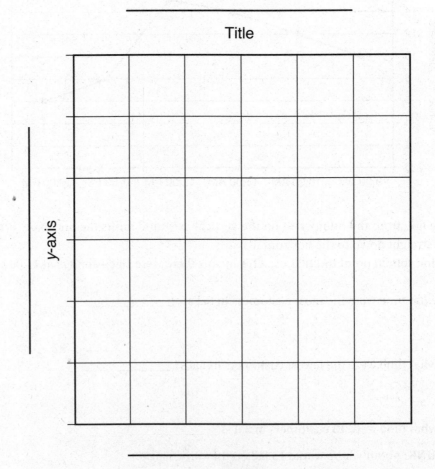

RAINFALL BY MONTH

January	4.0
February	2.0
March	4.0
April	6.0
May	6.0
June	8.0

All rainfall totals are in inches.

Title

y-axis

x-axis

UNIT 2: MATHEMATICS

Recognizing Trends in Line Graphs

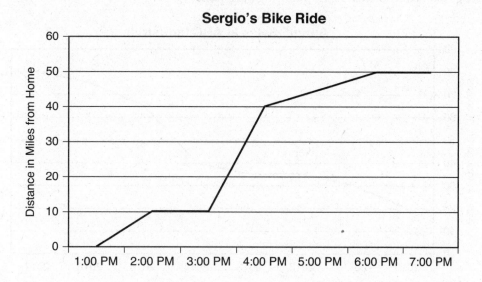

Sergio's Bike Ride

Before we begin, make sure you identify the following:

8. What is the graph about?

_____

9. What information is on each axis?

_____

10. What is the overall trend?

_____

TIP

Flat lines on a line graph mean there has been no change.

TREND #1, THE FLAT LINE

On this graph, we see that Sergio starts riding his bike at 1:00. At that point, he is at zero miles in distance because he hasn't left home yet. An hour later, at 2:00, he is 10 miles away. Then the line flattens out between 2:00 and 3:00. What does that mean?

This means that between 2:00 and 3:00, his distance didn't move at all even though one hour passed. In other words, Sergio must have stopped riding for an hour.

According to the graph, between what two hours does Sergio stop again?

TIP

The steepest part of a line graph shows the greatest increase.

TREND #2, THE GREATEST INCREASE

Another trend you will need to be able to spot on line graphs is where the greatest increase occurs. It may seem like the greatest increase occurs between 6:00 and 7:00 because that is the highest point on the graph. But look again, that is actually a flat line, and that means there was <u>no</u> increase during that time.

Instead, we are looking for the steepest line. Take a look at the time between 3:00 and 4:00. The distance jumps from 10 miles at 3:00 to 40 miles at 4:00. That is a total of 30 miles in 1 hour, and that is the greatest increase.

Practice Exercises—Using Graphs in Math

Use the graph below to answer the following questions.

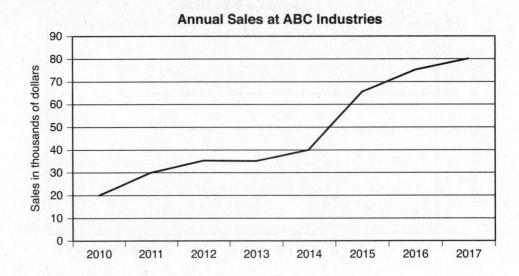

Annual Sales at ABC Industries

1. What is the overall trend of the graph?
   (A) Sales have generally risen over time at ABC Industries.
   (B) Sales have generally decreased over time at ABC Industries.
   (C) Sales peaked in 2017.
   (D) Sales rose and fell between 2010 and 2017.

2. Between what years did annual sales stay the same?
   (A) 2010–2011
   (B) 2011–2012
   (C) 2012–2013
   (D) 2013–2014

3. What was the amount of annual sales in 2014?
   (A) $40
   (B) $40,000
   (C) $35
   (D) $35,000

4. What was the approximate amount of sales in 2016?
   (A) $60,000
   (B) $65,000
   (C) $70,000
   (D) $75,000

5. When did the greatest increase in sales occur?
   (A) 2013–2014
   (B) 2014–2015
   (C) 2015–2016
   (D) 2016–2017

MULTIPLE LINE GRAPHS

Some graphs will have more than one line. This means that there are two or more sets of data on the graph, one for each line. The graph below is the same as the one used in the previous questions, with one major difference: now a second company, XYZ Industries, has been added to the graph.

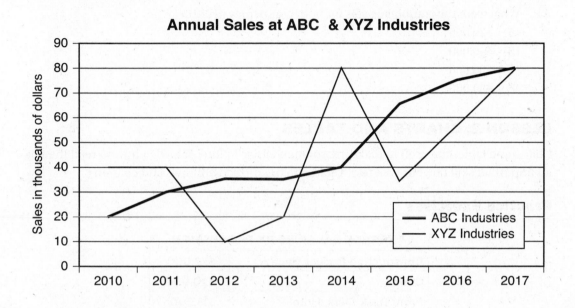

Annual Sales at ABC & XYZ Industries

6. What is the overall trend for XYZ Industries?
   (A) Sales generally rise over time.
   (B) Sales generally fall over time.
   (C) Sales rise and fall over the years.
   (D) Sales are highest in 2014.

7. What were the annual sales for XYZ Industries in 2011?
   (A) $30,000
   (B) $40,000
   (C) $50,000
   (D) $60,000

8. How much higher were ABC Industries sales than XYZ's sales in 2012?
   (A) $45,000
   (B) $35,000
   (C) $25,000
   (D) $10,000

9. In what year were the sales for ABC and XYZ the exact same?
   (A) 2014
   (B) 2015
   (C) 2016
   (D) 2017

UNIT 2: MATHEMATICS

10. During what 2-year period did sales neither rise nor fall for XYZ Industries?
   (A) 2010–2011
   (B) 2011–2012
   (C) 2012–2013
   (D) 2013–2014

11. What were the combined sales for both companies in 2010?
   (A) $20,000
   (B) $40,000
   (C) $60,000
   (D) $80,000

LESSON 2: CHARTS AND TABLES

Charts and tables are used to make information easier to find. Knowing how to read them is an important skill on your HSE test. Tables are organized with rows and columns.

Practice Exercises

AVERAGE SALARIES BY PROFESSION

Construction Project Manager	$72,000
Cook	$20,000
Front Desk Clerk, Hotel	$18,500
Lawyer	$75,000
Mail Carrier	$44,000
Registered Nurse	$55,000
Retail Store Manager	$41,000
Software Developer	$92,000
Teacher	$40,000

1. Every table will have a title. What is this table about?

   _____

2. Which profession has the highest average salary?

   _____

3. Which profession has the lowest salary?

   _____

4. How much more does a registered nurse earn than a retail store manager?

   _____

5. How much would a construction project manager earn per month?

   (**THINK:** How many months are in a year? What key word can help with what operation to choose?)

   _____

Some charts will show multiple types of information. Use the chart below for the following questions.

VOTER DATA BY COUNTY

County	Number of Voters	% Male	% Female
Appleton	5,500	48%	52%
Bazemore	10,100	49%	51%
Clark	6,000	61%	39%
Douglas	25,000	50%	50%

6. What categories are being compared on this chart?

_____

7. Which county had the greatest number of voters?

_____

8. Which county had the lowest percentage of female voters?

_____

9. How many males voted in Clark County?

   (**THINK:** How can you find the actual number from a percent?)

_____

Some charts require you to look carefully at both the rows and the columns. That is to say, you will need to read both the top and the side of the chart to find the correct information. In that way, some charts are a lot like line graphs. Take a look at the chart below.

DEW POINT CHART

Air Temp °F	% Relative Humidity																		
	100	95	90	85	80	75	70	65	60	55	50	45	40	35	30	25	20	15	10
110	110	108	106	104	102	100	98	95	93	90	87	84	80	76	72	65	60	51	41
105	105	103	101	99	97	95	93	91	88	85	83	80	76	72	67	62	55	47	37
100	100	99	97	95	93	91	89	86	84	81	78	75	71	67	63	58	52	44	32
95	95	93	92	90	88	86	84	81	79	76	73	70	67	63	59	54	48	40	32
90	90	88	87	85	83	81	79	76	74	71	68	65	62	59	54	49	43	36	32
85	85	83	81	80	78	76	74	72	69	67	64	61	58	54	50	45	38	32	
80	80	78	77	75	73	71	69	67	65	62	59	56	53	50	45	40	35	32	
75	75	73	72	70	68	66	64	62	60	58	55	52	49	45	41	36	32		
70	70	68	67	65	63	61	59	57	55	53	50	47	44	40	37	32			
65	65	63	62	60	59	57	55	53	50	48	45	42	40	36	32				
60	60	58	57	55	53	52	50	48	45	43	41	38	35	32					
55	55	53	52	50	49	47	45	43	40	38	36	33	32						
50	50	48	46	45	44	42	40	38	36	34	32								
45	45	43	42	40	39	37	35	33	32										
40	40	39	37	35	34	32													
35	35	34	32																
32	32																		

We can tell from the title that this chart is about dew point. The dew point is the temperature at which water condenses from the air. Have you ever walked outside in the morning and noticed that the ground, parked cars, and other objects are damp even though it did not rain? This is the result of condensation when the temperature reaches the dew point. The dew point changes with temperature and relative humidity.

10. Which side of the chart lists the air temperature, and which side lists the relative humidity?

    _____

11. Use the chart to find the dew point if the air temperature is 75 degrees, and the relative humidity is 35%.

    _____

(STEP 1) Find the air temperature of 75 degrees on the left. Now find 35% relative humidity on the top.

(STEP 2) Put your finger on the 75 degrees. Now move it directly to the right until it lines up with the 35% relative humidity column.

(STEP 3) Where the 75 degree row and the 35% column meet is your answer. The dew point is 45 degrees.

12. If the air temperature is 100 degrees and the relative humidity is 50%, what is the dew point? _____

13. If the air temperature is 35 degrees and the relative humidity is 90%, what is the dew point? _____

14. If the air temperature is 90 degrees and the relative humidity is 35%, what is the dew point? _____

15. If the air temperature is 60 degrees and the *dew point* is 52, what is the relative humidity? _____
    (THINK: Read carefully, this requires you to use the chart differently than before.)

16. If the relative humidity is 75% and the *dew point* is 71, what is the air temperature?

    _____

LESSON 3: PIE CHARTS

Pie charts, also known as circle graphs, are used to show how something is divided. They are commonly used with percentages and can be a great way to compare different amounts to each other. Take a look at the two charts below.

Sam's Monthly Budget

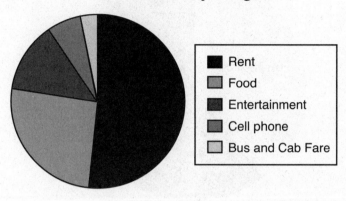

- Rent
- Food
- Entertainment
- Cell phone
- Bus and Cab Fare

Sam's Monthly Budget	Dollar Amount
Bus and Cab Fare	$50
Rent	$800
Cell Phone	$100
Entertainment	$200
Food	$400

Which one is easier to read? If you were looking for a specific amount, the chart above is easier to use. However, if you were trying to see how much Sam spends on rent compared to everything else, then the pie chart is easier to read. We can clearly and easily see that rent is over half of the budget.

Practice Exercises

Use the chart below to answer the following questions.

Types of Vehicles on Main Street

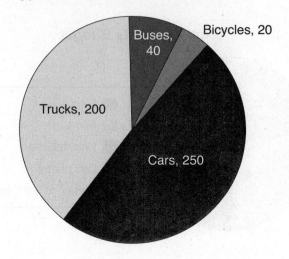

The Department of Transportation counted all of the vehicles that used Main Street between 4 P.M. and 6:00 P.M. on Monday. The chart above displays the data.

1. Which type of vehicle was used the least? _____

2. How many trucks used Main Street? _____

3. How many more people drove a car than drove a truck? _____

4. If ten people were on each bus, how many people rode the bus on Main Street? _____

Use the chart below to answer the following questions.

Flavors of Ice Cream Sold

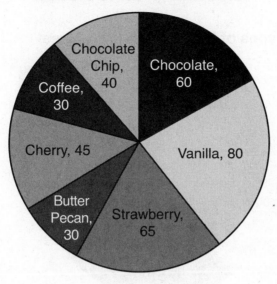

5. Which two flavors sold the exact same amount? _____

6. How many more strawberry and butter pecan were sold than vanilla? _____

7. What is the sum of all the flavors sold? _____

PIE CHARTS AND PERCENTAGES

Another popular use of pie charts is to compare percentages. Take a look at the graph below.

Types of Vehicles on Main Street

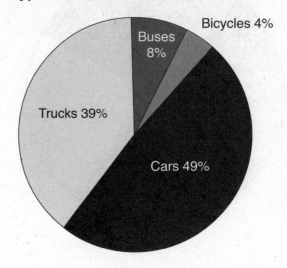

8. What percent of vehicles on Main Street were bicycles? _____

9. What is the difference in percentage between the number of cars and trucks. _____

Use the chart below to answer the following questions.

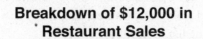

**Breakdown of $12,000 in
Restaurant Sales**

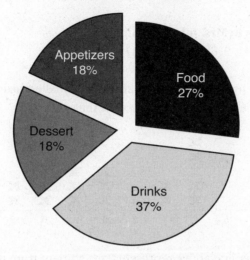

10. What percent of restaurant sales were food and drinks combined?

   (A) 27%

   (B) 37%

   (C) 55%

   (D) 64%

11. What was the *dollar amount* of dessert sales?

   (**THINK:** If the total sales were $12,000 how can you find 18% of that?)

   (A) $18

   (B) $666

   (C) $2,160

   (D) $11,912

12. What was the dollar amount of food sales?

   (A) $324

   (B) $3,240

   (C) $8,760

   (D) $11,973

13. What is the difference in the dollar amount of food sales and drink sales?

   (**THINK:** We need to find the dollar amount for each item.)

   (A) $1,200

   (B) $3,240

   (C) $4,440

   (D) $7,640

LESSON 4: DOT PLOTS

Dot plots are another way to organize numbers visually. They are useful to see where numbers group together and where any outliers may be.

Take a look at the following list of numbers:

Student Shoe Sizes in Mrs. Johnson's Class
6, 10, 12, 7, 9, 6, 8, 11, 9, 6, 10, 7, 12, 6, 11, 9, 6, 13, 4, 10

Which shoe size was the most common? What was the smallest size? It is difficult to tell by looking at the list. Now let's use a dot plot to view the same data.

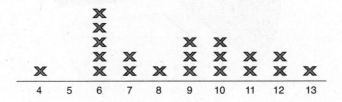

Each mark on the number line above represents one student from the list. Because there are five X marks over the number 6, that means five people had a shoe size of 6.

Practice Exercises

Use the dot plot below to answer questions 1–5.

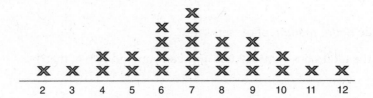

Jerry rolled the dice 25 times. He recorded the results on the dot plot above.

1. How many times did Jerry roll a 5?
   (A) 2
   (B) 3
   (C) 4
   (D) 5

2. What number was rolled the most times?
   (A) 5
   (B) 7
   (C) 10
   (D) 12

3. How many more times was an 8 rolled than a 5?

   (A) 1
   (B) 2
   (C) 3
   (D) 4

4. Which number was rolled exactly twice as many times as a four was rolled?

   (A) 5
   (B) 6
   (C) 7
   (D) 8

5. How many times did Jerry roll a ten or higher?

   (A) 4
   (B) 6
   (C) 8
   (D) 10

6. Use the information below to create a dot plot.

   Mrs. Johnson asked her class to write down the number of children in their family. Here are the results:

   3, 3, 1, 5, 4, 2, 2, 2, 1, 3, 5,

   ```
   _____
        1        2        3        4        5
   ```

LESSON 5: COORDINATE PLANE

Take a look at Map A below. How could you describe where the tree is located? It is hard to say exactly when the rest of the map is blank.

Map A

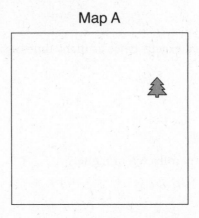

Now take a look at Map B How could you describe where the tree is now?

The tree is clearly located in the top half of the map, and above the number 4.

Map B

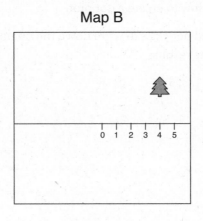

Map C

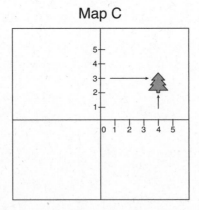

Using Map C allows us to precisely locate the tree. We could say it is four spaces to the right, and up three spaces.

This is the system used by the **coordinate plane**. The coordinate plane uses two number lines to locate points. The horizontal, or sideways, number line is the *x*-axis. The vertical, or up and down, number line is the *y*-axis.

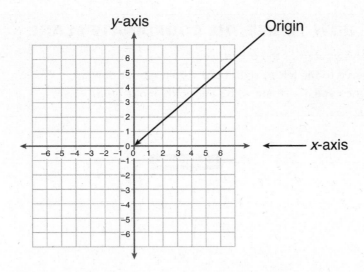

So, the coordinate plane is like a map. You can use it to find your way around, or give directions.

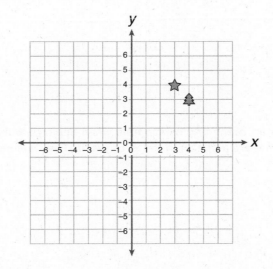

Everything on coordinate plane starts at the **origin**, or the intersection in the middle marked zero. This is where the x- and y-axis meet.

So the tree is located four spaces to the right. This is the x-coordinate. The tree is also located three spaces up. That is the y-coordinate. When we write the x- and y-coordinates together, it is called an **ordered pair**. Ordered pairs are written in parentheses. NOTE: The x-coordinate is always first!

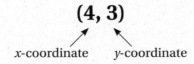

Now look where the star is on the coordinate plane. It is three spots to the right, and four spaces up. So, we can write its location as an ordered pair, (3, 4). Notice how similar that is to where the tree is located? It is very important to remember that the x-value always comes before the y. Otherwise, you may wind up at the wrong point!

TIP

Remember you have to take a taXi before you flY. In other words, you have to use your *x*-coordinate before your *y*-coordinate!

UNIT 2: MATHEMATICS

HOW TO USE THE COORDINATE PLANE

1. Always start at the origin.
2. Move to the left or right before going up or down.
3. Once you are in line with your point, move up or down.

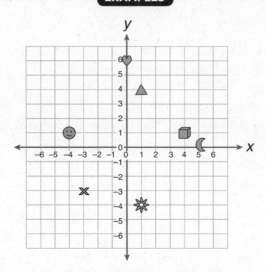

Remember, always start at the origin each time when finding a point. Pay special attention to points that are actually on the *x*- or *y*-axis. They will have a zero in the ordered pair.

Heart (0, 6)
Triangle (1, 4)
Smiley face (−4, 1)
Moon (5, 0)
X (−3, −3)
Sun (1, −4)
Box (4, 1)

UNIT 2: MATHEMATICS

Practice Exercises—Coordinate Plane

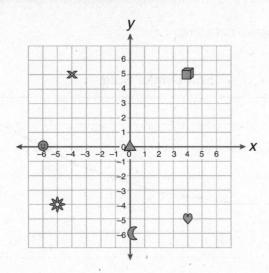

1. Write the ordered pair for each symbol:

   Heart _____

   Triangle _____

   Smiley face _____

   Moon _____

   X _____

   Sun _____

   Box _____

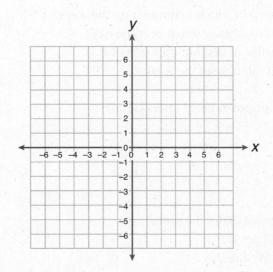

2. Write each letter on the coordinate plane

   A (0, 5)   *B* (6, –2)   *C* (2, 2)   *D* (–6, 2)   *E* (5, 0)   *F* (–3, –1)   *G* (4, 1)   *H* (0, 0)

Use the graph below to answer questions 1 through 5.

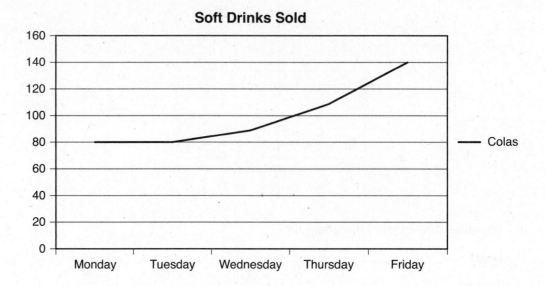

Soft Drinks Sold

—— Colas

1. On what day was the most amount of colas sold?
   (A) Tuesday
   (B) Wednesday
   (C) Thursday
   (D) Friday

2. What is the overall trend of the graph?
   (A) Cola sales generally increase throughout the week.
   (B) Cola sales do not change much over the week.
   (C) Cola sales decline at first but then increase.
   (D) Cola sales fall throughout the week.

3. On what day were approximately 110 colas sold?
   (A) Monday
   (B) Wednesday
   (C) Thursday
   (D) Friday

4. On what days were cola sales the same?
   (A) Monday and Tuesday
   (B) Tuesday and Wednesday
   (C) Wednesday and Thursday
   (D) Thursday and Friday

5. What is the difference between cola sales on Monday and Friday?
   (A) 60
   (B) 80
   (C) 120
   (D) 200

Use the graph below to answer questions 6 through 10.

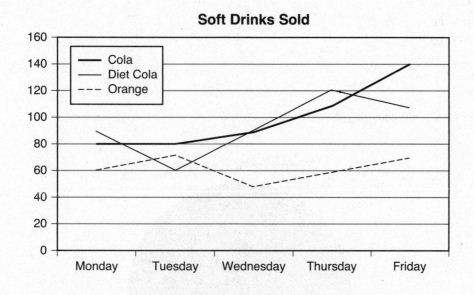

Soft Drinks Sold

6. How many orange sodas were sold on Thursday?
   (A) 60
   (B) 100
   (C) 110
   (D) 120

7. On what day were the least amount of soft drinks sold?
   (A) Monday
   (B) Tuesday
   (C) Wednesday
   (D) Thursday

8. On what day were cola and diet cola sales the same?
   (A) Monday
   (B) Tuesday
   (C) Wednesday
   (D) Thursday

9. On what day were diet cola sales higher than other soft drinks?
    (A) Monday
    (B) Tuesday
    (C) Wednesday
    (D) Thursday

10. Approximately how many total soft drinks were sold on Monday?
    (A) 60
    (B) 80
    (C) 90
    (D) 230

Use the chart below to answer questions 11 and 12.

Types of Books Sold

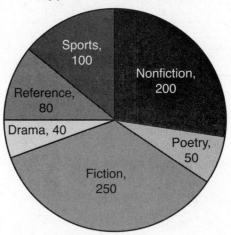

11. What type of book sold fewer copies than poetry?
    (A) Sports
    (B) Reference
    (C) Drama
    (D) Nonfiction

12. Which two categories combined sold the same amount as fiction?
    (A) Sports and reference
    (B) Nonfiction and poetry
    (C) Reference and nonfiction
    (D) Drama and poetry

Use the chart below to answer questions 13 through 15.

Eye Color Survey of 500 People

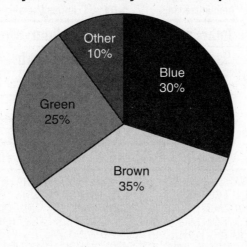

13. What percent of the people surveyed had brown or blue eyes?
    (A) 30%
    (B) 35%
    (C) 60%
    (D) 65%

14. What number of people (not percent) surveyed had green eyes?
    (A) 10
    (B) 50
    (C) 100
    (D) 125

15. How many people surveyed had brown eyes?
    (A) 25
    (B) 50
    (C) 100
    (D) 175

UNIT 2: MATHEMATICS

Use the table below to answer questions 16 and 17.

Nutrition Facts	Amount/serving	%DV*	Amount/serving	%DV*
Serv. Size 1 cup (249g)	**Total Fat** 12g	**18**%	**Sodium** 940mg	**39**%
Servings About 2	Sat. Fat 6g	**30**%	Total Carb. 24g	**8**%
Calories 250	Polyunsat. Fat 1.5g		Dietary Fiber 1g	**4**%
Fat Cal. 110	Monounsat. Fat 2.5g		Sugars 1g	
*Percent Daily Values (DV) are based on a 2,000 calorie diet.	**Cholest.** 60mg	**20**%	**Protein** 10g	**20**%

Vitamin A 0% • Vitamin C 0% • Calcium 6% • Iron 8%

INGREDIENTS: WATER, CHICKEN STOCK, ENRICHED PASTA (SEMOLINA WHEAT FLOUR, EGG WHITE SOLIDS, NIACIN, IRON, THIAMINE MONONITRATE (VITAMIN B1), RIBOFLAVIN [VITAMIN B2] AND FOLIC ACID), CREAM (DERIVED FROM MILK), CHICKEN, CONTAINS LESS THAN 2% OF: CHEESES (GRANULAR, PARMESAN AND ROMANO PASTE (PASTEURIZED COW'S MILK, CULTURES, SALT, ENZYMES), WATER, SALT, LACTIC ACID, CITRIC ACID AND DISODIUM PHOSPHATE), BUTTER (PASTEURIZED SWEET CREAM [DERIVED FROM MILK] AND SALT), MODIFIED CORN STARCH, SALT, WHOLE EGG SOLIDS, SUGAR, DATEM, RICE STARCH, GARLIC, SPICE, XANTHAN GUM, CHEESE FLAVOR (PARTIALLY HYDROGENATED SOYBEAN OIL, FLAVORINGS AND SMOKE FLAVORING), MUSTARD FLOUR, ISOLATED SOY PROTEIN AND SODIUM PHOSPHATE.

16. What percent of the daily value of sodium is listed?
    - (A) 18%
    - (B) 24%
    - (C) 39%
    - (D) 940%

17. What is the difference in grams (g) between polyunsaturated fat and monounsaturated fat?
    - (A) 1
    - (B) 1.5
    - (C) 2.5
    - (D) 4

Use the chart below to answer questions 18 through 20.

Wind Chill Factor

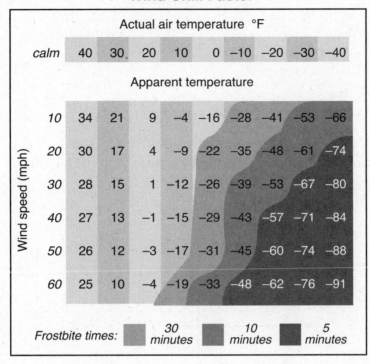

Actual air temperature °F

| calm | 40 | 30 | 20 | 10 | 0 | −10 | −20 | −30 | −40 |

Apparent temperature

Wind speed (mph)	40	30	20	10	0	−10	−20	−30	−40
10	34	21	9	−4	−16	−28	−41	−53	−66
20	30	17	4	−9	−22	−35	−48	−61	−74
30	28	15	1	−12	−26	−39	−53	−67	−80
40	27	13	−1	−15	−29	−43	−57	−71	−84
50	26	12	−3	−17	−31	−45	−60	−74	−88
60	25	10	−4	−19	−33	−48	−62	−76	−91

Frostbite times: □ 30 minutes ■ 10 minutes ■ 5 minutes

18. If the wind speed is 40 mph and the actual air temperature is 20 degrees, what is the apparent temperature?
    (A) −1
    (B) 0
    (C) 1
    (D) 27

19. If the wind speed is 20 mph and the actual air temperature is 0 degrees, what is the apparent temperature?
    (A) 4
    (B) −9
    (C) −16
    (D) −22

20. If the wind speed is 50 mph and the *apparent air temperature* is 12, what is the actual air temperature?
    (A) 40
    (B) 30
    (C) 20
    (D) 10

21. Use the information below to create a dot plot.

For each pair of shoes sold at Paymore Shoes, the salesman wrote down the size. At the end of his shift, he recorded the following data: 10, 12, 8, 9, 9, 10, 12, 11, 8.

22. Use the coordinate plane below to mark a point at (4, 0) and (−1, −3).

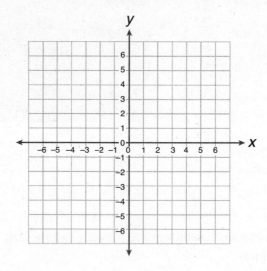

23. What are the coordinates of the point shown below?

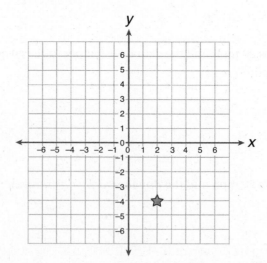

CHAPTER 12 ANSWER EXPLANATIONS

Lesson 1: Reading Graphs in Math (Page 298)

1. Number of customers
2. Time of day
3. The overall trend is that the number of customers rises before falling sharply after 12:00
4. 12:00
5. 2:00
6. 12:00
7. (C)

RAINFALL BY MONTH

January	4.0
February	2.0
March	4.0
April	6.0
May	6.0
June	8.0

All rainfall totals are in inches.

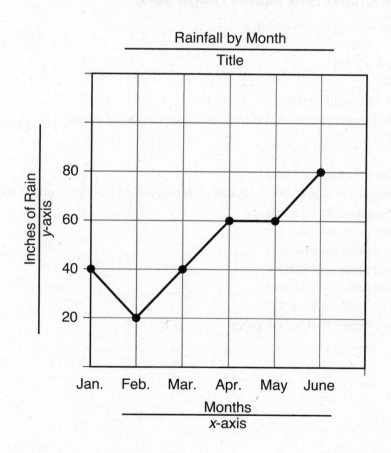

8. The distance Sergio rides his bike by hour.

9. *x*-axis (horizontal) shows time by hour, *y*-axis (vertical) shows distance in miles.

10. Sergio's distance increases throughout the day.

PRACTICE EXERCISES—USING GRAPHS IN MATH (PAGE 302)

1. **(A)**

2. **(C)**

3. **(B)**

4. **(D)**

5. **(B)** The greatest increase is the steepest part of the line and not the highest point.

6. **(C)**

7. **(B)**

8. **(C)** ABC sales in 2012 were $35,000, XYZ sales in 2012 were $10,000. The difference between those numbers is $25,000.

9. **(D)** In 2017, the lines meet.

10. **(A)** From 2010–2011, the line for XYZ is flat, meaning that there was no change in sales.

11. **(C)** XYZ sales were $40,000, and ABC sales were $20,000. Combined sales equal $60,000.

Lesson 2: Charts and Tables (Page 304)

1. Average salaries by profession

2. Software developer

3. Front desk clerk

4. $14,000

5. $6,000. 72,000 divided by 12.

6. Percent of men and women voters, and total number of votes.

7. Douglas

8. Clark

9. 3,600. 61% of 6,000 is 3,660.

10. The vertical left side of the chart lists air temperature; the horizontal top side of the chart lists the relative humidity.

11. The dew point is 45 degrees.

12. The dew point is 78 degrees.

13. The dew point is 32 degrees.

14. The dew point is 59 degrees.

15. The relative humidity is 75%.

16. The air temperature is 80 degrees.

Lesson 3: Pie Charts (Page 308)

1. Bicycles
2. 200
3. 50. 250 − 200 = 50
4. 400. 10 × 40 = 400
5. Coffee and butter pecan each sold 30.
6. 15. Strawberry and butter pecan total 95 sales, vanilla 80. The difference between those two numbers is 15.
7. 350
8. 4%
9. 10%. 49 − 39 = 10%
10. **(D)**
11. **(C)** 18% of 12,000 is $2,160
12. **(B)** 27% of 12,000 is $3,240
13. **(A)** Food sales are 27% or $3,240. Drink sales are 37% or $4,440. The difference between those amounts is $1,200.

Lesson 4: Dot Plot (Page 312)

1. **(A)** The two X marks over the five show that a five was rolled twice.
2. **(B)** The greatest number of X marks appear over the seven.
3. **(A)** Two X marks appear above the five, and three X marks appear above the eight. The difference between the two is one.
4. **(B)** The number four was rolled two times, and the number six was rolled four times. The number seven was rolled more than four times, but the question asked for which was rolled exactly twice as many times.
5. **(A)** Ten was rolled twice, eleven once, and twelve once for a total of four.
6.

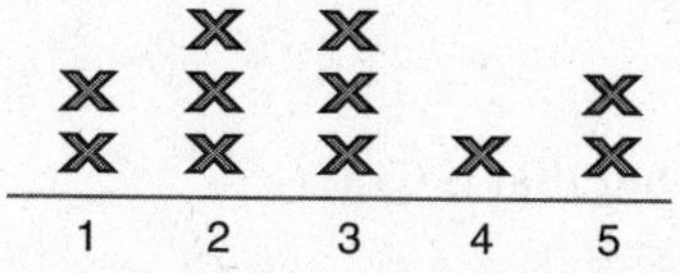

```
        X   X
    X   X   X       X
    X   X   X   X   X
   ─────────────────────
    1   2   3   4   5
```

Lesson Five: Coordinate Plane

PRACTICE EXERCISES—COORDINATE PLANE (PAGE 317)

1. Heart (4, −5)
   Triangle (0, 0)
   Smiley face (−6, 0)
   Moon (0, −6)
   X (−4, 5)
   Sun (−5, 4)
   Box (4, 5)

2.

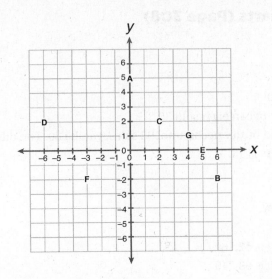

End-of-Chapter Questions (Page 318)

1. **(D)**
2. **(A)**
3. **(C)**
4. **(A)**
5. **(A)** 140 − 80 = 60
6. **(A)**
7. **(B)** The total for Tuesday of all beverages sold is 210, and that is lower than any other day.
8. **(C)** The lines for cola and diet cola meet on Wednesday.
9. **(D)**
10. **(D)**
11. **(C)**
12. **(B)**
13. **(D)** 30% had blue and 35% had brown. Added together that is 65%.
14. **(D)** 25% of 500 is 125.
15. **(D)** 35% of 500 is 175.
16. **(C)**
17. **(A)** Monounsaturated fat is 2.5 grams, and polyunsaturated fat is 1.5. The difference between the two numbers is 1.
18. **(A)**
19. **(D)**
20. **(B)**
21.

```
        X    X         X
   X    X    X    X    X
  ─────────────────────────
   8    9   10   11   12
```

22.

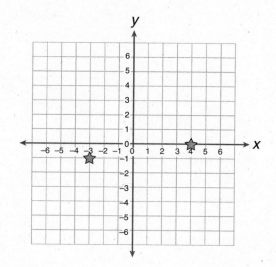

23. $(2, -4)$

Mathematics Posttest

The mathematics posttest has 54 questions. After you review the material in this unit, you can use this test to get a sense of what areas you still need to study. Make sure you have at least 60 minutes of quiet time available to complete the test. Read each question carefully, and do your best. It is better if you do not guess on these questions. If you don't know the answer to a question, simply skip it and go on to the next one. The purpose of this test is to find out what areas you still need to work on, and random guessing might throw you off course.

Once you have finished, check your answers on pages 342–344, and complete the posttest evaluation chart on page 340 by circling the number of each question you answered correctly. This way you can easily see your strengths and weaknesses as well as where information on each question you missed is located in the book.

If you score very well on the posttest, it is a great sign that you have a solid foundation in math, and you should be ready to begin studying higher-level material.

1.   14
    × 22

    (A) 56
    (B) 208
    (C) 308
    (D) 408

2. $7\overline{)483}$

    (A) 49
    (B) 69
    (C) 490
    (D) 690

3. Rewrite the number 36,241 by switching the hundreds digit with the ten thousands digit to create a new number.

4. Round the following number to the nearest hundred: 4,521

5. Round the following number to the nearest thousand: 348,973

6. What is the quotient of 24 and 6?
    (A) 4
    (B) 18
    (C) 30
    (D) 144

Use the table below to answer questions 7 through 9.

	Table	Chair	Table and Chair Combo
A1 Furniture	$150	$75	$215
Ben's Home Goods	$125	$90	$210
Cal's Couches and More	$160	$55	$205

The three stores listed above are selling the same models of tables and chairs. They are sold individually or together at a discount.

7. How much would you save by purchasing the table and chair combo at Ben's Home Goods instead of buying the table and chair individually?
    (A) $5
    (B) $35
    (C) $215
    (D) $25

UNIT 2: MATHEMATICS

8. How much would you save if you bought a table at Ben's and a chair at Cal's instead of purchasing the table and chair combo at A1?
   (A) $35
   (B) $70
   (C) $180
   (D) $390

9. How much would two chairs from A1 and three tables from Cal's cost?
   (A) $330
   (B) $150
   (C) $480
   (D) $630

10. Rewrite the number 7.0812 by switching the tenths digit with the hundredths digit to create a new number.

11. Which of the following correctly expresses four and seven hundred ninety two thousandths?
    (A) .4792
    (B) 4.792
    (C) 47.92
    (D) 479.2

12. Round the following number to the nearest tenth: 3.890

13. Round the following number to the nearest thousandth: .9911

14.   150
    $\times .25$

15. 33.875 + 17.98

16.   55.4
     $- 4.8$

17. Rob bought five tee shirts for $9.19 each and two magnets for $1.99 each at the beach. *Approximately* how much did he spend?
    (A) $45
    (B) $54
    (C) $65
    (D) $70

18. Four plane tickets cost $583.70. *Approximately* how much does each ticket cost?
    (A) $100
    (B) $150
    (C) $200
    (D) $250

19. Arrange the following fractions in order from least to greatest.

$$\frac{1}{2} \qquad \frac{1}{3} \qquad \frac{2}{3} \qquad \frac{3}{4} \qquad \frac{1}{10}$$

20. On the ruler below, place a mark at $1\frac{1}{4}$ inches.

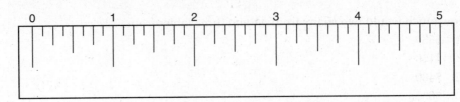

21. Write the following mixed number as an improper fraction: $2\frac{1}{2}$

22. Write the following improper fraction as a mixed number: $\frac{10}{3}$

23. $\frac{4}{5} + \frac{1}{3}$

24. $1\frac{3}{4} - \frac{1}{2}$

25. Reduce the following fraction to lowest terms: $\frac{4}{16}$

26. $\frac{1}{2}$ is the simplest term for which of the following fractions?

    (A) $\frac{3}{4}$

    (B) $\frac{6}{9}$

    (C) $\frac{5}{12}$

    (D) $\frac{15}{30}$

Use the following information to answer questions 27 and 28.

At the office there are eight women and six men currently employed.

27. What is the ratio of men to women?

28. What is the ratio of women to total employees?

29. Solve for the missing term in the proportion:

$$\frac{?}{9} = \frac{40}{45}$$

30. Solve for the missing term in the proportion:

$$\frac{3}{4} = \frac{?}{24}$$

31. On the map, Springville and Capital City are 5 inches apart. If the map scale reads that 1 inch equals 20 miles, how far apart are the two cities?
    (A) 4
    (B) 15
    (C) 25
    (D) 100

32. A recipe calls for two eggs and one cup of milk for every four people served. If 20 people are expected for a surprise dinner, how many eggs will be needed?
    (A) 4
    (B) 8
    (C) 10
    (D) 26

33. What is $\frac{3}{4}$ written as a percent?
    (A) 3.4%
    (B) 34%
    (C) 75%
    (D) 133%

34. How can 33% be expressed as a fraction?
    (A) 1/3
    (B) 2/3
    (C) 3/3
    (D) 33/1

35. Find 10% of 60.
    (A) 6
    (B) 10
    (C) 16
    (D) 600

36. What is 25% of 200?
    (A) 2.5
    (B) 50
    (C) 100
    (D) 150

37. Internet sales account for 40% of the sales at Sports Express. If the store made $6,000 in total sales last week, how much came from Internet sales?
    (A) 240
    (B) 2,400
    (C) 3,000
    (D) 3,600

38. A sales tax of 5% is added to every purchase. If you buy $80 worth of goods at the store, what will your total be with tax?
    (A) 4
    (B) 5
    (C) 76
    (D) 84

39. Peter has a coupon for 10% off any purchase of $50 or more. If he buys $70 worth of goods, what will be his total after using the coupon?
    (A) 7
    (B) 60
    (C) 63
    (D) 77

CALCULATOR USE ALLOWED FOR QUESTIONS 40 THROUGH 50.

40. $\dfrac{3}{4} \times \dfrac{5}{6}$

41. 45% of 280

Use the graph below to answer questions 42 through 44.

Pet Ownership in a Neighborhood

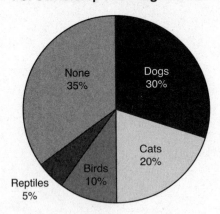

None 35%
Dogs 30%
Cats 20%
Birds 10%
Reptiles 5%

42. What percent of people have at least one pet?
    (A) 30%
    (B) 35%
    (C) 50%
    (D) 65%

43. Which two types of pets combined equal the percent of people who own no pets?
    (A) Reptiles and birds
    (B) Birds and cats
    (C) Cats and dogs
    (D) Dogs and reptiles

44. If 500 people live in the neighborhood, how many people have cats?
    (A) 35
    (B) 100
    (C) 325
    (D) 400

Use the graph below to answer questions 45 through 48.

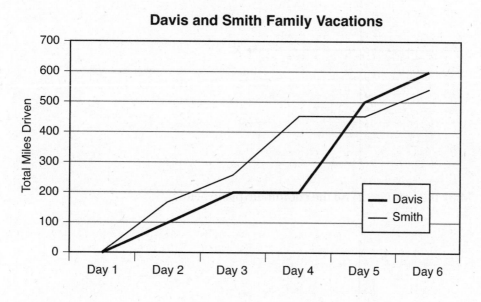

Davis and Smith Family Vacations

45. How many total miles had the Davis family driven by Day 6?
    (A) 200
    (B) 500
    (C) 550
    (D) 600

46. On what day did the Davis family pass the Smith family in total miles driven?
    (A) Day 2
    (B) Day 3
    (C) Day 4
    (D) Day 5

47. Between what days did the Smith family not drive at all?
    (A) Days 2 and 3
    (B) Days 3 and 4
    (C) Days 4 and 5
    (D) Days 5 and 6

48. Between what days did the greatest increase in miles driven occur for the Davis family?

(A) Days 2 and 3

(B) Days 3 and 4

(C) Days 4 and 5

(D) Days 5 and 6

49. Mark the point (2,–4) on the coordinate plane below.

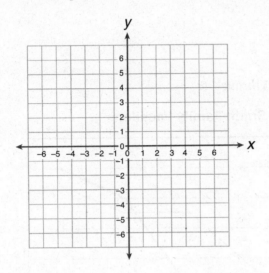

50. Mark the point (–3,1) on the coordinate plane below.

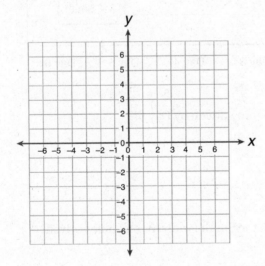

Use the information below to answer questions 51 through 54.

Yusef made a chart of how many times he heard his favorite song on the radio.

Monday	4
Tuesday	2
Wednesday	4
Thursday	3
Friday	1
Saturday	3
Sunday	4

51. What is the average number of times he heard the song each day?
    (A) 1
    (B) 2
    (C) 3
    (D) 4

52. What is the median number of times Yusef heard his favorite song?
    (A) 1
    (B) 2
    (C) 3
    (D) 4

53. For the table above, what is the mode?
    (A) 1
    (B) 2
    (C) 3
    (D) 4

54. Use the song data for the week to create a dot plot. Place an X over each number as many times as you need.

```
_____
      1       2       3       4       5
```

POSTTEST EVALUATION CHART

After checking your answers on the following pages, circle the numbers of the questions you got correct in Column B. Record the number of correct questions for each skill in Column C. Column D gives you the number of correct questions you need to answer correctly to indicate that you have a good understanding of the skill. If you got fewer correct answers than shown in Column D, study the pages shown in Column E. Using this analysis will allow you to focus on your challenges and use your study time more effectively.

A Skill Area		B Questions	C Number of Correct Answers	D Number Correct to Show a Good Understanding	E Pages to Study
Whole Numbers	Multiplication	1			126–131
	Division	2			131–134
	Place Value	3			119–121
	Rounding	4, 5			135–139
	Total		____ /5	5	
Understand Word Problems	Key Words	6			148–149
	Multistep	7, 8, 9			153–155
	Total		____ /4	3	
Decimals	Place Value	10, 11			163–165
	Rounding	12, 13			166–168
	Multiplication	14			171–173
	Addition	15			169–170
	Subtraction	16			169–170
	Estimation	17, 18			166–168
	Total		____ /9	8	
Fractions	Ordering	19			192
	Measurement	20			188–189
	Improper Fractions and Mixed Numbers	21, 22			194–197
	Addition	23			198–202
	Subtraction	24			198–202
	Reducing	25, 26			189–191
	Total		____ /8	7	

	A	B	C	D	E
	Skill Area	Questions	Number of Correct Answers	Number Correct to Show a Good Understanding	Pages to Study
Ratios and Proportions	Write a Ratio	27, 28			219
	Solve Proportion	29, 30			223–224
	Map Scale	31			221
	Word Problem	32			224–231
	Total		____ /6	5	
Percentages	Percent Conversion	33, 34			248–252
	Find %	35, 36			256–261
	% Word Problem	37, 38, 39			262–264
	Total		____ /7	6	
Calculator Use	Fraction and percentage	40, 41			277–283
	Total		____ /2	2	
Graphic Materials	Pie Chart	42, 43, 44			307–311
	Line Graph	45, 46, 47, 48			297–304
	Coordinate Plane	49, 50			314–317
	Dot Plot	54			312–313
	Total		____ /9	8	
Standard Deviation	Mean, Median, Mode	51–53	____ /3	3	285–292
	Total		____ /		
	TOTAL		____ /54	47	

If you have correctly answered more than the number of questions in the Column D TOTAL, you are ready for HSE-Level Math!

POSTTEST ANSWER EXPLANATIONS

1. **(C)**
2. **(B)**
3. 26,341
4. 4,500
5. 349,000
6. **(A)** Quotient is a key word to divide.
7. **(A)** $215 - 210 = 5$
8. **(A)** $215 - 180 = 35$
9. **(D)** $150 + 480 = 630$
10. 7.8012
11. **(B)**
12. 3.9
13. .991
14. 37.5
15. 51.855
16. 50.6
17. **(B)** $5 \times 10 = 50$, $2 \times 2 = 4$, $50 + 4 = 54$
18. **(B)** $600 \div 4 = 150$
19. $\dfrac{1}{10}$, $\dfrac{1}{3}$, $\dfrac{1}{2}$, $\dfrac{2}{3}$, $\dfrac{3}{4}$

20.

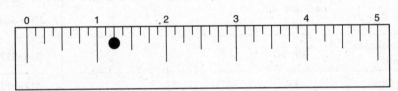

21. $2 \times 2 = 4$, $4 + 1 = 5$. This is the top number (numerator); the bottom number (denominator) stays the same.

$$\frac{5}{2}$$

22. $10 \div 3 = 3$, remainder 1.

$$3\frac{1}{3}$$

23. $\dfrac{4}{5}$

$$\begin{array}{rcl} \frac{4}{5} & \times\, 3 = & \frac{12}{15} \\ + & & + \\ \frac{1}{3} & \times\, 5 = & \frac{5}{15} \\ \hline & & \frac{17}{15} \text{ or } 1\frac{2}{15} \end{array}$$

24. $1\frac{3}{4} = \frac{7}{4}$

$\frac{1}{2} = \frac{2}{4}$
_____
$\frac{5}{4}$

-OR-

$1\frac{1}{4}$

25. $\dfrac{4 \div 4 = 1}{16 \div 4 = 4}$

26. **(D)** $\dfrac{1}{2}$ is the lowest term for $\dfrac{15}{30}$.

27. 6:8, or 3:4

28. 8:14, or 4:7

29. $9 \times 40 = 360$
$360 \div 45 = 8$

30. $3 \times 24 = 72$
$72 \div 4 = 18$

31. **(D)**

$\dfrac{1}{20} = \dfrac{5}{?}$

$20 \times 5 = 100$
$100 \div 1 = 100$

32. **(C)**

$\dfrac{2}{4} = \dfrac{?}{20}$

$2 \times 20 = 40$
$40 \div 4 = 10$

33. **(C)**

34. **(A)**

35. **(A)**
$60 \times .10 = 6$

36. **(B)**
$200 \times .25 = 50$

37. **(B)**
$6,000 \times .40 = 2,400$

38. **(D)**
$80 \times .05 = 4$
$80 + 4 = 84$

39. **(C)** $70 \times .10 = 7$, $70 - 7 = 63$.

40. $\dfrac{5}{8}$

41. 126

42. **(D)**

43. **(D)** Dogs are 30% and reptiles are 5%. 30% + 5% = 35%.

44. **(B)** 20% of 500 is 100.

45. **(D)**

46. (D) This is the day where the line for the Davis family passes the Smith family.

47. (C) The flat line indicates that no distance was gained. This means they did not drive at all.

48. (C) The steepest line shows the greatest change or increase.

49.

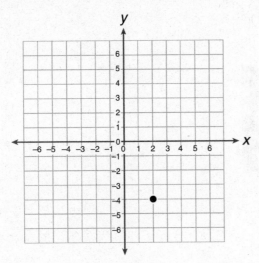

50.

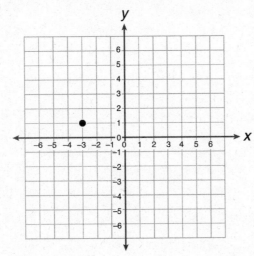

51. (C) To compute the average, first add up all of the numbers. The numbers on the table add up to 21. Then divide that amount by how many numbers you added.

$21 \div 7 = 3$.

52. (C) To find the median, order the numbers from least to greatest, then choose the number in the middle.

53. (D) The mode is the number that appears the most. 4 appears more than any other number on the table.

54.

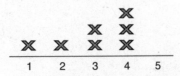

UNIT 3

Science

Science Pretest

The science pretest has 30 questions. It is organized into groups of questions that follow the chapters in the science unit. The science unit is divided into chapters on life science, earth and space science, and the physical sciences. You can use this test to get a sense of which areas you need to study. Make sure you have at least 30 minutes of quiet time available to complete the test. Read each question carefully, and do your best. However, do not guess on these questions. If you don't know the answer to a question, simply skip it and go on to the next one. The purpose of this test is to find out what areas you need to work on, and random guessing might throw you off course.

Some questions on this test will ask about your comprehension of the passages you read. Other questions will test your critical thinking skills, like being able to draw conclusions or make predictions.

Once you have finished, check your answers on pages 360–362 and complete the pre-test evaluation chart on page 358 by circling the number of each question you missed. This way you can easily see your strengths and weaknesses as well as where information on each question you missed is located in the book.

If you score very well on the pretest, that is a great sign that you have a solid foundation in the different areas of science. Still, make sure to check out the end-of-chapter questions for each topic. These pages will include several questions focusing on the thinking skills you will need to get a high score on the science test. You'll want to make sure your skills are sharp before moving on to the next section.

Life Science

Questions 1 through 3 are based on the following diagram and passage.

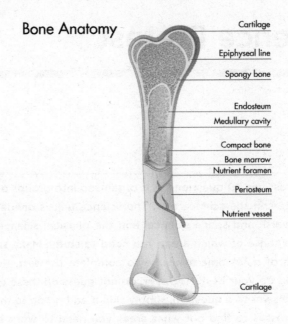

Bone Anatomy

Cartilage
Epiphyseal line
Spongy bone
Endosteum
Medullary cavity
Compact bone
Bone marrow
Nutrient foramen
Periosteum
Nutrient vessel
Cartilage

Many people assume that their bones are hard, dry, and solid all the way through, but this is a misconception. Bones contain spongy tissues called **bone marrow**. The bone marrow in larger bones, such as the large leg bones, produces blood cells. Any disease that reaches the bone marrow can interfere with healthy blood production. Leukemia, for example, a type of cancer, affects white blood cell production and can seriously **jeopardize** a person's ability to fight off infection.

1. What is the main idea of the above passage and diagram?
   (A) Leukemia is a deadly disease.
   (B) Bone marrow plays an important part in keeping a person healthy.
   (C) Bone marrow is inside your bones.
   (D) When bone marrow is diseased, it is easier to break a bone.

2. Which of the following is produced by the bone marrow?
   (A) Antibodies
   (B) Viruses
   (C) Red blood cells
   (D) Mucus

3. Which of the following is the best definition of jeopardize?
   (A) Help
   (B) Put in danger
   (C) Improve
   (D) Examine

Questions 4 and 5 are based on the following diagram and passage.

Animal and plant cells share many of the same characteristics. Plant cells, however, have elements that animal cells do not. The cell wall in a plant cell gives the plant support in the same way that bones support many animals. Chloroplasts contain the colors, green in particular, that allow the plant to feed through photosynthesis.

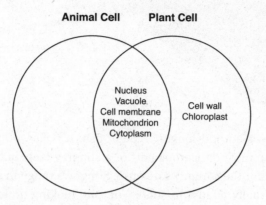

Animal Cell   **Plant Cell**

Nucleus
Vacuole
Cell membrane
Mitochondrion
Cytoplasm

Cell wall
Chloroplast

4. Which of the following pairs are shared by both animal and plant cells?
    (A) Cell walls and chloroplasts
    (B) Cytoplasm and chloroplasts
    (C) Cell membrane and vacuoles
    (D) Cell walls and mitochondrion

5. Which of the following pairs is found only in plant cells?
    (A) Cell walls and chloroplasts
    (B) Cytoplasm and chloroplasts
    (C) Cell membrane and vacuoles
    (D) Cell walls and mitochondrion

Read the following passage and answer questions 6 and 7.

Zack and Jason were changing the oil in a customer's car. Each of them received a small cut on the arm. Zack immediately covered his with a bandage. Jason washed his cut with soap and water before applying a bandage. When Zack removed his bandage several days later, the cut was red and sore. Jason's arm felt fine.

6. What is the most likely cause of the different rate of healing of the mens' arms?
    (A) Zack's arm is healing more slowly because he is not as healthy as Jason.
    (B) Jason probably used a better quality bandage.
    (C) Zack's arm became infected because he did not clean the cut.
    (D) Jason is stronger than Zack.

7. What is the best thing for Zack to do now?
    (A) Cover the arm back up.
    (B) Clean the cut and cover it. Make an appointment with the doctor.
    (C) Bring a lawsuit against the customer who owned the car Zack was working on when he was hurt.
    (D) Leave it alone. It's just a small cut.

The marine stingray is an odd-looking type of fish. It is flat, boneless, and has eyes on the top of its head. The most dangerous part of a stingray is its tail, which sometimes has poisonous spines on it for the stingray's defense. Stingrays range in size from 4 inches to 22 feet wide. They are actually related to sharks, despite looking quite different. Like sharks, stingrays are carnivores.

8. What conclusion can you make about stingrays?
   (A) It is wise to approach stingrays with caution until you know if they are poisonous or not.
   (B) A stingray lives mainly in riverbeds.
   (C) A stingray can bite as hard as a shark.
   (D) The smaller stingrays would make good pets.

9. Kaylie and Brian both have brown eyes. Their baby, Kabrina, has blue eyes. How is this possible genetically?
   (A) Kaylie wore blue contact lenses during pregnancy.
   (B) Although brown-eyed, both parents carry a blue-eyed gene.
   (C) Although blue-eyed, Kabrina carries brown-eyed genes.
   (D) Both parents had blue eyes as babies, and then their eyes turned brown.

10. In 1505, humans landed on the island of Mauritius for the first time. They noticed that one bird in particular was not afraid of them. The Dodo made no attempts to avoid people or to hide its nests and eggs. As the Dodo was a good source of meat, it was soon hunted to extinction. By the end of the 17th century, there were no more.

    What is the best explanation for why Dodos were not afraid of people?
    (A) The Dodo was not intelligent enough to know that people were dangerous.
    (B) Because it had evolved on an uninhabited island, it did not recognize humans as predators.
    (C) Because the Dodo had evolved on an uninhabited island, the Dodo assumed that the humans would soon leave.
    (D) The Dodo could not run or fly fast enough to escape humans.

Earth and Space Science

Read the following passage and answer questions 11 and 12.

For generations, schoolchildren have made models of the nine planets, Mercury, Venus, Earth, Mars, Jupiter, Saturn, Uranus, Neptune, and Pluto. Then in 2006, the IAU (International Astronomical Union) issued a press release: There were now only eight planets! Pluto's status had been changed to that of "dwarf planet."

Two reasons were given for this change: one, Pluto was no longer considered large enough to be classified as a planet, and two, Pluto did not travel alone in its orbit—there were many more objects of the same size as Pluto that traveled with it. These objects, together with Pluto, form a sort of "belt" called the Kuiper Belt.

This is actually not the first time a planet has had its status changed. The dwarf planet Ceres has had its status changed twice! Upon its discovery in 1801, it was briefly considered a planet. Later, astronomers changed Ceres's classification to asteroid. Now, it is considered a dwarf planet along with Pluto.

11. What is one difference between a planet and a dwarf planet?
   (A) A dwarf planet is farther from the sun.
   (B) A dwarf planet is smaller than an asteroid.
   (C) A dwarf planet is smaller than a planet.
   (D) A dwarf planet has no gravity.

12. What is the most likely reason the IAU decided to change Pluto's classification?
   (A) They wanted to confuse everybody.
   (B) They felt this new classification reflected new knowledge about the solar system.
   (C) They felt that all the old astronomers were wrong.
   (D) They felt this new classification would be easier to learn than the old one.

Question 13 is based on the following passage.

Two of the motions that continents make are **converging** and **diverging**. The two often happen at the same time, on different sides of a continent. When a crack appears in the ocean floor, lava from underneath the surface pushes up and causes continental plates on both sides to push apart. A continental plate that is being pushed in one ocean will converge with a plate in another ocean—just as if a person on your right were to bump you and push you into a person standing on your left.

13. Based on the above passage, which of the following is the most likely definition of diverge?
   (A) To move sideways
   (B) To stay stationary
   (C) To push together
   (D) To be pushed apart

Questions 14 through 16 are based on the following map and passage.

The Arctic biome encompasses a vast amount of land, with its center at the North Pole. Many different species, habitats, and ecosystems depend on the continued stability of the arctic environment for survival. One of these is the polar bear. Polar bears spend much of their lives on the ice and in the sea, hunting seals and other mammals.

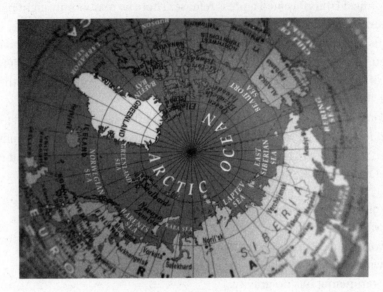

The biggest threat to the polar bear today are rising temperatures due to climate change and global warming. Rising temperatures in the arctic means melting ice. With no ice to live and hunt on, polar bears are in danger of dying off, or becoming extinct. Another problem is that without open ice to resort to, hungry polar bears come into much more frequent contact with populated areas—dangerous for them and for us.

14. What is an unstated assumption that the author makes about polar bears?
    (A) That they are dangerous.
    (B) That they are endangered by global warming.
    (C) That they live in an arctic environment.
    (D) That humans do not want polar bears to become extinct.

15. Which of the following is an opinion about the information in the passage and on the map?
    (A) The northernmost parts of Russia and Canada lie within the Arctic Circle.
    (B) Polar bears should not be allowed to die out.
    (C) Scientists will probably be able to reverse global warming in the future.
    (D) Polar bears are the only arctic animals that are endangered.

16. Which of the following is a fact based on the information in the passage and on the map?
    (A) The northernmost parts of Russia and Canada lie within the Arctic Circle.
    (B) Polar bears should not be allowed to die out.
    (C) Scientists will probably be able to reverse global warming in the future.
    (D) Polar bears are the only arctic animals that are endangered.

Questions 17 and 18 are based on the following passage.

Lauren's little sister asked her one day why the sky was blue. Lauren didn't know, so she asked her teacher. This is what the teacher told her:

Sunlight, or white light, is actually made up of all the colors of the rainbow. The sunlight has to travel through Earth's atmosphere before it gets to us on the planet. Blue light has a very high frequency, or wavelength. The particles in our atmosphere scatter blue light more than any of the other colors. This makes blue much easier to see. During a sunset, the sunlight has to travel through more of the atmosphere and other wavelengths of light (red, orange, yellow, green, and violet) are scattered as well. This accounts for the beautiful reds, oranges, and other colors that we see.

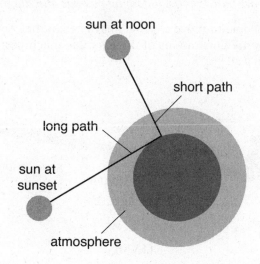

17. What is the difference between the path to Earth sunlight takes at noon and the path it takes at sunrise?
    (A) At sunrise the Sun is weaker.
    (B) The Sun's rays travel through less of the atmosphere at sunrise.
    (C) The Sun's rays travel through more of the atmosphere at noon.
    (D) The Sun's rays travel through more of the atmosphere at sunrise.

18. Which of the following is an unstated assumption made by the author?
    (A) That the reader has seen a sunset.
    (B) That the reader likes sunsets.
    (C) That the reader doesn't get up early enough to look at sunrises.
    (D) That blue light is scattered by atmospheric particles.

19. A tree grows on the side of the hill. Every time it rains, more dirt and rocks are washed away from the tree's roots until the roots are left exposed. Finally a big storm arrives. High winds uproot the tree, and it falls down the hill. What two natural processes have caused these events?

(A) Chemical weathering and erosion
(B) Chemical weathering and physical weathering
(C) Erosion and climate change
(D) Physical weathering and erosion

Physical Science

Questions 20 through 22 are based on the following passage and diagrams.

Simple machines help people to move weights heavier than they could lift, carry, push, or pull on their own. Below are illustrations of three simple machines: the lever, the inclined plane, and the wheel and axle.

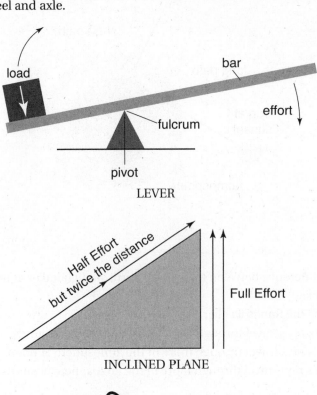

LEVER

INCLINED PLANE

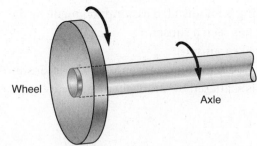

WHEEL AND AXLE

20. Which of the following is an example of a wheel and axle?
    (A) A wheelchair ramp
    (B) A screwdriver
    (C) Scissors
    (D) A pulley

21. Which of the following is an example of an inclined plane?
    (A) A wheelchair ramp
    (B) A screwdriver
    (C) Scissors
    (D) A pulley

22. Which of the following is an example of a lever?
    (A) A wheelchair ramp
    (B) A screwdriver
    (C) Scissors
    (D) A pulley

Read the following passage and answer questions 23 and 24.

Jenna's teacher gave a lesson on mixtures and solutions and then gave the class a homework assignment. Jenna filled two containers with the same amounts of water. Into one container she emptied ½ cup of salt. Into the other container she emptied ½ cup of sand. She stirred both. She then attempted to remove the salt from the first container. This was impossible, as the salt and water had become salt water. She was able to drain the water from the second container and remove the sand. In her notebook, Jenna labeled the salt and water a solution and the sand and water a mixture.

23. Based on Jenna's experiment, what can you conclude about solutions?
    (A) Once they are combined, they cannot be separated.
    (B) They are usually messy.
    (C) Once they are combined, they are usually able to be separated.
    (D) A substance can be both a mixture and a solution.

24. Which of the following combinations would also be considered a solution?
    (A) Popcorn and milk
    (B) Grapes and water
    (C) Lemonade mix and water
    (D) Nuts and raisins

Carbon monoxide is a colorless, odorless gas composed of one carbon atom (C) and one oxygen atom (O). Carbon monoxide (CO) is toxic to humans if they are exposed to it in conditions where there is little or no ventilation. However, CO is a gas expelled by most cars and trucks. Because of this, people are cautioned to avoid running their cars in enclosed spaces (like garages) for long periods of time.

Carbon dioxide, on the other hand (formed by adding two oxygen atoms to one carbon atom), is part of the natural life cycle. Humans and animals exhale carbon dioxide, which plants take in during photosynthesis. Carbon dioxide is also used in the production of some beverages, such as soft drinks and wines.

One little oxygen atom can make a big difference!

25. Carbon dioxide has one more oxygen atom than carbon monoxide (CO). What is the most likely chemical symbol for carbon dioxide?
    (A) CO_2
    (B) H_2O
    (C) Na
    (D) H_2O_2

26. In the passage above, what is the most likely definition of the word toxic?
    (A) Annoying
    (B) Deadly
    (C) Expensive
    (D) Common

In the first century B.C., Archimedes, a Greek inventor, discovered a way to measure the volume of an irregularly shaped object (in Archimedes's case, a crown or wreath of gold leaves). In his bath, Archimedes noticed that as he immersed himself deeper in the water, the water level rose. He realized that if he did the same with the wreath, the level of the water that rose would have the same volume as the wreath.

27. What is the main idea of this passage?
    (A) Archimedes was a scientist who lived a long time ago.
    (B) People in Archimedes's time had no way to measure the volume of any object.
    (C) By making an observation of everyday life, a scientist discovered a useful method of measurement.
    (D) Archimedes was one of the world's first geniuses.

28. What was the cause of the water level in Archimedes's bathtub rising?
    (A) The volume of Archimedes's body displaced it in the tub.
    (B) Archimedes had filled his bathtub too full.
    (C) The volume of the wreath displaced it in the tub.
    (D) Archimedes was the first to discover how to measure objects by this method.

Read the following passage and answer questions 29 and 30.

Ted and Bill are building houses in New Mexico. They have both decided to take advantage of the dry, sunny climate to incorporate solar power into their designs. However, Ted is including backup sources of energy such as electricity and gas. Bill wants to go "off the grid" entirely and use only renewable energy. Both have included storage capabilities in the solar power systems that will keep the energy flowing overnight or over one cloudy day at most.

Soon after Ted and Bill move into their houses, New Mexico is hit by an unusual spell of several days of cloudy and rainy weather.

29. What do you predict will happen at Ted and Bill's houses?
    (A) Ted will not have power some of the time; Bill will have power all the time.
    (B) Bill will not have power some of the time; Ted will have power all the time.
    (C) They will both be out of power for some of the time.
    (D) Neither of them will run out of power.

30. After the cloudy spell is over, what solution would ensure that both houses are powered all the time?
    (A) Bill should run lines to Ted's house so he can borrow power when he needs it.
    (B) Bill should buy more solar panels.
    (C) Ted should buy more solar panels.
    (D) Bill should invest in a backup power source.

PRETEST EVALUATION CHART

After checking the answers on the following pages, circle the numbers of the questions you got correct in Column B. Record the total number of correct questions for each skill in Column C. Column D gives you the number of correct questions you need to answer correctly to indicate that you have a good understanding of the skill. If you got fewer correct answers than shown in Column D, study the pages shown in Column E. Using this analysis will allow you to focus on your challenges and use your study time more effectively.

A		B	C	D	E
Skill Area		Questions	Number of Correct Answers	Number Correct to Show a Good Understanding	Pages to Study
Main Idea	Life Science	1			
	Earth and Space		____/2	2	363–478
	Physical Science	27			
Compare/ Contrast	Life Science	4, 5			
	Earth and Space	11, 17	____/4	3	
	Physical Science				
Cause and Effect	Life Science	9, 10			
	Earth and Space	19	____/4	3	
	Physical Science	28			
Making Predictions	Life Science	7			
	Earth and Space		____/2	2	
	Physical Science	29			
Drawing Conclusions	Life Science	8			
	Earth and Space		____/3	2	
	Physical Science	23, 30			

	A	B	C	D	E
	Skill Area	Questions	Number of Correct Answers	Number Correct to Show a Good Understanding	Pages to Study
Making Inferences	Life Science				
	Earth and Space	12	____ /3	2	
	Physical Science	24, 25			
Fact and Opinion	Life Science				
	Earth and Space	15, 16	____ /2	2	
	Physical Science				
Unstated Assumptions	Life Science				
	Earth and Space	14, 18	____ /2	2	
	Physical Science				
Content	Life Science	2, 3			
	Earth and Space	13	____ /7	5	
	Physical Science	20, 21, 22, 26			
TOTAL			____ /29	23	

If you answered enough of the questions in Column D for a skill, you know enough about that skill already. You may want to do the Review at the end of these skill areas as a check.

To use your study time wisely, improve your skills in the other areas by studying the pages noted in Column E.

PRETEST ANSWER EXPLANATIONS

1. **(B)** *Bone marrow plays an important part in keeping a person healthy.* The passage defines bone marrow and explains its function. (A) Leukemia is a serious disease, but not always deadly. It is only mentioned in the last sentence of the passage, nowhere else. (C) is a detail of the passage and diagram. (D) is not supported by anything in the passage.

2. **(C)** *Red blood cells.* The passage states that marrow in large bones produce blood cells. This includes red blood cells. None of the other choices are mentioned in the passage.

3. **(B)** *Put in danger.* The passage states that leukemia can jeopardize, or endanger, a person's immune system. (A) and (C) Having cancer will not help or improve anyone's health. (D) A disease cannot examine, only a doctor can.

4. **(C)** *Cell membranes and vacuoles.* Any items placed in the center of a Venn diagram are characteristics shared by both circles. (A) These characteristics appear only in the plant circle, not in the animal circle or shared space. (B) Chloroplasts appear only in the plant circle. (D) Cell walls appear only in the plant circle.

5. **(A)** *Cell walls and chloroplasts.* These characteristics appear only in the plant circle, not in the animal circle or shared space. (B) Chloroplasts appear only in the plant circle. (C) Any items placed in the center of a Venn diagram are characteristics shared by both circles. (D) Cell walls appear only in the plant circle.

6. **(C)** *Zack's arm became infected because he did not clean the cut.* All cuts, no matter how small, should be cleaned immediately to prevent infection. Redness and soreness are signs of infection.

7. **(B)** *Clean the cut and cover it. Make an appointment with the doctor.* A small cut with signs of infection may heal if cleaned thoroughly with an antiseptic. However, a doctor should be consulted to be safe.

8. **(A)** *It is wise to approach stingrays with caution until you know if they are poisonous or not.* The passage states that stingrays are *sometimes* poisonous but does not reveal a method for telling safe fish from dangerous ones. Therefore, it is a good idea to approach any stingray with caution. (B) A marine animal lives in saltwater, not freshwater. (C) is not supported by the passage. (D) is an opinion and a dangerous one.

9. **(B)** *Although brown-eyed, both parents carry a blue-eyed gene.* (A) Contact lenses do not affect a person's genes. (C) This is irrelevant; Kabrina's blue-eyed genes determine her eye color. (D) Many babies at birth have lighter eyes, which change color or become darker later. This is unrelated to their genetic inheritance.

10. **(B)** *Because the Dodo had evolved on an uninhabited island, it did not recognize humans as predators.* (A) and (C) Fleeing predators is a matter of instinct, not intelligence or reasoning. (D) The Dodo still has the option to hide, which it did not do.

11. **(C)** *A dwarf planet is smaller than a planet.* The passage states that Pluto is too small to be considered a planet under the new classification. (A) Even though Pluto is very far from the Sun, the passage does not give distance as a reason for the change. (B) No information is given on the size relationship between dwarf planets and asteroids. (D) is false; all bodies have gravity.

12. **(B)** *They felt this new classification reflected new knowledge about the solar system.* The IAU was responding to knowledge that astronomers have discovered since Pluto's classification. This does not mean that (C) all old astronomical knowledge is wrong. (A) Scientists' jobs are to make things clearer, not to confuse. (D) The new classification

actually adds more than it takes away, since a new category must be learned: dwarf planets.

13. **(D)** *To be pushed apart.* The passage states that plates *converge with* one another when they are pushed apart on the other side. Thus, pushing apart (diverging) must be the opposite of converging.

14. **(D)** *That humans do not want polar bears to become extinct.* The author speaks of extinction as a possible *problem.* She assumes people will want to solve (prevent) it. (A), (B), and (C) are directly stated in the passage.

15. **(B)** *Polar bears should not be allowed to die out.* The word *should* normally signals an opinion. (A) is a fact supported by the map. (C) is a prediction. (D) is false and not supported by the passage.

16. **(A)** *The northernmost parts of Russia and Canada lie within the Arctic Circle.* This fact can be verified by looking at the map. (B) The word *should* normally signals an opinion. (C) is a prediction. (D) is false and not supported by the passage.

17. **(D)** *The Sun's rays travel through more of the atmosphere at sunrise.* The diagram shows a longer path for the Sun's rays at sunset. The Sun at sunrise is in the same position relative to the horizon and viewers on Earth.

18. **(A)** *The reader has seen a sunset.* The author mentions *the colors that we see* at sunset but does not fully explain what happens then. She assumes the reader is familiar with sunsets. (B) and (C) Neither of these conditions need to be true to understand the passage. (D) This is a fact stated in the passage.

19. **(D)** *Physical weathering and erosion.* (A) and (B) The tree, soil, and rocks do not change their substance; they simply change shape and move. (C) Climate change is a more global phenomenon than simple local weather changes.

20. **(B)** *A screwdriver.* A screwdriver uses a turning motion. The handle of the screwdriver functions as the wheel and the blade as the axle. Force applied to the handle is increased by the blade (axle). (A) A wheelchair ramp is an inclined plane. (C) Scissors are two levers that work together with the fulcrum at the fastening. (D) A pulley is a different type of simple machine, not pictured here.

21. **(A)** *A wheelchair ramp.* It is easier to roll the chair up a ramp than to lift it and its owner straight up off the ground. (B) A screwdriver uses a turning motion. The handle of the screwdriver functions as the wheel and the blade as the axle. (C) Scissors are two levers that work together with the fulcrum at the fastening. (D) A pulley is a different type of simple machine, not pictured here.

22. **(C)** *Scissors.* Scissors are two levers that work together with the fulcrum at the fastening. (A) A wheelchair ramp is an inclined plane. It is easier to roll the chair up a ramp than to lift it and its owner straight up off the ground. (B) A screwdriver uses a turning motion. The handle of the screwdriver functions as the wheel and the blade as the axle. (D) A pulley is a different type of simple machine, not pictured here.

23. **(A)** *Once they are combined, they cannot be separated.* Jenna labeled the saltwater as a solution. Once the salt and water were combined, the salt could not be taken back out of the water.

24. **(C)** *Lemonade mix and water.* This is considered a solution because the mix crystals cannot be taken back out of the drink. (B) Putting grapes into water does not create a solution because it is possible to take the grapes out again. (A) It is also possible to remove popcorn from milk (although it will be quite soggy!). (D) Nuts and raisins can be easily separated.

25. **(A)** CO_2. Carbon dioxide has one carbon atom (C) and two oxygen atoms (O_2). H_2O is the symbol for water. Na is the symbol for sodium. H_2O_2 is the symbol for hydrogen peroxide.

26. **(B)** *Deadly*. The definition of the word toxic is (B) *deadly*. A context clue for this is that people are advised not to breathe carbon monoxide in enclosed spaces.

27. **(C)** *By making an observation of everyday life, a scientist discovered a useful method of measurement.* (A) is a detail of the passage. (B) The passage says it was only *irregularly* shaped objects that scientists could not measure. (D) This is an opinion.

28. **(A)** *The volume of Archimedes's body displaced it in the tub.* (B) This is an opinion. (C) Archimedes did not lower the wreath into his bath; he thought about or *realized* he could measure it by doing so. (D) is a conclusion based on the first sentence of the passage.

29. **(B)** *Bill will not have power some of the time; Ted will have power all the time.* (A) This is unlikely, since it is Ted who has the backup power sources. (C) and (D) Neither of these is likely. The two men will not experience the same results, since the power supply to their houses differs.

30. **(D)** *Bill should invest in a backup power source.* (A) This might work for Bill, but Ted might object. (B) and (C) More solar panels will not help in cloudy weather.

Life Science

E arth is sometimes referred to as a closed system. What does this mean? Well, when scientists and other people use this term, they mean that matter or solid things on Earth stay on Earth and do not travel into space. Things that exist outside of Earth tend to stay outside.

In actual fact, this closed system is not completely closed. Energy enters and leaves Earth's atmosphere all the time. Meteors have visited and left marks of their existence. Scientists send probes and satellites into space to gather information and assist technology (your cell phone depends on one such satellite). A few brave humans have even left our planet to walk in space.

However, when it comes to living things—plants and animals—we see the importance of keeping a closed community balanced and healthy. All living things depend upon each other to form a functioning global ecosystem. If the air of Earth becomes too polluted to breathe, there is no stopping the planet and getting off!

HOW THIS CHAPTER IS ORGANIZED

Lesson 1: Plants and Animals

This chapter presents cells—the foundation of all life—and reviews the process of photosynthesis that plants go through.

Lesson 2: The Human Body

You are more complex than the most hi-tech computer—find out why!

Lesson 3: Organ Systems

Human organ systems, though labeled and studied separately, must work together to ensure your health.

Lesson 4: Heredity

All living things pass traits from generation to generation.

Lesson 5: Evolution

All living things change and adapt.

Lesson 6: Scientific Method

Experimentation and observation are the key elements in forming strong hypotheses.

Lesson 7: Graphic Materials

Practice your comprehension of scientific information in the forms of tables, diagrams, and graphs.

Lesson 8: Critical Thinking Skills

Lesson 8 gives you the opportunity to practice the skills of finding the main idea, drawing conclusions from details, making predictions, and identifying cause and effect.

LESSON 1: PLANTS AND ANIMALS

One of the best ways to keep ourselves (and our environment) healthy is to find out as much as possible about the systems and structures that make life possible—that keep it active and productive. One of the most basic of these structures is the cell.

The Cell

A common nickname for the cell is the "building block of life." All living things are formed from cells. Organisms may be simple, made up of one or a few cells, or they may be multicellular. You yourself, as you read this, are composed of many different types of cells. This is a common bond you have with the student next to you, the trees in the rain forest, the birds outside, and anything that is or ever was alive.

Cells are **distinguished** or separated from the rest of the natural world by the fact that they reproduce themselves. Because life is made of cells, this is an ability that is special to living things. In other words, a rabbit can produce another rabbit, but a chair is never going to produce another chair (or a rabbit).

Both animal and plant cells have a **nucleus**, a small, round "command center," inside them, where many of their important functions are carried out. However, there are some key differences between animal and plant cells.

ANIMAL CELLS

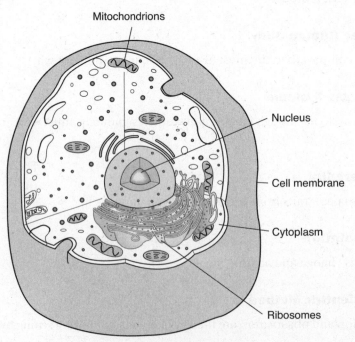

The diagram on page 364 gives you an idea of the structure of an animal cell. The cell **membrane** covers the outside of each cell. It is not skin, but it functions somewhat as your skin does; it lets in things the cell needs (like water and oxygen) and protects the cell.

In addition to being the control center of the cell, the round nucleus carries important **hereditary** information. In other words, each nucleus holds information necessary for reproduction or making another cell.

Between the membrane and the nucleus is the cytoplasm, a fluid that performs several important functions. With so much fluid in your cells, you can see why it is important to drink enough water to stay **hydrated**!

PLANT CELLS

One difference between animal and plant cells is that plants have a cell wall in addition to a membrane. The cell wall provides support for the plant, much as our bones support us. However, the cell wall still allows water, light, and essential nutrients to reach the cell. Another structure that helps the plant cell support itself is a large **vacuole** (fluid-filled sac) inside the membrane. While animal cells also have vacuoles, they are small and mostly assist in processing food and water.

If you look at plant cells under a microscope or search for a photo of plant cells on your computer, you will see something else interesting. The plant cells are likely to be covered with lots of round green dots. These dots are called **chloroplasts**. Can you locate them on the diagram below?

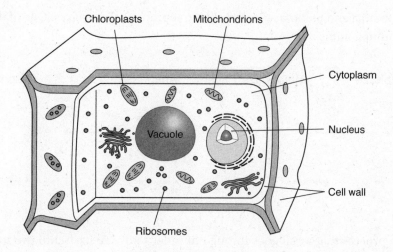

Animal cells do not have chloroplasts. That's because plant cells have a job to do that animal cells do not. Plant cells have to manufacture food directly from the Sun's light. The green color that we see on grass, trees, and the leaves of flowers is actually helping them eat! The process by which plants turn light into food is called **photosynthesis**.

Photosynthesis

Photosynthesis is a compound word from photo (light) and synthesis (make or made). During the process of photosynthesis, plants take the Sun's light and combine it with carbon dioxide that they find in Earth's atmosphere. The chloroplasts in their leaves begin to transform this combination into food.

However, even though sunlight is the main source of food for most plants, they cannot exist on light alone. Like all living things, plants need a constant supply of water. Even plants that are able to store water for long periods of time (like cactus) need to replenish their supply at regular intervals. Water is the third ingredient plants need to complete the process of photosynthesis.

Have you ever had a backyard garden? Then you know that plants also need soil, which has the right mixture of nutrients for them. Pineapple growers in Hawaii, for instance, know that iron is crucial for a good pineapple crop. Blue Spruce trees like acid soil, while asparagus prefers soil that is **alkaline**.

Do all plants use photosynthesis to make food? The answer to this question was once no. There were a group of plants called **fungi**. Fungi include many mushrooms familiar to us. You may have some in your refrigerator right now! Fungi cannot transform light into food. However, scientists have now reclassified fungi into their own kingdom, separate from plants.

Did you know that when plants take in carbon dioxide during photosynthesis they give off oxygen? Do you know or can you guess what you breathe out when you breathe oxygen in?

If you wrote carbon dioxide, you are correct. These two facts are a good example of the interconnectedness of life on our planet.

Mitosis

Cells, both animal and plant, need to be able to reproduce themselves. One of the ways they do this is through mitosis.

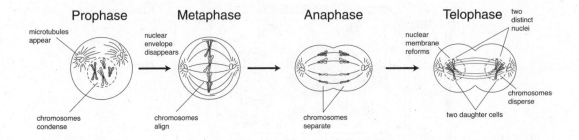

Mitosis is a process that a cell goes through in order to divide itself into two identical cells. These two cells have the ability to divide again, until one original cell can have many, many duplicates.

Mitosis takes five steps. The four active stages:

- Prophase
- Metaphase
- Anaphase
- Telophase

are pictured here. The fifth stage, **Interphase**, is a resting stage. A cell undergoing division always ends in Interphase. Likewise, a cell in Interphase always has the ability to begin dividing.

In Prophase and Metaphase, the cell is duplicating the important information it carries in its interior (**DNA**) so that each cell has a copy. Things begin moving around inside the cell to be in proper position before the actual division begins.

In Anaphase, two sets of **chromosomes**, or genetic information, move to opposite ends of the cell.

In Telophase, the cell membrane, or wall, finally splits and the two cells are now separate. Both cells immediately go into Interphase, to repeat the whole process sometime in the future.

WHERE CAN I SEE EXAMPLES OF MITOSIS?

Right under your nose!

Skin and hair cells, as well as other body cells, reproduce through mitosis.

Practice Exercise 1

Match the term on the left with its correct definition on the right.

_____ 1. Cell membrane

_____ 2. Hereditary

_____ 3. Hydrated

_____ 4. Vacuole

_____ 5. Chloroplast

_____ 6. Photosynthesis

_____ 7. Alkaline

_____ 8. Fungi

(A) Plants that do not synthesize their own food

(B) The opposite of acid; not acidic

(C) Covering of a cell that lets nutrients pass through

(D) Process by which plants create food from light and carbon dioxide

(E) Passed from parent to offspring

(F) Filled with enough water

(G) Green objects in plant cells that help convert light to food.

(H) Fluid-filled sacs found in plant and animal cells.

Exercise

In the last 20 years, researchers have proposed that by eating foods containing more **antioxidants**, people can reduce cell damage that occurs as a natural effect of daily life. Two of the antioxidants recommended are beta-carotene and lycopene, most common in orange and red fruits and vegetables.

Practice Exercise 2

Read the following passage and answer the question.

Cancer is a disease in which cells in the body grow and reproduce unnaturally quickly. If detected early, cancer can often be successfully treated. If left unchecked, though, dangerous tumors (large growths) can develop. Doctors like to know a patient's family medical history because cancer often has a genetic component. However, environmental factors—diet and lifestyle, for example—can be important in helping a person avoid or continue in remission from this disease.

1. Lung cancer is one of the deadliest cancers in the United States. What might be a contributing environmental factor for this?
    (A) Water in many cities that is unsafe to drink
    (B) Inhaling smoke from other people's cigarettes
    (C) Improperly cooked meat
    (D) Chewing tobacco

Read the following passage and answer the question.

In some parts of the country, the leaves of many trees turn different colors during the autumn. Eventually, the leaves fall, and the tree is left with bare branches. People often assume this process is a response to the colder weather. In reality, each tree is responding to shorter days and fewer daylight hours. The green chlorophyll that helped the tree make food all summer is no longer needed and fades away. A healthy tree is well able to wait out the cold winter until it can put out buds in the spring.

2. What is a fact that you can infer from the above passage?
    (A) Trees are probably cold in winter.
    (B) During the short winter days, the tree lives on energy it has stored during the summer.
    (C) If there was a very mild winter, the trees would not lose their leaves.
    (D) The tree is mainly responding to the lack of light, but probably also a little to the cold as well.

LESSON 2: THE HUMAN BODY

A person's body, when healthy and functioning properly, has sometimes been referred to as "a well-oiled machine." Of course, people are not machines! The human body, with all its **interconnected** systems, is more complex than even the smallest microprocessor. However, like a machine, all systems must be working for the body to do its job. What is that job? It is to let its owner work, relax, exercise, and enjoy life as fully as possible.

Another similarity between people's bodies and machines is that both require maintenance. Your car, if you drive one, needs the oil checked every three thousand miles. A home heating system must be inspected every fall to make sure it is ready for winter. You and your body also need to see your doctor regularly to make sure you stay healthy. If your doctor recommends further treatment or tests, there are **specialists** who have experience with individual body systems. **Cardiologists**, for example, treat diseases of the heart and blood vessels. An **orthopedic** doctor works with bones and bone injuries.

In this lesson and the next, you will learn about some of the systems that support you in your daily life. If you keep them healthy, they will keep you active!

Blood Vessels

You have trillions of cells in your body. Each of them needs oxygen and nutrients. How are they supplied? The answer is in your blood! Blood is the transportation and delivery system of the body. It travels to every cell inside you through tiny tubes called **blood vessels**. Blood vessels are not all the same size; there are larger vessels, called **veins** and **arteries** and smaller vessels called **capillaries**. But they all share the same job. Blood vessels all:

✔ Supply cells with oxygen
✔ Supply cells with nutrients to make energy
✔ Take away waste products (like carbon dioxide) from cells

For a blood vessel to work properly, it is important that the inside is clear for red and white blood cells to travel through. One of the main dangers to healthy blood flow is the build-up of **plaque**. Plaque sticks to the inside of arteries and narrows the pathway, blocking some of the "traffic lane." If the artery become completely blocked, serious results—heart attack or stroke—may occur.

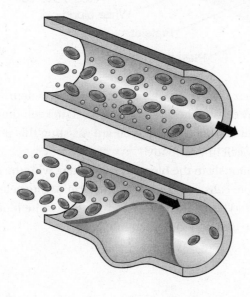

Practice Exercise 3

1. Some of the risk factors for plaque build-up in the arteries have been identified as smoking, eating foods high in LDL ("bad") cholesterol, having high blood pressure, and eating foods high in sugar and fat. Which of the following activities would doctors target as contributing to a patient's plaque build-up problem? (Check all that apply).

   (A) _____ Starting an exercise program.

   (B) _____ Eating a slice of cheesecake every night.

   (C) _____ Having a family history of high blood pressure.

   (D) _____ Switching from sweetened to unsweetened iced tea.

   (E) _____ Smoking, but only on work breaks and after dinner.

   (F) _____ Using olive oil in cooking and on salads.

Cheesecake has both sugar and unhealthy fats. Having a family medical history that includes high blood pressure puts you at risk for having it too. Only your doctor can tell you if you have inherited the actual condition or not. Finally, smoking occasionally, while healthier than smoking two packs a day, is still enough to contribute to a higher risk for plaque.

Two different types of blood cells use the vessels as their streets and highways. They are **red blood cells** and **white blood cells**.

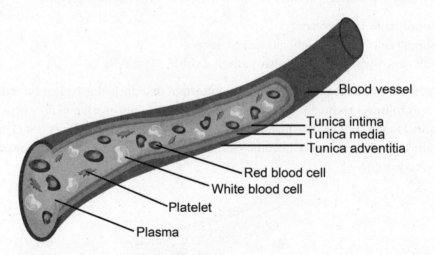

Red blood cells circulate oxygen to all your cells. A cell that is deprived of oxygen will soon die. Red cells also take away carbon dioxide from each cell to keep the body clean. When you breathe in (oxygen) and out (carbon dioxide) you are assisting this process. Breathe deep—you are breathing for every cell in your body!

White cells travel continuously in the **bloodstream**, along with the red cells. As part of the body's defense system, white cells' job is to fight infection. White cells can also help doctors by being a warning system. When a doctor sees a patient's white blood cell count increase, he or she can be pretty sure that patient has an infection.

Practice Exercise 4

Match the terms on the left below with the correct definitions on the right.

_____ 1. Plaque   (A)   Cells in the blood that fight infection

_____ 2. Capillaries   (B)   The flow of blood through your body

_____ 3. White cells   (C)   An unhealthy buildup inside blood vessels

_____ 4. Veins   (D)   Cells that carry oxygen to your body

_____ 5. Red cells   (E)   Small blood vessels

_____ 6. Blood vessels   (F)   Large blood vessels

_____ 7. Bloodstream   (G)   Tubes that blood flows through

Bones and Muscles

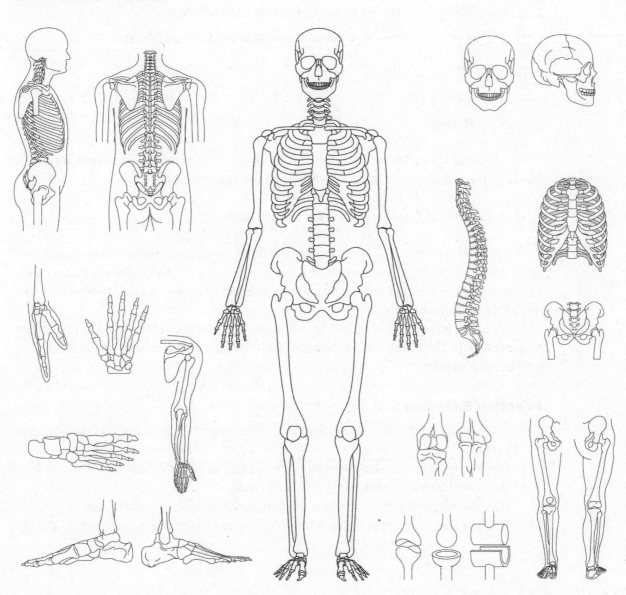

Have you ever seen a tent collapse? Tents can be supported with only one or two tent poles. Yet those poles are **crucial**. Take them away and the tent loses its shape and falls to the ground.

Like the tent, the human body needs a framework. The human skeleton has 206 bones. These do more than just support and protect our organs. They allow us to move in an incredible variety of ways. The rib cage, for example, protects the heart, lungs, and other organs in your chest. However, the rib cage is also constructed to move with each breath. If you are running and need deeper breaths, the rib cage will not get in the way of your lungs!

There are likewise several different types of **joints** (places where bones meet) in the human body.

Practice Exercise 5

Can you match each type of joint to the appropriate body part?

Hint: some letters are used more than once.

_____ 1. Elbow   (A) Pivot joint—can turn from side to side

_____ 2. Hip   (B) Ball and socket—can swing in many directions

_____ 3. Neck   (C) Hinge joint—can straighten or bend only

_____ 4. Knee

_____ 5. Shoulder

Two types of strong tissue, **cartilage** and **ligament**, help to connect and cushion joints. The cartilage and ligaments in your body give it even more flexibility.

Read the following passage and answer the question.

The human skull is designed to protect the brain and **sense organs** (those organs that allow us to hear, smell, see, and taste). It is not one bone, but is made of many bones **fused**, or connected. The skull has no moving parts. It generally provides adequate protection for us during the activities of daily life.

Many states, however, now require at least some part of the motorcycle riding population to wear helmets. These decisions were made after reviewing statistics of motor accidents over the last 30 to 40 years.

Practice Exercise 6

1. What do you think is the main reason state governments want motorcycle riders to wear helmets?
   (A) The head of the rider might hit a hard surface at a high speed.
   (B) The rider might not be able to brake in time.
   (C) The helmet filters out traffic noise and allows the rider to better focus.
   (D) The states are trying to cut down on the number of accident cases that go to trial.

Practice Exercise 7

Match the terms on the left with the correct definitions on the right.

_____ 1. Skeleton   (A) Framework of connected bones

_____ 2. Bone   (B) Joint that can straighten or bend

_____ 3. Joint   (C) Hard, supportive tissue

_____ 4. Pivot   (D) Connected and non-moving

_____ 5. Hinge   (E) Tissue that cushions and supports bone

_____ 6. Ball and socket   (F) Where two bones connect

_____ 7. Cartilage   (G) Joint that can swing in many directions

_____ 8. Fused   (H) Joint that turns from side to side

Muscles

Muscles are the lifters and movers for the body, and are attached to your bones by **tendons**. They work in pairs. For example, when you bend your elbow, one muscle in your arm is **contracting**, or tightening, and the muscle opposite is **expanding**, or getting longer. People who go to the gym use several different machines for their arms to exercise all the muscle groups. They must do the same thing with any other areas they wish to strengthen.

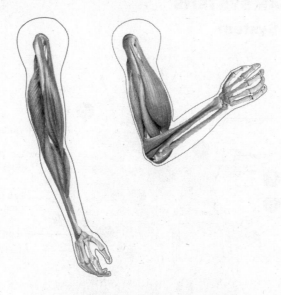

Contracting/expanding muscle pair.

Muscle movement is classified as **voluntary** or **involuntary**. A voluntary movement is one controlled by you, such as standing up or reaching for a pencil. Involuntary muscle movement is something the body does on its own (like breathing or shivering).

Proper diet and exercise are key factors to maintaining healthy bones and muscles, veins, arteries, and capillaries. However, it is important to remember that what works for one person may not be the best practice for another. Know your family medical history, so that you may work with your doctor on developing your own personal healthy lifestyle.

Practice Exercise 8

Classify the following muscle movements as voluntary (V) or involuntary (I).

_____ 1. Lifting your arm above your head.

_____ 2. Your heart beating

_____ 3. Bending over to pick up a shoe

_____ 4. Jumping

_____ 5. Blinking

_____ 6. Sneezing

LESSON 3: ORGAN SYSTEMS
The Circulatory System

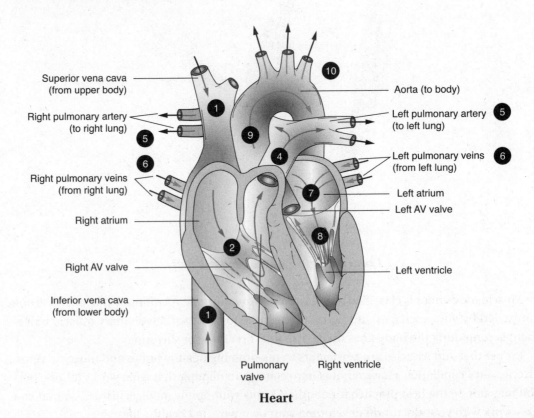

Superior vena cava (from upper body)

Right pulmonary artery (to right lung)

Right pulmonary veins (from right lung)

Right atrium

Right AV valve

Inferior vena cava (from lower body)

Aorta (to body)

Left pulmonary artery (to left lung)

Left pulmonary veins (from left lung)

Left atrium

Left AV valve

Left ventricle

Pulmonary valve

Right ventricle

Heart

Remember the blood cells from Lesson 1? How does your blood keep refreshing your cells with the oxygen and nutrients they need? The key to the health of your **circulatory** system is your heart. Your heart is an involuntary muscle that never stops moving, or **beating**. As it beats, it pushes the blood in a closed path through your body—somewhat the same way that race cars travel on a track. The blood leaves your heart full of oxygen. It travels away from the heart through **arteries**, and eventually reaches the cells in your body through smaller **capillaries**.

As the cells are being nourished, they deposit their wastes (such as carbon dioxide) in the blood. These waste products are carried back to the heart through the **veins**. Once at the heart, the blood is cleaned and the whole process starts again!

Practice Exercise 9

Match the terms on the left with the correct definitions on the right.

_____ 1. Circulation

_____ 2. Vein

_____ 3. Artery

_____ 4. Capillary

_____ 5. Beat

_____ 6. Carbon dioxide

(A) A single movement of the heart

(B) Movement of blood throughout the body

(C) A waste product in the blood

(D) A vessel that carries blood away from the heart

(E) A vessel that carries blood toward the heart

(F) A small vessel that carries blood to the cells

TAKE IT HOME

Take your own pulse! You will need a clock or watch with a second hand. Place your forefinger and second finger on the side of your neck under your chin until you feel a gentle beating. That is your pulse! Have a friend tell you when 10 seconds starts and stops. In between that time, count how many beats you feel. Multiply whatever number you get by 6. That is your pulse or heart rate.

Digestive System

Unlike plants, humans cannot make their own food out of sunlight! Not only do we need to eat, we need to eat the right balance of nutrients to stay healthy.

Digestion begins in the mouth. While some other animal species (like snakes) are able to swallow their food whole, humans must use their teeth to grind food into tiny pieces before they swallow it. After food is swallowed, it passes down a long tube (the **esophagus**) to the stomach. Your stomach is filled with **acidic** juices to further break down food so that the body can use it (anybody who has ever had heartburn after a big meal has felt that acid in action!).

Food only stays in your stomach a few hours before passing into the **small intestine**. This long, coiled, organ takes everything your body needs from the food. The **gallbladder**, **liver**, and **pancreas** are also vital to this process. All the nutrition is absorbed into your circulatory system (your blood) through the walls of the small intestine. Any solid waste your body does not need moves on to the **large intestine** (liquid waste is filtered through the kidneys and leaves the body through the **urethra**.) A healthy digestive system eliminates solid waste from the **rectum** (anus) every 1–2 days.

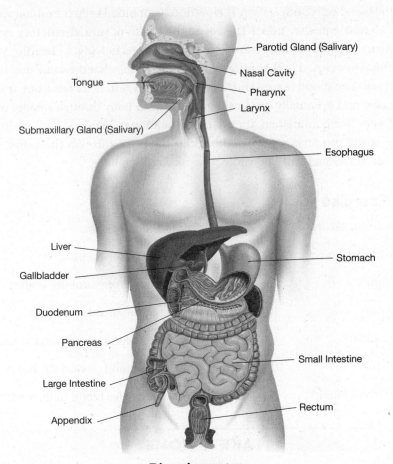

Digestive system

Fiber is part of many different fruits, vegetables, and cereals. It cannot be digested, but aids in keeping the digestive process healthy. The American Dietetic Association recommends adults consume 20–35 grams of fiber per day.

Practice Exercise 10

1. Lillian wants to increase her fiber intake. Which breakfast should she have?

Sturdy O's	Sugar Crunch	Slim Snips
Calories: 160	Calories: 110	Calories: 90
Fat: 1.5 g	Fat: 0 g	Fat: 0.5 g
Sugar: 6 g	Sugar: 11 g	Sugar: 5 g
Fiber: 13 g	Fiber: 1 g	Fiber: 5 g

Immune System

Your immune system is a complex network that puts your whole body on alert when threatened by disease or infection. As such, your immune system has two main jobs: remember infections and diseases you had in the past so your body can recognize them again and actively fight any current threats.

Your body keeps a "record" of past illnesses so that it knows just what weapons to use if you should come in contact with one again. For example, did you know that there is not just one type of common cold? There are over 100 cold viruses! Every time you recover from a cold, you are then immune from that particular virus. Your body will remember it in the future and create **antibodies** to keep it from infecting you. But (unfortunately for you) there are still over 99 varieties of common cold your body could still be **susceptible** to!

What creates antibodies? Who are the soldiers in your body's defense system?

The white blood cells (**leukocytes**). They travel throughout the body, ready to attack bacteria or any other foreign substance. When we receive **immunizations** as children, for example, the doctor injects a weakened form of a virus (say measles) into the body. The white blood cells fight off the virus and remember its structure. If your body ever meets measles in its full strength, it will already have **immunity**.

Practice Exercise 11

Read the following passage and answer the questions.

Concern about the spread of the H1N1 Flu virus caused the United States CDC (Center for Disease Control) to declare a national public health emergency in 2009. Suggested safety measures were posted in schools, hospitals, and other buildings to remind people to take **hygienic** precautions. Some of the suggestions included: washing hands for 15–20 seconds, coughing or sneezing into the elbow (not the hands), and **refraining** from touching the eyes or nose.

1. Based on the context, which two words best define **hygienic**?
   (A) Clean and healthful
   (B) Expensive and unnecessary
   (C) Illegal and dangerous
   (D) Restrictive and monitored.

2. Which of the following actions would likely **NOT** help stop the spread of the H1N1 flu virus?
   (A) Staying home from work when you have the flu.
   (B) Getting a flu shot.
   (C) Using individual glasses in your home bathroom.
   (D) Spraying air freshener in the company bathroom.

3. If you were to catch the flu, in spite of all precautions, which of the following is most likely NOT recommended?
   (A) Stay home and get plenty of rest.
   (B) See your doctor.
   (C) Drink fluids.
   (D) Try to keep going to work until you just can't get out of bed anymore.

LESSON 4: HEREDITY

Before you were born, your body had already received a specific set of instructions—a kind of code. Half of this code came from your mother and half from your father. These instructions created a unique individual—you!

Heredity is still not completely understood by scientists, but they are learning more all the time. Heredity is the passing of **traits** from parents to offspring. What are traits? They are your characteristics. Some obvious traits are eye and hair color, tallness, and facial features. Less obvious traits—that might not be apparent right away or need to be tested for—are certain diseases or health problems. Sickle-cell anemia, for example, is passed from parent to child. So is Hemophilia. Both of these blood disorders can make a person very ill if a doctor is not monitoring the disease.

Heredity is not just a human occurrence. Whenever life reproduces itself, heredity plays a role—a major role. Plants were instrumental in first helping people understand heredity—specifically pea plants.

In the 19th century, a monk named Gregor Mendel had a garden. Mendel was a keen observer. Following the scientific method (which you will learn more about in Lesson 6), he noticed things about his plants. He hypothesized that they were passing traits down to their offspring. He then experimented and found that by **cross-pollinating** one plant with another he could predict the chance of certain traits (tallness or colored flowers) appearing. Cross-pollinating means fertilizing one plant with the pollen of another.

How did nature decide which traits your parents passed on to you? A human is much more complex than a pea plant.

The average human has 46 **chromosomes.** A chromosome is a type of blueprint or instruction manual. Each person's is different. This blueprint is carried in the nucleus of each of his or her cells. When a baby is conceived, the baby receives 23 chromosomes from one parent and 23 from the other. The chromosomes carry your **genes**, and your genes are what make you tall, short, brown-eyed, broad-shouldered, and many other things.

> ### FUN FACT
> Identical twins are the only humans who can have the exact same genetic make-up as another human being. In fact, if twin sisters married twin brothers, their two sets of children would be genetically brothers and sisters!

Yes, you may say, but why am I green-eyed when everyone else in my family is brown-eyed? Is my musical ability inherited?

Scientists do not know all the answers yet. One thing they have discovered, though, is that some traits are **dominant** (strong) and some are **recessive** (weaker). Some traits, like the Rh factor in our blood, are controlled by one gene. Others (like eye color) may be controlled by several.

One way to understand the chance of a child or offspring inheriting a particular gene is to use a table called a **Punnett Square,** invented by biologist Reginald Crundall Punnett in the early 20th century. An empty Punnett Square looks like this:

The top row here is for the male (father)'s genetic information. The left column is for the female (mother)'s information. Let's look at the case of Anne and Fred who both have—freckles! The freckle gene is a dominant one. Let's represent it with **F.** Each parent also carries a nonfreckle gene (NF). This means that back in the past some of the relatives in both families did not have freckles. However, since the freckling gene is stronger, when we look at Ann and Fred they both have freckles:

Here is a Punnett Square with Anne and Fred's genetic freckle information filled in.

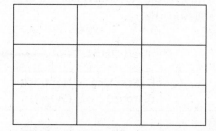

	F (Freckle) (Strong)	Nonfreckle (Weak)
F (Strong)		
NF (weak)		

What goes in the four empty boxes? If you think of the Punnett Square as working on the same principle as a multiplication table, you may be able to fill it in without looking below. The four empty boxes should be filled in like this:

FF	F/NF
F/NF	NF/NF

The boxes above show the possible freckle/nonfreckle gene combinations that each of Fred and Anne's children could inherit. This does not mean the couple will have four children or has to have four children. Think of a spinner being attached to the table above.

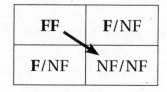

Every time Fred and Anne have a child, it is as if the spinner spins. There is a one in four chance that the child will carry only NF genes. That child will have no freckles and will not be able to pass them on to future generations. There is a two in four chance that the child will inherit the **F/NF** gene. That child would have freckles, but also might have children with no freckles. Here is the whole table together:

Anne (mother)   Fred (father) ⟶

	F (Freckle) (Strong)	Nonfreckle (Weak)
F (Strong)	FF	F/NF
NF (weak)	F/NF	NF/NF

And this is only one trait out of the many possibilities of 46 chromosomes!

Practice Exercise 12

Match the terms on the left with the correct definitions on the right.

_____ 1. Chromosomes   (A) The fertilization of one plant by another

_____ 2. Cross-pollination   (B) Weak

_____ 3. Dominant   (C) The passing of traits from parents to offspring

_____ 4. Traits   (D) Strong

_____ 5. Genes   (E) You receive 23 from each parent

_____ 6. Heredity   (F) A feature inherited from either parent

_____ 7. Recessive   (G) Instructions in your chromosomes that determine your traits

Practice Exercise 13

Fred and Anne have three children. Delilah, the eldest, has no freckles. Samson and Hercules, identical twins, have freckles. Answer the following questions about Fred and Anne's family.

1. According to the Punnett Square above, which one of the genetic combinations must Delilah have?
   (A) FF
   (B) F/NF
   (C) NF/NF
   (D) It is not possible to know just by looking at her.

2. According to the Punnett Square, which of the following statements is the only one that **cannot** be true of the twins?
    (A) They have no freckle genes at all (NF/NF).
    (B) Being identical twins, they must carry the same freckle genes.
    (C) They may both carry a freckle gene (F) and a nonfreckle gene (NF).
    (D) They may both carry two freckle genes (FF).

LESSON 5: EVOLUTION

For thousands of years, people have wondered about the rich **diversity** of life that we see around us. How did all this variety begin? Where did all these life forms come from? Many people believed that all **species** (types or families of living things) came into being exactly as they appear now and have never changed. But not everyone believed this.

Charles Darwin was a 19th century scientist. Darwin had traveled **extensively** all over the world. He had been in different environments and seen many strange plants and animals. In 1859, he published a book called *On the Origin of Species by Means of Natural Selection*. In it he introduced the public to concepts unfamiliar to most: natural selection and evolution.

The basic principle behind both these ideas is that species do not stay the same forever; they change and **adapt** to their environments. These changes are so gradual that to see their progress scientists must compare present-day plants and animals to the **fossils**, or remains, of those who lived long ago.

Natural selection means that living things that are adapted well to the world around them tend to live longer and have more **offspring** (babies). Living things that are not as well adapted do not live as long or reproduce as well and eventually die out. For example, a bird that eats nuts with hard shells would need a strong beak to crack them. Naturally the bird does not think, "I'm going to grow a stronger beak." What happens is that the birds with slightly stronger beaks get more food, live longer, and reproduce with other strong-beaked birds. Over time (thousands of years!), the offspring of strong-beaked birds develop even stronger beaks. The end result of this process—the constant, gradual changes all species go through—is called **evolution**.

Practice Exercise 14

Match the vocabulary word on the left with its definition on the right.

_____ 1. species   (A) Children, babies, or young of a species

_____ 2. extensively   (B) A lot; largely; much

_____ 3. natural selection   (C) The remains of a formerly living creature

_____ 4. evolution   (D) To change or adjust to the environment

_____ 5. adapt   (E) A group of related living things

_____ 6. fossil   (F) The gradual change of all living things

_____ 7. offspring   (G) The process by which a species evolves

Many behavioral traits that have been developed by natural selection are passed down by what is called **instinct.** Instinct means to react to the environment in a way that is beneficial for the organism, but without necessarily thinking about it or knowing why. For example, a domestic cat, which has never had to hunt for its food, still has a hunting instinct. If it sees a mouse, it will **instinctively** want to catch or even eat it.

Practice Exercise 15

1. Jessica has a rabbit that lives in a hutch in the backyard. Jessica notices that whenever a hawk flies overhead, the rabbit freezes (remains motionless) even though the hawk cannot get into the hutch. What is the most likely reason for the rabbit's behavior?
   (A) The rabbit is afraid the hutch door is unlocked.
   (B) The rabbit is injured.
   (C) The rabbit's ancestors stayed safe from danger by staying still and hiding.
   (D) The rabbit's ancestors were all eaten by hawks.

2. The Giant Anteater of Central and South America eats ants—hence its name. Below is a list of some of the attributes of the Anteater.

   - Sharp claws
   - Poor eyesight
   - Long tongue
   - Good sense of smell
   - Long **snout** (nose)
   - No teeth

   Which combinations of traits are logically the most helpful to the Giant Anteater in finding ants underground?
   (A) Sharp claws, poor eyesight, and long tongue
   (B) No teeth, long tongue, and good sense of smell
   (C) Sharp claws, long snout, and no teeth
   (D) Sharp claws, long snout, and good sense of smell

Humans are products of evolution as well as other living beings. Humans have developed and changed greatly over thousands of years. We have adapted successfully to environments all over the globe. One of the biggest factors in our success is our ability to think, reason, and problem-solve in new situations.

Practice Exercise 16

Harland lives on a quiet street in a small town. One cold night, in the middle of winter, he hears a loud bang outside. He runs out of the house in his stocking feet with no coat on. He leaves his keys inside and accidentally locks the front door. He does, however, have his phone in his pocket.

Suggest some ways that Harland could use problem-solving skills to help himself out of his **predicament** (bad situation).

_____

_____

_____

_____

One of the ways humans use their brains to their advantage is by inventing **tools** that greatly increase their chances of survival. Although there are examples in the animal kingdom of using and even making tools, human tool making is incredibly varied and complex.

Practice Exercise 17

1. Humans, unassisted by their inventions, can comfortably exist in a very narrow range of climates. However, humanity in modern times has expanded to every continent and environment on Earth. List some of the tools and inventions (old and new) that make this possible:

_____

_____

_____

_____

_____

_____

_____

_____

2. Which of the following is an example of tool use in animals?
   (A) A bird uses its beak to crack seeds.
   (B) A chimpanzee uses a twig to fish for termites.
   (C) A bear uses its claws to catch a salmon.
   (D) A fish uses its tongue to lure smaller fish.

LESSON 6: SCIENTIFIC METHOD

In Lesson 5 you learned about classification of animals. Now you will use those skills to classify—statements! When you understand how scientists classify information, you will take the first step toward discovering the **scientific method**—the procedure used to make great discoveries like Jonas Salk's polio vaccine and Albert Einstein's Theory of Relativity.

Scientists classify each statement as fact, hypothesis, or opinion.

A **fact** can be proven with evidence. Carol has successfully passed the GED. She has her certificate, and there are state records to prove it.

A **hypothesis** is a theory, or guess, based on some observation. It requires more observation to be proved true or false. Carol believes the GED is a valuable career tool. She bases this on her own experience. She could test this by interviewing other GED recipients. Hypotheses often include the words *might* or *may*.

An **opinion** cannot be proved or disproved. Carol thought GED class should have been held at 5:00 P.M., not 4:30. Others may have thought differently. Opinions often contain the words *ought to, too much, not enough*, and other words that indicate judgment.

Practice Exercise 18

Read the following sentences and decide whether each is a fact (F), hypothesis (H), or opinion (O).

_____ 1. Nguyen thinks he might be able to get to work faster if he takes I-95 instead of the Expressway.

_____ 2. Only children should drink milk.

_____ 3. The Monarch butterfly is the most beautiful of all butterflies.

_____ 4. A hummingbird's wings beat up to 90 times each second.

_____ 5. The presence of water on a planet other than Earth might indicate the presence of life as well.

_____ 6. The nervous system is the communication system of the human body.

_____ 7. If Denise walks one mile every day, in addition to dieting, it may help her to lose weight faster.

_____ 8. Watching a movie is more fun than cleaning the garage.

The scientific method, which is used to make new discoveries, has five steps. Let us look at Nguyen, above, who is interested in finding a faster way to get to work.

1. **ASK A QUESTION BASED ON OBSERVATION.** Nguyen passes a section of I-95 when he takes the Expressway to work. He notices there often seems to be less traffic on I-95. He asks himself, "Would it be quicker if I took I-95 to work instead of my current route?"

2. **GATHER INFORMATION.** Nguyen listens to traffic reports for one week to see if traffic jams are a problem on I-95. He also plots his work route both ways online to see if the distance is the same.

3. **FORMING A HYPOTHESIS.** Nguyen states to himself: "It might take less time to get to work if I took I-95."

4. **TESTING THE HYPOTHESIS.** Nguyen takes I-95 to work every day for a week. He keeps a record of the time he leaves his house and the time he gets to work each day. He compares this to his leaving and arrival times for one week using the Expressway.

5. **DRAWING CONCLUSIONS.** Nguyen finds that on average he saves 10 minutes in the morning by using I-95 instead of the Expressway. He therefore decides to change his work route.

Sometimes when scientists test their hypotheses, their conclusions are not so exact. Suppose Nguyen had found out that he saved time from Monday to Thursday, but he actually lost time on Friday? He would have to do further testing to determine whether this was a one-day event or a traffic pattern that occurred every Friday.

Practice Exercise 19

Read the following passage and answer the question.

Adwoa is interested in switching to nontoxic household products to clean. She feels that using natural products like lemon, vinegar, and baking soda will be better for the environment and safer for her children. One thing she doesn't know is: will natural products clean as well as the brands she is used to? Adwoa goes to several **reputable** environmental websites and reads about how to best use nontoxic products. She thinks they might work for her. What is the next best step for Adwoa to take?

(A) Buy all of the products the websites recommend and throw out all her old supplies.
(B) Alternate between using natural and her usual products to make sure everything is really clean.
(C) Experiment with some of the recommended natural products to see if they clean satisfactorily.
(D) Mix the natural products and her usual cleaners together.

Design an Experiment for Lalita!

Lalita has always kept her potatoes in the refrigerator because her mother once told her that potatoes left in a cupboard could sprout. Lalita wonders if this is really so. She always thought that plants needed sunlight to grow. It occurs to her that the refrigerator is dark like the cupboard. The refrigerator is colder than the cupboard, of course. Could that make the difference? Will potatoes in a dark, warm place sprout faster than potatoes in a dark, cold place?

Lalita's question, based on observation, is the first step of the scientific method. Using Nguyen's example and the prompts below, design an experiment to help Lalita find out what she wants to know.

(STEP 2) Gather information

_____

_____

_____

_____

_____

STEP 3 Form a hypothesis

_____

_____

_____

_____

STEP 4 Test the hypothesis

_____

_____

_____

_____

_____

STEP 5 Draw a conclusion

_____

_____

_____

_____

_____

ANSWERS TO "DESIGN AN EXPERIMENT FOR LALITA"

STEP 2 Gather information: Lalita looks at a few gardening websites (or other reputable gardening information sources) to find out what plants need in general. She also researches whether potatoes have any special requirements.

STEP 3 Form a hypothesis: Lalita states to herself, "I think potatoes will sprout quicker in a cupboard than in the refrigerator."

STEP 4 Test the hypothesis: Lalita takes out two organic potatoes from the same bag. She places one in the vegetable drawer in the refrigerator (where she usually keeps her potatoes). She places the other in the cabinet under her sink. She monitors them once a day for two months.

STEP 5 Draw a conclusion: Lalita finds that the potato in the cupboard begins to sprout between 30 and 40 days into her experiment. She concludes that the refrigerator is the best place to store potatoes after all. Mom was right!

LESSON 7: GRAPHIC MATERIALS

One of the best ways to illustrate **quantitative** information—information that depends on numbers and measurement—is with a **graphic**. A graphic is a pictorial representation of the information. In this lesson, we will look at diagrams, charts/tables, and different types of graphs.

Just like a paragraph, a table has a main idea and supporting details. The following table provides dates for the first five large mammals domesticated by humans.

First Five Large Domestic Mammals (Approximate Dates)

Species	Date (B.C.)	Place
Dog	10,000	Southwest Asia, China, North America
Sheep	8,000	Southwest Asia
Goat	8,000	Southwest Asia
Pig	8,000	China, Southwest Asia
Cow	6,000	Southwest Asia, India, North Africa

—based on a chart by Jared Diamond in *Guns, Germs and Steel*

The main idea of a table is contained in the **header.** How can you express this header in your own words?

_____

_____

You might have said that these are the first five animals that were bred and trained to live and work with people.

The horse is a common domesticated large animal in many parts of the world. Why do you think that the horse is not on this list?

_____

_____

The most logical conclusion is that the horse was domesticated after 6,000 B.C.

A longer version of this table lists nine other mammals. Would you expect to find the chicken on this list? Why or why not?

_____

_____

A chicken would not be part of a longer table. While it is a useful domestic animal, it is not a mammal, and it is not large.

Tables and charts can also help to organize classifications. Look at the following table of human body systems, and use it to complete the exercise on page 388.

Human Body Systems and Functions

System	Function
Respiratory/Circulatory	Transport oxygen and nutrients to all cells
Skeletal	Support the body
Digestive	Digest food, pass nutrients to the body and waste to the outside
Immune	Fight infection
Nervous	Provide a communication network
Reproductive	Create offspring (children)
Muscular	Move the body

Practice Exercise 20

For each statement below, enter a (T) for true or an (F) for false.

_____ 1. A strong immune system keeps you healthy.

_____ 2. Bones do not need muscles to move.

_____ 3. The nervous system is the transportation system of the body.

_____ 4. Your digestive system can tell the difference between nutrients and waste.

_____ 5. Respiratory and circulatory systems work together to get oxygen to your cells.

_____ 6. Your reproductive system can fight infection on its own.

Diagrams can also be used to present information. The diagram below is called a **Venn diagram**. It is used when comparing different groups, some of whom share the same characteristics. In this particular diagram, the left circle represents plants that reproduce asexually. Two examples are tulips, which reproduce through bulbs, and potatoes, which reproduce through tubers. Neither require pollination. The right circle represents plants that reproduce sexually, through pollination. Examples are geraniums, corn, and roses. The center section holds mosses and ferns, plants that share characteristics of BOTH circles. They are known to reproduce sexually and asexually.

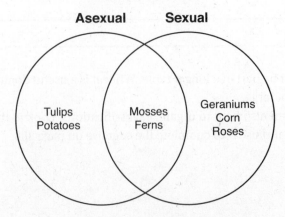

Plant Reproducers

The following is an example of a different, more complex type of Venn Diagram.

Methods of Animal Locomotion

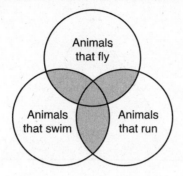

The circles interconnect because each group of animals has members that fit into one or more categories. For example, fish would be placed in the "animals that swim" circle. But what about alligators? They swim and run. They are placed in the **dark** area between "animals that swim" and "animals that run."

The following Venn diagram uses the same categories as the one above. Place the animals correctly. The first three are done for you.

Methods of Animal Locomotion

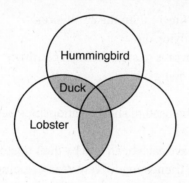

(1) Lobster	(6)	Cheetah
(2) Hummingbird	(7)	Ostrich
(3) Duck	(8)	Horses
(4) Giraffe	(9)	Great white shark
(5) Eagle	(10)	People

How did you fill out your diagram? What did you discover? You may have noticed several animals that swim and run, a few that swim and fly, and none that fly and run. A lobster swims and can crawl on land, but it cannot run. A hummingbird's feet are not designed to paddle or to support its weight on the ground. Giraffes run but have never been observed swimming. These three animals go in the separated, light sections of the diagram. A duck can swim and fly, so it fits in the dark area between "animals that swim" and "animals that fly." Ducks do not run; they waddle. Eagles fly, but they do not run or swim. Cheetahs and ostriches, although they do not like to swim, can do it if necessary. Put them in the dark area between "animals that run" and "animals that swim." Horses can swim

Trivia Point

A few creatures on Earth can run, swim, and fly. One of these is the pink flamingo.

and run and are very good at both. They are classified with the cheetahs and ostriches. Great white sharks do not run or fly (and it is a lucky break for us that this is so!). People can run and swim. Flying by airplane or helicopter does not count.

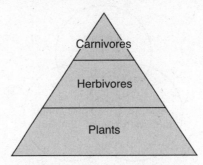

The Food Chain (Simplified)

Diagrams can be used to show relationships of size or quantity between groups. The pyramid diagram above is a simplified representation of part of the food chain. Carnivores (meat eaters) eat herbivores, which, in turn, eat plant foods.

Practice Exercise 21

1. What does the shape of the pyramid imply about the relationship between herbivores and carnivores?
   - (A) The herbivores are bigger than the carnivores.
   - (B) The carnivores are dying out.
   - (C) It takes many herbivores to support each carnivore.
   - (D) The herbivores are dying out.

Another diagram that can be used to show relationships between groups or individuals is the multiline graph.

Molly, Sara, and Danielle have each been told by their doctors to lose 10 pounds for health reasons. In January, the three friends made New Year's resolutions together to live healthier lifestyles. Molly limited desserts to once a week. In March, she added ½ hour of exercise twice a week. Sara started January exercising 1 hour daily, eating no desserts, and severely limiting her fat intake. However, her schedule kept her from maintaining her exercise and diet plan in March. In April, Sara started a new diet approved by her doctor and began exercising ½ hour three times a week. Danielle limited desserts to twice a week, monitored her meal portions, and exercised 25 minutes every day.

Below is a **multiline** chart of the friends' weight loss progress for 4 months. Before you begin to compare lines, however, it is important to read the title of the chart, and the information along the **vertical** (going up) and **horizontal** (going sideways) axes. The title at the top of the chart reads *Weight Loss per Month*. The numbers or scale along the left-hand vertical axis shows number of pounds. The horizontal axes lets you know the **time frame** or number of months the chart gives results for. Different multiline charts will have different scales along the axes; the horizontal axis is not always time, and the vertical is not always numbers. That is why it is important to thoroughly read each chart you find. Each line tracks one of the three friends' progress in losing weight. The key tells you that Molly's line is solid, bold, Sara's is dashed, and Danielle's is thin and solid. The higher the line reaches, the faster each girl is achieving her goal.

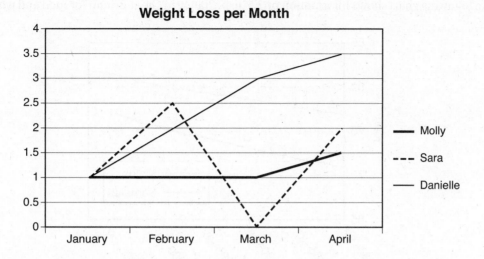

Weight Loss per Month

How much weight did Molly lose in January?

_____

The answer is 1 pound. Sara and Danielle also each lost a pound in January. You can confirm this by finding the word January on the chart. If you trace a line with your finger straight up, you will see that all lines rest at the number 1 line.

How much weight did Sara and Danielle each lose in February?

_____

_____

The dotted line is at 2.5 right above the word February. That means Sara lost 2.5 pounds in February. The skinny solid line (Danielle) is crossing the 2 line in February, so Danielle lost 2 pounds.

Practice Exercise 22

1. How much total weight has each friend lost? (Hint: find out how much each friend lost per month and add each girl's monthly losses together.)

    Molly   _____

    Sara   _____

    Danielle   _____

2. If the friends continue to lose weight at the same rate that they do in April (in other words, not increasing their rate) about what month will each one have lost 10 pounds?

    Molly   _____

    Sara   _____

    Danielle   _____

The following chart shows information on life expectancy in Great Britain for men and women.

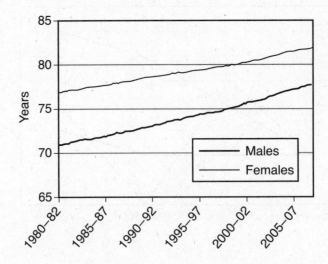

3. What do the numbers going up the left axis represent?

_____

4. What does the bottom axis show?

_____

_____

5. The chart's 2-year groups show you which years the data were researched. The graph does not give us any information for the years 1978 or 2011. How do we know that?

_____

_____

6. Which line represents males in Great Britain between the years 1980 and 2007?

_____

7. What is the life expectancy of a woman in Great Britain between the years 1985–1987?
   (A) 65 years
   (B) Between 70 and 75 years
   (C) Between 75 and 80 years
   (D) Between 80 and 85 years

8. What is the life expectancy of a man in Great Britain between the years 1985–1987?
   (A) 65 years
   (B) Between 70 and 75 years
   (C) Between 75 and 80 years
   (D) Between 80 and 85 years

9.   What is a conclusion that you can draw from the above graph?
     (A) Life expectancy is always increasing.
     (B) Life expectancy for both men and women in Great Britain increased between the
          years of 1980 and 2007.
     (C) Women always live longer than men.
     (D) Men always live longer than women.

LESSON 8: CRITICAL THINKING SKILLS
Main Idea

A piece of writing is like a bridge. The main point (or main idea) of a bridge is the road on top
that gets people places. One way to find the main idea is to ask yourself, "What is the most
important piece of information in this passage? What is the BIG message the author wants
me to get?"

   A bridge must be sturdy, so it relies on supports. A piece of writing relies on supporting
details. Look for the main idea and the details (or supports) that it stands on in each of the
readings in this section.

Practice Exercise 23

Questions 1 through 3 are based on the following passage.

What Do These Cells Do For Us?

Humans are made up of trillions of tiny cells. However, these cells do not all look alike. They
are specialized by **function**. Muscle cells do not look like bone cells, and blood cells do not
look like skin cells.

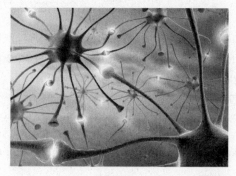

Neuron

   Brain cells or neurons' job is to communicate. Neurons have a particular adaptation that
allows them to do their jobs. Each neuron has a long extension called an **axion** to transmit

information and many short extensions called **dendrites** to receive it. As neurons in your brain send messages to each other they create pathways. Creating pathways and connections between neurons is one of the most important things a person can do to keep his or her mind keen and active, since new neurons cannot be created when old neurons die. We create pathways by using our brains. You have 100 billion neurons—think of the pathways you can create by keeping all of them healthy!

1. What is the main idea of the first paragraph?
   (A) Every cell in the human body looks different.
   (B) Human cells look different depending on what job they do.
   (C) Humans are made up of cells.
   (D) There are 50 trillion cells in the human body.

2. Which sentence best expresses the main idea for the second paragraph?
   (A) We create pathways by using our brains.
   (B) As neurons in your brains send messages to each other, they create pathways.
   (C) Brain cells or neurons' job is to communicate.
   (D) Neurons have a particular adaptation that allows them to do their job.

Questions 3 through 5 are based on the following chart.

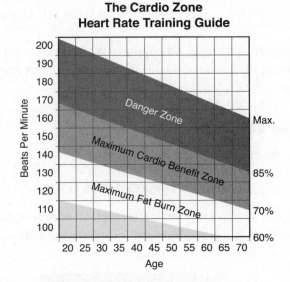

3. What is the main purpose of the above chart?
   (A) It helps people target the best heart rate for their exercise sessions.
   (B) It warns people when they should go to the doctor.
   (C) It tells people how much weight they should lose.
   (D) It shows people at what age they should be doing each type of exercise.

4. Where is the most likely place on the chart for the main idea to be displayed?
   (A) Along the vertical axis
   (B) In the title at the top
   (C) Along the horizontal axis
   (D) In the key

5. Where on the chart are you most likely to find the main idea?
    (A) On the vertical axis
    (B) In the title at the top of the chart
    (C) Under the horizontal axis
    (D) In the key

Question 6 is based on the following passage.

What Do We Know About These Creatures?

The **pterodactyl** is one of the most misunderstood of all ancient creatures. The pterodactyl or **pterosaur** (winged lizard), was not, as many people think, a flying dinosaur. Dinosaurs are defined as standing upright and living on land. Pterosaur did neither. Nor was it the ancestor of today's birds. It had some similarity to modern birds—wings and hollow bones—but by the Cretaceous period (144–65 million years ago), these flying reptiles were far more massive than today's eagles and condors. In fact, the largest pterosaur **fossil** ever found, **Quetzalcoatlus**, had a wingspan almost 36 feet wide!

6. What would the best title for this passage be?
    (A) The Flying Dinosaur
    (B) Ancestor to our Modern Birds
    (C) The Cretaceous Period
    (D) Some Surprising Facts about Pterosaurs

Questions 7 and 8 are based on the following graphic and passage.

In 2011, the U.S. Department of Agriculture adopted the "Choose My Plate" graphic to help educate and encourage Americans to eat healthy. The plate graphic replaced a Food Pyramid design that many people found confusing. The USDA's original Public Education graphic, the Four Food Groups, was developed in 1956. It was abandoned in 1992 because of concern that it promoted **obesity** and cholesterol problems.

7. What is the primary message of the USDA's Choose My Plate graphic?
    (A) Eat balanced and healthy meals.
    (B) Only drink milk with meals.
    (C) Eat meat with every meal.
    (D) Always have five food groups at every meal.

8. What is the main idea of the passage below the graphic?
    (A) The USDA can't seem to find a good food picture.
    (B) The USDA listens to consumers and researchers when adapting its graphics.
    (C) In 1956, there was far more of a problem with obesity than there is today.
    (D) In 1956, there was far less of a problem with obesity than there is today.

Details and Conclusion

On the test (and in life), you will often be asked to look at or **evaluate** information and come to a conclusion, or make a decision. This is part of what we call critical reasoning, and is a crucial life and workplace skill.

As you work through the following passages and questions, tap into your life skills and experiences. Use your logic. If you are working in the classroom, take advantage of that fact to pool the knowledge of your classmates and work some questions in teams.

END-OF-CHAPTER QUESTIONS

Questions 1 through 3 are based on the following passage and diagram.

One of the most commonly used diagrams in genetic study is the Punnett square. The Punnett square can be used to show simple heredity in plants as well as humans. The square displays **genotype** (that is, what genes parents and offspring carry) and indicates **phenotype** (how the gene affects the appearance or behavior of the organism).

The Punnett square below shows results achieved by Gregor Mendel, a scientist who did groundbreaking work in genetics in the 19th century. Mendel crossed two pea plants, each with one dominant round pea gene (R) and one recessive wrinkled pea gene (w). The shaded squares represent potential genetic combinations for offspring.

	R	w
R	RR	Rw
w	Rw	ww

1. Since R (round) is dominant, any plant with this gene will have peas with a round appearance or phenotype. Of the above gene combinations, which will result in a pea plant with wrinkled peas?
    (A) RR
    (B) ww
    (C) Rw
    (D) None of the above

2. Genetic inheritance can also be expressed as a ratio. What is the chance that any particular offspring of these two plants will carry the R and w gene?
    (A) One in four
    (B) One in two
    (C) Three in four
    (D) Four in six

3. What conclusion can you make about a man who possesses both the genotype and phenotype for freckles?
   (A) He does not have freckles himself but could pass them on to his children.
   (B) He has freckles himself but cannot pass them on to his children.
   (C) He has freckles himself and could pass them on to his children.
   (D) He does not have freckles and cannot pass them on to his children.

Questions 4 and 5 are based on the following passage.

How Have These Creatures Survived?

Most of us shudder when we hear the word cockroach, but these little pests are marvels of adaptation. Cockroaches are some of the oldest inhabitants of the planet. They have been here for over 300 million years and have outlived countless other species. One reason is that many cockroaches will eat both **organic** (living) foods and **inorganic** foods like paste and paper. If no food is available, they are able to **fast** for several weeks. Cockroaches reproduce incredibly quickly. A female only needs to mate once and can produce up to 400 offspring in her lifetime. These **resourceful** creatures are also capable of surviving in stressful situations: they can go 45 minutes without breathing and withstand high levels of radiation.

4. What is the best concluding sentence for this passage?
   (A) No matter how incredible cockroaches are, they're still disgusting.
   (B) The cockroach is one of the most successful creatures Earth has ever produced.
   (C) Cockroaches will probably be here after humans are gone.
   (D) Cockroaches can withstand more radiation than other insects.

5. Based on the above details, which pest control measures would be most effective in your kitchen?
   (A) Washing dishes once a day
   (B) Dumping water on roaches to drown them
   (C) Storing only paper bags and boxes in lower cabinets
   (D) Spraying with an insecticide safe for children and pets

Questions 6 through 8 are based on the following passage.

What Do Scientists Hope to Find?

Where could the next long-awaited cure for cancer come from? What about the bottom of the sea?

Bioprospecting is the search for organic (living) material that can be used to develop new drugs. Most of the drugs we use today were developed from terrestrial sources. Both the willow tree and the herb meadowsweet, for example, contributed to the development of aspirin. Marine (saltwater) bioprospecting, however, is the new hot area for pharmaceutical companies seeking the next miracle drug. Marine bioprospecting focuses on sampling plants and animals from ocean ecosystems, in hopes of their yielding the next great discovery. No drugs are on the market yet, but about 25 continue to be tested for safety and effectiveness.

6. What conclusion can you make about terrestrial (land) and marine sources for new drugs, based on the information in this passage?
   (A) Marine ecosystems are currently more promising candidates for new drug sources than terrestrial ecosystems.
   (B) Drugs from terrestrial sources are dangerous.
   (C) Prescription drugs became much more expensive in the last century.
   (D) Drugs from marine sources are cheaper.

7. What is a conclusion that is NOT supported by the passage's details?
   (A) Leads for drug sources on dry land may open up again.
   (B) The ocean is a rich untapped source for new medical discoveries.
   (C) Further investigation into marine sources for drugs are yielding rich discoveries.
   (D) This is an exciting time in pharmaceutical research.

8. Based on the evidence in the passage, is it reasonable to conclude that marine bioprospecting has been successful?
   (A) Yes—it has yielded many possibilities for future treatments.
   (B) Yes—it has yielded many treatments that are in use today.
   (C) No—it has been much more expensive than bioprospecting on land.
   (D) No—marine bioprospecting could pollute the oceans and endanger marine wildlife.

Questions 9 through 11 are based on the following table and passage.

Blood Types	O	A	B	AB
Can donate blood to:	All	A, AB	B, AB	AB
Can receive blood from:	O	O, A	O, B	All

The above table shows the four major blood types. In an emergency, it is crucial for medical personnel to know a patient's blood type. A patient who loses blood due to severe **trauma** (injury) may require a **transfusion** of blood from another person.

In addition to knowing if your blood type is A, B, AB, or O, you should know if you belong to a positive or negative blood group. Most hospitals will not risk complications that might arise from giving positive blood to a type negative patient.

It is a wise precaution to carry a card in your wallet with your blood type and significant medical information on it. Although hospitals have safety procedures in place to minimize the chance of giving a patient the wrong blood or medicine, such information could save valuable time in an emergency situation.

9. What do you think the result would NOT be if a type O patient were given type AB blood?
   (A) He would get a little sick.
   (B) He would get dizzy and have to lie down.
   (C) The doctors would have to get the blood back out of him.
   (D) He would need to be watched in case of a severe reaction.

10. Two brothers come to an emergency room. One has had an accident and needs a transfusion. The other volunteers as a blood donor for his brother. What is one of the first things you think the doctor will do?

(A) Tell the brother to go away—the hospital has enough blood.

(B) Have the brother's blood tested to see if it is compatible with the patient's.

(C) Assume the brother is okay as a donor—after all, they're brothers!

(D) Make them both wait in the waiting room.

11. A patient comes to the hospital needing a rare type of blood, of which the hospital has very little. What do you think the hospital administration will do?

(A) Admit him and start contacting nearby hospitals to add to the needed supply.

(B) Tell him to go away—there are other hospitals.

(C) Admit him but tell him he will have to find his own donor.

(D) Admit him and hope the supply on hand is enough.

Questions 12 and 13 are based on the following passage.

What Is the Best Way to Be Safe?

Once a year, in December, many households follow a tradition of cutting down a **coniferous** tree and bringing it into the house for the holidays. Most people do not think of their holiday tree as a living thing. Very few probably know that half a tree's weight consists of water, and when in the ground it requires an inch of water a week. The National Christmas Tree Association recommends that anyone with a live tree inside provide a constant one quart of water per inch of stem diameter. That means for a tree with a trunk 4 inches wide, 4 quarts of water should be in the stand AT ALL TIMES.

12. What do you predict might happen if people neglect to follow the NCTA's recommendations?

(A) The NCTA will come and take their tree away.

(B) The tree might fall over.

(C) The tree could become a fire hazard.

(D) The tree could begin to mold.

13. Conifer forests are important **carbon sinks**—that is, they absorb more carbon from the atmosphere than they emit. What do you think might be the global impact if too many conifer forests were cut down?

(A) There would be more forest fires.

(B) There would be fewer forest fires.

(C) Global atmospheric carbon levels would rise.

(D) Global atmospheric oxygen levels would rise.

How Does the Snow Buttercup Survive?

Heliotropic plants move their flowers from east to west every day to follow the Sun in its path (helio = sun, tropic = to turn). Flowers that track the Sun often grow in cold climates, like high mountain ranges. An example is the snow buttercup. The practice of solar tracking helps the snow buttercup to capture the heat and light necessary to survive in its rocky, sometimes icy environment.

14. Heliotropic flowers move from east to west to follow the sun during the day. How do you predict they move their petals at night?
    (A) They stay still.
    (B) They wait to see if it will be cloudy the next day.
    (C) They turn so they will be facing east in the morning.
    (D) They close up tight so that insects inside will not escape.

15. Insects like bees often warm themselves inside the petals of heliotropic flowers. This benefits insects that need outside heat sources to warm up. After an insect has been warmed inside a snow buttercup, what will it probably do that benefits that plant?
    (A) Leave some honey.
    (B) Fly away without stinging the plant.
    (C) Carry the flower's pollen to another flower.
    (D) Chase harmful insects away from the plant.

16. It generally takes several hours for an insect to raise its body temperature high enough to be active. If you were to disturb a bee on an arctic poppy at dawn, what do you predict its response would be?
    (A) It would sting you as many times as possible.
    (B) It would appear **sluggish** and unresponsive, as if in a coma.
    (C) Other bees would come to its rescue.
    (D) The flower would close up.

Questions 17 and 18 are based on the following passage.

How Can We Keep from Getting Sick?

When food contains high enough levels of bacteria to make it dangerous for human **consumption**, we often refer to it as "spoiled." Some foods spoil more quickly than others and should be handled more carefully: Eggs, for example, and egg products like mayonnaise or meringue can spread **salmonella** bacteria if not handled properly.

One way to **inhibit**, or slow down spoilage, is to keep foods at a low temperature, as in a refrigerator or freezer. Milk, for example, will spoil in a matter of hours at room temperature, but can last up to a week in a refrigerator set at 45 degrees or colder.

17. On Wednesday, Edith brings her lunch to work: a tuna salad sandwich, chips, apple, and two oatmeal-raisin cookies. She leaves her lunch bag in her desk all morning instead of putting it in the office refrigerator. Edith feels fine after she eats lunch, but that night she feels nauseous and has a headache and low fever. What is most likely the cause?

    (A) The unrefrigerated mayonnaise in the tuna salad has given Edith food poisoning.

    (B) Edith needs to call the doctor before her symptoms get worse.

    (C) Edith is allergic to apples.

    (D) The bread in Edith's sandwich was stale.

18. What is the most likely explanation of the effect of refrigeration upon the growth of bacteria?

    (A) Refrigeration slows bacteria growth, which preserves food.

    (B) Refrigeration kills all bacteria.

    (C) Refrigeration will make spoiled food fresh again.

    (D) Refrigeration is not as good as freezing.

Questions 19 and 20 are based on the following passage.

NIH (The National Institutes of Health) posts the following informational warning on its website:

Osteoporosis makes your bones weak and more likely to break. Anyone can develop osteoporosis, but it is common in older women. As many as half of all women and a quarter of men older than 50 will break a bone due to osteoporosis.

Risk factors include

- Getting older
- Being small and thin
- Having a family history of osteoporosis
- Taking certain medicines
- Being a white or Asian woman
- Having **osteopenia**, which is low bone mass

Osteoporosis is a silent disease. You might not know you have it until you break a bone. A bone mineral density test is the best way to check your bone health. To keep bones strong, eat a diet rich in calcium and vitamin D, exercise and do not smoke. If needed, medicines can also help.

19. Which of the following is NOT a cause of osteoporosis?

    (A) Having a small build

    (B) Having low bone mass

    (C) Having family members with osteoporosis

    (D) Having a family history of asthma

20. The NIH contains another page that lists triggers (causes) of a different condition. These triggers include:

- Anxiety
- Lack of food or sleep
- Exposure to light
- Hormonal changes

Is this condition likely to be:

(A) A broken bone
(B) A nosebleed
(C) A migraine headache
(D) An infection

Questions 21 and 22 are based on the following passage.

What Is Wrong at Rock Point Bay?

In 1 year, three new factories were built on the shores of Rock Point Bay. After 6 months, environmental biologists noticed that the fish population of the lake had decreased by 25%. Samples of lake water taken for testing also contained amounts of industrial fuels and chemicals harmful to humans.

21. What is the likely cause of these two phenomena?
(A) Employees of the factory are throwing their trash into the bay.
(B) Pollution from the factory workers' cars is contaminating the bay.
(C) Liquid run-off from the factories is contaminating the bay.
(D) Nearby townspeople are overfishing the bay.

22. As weather grew warmer in the Bay area, biologists noticed an **algae bloom** (large mass of algae) covering part of the bay for the first time. What is the most likely explanation?
(A) The factories became busier in the hot weather.
(B) The heat combined with the pollutants to create a good environment for algae.
(C) The algae were killing the fish.
(D) The algae would go away once the weather turned colder.

Questions 23 and 24 are based on the following passage.

How Does This Benefit Humankind?

People who require artificial heart valves may choose from either mechanical or biological implants. Mechanical valves' chief advantage is their **durability**; most will not wear out in a patient's lifetime. However, the patient must constantly take medications to keep the valve from triggering dangerous **clotting**, or clumping of blood cells. Biological, or animal implants require the patient to take fewer maintenance drugs. They do not trigger clotting. Biological valves, unfortunately, will not last as long as metal valves; under normal circumstances, they need to be replaced every 10–15 years, the lifespan of most donor animals. Although biological valves are easily obtainable (one of the animals most often used is the pig), the stress of major surgery every 10 years on the patient should be taken into consideration at the time of decision.

23. Why is it necessary for patients with biological valves to undergo surgery every 10–15 years?
    (A) Because the body begins to reject the biological valve.
    (B) Because the biological valves wear out at that time.
    (C) The doctors just want to look at the valve to make sure it's working.
    (D) Because the biological valves begin to cause blood clots.

24. What is the most likely reason that a biological valve would wear out in 10–15 years?
    (A) Because the patient does not follow his or her doctor's recommendations.
    (B) The doctor may not have inserted the valve properly.
    (C) The patient does not exercise enough; the valve cannot strengthen itself.
    (D) The valve was only meant to last for the natural lifespan of the donor animal.

CHAPTER 13 ANSWER EXPLANATIONS

Lesson 1: Plants and Animals

PRACTICE EXERCISE 1 (PAGE 367)

1.	C	5.	G
2.	E	6.	D
3.	F	7.	B
4.	H	8.	A

PRACTICE EXERCISE 2 (PAGE 368)

1. **(B)** is correct, since of the four choices, only "second-hand smoke," as it is called, enters the lungs. Impure water and raw food can be dangerous, but they pass through the digestive system. Chewing tobacco can cause cancer, but it is cancer of a different type.

2. **(B)** During the short winter days, the tree lives on energy it has stored during the summer. (A) There is no known test to determine if trees feel the cold, although they do not have the same nervous systems that animals do. (C) In a mild winter, trees would still respond to the change in light and shed their leaves. (D) is not supported by the passage.

Lesson 2: The Human Body

PRACTICE EXERCISE 3 (PAGE 370)

1. Your answers should have been (B), (C), and (E).

PRACTICE EXERCISE 4 (PAGE 371)

1.	C	5.	D
2.	E	6.	G
3.	A	7.	B
4.	F		

PRACTICE EXERCISE 5 (PAGE 372)

1. **C**
2. **B**
3. **A**
4. **C**
5. **B**

PRACTICE EXERCISE 6 (PAGE 372)

1. **(A)** is the most logical answer. The passage states that new laws were passed after the states had reviewed accounts of accidents; therefore, (D) is not relevant. (C), if it is true, is a secondary benefit—the primary function of the helmet is protecting the head. (B) does not address the question.

PRACTICE EXERCISE 7 (PAGE 373)

1. **A**
2. **C**
3. **F**
4. **H**
5. **B**
6. **G**
7. **E**
8. **D**

PRACTICE EXERCISE 8 (PAGE 374)

1. **V**
2. **I**
3. **V**
4. **V**
5. **I**
6. **I**

Lesson 3: Organ Systems

PRACTICE EXERCISE 9 (PAGE 375)

1. **B**
2. **E**
3. **D**
4. **F**
5. **A**
6. **C**

PRACTICE EXERCISE 10 (PAGE 376)

1. The best choice for Lillian is Sturdy O's. It has over twice the amount of fiber as Slim Snips and more than ten times as much fiber as Sugar Crunch.

PRACTICE EXERCISE 11 (PAGE 377)

1. **(A)** Clean and healthful. The examples that follow, washing hands and sneezing correctly, and avoiding touching the face, are examples of clean and healthy behavior.
2. **(D)** Spraying air freshener in the company bathroom. Air freshener, unless it contains disinfectant, will not kill germs.
3. **(D)** Try to keep going to work until you just can't get out of bed anymore. This action would not only be dangerous for you, but could spread the flu virus throughout your workplace. As soon as you know you are ill, you should stay home and concentrate on your recovery.

Lesson 4: Heredity

PRACTICE EXERCISE 12 (PAGE 380)

1. E
2. A
3. D
4. F
5. G
6. C
7. B

PRACTICE EXERCISE 13 (PAGE 380)

1. **(C)** *NF/NF.* Any other combination includes a freckle gene (F). Since the freckle gene is strong, even if Delilah had just one she would show freckles. (D) is wrong because it is possible to tell from Delilah's appearance (no freckles!) that she has no F gene.

2. **(A)** *They have no freckle genes at all (NF/NF).* This is the only statement that cannot be true. (C) and (D) The twins exhibit freckles. Therefore, they must have at least one freckle gene (F/NF). They may have two genes each for freckles (FF). (B) Identical twins must carry the same genetic blueprint.

Lesson 5: Evolution

PRACTICE EXERCISE 14 (PAGE 381)

1. E
2. B
3. G
4. F
5. D
6. C
7. A

PRACTICE EXERCISE 15 (PAGE 382)

1. **(C)** (A) Animals' actions are largely guided by instinct, not reasoning. (B) If so, the rabbit would not stop exhibiting distress when the hawk goes away. (D) This is illogical; if all the rabbit's ancestors were eaten, the rabbit would not exist.

2. **(D)** The claws help the anteater dig; the sense of smell leads it to food; the long snout and tongue help it to eat the insects.

PRACTICE EXERCISE 16 (PAGE 382)

Several suggestions follow:

- Harland could phone a friend to bring him extra clothes or an extra set of keys.
- Harland could knock on a neighbor's door and call a locksmith from there.
- Harland could phone a friend and ask to stay at the friend's house.

PRACTICE EXERCISE 17 (PAGE 383)

1. There are a great many tools and inventions that could be listed here.

Examples of ancient tools:	Examples of modern tools:
The wheel	The combustion engine
The axle	Airplanes and flying machines
Firemaking	Indoor heating and plumbing
The pulley	Vaccines/medicines
Cloth and clothes making	
Cooking and preserving food	

2. **(B)** This is tool use. All the other examples involve animals using or manipulating their own body parts.

Lesson 6: Scientific Method

PRACTICE EXERCISE 18 (PAGE 384)

1.	**H**	**5.**	**H**
2.	**O**	**6.**	**F**
3.	**O**	**7.**	**H**
4.	**F**	**8.**	**O**

PRACTICE EXERCISE 19 (PAGE 385)

1. **(C)** If Adwoa is using the scientific method to test her hypothesis, the next step is to test the new cleaners by themselves to see if they work. She should not throw out her old products—in case her hypothesis is false, she might need them!

Lesson 7: Graphic Materials

PRACTICE EXERCISE 20 (PAGE 388)

1.	**T**	**4.**	**T**
2.	**F**	**5.**	**T**
3.	**F**	**6.**	**F**

PRACTICE EXERCISE 21 (PAGE 390)

1. **(C)** It takes many herbivores to support each carnivore. The pyramid implies that each layer below must contain a bigger population to feed the one above. One lion must eat many antelope, and one antelope must eat many plants for each to survive.

PRACTICE EXERCISE 22 (PAGE 391)

1. Molly has lost 4.5 pounds, Sara has lost 5.5, and Danielle has lost 9.5.
2. Molly will achieve her goal in August, Sara in July, and Danielle in May.
3. They represent the possible ages each individual can reach (the label is years).
4. These are also years. Notice how they are arranged in 2-year groups (1980–1982, etc.).
5. The answer is because the graph only shows information between the years 1980 and 2007.
6. The thick line represents males, and the thin line represents females.
7. **(C)** Between 75 and 80 years. The thin line (women) above the label 1985–1987 is half-way between the 75 and 80 lines.

8. **(B)** Between 70 and 75 years. The thick line (men) is between the 70 and 75 lines above the same years.

9. **(B)** Life expectancy for both men and women in Great Britain increased between the years of 1980 and 2007. The line for women in 2007 is between 80 and 85, as compared to between 70 and 75 in 1980. The line for men is between 75 and 80 in 2007. In 1980, it is almost at 70 years. (A) and (C) are broad generalizations. (D) is disproved by the graph.

Lesson 8: Critical Thinking

PRACTICE EXERCISE 23 (PAGE 393)

1. **(B)** The paragraph emphasizes that human cells look differently based on their function, or job.

2. **(C)** Every other choice is a detail supporting the main idea of the paragraph.

3. **(A)** (B) The chart does not mention doctors. (C) The chart gives an optimal heart rate for fat-burning, but provides no guidelines on how much weight to lose. (D) The chart offers no advice on aging and exercise except what heart rate to maintain.

4. **(B)** This is the area where the most people would immediately benefit from the information.

5. **(B)** Because this is usually where the main idea of a chart is displayed, it is crucial to read the title first. (A) and (C) It is important to understand what the vertical and horizontal axes measure, but they each contain only part of the chart's information. (D) Some charts do not contain keys, but instead label the lines or bars being compared. Keys and labels should be read at the same time as the axes; however, they do not convey the main idea of a chart.

6. **(D)** (A) and (B) The passage states that Pterosaurs are not classified as dinosaurs, nor are they ancestors to today's modern birds (who are, in fact, descended from dinosaurs). (C) The passage does not focus on the Cretaceous period, except to say that Pterosaurs existed at that time.

7. **(A)** The USDA wants you to *eat balanced and healthy meals*. The other choices are too restricting—you are allowed some variety in your diet!

8. **(B)** The passage indicates that the government weighs input from several sources before changing public education diagrams.

End-of-Chapter Questions (Page 396)

1. **(B)** Only a plant with no round gene (R) will have wrinkled peas. Since R is a dominant gene, even a plant with one R gene will have all round peas and no wrinkled peas.

2. **(B)** *One in two.* The Punnett square shows two out of four offspring possibilities have the Rw combination. 2:4 reduces to 1:2.

3. **(C)** Having the genotype for a trait means it may be passed to one's children. Having the phenotype means one shows the trait oneself.

4. **(B)** In terms of **longevity** (number of years on Earth) and adaptability (ability to change to fit the environment), this is true. (A) is an opinion. (C) is a prediction. (D) is not substantiated by the passage.

5. **(D)** None of the other methods is likely to cure an infestation problem. Cockroaches do not drown easily, and they may eat or live in bags and boxes. Leaving unwashed dishes in the sink all day will only encourage them.

6. **(A)** The passage states that marine bioprospecting is a "new hot area." (B) The terrestrial example given (aspirin) is not dangerous. (C) and (D) are not supported by the passage. No mention is made of cost, only of medical possibilities.

7. **(A)** The article does not speculate on the future of land-based leads for drug sources.

8. **(A)** *Yes*—Scientists are currently testing marine-based drugs for "safety" and "effectiveness" but not releasing them to the public yet. (B), (C), and (D) are not supported by the passage.

9. **(C)** Once a transfusion has been performed, there is no way to separate the donated blood out again. (A), (B), and (D) are all possible reactions.

10. **(B)** Close family members are not necessarily compatible blood types. The passage states that hospitals take safety precautions to avoid making anyone sick.

11. **(A)** Hospitals already have such networks in place. All the other possible choices are irresponsible.

12. **(C)** A tree is made of wood, and when it becomes overly dry, it may catch fire. (B) and (D) It will not fall over or mold (things mold when they are damp). The NCTA is not a policing agency and does not confiscate dry trees.

13. **(C)** If the forests are not there to absorb carbon, there will be more carbon trapped in the atmosphere.

14. **(C)** If heliotropic flowers begin each day facing east, then logically, this must be so.

15. **(C)** (A) Only bees make honey, and they do not take it out of the hive. (B) Insects do not sting plants; stinging is a defense when an insect feels another animal is attacking. (D) Insects do not protect flowers. They protect themselves and their nests or hives.

16. **(B)** The passage states that insects must be warmed by the Sun before becoming active. At dawn, the bee would still be too cold to react strongly.

17. **(A)** The passage states that egg products are prone to spoilage. (B) is a recommendation, not a cause. (C) Edith's discomfort is more symptomatic of salmonella poisoning than an allergic reaction. (D) Stale bread does not cause headache or fever.

18. **(A)** (B) and (C) are untrue. Killing bacteria is known as **sterilization**, and there is no known way as yet to make spoiled food fresh. (D) is an opinion.

19. **(D)** Asthma is a respiratory ailment, unrelated to bone mass. The other three choices are restatements of risk factors mentioned in the passage.

20. **(C)** These are possible triggers of *a migraine headache*. (A) A broken bone results from **impact** (a fall or a blow). (B) A nosebleed can have several triggers, but light and lack of food are not usually among them. (D) An infection requires an outside agent, such as bacteria.

21. **(C)** (A) There is no reason to suppose factory employees are any less responsible with their trash than other people, and they would not be likely to be able to generate enough waste to kill a large percentage of the bay's marine life. (B) Cars pollute the air. (D) Overfishing does not explain the presence of industrial chemicals.

22. **(B)** (A) If the factory alone did not cause the algae bloom before the hot weather, then an added factor is likely. (C) This is not supported by the passage. (D) This is a prediction.

23. **(B)** (A) and (D) These are defects of mechanical valves, not biological ones. (C) Major surgery is risky for the patient. A doctor would not recommend it simply to check on a valve. There are other, less invasive ways to tell if the valve is working properly.

24. **(D)** None of the other choices are supported by the passage, which states that biological valves will need to be replaced every 10–15 years *under normal circumstances*. The fact that they wear out does not indicate that the patient neglected his health or the doctor did not do the surgery correctly.

Earth and Space Science

14

On viewing a photograph of Earth from space:

> "From this distant vantage point, the Earth might not seem of any particular interest. But for us, it's different. Look again at that dot. That's here, that's home, that's us. On it everyone you love, everyone you know, everyone you ever heard of, every human being who ever was, lived out their lives."
>
> —Carl Sagan

This unit is all about our home—not only our home planet, but our home system! As you read about the past and present of Earth and the Solar System, think about the future of both. Our futures as individuals are not separate from it.

HOW THIS CHAPTER IS ORGANIZED

Lesson 1: Geology

Geology is the study of the stuff our planet is made from. Think a rock just sits there? You'd be surprised!

Lesson 2: Ecosystems

There are two ecosystems an Earth, terrestrial (land) and aquatic (water). Both interact to form our global environment.

Lesson 3: Weather

Weather is the study of the changes in our atmosphere and how they affect us.

Lesson 4: The Solar System

Earth and all our neighboring planets revolve around the Sun. This chapter is about our local neighborhood in space.

Lesson 5: Graphic Materials

Practice your comprehension of science information in the form of maps, bar graphs, and diagrams.

Lesson 6 gives you the opportunity to practice the skills of distinguishing fact and opinion, recognizing unstated assumptions, and comparing and contrasting information.

LESSON 1: GEOLOGY

Plate Tectonics

You may have heard that geology is the study of rocks. More specifically, it is the study of the physical history of the Earth and the changes it goes through. Some 200 million years ago, a map of the continents would have looked like this:

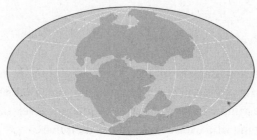

200 million years

135 million years ago, they began to separate:

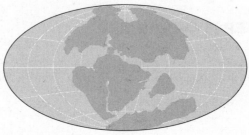

120 million years

And today they look like this:

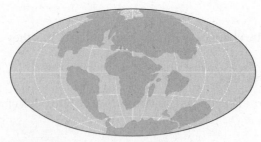

Present day

How can this be? How can an entire continent move across the ocean like a ship?

The Earth's Crust

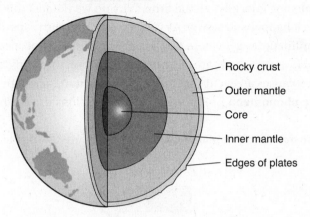

- Rocky crust
- Outer mantle
- Core
- Inner mantle
- Edges of plates

The Earth is not one solid mass all the way through. It is composed of many layers of different type of rock in different forms (think of the layers of an onion). The outermost layer is called the **crust.** Continents sit on **plates** on the crust. The study of the movement of the plates is called **plate tectonics**.

Now instead of an onion, let's think of an apple. If the Earth's crust was like the skin on an unpeeled apple, it would never move. But suppose someone peeled the apple and then tried to put the skin back on? The peel might cover the apple, but it would not be as stable as before. It would slip and slide.

Continents on crustal plates slip and slide against each other. The crustal plates ride on top of the softer **mantle** layer. Because they grind and push each other, they often change shape or become smaller as they destroy each other's edges.

Meanwhile, under the ocean, new crust is being formed by **magma**, hot liquid rock that pushes up from the mantle and cools. The magma fills cracks formed when two ocean plates are pulled apart.

Practice Exercise 1

Label the following statements true (T) or false (F).

_____ 1. Magma is extremely hot liquid rock.

_____ 2. Plate tectonics is the study of the movement of crustal plates.

_____ 3. Geology includes the study of weather conditions.

_____ 4. The mantle is the outermost layer of rock on the Earth.

_____ 5. The crust is the outermost layer of rock on the Earth.

_____ 6. Plates are only under continents, not under the ocean.

Earthquakes and Volcanoes

The Earth's plates are pulling apart (**diverging**), pushing together (**converging**), and sliding past each other (moving **laterally**) all the time. Why do we not feel this movement?

Mostly because it happens so slowly. As you can see from the maps above, it took millions of years for the continents to get where they are today. They do not speed around the oceans like powerboats! However, there are occasions when pressure builds up at or under the Earth's surface and causes an event that can affect large numbers of people and other living things. Two of the **phenomena** produced by these occasions are earthquakes and volcanic activity.

Earthquakes are most likely in places where two plates are sliding past each other in opposite directions.

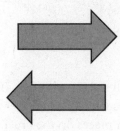

Some of the areas of the globe most prone to earthquakes are those around the **Pacific Rim.** The Pacific Rim is a ring around the Pacific Ocean. Here, the large plate that the ocean rides on meets all the plates that surround it.

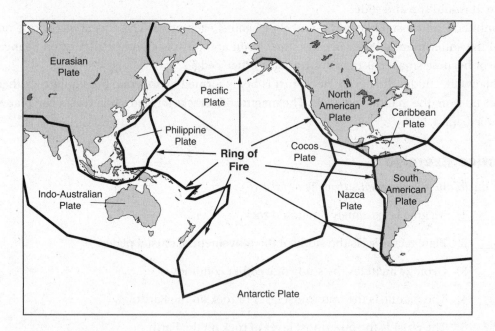

Cities in Japan, the west coast of the United States, and other countries that surround the Pacific Ocean often have extra-preparedness procedures in place because these areas experience earthquakes more often than areas elsewhere.

The Pacific Rim (or Ring of Fire, as it is sometimes called) is also prone to **volcanoes**. Volcanoes are mountains that may **erupt** and **spew** hot ash, gases, and liquid rock (**lava**) from the mantle into the environment.

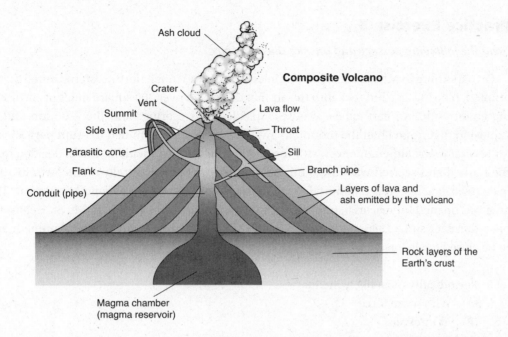

Composite Volcano

Ash cloud

Crater

Vent

Summit

Side vent

Parasitic cone

Flank

Conduit (pipe)

Magma chamber
(magma reservoir)

Lava flow

Throat

Sill

Branch pipe

Layers of lava and
ash emitted by the volcano

Rock layers of the
Earth's crust

A volcano may lay **dormant**, or quiet, for many years. In the past, people had few ways to predict when a volcano might erupt. In 79 A.D., in ancient Rome, Mt. Vesuvius erupted after being dormant for centuries. It buried the nearby towns of Pompeii and Herculaneum in hot ash. Today, an active volcano like Mt. St. Helens in the northwestern United States is monitored by **seismologists**. Seismologists study underground motion that can trigger earthquakes, volcanoes, and **tsunamis** (giant waves). In the event of the possibility of any of these events, emergency procedures can be enacted, and many lives can be saved.

> **Trivia**
>
> The largest volcano in our solar system is not on Earth—it is on Mars!

Practice Exercise 2

Match the terms on the left with the correct definitions on the right.

_____ 1. Volcano

_____ 2. Lava

_____ 3. Dormant

_____ 4. Ring of Fire

_____ 5. Seismologist

_____ 6. Erupt

_____ 7. Tsunami

(A) Quiet; Inactive

(B) Rim of the Pacific plate, where volcanoes are most active

(C) A giant wave

(D) A scientist who studies the motion of the Earth.

(E) Liquid rock spewed from a volcano

(F) To burst forth; to break out

(G) A mountain that emits hot gas, ash, and liquid rock.

Practice Exercise 3

Read the following passage and answer the questions:

On a morning in May in 1980, Mt. St. Helens, a volcano in the northwestern United States, erupted, blowing ash and rock into the air that destroyed over 200 square miles of surrounding countryside. An earthquake was responsible for triggering both the eruption and an explosion that ripped half the mountain away. The volcano continued to erupt **periodically** for several years, although never with the violence of the first incident. It was decided to let the burned and scarred wilderness on the mountain recover naturally on its own. In 1982, over 100,000 acres on the mountain were declared the National Volcanic Monument. This area was opened for research, public education, and recreation. Although Mt. St. Helens has been dormant since 1986, public safety scares have sometimes caused the Monument area to be closed to visitors.

1. **Periodically** most likely means
   (A) With more force
   (B) At intervals
   (C) Beautifully
   (D) Legally

2. Some people who lived on the mountain refused to leave, even when warned an explosion was **imminent** (about to happen). Sadly, they did not survive. Why do you think they chose to stay? What would you do if you were told you needed to leave your home immediately due to natural disaster?

   _____

   _____

   _____

LESSON 2: ECOSYSTEMS

An **ecosystem** is a balance of many living things—for example, plants, animals, and bacteria—which all benefit from their interaction. An ecosystem's health is dependent on getting the right amount of water, heat, light, and nutrients for all its members. What is the right amount? That **varies** for each individual system.

Ecosystems can be large or small. **Tide pool** ecosystems exist only in shallow puddles on the edges of oceans. They contain all kinds of specialized life forms. Tide pools are very fragile and easily destroyed. The seas around Antarctica, however, (an entire continent) are also considered one ecosystem.

Terrestrial Ecosystems

When several similar ecosystems combine together to create a larger system, we call that a **biome**. Two examples of **terrestrial** (land) biomes are desert and tropical rain forest, both of which contain many smaller ecosystems. The table below lists some of the major terrestrial biomes and some of their occupants:

Biome	Plants	Animals
Desert	Cactus, yucca, Joshua tree	Lizards, snakes, rodents
Mountains	Conifer trees, alpine flowers	Mountain goats, alpaca, snow leopard
Tropical rain forest	Coconut, durian, bamboo	Jaguars, parrots, bats
Tundra	Short shrubs, grasses, and flowers.	Arctic hare, caribou, reindeer

An important contributing factor to the health of all biomes on Earth is the planet's **water cycle**. Water is never used up completely—that is, it never disappears from the Earth. It is constantly recycled, up into the atmosphere, down into the **groundwater**, and into and out of rivers, streams, and oceans. This is necessary, as there are no water deliveries coming to us from anywhere else in the universe! Look at the diagram below:

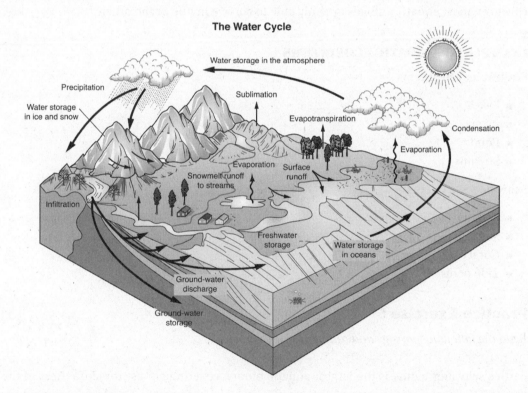

The Water Cycle

This diagram shows how important it is for all of us to work to keep our local water supply as clean as possible. **Contaminants** that get into the water in one area can easily be spread farther by the action of the water cycle.

TAKE IT TO YOUR COMMUNITY

What is the level of water safety in your community? Who is responsible for making sure the water supply is safe to drink? What precautions would you and your neighbors need to take if the water became temporarily undrinkable? Find out, and report back to the class.

Practice Exercise 4

Read the following statements and label them true (T) or false (F):

_____ 1. A terrestrial ecosystem exists on land.

_____ 2. A biome is usually composed of more than one ecosystem.

_____ 3. Coconut trees are often found in the desert.

_____ 4. A healthy ecosystem is a balanced community of living things.

_____ 5. Contaminants in one part of the water cycle will not spread to other parts.

Aquatic Ecosystems

There are two aquatic biomes on Earth: freshwater and saltwater (**marine**). Each biome contains a staggering variety of life forms, spread throughout many different ecosystems. Some few creatures, like the salmon, travel back and forth between fresh and saltwater homes. However, most **aquatic** animals are only able to survive in one or the other.

EXAMPLES OF AQUATIC ECOSYSTEMS

Freshwater ecosystems

- Lakes
- Rivers
- Ponds
- Streams

Saltwater ecosystems

- Oceans
- Salt marshes
- Coral reefs
- Tide pools

Practice Exercise 5

Read the following passage and answer the questions.

Earth's saltwater biome is the largest aquatic biome, covering almost three-quarters of the planet. The coral reef is an example of one of its tropical ecosystems. Coral reefs require very specific conditions to **thrive**. They do best in warm, shallow waters. The reefs are built by a fascinating creature called the **coral**, which has properties common to both plants and animals. Corals can **synthesize** food from sunlight through photosynthesis as plants do. They also catch food as a **predator** does. Corals cannot move, but they have **tentacles** to reach out and grab any small fish or organism that gets too close to the reef. Today many coral reefs are in danger. Their **fragility** makes them some of the most common victims of waterborne contaminants and diseases.

1. Which of the following is a fact stated in the passage?
    (A) The ocean covers almost 75% of the Earth.
    (B) The author has recently visited a coral reef.
    (C) The author thinks all coral reefs could disappear in the near future.
    (D) The author finds corals fascinating.

2. Which of the following is an opinion voiced in the passage?
    (A) The ocean covers almost 75% of the Earth.
    (B) The author has recently visited a coral reef.
    (C) The author thinks all coral reefs could disappear in the near future.
    (D) The author finds corals fascinating.

Practice Exercise 6

Match the terms on the left with the correct definitions on the right.

_____ 1. Marine (A) Grow and develop healthily

_____ 2. Aquatic (B) Make

_____ 3. Thrive (C) Saltwater; from a saltwater environment

_____ 4. Synthesize (D) Easily broken or hurt

_____ 5. Coral (E) Water; from a water environment

_____ 6. Fragile (F) A small marine animal that lives in warm, shallow waters

  Aquatic and terrestrial biomes are **interconnected** on a global level. All life forms on land need water, after all. Many terrestrial **inhabitants** like bears, humans, and sea birds take part of their diet from lakes and oceans. Some animals like turtles and seals spend equal amounts of time on land and in the water. **Algae** communities in the ocean act as carbon sinks in much the same way terrestrial forests do: The oxygen these tiny creatures produce is vital for the planet's well-being. It is important for future generations that we recognize the need to keep all our biomes as clean and healthy as possible.

> **Trivia**
>
> Did you know that most home aquariums and fish tanks are freshwater environments? Saltwater tanks can be set up in the home, but they are generally more expensive and require more maintenance than freshwater systems.

The Flow of Energy in Ecosystems

The **energy flow** through an ecosystem is a circle, and it all starts with the Sun.

The Sun is the ultimate source of energy for Earth's life forms. Some organisms—like plants—depend solely on the Sun for their energy. We call these organisms **producers**.

Other living things are called **consumers**. They must eat plants or other animals to gain energy. Humans are consumers. We cannot exist on sunlight alone! We need to eat to live, like other consumers.

The pattern of who eats what in nature is often called the **food chain**.

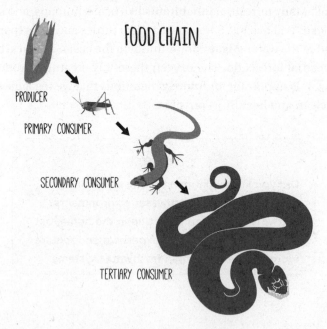

FOOD CHAIN

PRODUCER

PRIMARY CONSUMER

SECONDARY CONSUMER

TERTIARY CONSUMER

Animals who are 'higher up' on the food chain like humans or large **carnivores** do not have as much to fear from other animals as smaller or weaker animals like deer or rabbits. However, all animals eventually die and **decompose**. Then they feed producers by becoming part of the soil.

For an ecosystem to be healthy, the flow of energy must be balanced and work to the benefit of all organisms involved. This is hard to see on an individual level; how is it to the field mouse's advantage to be eaten by a hawk? On a larger level, however, that ecosystem works as a home for the field mouse population as a whole. When, as sometimes happens, a predator is eliminated or a new species is introduced, the balance is upset and the effects can be disastrous.

WRITING PROMPT

On Lake Hikoweehee, a certain type of frog that eats flies and mosquitoes is being killed off by pollutants introduced by a new development of vacation cottages. What do you think that will mean for the insect population? Write a paragraph in which you answer the question and speculate on how that might affect the people who now live on the lake.

ANSWER TO FLOW OF ENERGY WRITING PROMPT

The answer should predict that without the frogs to keep them in check, the fly and mosquito population will soon grow. This will most likely be an annoyance to the lake's community, but it could also be a health hazard, as flies and mosquitoes are disease carriers. The student may think of additional possible consequences.

LESSON 3: WEATHER

Atmosphere and Latitude

Weather refers to changes in Earth's **atmosphere**. The changes that we notice every day are those in temperature, wind speed, cloudiness, air pressure, and **humidity** (wetness). Some of Earth's **climates** experience fairly constant weather conditions from day to day. The island of Aruba has an average temperature of about 82 degrees year round and seldom gets rain. Other areas may register quite large daily or **seasonal** weather differences. Australia, for example, a country that inhabits an entire continent, experiences **monsoons** (severe storms), seasonal changes, and wide ranges of temperature. Australia's desert region may go for years without rain and then be **drenched** by downpours.

One significant factor in weather conditions is the **latitude** of a region. Latitude means how far north or south a region is.

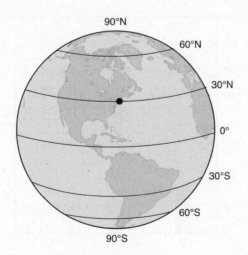

Regions near the **equator** (0 degrees) will be warmer year round because they get more direct sunlight. Regions closer to the poles (90 degrees north and south) have colder weather and harsher winters.

Practice Exercise 7

Match the terms on the left with the correct definitions on the right.

_____ 1. Atmosphere   (A)   Wetness; moisture level

_____ 2. Humidity   (B)   Completely soaked with water

_____ 3. Climate   (C)   0 degrees latitude

_____ 4. Latitude   (D)   Number of degrees north or south

_____ 5. Monsoon   (E)   The weather of a region

_____ 6. Drenched   (F)   A severe storm

_____ 7. Seasonal   (G)   The envelope of air surrounding the Earth

_____ 8. Equator   (H)   Referring to periodic changes in weather throughout the year

Climate Change

You may have heard the term "global warming" at some time in the past. **Global warming** is a phrase sometimes used to describe the negative effects of pollution on our Earth's atmosphere. It is misleading because it suggests that the only effect humans are having on Earth is to make it warmer.

A better term would be **climate change**. Earth's climate has changed naturally several times in its 4-billion-year history. However, scientists are now concerned that the effects of industrial development (such as burning coal and oil) are hurting our environment.

Carbon dioxide, methane, and nitrous oxide are just some of the harmful chemicals released into the air in the last few hundred years. Take a look at the following bar chart. Make sure to read the title, the scale on the left axis, and the scale that runs along the bottom of the chart and labels the bars. Then note the height that each bar reaches to.

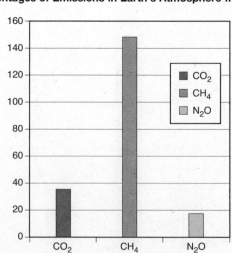

Rising Percentages of Emissions in Earth's Atmosphere from 1750–2011

Scientists estimate that total harmful **emissions** produced by human industrial activity have risen 17% in the last 20 years. They predict a continued increase of 1% a year.

What does this mean for us and future generations? What effects do these weather changes have on our lives?

The warming of the planet through **greenhouse gases** (such as those above) trapped in the atmosphere can lead to rising sea levels, more intense storm activity, and more frequent heat waves and **droughts**. An especially harmful effect of the use of CFCs (chemicals used in cooling and aerosol sprays) has been the depletion of the **ozone**. The ozone is a layer of the atmosphere that protects the Earth from UVB (ultraviolet) sunlight. UVB rays are thought to be factors in certain types of skin cancers.

Practice Exercise 8

Read the following passage, and answer the questions.

The phrase "think globally, act locally" means that what we do in our daily lives, in our communities, can help keep the whole planet healthy. One of the best ways to conserve energy and resources is to recycle. Many cities collect plastic, glass, and paper separately from other trash. If your community does not, why not work together with neighbors to see if you can get a recycling program started?

1. Which of the following is NOT a useful suggestion to avoid using **fossil fuels**?
   (A) Set the thermostat higher (warmer) on your air conditioner.
   (B) Replace regular light bulbs with long-lasting CFL bulbs.
   (C) Wash your car every week.
   (D) Turn the water temperature down on your water heater.

Practice Exercise 9

Read the following statements, and mark each one fact (F) or opinion (O).

_____ 1. Everyone should be able to conserve energy.

_____ 2. Adding insulation to your house will help you conserve energy.

_____ 3. Nitrous oxide emissions have risen almost 20% in the last 200 years.

_____ 4. It is better to bike to work than to drive a car.

_____ 5. Earth's climate sometimes changes on its own.

_____ 6. Fossil fuels should be banned.

Weathering

Weathering is the effect of different aspects of weather or the environment on the land. Water, wind, temperature—these all contribute to the breaking down of rocks. In this process, rocks, dirt, and sand often move from their original location. We call this **erosion**.

Some effects of weathering can be observed within a human lifespan. Others happen over millions of years. People who live in beach towns, for instance, know that the ocean may take rocks and sand from one beach, while it deposits land in another. The beach in Town

A seems to shrink, while that of Town B gets wider. However, the Grand Canyon in Arizona has been millions of years in the making. Its awesome beauty is proof of the eroding power of the Colorado River.

There are two types of weathering—**chemical** and **mechanical**. Chemical weathering actually changes one substance into another. A good example is when iron changes into rust upon being **exposed** to oxygen and water.

Mechanical weathering breaks rocks down through pressure, but the rocks themselves remain the same—only smaller. Examples of mechanical weathering are when glaciers break rocks as they move, or waves wear away rock on a **coastline**.

Practice Exercise 10

Connect the following vocabulary words with their definitions.

_____ 1. Weathering

_____ 2. Chemical

_____ 3. Mechanical

_____ 4. Erosion

_____ 5. Exposed

_____ 6. Coastline

(A) Left in the open air

(B) Movement of land or rock from one place to another

(C) The action of weather on rock or land

(D) Where land meets water

(E) The basic composition and substance of matter (things)

(F) Physical or of movement

LESSON 4: THE SOLAR SYSTEM

Planets

The **Solar System** is our local neighborhood in space. Eight planets and other celestial bodies (such as **asteroids**) **orbit** around the Sun, a class G2 star in the center. The planets in order of their distance from the Sun are Mercury, Venus, Earth, Mars, Jupiter, Saturn, Uranus, and Neptune. Pluto, formerly classified as a planet, is now considered a **dwarf planet**.

A total **revolution** around the Sun is called a year. Earth's year is approximately 365¼ days long, but other planets vary. Neptune's year, for example, is about 165 Earth years long!

Each planet also **rotates** or spins on its **axis**. Earth's rotation time is 24 hours—a day and a night.

Mercury, the closest planet to the Sun, has little to no atmosphere. It also has a rotation almost equal to its revolution, making Mercury's days and nights each roughly 59 Earth days long. These two conditions combine to make temperatures extreme on the little planet. In the daylight, Mercury can reach 800 degrees Fahrenheit. Compare that to its nighttime temperature of more than –200 degrees!

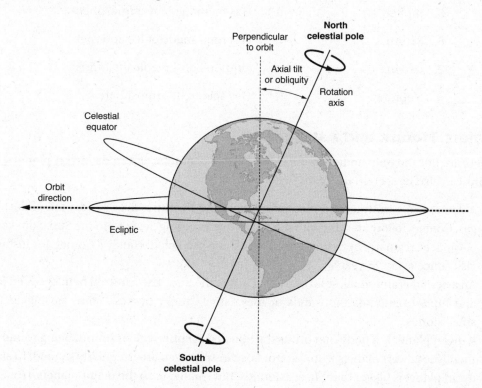

Venus, the second planet, is the closest in size to Earth. However, its surface is anything but inviting to Earth life forms! Venus has a hot, thick, poisonous atmosphere, full of **sulphuric** acid and carbon dioxide.

After our own planet, the next planet is **Mars**. Scientists have long been curious about Mars and for many years hoped to find life there. One of the reasons was that there is water on Mars. The water is frozen now, but some scientists see evidence that it once flowed over Mars's surface. Water is necessary to all life as we know it. Although probes have been sent to investigate Mars's surface, no indications of Martian life have yet been found.

Jupiter and **Saturn** are the giants of our Solar System. Composed of mostly gas rather than rock (as the smaller planets are), they both **radiate** more heat than they absorb from the Sun. Saturn, the smaller of the two, is **encircled** by rings made of ice and rock.

Uranus and **Neptune** are blue planets. Because they have so much methane in their atmospheres, red light cannot escape. They are the third and fourth largest planets in the Solar System and like Jupiter and Saturn, they are gas giants. Neptune is the planet farthest from the Sun at about 2.8 billion miles out. Like Saturn, it also has rings. Neptune radiates heat like the larger gas giants, but Uranus does not. Uranus's average temperature is about –350 degrees Fahrenheit!

Practice Exercise 11

Match each planet with the correct description.

_____ 1. Mercury   (A)   Has water on its surface

_____ 2. Venus   (B)   Is furthest from the Sun

_____ 3. Earth   (C)   Is the largest of the planets

_____ 4. Mars   (D)   Experiences extreme temperatures

_____ 5. Jupiter   (E)   Has methane in its atmosphere

_____ 6. Saturn   (F)   Has rings made of ice and rock

_____ 7. Uranus   (G)   Supports observable life forms

_____ 8. Neptune   (H)   Has acid in its atmosphere

Comets, Moons, and Asteroids

Planets are not the only bodies in our Solar System. **Comets**, **asteroids**, **dwarf planets,** and **moons** can also be seen in the night sky.

- A comet has a central solid mass of ice, gas, and dust (the head) and a tail of dust and gas. Comets follow an orbit with the tail always pointing away from the Sun. Some comets appear regularly in Earth's skies and can be predicted; Halley's Comet, for instance, visits once every 75 years.
- An asteroid is any small, solid body that orbits the Sun. The **asteroid belt**, between Mars and Jupiter, contains thousands of these small, rocky bodies—some no bigger than small stones.
- A dwarf planet is a body that orbits the Sun and is **spherical**, or round. Being round distinguishes dwarf planets from asteroids, many of which are irregularly shaped. In size, a dwarf planet is bigger than most asteroids, but smaller than the major planets. Our Solar System contains three dwarf planets: **Ceres, Pluto**, and **2003 UB313**.
- A **moon** does not orbit the Sun but another celestial body. Earth has one moon, which is about 25% of its size. This is actually a bit unusual. Many of the other planets have several moons (Jupiter and Saturn have more than 60 each!). The moons that circle around the other planets are also much smaller in comparison to the planets they orbit.

Practice Exercise 12

Read the following passage, and answer the questions.

When humans finally colonize space, it may not be a planet they first settle on—it may be a moon. One of Jupiter's largest moons, Europa, is about the same size as Earth's moon. Europa is rocky rather than gaseous like Jupiter and has an ocean of liquid water under an outer shell of ice. Furthermore, there is oxygen on Europa, not only in the water but in its atmosphere.

Even if Europa should eventually prove **inhospitable** to colonization, it would still be one of the best candidates for supporting extraterrestrial life in the Solar System. Scientists theorize that its oceans could support some of the same life forms found in deep sea habitats here on Earth.

1. Why does the author feel Europa would be a good place for an Earth colony?
   (A) It has liquid water and oxygen.
   (B) The gravity is the same as on Earth.
   (C) Europa is closer to Earth than any other celestial body.
   (D) Europa is bigger than the Earth; there would be more room for people.

2. Based on the context, what is the best definition of **inhospitable**?
   (A) Just right
   (B) Perfect
   (C) Not hostile
   (D) Not welcoming

3. An **unstated assumption** is a fact that an author assumes must be true in order to support the information in a passage. Which of the following is an unstated assumption made by the author?
   (A) People will never colonize space.
   (B) Extraterrestrial life needs water as much as life on Earth does.
   (C) Europa is one of Jupiter's largest moons.
   (D) Europa is larger than the Earth's moon.

LESSON 5: GRAPHIC MATERIALS

Maps

To get the full benefit of information from a map, it is important to read EVERYTHING on the map. This includes the title and information in the **key**. Key information is usually found in a small box on the map. It tells you what the symbols mean that are used on that particular map.

Practice Exercise 13

Read the following passage and map, and answer the questions.

Costa Rica is famous for its many volcanoes, although few are still active today. The map on page 426 shows the major volcanoes of Costa Rica. Each volcano is represented by a mountain ridge. There is no key, but there is a **scale**. This particular scale shows distance using **metric (kilometers)** and **imperial (miles)** measurements.

Major Volcanoes of Costa Rica

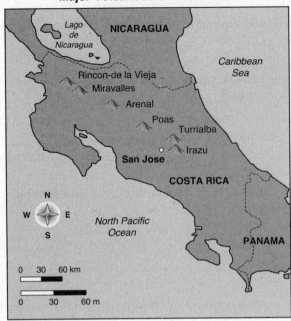

1. The Arenal Volcano is Costa Rica's most famous active volcano and a popular tourist attraction. Which volcano(es) would a tourist from the city of San Jose pass to get to the Arenal?

    _____

    _____

2. Which of the following can you infer from the fact that the Costa Rican authorities encourage tourism at all the volcanic sites marked on the map?
    (A) The Costa Rican government considers these sites safe for the public.
    (B) The volcanoes themselves are not that spectacular.
    (C) Too many visitors to the volcanoes is not good for the Costa Rican economy.
    (D) The volcanoes are off limits to all but scientists.

3. In kilometers (km), about how far is the distance between Arenal and the next volcano (Miravalles)?
    (A) 20 km
    (B) 60 km
    (C) 70 km
    (D) 100 km

Penny's science class is learning about **floodplains**. A floodplain is the land surrounding a waterway that can become flooded when the creek, stream, or river is too full. Penny's teacher asked the students to draw maps of their neighborhoods. He also directed the students to Internet sources to learn if any student's house lay within a floodplain. Penny lives close to Arundal Creek (her map is reproduced below). She found that the floodplain behind her house had advanced toward her house in the last fourteen years.

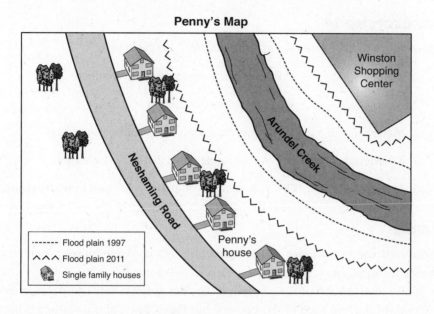

Penny's Map

4. What does the dashed line on the map represent?
    (A) The edge of the flood plain in 1997
    (B) The edge of the flood plain in 2011
    (C) The edge of public property owned by Arundel Township
    (D) The place where flooding will stop in 2012

5. Which of the following areas does the map NOT indicate?
    (A) Penny's neighborhood
    (B) Part of the Winston Shopping Center
    (C) Penny's school
    (D) The Winston Shopping Center parking lot

6. The Winston Shopping Center was built in 2002. Which of the following is a logical hypothesis that Penny's teacher could suggest?
    (A) The building of the shopping center caused the floodplain to shrink.
    (B) The building of the shopping center caused the floodplain to increase.
    (C) Penny and her parents will soon be moving to another house.
    (D) It is never safe to build a huge complex so close to water.

7. If Penny and her teacher believe that the shopping center has affected the floodplain, what is the next logical step to prove their hypothesis?
   (A) Refuse to buy anything at the Winston Shopping Center
   (B) Send a letter of protest to the shopping center's management
   (C) Gather more information
   (D) Waterproof the basements of all the houses on Neshaminy Road

Practice Exercise 14

Match the terms on the left with the correct definitions on the right.

_____ 1. Key   (A) A metric measurement of distance

_____ 2. Scale   (B) To evaluate or judge

_____ 3. Metric   (C) A box on a map that explains symbols

_____ 4. Kilometers   (D) A tool to measure distances on a map

_____ 5. Assess   (E) A system of measurement used in many countries

Bar Graphs

A **bar graph** helps you to **compare** and **contrast** different pieces of information. To compare means to look for similarities; to contrast means to look for differences.

Remember to read the title of the graph first. The bar graph below compares and contrasts rotation (length of day) on each of the planets and Pluto. Each of the planets is listed along the bottom (**horizontal**) **axis**. The number of Earth days is listed **vertically** on left side. It is important to read the information on both axes of a bar graph.

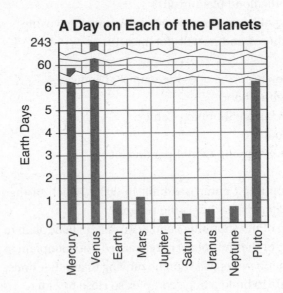

A Day on Each of the Planets

Practice Exercise 15

Use the graph on page 428 to answer the following questions.

1. A. Which planet has the longest rotation? _____

    B. Which planet has the shortest rotation? _____

    C. Which planet has a rotation of just over 1 Earth day? _____

2. This chart does not show any dwarf planets, moons, or asteroids. Which of the following is the most probable reason?
    (A) Planets are the only celestial bodies that rotate (experience day and night).
    (B) Planets are more important than asteroids or moons.
    (C) Because the chart's title specifies it is about planets, information on other bodies will not be listed there.
    (D) Astronomers generally have to guess at rotation times for bodies other than planets.

Questions 3 through 7 are based on the following graph.

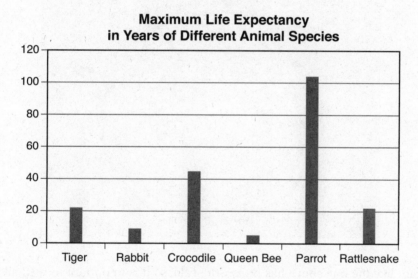

3. What does the scale of numbers on the left axis represent?
    (A) Years
    (B) Months
    (C) Days
    (D) Pounds

4. What does each individual bar represent?

    _____

    _____

5. Which animal on the chart has the longest life span?

    _____

6. Which animal on the chart has the shortest life span?

_____

7. The parrot can live up to 104 years. What implications does this have for someone who is thinking of keeping a parrot as a pet?

_____

_____

Diagrams and Illustrations

"A picture is worth a thousand words." Sometimes the best way to grasp a concept is to see it illustrated! This is especially the case when a situation involves many interconnected relationships. The illustration below shows the **Greenhouse Effect**, which demonstrates how light and heat from the Sun interact with our atmosphere.

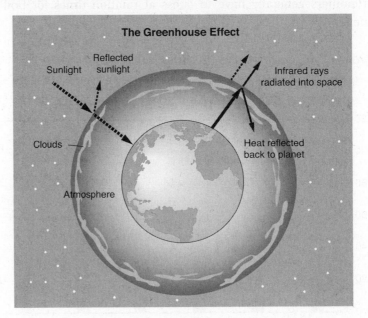

A diagram like the one above has no key or scale, so it is important to read all the labels carefully. The arrows above show the source and destination of heat and light. Light gray represents the atmosphere; dark gray represents space.

Practice Exercise 16

Answer the following question based on the above diagram.

1. One effect of pollution is the buildup of "greenhouse gases" that cause the atmosphere to retain more heat from the Sun and release less out into space. How would you show this shift toward retaining more heat in the above diagram?
   (A) The "heat reflected" solid, black arrow should be larger.
   (B) There should be no solid, black arrow pointing to space from Earth.
   (C) All the arrows should be smaller.
   (D) The "sunlight" dashed arrow should be larger.

The diagram below shows inhabitants of a polar ecosystem. Each animal is placed in its particular **niche** or section of the ecosystem. The polar bear is shown on top of the ice because that is where it spends most of the time. Polar bears are, in fact, excellent swimmers. However, to show the bear in the water would suggest that it spends the majority of its life cycle there. Likewise, creatures under the ice are shown at the level of water they live in the most.

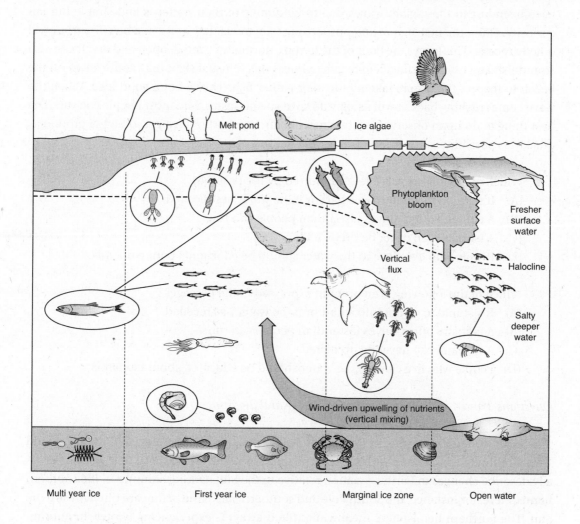

2. The word **halocline** labels a largely horizontal dotted line in the above diagram. Based on some of the other labels, what do you think is the best definition of halocline?
   (A) The depth at which the ice melts
   (B) The line where cold water meets warmer water
   (C) The line where saltwater meets fresh water
   (D) The depth to which the whale will dive

UNIT 3: SCIENCE

Questions 1 and 2 refer to the following passage.

People who live by the shore should be educated about the nature of tsunamis. Many lives have been lost to these giant waves due to ignorance of their patterns and simple human curiosity. Often the first sign of an approaching tsunami is that water in a bay or harbor will quietly **recede**. This leaves the floor of the harbor, normally covered, open and dry. It can also strand fish and other sea life. People who witness this unusual sight may come down on the beach to inspect the beach, take pictures, or gather fish. This is not a good idea. When the wave comes rushing back, it will usually do so at speeds faster than most people can run. The best thing to do upon observing waters receding from a harbor is to get to higher ground as quickly as possible.

1. Which of the following is a fact supported by the passage?
    (A) It's stupid to go out into a harbor if the water has receded.
    (B) A tsunami often moves faster than people can run.
    (C) A tsunami can never be predicted.
    (D) People who live close to the water should be educated about tsunamis.

2. Which of the following is an opinion expressed in the passage?
    (A) It's stupid to go out into a harbor if the water has receded.
    (B) A tsunami often moves faster than people can run.
    (C) A tsunami can never be predicted.
    (D) People who live close to the water should be educated about tsunamis.

Questions 3 and 4 refer to the following passage and diagram.

The Earth's tilted axis results in four separate seasons, spring, summer, fall (autumn), and winter. Although associated with weather changes in many areas, these four seasons actually describe changes in Earth's position relative to the Sun. During summer in the southern **hemisphere**, for instance, the South Pole and southern half of the planet are tilted toward the Sun. The northern hemisphere meanwhile (tilted away) is experiencing winter. In autumn and spring, the two hemispheres experience equal sunlight intensity.

The following diagram shows the seasons in the northern hemisphere:

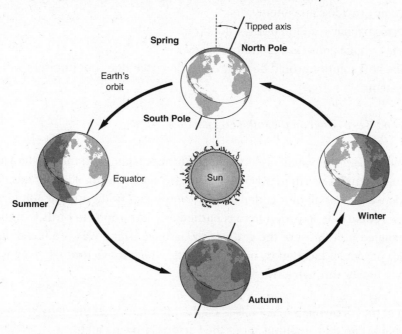

3. Which of the following is a fact based on the information in the passage and diagram?
   (A) Summer is hotter in the southern hemisphere than in the northern.
   (B) Summer is better than winter.
   (C) When it's autumn in the southern hemisphere, it's spring in the northern hemisphere.
   (D) It takes Earth 365¼ days to go around the Sun.

4. Which of the following is an opinion based on the information in the passage and diagram?
   (A) Summer is hotter in the southern hemisphere than in the northern.
   (B) Summer is better than winter.
   (C) When it's autumn in the southern hemisphere, it's spring in the northern hemisphere.
   (D) It takes Earth 365¼ days to go around the Sun.

Questions 5 and 6 refer to the following passage.

Building a dam is an example of a situation where changes to a water environment affect the terrestrial ecosystems around it. When a dam is built on a river, water levels behind it rise. Areas that were once above the water line can be flooded and end up deep underwater. People and animals that live below the dam may lose all or part of their access to water they need. In addition, the dam can act as a barrier separating those animals that live downstream from those who live upstream and blocking **migrating** species from making their **instinctual** journeys.

5. Which of the following is a fact based on the above passage?
   (A) Dams provide clean energy.
   (B) Dams usually result in upriver flooding.
   (C) The Canada goose is a migratory species.
   (D) The best solution would be to design a dam that does not interfere with local ecosystems.

6. Which of the following is an opinion based on the above passage?
   (A) Dams provide clean energy.
   (B) Dams usually result in upriver flooding.
   (C) The Canada goose is a migratory species.
   (D) The best solution would be to design a dam that does not interfere with local ecosystems.

Questions 7 and 8 are based on the following passage.

The Great Pacific Garbage Patch, also known as Garbage Island and the Pacific Trash Vortex, is several hundred miles worth of trash in the North Pacific Ocean. Some of it is floating and some is underwater, but all of it is dangerous (even toxic) to the marine life forms around it. The plastic **refuse** that is carried here is particularly hazardous to birds that may eat it or become entangled in it. Most of the garbage in Garbage Island was produced on land. It is carried to this particular location by ocean currents, which move through deep water somewhat as a river moves through a riverbed.

7. Which of the following is a fact based on the information in the above passage?
   (A) People can't do anything about the Pacific Garbage Patch.
   (B) Ocean currents transport man-made trash to one particular spot.
   (C) It will take decades to clean up the Pacific Garbage Patch.
   (D) Governments of the countries around the North Pacific should do something to stop Garbage Island from growing.

8. Which of the following is an opinion based on the above passage?
   (A) People can't do anything about the Pacific Garbage Patch.
   (B) Ocean currents transport man-made trash to one particular spot.
   (C) It will take decades to clean up the Pacific Garbage Patch.
   (D) Governments of the countries around the North Pacific should do something to stop Garbage Island from growing.

Questions 9 and 10 are based on the following passage.

When wind blows fumes from the active Kilauea volcano in Hawaii to the surrounding national park, The National Park Service offers the following safety advice to visitors:

- If you are indoors (museum, visitors center, etc.)—stay indoors with windows closed and air conditioning or air filter turned on—until conditions improve. You may be asked to **evacuate**.
- If driving a car: Keep vehicle windows closed and run your car air conditioner until you leave the area.

9. What assumption do these safety instructions make?
   (A) Closing windows will keep lava out of the house.
   (B) Breathing fumes from the volcano is dangerous.
   (C) You may be asked to evacuate.
   (D) People should not play around with volcanoes.

10. Which of the following is also assumed but not stated?
    (A) In case of volcanic activity, there will be time to evacuate visitors.
    (B) Safety procedures may be discontinued when conditions improve.
    (C) The Kilauea volcano is a beautiful sight.
    (D) It's worth braving a little danger for the sight of the Kilauea volcano.

Questions 11 and 12 are based on the following passage and graphics.

The Earth's crust or **lithosphere** is broken up into plates. Some, like the African or Antarctic plates, are quite large. Others, like the Juan de Fuca plate, are smaller. Crustal plates move in one of three ways:

■ **Diverging**, or moving away from each other.

This generally happens under the ocean, when new rock is pushing up from the **mantle**.

■ **Converging**, or pushing together.

Convergent motion can result in mountain ranges or volcanoes being formed.

■ Moving **laterally** or sideways.

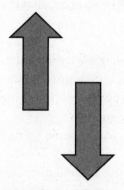

Lateral movement and occasional plate **slippage** is a major cause of earthquakes.

11. What is an unstated assumption made by the author?
    (A) Plate slippage causes earthquakes.
    (B) Plates cannot converge and diverge at the same time.
    (C) All crustal plates move.
    (D) The mantle is underneath the crust.

12. What is an assumption NOT made by the author?
    (A) People living on the plates can feel all three types of motion.
    (B) All crustal plates move.
    (C) The mantle is underneath the crust.
    (D) Plate convergence sometimes forms volcanoes.

Questions 13 and 14 are based on the following passage and diagram.

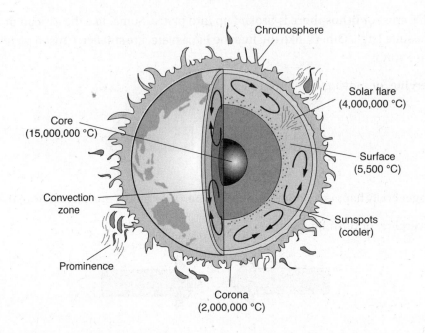

Our Sun is a yellow star. Like all stars, it burns hydrogen and helium in its core to maintain its enormous heat. When the gases in its core are all burned away, the Sun will expand into a **red giant**. At that point, its size will be so great, that it will expand into the space currently occupied by its orbiting planets.

13. What is an unstated assumption made by the author of the passage?
    (A) The core of our Sun is hotter than the corona.
    (B) People will not be around any longer when the Sun expands.
    (C) The Sun is not a very large star.
    (D) The hydrogen and helium will, at some point, be used up.

14. What is an assumption of the passage and diagram together?
    (A) The interiors of all yellow stars are similar to that of the Sun's.
    (B) Larger stars do not turn into red giants.
    (C) Humans will someday land on the Sun.
    (D) When the Sun begins to expand, humans will be able to travel to another Solar System.

Questions 15 and 16 are based on the following passage.

Although we tend to think of air as weightless, it is affected by gravity. The weight of the air in the atmosphere pushing on our planet is called **air pressure**. Air pressure is greatest at sea level and decreases as you go to a higher **altitude** (or up into the atmosphere). Barometric pressure is another term for air pressure. The instrument that measures air pressure is called a **barometer**. If you look at your barometer in the morning, you can tell whether the pressure in your area has risen or fallen overnight. Lower air pressure and lower oxygen levels are why people do not feel well when they travel up into the mountains. Altitude sickness symptoms can resemble those of the flu. They can be relieved by moving back down to a lower altitude.

15. What is one assumption the author makes about people who travel to a higher altitude?
    (A) They don't know anything about altitude sickness.
    (B) They all experience altitude sickness.
    (C) None of them have ever been to the mountains before.
    (D) People only get altitude sickness the first time they go to the mountains.

16. What is an assumption the author makes about the reader?
    (A) The reader knows what a barometer is.
    (B) The reader has had altitude sickness before.
    (C) The reader has a barometer.
    (D) The reader lives at sea level.

Questions 17 and 18 are based on the following passage and table.

Chris wants to set up a home aquarium. To decide whether to set up a freshwater or saltwater system, he went to his local pet store for information. The following table shows information that Chris received about both systems.

System Details	Freshwater	Saltwater
Size	40 gallons	55 gallons
Electrical needs	3 outlets	4 outlets
Setup/wait time	24–48 hours	24–48 hours
Marine salt	No	Yes
Cost	$75.00	$150.00
Maintenance time required	1–2 hours/week	3–4 hours/week

17. Chris found that the cost of the freshwater system he looked at was half that of a saltwater system. According to his chart, what might be one factor in the lower cost?
    (A) Freshwater fish are smaller than saltwater fish.
    (B) The freshwater tanks are always on sale.
    (C) The freshwater tank Chris looked at is smaller than the saltwater tank.
    (D) The saltwater tank will last longer.

18. Which tank will use more electricity?
  (A) The freshwater tank
  (B) The saltwater tank
  (C) They will both use the same amount.
  (D) It is impossible to tell from the table.

Question 19 is based on the following graph and passage.

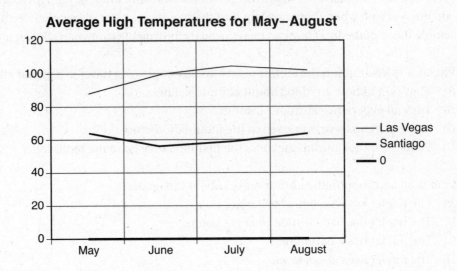

Average High Temperatures for May–August

Mia lives in Las Vegas, Nevada. Her friend Charles lives in Santiago, Chile. The two of them email frequently. Mia knows that in the southern hemisphere, where Charles lives, it is winter when it is summer in Las Vegas. Mia decides to keep a record to compare temperatures in the two cities for the months of May to August. The chart above shows her results.

19. Which of the following conclusions is true based on a comparison of the information from both cities?
  (A) The average temperature of Santiago is almost 40 degrees higher than the average temperature of Las Vegas for these 4 months.
  (B) The average temperature of Las Vegas is almost 40 degrees higher than the average temperature of Santiago for these 4 months.
  (C) The average temperature of Las Vegas is almost 40 degrees lower than the average temperature of Santiago for these 4 months.
  (D) The average temperature of Santiago is much higher in the months of January to April.

Questions 20 through 23 are based on the following passage.

Earth rocks are generally classified into one of three categories.

- **Igneous** rocks form from slow-moving liquid rock (magma) that cools and solidifies. An example of igneous rock is granite.
- **Metamorphic** rock is formed by intense heat and/or pressure. Marble and jade are two types of rock formed by metamorphosis.
- **Sedimentary** rocks are formed when other materials (for example, sand) fuse together under pressure. Limestone and sandstone are sedimentary rocks.

20. What is one difference between metamorphic rock and sedimentary rock?
    (A) Sedimentary rock does not need heat to form, while metamorphic rock does.
    (B) Sedimentary rock is softer than metamorphic rock.
    (C) Metamorphic rock does not need heat to form, while sedimentary rock does.
    (D) Metamorphic rock is more valuable than sedimentary rock.

21. What is one difference between metamorphic rock and igneous rock?
    (A) Metamorphic rock does not need pressure to form, while igneous rock does.
    (B) Metamorphic rock does not need heat to form, while igneous rock does.
    (C) Igneous rock does not need pressure to form, while metamorphic rock does.
    (D) Igneous rock does not need heat to form, while metamorphic rock does.

22. Which type of rock would you most likely find near a beach and which would you likely find near a volcano?
    (A) Igneous rock appears on beaches and metamorphic rock appears near volcanoes.
    (B) Sedimentary rock appears on beaches and igneous rock appears near volcanoes.
    (C) Metamorphic rock appears on beaches and sedimentary rock appears near volcanoes.
    (D) Igneous rock appears on beaches and sedimentary rock appears near volcanoes.

23. Alexander found a small **meteorite** (a rock that falls to Earth from outside the atmosphere). He took it to his teacher to classify it. What type of rock did the teacher say it was?
    (A) Igneous rock
    (B) Sedimentary rock
    (C) Metamorphic rock
    (D) None of the above

Question 24 is based on the following bar chart and passage.

In March of 2011, a 97-foot high tsunami wave hit the coast of Japan. The tsunami was triggered by a 9.0 earthquake, the largest quake ever to hit Japan. The wave caused incredible havoc, including the loss of many lives and the meltdown of the Fukushima Nuclear Power Plant.

The island nation of Japan, on the edge of the Pacific Rim, has a long history of and experience with earthquakes, tsunamis, and **megatsunamis** (tsunamis much higher than average). The chart below measures selected tsunami height to hit coastal Japanese communities from the 18th century to the present.

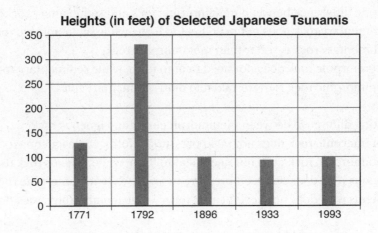

24. Which tsunami recorded above is likely to be labeled a **megatsunami** by scientists?
    (A) 1771
    (B) 1792
    (C) 1896
    (D) 1993

CHAPTER 14 ANSWER EXPLANATIONS

Lesson 1: Geology

PRACTICE EXERCISE 1 (PAGE 411)

1. T
2. T
3. F
4. F
5. T
6. F

PRACTICE EXERCISE 2 (PAGE 413)

1. G
2. E
3. A
4. B
5. D
6. F
7. C

PRACTICE EXERCISE 3 (PAGE 414)

1. **(B)** At intervals. There were periods of time between the later eruptions. (A) does not make sense because the passage says the eruptions were less violent. (C) and (D) do not fit the sense of the sentence.
2. Answers will vary.

Lesson 2: Ecosystems

PRACTICE EXERCISE 4 (PAGE 416)

1. T
2. T
3. F
4. T
5. F

PRACTICE EXERCISE 5 (PAGE 416)

1. **(A)** is a fact stated in the first sentence of the passage. 75% and three quarters are equal. (D) is an opinion; the adjective fascinating describes how the author feels about corals, but we may not share her fascination. (B) is not supported by the passage. (C) is an exaggeration of the author's statement. She mentions that many coral reefs are threatened, not all.
2. **(D)** is an opinion; the adjective fascinating describes how the author feels about corals, but we may not share her fascination. (A) is a fact stated in the first sentence of the passage. 75% and three quarters are equal. (B) is not supported by the passage. (C) is an exaggeration of the author's statement. She mentions that many coral reefs are threatened, not all.

PRACTICE EXERCISE 6 (PAGE 417)

1. C
2. E
3. A
4. B
5. F
6. D

Lesson 3: Weather

PRACTICE EXERCISE 7 (PAGE 420)

1.	G	5.	F
2.	A	6.	B
3.	E	7.	H
4.	D	8.	C

PRACTICE EXERCISE 8 (PAGE 421)

1. **(C)** Wash your car every week is the only choice that will not save energy.

PRACTICE EXERCISE 9 (PAGE 421)

1.	O	4.	O
2.	F	5.	F
3.	F	6.	O

PRACTICE EXERCISE 10 (PAGE 422)

1.	C	4.	B
2.	E	5.	A
3.	F	6.	D

Lesson 4: The Solar System

PRACTICE EXERCISE 11 (PAGE 424)

1.	D	5.	C
2.	H	6.	F
3.	G	7.	E
4.	A	8.	B

PRACTICE EXERCISE 12 (PAGE 424)

1. **(A)** It has liquid water and oxygen. People need both to survive. (B) and (D) are untrue. Europa is about the size of the Moon, and its gravity is less than Earth's. (C) This is untrue; the Moon is our closest neighbor in space.

2. **(D)** Not welcoming. All the other choices describe conditions that would encourage colonization.

3. **(B)** Extraterrestrial life needs water as much as life on Earth does. (A) The author says when people colonize space; he, therefore, assumes they will. (C) is a fact from the passage. (D) This is an untrue statement. The author says the two bodies are about the same size.

Lesson 5: Graphic Materials

PRACTICE EXERCISE 13 (PAGE 425)

1. To get to the Arenal, a tourist from San Jose would only need to pass the Poas Volcano. Rincon de la Vieja and Miravalles are farther up past Arenal. Turrialba and Irazu are in a different direction.
2. **(A)** (B), (C), and (D) are all good reasons why the volcanoes would NOT be visited.
3. **(B)** The scale shows that the distance between Arenal and Miravalles is about 60 km. One good technique to measuring distance on a map is to mark the distance between two points on something handy, like a pencil or piece of paper. Then hold the pencil or paper next to the key to better assess the distance.
4. **(A)** The key identifies the dashed line as the edge of the floodplain in 1997.
5. **(C)** Penny's school is not labeled on the map, nor is it mentioned in the key.
6. **(B)** This hypothesis is possible based on the facts Penny has observed. (A) is incorrect because the floodplain has not shrunk; it has grown. (C) is a prediction. (D) is an opinion.
7. **(C)** A hypothesis cannot be proven until facts that support it are gathered. The actions in (A) and (B) are forms of protest. They do not prove anything; furthermore if it demonstrated that the shopping center did not cause the floodplain's growth, these protests are misguided. (D) is a safety measure. While waterproofing may be wise, it does not in itself prove anything.

PRACTICE EXERCISE 14 (PAGE 428)

1. C
2. D
3. E
4. A
5. B

PRACTICE EXERCISE 15 (PAGE 429)

1. Your answers should be (A) Venus, (B) Jupiter, and (C) Mars.
2. **(C)** This chart's title indicates that it is not meant to provide complete information for all celestial bodies in the solar system—the title specifies that only planets are shown here.
3. **(A)** Years. Although there is no label on the left-hand axis, the sentence above specifies that the measure is years.
4. Each individual bar represents the life span of the animal label below the bar.
5. The animal with the longest bar (the parrot) has the longest life span.
6. The animal with the shortest bar (the queen bee) has the shortest life.
7. One of the unique things parrot owners must consider is that their pets may outlive them! Parrot owners are often encouraged to provide for their pets (for example, in the owner's will) in case of sickness, accident, or death.

PRACTICE EXERCISE 16 (PAGE 430)

1. **(B)** is correct. If more heat is being reflected back to Earth, the "heat reflected" arrow should be larger.

2. Hopefully you picked **(C)**. The line where saltwater meets freshwater. Your clue is that above the word "halocline" and the line, the water is labeled fresher surface water. Below the line the water is labeled salty deeper water.

End-of-Chapter Questions (Page 432)

1. **(B)** (A) and (D) are opinions. (C) is untrue.

2. **(D)** This opinion is voiced by the author in the first sentence. "Should" is a key opinion clue. (A) The author does not call anyone stupid. He observes that it is not a good idea to walk out into the harbor. (B) This is a fact, not an opinion. (C) is untrue.

3. **(C)** The passage explains that the seasons in the two hemispheres are reversed. Based on that information, this fact is a conclusion that the reader can draw. (A) is untrue. (B) is an opinion. (D) is a fact unrelated to the information about seasons in the passage and diagram.

4. **(B)** A judgment word like "better" is a key clue that this is an opinion. (A) is untrue. (C) is a conclusion that the reader can draw based on the information in the passage. (D) is a fact unrelated to the passage and diagram.

5. **(B)** The author states that areas behind the dam can end up underwater. (A) and (C) are unsupported by any information in the passage. (D) is an opinion; the key word is "best."

6. **(D)** The word "best" indicates that this is an opinion. (A) and (C) are unsupported by the passage. (B) is a fact.

7. **(B)** The passage states that the garbage "is carried to this particular location by ocean currents." (A) is not supported by anything in the passage and not a proven fact. (C) is a prediction. (D) is an opinion; "should" is the key word.

8. **(D)** "Should" is the key word that this is an opinion. (A) is unsupported by the passage and is an unproven statement. (B) is a fact. (C) is a prediction.

9. **(B)** The warning correctly assumes that fumes in the air are bad for people. By using the word "improve," it indicates that fumes are bad, clear air is good. (A) Lava travels over the ground, not through the air. (C) is not an assumption. It is directly stated in the passage. (D) is an opinion. However, the passage indicates that people are welcome to visit the volcanoes in the park if they follow safety procedures.

10. **(A)** There are no instructions for visitors in the event of a failed evacuation. Therefore, the passage assumes that evacuations will be successful. (B) is a fact stated in the passage. (C) and (D) are opinions.

11. **(C)** The author gives no examples of stationary plates, only of different directions in which plates may move. (A) is a fact directly stated in the passage. (B) is not true; a plate may be converging with another plate on one side and diverging from a plate on the other side. (D) This is a conclusion the reader may draw from the statement *new rock is pushing up from the mantle.*

12. **(A)** The author does not assume or state anything related to humans' perceptions of the motion. She does mention earthquakes from slippage. We know people can feel earthquakes. However, this is only one type of plate movement. (B) is an assumption made by the author. (C) This is a conclusion the reader may draw from the statement new rock is pushing up from the mantle. (D) This is a fact directly stated in the passage.

13. **(D)** The author says *WHEN the gases in its core are burned away.* It is assumed that there is no possibility of their being replenished. (A) This is a fact demonstrated by the

diagram. (B) The author does not mention the state of humanity at the time of the Sun's expansion. (C) The author does not clarify the Sun's size in relation to other stars.

14. **(A)** By classifying the Sun as a yellow star, the author indicates that they have the same properties. (B) As the passage does not state the size of yellow stars relative to other stars, we have no way of knowing if this is true or not. (C) and (D) These are both predictions. The author makes no mention of the state of humanity in the future.

15. **(B)** The author states that *people do not feel well when they travel up into the mountains.* No exception is made for those who might not be affected by altitude sickness. None of the other choices are supported by the passage.

16. **(C)** The author mentions experimenting with *your barometer.* Yet somewhat oddly, the author presumes the reader does not know what his barometer is for, and explains its function (A). (B) The passage explains altitude sickness; it does not presume the reader is familiar with it. Neither does it presume the reader lives at sea level (D).

17. **(C)** Differences in size could account for a difference in price. (A) and (D) are not true. (B) No mention of a sale is made on the table or in the passage.

18. **(B)** *The saltwater tank* requires four outlets, where the freshwater tank only requires three (see table).

19. **(B)** According to the chart, the temperatures for Las Vegas range from about 84 degrees to 105 degrees; those of Santiago range from about 62 to 58 degrees.

20. **(A)** The definition for metamorphic rock formation lists "heat" as a factor, while the definition for sedimentary rock does not. (B), (C), and (D) are not supported by the passage.

21. **(C)** The passage states that igneous rock forms from lava on the surface of the Earth. Therefore, there is no pressure other than ordinary air pressure. Metamorphic rock requires pressure by definition.

22. **(B)** The passage gives the example of sand as one of the materials that can be compressed to form sedimentary rock. Beaches have sand in abundance. The passage also states the igneous rock is formed from magma (lava). Lava comes from volcanoes.

23. **(D)** The author of the passage makes it clear in the first sentence that these are classifications of *Earth* rocks. Meteorites, being extraterrestrial, fall into a different category altogether.

24. **(B)** The 1792 wave reaches over 300 feet, much higher than the other waves. Megatsunamis, according to the passage, are waves much higher than the average tsunami.

Physical Science

"The whole of science is nothing more than a refinement of everyday thinking."

—Albert Einstein

Physical science deals with **inanimate** (non-living) **matter** and **energy**. Matter is the substance (solid, liquid, or gas) of which every physical object is made. Energy is the **capacity** or ability for power, movement, or work. Everything on Earth and in the Universe is made of one or the other. In your body, matter and energy work together. Your muscles and bones are made of matter, but you need energy to move them. The food (matter) that you eat is **transformed** or changed into energy that you use to walk, think, and live your life with.

HOW THIS CHAPTER IS ORGANIZED

In this unit, you will discover the ways energy and matter work together to make up the world we see around us.

Lesson 1: Building Blocks

Atoms and molecules are the foundations of everything we know.

Lesson 2: Matter

How is matter classified? How do different forms of matter interact?

Lesson 3: Newton's Laws

Three principles discovered in the 17th century still hold true today.

Lesson 4: Types of Energy

What is energy? Where does it come from?

Lesson 5: Graphic Materials

Practice your comprehension of science information in the form of tables, pictographs, and pie charts.

LESSON 1: BUILDING BLOCKS
Atoms

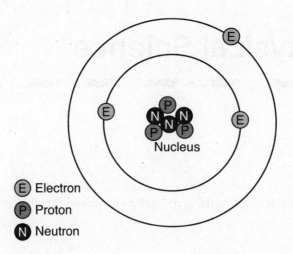

All matter is **composed** of atoms. An atom is the smallest **component** or part of a substance possible. The **substance** gold, for example, is made up of atoms of pure gold and nothing else. Most of the weight of an atom is in its **nucleus** or center. The nucleus is composed of **protons** and **neutrons**. A proton has a positive electrical charge. A neutron has no charge (it is **neutral**). Around the nucleus of an atom are clouds of **electrons**, which remain connected to it. Electrons are much smaller than protons or neutrons, and they have negative charges.

Not all atoms have the same number of protons, neutrons, or electrons. The illustration above, for example, shows a **lithium** atom. It has three protons, three neutrons, and three electrons. Lithium atoms will always have three protons and three electrons. The number of neutrons may vary. A **hydrogen** atom, however, contains one proton and one electron.

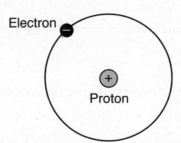

Some atoms have many electrons orbiting at different distances or **energy levels**.

For many years, it was thought impossible to divide the parts of an atom. In the mid-twentieth century, scientists discovered how to trigger nuclear **fission**, or the splitting of an atom. In doing so, they released an enormous amount of energy, including **radioactive** energy. **Radioactive** energy is harmful to humans and other life forms.

After scientists split the atom, atomic bombs and nuclear reactors became possible. The beginning of the "nuclear age," in fact, gave people some important **ethical** questions to decide. Under what circumstances should such power be used? The horrifying destruction of Hiroshima and Nagasaki by atomic bombs during World War II demonstrated that the power of the atom was too great to be used carelessly.

WRITING EXERCISE

You are a member of the city council of Little Eden, PA. An energy company has requested permission to build a nuclear power plant just outside your town. The company claims their nuclear energy will be cheap, reliable, and safe. They are willing to pay a fee to establish themselves in your community and would also provide jobs for your citizens.

You have heard about the problems of contamination and waste disposal associated with nuclear power. This particular company, however, has no history of accidents at any of their plants.

Go online to research the pros and cons of nuclear power. Then write a paragraph explaining your position as a city councilperson.

Molecules

In nature, atoms combine with other atoms to form **molecules**. How do they do this?

They use their electrons. Molecules are formed when atoms share one or more electrons. The electrons then **orbit** or revolve around the nuclei of both atoms.

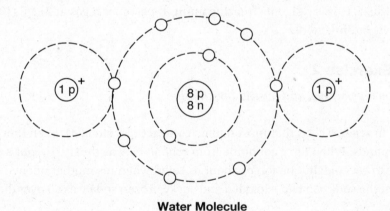

Water Molecule

Atoms can combine with **like** (identical) atoms or different atoms. In the diagram above, the electrons in the outer shell of the oxygen atom are also orbiting each of the hydrogen atoms. Water, one of the most plentiful substances on the planet, is formed by this connection.

Practice Exercise 1

Match the terms on the left with the correct definitions on the right.

_____ 1. Atom	(A)	A positively charged particle in the nucleus
_____ 2. Nucleus	(B)	A negatively charged particle outside the nucleus
_____ 3. Component	(C)	The smallest part of a substance
_____ 4. Proton	(D)	A neutral particle in the nucleus
_____ 5. Fission	(E)	An energy dangerous to life forms
_____ 6. Neutron	(F)	Splitting apart of an atom
_____ 7. Electron	(G)	To revolve or circle around
_____ 8. Energy levels	(H)	Different distances of electrons from the nucleus
_____ 9. Radioactive	(I)	The central part of an atom
_____ 10. Molecule	(J)	Part of something
_____ 11. Orbit	(K)	Object formed by the combination of two or more atoms.

LESSON 2: MATTER

Matter has three main states, solid, liquid, and gas. Matter changes states or **phases** when pressure or temperature is changed. Water, for instance, becomes solid (ice) below 32° Fahrenheit (0° Celsius). This is called its **freezing point**. It becomes a gas at 212°F (100° Celsius). This is called its **boiling point**.

TIP
Not all matter freezes or boils at the same temperature. Mercury does not freeze until the thermometer gets to almost –38°F and boils at over 600°F (over 300°C)!

Practice Exercise 2

Read the following passage, and answer the question.

Jerry learned in science class that most liquids **contract** (get smaller) when they freeze, but that water **expands**. When Jerry got home from school, he was thirsty. He put a can of soda in the freezer to get cold, but he forgot about it. Later, when his mother opened the freezer, she found that the soda can had exploded and sticky, frozen soda was all over the freezer.

1. What is the most likely explanation?

_____

_____

_____

Elements

An **element** is a substance that cannot be divided into a simpler substance by chemical means. The element iron (Fe) is made up of nothing but iron. You can divide a piece of iron into smaller and smaller parts until you reach single atoms, and you will never find anything but iron. Even if you split iron's atoms, you will not form a new element; you will only end up with separated neutrons, protons, and electrons.

Currently, scientists know of a little over 100 elements. Many, like hydrogen (H) and Nitrogen (N), occur naturally and are very common. Others, like **Roentgenium (Rg)** or **Copernicium (Cn)** are **synthetic** (man-made) and very rare.

How do scientists keep track of, or **classify** all these different elements? They use a table called the **Periodic Table of Elements**. Although many scientists were involved in its development, Russian chemist Dmitri Mendeleev is usually credited as the "Father of the periodic table." The table shows similarities that different elements share. Each element on the periodic table is represented by a box that shows the symbol for the element, its **atomic number** (number of protons) and its **atomic weight**. Other information, such as the number of electrons in each shell of the element's atom, may also be included. Below is an illustration of the box that identifies silver on the periodic table.

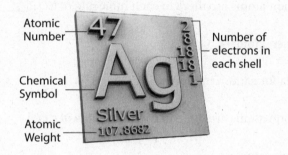

Practice Exercise 3

Match the term on the left with the correct definitions on the right.

_____ 1. Atomic number   (A) The classification of all known elements

_____ 2. Atomic weight   (B) Point at which a liquid turns to gas

_____ 3. Periodical table of elements   (C) Man-made

_____ 4. Element   (D) Number of protons in an element's atoms

_____ 5. Boiling point   (E) Average weight of an atom of an element

_____ 6. Freezing point   (F) Combination of two or more atoms

_____ 7. Synthetic   (G) Point at which a liquid turns to solid

_____ 8. Molecule   (H) Substance that cannot be divided into simpler substances.

Compounds

A **compound** is a chemical substance that consists of two or more elements in combination. In the previous section on molecules, you read about the common compound water, which consists of hydrogen and oxygen. One of the properties of compounds is that they cannot be separated into their elements physically. You cannot, for example, pour a glass of water and then pick all of the hydrogen out of it!

Compounds are identified by their **chemical formulas**. Below is the chemical formula for water:

$$\text{HYDROGEN (H) + HYDROGEN (H) + OXYGEN (O)} = H_2O$$

The small "2" behind the H means that there are two hydrogen atoms in a water molecule. There is no number after the O; that means there is only one oxygen atom in a water molecule. H_2O represents one molecule of water.

The **chemical formula** for carbon dioxide is CO_2. C represents carbon and O represents oxygen.

Practice Exercise 4

1. How many carbon atoms are there in each molecule of CO_2? _____

2. How many oxygen atoms? _____

The chemical formula for carbon monoxide is CO.

3. How many carbon atoms are there in each molecule of CO? _____

4. How many oxygen atoms? _____

There is one atom of carbon and one atom of oxygen in carbon monoxide. What a difference one atom of oxygen makes! Carbon dioxide is exhaled by humans as part of the natural respiration cycle between plants and animals. It is also used in the production of many foods and beverages. Carbon monoxide is extremely toxic and should never be inhaled.

When scientists want to indicate more than one molecule, they do so by putting a number in front of the chemical formula. Sodium (Na) and Chloride (Cl) combine to create one molecule of table salt (NaCl). Two molecules of table salt would be indicated 2NaCl.

The diagram below shows three molecules of water.

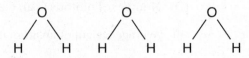

> **TIP**
>
> Little numbers underneath are for atoms—big numbers in front are for molecules!

The chemical formula for these three molecules together is $3H_2O$. Since there are two hydrogen atoms in each molecule and there are three molecules, the total number of hydrogen atoms in three molecules of water is six.

This is a molecule of H_2O_2, also known as hydrogen peroxide.

```
   H         H
    \       /
     O --- O
```

Hydrogen peroxide is most familiar to us as the mild cleaning agent sold in a brown bottle in pharmacies and food stores.

Practice Exercise 5

1. With the help of your own diagram, see if you can figure out how many atoms of oxygen there are in four molecules of H_2O_2.

_____

A quick way to find this out without having to draw a diagram is to multiply the big number in front of the formula by the little numbers behind the atoms. $4H_2O_2$ means 4×2 hydrogen atoms (8) and 4×2 oxygen atoms (8).

Practice Exercise 6

Match the following chemical formulas with their descriptions.

_____ 1. C_3H_8 (propane)

(A) One hydrogen atom and one chloride atom

_____ 2. Na_2O (sodium oxide)

(B) Two sodium atoms and one oxygen atom

_____ 3. HCl (hydrogen chloride)

(C) One carbon atom and four hydrogen atoms

_____ 4. CH_4 (methane)

(D) Three carbon atoms and eight hydrogen atoms

Practice Exercise 7

Read the following passage, and answer the question.

Sidney has smoke detectors in his home, but he has read about the dangers of carbon monoxide (CO) poisoning and wants to protect his family. After doing some research, he installs a CO alarm that meets current safety standards. The instructions for the alarm state that if it sounds, all residents should **evacuate** the premises and 911 should be called. Late one night, after Sidney's family is in bed, the alarm goes off.

1. What is the safest thing the family can do?
   (A) Disable the alarm; it's probably defective.
   (B) Go back to sleep, and deal with the problem in the morning.
   (C) Get up and go around the house to try to find the source of the CO.
   (D) Get outside to fresh air immediately.

TIP

Batteries in smoke and CO detectors should be kept charged and checked regularly.

LESSON 3: NEWTON'S LAWS

Sir Isaac Newton was a great scientist and mathematician who lived in England from 1643–1727. One of his greatest contributions to science was the formulation of Newton's Three Laws of Motion.

Newton's First Law

Newton's first law states that an object at rest will not move unless an outside **force**, or pushing motion, makes it; likewise an object in motion will stay in motion unless an outside force stops it or changes its direction.

What does this mean? Imagine a ball stopped on the ground. The ball will not start rolling by itself. **Something else** must start it rolling. A child might kick it or pick it up and throw it. Now imagine that ball rolling. It will keep rolling forever until someone or something stops it. But, you may say, I've often seen balls and shopping carts and things rolling to a stop on their own. In those cases it is **friction** with the ground that stops those shopping carts from moving. Friction is surface resistance. It is stronger on rough surfaces than smooth, and one of the reasons we do not bowl on alleys covered with carpet!

This first law is often called the definition of **inertia**. Inertia is the resistance of any object to a change in its state of motion or rest.

Newton's Second Law

Newton's second law tells us that how fast an object moves depends on how much mass it has and how much force it is pushed with. A simple restatement of this law (called the law of **acceleration**) is that

(A) Bigger things take more force to move

— AND —

(B) If a small object and a big object are pushed with the same force,
the small object will go farther.

EXAMPLE A

How far can you push a toy truck? Or even throw a toy truck? 6 feet? 7 feet? More? How much energy did it take? Could you do it again right away? Now how far can you push a full-size truck? (Let's not even consider throwing it.) You might be able to move it a few feet if you are very strong and the truck is not in gear. However, it is probably not something you would care to do all day. You would expend a great deal of energy.

EXAMPLE B

If you have ever gone bowling, you may have noticed that the bowling alley provides balls of different sizes. If you are used to an 8-pound bowling ball and pick up a 12-pound ball by mistake, you will soon figure out what you did! To make the larger ball go as far as the smaller one, you will have to expend more energy.

It is not always easy to see pure, unaffected examples of Newton's laws in the real world because there are so many other variables to consider. If you were doing an experiment on Newton's second law outside, for instance, you would have to take wind speed and direction into account. However, the understanding of the theory of these laws has made many technological advances possible.

Newton's Third Law

Newton's third law states that for every action, there is an equal and opposite reaction. During a fire, for example, many firemen may be needed to hold the fire hoses firmly. That is because the force that shoots the water out also pushes the hose back.

Practice Exercise 8

Read the following descriptions. Decide which of Newton's laws is applicable.

1st   2nd   3rd

_____ 1. A cinderblock and a marble are dropped at the same time from the same height. The marble hits the ground first.

_____ 2. It is easier to roller skate on a hard surface than on carpet.

_____ 3. Marc is learning to shoot at a rifle range. Every time he fires, he feels the gun push back into his shoulder.

_____ 4. A bowling ball rolls down the alley until it hits the pins and stops.

_____ 5. When Irina jumps up off the diving board to start her dive, she pushes the board down.

_____ 6. A basketball player throws a basketball. A baseball player standing next to him throws a baseball with the same force. The baseball goes farther.

Because the marble is smaller and dropped with the same force, Newton's second law predicts it will move faster. You can roller skate better on a smooth surface (rather than a rug) because there is less friction to slow your wheels down. Marc is experiencing the **reaction** of the gun every time a bullet is fired (**action**). If the bowling ball was not slowed by friction from the alley and stopped by the pins, it would continue rolling forever. The board moves down as a reaction to Irina's moving up. Finally, the two athletes throw two balls with the same amount of force, but the baseball goes farther because it is smaller.

Practice Exercise 9

Read the following passage, and answer the questions.

Do you ever think about the fact that when your car is moving, everybody and everything in the car is moving at the same speed? If you are driving at 55 mph, your body is also moving at 55 mph. In normal traffic this is not a problem, since there is usually enough time to **decelerate** (slow down). However, in case of an accident or a sudden stop, inertia will cause everything in the car to be flung forward until it hits something.

1. Which of Newton's laws predicts the action of the contents of the car in case of a sudden stop?
   (A) Newton's first law
   (B) Newton's second law
   (C) Newton's third law

The key word is inertia, since the First Law is often called the Law of Inertia. Because the initial impact touches only the outside of the car, everything inside will keep moving forward until some other object causes it to stop as the car did.

2. What is the safest way to keep your body in place in case of an accident?
   (A) Hold on to the door handle.
   (B) Buy a non-breakable windshield.
   (C) Wear a seat belt and install airbags.
   (D) Brace your feet against the floor of the car.

LESSON 4: TYPES OF ENERGY

Energy is power. It is all around us and in us. It cannot be created or destroyed. It can, however, be transformed from one state to another. This is called **The Law of Conservation of Energy**.

To move anything it is necessary to **expend** energy. Expended energy does not disappear, but it is changed from a form that we can use to a form that we can't. When you eat food, for example, it gives you energy to exercise. Exercising your muscles creates heat. Your body cannot reuse that heat; instead it requires more food. When you drive a car, you use up the energy from the gasoline you put in the tank. Eventually you will need to buy more gas. With so much energy on Earth being expended all the time, is it any wonder we are concerned that we have enough of the right kind when we need it?

Potential and Kinetic Energy

There are two basic types of energy: **potential** and **kinetic**.

Potential means something hasn't happened yet, but it could happen. Potential energy hasn't been released yet, but it can be. Think of a roller coaster at the top, waiting to go down. There is a moment when it is motionless. Yet it is filled with potential energy, enough energy to send the cars speeding downhill and around the loop.

When you pull back a rubber band, it is filled with potential energy until it breaks or you let it go. Potential energy, in other words, is stored energy.

Kinetic energy is energy in action. When the roller coaster finally goes down and around the loop, that is kinetic energy. When the rubber band snaps, that is also kinetic energy. Kinetic energy is the runner running, the bird flying, the ball falling down the stairs.

Practice Exercise 10

Identify the following situations as examples of potential (P) or kinetic (K) energy.

_____ 1. 1. An arrow is flying through the air toward its target.

_____ 2. A bus is moving down the street.

_____ 3. A batter is up to bat, waiting for the pitcher to throw.

_____ 4. The batter hits the ball.

_____ 5. A diver stands on a platform, ready to dive into the water.

Sources of Energy in Our World

When we discuss sources of energy, one of the important questions to ask is: Energy for what? If the answer is energy to power our bodies, the answer is simple: we need food. Food can be meat from animals, which get their energy from eating other animals or plants. Food can also be plants (vegetables, fruit, and cereals), which receive their energy directly from the Sun.

However, when scientists and others discuss energy sources, they are usually interested in sources that power our technology. What sources heat our homes, move our bulldozers, and power our computers and cellphones?

Energy sources can be either **renewable** or **nonrenewable**.

Renewable energy sources never run out. Two good examples are **solar** (Sun) and **wind energy**. As long as Earth exists, there will always be Sun and wind. These two energy sources are clean as well. So why not use them more? This is a complicated question. One of the problems is that, although **inexhaustible**, solar and wind power do not have steady outputs. When it is cloudy, solar panels cannot receive energy from the Sun. When the wind does not blow, wind turbines stop turning.

Perhaps someday scientists will invent a system to take full advantage of these clean, abundant energy sources.

Nonrenewable energy sources come out of the ground. Most of them are **fossil fuels**: They are formed from the bodies of creatures that died millions of years ago. As you can imagine, these supplies are not inexhaustible. They will someday run out. This is going to create a big problem if we do not do something about it now, as so much of our energy today comes from fossil fuels. This problem is often called the **energy crisis**.

Petroleum is a fossil fuel. We use petroleum to run our cars, heat our houses, and make many common products. Drilling for petroleum (or oil) carries a risk to the environment. Mistakes and accidents can cause oil spills, which damage the surrounding environment and hurt or kill wildlife. Yet we have not, to this date, found a substitute for oil that is as useful or economical.

Natural gas is used to heat homes and power stoves for cooking. It is one of the cleanest fossil fuels. One of the more **controversial** aspects of natural gas is **fracking**, or extracting gas from rock. Fracking can cause problems, including making the land nearby unstable.

Coal was commonly used to heat homes many years ago. Today it is more often used to power **electricity**. Coal is a fossil fuel that is particularly dangerous to **mine** or get out of the Earth. It also burns less cleanly than other fossil fuels.

Finally, **nuclear energy** is energy that results from the tremendous power released when atoms are split. Nuclear energy is clean, but the process of making it is dangerous and complex. If a mistake is made, the possibility exists of the whole area becoming **radioactive**. **Radioactivity** can make people and animals very sick.

Practice Exercise 11

Match the following terms with their definitions.

_____ 1. Renewable energy   (A) Fuels formed from creatures that lived long ago

_____ 2. Fossil fuels   (B) Energy that results from splitting atoms

_____ 3. Radioactive   (C) To dig out of the earth

_____ 4. Fracking   (D) Energy that is inexhaustible

_____ 5. Mine   (E) A method of extracting natural gas from rock

_____ 6. Energy crisis   (F) The concern over using up nonrenewable energy sources

_____ 7. Nuclear energy   (G) Emitting radiation harmful to life forms

Practice Exercise 12

1. Which of the houses below would be the best candidate for solar panels?
   (A) A house in a city where it rains 155 days a year.
   (B) An apartment on the fourth floor of a six-floor building.
   (C) A house in the Arizona desert.
   (D) A house deep in the forest.

LESSON 5: GRAPHIC MATERIALS

One of the best ways to illustrate quantitative information—information that depends on numbers and measurement—is with a graphic. A graphic is a pictorial representation of the information. In this lesson, we will look at pie charts, tables, and pictographs.

Pie Charts

Pie charts can be useful in showing parts and their relation to a whole. The pie chart below shows the elemental composition of the Earth.

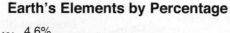

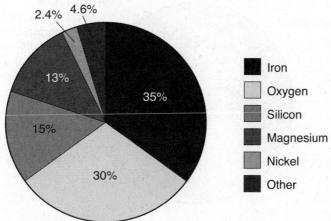

Earth's Elements by Percentage

2.4% 4.6%
13%
35%
15%
30%

- Iron
- Oxygen
- Silicon
- Magnesium
- Nickel
- Other

To correctly show relationships, all the percentages in a pie chart must add up to a total of 100%. Add the percentages together in the chart above, and see if this chart is accurately constructed! As with all illustrations and diagrams, reading THE WHOLE CHART thoroughly is the secret to comprehension. This includes titles and all information on and around the pie sections.

Practice Exercise 13

Questions 1 through 5 are based on the chart above.

1. What is the title of the chart? Where is it on the chart?

   _____

2. How is the relationship between different elements in the Earth demonstrated?

   _____

   _____

3. Which is the most abundant element in the Earth's composition?

   _____

4. Which two elements together make up half of the Earth's composition?

_____

5. What element in the above chart also makes our atmosphere breathable?
(Hint: you are breathing it now)

_____

Questions 6 through 8 are based on the following chart.

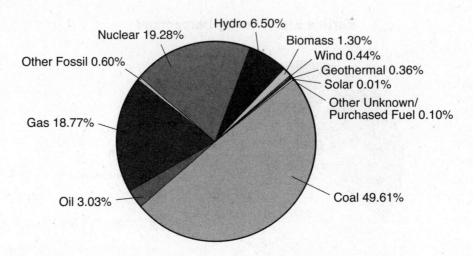

The above pie chart is shown on the website of the Environmental Protection Agency. It compares the percentages of different types of fuels used to generate electricity in the United States. As on the previous chart, the size of each wedge corresponds to the size of the percentage it represents. In other words, the largest percentage (in this case, coal at 49.61%) has the largest wedge. This means that coal is used as fuel for 49.61% of all electricity use and is its most common source of fuel.

6. Which fuel has the smallest wedge in the pie chart?

_____

7. What does this say about that fuel source?

_____

_____

8. What are the two largest fuel sources of electricity in the United States?
   (A) Coal and gas
   (B) Coal and nuclear
   (C) Oil and nuclear
   (D) Nuclear and gas

Tables

Just like a paragraph, a table has a main idea and supporting details. The table below shows the effect of wind chill factors. Wind chill is a term often used in weather forecasts. Wind **velocity** or speed can make temperatures feel colder than they are. The stronger the wind, the colder it "feels like."

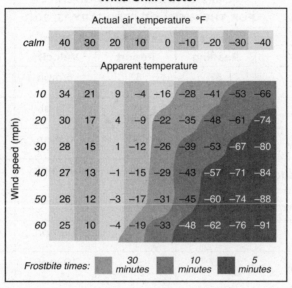

Wind Chill Factor

Actual air temperature °F

| calm | 40 | 30 | 20 | 10 | 0 | –10 | –20 | –30 | –40 |

Apparent temperature

Wind speed (mph)									
10	34	21	9	–4	–16	–28	–41	–53	–66
20	30	17	4	–9	–22	–35	–48	–61	–74
30	28	15	1	–12	–26	–39	–53	–67	–80
40	27	13	–1	–15	–29	–43	–57	–71	–84
50	26	12	–3	–17	–31	–45	–60	–74	–88
60	25	10	–4	–19	–33	–48	–62	–76	–91

Frostbite times: 30 minutes   10 minutes   5 minutes

Practice Exercise 14

1. What is the title (main idea) of the table above?

   _____

2. What do the numbers running up the left axis indicate?

   _____

3. What do the numbers across the top indicate?

   _____

Using this table is not unlike using a multiplication table! Where the wind speed and calm temperature meet, there is the windchill factor. For example, suppose the calm temperature on a given day is 10° and the wind speed is 20 mph. Follow the 10° column down until your finger is across from 20 on the left axis. The wind chill factor is –9°. That is what it "feels like" outside.

4. What is the windchill on a 10° day when the wind is blowing at 30 mph?
   (A) –4°
   (B) –9°
   (C) –11°
   (D) –12°

Tables can be used to compare information gathered over time. Using the windchill information above, Erin tracked the weather in her city for a week in February. She measured the temperature in an area protected from wind and compared her readings to the daily weather report on television. She also noted wind velocity and windchill factors reported by the weatherperson each day. The table below shows her data (temperatures are in Fahrenheit:

TEMPERATURES AND WINDCHILL
FOR THE WEEK OF FEBRUARY 13, 2011

Day	Erin's Reading	Television Report	Wind Velocity	Windchill
Sunday	37	35	5 mph	31
Monday	43	40	5 mph	36
Tuesday	22	20	0 mph	20
Wednesday	22	20	20 mph	4
Thursday	28	25	25 mph	9
Friday	42	40	15 mph	32
Saturday	37	35	10 mph	27

Practice Exercise 15

Look carefully at the title, axes, and information boxes on Erin's table.

1. What is a trend you notice when comparing Erin's temperatures to the weather report's temperatures?
   (A) They are always the same.
   (B) Erin's temperatures are always slightly higher.
   (C) Erin's temperatures are always slightly lower.
   (D) The weather report's temperatures are always slightly higher.

2. On Tuesday and Wednesday, the TV station weatherperson reported the same temperature. However, the windchill on Wednesday was much lower. What information on Erin's table explains this difference?

_____

_____

Pictographs

A pictograph is a chart or graph that uses symbols or pictures instead of bars, lines, or circles. For example, a graph that compares the number of households in different cities who use solar energy might use the picture of a house 🏠 to represent 100, 1,000, or even a million households. Let us say the house represents 1,000 households. Then three houses represent 3,000 households. A half a house 🏠 represents 500 households. The KEY is your guide to tell you what each symbol stands for. Reading the key is especially crucial when **deciphering** a pictograph, as the pictures are sometimes small and hard to see.

Getting the picture? Let's look at the following pictograph on the development of nuclear power worldwide.

Countries with the Most Nuclear Power Plants

Country	Every 🏭 represents 10 power plants
USA	🏭🏭🏭🏭🏭🏭🏭🏭🏭🏭🏭
France	🏭🏭🏭🏭🏭🏭
Japan	🏭🏭🏭🏭🏭
Russian Federation	🏭🏭🏭🏭
Korea Republic	🏭🏭🏭

Practice Exercise 16

1. What is the title of the above pictograph?

_____

2. What information does the left vertical axis of the pictograph show?

_____

3. How many nuclear power plants does each symbol represent? Where did you find this information?

_____

4. Which country on the pictograph has the most power plants? Which country has the least?

_____

_____

The following pictograph compares the electrical consumption of different types of house-hold cooling systems. Look carefully at the title, the key, and the list of cooling units along the left-hand axis.

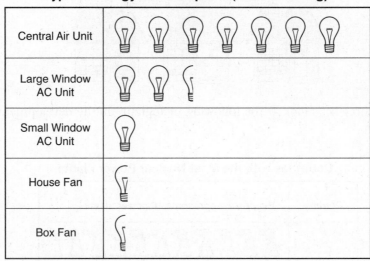

Typical Energy Consumption (when running)

= 500 watts

5. What does each lightbulb represent?

_____

6. The House Fan pictograph is slightly less than one full lightbulb. What does this indicate?

_____

7. The title of the chart includes the words *when running*. What does this imply?
   (A) All these appliances are running all the time.
   (B) When the appliance is running, it uses this level of electricity.
   (C) When the appliance is running, it does not use this level of electricity.
   (D) When the appliance is not running, it does not use this level of electricity.

8. Jan is trying to decide between installing central air and buying both a large and small window AC unit. Which choice would cost her more in electricity?
   (A) The central air
   (B) The large and small window unit
   (C) The cost would be the same
   (D) If she installed central air, she would not need to run it as often as the window units.

Critical Reading Skills

INFERENCE

Inference—sometimes called "reading between the lines"—is the skill of getting information from what the author does NOT say. Sound complicated? You've probably been doing it all your life. What is the difference between **inferring** and **implying**? These two things often happen together. To imply means to communicate something without saying it directly. To infer means to understand something that is not stated directly. For example, what can you infer from the following passage?

Andie has several houseplants. Recently she went on a trip. While she was away, a neighbor came in every other day to water the plants. When Andie came back, the plants looked great. Andie brought her neighbor a souvenir from the trip to thank her.

You can infer that Andie specifically asked the neighbor to water the plants. You can also infer that the neighbor had a key to get into Andie's house. This is partly because it is unlikely that the neighbor was peering in the window, saw the dying plants, and broke in to water them (normal neighbors do not do that!). It is also inferred from the fact that Andie knew her neighbor was watering the plants. She thought about it on vacation and bought a souvenir in advance.

END-OF-CHAPTER QUESTIONS

Read the following passage, and answer questions 1 through 3.

The Great Pyramids of Egypt are the only one of the seven wonders of the ancient world left standing. For centuries, people have wondered how these massive structures were built without modern technology. Today, many historians believe that the Egyptians used a simple machine, **the inclined plane**, to help them push the huge blocks of limestone into their intended places. What is an inclined plane? It is a slope or a ramp that enables people to move heavy loads up. The Greek historian Herodotus mentions "machines made of short wooden planks." Some modern engineers have theorized that these machines pushed the blocks up inclined planes from one level of the pyramid to the next, until they were fitted in place.

1. Which of the following is an inference made by the author of the passage?
   (A) The blocks the Egyptians used were much too heavy for any group of men to lift and carry them.
   (B) The men who worked on the pyramids were not strong.
   (C) The men who worked on the pyramids were well paid.
   (D) Herodotus visited while the pyramids were being built.

2. What does the author infer about the other six wonders of the ancient world?
   (A) They were destroyed.
   (B) They were not as great as the pyramids.
   (C) They were also built with inclined planes.
   (D) They were all in Egypt.

3. Which of the following jobs can you infer an inclined plane would NOT be useful for?
   (A) Creating a wheelchair-accessible entrance to a building.
   (B) Loading cars onto a truck.
   (C) Sliding a boat into the water.
   (D) Pulling a tree stump out of the ground.

Read the following passage and diagram and answer question 4.

Voltage is a measure of electricity. The higher the voltage, the more dangerous the source can be to touch. The symbol below is the international high voltage safety symbol, which warns people of the possibility of electric shock.

Contact with high voltage can result in serious burns, heart problems, or electrocution. It can be fatal. Voltage of only 50 V (volts) is often sufficient to do physical damage to human beings.

4. Which of the following is inferred by the above passage?
   (A) Humans who come into contact with high voltage will instantly die.
   (B) Humans who come into contact with high voltage are usually protected by their clothing.
   (C) People who are near or work with high voltage need to be extremely careful about their safety.
   (D) It is not necessary to take safety precautions when using the appliances in your home as they are so low in voltage.

Read the following passage, and answer questions 5 and 6.

Alchemy is the transforming of ordinary materials into something of value. In the Middle Ages, when many modern principles of chemistry had not yet been discovered, alchemists worked to find the secret of turning ordinary metal into gold or plain water into an **elixir** that would make them immortal. Alchemy, although flawed in many of its assumptions and practices, is sometimes seen as the father of modern chemistry, particularly, in many alchemists' practice of experimentation. In the 17th and 18th centuries, alchemy all but disappeared as modern chemistry began to emerge.

5. What does the author infer in the second sentence?
    (A) The alchemists were foolish.
    (B) In the Middle Ages, gold was more valued than other metals.
    (C) The alchemists would have succeeded if they had had modern equipment.
    (D) An elixir of immortality is impossible to create.

6. In the last sentence, what does the author infer?
    (A) Chemists threatened alchemists.
    (B) In the 17th and 18th centuries, alchemy was outlawed.
    (C) In the 17th and 18th centuries, many people became chemists rather than alchemists.
    (D) Alchemy was so dangerous that many alchemists died.

Read the following passage, and answer questions 7 and 8.

Gravity is the force that attracts any two objects in the universe together. The larger an object is, the stronger the gravitational force it exerts. Everything on Earth is attracted to (held on to) the planet by the force of gravity. Without it, there would be nothing to prevent us, our houses, and everything else from floating off into space.

Not all bodies in the Solar System exert the same gravitational pull. The gravity on Jupiter, for example, is over 200% greater than on Earth. The Moon, on the other hand, has a little over 1/6 of Earth's gravity. A person who weighs 150 lb. on Earth weighs about 26 lb. on the Moon!

7. What inference can you make about the size of Jupiter in relation to Earth?
    (A) It is larger.
    (B) It is smaller.
    (C) They are the same size.
    (D) No inference can be made.

8. What inference can you make about the size of the Moon in relation to Earth?
    (A) It is larger.
    (B) It is smaller.
    (C) They are the same size.
    (D) No inference can be made.

SUMMARIZING

To summarize (say or write something in a shorter form) is a useful skill. As a student and effective reader, you need to express the meaning of passages and graphics in one or two insightful sentences. A good summary will include the information in the main idea sentence and major supporting details. A summary of a graphic takes into account the title, information on the left and bottom axes, and the relationship of the different items presented.

Read the following passage, and graph and answer questions 9 and 10.

The International Association of Electrical Inspectors is an agency that has been in existence since 1928. In their concern for electrical safety, the IAEI conducts safety trainings and seminars, promotes safe electrical products, and regularly publishes statistics on electrical safety.

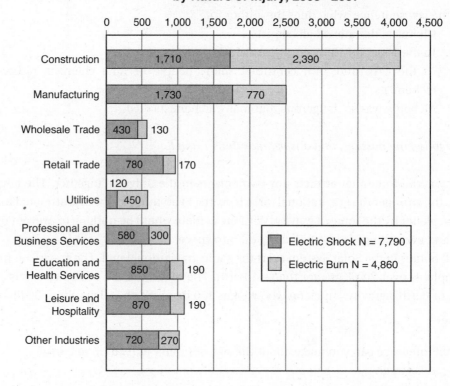

Nonfatal Electrical Injuries, Private Industry, by Nature of Injury, 2003–2007

9. Which of the following is the best summary of the information presented in the chart above?
   (A) The dark gray bar is for electric shock, and the light gray bar is for electric burns.
   (B) The chart compares frequency and severity of electrical injury in different private industries.
   (C) There were fewer electrical injuries from 2003–2007 than in the years before.
   (D) The most dangerous industry to work in is Leisure and Hospitality.

10. Which of the following is the best summary of the passage?
    (A) The IAEI is an organization dedicated to industry safety.
    (B) The IAEI is an organization open to anybody.
    (C) IAEI conducts safety trainings.
    (D) Electrical inspectors have to go through a lot of training.

Questions 11 through 13 are based on the following passage.

Newton's first law states that an object at rest will not move unless an outside force, or pushing motion, makes it; likewise an object in motion will stay in motion unless an outside force stops it or changes its direction.

Newton's second law, the law of acceleration, tells us that how fast an object moves depends on how much mass it has and how much force it is pushed with. Bigger things take more force to move; when a small object and a big object are pushed with the same force, the small object will go farther.

Newton's third law states that anybody that exerts a force on another body will be affected by the same amount of force. A wrestler, for example, pushing on another wrestler, is encountering the same amount of force directed back at him.

11. Which of the following is the best summary of Newton's first law?
    (A) For every action there is an equal and opposite reaction.
    (B) All motion is relative.
    (C) An object's speed depends on its size and how hard it is pushed; smaller things are easier to push farther than larger things.
    (D) Objects cannot move, stop, or change direction by themselves.

12. Which of the following is the best summary of Newton's second law?
    (A) For every action there is an equal and opposite reaction.
    (B) All motion is relative.
    (C) An object's speed depends on its size and how hard it is pushed; smaller things are easier to push farther than larger things.
    (D) Objects cannot move, stop, or change direction by themselves.

13. Which of the following is the best summary of Newton's third law?
    (A) For every action there is an equal and opposite reaction.
    (B) All motion is relative.
    (C) An object's speed depends on its size and how hard it is pushed; smaller things are easier to push farther than larger things.
    (D) Objects cannot move, stop, or change direction by themselves.

Horseshoe Magnet   Bar Magnet

   Two of the most common shapes of household magnets are the bar magnet and the horse-shoe magnet. Their shapes may be different, but their properties are essentially the same. Both have north and south poles, which create magnetic lines of force. Magnetic lines of force always flow from one pole to the other. The lines of force around the bar magnet, therefore, completely surround it, as each line flows from one pole to the other. The magnetic lines of the horseshoe magnet have a much shorter distance to travel. Its magnetic field is, therefore, more contained.

14.   What is the best title for the passage above?
      (A)   Bar magnets are more effective than horseshoe magnets.
      (B)   Horseshoe magnets are more effective than bar magnets.
      (C)   A comparison of two different types of magnet.
      (D)   An explanation of magnetic fields.

Questions 15 and 16 refer to the following passage.

   Many of the elements we know today had already been documented before the mid-nineteenth century. However, no one scientist had developed a satisfactory comprehensive organization of them, although chemists realized that certain elements were more similar to each other than other elements. A Russian chemist, Dimitri Mendeleev, is often credited as the father of the periodic table. The periodic table lists the elements in order of their atomic mass, or weight. Today's periodic table is somewhat different than Mendeleev's. Elements are listed by atomic number (number of protons), for example, rather than atomic mass. The periodic table has proved useful not only to classify known elements but to predict the existence of unknown ones.

15.   What is the best title for the above passage?
      (A)   A Brief History of the Periodic Table
      (B)   The Life of Dimitri Mendeleev
      (C)   Where Mendeleev Went Wrong
      (D)   Atomic Number vs. Atomic Mass

16. Which of the following choices best summarizes the passage?
    (A) The periodic table is confusing and should be redone.
    (B) Scientists are always changing each other's work.
    (C) The periodic table could be used to classify things other than elements.
    (D) The periodic table has gone through many changes to get to its current form.

Questions 17 through 20 are based on the following diagram and passage.

Mineral	Mohs Hardness Scale
Diamond	▽▽▽▽▽▽▽▽▽▽
Emerald	▽▽▽▽▽▽▽▽
Topaz	▽▽▽▽▽▽▽▽
Quartz	▽▽▽▽▽▽▽
Fluorite	▽▽▽▽
Gypsum	▽▽
Talc	▽

▽ = 1 level of hardness

Alexis needed a project for the school fair. She learned in science class about the Mohs hardness scale, developed in 1812 to evaluate the hardness (defined as resistance to scratching) of different gems and minerals. Alexis created the above pictograph to display at the fair. She also wrote a report about her experiments scratching some of the minerals against each other.

17. What conclusion can you draw about diamonds from the above chart?
    (A) A diamond will probably cut glass.
    (B) Diamonds are the hardest substance of the seven substances shown on the chart.
    (C) Diamonds are the hardest substance on Earth.
    (D) The diamond is the most valuable stone shown on the chart.

18. Which of the following is NOT a conclusion you can make based on the chart?
    (A) Talc is the easiest mineral on the chart to use in powder form.
    (B) The Mohs hardness scale makes it easier to compare the scratch resistance of different minerals.
    (C) Minerals that are harder probably cost more.
    (D) Alexis's report was accepted for inclusion in the fair.

19. Which of the following can you conclude about Alexis's report?
    (A) Alexis knows nothing about the scientific method.
    (B) Alexis used some of her mother's jewelry in her experiments.
    (C) Alexis asked another student to help her with her drawing.
    (D) Alexis used some of the same minerals in her experiments that she listed on the chart.

20. Alexis wants to add ruby to her pictograph. A ruby has a Mohs number of 9. What can you conclude about the scratch resistance of a ruby?
    (A) It is harder than quartz and softer than topaz.
    (B) It is harder than an emerald and softer than a diamond.
    (C) It is harder than talc and softer than gypsum.
    (D) It is harder than topaz and softer than an emerald.

Questions 21 and 22 are based on the following passage.

Two workers at a construction company are each lifting 100-lb. loads. Ramon is using a moveable pulley, which gives an advantage of 2:1. Stanley is using a fixed pulley, which gives no mechanical advantage (1:1).

21. What can you conclude about the force Ramon must expend to lift the 100-lb. load?
    (A) Ramon only needs to expend 50 lbs. of force to lift 100 lb.
    (B) Ramon needs to expend 200 lb. of force to lift 100 lb.
    (C) Ramon needs to expend 100 lb. of force to lift 100 lb.
    (D) Ramon will expend less force if he uses the fixed pulley.

22. What can you conclude about the force Stanley must expend to lift the 100-lb. load?
    (A) Stanley only needs to expend 50 lb. of force to lift 100 lb.
    (B) Stanley needs to expend 200 lb. of force to lift 100 lb.
    (C) Stanley needs to expend 100 lb. of force to lift 100 lb.
    (D) Stanley will expend more force if he uses the mechanical pulley.

Questions 23 and 24 are based on the following diagram and passage.

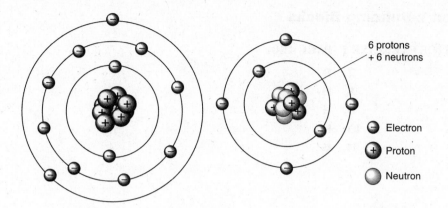

6 protons
+ 6 neutrons

⊖ Electron

⊕ Proton

◯ Neutron

The magnesium atom has 12 protons and 12 neutrons in its nucleus. It also has 12 electrons: two in the first shell, eight in the second shell, and two in the outer shell.

The carbon atom has six protons and six neutrons in its nucleus. It has six electrons: two in the inner shell and four in the outer shell.

23. What conclusion can you draw about the diagram based on the descriptions in the passage?
    (A) The atom on the left is carbon and the atom on the right is magnesium.
    (B) Both of the atoms are carbon atoms.
    (C) The atom on the left is magnesium, and the atom on the right is carbon.
    (D) Both of the atoms are magnesium atoms.

24. What conclusion can you draw from the fact that the magnesium atom has more shells?
    (A) The magnesium atom is better than the carbon atom.
    (B) The magnesium atom can be seen with the naked eye because it is larger than the carbon atom.
    (C) The magnesium atom can fit more electrons into the same amount of shells as the carbon atom.
    (D) The magnesium atom needs more shells to accommodate more electrons.

CHAPTER 15 ANSWER EXPLANATIONS

Lesson 1: Building Blocks

PRACTICE EXERCISE 1 (PAGE 450)

1. C
2. I
3. J
4. A
5. F
6. D
7. B
8. H
9. E
10. K
11. G

Lesson 2: Matter

PRACTICE EXERCISE 2 (PAGE 450)

1. Soda cans and bottles in the freezer explode because the water in the soda starts to expand as it gets colder. This puts pressure on the inside of the container, which is designed to hold a certain volume of unfrozen liquid. When the container cannot resist the pressure anymore, it breaks open and presto! Frozen soda all over tomorrow's hamburger.

PRACTICE EXERCISE 3 (PAGE 451)

1. D
2. E
3. A
4. H
5. B
6. G
7. C
8. F

PRACTICE EXERCISE 4 (PAGE 452)

1. One
2. Two
3. One
4. One

PRACTICE EXERCISE 5 (PAGE 453)

1. There are eight oxygen atoms in four molecules of hydrogen peroxide.

PRACTICE EXERCISE 6 (PAGE 453)

1. D
2. B
3. A
4. C

PRACTICE EXERCISE 7 (PAGE 453)

1. **(D)** Get outside to fresh air immediately. CO alarms are set to sound before residents begin to feel any symptoms of CO poisoning (headache, fatigue, nausea, shortness of breath, and dizziness). The longer the family stays in the house, the more likely they are to experience these and even more severe symptoms.

Lesson 3: Newton's Laws

PRACTICE EXERCISE 8 (PAGE 455)

1. 2nd
2. 1st
3. 3rd
4. 1st
5. 3rd
6. 2nd

PRACTICE EXERCISE 9 (PAGE 456)

1. **(A)** Newton's first law.
2. **(C)** Wear a seat belt and install airbags. (A) and (D) depend on the strength of the driver or passenger. This will never be greater than the force of the impact. (B) Any windshield, breakable or not, is a hard surface. It will damage a person who hurtles into it.

Lesson 4: Types of Energy

PRACTICE EXERCISE 10 (PAGE 457)

1. K
2. K
3. P
4. K
5. P

PRACTICE EXERCISE 11 (PAGE 458)

1. D
2. A
3. G
4. E
5. C
6. F
7. B

PRACTICE EXERCISE 12 (PAGE 458)

1. **(C)** A house in the Arizona desert is the best answer. (A) A house in a rainy area will not be able to collect enough sunlight to run exclusively on solar energy. (B) The apartment has no roof space and not enough outside wall space to affix solar panels. (D) A house in the forest will find much of its sunlight blocked by trees.

Lesson 5: Graphic Material

PRACTICE EXERCISE 13 (PAGE 459)

1. The title is *Earth's Elements by Percentage*. The title is found at the top of the chart.
2. The relationship between the amounts of each element is demonstrated by shading and the size of each pie wedge. Individual pie wedges are also labeled with their percentages. The chart does not indicate that all percentages added together equal 100; this is assumed.
3. Iron. It has the largest wedge and biggest percentage (35%).
4. Iron (35%) and Silicon (15%). Even though their wedges are not next to each other, you should realize that adding their percentages equals 50%. 50% is ½.
5. Oxygen!
6. The smallest wedge of the pie chart is solar energy (0.01%).
7. This tells us that solar energy provides less electricity than any other fuel source.
8. **(B)** Coal and nuclear. Coal accounts for 49.61% (almost half) of all electrical power. It also has the largest wedge by far. The next largest wedge is nuclear at 19.28%. Because this wedge is so close in size to the gas wedge, it is necessary to look carefully at the numbers to confirm which is bigger.

PRACTICE EXERCISE 14 (PAGE 461)

1. The title is *Windchill Factor*. A title is often at the top of a table, written in larger letters than the rest of the information.
2. The numbers up the left axis show wind speeds in miles per hour (mph).
3. The numbers across the top indicate actual air temperatures (temperatures with no wind).
4. **(D)** −12°.

PRACTICE EXERCISE 15 (PAGE 462)

1. **(B)** Erin's temperatures are always slightly higher.
2. Although the temperatures were the same on both days, on Wednesday there was a 20 mph wind, which would have accounted for the greater windchill.

PRACTICE EXERCISE 16 (PAGE 463)

1. The title, which is at the top of the pictograph, is *Countries with the Most Nuclear Power Plants*.
2. The left vertical axis shows the names of the countries being compared.
3. Each symbol represents ten nuclear power plants. The key is directly under the title.
4. The United States has the most power plants. There are ten complete symbols in the United States column and one incomplete symbol. 10 × 10 = 100. The incomplete symbol accounts for one to five more (it is less than half of the picture). Therefore, the United States has about 104 power plants.

   The Korea Republic has two full symbols and a partial symbol. 2 × 10 = 20. The partial symbol is barely there so it represents one to three power plants. The Korea Republic has about 21 power plants.
5. The key indicates that each lightbulb represents 500 watts. A pictograph that is not complete indicates some fraction of 500 watts being used.

6. The House Fan pictograph represents about 300–400 watts, since the lightbulb is nearly complete.

7. **(B)** "When running" means that this chart is accurate ONLY when the appliances are actively in use.

8. **(A)** The Central Air. The Central Air unit uses seven icons (pictures of lightbulbs). $7 \times 500 = 3,500$ watts. The Large and Small Window Units use, added together, is less than four icons (2,000 watts).

End-of-Chapter Questions (Page 465)

1. **(A)** (B) The workers could not lift the blocks because the blocks were huge. It did not mean the men were weak in comparison to other people. (C) The passage does not address how the workers were treated. (D) Herodotus was a historian, which means he could have been writing at any time after the pyramids were built.

2. **(A)** The author says that the pyramids are the last remaining ancient wonders. (B) The author does not rank or compare the ancient wonders. There is also no reference to building techniques (other than those used at the pyramids) or locations for the other wonders. They cannot all be assumed to be in Egypt.

3. **(D)** A tree stump is anchored to the ground by roots and needs a lever (like a crowbar or shovel) to dislodge it. (A) and (B) are examples of wheeled transportation that can be rolled up a ramp. (C) slides and may be pushed or pulled up a ramp.

4. **(C)** The whole passage emphasizes the danger of electricity and the possible results of carelessness. All of the other answer choices are untrue. People who come into contact with high voltage may survive, although seriously injured. Clothing does not insulate a person from electric shock. Even though these are workplace statistics, accidents happen at home as well. Safety procedures should be observed everywhere.

5. **(B)** Alchemists would not have spent time and energy trying to make gold in laboratories if they did not value it highly. (A) is an opinion. (C) and (D) are predictions.

6. **(C)** In the 17th and 18th centuries, many people became chemists rather than alchemists. The author indicates that chemistry was growing while alchemy was dying. Therefore, people interested in science were choosing the first over the second. Neither (A), (B), nor (D) is supported by the passage.

7. **(A)** Jupiter's gravitational pull is stronger than Earth's. Larger bodies have a stronger gravitational pull. Therefore, Jupiter is larger than Earth.

8. **(B)** The Moon's gravitational pull is weaker than Earth's. Smaller bodies have a weaker gravitational pull. Therefore, the Moon is smaller than Earth.

9. **(B)** This answer is supported by the title and the list of private industries along the left vertical axis. (A) is a detail of information found in the key. (C) The chart does not address years before 2003. (D) contradicts the information on the chart and is an incorrect conclusion.

10. **(A)** (B) IAEI is a trade organization specifically for electrical inspectors. No one else has any reason to join. (C) is a detail. (D) The trainings are for general safety purposes. They are not education toward a career. This choice is not necessarily false, but it is unrelated to the subject of the passage.

11. **(D)** Objects cannot move, stop, or change direction by themselves. (A) This is a summary of Newton's third law. (B) This is unrelated to the laws altogether. It is a principle of Einstein's theory of relativity. (C) is a summary of Newton's second law.

12. **(C)** (A) This is a summary of Newton's third law. (B) This is unrelated to the laws altogether. It is a principle of Einstein's theory of relativity. (D) is a summary of Newton's first law.

13. **(A)** (B) This is unrelated to the laws altogether. It is a principle of Einstein's theory of relativity. (C) is a summary of Newton's second law. (D) is a summary of Newton's first law.

14. **(C)** *A comparison of two different types of magnets.* The passage describes the similarities and differences between bar magnets and horseshoe magnets.

15. **(A)** The passage traces the development of the periodic table. (B) Mendeleev is mentioned once. Details of his life are not provided. (C) The passage discusses Mendeleev's success, not his failures. (D) This choice has no application to the subject of the passage. Atomic number and mass are terms used in the description, but they are not its focus.

16. **(D)** (A) is an opinion. (B) Although scientists have modified the periodic table at times, it has also remained unchanged for long amounts of time. (C) is an unlikely prediction.

17. **(B)** (C) This statement assumes too much about substances that are not shown on the chart. (A) is a prediction, and (D) is an opinion.

18. **(C)** The chart give no information about the price or cost of a sample of each mineral. (A) Since talc is the softest material, it would be the easiest to grind into a powder. (B) The Mohs hardness scale is an example of classification, which scientists often do to clarify (make clear) relationships. (D) Since Alexis presented in the fair, her report must have been accepted.

19. **(D)** (A) Alexis used the scientific method when she tested what she had learned. (B) The passage does not state where her samples came from. (C) The passage does not mention any other student involved in the project.

20. **(B)** Emerald has a score of 8 and diamond has a score of 10. Therefore, ruby should be listed between the two.

21. **(A)** Since Ramon's moveable pulley gives him a 2:1 (doubled) mechanical advantage, he only needs to expend ½ the force necessary to move the load with no help. ½ of 100 lb. is 50 lb.

22. **(C)** Since Stanley's pulley gives him no mechanical advantage, he must expend the same amount of force as the load he needs to move (100 lb.)

23. **(C)** This choice matches the two different descriptions of magnesium and carbon.

24. **(D)** (A) This is an opinion. (B) and (C) are unsupported by any information in the passage or diagram.

Science Posttest

The science posttest has 54 questions. After you review the material in this unit, you can use the test to get a sense of what areas you still need to study. Make sure you have at least 120 minutes of quiet time available to complete the test. Read each question carefully and do your best. As with the pretest, it is better if you do not guess on these questions. If you don't know the answer to a question, simply skip it and go on to the next one. The purpose of this test is to find out what areas you still need to work on, and random guessing might throw you off course.

Once you have finished, check your answers on pages 498–500, and complete the posttest evaluation chart on page 496 by circling the number of each question you answered correctly. This way you can easily see your strengths and weaknesses as well as where information on each question you missed is located in the book.

If you score very well on the posttest, it is a great sign that you have a solid foundation in the different study areas of science. You are ready to begin studying higher-level material in this subject.

Life Science

Questions 1 and 2 are based on the following passage.

Unlike plant cells, which have cell walls, the animal cell is protected only by a thin cell membrane. This cell membrane is **semipermeable**—that is, it will allow some things to pass through (like nutrients) and not others. The cell membrane is made up of protein and fat tissues and allows the animal cell greater flexibility than the plant cell.

1. What is an example of something that will NOT pass through a cell membrane?
   - (A) Water
   - (B) Oxygen
   - (C) Glucose (sugar)
   - (D) Another cell

2. Which of the following is the best definition for semipermeable?
   - (A) Rigid
   - (B) Partially porous
   - (C) Hard
   - (D) Unable to be penetrated

Questions 3 through 5 are based on the following diagram and passage.

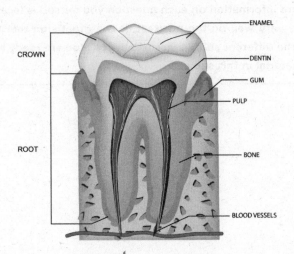

Healthy teeth are crucial to a person's well-being. A tooth has several components, all of which need to be maintained and checked regularly by a dentist. The outer part (the part we see) is made of enamel. If the enamel wears away and exposes the root, this can prove painful. Holes in the enamel are called **cavities**. Cavities are caused by decay, which, in turn, can be caused by a person's diet and care of his or her teeth. Cavities should be treated immediately, so they do not worsen and cause more pain and more extensive (and expensive!) dental work.

3. According to the diagram, what is the layer just under the enamel of a tooth called?
   (A) Dentin
   (B) The crown
   (C) The gum
   (D) The nerve

4. According to the passage, what is the best thing to do if you think you have a cavity?
   (A) Leave it alone; it will go away.
   (B) Make an appointment with your dentist right away.
   (C) Chew only on the other side.
   (D) Poke at the tooth to try to find the cavity yourself.

5. What does the passage say is the probable effect of ignoring a cavity?
   (A) It will go away.
   (B) It will stay the same.
   (C) It will get worse
   (D) It will cure itself.

Question 6 is based on the following passage.

Inherited characteristics are those that can be passed from parents to children. Examples of inherited characteristics would be eye color or height. Acquired characteristics cannot be passed to children. Acquired characteristics only affect the person who acquires them. A man who has developed strong arm muscles will not automatically have children with strong arm muscles unless he carries that gene.

6. Tanya does not carry a gene for blondness. Neither does her husband. Tanya regularly dyes her hair blonde. What are the chances that she will have blonde children?
   (A) 0%
   (B) 25%
   (C) 50%
   (D) 100%

Questions 7 and 8 are based on the following passage.

Many people in ancient times, including the philosopher Aristotle, believed in the principle of **spontaneous generation**. Spontaneous generation was a theory that proposed that life could emerge from non-living objects. People thought mice and rats, for example, could be formed from mud. One of the first scientists to challenge this way of thinking by experiment was Francesco Reid in 1668. Reid placed jars of uncovered meat on a table. Next to them, he placed jars of the same meat, but covered them tightly. Maggots (fly larvae) appeared in the open jars but not in the covered jars.

7. What conclusion can you draw based on Reid's experiment?
   (A) That living things are not created from non-living things.
   (B) That living things are not created from other living things.
   (C) That covered meat lasts longer.
   (D) That flies don't like meat.

8. What can you infer is the most likely reason that people believed in spontaneous generation?
   (A) They had made careful observations and experiments.
   (B) They misinterpreted what they saw.
   (C) Spontaneous generation used to exist, but it does not anymore.
   (D) Nobody ever did experiments on anything.

Questions 9 through 12 are based on the following passage, illustration, and chart.

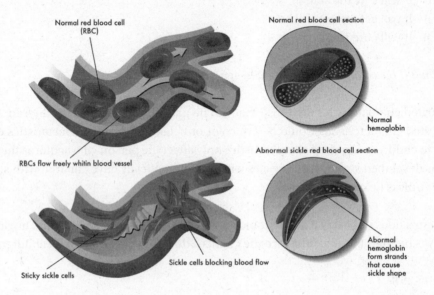

Sickle cell disease is a serious inherited condition that affects roughly one out of every 400 African-American children born. This condition causes some red blood cells to be shaped like sickles, or half-moons, instead of the normal round shape. It is harder for sickle-shaped cells to pass through the blood vessels, and there is a higher likelihood that they will clump and form clots. These clots can be life-threatening. Some of the signs of sickle cell clumping are listed below.

Part of the Body Affected	Symptom
Brain	Stroke or severe headache
Eye	Problems with vision
Hands or feet	Pain and swelling

9. Which of the following is an opinion about sickle cell disease?
   (A) Sickle cell is caused by irregularly shaped blood cells.
   (B) Sickle cell affects primarily Asian-Americans.
   (C) You can catch sickle cell from someone who has it.
   (D) Sickle cell is a terrible, painful disease.

10. Which of the following is a fact about sickle cell disease?
    (A) Sickle cell is caused by irregularly shaped blood cells.
    (B) Sickle cell affects primarily Asian-Americans.
    (C) You can catch sickle cell from someone who has it.
    (D) Sickle cell is a terrible, painful disease.

11. What is the difference between sickle cells and normal red blood cells?
    (A) Normal cells are round, and sickle cells are a half-moon shape.
    (B) Sickle cells are round, and normal cells are a half-moon shape.
    (C) Sickle cells are bigger.
    (D) Red blood cells are smaller.

12. What can you conclude is the safest course of action for parents if their child with sickle cell experiences sudden vision problems?
    (A) Make an appointment in a few weeks to see if the child needs glasses.
    (B) Give the child eye drops.
    (C) Contact the child's doctor immediately.
    (D) Tell the child's teacher to let him sit in the front row to see the board.

Questions 13 and 14 are based on the following passage.

Scurvy is a sometimes fatal disease caused by a lack of enough Vitamin C. Some of its symptoms are spots on the skin, soft gums and loss of teeth, and fever. For hundreds of years, scurvy was a common complaint among sailors, who were unable to get proper nutrition during long voyages. It was noticed that fresh fruits and vegetables usually helped or prevented scurvy, but James Lind in 1747 was the first to discover the specific link to Vitamin C. Because of the modern availability of fresh foods and vitamin-fortified foods, scurvy is rare today. However, it does occasionally occur in people with poor diets.

13. Which of the following foods would NOT likely help prevent scurvy?
    (A) Orange juice
    (B) Lemons
    (C) Broccoli
    (D) Bread

14. Which of the following is the most likely cause of sailors being so prone to scurvy?
    (A) They didn't get enough exercise.
    (B) It was too expensive for captains to buy enough fresh food for all the crew.
    (C) It was hard to store fresh fruits and vegetables for long periods at sea.
    (D) The sailors didn't like fresh fruits and vegetables.

Ken learned in school that there are six kingdoms in the natural world. After class, he listed the kingdoms in the following way:

ANIMAL—members of the animal kingdom are multicellular (made up of more than one cell). They cannot photosynthesize or make their own food. They are able to move themselves about.

PLANTS—Plants are also multicellular, but they feed themselves by converting the Sun's energy into food. Although they can move to a limited extent (opening and closing flowers, for instance) they are not considered mobile.

FUNGI—Fungi do not feed themselves through photosynthesis, but they reproduce like plants. Mushrooms are an example of fungi.

PROTIST—Protists are single-celled organisms that contain a nucleus.

EUBACTERIA—Eubacteria is the scientific name for most common forms of bacteria, including those that cause infection in humans and animals.

ARCHAEBACTERIA—Archaebacteria are one-celled organisms living in extreme environments. Except for scientists who study them, most people do not come into contact with these organisms.

15. What is the main idea of the passage above?
    (A) Bacteria are more numerous than plants or animals.
    (B) Animals are the only kingdom who can move themselves on their own.
    (C) Living things are classified into six different categories.
    (D) Plants can feed themselves through photosynthesis.

16. Scientists find a one-celled organism living in boiling water in a natural hot spring. In which kingdom do you predict that this organism probably be classified?
    (A) Eubacteria
    (B) Animals
    (C) Protist
    (D) Archaebacteria

17. Paul has a bacteriological infection. What classification of organism is most likely the cause?
    (A) Eubacteria
    (B) Animals
    (C) Protist
    (D) Archaebacteria

18. Amoebas are single celled but contain a nucleus. What can you infer is their classification?
    (A) Eubacteria
    (B) Animals
    (C) Protist
    (D) Archaebacteria

19. Mitosis is the process by which a cell creates an identical reproduction of itself. Julio cuts himself by accident at work. After the cut heals, there is no scar. What conclusion can you draw about how Julio's body has healed itself?

(A) Julio should be more careful.

(B) The cut did not get infected because Julio cleaned and bandaged it right away.

(C) Julio's skin cells reproduced themselves to heal and cover the wound.

(D) Hair cells can also reproduce by mitosis.

Earth and Space Science

Questions 20 and 21 are based on the following passage and map.

Earthquakes are measured on a scale called the Richter scale. The higher the number registers on the scale, the stronger the earthquake. An earthquake with a Richter magnitude of 2 might pass unnoticed by many people and probably would not do much damage. A quake with a magnitude of 7 could cause a great deal of damage indeed, and be very dangerous to any people in the area.

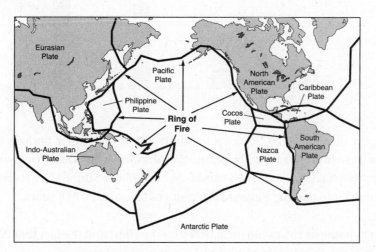

One area of the Earth that is susceptible to earthquakes is called the Pacific Rim. The state of California is part of the Pacific Rim. Many Californians are familiar with basic safety precautions during an earthquake. These include having an earthquake-readiness plan, staying indoors until the shaking has stopped, avoiding operating heavy machinery (such as a car), and staying away from windows or anything that might fall on you.

20. Which of the following would be a wise safety precaution during an earthquake?

(A) Running outside, and shouting to alert your neighbors.

(B) Hiding under your bed.

(C) Pulling over to the side of the road if you are driving.

(D) Looking out the window to see what is happening.

21. The Pacific Rim, where earthquakes are common, extends all the way around the Pacific Ocean. In what other country is earthquake safety likely to be an important public safety issue?
    (A) Egypt
    (B) Japan
    (C) France
    (D) Greenland

Questions 22 and 23 are based on the following bar chart and passage.

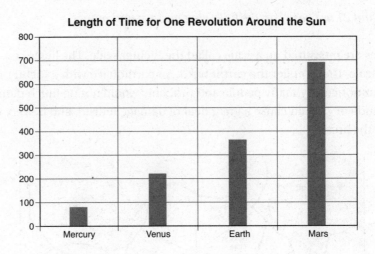

Length of Time for One Revolution Around the Sun

The four inner planets of the Solar System have the most similar periods of revolution. Planets farther out—Jupiter, Saturn, Neptune, and Uranus—take much longer to complete a revolution. Neptune takes almost 165 years to go around the Sun! Before its reclassification as a dwarf planet, Pluto had the longest revolution of all—almost 248 years.

22. What is a hypothesis you could form based on the chart and the fact that Pluto, the body farthest out, has the longest revolution?
    (A) Pluto takes a long time because it is small.
    (B) The inner planets are less heavy than the outer planets.
    (C) The farther a planet is from the Sun, the longer its revolution.
    (D) The outer planets are less heavy than the inner planets.

23. What is one way you could go about testing your hypothesis?
    (A) Go outside, and look up at the night sky every night for at least a year.
    (B) Research information on all the planets to see if it supports or negates your theory.
    (C) Buy a telescope, and track the planets from your window or backyard.
    (D) Assume your hypothesis is correct.

The classification of a wave as a tsunami depends on two things: its size and the way it was created. Regular common waves on the water are caused by wind friction. Tsunamis are caused by underwater earthquakes, volcanoes, or landslides. They may also be caused (rarely) by asteroids or other extraterrestrial bodies falling into the ocean. Tsunamis travel more than 10 times faster than ordinary waves. They also have a much longer wavelength than average.

24. What is the best title for the above passage?
    (A) Causes of Megatsunamis
    (B) The Likelihood of an Asteroid Crashing to Earth
    (C) The Deadly Tsunami
    (D) A Comparison of Tsunamis with Ordinary Waves

25. What is one way the passage contrasts ordinary waves and tsunamis?
    (A) It states that waves and tsunamis are caused by different things.
    (B) A giant tsunami is called a megatsunami.
    (C) Tsunamis can move at over 600 mph.
    (D) Tsunamis are caused by wind friction.

26. What is an example of an extraterrestrial body?
    (A) A meteoroid
    (B) An iceberg
    (C) Earth
    (D) A whale

Questions 27 through 30 are based on the following passage.

In 1967, scientist John Wheeler applied the term "black hole" to bodies so massive that not even light could escape their gravitational fields. Such bodies had been suspected for hundreds of years but never officially named before. Scientists believe that a black hole is the result of the death of a giant star (at least three times as big as our Sun). Every star has a life cycle the length of which depends on how much hydrogen and helium it has to burn. As a giant star runs out of these elements, it swells to become a huge red supergiant. The most massive stars then collapse and explode in supernovas. Finally, it becomes a black hole.

27. Which of the following is a prediction based on the above passage?
    (A) Black holes result from the collapse of giant stars.
    (B) Scientists will one day figure out how to visit black holes.
    (C) All stars go through life cycles.
    (D) Studying the stars really isn't very useful.

28. Which of the following is NOT addressed by the passage?
    (A) What type of stars become black holes.
    (B) What stars burn in their cores.
    (C) When the term "black hole" was coined.
    (D) How a star is born.

29. What is a conclusion you can make based on the above information?
    (A) Our Sun will never become a black hole.
    (B) Any star can become a black hole.
    (C) When we travel to distant stars, we might find other life forms.
    (D) A red supergiant is three times more massive than our Sun.

30. What is the main idea of the passage above?
    (A) To describe the nature and origin of black holes.
    (B) To compare our Sun with other stars.
    (C) To warn people of the time when our Sun will become a black hole.
    (D) To describe the life cycle of all stars.

Questions 31 through 33 are based on the following passage.

Galileo was an Italian astronomer who lived about 400 years ago. He was one of the first scientists to look at the sky through a telescope. In doing so, he made many major discoveries: the rings of Saturn, the moons of Jupiter, and others. Galileo's observations convinced him that the Earth revolved around the Sun (as had been earlier proposed by Nicolaus Copernicus) and not the other way around, as was commonly thought. Galileo began to publish books on his theories. The church in Italy was upset with his findings and threatened him. He died under house arrest in 1642.

31. What is the best title for the above passage?
    (A) A Comparison of Astronomers Galileo and Copernicus
    (B) The Life of Nicolaus Copernicus
    (C) Galileo's Contribution to Science
    (D) The Italian Church in 1642.

32. Why was Galileo able to see things in the sky that other scientists couldn't?
    (A) His eyesight was better.
    (B) He used a telescope.
    (C) He was able to prove that the Earth went around the Sun.
    (D) He kept notes on everything he saw.

33. *Heliocentric* means to circle the Sun. Most people at the time believed the universe was *geocentric*. What is the most likely meaning of geocentric?
    (A) Circling around Earth
    (B) Circling around Saturn
    (C) Empty
    (D) Old

Questions 34 through 36 are based on the following passage and pie chart.

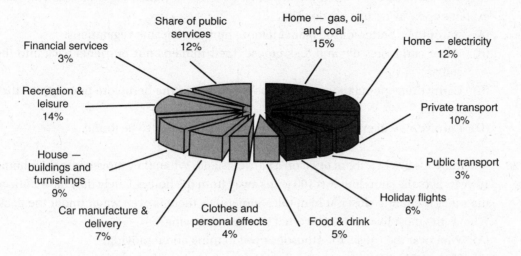

Financial services
3%

Share of public
services
12%

Home — gas, oil,
and coal
15%

Home — electricity
12%

Recreation &
leisure
14%

Private transport
10%

House —
buildings and
furnishings
9%

Public transport
3%

Car manufacture &
delivery
7%

Clothes and
personal effects
4%

Food & drink
5%

Holiday flights
6%

www.carbonfootprint.com

In 2006, presidential candidate Al Gore produced the movie *An Inconvenient Truth* about the effects of pollution on the environment. Included in the film were tips for reducing each individual's **carbon footprint**. What is a carbon footprint?

It is the amount of carbon each of us is responsible for emitting into the atmosphere. There is a small natural amount of carbon in the atmosphere, but the extra amounts being contributed by industry and our lifestyles are contributing to global climate change.

Some ways to reduce our carbon footprints are

- Buy organic local food.
- Use a water filter instead of bottled water.
- Make your home as energy-efficient as possible.

34. According to the chart, which two areas emit the most carbon into the atmosphere?
    (A) Home-gas, oil, and coal and Home-electricity
    (B) Home-electricity and Share of public services
    (C) Home-gas, oil, and coal and Recreation and leisure
    (C) Home-electricity and Private transport

35. Which two areas emit the least carbon?
    (A) Public transport and Clothes and personal effects
    (B) Public transport and Financial services
    (C) Financial services and Clothes
    (D) Clothes and Food and Drink

36. Which of the following is NOT a way to reduce your personal carbon footprint?
    (A) Take public transportation instead of driving.
    (B) Carpool instead of driving alone.
    (C) Put your air conditioner on the coldest setting.
    (D) Buy food from a local organic co-op.

37. The flow of energy in ecosystems moves in a circle. Plants nourish herbivores (plant eaters). Herbivores nourish carnivores and omnivores (meat eaters and animals that eat both). Carnivores in turn nourish plants. Which of the following choices is a fact that explains one way carnivores do this?
    (A) It would be better for the planet if more humans became vegetarians.
    (B) When carnivores die and decompose, their remains put nutrients back into the soil.
    (C) Carnivorous populations are always smaller than the herbivore populations they feed on.
    (D) Carnivores will exist on a plant diet if there is no meat to be found.

38. The Hudsons live in a shore town on a barrier island. When they moved into their home 10 years ago, the shoreline was 100 yards away from the house. Lately they have noticed the water is coming closer at high tide. Sometimes there is even water under the deck! What is the most likely cause for what they are observing?
    (A) Whatever the cause, the Hudsons need to think about moving.
    (B) The next big storm may actually bring water up into the house.
    (C) Physical weathering is changing the landscape of the barrier island.
    (D) Chemical weathering is changing the landscape of the barrier island.

Physical Science

Question 39 is based on the following passage.

When replacing a light bulb, always use one of the recommended wattage or lower. Most manufacturers affix a sticker or a tag to their products to let the consumer know what wattage to use. Using a higher wattage than recommended can cause the lamp or light fixture to overheat and become a fire hazard.

39. In a lamp that has a wattage recommendation of 60 watts, which of the following bulbs is NOT safe to use?
    (A) 25 watts
    (B) 40 watts
    (C) 60 watts
    (D) 100 watts

Questions 40 through 42 are based on the following passage.

All sugar is made up of carbon, hydrogen, and oxygen. Two common forms of sugar are lactose ("milk sugar" found mainly in dairy products) and fructose (fruit sugar). The chemical symbol for lactose is $C_{12}H_{22}O_{11}$. The chemical symbol for fructose is $C_6H_{12}O_6$.

40. How many oxygen atoms are there in fructose?
    (A) 6
    (B) 11
    (C) 12
    (D) 22

41. How many more carbon atoms are there in lactose than fructose?
    (A) 6
    (B) 11
    (C) 12
    (D) 22

42. How many hydrogen atoms are there in three molecules of lactose ($3C_{12}H_{22}O_{11}$)?
    (A) 22
    (B) 33
    (C) 36
    (D) 66

Questions 43 and 44 are based on the following passage and illustration.

A lever moves a weight (load) by pivoting on a fulcrum using a force. A pair of pliers consists of two levers fastened together.

43. You are using a pair of pliers to pull a nail out of a piece of wood. What is the load?
    (A) Your hand
    (B) The pliers
    (C) The fastening holding the pliers together
    (D) The nail

44. In the situation in question 43, what is the force?
    (A) Your hand
    (B) The pliers
    (C) The fastening holding the pliers together
    (D) The nail

A compass is an instrument that takes advantage of the Earth's magnetic field to help people find directions. The needle of the compass always points toward the magnetic North Pole, a spot very near the actual North Pole. By aligning that needle with the N on the dial, a user can tell which ways are north, east, south, and west. Compasses are especially useful in places where there are no other landmarks, such as deep in the woods or a desert.

45. You are standing in the woods, holding your compass in front of you. The arrow points at the N, straight ahead. Which way will you need to walk to go east?
    (A) Left
    (B) Right
    (C) Straight ahead
    (D) Behind you

46. What is the best summary of the above passage and illustration?
    (A) A compass is a magnetic instrument that helps people to find directions.
    (B) A compass's needle always points to the North Pole.
    (C) Many people take compasses with them on trips.
    (D) A compass is a useful tool to pack on a camping trip.

47. What is a conclusion you can draw from the above passage and illustration?
    (A) A compass is a magnetic instrument that helps people to find directions.
    (B) A compass's needle always points to the North Pole.
    (C) Many people take compasses with them on trips.
    (D) A compass is a useful tool to pack on a camping trip.

A wedge is a simple machine that is used to split or separate something. It has one pointed end and one thicker end. The mechanical advantage of a wedge depends on its slope divided by its thickness. In other words, the longer and narrower the wedge, the more advantage it will give the user.

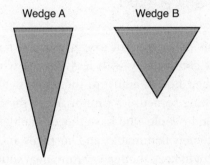

Wedge A   Wedge B

48. Wedge A above on the left has a slope 6 inches long and a width of 3 inches. Wedge B on the right has a slope 4 inches long and a width of 4 inches. Which wedge gives the greater mechanical advantage?
    (A) Wedge A
    (B) Wedge B
    (C) Neither
    (D) It is impossible to tell.

49. Bob is chopping firewood. He needs to fix a wedge facing downward into a split in the wood before hitting it with a chopping tool. Which wedge will make it easier for him to split the log?
    (A) Wedge A
    (B) Wedge B
    (C) Neither
    (D) It is impossible to tell.

People sometimes think that the air that we breathe is 100% oxygen, but in point of fact, the percentage of oxygen in our atmosphere is much lower—about 21%. The most abundant gas in the atmosphere is nitrogen at 78%.

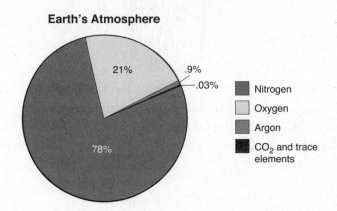

Earth's Atmosphere

For a healthy person, this percentage of oxygen is quite sufficient. People who live at high altitudes actually exist comfortably with less (people who travel to higher altitudes often don't feel well until their bodies adjust to the difference). However, people who are sick or have difficulty breathing sometimes cannot get all the oxygen they need out of the air. Doctors often recommend people who have this difficulty breathe pure oxygen from a canister. Pure oxygen is extremely flammable, and hospitals and patients who use and store these canisters must take care to keep them away from heat sources.

50. What is the main idea of the pie chart?
    (A) Nitrogen is the most abundant element in the atmosphere.
    (B) Four main elements and some trace elements compose Earth's atmosphere.
    (C) People who are sick often need to breathe pure oxygen.
    (D) The CO_2 and trace elements really don't affect humans at all.

51. What is the danger of storing oxygen too near a heat source?
    (A) The oxygen could be contaminated.
    (B) The oxygen might not be effective.
    (C) The oxygen could spoil.
    (D) The oxygen might spark and ignite.

52. Which of the following should you never do within 5 feet of an oxygen canister?
    (A) Eat
    (B) Move heavy furniture
    (C) Light a cigarette
    (D) Fall asleep

Question 53 is based on the following passage and illustration.

Many household cleaning products are more dangerous than people realize. Bleach and ammonia, in particular, should never be mixed. Once together, they release toxic fumes that can render a person unconscious and unable to get to safety.

53. Which of the following is NOT a safety precaution in the case of bleach and ammonia accidentally being mixed?
    (A) Get away from the area immediately.
    (B) Call 911.
    (C) Call Poison Control.
    (D) Continue cleaning. Only open windows if it is not cold out.

Figure A

Figure B

54. Figures A and B show two roller coasters. A is waiting at the top of the structure; B is on its way down. What type of energy does each display?
    (A) A shows kinetic energy and B shows potential energy.
    (B) B shows kinetic energy and A shows potential energy.
    (C) The force of a moving roller coaster cannot be measured accurately.
    (D) Both roller coasters are capable of kinetic and potential energy states.

POSTTEST EVALUATION CHART

After checking the answers on the following pages, circle the numbers of the questions you got correct in Column B. Record the total number of correct questions for each skill in Column C. Column D gives you the number of correct questions you need to answer correctly to indicate that you have a good understanding of the skill. If you got fewer correct answers than shown in Column D, study the pages shown in Column E. Using this analysis will allow you to focus on your challenges and use your study time more effectively.

A		B	C	D	E
Skill Area		Questions	Number of Correct Answers	Number Correct to Show a Good Understanding	Pages to Study
Main Idea	Life Science	15	____/5	4	363–478
	Earth and Space	24, 30, 31			
	Physical Science	50			
Compare/ Contrast	Life Science	11	____/2	2	
	Earth and Space	25			
	Physical Science				
Cause and Effect	Life Science	14, 17	____/3	2	
	Earth and Space	38			
	Physical Science				
Making Predictions	Life Science	5, 13, 16	____/8	6	
	Earth and Space	21, 27			
	Physical Science	45, 49, 52			
Drawing Conclusions	Life Science	7, 12, 19	____/8	6	
	Earth and Space	22, 29			
	Physical Science	43, 44, 47			

A		B	C	D	E
Skill Area		**Questions**	**Number of Correct Answers**	**Number Correct to Show a Good Understanding**	**Pages to Study**
Making Inferences	Life Science	8, 18			
	Earth and Space	20, 23	____ /6	4	
	Physical Science	39, 51			
Fact and Opinion	Life Science	9, 10			
	Earth and Space	37	____ /3	2	
	Physical Science				
Summarization	Life Science				
	Earth and Space		____ /1	1	
	Physical Science	46			
Content	Life Science	1, 2, 3, 4, 6			
	Earth and Space	26, 28, 32, 33, 34, 35, 36	____ /18	15	
	Physical Science	40, 41, 42, 48, 53, 54			
TOTAL			____ /54	42	

If you have correctly answered more than the number of questions in the Column D TOTAL, you are ready for HSE-Level Science!

POSTTEST ANSWER EXPLANATIONS

1. **(D)** All the other options are nutrients, which the passage states are able to pass through the cell membrane. Another cell is not a nutrient.

2. **(B)** Even if you are not sure of the meaning of porous, process of elimination rules out all the other choices. Semipermeable means able to be permeated by some things. *Hard* and *rigid* mean the same thing. *Unable to be penetrated* is the opposite of permeable.

3. **(A)** The label that identifies this layer is above the gum on the left-hand side of the diagram.

4. **(B)** *The passage says cavities should be treated immediately.* Immediately means right away. (A) and (C) The passage says ignoring cavities may cause them to get worse. (D) Never attempt to do dental work on yourself; you could injure your mouth.

5. **(C)** The passage says *cavities should be treated immediately so they do not worsen.*

6. **(A)** 0% Dyed blonde hair is an acquired characteristic and will not be passed on to offspring.

7. **(A)** Reid proved that meat alone could not produce larvae (baby flies). Only adult flies, feeding on the meat in the open containers, could produce larvae.

8. **(B)** People constantly saw mice coming out of the mud and maggots hatching in old meat. They made the mistaken assumption that one thing (mud) gave birth to the other (mice). (A) Scientists who did make careful observations ultimately realized the truth. (C) is untrue. (D) is too broad; experiments were done in many areas, but Reid was the first one to prove this particular fact.

9. **(D)** The word *terrible* is a judgmental adjective. (A) This is a fact, not an opinion. (B) is false; the passage says the African-American community is affected. (C) is incorrect. The passage states that sickle cell is inherited.

10. **(A)** This is a fact stated in the passage. (B) is false. The passage says the African-American community is affected. (C) is incorrect. The passage states that sickle cell is inherited. (D) This is an opinion. The word terrible is a judgmental adjective.

11. **(A)** Although the two different types of cells are not labeled in the diagram, the passage states that round is normal and half-moon shapes are caused by the condition of sickle cell.

12. **(C)** Vision problems can be a symptom of a clot in the eye according to the chart. The passage states that clots can be life threatening. Any of the other choices would be inadequate, to say the least.

13. **(D)** Bread does not qualify as a fresh fruit or vegetable. All the other choices do.

14. **(C)** Hundreds of years ago there was no refrigeration and few ways to preserve food properly. (A) Sailors were workers, not passengers. They had ample opportunity to exercise. (B) Cost is not mentioned in the passage. In fact, once captains realized what was making men sick, every effort was made to provide a proper diet. (D) This is not supported by the passage.

15. **(C)** There is no evidence for choice (A) or (B) in the passage. (D) is a fact (detail) from the passage.

16. **(D)** Archaebacteria live in extreme environments. Boiling water is an extreme environment.

17. **(A)** This is the category for most common forms of bacteria, including those that infect humans.

18. **(C)** An amoeba is a single-celled organism with a nucleus. This is the definition of the members of the protist group.

19. **(C)** This is an example of the process of mitosis explained in the paragraph. (A) is an opinion. (B) is an assumption; no mention is made of how the cut was treated. (D) is an unrelated fact.

20. **(C)** Pulling over to the side of the road if you are driving is the safest choice here. The passage states that staying indoors is important, so (A) is not a good idea. (B) Hiding under a bed, or anything heavy, is dangerous. (D) The passage recommends staying away from windows.

21. **(B)** Japan is the only country on or close to the Pacific Ocean.

22. **(C)** Each planet on the chart is farther than the one on its right and has a longer revolution period. Pluto, the farthest body out, has the longest revolution. There is enough evidence to create a hypothesis that the planets not on the chart follow the same pattern. Such a hypothesis would need to be proved with evidence before it could be stated as a fact.

23. **(B)** Statistics for the Solar System can be easily found at the library or online. (A) and (C) Not all of the planets can be seen at night by the unaided eye or even a commercial telescope. In any event, one Earth year is not enough to observe the full revolutions of the farther planets. (D) This choice does not follow the rules of the scientific method.

24. **(D)** The passage compares and contrasts two different types of waves. (A) Megatsunamis are not mentioned. (B) The example of an asteroid is a supporting detail, not the main idea. (C) This title ignores details presented about ordinary waves.

25. **(A)** (B), (C), and (D) only address tsunamis, not ordinary waves.

26. **(A)** A meteoroid is a piece of rock that enters Earth's atmosphere from space. *Extraterrestrial* means outside of Earth. All of the other choices have their origins on our planet.

27. **(B)** The word "will" marks this as a prediction. (A) and (C) are facts. (D) is an opinion.

28. **(D)** (A) The passage says giant stars become black holes. (B) The passage states stars burn hydrogen and helium. (C) According to the passage, in 1967.

29. **(A)** The passage states that our Sun is not big enough. (B) is false. (C) is a prediction. (D) is a detail from the passage.

30. **(A)** (B) The Sun is only briefly mentioned. (C) is incorrect; the passage states that only stars 3 times bigger than the Sun can become black holes. (D) is too broad. Only giant stars are described.

31. **(C)** Events from Galileo's career are the focus of the passage. Copernicus and the Italian church are only mentioned in relation to him.

32. **(B)** The passage states that he was one of the first to do so.

33. **(A)** *Geo* means Earth. Also the passage states that this was the common belief of the time.

34. **(C)** Home-gas, oil, and coal emits 15%. Recreation and leisure emits 14%. These are the two largest sections of the pie.

35. **(B)** *Public transport and Financial services.* These are the two smallest sections, with only 3% each.

36. **(C)** Using a warmer air conditioning setting saves energy and money. All of the other choices will also do so.

37. **(B)** (A) is an opinion. (C) is an unrelated fact. (D) is incorrect.

38. **(C)** (A) is an opinion. (B) is a prediction. (D) is incorrect. Chemical weathering would change the substance of the land, not just its shape.

39. **(D)** Using a light bulb of more than recommended wattage creates a risk of fire.

40. **(A)** 6. The small subscripted number after the (O_6) denotes the number of oxygen atoms.

41. **(A)** 6. There are 12 carbon atoms in lactose (C_{12}). There are six carbon atoms in fructose (C_6). $12 - 6 = 6$.

42. **(D)** Three molecules with 22 atoms of hydrogen in each one = 66.

43. **(D)** The load is always the weight you are trying to move—in this case, a nail.

44. **(A)** The force supplies the energy to move the load. Your hand is the only thing moving the pliers.

45. **(B)** By looking at the diagram, you can see that if N (north) is straight ahead, east is on the right, west is on the left, and south is behind you.

46. **(A)** (B) is a fact (detail) from the passage. (C) is an unproven observation. It is not supported by any information in the passage. (D) is a conclusion drawn from the facts in the passage.

47. **(D)** The passage states that compasses are especially useful where there are no landmarks. (A) is a summary of the whole passage. (B) is a fact (detail) from the passage. (C) is an unproven observation. It is not supported by any information in the passage.

48. **(A)** *Wedge A* has a slope 2 inches longer than Wedge B and is 1 inch narrower. The passage states that a longer, narrower wedge will give more advantage than a shorter, wider one.

49. **(A)** *Wedge A* has a slope 2 inches longer than Wedge B and is 1 inch narrower. The passage states that a longer, narrower wedge will give more advantage than a shorter, wider one. Having a greater mechanical advantage means it increases Bob's force more than Wedge B will.

50. **(B)** (A) and (C) are details from the passage. (D) is not supported by the passage. CO_2 is, in fact, part of the natural global life cycle.

51. **(D)** The passage states that oxygen is *flammable*. Flammable means able to burn. (A), (B), and (C) are not supported by the passage.

52. **(C)** A cigarette is a heat source. None of the other choices would create a dangerous situation.

53. **(D)** If you are in the vicinity of toxic fumes from a mixture of bleach and ammonia, get out immediately. Do not stop to open windows no matter what the temperature. The room can be aired and cleared later by emergency personnel. (A) This is always the first step in this particular emergency. (B) and (C) 911 and Poison Control will both assist callers who alert them to dangerous fumes.

54. **(B)** Kinetic energy is exhibited when things move; potential energy is an attribute of things about to move.

UNIT 4
Social Studies

Social Studies Pretest

The social studies pretest has 28 questions. It is organized into groups of questions that follow the chapters in the social studies unit. The social studies unit is divided into chapters on U.S. history, government, world history, geography, and economics. You can use this test to get a sense of which areas you need to study. Make sure you have at least 30 minutes of quiet time available to complete the test. Read each question carefully, and do your best. However, *do not guess on these questions*. If you don't know the answer to a question, simply skip it, and go on to the next one. The purpose of this test is to find out what areas you need to work on, and random guessing might throw you off course.

Some questions on this test will ask about a specific fact in one of the social studies content areas, such as world history. Other questions will test your critical thinking skills, like identifying a fact from an opinion or analyzing information from a graph.

Once you have finished, check your answers on page 514, and complete the pretest evaluation chart on page 512 by circling the number of each question you answered correctly. This way you can easily see your strengths and weaknesses as well as where information on each question you missed is located in the book.

If you score very well on the pretest, that is a great sign that you have a solid foundation in social studies. Still, make sure to check out the end-of-chapter questions for each topic. These pages will include several questions focusing on the thinking skills you will need to get a high score on the social studies test. You'll want to make sure your skills are sharp before moving on to the next chapter.

1. What was a major difference between the northern colonies and the southern colonies in America before the Revolutionary War?
   (A) Slavery was more popular in the North than in the South.
   (B) The northern colonies were originally established by the Canadians, while the southern colonies were originally settled by the French.
   (C) Northern colonies developed more manufacturing than the more agricultural southern colonies.
   (D) More southern colonies were founded for religious reasons than the northern colonies.

2. During World War II, the United States was allied with which nations?
   (A) Great Britain and the Soviet Union
   (B) Germany and France
   (C) France and Italy
   (D) Japan and Germany

Use the graph below to answer question 3.

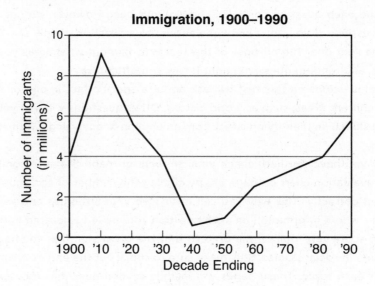

3. Approximately how many people immigrated to the United States in 1980?
   (A) 2 million
   (B) 4 million
   (C) 5.5 million
   (D) 9 million

Use the passage below to answer questions 4 and 5.

American colonists frequently conflicted with Native Americans over land and resources. Later, as the United States grew and expanded west, this trend continued. Settlers pushed across the continent eventually establishing states from the Atlantic Ocean to the Pacific Ocean. During the 19th century, the overall population grew from under 10 million to approximately 80 million. At the same time, the number of Native Americans declined by over 50%.

4. What was an effect of American expansion west?
   (A) Wars with foreign countries
   (B) A decline in the overall U.S. population
   (C) A decline in the Native-American population
   (D) Fewer conflicts with Native Americans over land and resources

5. Which statement best restates the information from the paragraph?
   (A) Despite conflicts, the United States grew rapidly during the 19th century.
   (B) Native Americans prospered in the 19th century.
   (C) The United States gradually spread from west to east.
   (D) No states were created along the Pacific Ocean in the 19th century.

6. The Supreme Court of the United States is in which branch of government?
   (A) Legislative
   (B) Judicial
   (C) Executive
   (D) Congress

7. Which statement is true about a representative democracy?
   (A) People vote directly to change a law.
   (B) The king or queen makes the final decisions for the government.
   (C) The government is run by a totalitarian ruler.
   (D) People elect officials like senators to vote on issues for them.

8. Why are political parties important in elections?
   (A) The parties are held on election day, and the party guests are encouraged to vote.
   (B) Political parties help candidates with elections.
   (C) Political parties determine how many members serve in Congress.
   (D) Political parties are not important to the election process.

9. Which statement below describes how the "checks and balances" of the United States government works?
   (A) Each branch of government is able to limit the power of the other branches.
   (B) The President may rule like a king and check the rest of government.
   (C) Checks are used to pay the government bills and balance the books.
   (D) The majority will rule and balance the minority in elections.

Use the image below to answer question 10.

10. Which statement best **summarizes** the cartoon?
    (A) The American colonies must come together.
    (B) The American colonies are like a dangerous snake.
    (C) The Boston Tea Party was justified.
    (D) Without help from the French, the colonists are unlikely to defeat the British.

11. Which statement below is an opinion?
    (A) The President is the commander in chief of the military.
    (B) The U.S. Constitution is the best form of government ever created.
    (C) The House of Representatives is based on population.
    (D) The Supreme Court is elected by the Senate.

Use the passage below to answer question 12.

One of the jobs of Congress is to introduce new laws. Once passed, the President can either enact the law or veto it. If the law is vetoed, a two thirds majority of Congress can overturn the veto and enact the law. Still, the Supreme Court can strike down any law they see as unconstitutional. Supreme Court justices are nominated by the President and approved by the Senate.

12. What can you infer from the passage?
    (A) The President is more powerful than the other two branches.
    (B) The Supreme Court can strike down any law as unconstitutional.
    (C) When the President vetoes a law it is gone forever.
    (D) The U.S. government values checks and balances between its branches.

13. Ancient river valley civilizations existed along the following rivers except:
    (A) Nile
    (B) Missouri
    (C) Indus
    (D) Tigris

14. Which of the following is true about the Renaissance?
    (A) People began to study the ancient Greeks and Romans.
    (B) Electricity was invented.
    (C) The great pyramids of Egypt were constructed.
    (D) Democracy spread throughout Europe.

Use the time line below to answer questions 15 through 17.

World War II Time Line

Hitler becomes Chancellor of Germany		Germany announces "union" with Austria		Germany invades Poland	
1933		**1938, March**		**1939, September 1**	
	1936		**1938, October**		**1939, September 3**
	German troops occupy the Rhineland		German troops occupy part of Czechoslovakia		Great Britain and France declare war on Germany

15. Which event occurred first?
    (A) German troops entered Czechoslovakia.
    (B) The Japanese bombed Pearl Harbor.
    (C) Great Britain and France declared war on Germany.
    (D) German troops occupied the Rhineland.

16. Which statement can be concluded from the information in the time line?
    (A) Hitler became Chancellor of Germany.
    (B) Poland instigated a war with Germany.
    (C) German expansion helped to cause World War II.
    (D) The United States was allied with Great Britain.

17. How do the events of 1936 and 1938 compare on the time line?
    (A) They are similar to the events of World War I.
    (B) They involve Germany.
    (C) They involve Czechoslovakia.
    (D) Great Britain and France declare war just before 1936.

18. World maps can typically be divided in half creating which of the following:
    (A) continents
    (B) countries
    (C) hemispheres
    (D) climates

Use the map below to answer question 19.

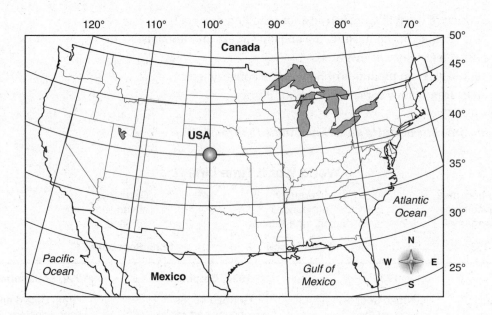

19. What is the latitude and longitude of the point on the map above?

_____

Use the map below to answer questions 20 through 22.

India

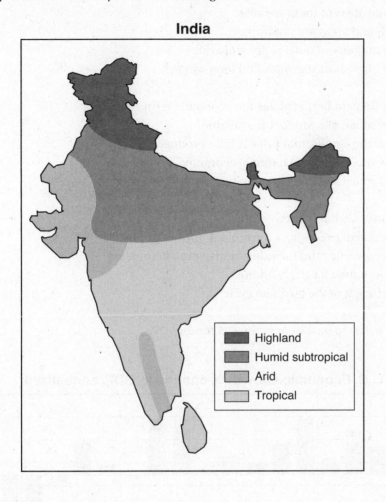

Highland
Humid subtropical
Arid
Tropical

20. What would be the best title for this map?
    (A) Climate Zones of India
    (B) The Different States of India
    (C) Mountain Regions of India
    (D) Industrial Zones of India

21. According to the map, where are the humid subtropical areas of India?
    (A) south
    (B) west
    (C) north
    (D) along the coasts

22. What can you infer from the map?
    (A) All the areas of India are alike.
    (B) Highland areas are not tropical.
    (C) The majority of India is dry and arid.
    (D) India has short summers and long winters.

23. Which statement best explains the economic term "demand?"
    (A) How much of a product is available
    (B) What the equilibrium price is for a product
    (C) How taxes affect the national economy
    (D) How much someone is willing to pay for a product

24. In economics, what is a recession?
    (A) A period of time where the gross domestic product shrinks
    (B) An economic term meaning "worse than depression"
    (C) A boom time for the economy
    (D) The height of the business cycle

Use the graph below to answer questions 25 through 27.

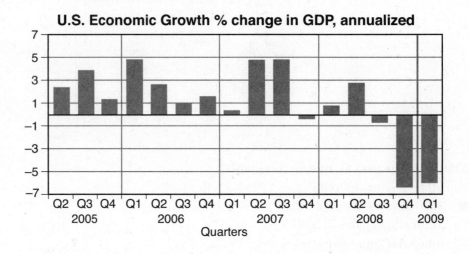

25. According to the graph, in which quarter did the largest change in GDP occur?
    (A) Q1 2006
    (B) Q2 2007
    (C) Q4 2008
    (D) Q1 2009

26. What would you predict would happen to U.S. economic growth in the next quarter?
    (A) It would be positive.
    (B) It would be negative.
    (C) There would be no change.
    (D) The economy will rise by 10%.

27. Which of the following is an unstated assumption based on the graph?
    (A) The economy grew by 5% in the 2nd quarter of 2007.
    (B) The economy grew faster in quarter two of 2008 than in quarter one.
    (C) The U.S. economy is expanding faster than any other nation in the world.
    (D) By 2009, the U.S. economy appears to be headed into a recession.

PRETEST EVALUATION CHART

After checking your answers on the following pages, circle the number of the questions you got correct in Column B. Record the total number of correct questions for each skill in Column C. Column D gives you the number of correct questions you need to answer correctly to indicate that you have a good understanding of the skill. If you got fewer correct answers than shown in Column D, study the pages shown in Column E. Using this analysis will allow you to focus on your challenges and use your study time more effectively.

A		B	C	D	E
Skill Area		**Questions**	**Number of Correct Answers**	**Number Correct to Show a Good Understanding**	**Pages to Study**
U.S. History	General Knowledge	1, 2	____ /5	4	515–538
	Line Graph	3			528–530
	Cause and Effect	4			519
	Restating Info	5			523
Government	General Knowledge	6, 7, 8, 9	____ /7	6	543–574
	Political Cartoon	10			558–560
	Fact and Opinion	11			565–567
	Inference	12			567–570
World History	General Knowledge	13, 14	____ /5	4	575–591
	Time Line	15			582–585
	Drawing Conclusions	16			588–591
	Compare and Contrast	17			586–588
Geography	General Knowledge	18, 19	____ /5	5	595–619
	Reading Maps	20			601–619
	Main Idea	21			612–619
	Restating Info	22			612–619

A		B	C	D	E
Skill Area		Questions	Number of Correct Answers	Number Correct to Show a Good Understanding	Pages to Study
Economics	General Knowledge	23, 24			623–638
	Graphic Material	25	____ /5	4	629–633
	Making Predictions	26			636–638
	Unstated Assumption	27			633–635
TOTAL			____ /27	23	

If you answered enough of the questions in Column D for a skill, you know enough about that skill already. You may want to do the Review at the end of these skill areas as a check.

To use your study time wisely, improve your skills in the other areas by studying the pages noted in Column E.

PRETEST ANSWER EXPLANATIONS

1. **(C)** Answers (A), (B), and (D) are untrue as stated in Chapter 16, Lesson 1.

2. **(A)** Answer (C) is incorrect because those are the nations the United States was allied with during World War I. This information is found in Chapter 16, Lesson 3.

3. **(B)** According to the graph, moving straight up from the number 80, the line is at 4 million.

4. **(C)** (A) is incorrect because no foreign nations are mentioned. (B) and (D) are incorrect because they are the opposite of the evidence in the passage.

5. **(A)** (B) is untrue and (C) is incorrect because the United States generally spread from east to west. (D) is incorrect because the passage mentions states created all the way to the Pacific Ocean.

6. **(B)** This information is found in Chapter 17, Lesson 2.

7. **(D)** Choice (A) describes a direct democracy, and choice (B) describes an absolute monarchy. Choice (C) describes a dictator instead of a democracy.

8. **(B)** Choice (A) describes an actual party as a social event instead of a political party. Choice (C) is incorrect because the number of Congressmen is set by the Constitution, and choice (D) is the opposite of the correct answer.

9. **(A)** Choice (B) describes a government without checks and balances where the President has the most power. Choice (C) describes the writing of actual checks instead of the system of checks and balances in government. Choice (D) is incorrect, the 13th amendment abolished slavery.

10. **(A)** All of the initials above the snake represent American colonies, such as New York. The title, "Join, or die," indicates that the colonies must come together.

11. **(B)** Answers (A), (C), and (D) are not opinions.

12. **(D)** (A) and (C) are untrue, and (B) is directly stated. Answer (D) is correct because it is directly stated, but it can be inferred from the passage. By allowing different branches of government partial power over other branches, a system of checks and balances is created.

13. **(B)** This information is found in Chapter 18, Lesson 1.

14. **(A)** This information is found in Chapter 18, Lesson 2.

15. **(D)** According to the time line, the Germans occupied the Rhineland in 1936. That is earlier than any other event listed.

16. **(C)** A conclusion sums up all of the details. In this case, we see that Germany is taking over, or expanding, into other territories before war is declared.

17. **(B)** The events of 1936 and 1938 are similar because they all mention Germany.

18. **(C)** The definition of hemisphere is half of a sphere. This information is found in Chapter 19, Lesson 1.

19. 40 degrees latitude, 100 degrees longitude.

20. **(A)** All of the categories in the map key relate to climate.

21. **(C)**

22. **(B)** (A) is incorrect because the map shows distinct climate differences. (C) is incorrect because the map shows that the majority of the nation is tropical and not arid. (D) is incorrect because there is no way to tell how long the seasons are from the map. Since the highlands areas directly border a tropical area, they must not be tropical otherwise they would be labeled as the same.

23. **(D)** This definition is found in Chapter 20, Lesson 1.

24. **(A)** This definition is found in Chapter 20, Lesson 2.

25. **(C)** According to the graph in Q4, 2008, the change was almost –7%. This is the largest bar on the graph.

26. **(B)** Since there have been three consecutive negative quarters, it is logical to think that the next quarter will be negative as well.

27. **(D)** (A) and (B) are incorrect because they are directly stated. (C) is incorrect because there is no way to compare the data with other nations. There were three consecutive quarters of negative economic growth in 2008, so the economy appears to be in a recession heading into 2009.

U.S. History

"Professor Johnston often said that if you didn't know history, you didn't know anything. You were a leaf that didn't know it was part of a tree."

—Michael Crichton, *Timeline*

What makes the United States different than other countries? You may be able to think of a few reasons. Here's one big difference historians have noticed: unlike many other countries, the **population** of the United States is made up of many different religions, **ethnicities**, and languages. This may not seem like a big deal now, but when the United States was created, this was a **radical** change in human history.

Although there have been many bumps in the road, the history of the United States is a story of an experiment to give all people **liberty** and equality. This unit will tell you part of the story of how we got to this point as well as about some major challenges the nation faced.

Studying U.S. history is important because we are united together by these ideals of freedom and justice. Though Americans may look and speak differently, we all now share this common heritage. In order to protect these values for the future, it is crucial to understand where these ideas came from as well as to know the struggles people endured to keep them. Otherwise, we would be like the leaf who didn't know he was even on the tree!

Studying U.S. history is also important for passing your HSE test. Twenty-five percent of the social studies test will be based on U.S. history. But don't be afraid, you won't have to memorize a bunch of facts in order to pass this test. The social studies section will test your ability to use different thinking skills to understand social studies information. For example, you may be asked to read a passage on the Civil War and then determine some causes and effects. Likewise, you may need to be able to restate information from different kinds of maps and graphs.

Still, these questions can be a lot easier if you already know a little about what the reading passage or map is about. This unit on U.S. history will familiarize you with some of the main events, people, and ideas of U.S. history.

Date Nation Was Founded	
Zimbabwe	1980
Brazil	1822
United States	1781
Spain	1523
United Kingdom	843
Japan	660 BCE
China	2100 BCE
Egypt	3150 BCE

HOW THIS CHAPTER IS ORGANIZED

Lesson 1: The Colonial Era

This lesson will highlight the period around the American Revolution. You will read about what life was like for the colonists, and how they were able to defeat the most powerful nation in the world (Great Britain).

UNIT 4: SOCIAL STUDIES

Lesson 2: The Civil War

This lesson will discuss the growing pains of an expanding nation as well as the bitter conflict between slavery and freedom. This question would be decided once and for all through the bloodiest war in American history.

Lesson 3: The World at War

This lesson jumps to the modern era and two of the defining events of the 20th century. World Wars I and II cost millions of lives and still affect the world today.

Lesson 4: Graphic Materials

This lesson focuses on different types of graphs that are likely to appear on your HSE. Many test questions involve visual information, and this section will focus on using bar, line, and circle graphs in social studies.

Lesson 5: Criticial Thinking Skills

This lesson will help you practice a few of the thinking skills you will find on your HSE test. Here, we will look at recognizing causes and effects as well as practicing restating information.

LESSON 1: THE COLONIAL ERA

The United States has been in existence since 1781. This may seem like a long time, but take a look at the chart on the previous page. Compared to some other nations and cultures the United States is barely even a teenager!

The 13 Colonies

Our study will begin with the colonial era. A **colony** is an area that is under the control of another country. In the 1700s, the land of North America was controlled by Great Britain and other European nations. Before the Europeans arrived, Native Americans **thrived** in North America for thousands of years. Using the map above, you can see that the colony names are the same as some of the current United States.

European explorers, men like Christopher Columbus, had been poking around North America, known as the "New World," for **centuries**. These explorers were hoping to find gold or another route to India from Europe. Eventually, a permanent English settlement was created at Jamestown, Virginia in 1609.

Early colonial life was difficult and dangerous. 50% of the colonists at Jamestown died the first year from disease and starvation. Were it not for the generosity of the local Native-American tribes (called the "Powhatans" by the colonists), Jamestown would have vanished. Instead, the Powhatans gave the early colonists food and taught them how to plant local crops like tobacco. Demand for tobacco grew quickly in Europe, and many more Europeans would arrive seeking to make their fortunes through tobacco and other cash crops. This trend would spell disaster for the Native Americans, whose traditional lands were now wanted by an increasing number of colonists.

The lure of money is only part of the colonial story. In 1620, a group of English men and women boarded a ship called the *Mayflower* headed for the New World. These people, later known as **pilgrims**, were seeking religious freedom. They wanted to leave behind the Church of England and worship as they pleased. The *Mayflower* landed in Plymouth, Massachusetts, and helped start the tradition of religious freedom that continues in America today. Massachusetts, and other colonies like Rhode Island, were known as the New England colonies.

There were also major geographic differences between the New England and the Southern colonies. This means that the type of land and even the weather helped determine the future of the colonies. Think about it: would you want to go north or south for a sunny and warm winter vacation? The warm weather and good soil meant that the southern colonies could grow a lot of crops like tobacco but the New England colonies could not. With a colder climate, New Englanders found other ways to make a living like fishing and manufacturing goods to sell in stores. Northern colonies slowly developed big cities like New York and Boston and grew in population. Southern colonies, on the other hand, remained **rural** and imported slaves from Africa to work the cash crops like tobacco, cotton, and sugar.

Use the Venn diagram below to chart the similarities and differences of the New England and Southern colonies. List things that only relate to New England on the left of the circle, and things that only happened to the Southern colonies on the right. Things that may apply to both groups can go in the middle.

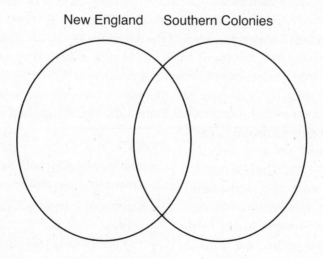

New England   Southern Colonies

Practice Exercise—Colonial Era Vocabulary

Write the letter of the correct match next to each problem.

_____ 1. Ethnicity

_____ 2. Radical

_____ 3. Liberty

_____ 4. Colony

_____ 5. Thrive

_____ 6. Century

_____ 7. Pilgrim

_____ 8. Rural

(A) Freedom

(B) A group of people linked by race or culture

(C) To live successfully

(D) Country: the opposite of urban

(E) One hundred years

(F) Extreme

(G) A person who travels for religious reasons

(H) A territory controlled by another nation

The American Revolution

The 13 original colonies grew rapidly. As they expanded, tensions mounted between colonists and various Native-American tribes. The colonists also butted heads with the French, who had also colonized neighboring parts of North America. Several wars erupted between all three of these groups. The British spent vast sums of money and manpower protecting their American colonies and eventually would become the dominant power in North America.

Heavily in debt after paying for decades of wars, the British felt that the colonists should chip in to help pay the bills. To do this, the British raised taxes in the colonies on everything from playing cards and dice to sugar and wine. But by the 1770s, the colonists were slowly beginning to see themselves more as Americans than as British subjects, and they detested all of these new taxes. To protest a new tax on tea, several colonists snuck on board three British ships in Boston harbor and dumped all of the tea into the water. This act of **defiance** would forever be known as the Boston Tea Party, and the ruling British reacted harshly to punish all of Boston. Before long, rebel colonists and British troops exchanged fire in Massachusetts and the American Revolution had begun!

The rebelling colonists didn't stand much of a chance at first. They were facing a professional army, the world's most powerful navy, and even about 20% of the colonists themselves sided with the British at the beginning. The Americans, however, did have some advantages. For one thing, they were fighting on their home turf. The British had to ship their troops and supplies across the Atlantic Ocean, a voyage that took about 2 months. Then, in July of 1776, Thomas Jefferson and others wrote the Declaration of Independence. This important document in American history would help to unify Americans against the British. The Americans were extremely lucky

Introducing...

George Washington—American general during the Revolution, became first President of the United States.

Thomas Jefferson—Primary author of the Declaration of Independence, became third President of the United States.

James Madison—Primary author of the Constitution, became fourth President of the United States.

- Colonists conflict with nearby Native-American tribes and French settlers
- The Declaration of Independence is written
- The British raise taxes on the colonists

to have some incredibly talented men (like Jefferson) who were in the right place at the right time. Finally, the Americans were able to persuade the French (who were the archenemies of the British) to aid their cause. The French supplied valuable land and sea forces against the British. After 8 long years of fighting, the American Revolution was over and a new nation, the United States of America, was born.

Being able to identify causes and effects is an important skill on the HSE tests. The simplest way to distinguish between the two is to remember that a cause explains *why* something happens, while an effect describes *what* happened.

American Revolution Time Line

1754–1763	French and Indian War
1764	Revenue Acts—new taxes on colonists
1765	Stamp Acts—more taxes on colonists
1773	Boston Tea Party
1775	Shots fired at Lexington, Massachusetts
1776	Declaration of Independence
1781	British surrender at Yorktown, United States begins
1783	American Revolution officially over

Practice Exercise—Cause and Effect

Choose events from the following list to fill in the chart. Causes go in the arrows on the left, and effects go in the stars on the right.

- Colonists conflict with nearby Native American tribes and French settlers
- The Declaration of Independence is written
- The British raise taxes on the colonists

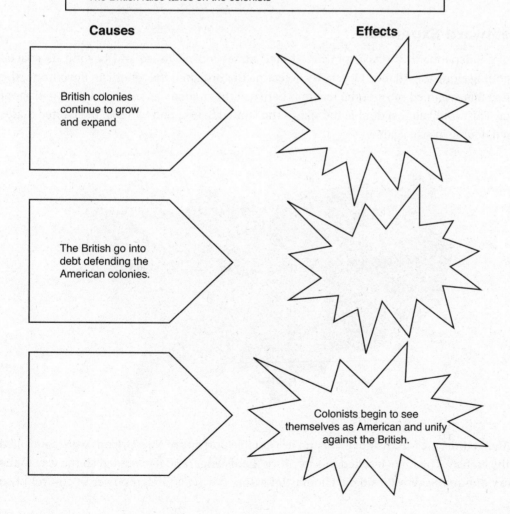

Causes

Effects

British colonies continue to grow and expand

The British go into debt defending the American colonies.

Colonists begin to see themselves as American and unify against the British.

LESSON 2: THE CIVIL WAR

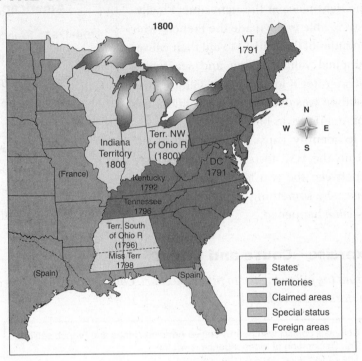

Westward Expansion

Finally independent, the fast-growing United States looked to expand beyond its coastal beginning along the Atlantic Ocean. By defeating the British in the American Revolution, the United States gained most of the territory between the original colonies and the Mississippi River. This would almost double the size of the United States, and by 1803, the United States would double in size again.

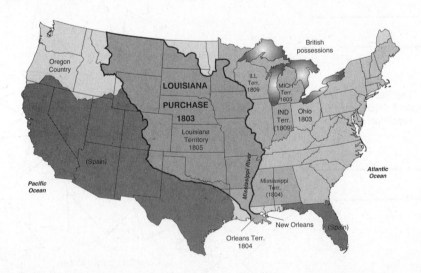

At that time, the Mississippi River and its valuable port city of New Orleans were controlled by the French. The French called this territory "Louisiana," and it extended all the way to the Rocky Mountains. For President Thomas Jefferson, having a foreign power in control of so much land was troubling. Hoping to avoid another costly war against a great power, Jefferson made the French an offer to buy the Louisiana Territory. Fortunately for Jefferson, he caught the French leader, Napoleon Bonaparte, at a good time. Napoleon had just lost thousands of troops fighting in Haiti, and he was preparing to conquer most of Europe. Eager to concentrate on Europe, Napoleon sold the entire Louisiana Territory to the United States for $15 million dollars. Known as the "Louisiana Purchase," this sale almost doubled the size of the United States. The Louisiana Purchase would also go down in history as one of the best deals of all time: Jefferson wound up paying approximately 3 cents an acre!

The American west was now officially open. California and parts of six other states would come under American control after a war with Mexico in 1846. America now stretched from coast to coast. New states would have to be created, but with them came some of the same problems from the colonial era. Native Americans, who had lived on these lands for generations, were forcibly and sometimes violently removed.

As you read in the previous lesson, there were large differences between the more industrialized northern colonies and the agricultural southern colonies. A **plantation** (large farm) system developed in the south to keep up with the growing demand for tobacco, cotton, and sugar. These crops were very labor intensive, which meant that they required a large number of people to work in the fields. This labor would largely come from African slaves.

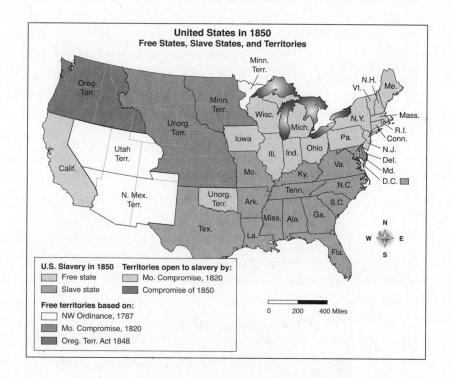

Slavery

Slavery had divided the nation since its founding. As the nation grew, the question would have to be answered: would each new state be a free or slave state? A series of compromises in the 1800s carefully balanced the number of free and slave states. This was important because it also balanced the power in Congress. Northern states were critical of slavery, and Southern states feared that slavery would be **abolished**. By 1860, the number of slaves in the South totaled nearly 4 million. A final showdown on the issue was inevitable. And when Abraham

Lincoln, who opposed slavery, was elected President in 1860, 11 Southern states left the United States to form their own country called The Confederate States of America.

What followed was the Civil War, which was by far the bloodiest war in American history. Taking place between 1861–1865, this war divided the nation and even individual families. Each side had unique advantages and disadvantages.

Advantages of the Northern States in the Civil War

Population
- 22 million people lived in the North to 9 million in the South.
- Close to four million of the Southern population were slaves.

Manufacturing
- The North had more factories and could produce more goods, like guns and uniforms.
- New York state alone produced twice as many manufactured goods as the entire South.

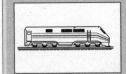

Transportation
- 75% of the railroad tracks were in the North
- The North controlled the Navy

Advantages of the Southern States in the Civil War

Defense
- The South didn't need to invade the North to win.
- The South only needed to tie to keep their territory.

Homefield Advantage
- Southerners knew their territory while the North did not.
- They had the determination to defend their homes.

Cotton
- Since cotton was so valuable, the South thought that England would join their side to keep receiving cotton.

In the end, the South simply could not keep up with the economic might of the North. Likewise, with such an advantage in population, the North could continually replace soldiers while the South could not. And while the North successfully blocked shipments of cotton to England, the British had stocked up before the war and would not intervene. In 1863, Abraham Lincoln issued the **Emancipation Proclamation**, which freed all of the slaves in the South. Thus, at a cost of over 600,000 lives, the Confederacy was finished, and the slavery question was settled once and for all.

Practice Exercise—Restating Information

On your HSE test you will need to recognize when information is being restated. In real life, you do this whenever you put something into your own words. Here's an example:

A. "10 out of 20 students were absent today with the flu."

B. "Because they were sick, half of the class missed school today."

The key with restating information is to make sure both statements mean the same thing. Both sentences here express the same idea, but they use different words. Try answering the following question using your own words.

1. What was the Louisiana Purchase?

   (**THINK:** Who was involved, and what did they do? What was the result for America?)

   _____

   _____

   _____

2. Which statement best restates the importance of the Emancipation Proclamation?
   (A) The Emancipation Proclamation freed all of the slaves in the north.
   (B) By writing the Emancipation Proclamation, Lincoln ended the Civil War.
   (C) The Emancipation Proclamation banned the sale of cotton to Europe.
   (D) The Emancipation Proclamation freed all of the slaves in the south.

The correct answer is (D). Notice the similarity between answer choices (A) and (D). When restating information, it is important to make sure that all of the information is restated correctly. The only difference is the last word, but that changes the entire answer. There were no slaves in the north, so Lincoln actually only freed the slaves in the south with the Emancipation Proclamation.

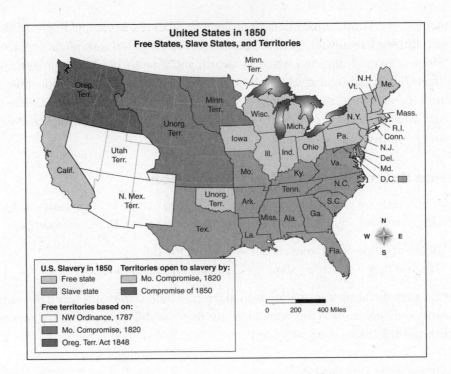

United States in 1850
Free States, Slave States, and Territories

U.S. Slavery in 1850   Territories open to slavery by:
- Free state
- Slave state
- Mo. Compromise, 1820
- Compromise of 1850

Free territories based on:
- NW Ordinance, 1787
- Mo. Compromise, 1820
- Oreg. Terr. Act 1848

0   200   400 Miles

3. Which statement best restates the information on the map above titled "United States in 1850?"
   (A) Slavery was not an issue before the Civil War.
   (B) Most states did not allow slavery.
   (C) All of the territories were open to slavery.
   (D) The number of free and slave states were fairly equal.

4. "Northern states were critical of slavery, and Southern states feared that slavery would be **abolished**." Knowing that the north and south would eventually go to war, what do you think best restates the meaning of the word **abolitionist**?
   (A) Someone who grew cotton
   (B) A person who wanted to end slavery
   (C) A supporter of the South during the Civil War
   (D) A person who supported slavery

LESSON 3: THE WORLD AT WAR

The United States grew and prospered after the Civil War. The frontier was explored, gold was mined, oil was discovered, and fields were planted. While the rest of Europe fought several wars, the United States was protected by two large natural allies: The Atlantic Ocean and the Pacific Ocean. Because of these natural barriers, the United States could stay isolated from the affairs of the rest of the world.

The United States was also quick to **industrialize**. By the early 1900s, American factories produced more goods than any other nation. "The business of America is business," said President Calvin Coolidge summing up an era. The United States was now unlikely to use its military unless its business interests were threatened.

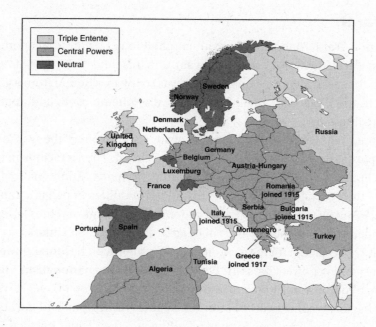

Legend:
- Triple Entente
- Central Powers
- Neutral

World War I

The new mix of modern machinery and warfare would have tragic consequences. World War I began in 1914 and ultimately would claim over 16 million lives from around the globe. Just as assembly lines allowed for new cars to be made quickly and cheaply, modern industry could now produce machine guns, tanks, and planes. These weapons had never been used in battle before, and they were dreadfully effective. At the Battle of the Somme in France, over 60,000 people were killed or wounded in 1 day. A lot had changed since the American Revolution.

Since the fighting was taking place in Europe, the United States was able to stay out of the conflict at first. But after a German submarine sank a British passenger ship killing 128 Americans, the United States entered the war with the British. Though only involved for the final year of the war, the United States helped turn the tide of the war, and over 117,000 Americans were killed. Germany surrendered in 1918, but the world was stunned at the terrible human cost of the war. At the time, it was not called World War I, but rather "the war to end all wars."

Practice Exercise—Reading Comprehension

1. According to the reading on pages 524 and 525, what was one reason the United States avoided European wars for so long?

_____

_____

_____

2. Reread paragraph two on page 524. If you knew that the United States invaded Cuba as part of the Spanish-American war in 1898, what do you think may have been a cause?
   (A) The British declaring war on the Spanish.
   (B) American business profits were at risk.
   (C) The loss of 128 American lives aboard a passenger ship.

World War II

Following World War I, Americans were in no mood to get involved in another conflict. Yet barely 20 years later, the world was at war again, and this time the United States would play a larger role. In the meantime, the United States was trying to rebound from a global economic **depression**. In the 1930s, 25% of all Americans were unemployed, and another 25% could only find part-time work!

So how could the world wind up fighting again so soon after "the war to end all wars?" The answer partially lies with the way World War I ended. The **victorious** nations, primarily Britain and France, wanted to shame the losing Germans. Additionally, they made the Germans pay the equivalent of hundreds of billions of dollars in penalties and give up their colonial lands. Add on top of this a global economic depression, and the Germans were ready for a new leader to restore their pride. This leader would be Adolf Hitler.

Hitler quickly became a **dictator**. A dictator is a ruler who has total power in a country, and they were gaining power across the world by appealing to **nationalism**. Hitler stressed an extreme form of patriotism, and blamed Germany's problems on others. He also built up his military and began invading nearby countries. Leaders from Japan and Italy began doing the same thing, and all three nations formed an **alliance**. When Hitler invaded Poland in 1939, the French and British declared war on Germany.

Still, the American people were **isolationist**, and the United States did not get involved in the war right away. All that changed on December 7, 1941, on a day President Frankin Roosevelt said would "live in **infamy**." The Japanese launched a successful surprise attack on the U.S. naval base at Pearl Harbor, Hawaii. By 1942, Germany had conquered most of Europe, and Japan held most of the Pacific.

Europe in 1938

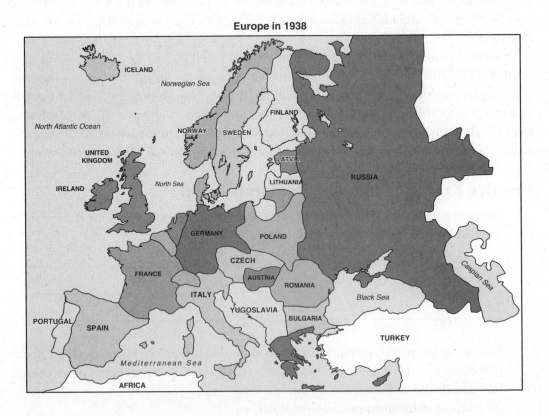

Known as the Allies, the United States, Great Britain, and the Soviet Union fought against Hitler in Europe. After launching an invasion from England in 1944 (known as D-Day), the Allies forced the Germans to surrender in 1945. Against Japan, the United States hopped from island to island across the Pacific in a series of battles. Hoping to end the war quickly, the United States used a devastating new weapon against Japan: the atomic bomb. After dropping two bombs on the Japanese cities of Hiroshima and Nagasaki, the Japanese surrendered in 1945. World War II was officially over; over 50 million lives were lost around the world due to the war.

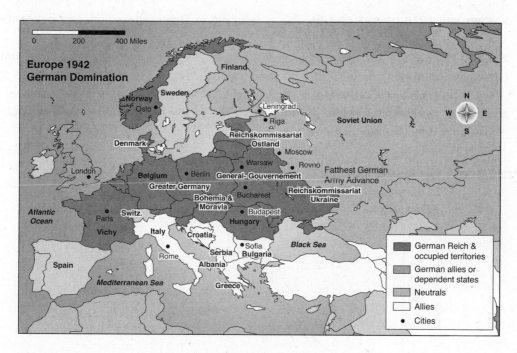

Practice Exercise—Sentence Completion

Use the words in the list below to complete the sentence.

isolationist	alliance	victorious	nationalism
infamous	industrialized	Depression	

1. The police and citizens formed an _____ to fight crime.

2. During the Olympics _____ is high because people are proud of their countries.

3. Between the world wars, the United States was _____ because it stayed out of European affairs.

4. With lots of factories making different things, you can tell this city is _____.

5. The economy was down during the Great _____ of the 1930s, and many people had a hard time finding work.

6. Because he always stays up late, John has become_____ for arriving late to work.

7. The Bears were_____ yesterday when they beat the Giants 35–14.

LESSON 4: GRAPHIC MATERIALS

Line Graphs

Graphs play an important role on HSE tests. Line graphs can be used to show how something changes over time. On the test, you will need to be able to look up information on a graph. You will also need to be able to describe the overall trend of a graph. Both of these skills are easy to do when you know the basics of reading graphs.

To get started, there are three things you must do with every line or bar graph.

1. **FIND THE TITLE OF THE GRAPH.** This is typically in larger letters above or below the graph.

2. **READ THE LABELS ON THE SIDES OF THE GRAPH.** When people are confused by line graphs, it is usually because they skipped this step. Using these labels will help us to easily find specific information.

3. **LOOK AT THE OVERALL TREND OF THE GRAPH.** This means to judge if the line is generally going up, down, or staying the same.

Practice Exercise—Reading Line Graphs

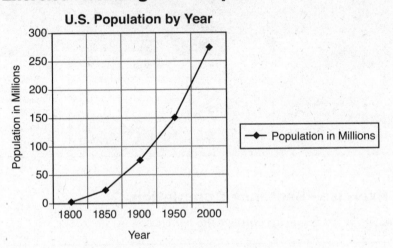

We can see that the title of the above graph is "U.S. POPULATION BY YEAR."

1. What information is found on the vertical axis?

   (**THINK:** The vertical line going up and down.)

2. What information is found on the horizontal axis?

   (**THINK:** The horizontal line is going sideways.)

3. What is the overall trend of the graph?

   (**THINK:** Is the line going up or down, and what does that mean for the U.S. population?)

Now that you know your way around this graph, let's use these skills to find some specific information.

Let's say you were asked to find the population of the United States in 1950. On this graph, we know that the years are on the horizontal axis, so let's start there. Once you find 1950, go straight up until you hit the line of the graph.

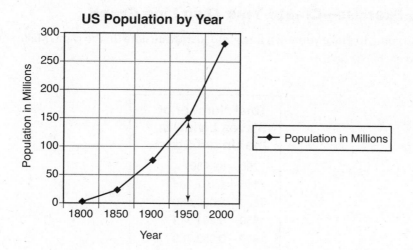

Once you hit that line, move straight over to the vertical axis on the left.

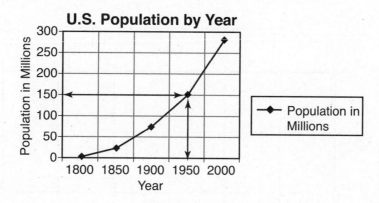

That's it! Using these techniques will help you with every line graph you see.

We can also use line graphs to **estimate**. We'll need to do this to *find out in approximately what year the U.S. population reached 200 million.* To begin, find 200 million on the population axis on the left, and then follow that straight over to the line.

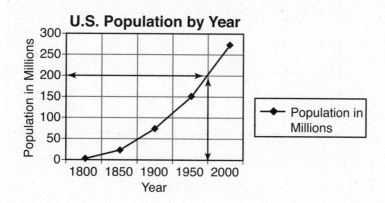

Now take that line straight down. Notice how this line does not fall exactly on one of the labeled years like 1950 or 2000? This means we will have to estimate. This line looks like it is about half way between 1950 and 2000. Since 1975 is half way between 1950 and 2000, the best answer would be around 1975.

Practice Exercise—Create Your Own Line Graph

Now you are going to make your own line graph using the data on the right. Make sure to label the title and each axis first.

Total Number of Slaves Living in the United States

1790 – 697,897
1810 – 1,191,364
1830 – 2,009,050
1850 – 3,204,313
1860 – 3,953,760

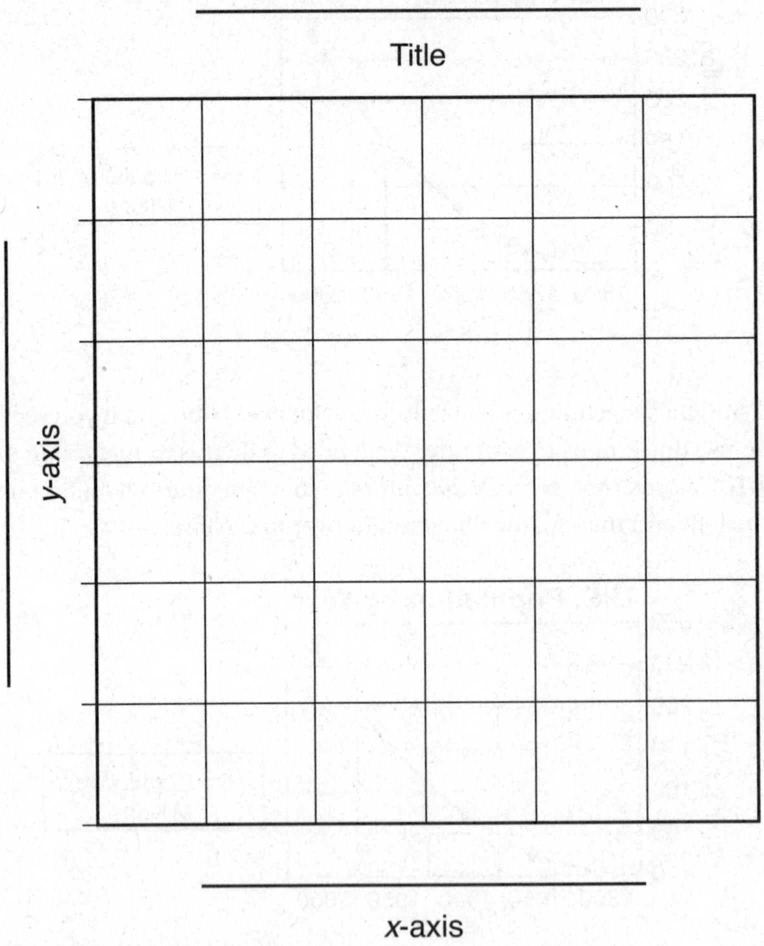

Title

y-axis

x-axis

1. How did the slave population change between 1790 and 1860?

   (**THINK:** What is the trend of the graph?)

Bar Graphs

Bar graphs are typically used to compare numbers. To understand them, you can use the same process you learned for line graphs. First find the title, then check the information on each axis, and finally try to figure out an overall trend.

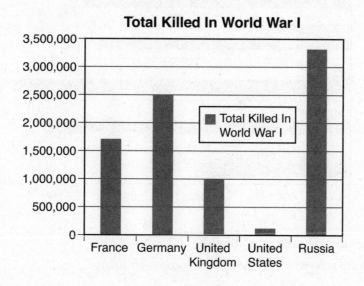

Practice Exercise—Reading Bar Graphs

1. What is the subject of this graph?

   _____

2. Each line on the graph represents how many people?

   _____

3. Approximately how many Germans were killed in World War I?

   _____

4. Which statement best restates the information on the graph?
   (A) Russia had more deaths than all of the other nations combined.
   (B) The United States lost fewer soldiers than other nations in World War I.
   (C) There were more injuries than deaths in World War I.
   (D) The Russians won World War I.

Bar graphs can also appear horizontally (from left to right).

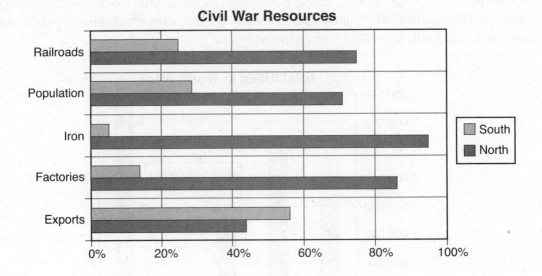

Civil War Resources

5. What information is being compared on this bar graph?

   (**THINK:** How do you know what this graph is about?)

   _____

6. In what area did the north have the largest advantage over the Confederacy?

   _____

7. In what area did the south have an advantage over the north?

   _____

8. Approximately what percent of United States lived in the north during the Civil War?

   _____

9. Which statement best restates the information on the graph?
   (A) The south had many advantages over the north.
   (B) Iron was unimportant in the Civil War.
   (C) The north had many advantages over the south.
   (D) The use of slaves in the south helped to balance the population with the north.

10. After 4 years of fighting, the south surrendered to the north. Using the graph above, what might have been a cause?
    (A) Slaves refused to fight for the South.
    (B) Southern factories handled agricultural items like cotton and sugar instead of guns and ammunition.
    (C) Southern military leaders could not agree on a war strategy.
    (D) With a larger population and more factories, the north could more easily replace troops and equipment than the south.

LESSON 5: CRITICAL THINKING SKILLS
Cause and Effect

On your HSE test, you will need to be able to identify causes and effects. A cause tells you *why* something happened. An effect tells you *what* happened.

For example, let's say you were very busy and skipped lunch at work. When you finally got home after work, you were really hungry. The cause was not eating lunch; the effect was feeling hungry.

In the next example, circle any key words that help you find causes and effects. The box to the right will help you.

"The colonial era was a time of great change. Since the colonists were looking for new land, they moved west. As a result, they conflicted with the Native Americans who were already living there. This pattern would continue when the United States expanded toward the west coast."

> **Cause Words**
>
> Because
>
> Since
>
> If
>
> When
>
> **Effect Words**
>
> Therefore
>
> Then
>
> So
>
> As a result
>
> Thus

Practice Exercise—Cause and Effect

Questions 1 and 2 are based on the following passage.

> In the year 1800, the United States was a small nation. The world was dominated by European Powers. When Napoleon lost thousands of troops in Haiti, he needed to raise money to concentrate on France. Thus, in 1803, he sold thousands of square miles to the United States for 15 million dollars. This deal was known as the Louisiana Purchase.

1. According to the passage, what was a cause of the Louisiana Purchase?

   (**THINK:** Which keywords can help you find the answer?)

   (A) In 1803, Napoleon sold thousands of square miles to the United States.
   (B) The world was dominated by European powers.
   (C) Napoleon lost thousands of troops in Haiti and needed to raise money.
   (D) None of the above.

2. According to the passage, what was one effect of the Louisiana Purchase?
   (A) In 1803, Napoleon sold thousands of square miles to the United States.
   (B) The world was dominated by European powers.
   (C) Napoleon lost thousands of troops in Haiti and needed to raise money.
   (D) None of the above.

Questions 3 and 4 are based on the following passage.

The United States industrialized rapidly. Since American factories produced goods cheaply, many Americans could then afford to buy new products. Everything from shoes, to guns, to automobiles could now be made faster and cheaper than ever before. Because the United States was protected by two large oceans from the rest of the world, the United States was able to stay out of European wars for many years. Therefore, the United States was free to concentrate on business.

3. According to the passage, what was one cause for the United States avoiding European wars?
   (A) American factories could produce goods cheaply.
   (B) Americans could afford to buy new products.
   (C) The United States was protected by the Atlantic and Pacific oceans.
   (D) The United States was free to concentrate on business.

4. According to the passage, what was one effect of industrialization in America?
   (A) Americans could afford to buy new products.
   (B) The United States was protected by the Atlantic and Pacific Oceans.
   (C) The United States was free to concentrate on business.
   (D) The United States stayed out of European wars.

Not all cause-and-effect questions will use the keywords like the examples above. *Remember, causes always happen before effects.* The following two questions are based on the American Revolution reading in Lesson 1.

5. According to the reading, what was one cause of the Boston Tea Party?
   (A) The British raised taxes on tea in the colonies.
   (B) The Declaration of Independence was written.
   (C) The French joined an alliance with the colonists.
   (D) Americans drank more coffee than tea.

6. According to the reading, what was one effect of the French helping the colonists against the British in the American Revolution?
   (A) The colonists were able to lower their taxes.
   (B) Shots were fired in Massachusetts to begin the American Revolution.
   (C) The British joined an alliance with Germany.
   (D) The additional French troops helped to end the war.

7. Before the Civil War, the economy of the northern states was based on manufacturing. Many people moved to cities. The southern states remained rural, and agriculture dominated the economy. Plantations developed to grow large amounts of crops like cotton.

   What is one effect of these differences between the north and south?

   (**THINK:** What happens before and after?)

   (A) Southern states made their own railroads.
   (B) Slavery developed in the south to work the crops.
   (C) Slavery grew in the cities of the north.
   (D) A strong demand for cotton and other crops.

Use the maps below to answer question 8.

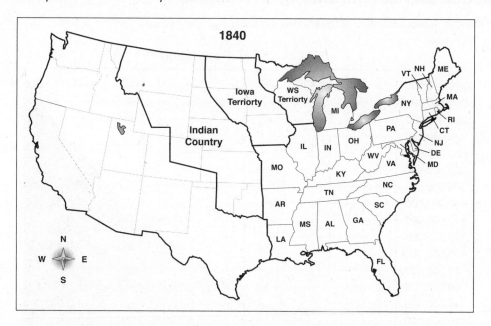

1840

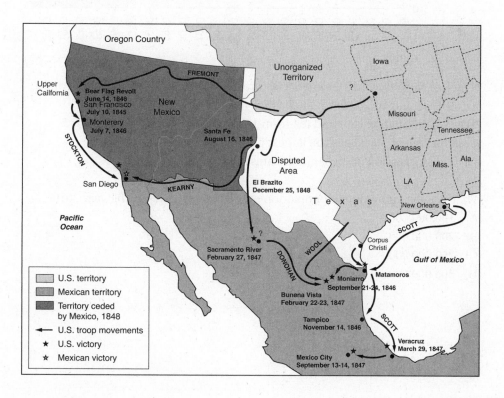

8. After comparing the two maps, what was one effect of the Mexican–American war in 1848?

(A) Mexico took over Texas.

(B) The United States gained territory.

(C) Americans no longer desired for territory to reach the Pacific Ocean.

(D) The United States lost territory.

Practice Exercise—Restating Information

Use the graph below to answer questions 1 and 2.

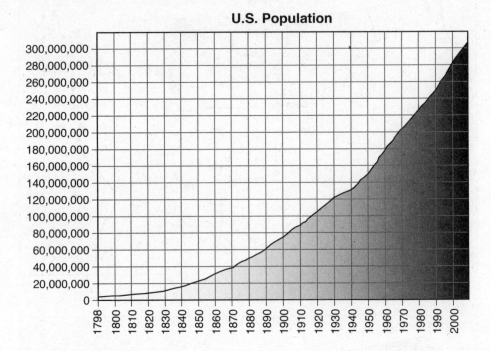

U.S. Population

1. Which of the following statements best restates the information on the graph?
   (A) U.S. population has remained steady over the years.
   (B) U.S. population rose and fell from 1800–1900.
   (C) The United States has the largest population of all countries.
   (D) The population of the United States has risen over time.

2. What was the approximate population of the United States in the year 2010?
   (A) 100,000,000
   (B) 200,000,000
   (C) 250,000,000
   (D) 300,000,000

Use the graph below to answer questions 3 and 4.

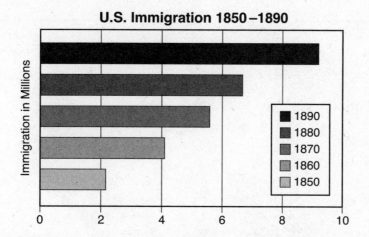

U.S. Immigration 1850–1890

Immigration in Millions

Legend:
■ 1890
■ 1880
■ 1870
■ 1860
■ 1850

0 2 4 6 8 10

3. Which of the following best restates the information on the graph?
   (A) Immigration to the United States increased over time.
   (B) Immigration did not occur before 1850.
   (C) Immigration has decreased in the United States over time.
   (D) Immigration numbers both increased and decreased over time.

4. According to the graph, approximately how many people immigrated to the United States in 1860?
   (A) 2 million
   (B) 4 million
   (C) 6 million
   (D) 7 million

Use the passage below to answer questions 5 and 6.

   When the United States began in the late 1700s, most of the country lived in rural areas. In fact, in 1790, less than 10% of the nation lived in an urban area. Fifty years later, in 1840, those numbers had barely moved. Nearly 90% of the country still lived in a rural area. But as the nation began to industrialize, people began to move to the cities in large numbers. Many came for the jobs available in cities. By 1920, 51% of the population lived in an urban area, and that trend continues today.

5. Which statement best restates the information in the passage?
   (A) The United States has always been a rural nation.
   (B) The United States quickly became an urban nation.
   (C) The population of the United States gradually moved from urban to rural areas.
   (D) People have traditionally moved to rural areas to find work.

6. Which of the following is the best restatement of the last sentence?
   (A) Most of the country still lived in a rural area.
   (B) Jobs were hard to find in rural areas.
   (C) In 1920, less than half of the population lived in an urban area.
   (D) Since 1920, more people have lived in urban areas than rural areas.

Use the map below to answer questions 7 and 8.

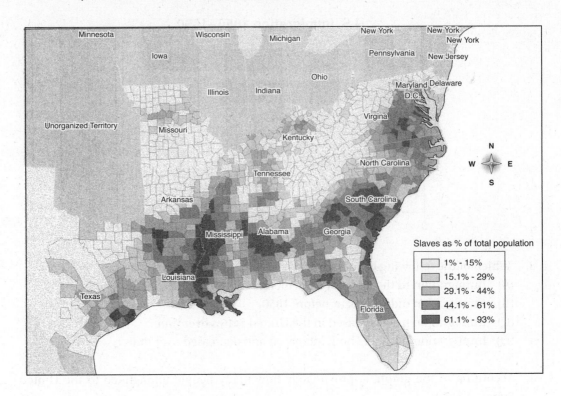

Slaves as % of total population

- 1% - 15%
- 15.1% - 29%
- 29.1% - 44%
- 44.1% - 61%
- 61.1% - 93%

7. Which of the following best restates the information on the map?
   (A) Most slaves in the United States lived in the south.
   (B) Slavery existed in large numbers in the north.
   (C) Slaves made up a majority of the population in Texas.
   (D) Fewer slaves lived in the east than in the west.

8. Which of the following best restates the information on the map for Mississippi?
   (A) Compared to northern states, few slaves lived in Mississippi.
   (B) More slaves lived in Missouri than in Mississippi.
   (C) In some areas of Mississippi, over 50% of the population were slaves.
   (D) Slavery did not exist in Mississippi in 1850.

CHAPTER 16 ANSWER EXPLANATIONS

Lesson 1: The Colonial Era

VENN DIAGRAM (PAGE 517)

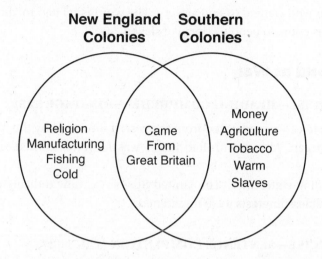

New England Colonies

Southern Colonies

Religion
Manufacturing
Fishing
Cold

Came
From
Great Britain

Money
Agriculture
Tobacco
Warm
Slaves

PRACTICE EXERCISE—COLONIAL ERA VOCABULARY (PAGE 518)

1. B
2. F
3. A
4. H
5. C
6. E
7. G
8. D

PRACTICE EXERCISE—CAUSE AND EFFECT (PAGE 519)

Cause: British colonies continue to grow and expand.
Effect: Colonists conflict with nearby Native-American tribes and French settlers.

Cause: The British go into debt defending the American colonies.
Effect: The British raise taxes on the colonists.

Cause: The Declaration of Independence is written.
Effect: Colonists begin to see themselves as American and unify against the British.

Lesson 2: The Civil War

PRACTICE EXERCISE—RESTATING INFORMATION (PAGE 523)

1. In 1803, President Thomas Jefferson purchased the territory of "Louisiana" from Napoleon Bonaparte of France. Napoleon needed money to fight a war, and sold all of the land for 15 million dollars. This territory, located west of the Mississippi River, doubled the size of the United States.

2. **(D)** The Emancipation Proclamation freed all of the slaves in the south. The Emancipation Proclamation did not affect the north, nor did it end the Civil War. It dealt with slavery and not cotton.

3. **(D)** The number of free and slave states were fairly equal. Looking at the shading of the map as found in the key, the number of slave states and free states are equal.

4. **(B)** A person who wanted to end slavery. The word is related to abolished, which the passage states refers to people critical of slavery.

Lesson 3: World at War

PRACTICE EXERCISE—READING COMPREHENSION (PAGE 525)

1. The United States was separated from the rest of the world by the Atlantic Ocean and the Pacific Ocean. Also, the United States was more concerned with business than foreign wars.

2. **(B)** The reading states that "The United States was now unlikely to use its military unless its business interests were threatened."

PRACTICE EXERCISE—SENTENCE COMPLETION (PAGE 527)

1. The police and citizens formed an *alliance* to fight crime.
2. During the Olympics *nationalism* is high because people are proud of their countries.
3. Between the world wars, the United States was *isolationist* because it stayed out of European affairs.
4. With lots of factories making different things, you can tell this city is *industrialized*.
5. The economy was down during the Great *Depression* of the 1930s, and many people had a hard time finding work.
6. Because he always stays up late, John has become *infamous* for arriving late to work.
7. The Bears were *victorious* yesterday when they beat the Giants 35–14.

Lesson 4: Graphic Materials

PRACTICE EXERCISE—READING LINE GRAPHS (PAGE 528)

1. Population in millions
2. Year
3. The line is going up, so the trend is that U.S. population is rising.

PRACTICE EXERCISE—CREATE YOUR OWN LINE GRAPH (PAGE 530)

1. The total number of slaves increased greatly.

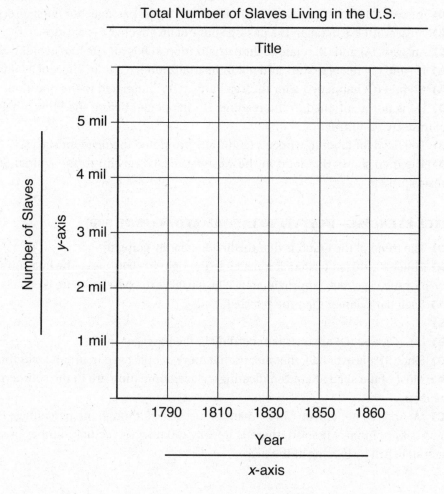

Total Number of Slaves Living in the U.S.

Title

PRACTICE EXERCISE—READING BAR GRAPHS (PAGE 531)

1. Total people killed in World War I
2. 500,000
3. 2,500,000
4. **(B)** The United States has the smallest line on the graph. Answers (C) and (D) aren't detailed on the graph. Answer (A) is incorrect because while Russia had the most deaths of any one nation, they do not have more than all the other nations added together.
5. Resources in the Civil War.
6. Iron. Here the bar for the north extends past 80%, while the southern bar is under 20%.
7. Exports. The southern bar is larger than the northern bar.
8. 70%. The bar for northern population is in between 60% and 80%.
9. **(C)** The bars for the north are larger than the south in all categories except exports.
10. **(D)** The effect of the northern resource advantage meant that it could produce more troops and equipment than the south. The graph does not tell how many slaves fought for either side, nor does it deal with southern war strategy, or what southern factories produced.

Lesson 5: Critical Thinking Skills

PRACTICE EXERCISE—CAUSE AND EFFECT (PAGE 533)

1. **(C)** Answer (A) is an effect. Answer (B) is a detail in the passage, but not a direct cause.
2. **(A)** Answer (B) is a detail in the passage but not an effect. (C) is a cause.
3. **(C)** Answers (A) and (B) relate to industrialization, (D) is an effect of avoiding wars.
4. **(A)** (B) and (D) relate to wars and not industrialization. (C) is an effect of avoiding war.
5. **(A)** (B) and (C) happened after the Tea Party, (D) is unrelated to the question.
6. **(D)** (A) is not mentioned in the reading. (B) happened before the French helped the colonists; (C) is untrue.
7. **(B)** The need for labor to work agriculturally prompted the need for slaves.
8. **(B)** The map shows that land in the west was ceded (given) to the United States by Mexico in 1848.

PRACTICE EXERCISE—RESTATING INFORMATION (PAGE 536)

1. **(D)** The trend of the graph is that the line is steadily going up.
2. **(D)** Though 2010 isn't listed, it must be to the right of 2000. Since the line continues to rise past the year 2000 (approximately 280,000,000), the best estimate is 300,000,000.
3. **(A)** Each bar is larger than the year before it.
4. **(B)**
5. **(B)** (A), (C), and (D) are untrue according to the passage.
6. **(D)** Since 51% is over half, that means that more people lived in urban areas than rural.
7. **(A)** Most of the shaded areas indicating a slave population are in the southern half of the map.
8. **(C)** (A) and (D) are untrue. (B) is incorrect because, although the percentage is higher in Mississippi than Missouri, there is no way to know the actual number of slaves in each state just by looking at the map.

Government 17

"The purpose of government is to enable the people of a nation to live in safety and happiness. Government exists for the interests of the governed, not for the governors."

—Thomas Jefferson

What do you know about government? You probably know more than you realize. We interact with different levels of government every day. For example, when the garbage truck empties your trash, that service is often handled by your local government. Likewise, the federal government may have built many of the roads and bridges you use in your daily routine. And who decides how many days of school are required in a school year? That decision is likely made by your state government.

Government is the system of rules and policies that regulate a society. As Thomas Jefferson explains above, it exists because we the people created it. Different countries utilize different forms of government. The United States uses a **federal** system. This means that power is divided between a national government (like the President of the United States), the states (like the Governor), and on a **local** level (like the Mayor.)

So who came up with all of this? Well, the tradition of **democracy** used by the United States and many other nations actually began about 2,500 years ago in ancient Greece. A democracy generally refers to "rule by the people," meaning that people vote in elections to make decisions about their government. This is different from something like a **monarchy**, where a king or queen makes all the decisions and the people have no say.

However, have you ever tried to pick a restaurant with a large group of friends? Sometimes voting on an issue can be difficult, and it is often hard to make a decision that pleases everybody. After all, can you imagine what life would be like in the United States if all 300 million people had to vote on changes to every law and policy? The United States, therefore, functions as a **republic.** A republic is a form of representative democracy where people vote in elections for representatives (like the president or school board) to make decisions in a government for them. The specific rules for the government of the United States are written in the **Constitution**.

HOW THIS CHAPTER IS ORGANIZED

Lesson 1: Historic Documents

This lesson will help prepare you to understand some of the historical papers that may appear on your HSE test. While these may seem difficult to understand at first, studying key themes in the Constitution and the Bill of Rights will make answering questions on those sources easier.

Lesson 2: Checks and Balances

This lesson will examine the foundation of the American Federal System. You will read about the crucial balancing of power between the three branches of the federal government, the legislative, executive, and judicial branches.

Lesson 3: Graphic Materials

This lesson will help you to comprehend a variety of visual resources. The HSE tests, like the real world we live in today, go beyond using just words on a page to transmit information. You will see many tables, charts, graphs, and even a few cartoons.

Lesson 4: Political Parties and Elections

This lesson explores the general differences between the two main parties in the United States, Democrats and Republicans, and the election process.

Lesson 5: Types of Government

This lesson describes several types of modern governments, including democracy, monarchy, dictatorship, and theocracy.

Lesson 6: Critical Thinking Skills

This lesson will concentrate on specific academic skills you will need to use on your high school equivalency test. The test will ask you a variety of critical reading questions. This means you will need to be able to recognize the difference between fact and opinion, cause and effect, and conclusions and supporting details. These questions are a lot easier to answer when you have the background knowledge from the previous units.

LESSON 1: HISTORIC DOCUMENTS
The Constitution

The Constitution is the supreme law of the land in the United States. It serves as the official, written plan for government. But, as Patrick Henry said, it also operates as a protection from the government. The Preamble, or introduction, to the Constitution is written below. On your HSE test you will need to analyze a historic document, and the Preamble is a great place to start.

We the People of the United States, in Order to form a more perfect Union, establish Justice, insure domestic Tranquility, provide for the common defence, promote the general Welfare, and secure the Blessings of Liberty to ourselves and our Posterity, do ordain and establish this Constitution for the United States of America.

Historic documents can be difficult to understand at first. They may use words that we are not familiar with in our modern culture. So, to figure out what is going on, we are going to read the document twice.

First, just read through the entire selection, and then think generally about the tone of the piece. This will help to put confusing parts in context.

Would you say the general tone of the Preamble to the Constitution is:

(A) Depressing
(B) Hopeful
(C) Warlike

The best answer is B. Even though you may not be familiar with all the words in the passage, or even what the Constitution is exactly, picking up on key words you do recognize can be helpful. Words like "perfect," "blessing," "liberty," and "justice" usually point to good things, so it makes sense that the rest of the Preamble will also be about the same themes.

Now let's tie in those context clues with the background knowledge you already have about the Constitution and reread the Preamble.

Practice Exercise—Context Clues

1. "We the People of the United States, in Order to form a more perfect Union,"
   What does the Preamble mean to form a more perfect union?

   (**THINK:** Why did the Framers write the Constitution? What does it do?)

   (A) Strengthen labor unions
   (B) Lower taxes
   (C) Create a better government
   (D) Declare war against the King

2. What does the word "Tranquility" mean in the Preamble?

   (**THINK:** What is the general tone? How might this word fit into that context?)

   (A) Peaceful
   (B) Militaristic
   (C) Poverty
   (D) Slavery

3. What can you infer about the authors of the Preamble?

   (**THINK:** When something is inferred it is hinted at but not directly stated.)

   (A) The Framers of the Constitution were Democrats.
   (B) They did not think the Constitution would last very long.
   (C) They wanted to promote the general welfare.
   (D) They had lofty goals for the new government.

Bill of Rights

Though the Constitution is still in use today, it was amended, or changed, almost immediately after it was written. Several colonies refused to accept the Constitution unless certain rights were specifically guaranteed. Therefore, the first ten **amendments**, known as the **Bill of Rights**, were attached to the Constitution. A copy of the Bill of Rights is printed below.

BILL OF RIGHTS

Amendment 1: Religion, Speech, Assembly, and Politics

Congress shall make no law respecting an establishment of religion, or prohibiting the free exercise thereof; or abridging the freedom of speech, or of the press, or the right of the people peaceably to assemble, and to petition the Government for a redress of grievances.

Amendment 2: Right to Bear Arms

A well regulated Militia, being necessary to the security of a free State, the right of the people to keep and bear Arms, shall not be infringed.

Amendment 3: Quartering (housing) of Soldiers

No Soldier shall, in time of peace be quartered in any house, without the consent of the Owner; nor in time of war, but in a manner to be prescribed by law.

Amendment 4: Search and Seizure

The right of the people to be secure in their persons, houses, papers, and effects, against unreasonable searches and seizures, shall not be violated, and no Warrants shall issue, but upon probable cause, supported by Oath or affirmation, and particularly describing the place to be searched, and the persons or things to be seized.

> "A Bill of Rights is what the people are entitled to against every government, and what no just government should refuse, or rest on inference."
>
> —Thomas Jefferson

Amendment 5: Self-Incrimination (pleading the 5th), Due Process

No person shall be held to answer for a capital, or otherwise infamous crime, unless on a presentment or indictment of a Grand Jury, except in cases arising in the land or naval forces, or in the Militia, when in actual service in time of War or public danger; nor shall any person be subject for the same offence to be twice put in jeopardy of life or limb; nor shall be compelled in any criminal case to be a witness against himself; nor be deprived of life, liberty, or property, without due process of law; nor shall private property be taken for public use without just compensation.

Amendment 6: Trial by Jury in Criminal Cases

In all criminal prosecutions, the accused shall enjoy the right to a speedy and public trial, by an impartial jury of the State and district wherein the crime shall have been committed; which district shall have been previously ascertained by law, and to be informed of the nature and cause of the accusation; to be confronted with the witnesses against him; to have compulsory process for obtaining witnesses in his favor; and to have the assistance of counsel for his defence.

Amendment 7: Trial by Jury in Civil Cases

In Suits at common law, where the value in controversy shall exceed twenty dollars, the right of trial by jury shall be preserved, and no fact tried by a jury shall be otherwise reexamined in any Court of the United States, than according to the rules of common law.

Amendment 8: Bail, Cruel and Unusual Punishment

Excessive bail shall not be required, nor excessive fines imposed, nor cruel and unusual punishments inflicted.

Amendment 9: Right Retained by the People

The enumeration in the Constitution of certain rights shall not be construed to deny or disparage others retained by the people.

Amendment 10: Powers Reserved to the States

The powers not delegated to the United States by the Constitution, nor prohibited by it to the States, are reserved to the States respectively, or to the people.

Practice Exercise—Bill of Rights

1. A right can be defined as a quality or virtue that a person has. What rights are guaranteed by the amendments listed here?

   (**THINK:** what specifically can people do, and what can governments not do?)

   _____

   _____

2. "Congress shall make no law respecting an establishment of religion." How does this line create a separation of Church and State (government)?

   (**THINK:** How does preventing the government from passing a law about something protect it?)

   _____

   _____

Practice Exercise—Know Your Rights

Match each situation with its appropriate amendment. Some answers may be used more than once.

_____ 1. I wrote a blog post critical of the President, and a week later, the Secret Service had me arrested.

(A) 5th Amendment

(B) 1st Amendment

_____ 2. I was arrested for stealing several DVDs. I was put on trial without a jury because the judge said it wasn't that serious, and I was sentenced to 1 week in jail.

(C) 6th Amendment

_____ 3. While on trial, the judge says that, if I don't answer all his questions, I will be put in jail.

(D) 3rd Amendment

(E) 2nd Amendment

_____ 4. The Governor wants to pass a law forbidding anyone from owning a shotgun.

(F) 8th Amendment

_____ 5. The U.S. Army wants to take over my house for the weekend to house a few soldiers.

_____ 6. While attending a public school, the teacher makes me pray before every class.

_____ 7. After I was arrested, the government kept me in jail for 10 years while I waited for my trial.

_____ 8. After being convicted for reckless driving, the judge made me mow his lawn for 2 years.

LESSON 2: CHECKS AND BALANCES

"The basic premise of the Constitution was a separation of powers and a system of checks and balances because man was perceived as a fallen creature and would always yearn for more power."

—Roy Moore

Imagine if the President ordered people over 5 feet 10 inches tall to pay a special $500 height tax. Or, what if Congress ordered everyone in the country to wear tuxedos. These are ridiculous examples because they could never happen in the United States. As outlined in the Constitution, the different powers of the federal government are divided between three branches of government: the legislative, executive, and judicial.

The framers of the Constitution, men like James Madison and Thomas Jefferson, thought long and hard about how to create a government that could prevent any one person or group from getting too powerful. For example, Congress writes the laws, but it takes the President to sign them into action. The Supreme Court can declare any law unconstitutional, which means that they can **repeal** or remove it. The President appoints judges to the Supreme Court, but Congress must approve them first. This system is often described as one of checks and balances because no one branch can dominate another.

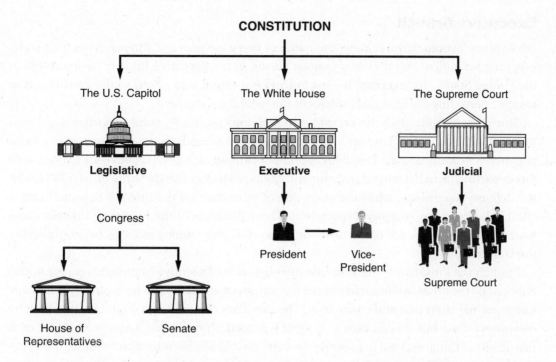

CONSTITUTION

The U.S. Capitol

Legislative

Congress

House of Representatives

Senate

The White House

Executive

President

Vice-President

The Supreme Court

Judicial

Supreme Court

The American federal system divides power between the national government in Washington, D.C. (often referred to as the federal government) and the 50 states. This chapter will investigate the relationship between the three branches of the federal government.

Checks & Balances

Judicial Branch
Upholds federal and state constitutions and other laws

Nominates federal judges

Can declare acts of the executive unconstitutional

Executive Branch
Enforces laws

Can declare laws unconstitutional

Can appoint or reject judicial nominations

Can veto laws made by the legislature

Can override executive's veto

Can reject judicial nominations

Legislative Branch
Writes laws

Executive Branch

While many people may not know the name of every member of Congress from their state, everyone is familiar with the most famous person in the Executive Branch: the President of the United States. To "**execute**" means to carry out or put into effect, so the President is in charge of enacting the laws and policies of the federal government.

This responsibility gives the President tremendous power. As **chief executive**, the President decides how to put laws into action, but this job is too large for any one person to do effectively. Accordingly, the President appoints a **cabinet**, or a group of advisors to head various departments in the federal government. Military services like the army or navy fall under the defense department, while the collection of taxes through the Internal Revenue Service (IRS) belongs to the Treasury Department. These divisions of the Executive Branch, along with dozens of others, are based in Washington, D.C. but employ millions of people across the United States.

Though the President is the supreme member of the Executive branch, his power is also checked by the other two branches of the federal government. As you have already read, only Congress may draft bills and create laws. The President can only sign them into law, or, if he disapproves of a bill, he can **veto** it. If a bill is vetoed it returns to Congress. Once there, if two-thirds of Congress vote to override the veto, the bill will become a law without the President's signature. This is another example of the checks and balances thoughtfully put into the Constitution.

One of the reasons the President is often thought of as one of the most powerful people in the world is because the job actually combines several other very important roles. The President is the **chief diplomat**, meaning that he is in charge of the nation's foreign policy and deals with the leaders of foreign countries. But perhaps most important of all, the President is also the **Commander-in-Chief**, which means he is personally in charge of all the armed forces.

Practice Exercise—Sentence Completion

Use the words in the list below to complete the sentence.

execute	Chief Diplomat	Cabinet
Chief Executive	Commander-in-Chief	veto

1. The President meets regularly with his _____ , who are the leaders of the most important government agencies.

2. When the President doesn't approve of a law sent from Congress, he may _____ it.

3. Because he is the most powerful member of the Executive Branch, the President is also known as the _____.

4. Through the role of _____ , the President represents the country to other nations around the world.

5. The Presidential oath states that the President will "faithfully _____ the office of the President of the United States."

6. As _____ , the President is the leader of the nation's armed forces.

WHAT A PRESIDENT CAN DO AND CANNOT DO

A President can:

- make treaties with the approval of the Senate
- veto bills and sign bills
- represent our nation in talks with foreign countries
- enforce the laws that Congress passes
- act as Commander-in-Chief during a war
- call out troops to protect our nation against an attack
- make suggestions about things that should be new laws
- lead his political party
- entertain foreign guests
- recognize foreign countries
- grant pardons
- nominate Cabinet members and Supreme Court Justices and other high officials
- appoint ambassadors
- talk directly to the people about problems
- represent the best interests of all the people

A President cannot:

- make laws
- declare war
- decide how federal money will be spent
- interpret laws
- choose Cabinet members or Supreme Court Justices without Senate approval

Source: *Trumanlibrary.org*

Judicial Branch

> "Presidents come and go, but the Supreme Court goes on forever."
> —William Howard Taft

Many people are familiar with the legal system through popular television shows like *Law and Order*, or in movies featuring dramatic courtroom scenes. And while these events are often "ripped from the headlines," the most important legal decisions in the United States are settled by the **Supreme Court**.

The Supreme Court is the only specific court outlined in the Constitution, and it quickly established itself as the ultimate authority to overturn or review any federal law or constitutional question. Because of this power, known as **judicial review**, decisions by the Supreme Court have long-lasting effects.

The Supreme Court does not handle the typical criminal cases you might see on T.V. Instead, it's **jurisdiction** (the power to interpret a law) generally covers possible violations of the Constitution. Such questions occur more often than you might think. The Constitution is intentionally vague in a lot of areas, such as the Elastic Clause. The Framers did this intentionally so that future leaders would have the flexibility to handle new situations as they developed. This means that there is often more than one **interpretation**, or way to read the Constitution.

For example, you probably know that when someone is arrested the person is told by the police that he or she has the right to remain silent, and the right to an attorney free of charge. But did you know that this did not happen before 1966? That is when the Supreme Court made its ruling in the case of *Miranda v. Arizona*, which states that suspects must be informed of their rights by the police or else their statements cannot be used in court.

That case happened over 40 years ago, and even though those specific rights are not mentioned in the Constitution, it is now the law of the land because of the Supreme Court decision. This is what President Taft meant when he said that the Court "goes on forever."

Practice Exercise—Judicial Review

1. What is judicial review?

   (**THINK:** What does this power allow the Supreme Court to do?)

   _____

   _____

2. What types of cases does the Supreme Court take?

   (**THINK:** What is the jurisdiction of the Supreme Court?)

   _____

   _____

3. Why are there controversies with the Constitution that the Supreme Court must solve?

   (**THINK:** What is it about the way the Constitution is written that leaves things up to interpretation?)

   _____

   _____

4. Do you think everyone in America agreed with the *Miranda v. Arizona* decision? Why might some people disagree with that ruling?

   _____

   _____

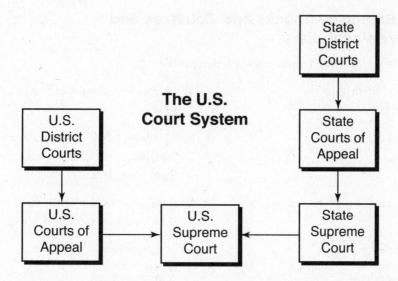

The U.S. Court System

U.S. District Courts → U.S. Courts of Appeal → U.S. Supreme Court

State District Courts → State Courts of Appeal → State Supreme Court → U.S. Supreme Court

5. Using the diagram, describe the path of a case that begins in a state district court to the Supreme Court.

_____

_____

Legislative Branch

Imagine you are the only chicken in a room full of wolves. You are about to vote on what is for dinner. How do you think that will turn out, and do you think that's fair for the chicken? The framers of the Constitution were thinking about just such principles when they created the legislative branch.

California is the most populous state in America, meaning that it has the most people. Wouldn't it make sense, then, that California has the most power in making national laws? Well, just like the wolves mentioned above, that would work out great for California, but it may not be fair to small states like Rhode Island. This is why the legislative branch created **Congress**, which is composed of the **Senate** and the **House of Representatives**.

To **legislate** means to create a law. Congress, then, writes the laws for the federal government. The House of Representatives is based on population. This means that the more people that live in a state, the more votes that state gets in the House. Texas, for example, has 30 members in the House, while Delaware only has one. This is balanced by the Senate, where each state gets two votes regardless of size. Both parts of Congress must agree on a **bill** (proposed law) for it to move to the executive branch. This process ensures that big states like New York have a lot of power, but it also protects the rights of small states like North Dakota.

The House and Senate have different duties defined by the Constitution. For example, the House has "the power of the purse," meaning that all bills involving money must start there. The Senate is in charge of approving Presidential appointments, such as Supreme Court nominations. According to the Constitution, there are 27 **expressed** powers of Congress. However, the Constitution also states that Congress has the power to create laws that are "necessary and proper" to carry out those duties. This is known as the "elastic clause," because its meaning can be stretched like elastic to include many topics beyond the original 27 written in the Constitution.

Practice Exercise—Checks and Balances and Legislative Vocabulary

Write the letter of the correct match next to each problem.

_____ 1. Constitution

_____ 2. Legislate

_____ 3. House of Representatives

_____ 4. Congress

_____ 5. Federal

_____ 6. Republic

_____ 7. Democracy

_____ 8. Local

_____ 9. Senate

_____ 10. Bill

_____ 11. Expressed

_____ 12. Monarchy

_____ 13. Repeal

(A) Relates to a smaller area like a city or a town.

(B) This level of government, located in Washington D.C., is superior to state and local governments.

(C) A form of government where power is held by a king or queen.

(D) To create laws.

(E) A proposed law.

(F) A document stating the principles by which a nation is governed.

(G) Government by the people; a form of government where people vote.

(H) In this house of Congress, each state gets two votes regardless of size.

(I) A form of representative democracy where people vote in elections for representatives.

(J) Specifically stated or put into words.

(K) To revoke or withdraw.

(L) In this house of Congress, the number of votes is determined by state population.

(M) The legislative branch consisting of both the House of Representatives and the Senate.

LESSON 3: GRAPHIC MATERIALS

Pictographs

In addition to reading passages, your HSE test will ask you to use a variety of visual materials. These resources can include everything from pictures and cartoons to maps and graphs. One type of graphic that may seem confusing at first is a pictograph, but with a little practice, these types of graphs are easy to understand.

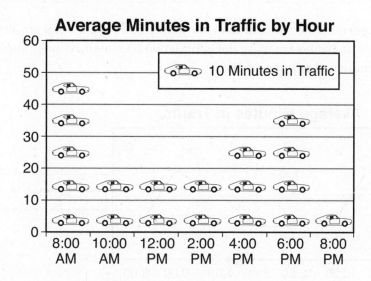

Average Minutes in Traffic by Hour

To better understand any graph, follow a few simple steps:

- What is the title of the graph?
- What are the symbols on the graph, and what do they represent?
- What information can be found on the *x*-axis (horizontal), and what information is represented on the *y*-axis (vertical)?

To read the graph correctly, multiply the number each symbol is worth (10 minutes for each car), by the number of times it appears. For example, we see, at 4:00 P.M. there are three cars. Since each car is worth 10 minutes of traffic, this means the average traffic time at 4:00 P.M. is 30 minutes (3 × 10).

Practice Exercise—Reading Pictographs

1. Based on the pictograph above, what time of day had the highest minutes in traffic? How many minutes were spent in traffic then?

   _____

2. What is the overall trend of the graph?

   (**THINK:** According to the graph, what happens to traffic throughout the day? How would you describe it to someone?)

   _____

Graphs are used because they make understanding information easier. Here is what the data from the pictograph looks like as a standard table. Both provide the same information, but with the graph, you can see at a glance the overall trend of traffic throughout the day.

	8:00 A.M.	10:00 A.M.	12:00 P.M.	2:00 P.M.	4:00 P.M.	6:00 P.M.	8:00 P.M.
Minutes in Traffic	50	20	15	15	30	40	10

Pictographs are really no different than the standard line graphs you are already used to. Pictographs just use symbols to make the information seem more visually appealing. Here's the same data presented as a line graph.

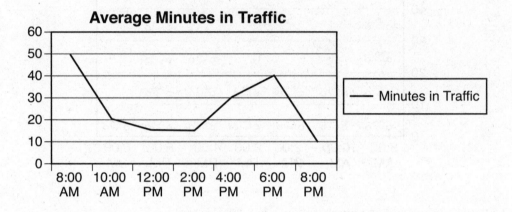

Practice Exercise—Data Interpretation

Use the graph below to answer questions 1 through 5.

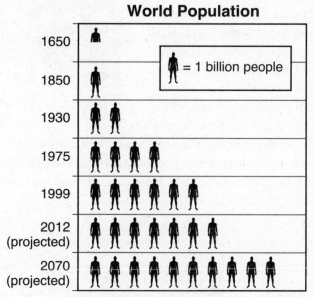

World Population

1650
1850
1930
1975
1999
2012 (projected)
2070 (projected)

= 1 billion people

Source: U.S. Census Bureau International Data Base

1. What was the world population is 1650?

   (**THINK:** How much does a whole person represent? What is half of that?)

   _____

2. According to the graph, for which years will the world population be over 6 billion?

   _____

3. Beginning in 1850, how long did it take for the world population to double?

   _____

4. What is the overall trend of the graph?

   _____

5. According to the graph, for which answer choice do you need more information to find?
   (A) The U.S. population in 1850
   (B) Projected world population in 2070
   (C) Which year had approximately 4 billion people
   (D) None of the above

Political Cartoons

Political cartoons are different than the cartoons you might find in a comic book or in the Sunday paper. Instead of being funny, they are drawn to make a point or express an opinion. Think of the saying "a picture is worth a thousand words." Political cartoons use symbols to create their message. Therefore, the first step to undestanding a political cartoon is analyze the symbols.

Two of the most common symbols used in political cartoons are the elephant and the donkey (top right.) These figures represent the two main political parties in the United States. The elephant represents the Republican Party, and the donkey represents the Democratic Party. Now take a look at the cartoon below.

Practice Exercise—Interpreting Political Cartoons

The main idea of the above cartoon can be hard to figure out at first, so let's start with some of the symbols. We see that there is a donkey, and elephant, and a setting Sun with some numbers written on it.

1. What does the Sun symbolize?

    (**THINK:** What do the numbers mean on the Sun?)

    (A) The year 1931 is almost over.

    (B) One party fell 1,931 votes short on election day.

The correct answer is (A). A setting Sun literally happens at the end of the day. In this case, because of the year 1931 written on it, we know that this Sun symbolizes the end of the year.

2. The donkey is saying "Cheer up! Remember your loss is my gain!" What can you infer happened to the Democrats?

   (**THINK:** What does the donkey represent?)

   (A) The Democrats defeated the Republicans in an election.
   (B) The Republicans defeated the Democrats in an election.

The correct answer is (A), the Democrats defeated the Republicans. Now let's put it all together.

3. What is the main idea of this political cartoon?
   (A) Democrats and Republicans in Congress are closer than ever before.
   (B) Neither the Democrats nor Republicans had a good year in 1931.
   (C) Democrats defeated the Republicans in an election in 1931.
   (D) Republicans won the Presidency in 1932.

The above cartoon was created by Benjamin Franklin who is known as one of the Founding Fathers of the United States. Franklin was an outspoken inventor and author who valued colonial unity and self-determination. These traits also guided him later in his life as an American Ambassador to France where he championed American *sovereignty* in a world dominated by European nations.

4. What symbols do you see in the cartoon?

   (**THINK:** What thing or object is pictured? What might the initials in the cartoon represent or stand for?)

   _____

5. Based on the passage and the cartoon, what does the word *sovereignty* mean?

   (**THINK:** Use context clues. What does it mean to champion something?

   According to the passage, what other ideas did Franklin champion?)
   (A) Loyalty to a king or queen
   (B) Political independence
   (C) A lower trade deficit
   (D) International fishing rights

6. Based on the passage, when was this cartoon created?

(**THINK:** What do you know about when Ben Franklin lived? Was it a long time ago?

Can you think of any other Founding Fathers and when they lived?)

(A) The Vietnam War
(B) During World War II
(C) The Presidential election of 1860
(D) Before the American Revolution

7. Which statement best **summarizes** the cartoon?

(**THINK:** What is the point of the drawing? Why did Ben Franklin draw it?)

(A) The American colonies must come together.
(B) The American colonies are like a dangerous snake.
(C) The Boston Tea Party was justified.
(D) Without help from the French, the colonists were unlikely to defeat the British.

Andrew Jackson was the seventh President
of the United States from 1829–1837

8. What symbols do you see in the above cartoon?

_____

_____

9. What is the point of view of the cartoon?
(A) Andrew Jackson was the nation's best president.
(B) Andrew Jackson was acting more like a king than an elected president.
(C) The Constitution was more powerful than the presidency.
(D) Andrew Jackson was loyal to the British King.

LESSON 4: POLITICAL PARTIES AND ELECTIONS

Imagine you wanted to run for President of the United States. How would people on the other side of the country find out about you? Unless you are already famous, it would be difficult to reach people across the nation, or even in your own town.

However, if you have good ideas about what to do in government, other people may want to help you get elected. This is the main job of a **political party**. A political party is a group of people who try to win elections. They work to get their **candidate** elected because they have similar goals and ideas about what the government should do.

In the United States, there are two main political parties, the Democrats and the Republicans. Though other parties exist, these parties usually do not win elections. Elections in the United States are usually winner takes all, where the one person with the most votes wins. This means that even though smaller parties may get some votes, they do not get to share power with the winner. The United States has had a two-party political system almost since its beginning.

The two main political parties today are the Democrats and the Republicans. So what are the differences between Democrats and Republicans? The views of each party change over time, but one big difference is in the role of government. Democrats believe the government should actively help people and regulate industries to keep things fair. This means Democrats typically favor spending more on things like schools, programs for the poor, and safeguards to make sure businesses do not pollute the environment. Doing all of these things costs money, however, so Democrats often support higher taxes to pay for these things.

Republicans, on the other hand, believe that government should be as small as possible. A smaller government costs less money to run, so Republicans support lowering taxes. They believe that too many rules and laws can make it difficult to run a business, so they look to reduce government regulations. If businesses do well, then they should be able to create more jobs, and that helps everyone. Likewise, Republicans believe that the government can provide too much support for people, and that this may prevent poor people from helping themselves.

> The ultimate rulers of our democracy are not a president and senators and congressmen and government officials, but the voters of this country.
>
> —Franklin D. Roosevelt

Practice Exercise—Political Parties

1. Organize the following ideas under the correct political party

   - Increase government spending to help people
   - Reduce laws that affect business
   - Lower taxes
   - Pass laws to protect the environment

DEMOCRAT	REPUBLICAN

The symbol of the Democratic Party is a donkey

The symbol of the Republican Party is an elephant

2. **Short answer question**: Which party do you believe would support raising the government-mandated minimum wage. Why do you think so?

Elections

Political parties play a big role in the election process. Parties create a **platform**, or a list of ideas and laws they support. This helps to focus the election and helps voters decide between candidates. Each party also works to **nominate** the one best candidate from their party for each election. This reduces the chance of an extremist winning an election because the two main parties try to appeal to the greatest number of voters.

If there is more than one person hoping to be nominated in a political party, then the parties may have a **primary election.** This is an election where all the candidates are from the same party. Whoever wins the primary election becomes the official candidate for that party. Both Republicans and Democrats use primaries when selecting someone to run for President. Whoever wins the primary does not become President but wins the support of his or her party in the national election for President.

In the United States, all citizen 18 years or older may vote in federal (President and Congress) elections. However, many states have laws that allow noncitizens to vote in local elections. State laws also vary on allowing prisoners and those convicted of serious crimes to vote. States are also allowed to make their own laws about what identification people need to have to be allowed to vote and how long they need to have lived in the area.

The election process is very expensive. Although it would not cost much for a small town candidate to reach his or her neighbors in a local election, state and national elections can cost millions of dollars. In fact, in recent presidential elections, the Democrat and Republican candidates each spent over one *billion* dollars! With the cost of running an election so high, it is easy to see why candidates need to have the support of one of the major political parties. It also may explain why **incumbents**, the people who are already in an elected office, get reelected more than 90% of the time. They usually have the huge financial support of the party.

So why do political parties need so much money, and where does it all come from? Most of the money goes to advertising. Political parties buy television ads for their candidates in all 50 states, and that costs a lot of money. They also must travel frequently to meet voters and pay their campaign staff to keep it all organized.

Almost all of the money comes from donations. Many individuals contribute small amounts to a candidate or party, and a few wealthy individuals can contribute millions of dollars. In addition, corporations or large businesses can also contribute millions of dollars. There is wide concern that the amount of money given by wealthy people or businesses may negatively influence elections.

U.S. Election Process

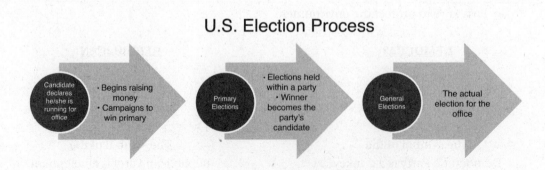

Candidate declares he/she is running for office
- Begins raising money
- Campaigns to win primary

Primary Elections
- Elections held within a party
- Winner becomes the party's candidate

General Elections
The actual election for the office

Practice Exercise—Political Party and Elections Vocabulary

Write the letter of the correct match next to each problem.

_____ 1. Political party

_____ 2. Candidate

_____ 3. Democrats

_____ 4. Republicans

_____ 5. Platform

_____ 6. Nominate

_____ 7. Primary

_____ 8. Incumbent

(A) An early election to nominate a candidate

(B) A party that supports using a large government to help people directly

(C) A party that supports smaller government and low taxes

(D) An organization that tries to win elections

(E) Someone who is currently in office

(F) To formally enter a candidate in an election

(G) The ideas and policies of a political party

(H) A person running for office

LESSON 5: TYPES OF GOVERNMENT

Have you ever wondered why we have a government? Many people ask that question when they pay taxes or when they get a parking ticket. It can seem like the government only causes problems for regular people. However, in the modern world, the government is an essential part of our daily lives. Nations without effective governments can be difficult places to live.

Simple governments began a long time ago as a form of protection. For example, instead of fighting invaders on your own, it would be easier to protect yourself if you worked with your neighbors to build a fort. But who would be in charge, and how would you pay for the fort? And how would you decide who did what job, lived in which house, or decided if someone was guilty of a crime? Answering questions like these still affect governments today. There are many kinds of government in the world today.

> "No one pretends that democracy is perfect or all-wise. Indeed, it has been said that democracy is the worst form of government except all those other forms that have been tried from time to time."
>
> —Winston Churchill

Monarchy

The most common form of government a long time ago was a **monarchy**. A monarch is a king or a queen, so a monarchy means rule by a king or a queen.

Early monarchies were often **absolute monarchies**. This means that the king or queen ruled absolutely; whatever they said was the law. These rulers never face elections so they often rule for life. When they died, power was usually given to a son or daughter who then became the absolute monarch.

However, as the saying goes, "absolute power corrupts absolutely." This means that people tend to abuse power when they are the only ones in charge. To protect against this, **constitutional monarchies** were developed. This means that the power of the monarch is limited instead of absolute. These powers are spelled out in a constitution like we have in the United States. Great Britain is a good example of a constitutional monarchy. Though there is a queen, the real power in Great Britain is with the **Parliament**, or legislature. The queen is unelected, but she is allowed to perform some tasks of government, like meeting foreign leaders. All other powers are decided by constitution and the elected Parliament.

Democracy

A democracy generally refers to rule by the people. This word comes from the Greek words *demos*, which mean "people" and *cracy* which means "power." This system of government typically involves people voting to make decisions. In a **direct democracy**, people vote directly on a policy or leader. This may sound like the best form of government, but it has its drawbacks. For example, say you needed to vote on new trade regulations with Argentina, or for who should be in charge of the Food and Drug Administration. Both of those issues are important votes, but the average citizen may not be able to, or even want to, vote on those issues.

Therefore, many nations, like the United States, use **representative democracy**. In this form of government, citizens elect representatives, like Senators or Governors, to vote and make decisions for them. This allows people to go about their daily lives without having to worry about every government matter. Voters who are unhappy with their representative's decisions can elect a new representative to serve.

Dictatorship

Another common form of modern government is a **dictatorship**. A dictatorship is much like an absolute monarch: one person has complete control of the government. This person dictates, or gives orders for the government. Many modern dictators are **totalitarian** rulers. This means that they totally control all aspects of life in a country. Totalitarian dictators control all of the political, economic, and social aspects of a nation. Adolf Hitler is an example of a totalitarian dictator.

Theocracy

Theocracy comes from the Greek words *theos* meaning "God" and *cracy* meaning "power." In these governments, religious leaders run the government, and the law is based on a religious text. Saudi Arabia is an example of a theocracy.

Practice Exercise—Types of Government

1. Place the correct form of government under each column.

    Democracy   Dictatorship   Absolute monarchy   Constitutional monarchy

One ruler with total power	Power shared by leaders through elections

2. Read each description of a nation. Write the type of government that matches the description in the blank.

A. While the king is meeting with the President of another nation, the Parliament is voting on a new law.

_____

B. A military general with total control of his nation cancels all elections.

_____

C. The high priest has declared that all schools and business must close at sundown to follow a religious tradition.

_____

D. The residents of a town vote to raise the local sales tax.

_____

E. The king decides that everyone in his nation must help to build him a new castle.

_____

LESSON 6: CRITICAL THINKING SKILLS
Fact or Opinion

A fact is something that can be verified, or looked up. An opinion is a point of view, or a judgment that may or not be true. For example, you may believe that "Star Wars" is the best movie ever, but someone else may disagree. That statement is an opinion rather than a fact.

Practice Exercise—Fact or Opinion

Questions 1 through 4 are based on the following map.

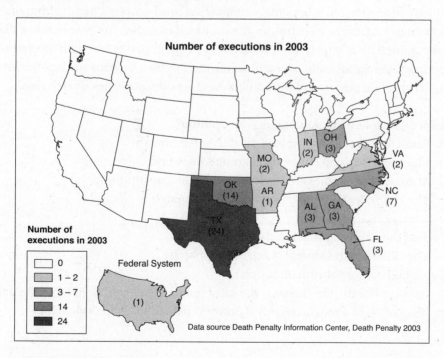

Number of executions in 2003

Number of executions in 2003

- 0
- 1 – 2
- 3 – 7
- 14
- 24

Federal System

(1)

Data source Death Penalty Information Center, Death Penalty 2003

1. Which of the following is a **fact** supported by the map?
   (A) More crimes are committed in the south.
   (B) Florida had more executions than Ohio.
   (C) There were no executions in Canada in 2003.
   (D) Texas had more executions than any other state.

2. Which of the following is an **opinion** based on the map?
   (A) More states should execute criminals.
   (B) Arkansas had the fewest executions of any state in 2003.
   (C) The federal system only executed one person.
   (D) More men were executed than women.

3. Which of the following **can be proven** by the information on the map?
   (A) More executions took place in 2003 than in any other year.
   (B) Oklahoma had the second highest total of executions.
   (C) South Carolina voters sided with the Democratic Party in 2003.
   (D) 2003 had less executions than 2002.

4. Which statement is an **opinion** based on the map?
   (A) Capital punishment is the most effective crime deterrent.
   (B) Zero people were executed in California.
   (C) Fewer executions took place in Washington State than in Indiana.
   (D) North Carolina executed more people than Virginia.

Use the following passage to answer questions 5 through 7.

Monarchies are one of the oldest and greatest forms of government in the world. In a monarchy, a king or queen is the head of the government. The most common form of monarchy is a hereditary monarchy. In a hereditary monarchy, royal power is passed from one family member to another. Dozens of countries use monarchies today. In some nations, like Great Britain, the monarchy is largely ceremonial, and political power lies with elected officials. Other countries, like Saudi Arabia, have absolute monarchies. This means that the royal family rules with absolute power, and the country has no political parties or elections.

5. Which of the following statements is an **opinion**?
   (A) Saudi Arabia is an example of an absolute monarchy.
   (B) Monarchies are no longer used around the world.
   (C) Absolute monarchies always follow a written constitution.
   (D) The U.S. federal system is superior to a monarchy.

6. Which of the following statements is a **fact**?
   (A) The United States should change to monarchy.
   (B) Monarchies are always unpopular.
   (C) In Great Britain, the Queen is the most politically powerful figure in the nation.
   (D) Most often in a monarchy, royal power is passed to a son or daughter.

7. Which sentence is an **opinion**?
   (A) Monarchies are one of the oldest and greatest forms of government in the world.
   (B) The most common form of monarchy is a hereditary monarchy.
   (C) In a hereditary monarchy, royal power is passed from one family member to another.
   (D) Dozens of countries use monarchies today.

Inferences

Something is inferred when it is suggested but not directly stated. For example, imagine if you came to class late, began coughing and sneezing, and then put your head down on the desk. The teacher may infer that you are sick even though you did not say so.

Practice Exercise—Inferences

Questions 1 and 2 are based on the following political cartoon.

In the cartoon above, Theodore (Teddy) Roosevelt is on the left, and George Washington is on the right.

1. What can be **inferred** from the political cartoon?
   (A) The constitutional system is the best system of government.
   (B) Theodore Roosevelt wants to be President for a third term.
   (C) George Washington was much taller than Teddy Roosevelt.
   (D) Teddy Roosevelt's policies are undemocratic.

2. What can be **inferred** from the political cartoon?
   (A) George Washington and Teddy Roosevelt were lifelong enemies.
   (B) George Washington appears to be a ghost in this cartoon.
   (C) George Washington was a better President than Teddy Roosevelt.
   (D) George Washington was against Presidents serving for more than two terms.

Use the passage below to answer questions 3 and 4.

The Constitution was written in 1787, and has served as the model for future governments all over the world. Influential and wise, the U.S. Constitution is the greatest political document ever written. Still, the Constitution was not ratified, or passed, by all of the states until 1790. During that time, James Madison, John Jay, and Alexander Hamilton published *The Federalist Papers* in support of the Constitution. These essays helped to explain the philosophy and goals behind the broad language used in the Constitution. For example, in *Federalist #10*, Madison argues that individual freedoms must always be protected against majority rule. These writings are considered a primary source for interpreting the Constitution.

3. Which statement can be **inferred** from the passage?
   (A) Influential and wise, the U.S. Constitution is the greatest political document ever written.
   (B) John Jay wrote some of the *Federalist Papers*.
   (C) Not all of the colonies were happy with the Constitution when it was first written.
   (D) George Washington wanted to be king.

4. Which statement can be **inferred** from the passage?
   (A) The meaning of Constitution can be interpreted in different ways.
   (B) The Constitution was written in 1787.
   (C) The Federalists were against the new form of government.
   (D) The Constitution is irrelevant to the modern world.

Use the maps below to answer question 5.

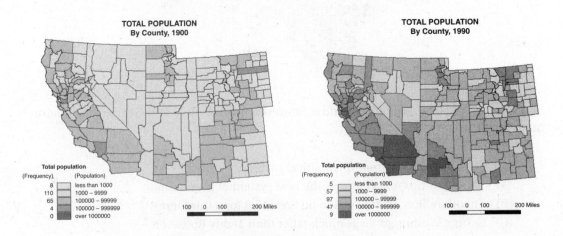

5. Which statement can be **inferred** from the above maps?
    (A) California had the most areas with populations over 1,000,000.
    (B) Many jobs were created in the southwest between 1900 and 1990.
    (C) New Mexico lost population between 1900 and 1990.
    (D) Arizona had one area grow to over 1,000,000 by 1990.

Use the political cartoon below to answer question 6.

ALL HAIL!

The man pictured in the cartoon is Theodore Roosevelt, America's 26th President.

6. What can be **inferred** from the cartoon?
    (A) Theodore Roosevelt was the first American King.
    (B) President Roosevelt liked large jewelry.
    (C) In wanting to be President for many terms, some people felt Roosevelt was acting like a king.
    (D) Roosevelt fought in the American Revolution.

Use the statement below to answer question 7.

Young people are frequently uninterested in politics, and are the most likely to be apathetic about elections.

7. What can be **inferred** about the above statement?
   (A) Young people are less likely to vote than older people.
   (B) Elections do not matter.
   (C) The democratic process is unfair.
   (D) Older people are less likely to vote than younger people.

CHAPTER 17 ANSWER EXPLANATIONS

Lesson 1: Historic Documents

PRACTICE EXERCISE—CONTEXT CLUES (PAGE 545)

1. **(C)** We know the Constitution is the written plan for the government of the United States, and we know from context clues like "perfect" that it is a good thing. Choice (A) is distracting because it has the word "union," but the Constitution is about government, so that is not a good choice.

2. **(A)** None of the other words make sense with the positive, hopeful tone of the Preamble.

3. **(D)** There is no way to know from the reading what political party the authors may have belonged to, so answer (A) is not a good choice. Choice (B) is incorrect because the word "posterity" means future generations, so the authors were hopeful the document would last. Choice (C) may seem like it is correct because it is written in the Preamble, but the question asks for an inference, and inferences are not directly stated. The Preamble lists the aspirations (goals) of the government like peace and liberty, so answer (D) is the best choice.

PRACTICE EXERCISE—BILL OF RIGHTS (PAGE 547)

1. Freedom of speech, religion, and assembly.
   Right to bear arms.
   Freedom from forcibly housing soldiers.
   Protection from search and seizure without a warrant.
   Trial by jury, and freedom from testifying against one's self.
   Protection from cruel and unusual punishment.

2. If the government cannot pass laws regarding religion, then the two will be separated. For example, this means that Congress cannot create a national religion or provide benefits for one religion over another.

PRACTICE EXERCISE—KNOW YOUR RIGHTS (PAGE 548)

1. B
2. C
3. A
4. E
5. D
6. B
7. C
8. F

Lesson 2: Checks and Balances

PRACTICE EXERCISE—SENTENCE COMPLETION (PAGE 550)

1. The President meets regularly with his *cabinet*, who are the leaders of the most important government agencies.
2. When the President doesn't approve of a law sent from Congress, he may *veto* it.
3. Because he is the most powerful member of the Executive Branch, the President is also known as the *Chief Executive.*
4. Through the role of *Chief Diplomat*, the President represents the country to other nations around the world.
5. The Presidential oath states that the President will "faithfully *execute* the office of the President of the United States."
6. As *Commander-in-Chief*, the President is the leader of the nation's armed forces.

PRACTICE EXERCISE—JUDICIAL REVIEW (PAGE 552)

1. The Supreme Court's ultimate authority to overturn and review any federal law or constitutional question.
2. The Supreme Court does not handle criminal cases. Instead, it takes on cases involving Constitutional questions.
3. Because the Constitution is written in vague language, there is more than one way to interpret it. This means that different people can read the same passage and arrive at different meanings.
4. Do you think everyone in America agreed with the *Miranda v. Arizona* decision? Probably not.
   Why might some people disagree with that ruling?
   Answers will vary. Some might think that the police are being too easy on suspected criminals.
5. There are two possible routes. (A). State District Courts to the State Courts of Appeal to the State Supreme Court. (B). U.S. District Courts to the U.S. Courts of Appeal.

PRACTICE EXERCISE—CHECKS AND BALANCES AND LEGISLATIVE VOCABULARY (PAGE 554)

1. F
2. D
3. L
4. M
5. B
6. I
7. G
8. A
9. H
10. E
11. J
12. C
13. K

Lesson 3: Graphic Materials

PRACTICE EXERCISE—READING PICTOGRAPHS (PAGE 555)

1. 8 A.M.: 50 minutes.
2. What is the overall trend of the graph?

   Traffic spikes in the morning, lessens during the day, and then increases later in the afternoon.

PRACTICE EXERCISE—DATA INTERPRETATION (PAGE 557)

1. Half a billion people, or 500 million.
2. 2012 and 2070.
3. In 1850, the population was 1 billion, and in 1930, it was 2 billion. Therefore, it took 80 years for the population to double.
4. World population growth is speeding up over time.
5. The correct answer is (D); all other choices can be found on the pictograph.

PRACTICE EXERCISE—INTERPRETING POLITICAL CARTOONS (PAGE 558)

1. **(A)** A setting Sun literally happens at the end of the day. In this case, because of the year 1931 written on it, we know that the Sun symbolizes the end of the year.
2. **(A)** The Democrats defeated the Republicans.
3. **(C)**
4. A snake appears in the cartoon, but it is cut into several pieces. The initials most likely represent the names of colonies. N.Y. means New York, N.C. means North Carolina, V. means Virginia, etc.
5. **(B)** The passage states that Franklin valued "self-determination," or the ability of a nation to make its own decisions. (A) is incorrect because Franklin "valued colonial unity" over European domination, and European nations had kings and queens. (C) and (D) are incorrect because they are not mentioned in the passage or the cartoon.
6. **(D)** Since the cartoon has to do with colonies, the best answer is the American Revolution. All of the other answer choices occur almost 100 years or more after the colonial era.
7. **(A)** This question asks you to apply the information about the author of the cartoon as a supporter of colonial unity to his drawing of the cut-up snake. None of the other answer choices are supported in the passage.
8. Possible answers include a crown, a scepter, and a ripped constitution on the floor.
9. **(B)** The caption states that Jackson was President, but the crown symbolizes royalty. Since he is standing on a ripped constitution, you can infer that he is acting more like a king than a President.

Lesson 4: Political Parties and Elections

PRACTICE EXERCISE—POLITICAL PARTIES (PAGE 561)

1.

Democrat	Republican
Increase government spending to help people	Lower taxes
Pass laws to protect the environment	Reduce laws that affect business

2. Democrats are more likely to support raising the minimum wage. Possible reasons why include that Republicans do not favor laws that affect business, so they would not support a law that mandated what an employer had to pay a worker. Also, Democrats support spending to help people, so although raising the minimum wage would cost businesses more money, it would put more money in worker's pockets.

PRACTICE EXERCISE—POLITICAL PARTY AND ELECTIONS VOCABULARY (PAGE 563)

1. **D**   5. **G**
2. **H**   6. **F**
3. **B**   7. **A**
4. **C**   8. **E**

Lesson 5: Types of Government

PRACTICE EXERCISE—TYPES OF GOVERNMENT (PAGE 564)

A. Constitutional monarchy
B. Dictatorship
C. Theocracy
D. Democracy
E. Absolute monarchy

Lesson 6: Critical Thinking Skills

PRACTICE EXERCISE—FACT AND OPINION (PAGE 565)

1. **(D)** With 24 executions, Texas had a higher number than any other state. Answer (A) is incorrect because the map only shows executions and not total crimes, so we do not know for a fact where more crimes were committed. (B) is incorrect because Florida and Ohio had the same number of executions. Since the map only shows the United States, (C) is incorrect because that cannot be determined from the map.
2. **(A)** This is an opinion because one person may believe that statement is true, while another may not. There is no way to look up the statement as a fact. Answers (B) and (C) are incorrect because they are facts that can be found on the map. Answer (D) is incorrect because it cannot be determined from the map, and is not an opinion statement.
3. **(B)** This is the only fact that can be proven by the map. Answers (A), (C), and (D) cannot be proven from the map.
4. **(A)** All other answer choices contain factual information that can be verified on the map.
5. **(D)** This is an opinion because one person may believe that statement is true, while another may not. There is no way to look up the statement as a fact. Answer (A) is a fact that may be found in the passage. Answer (B) is disproved in the passage, and there is no evidence to support (C).
6. **(D)** The correct answer is (D) because the passage states the power is passed from one family member to another. Answer (A) is an opinion. There is no evidence to support answer (B), and (C) is disproved in the passage.

7. **(A)** This is an opinion because there is no way to prove what form of government is the "greatest." All of the other answers are statement of facts in the passage.

PRACTICE EXERCISE—INFERENCES (PAGE 567)

1. **(B)** Answer (A) is incorrect because it is an opinion and not an inference. (C) is incorrect because, in the cartoon, George Washington is clearly taller than Roosevelt, so that is directly stated and not inferred. There is no evidence for answer (D). It can be inferred that the ghost of George Washington's anti-third term principle is against Roosevelt.

2. **(D)** There is no evidence to support (A), (B) is directly stated, and (C) is an opinion. (D) is correct because it says anti-third term directly on Washington.

3. **(C)** Because the Constitution was written in 1787 and not approved until 1790, we can infer it took 3 years to pass it, so some of the colonies must have initially disagreed. (A) is an opinion. (B) is a stated fact; there is no evidence to support (D).

4. **(A)** The passage states that the Federalist papers are used as sources to interpret the Constitution, so that means there is more than one way to interpret the document. (B) is fact stated in the passage, (C) and (D) are disproved in the passage.

5. **(B)** Since the map shows large population gains, it can be inferred that many of these people found jobs; otherwise, the population would not have risen. Answers (A) and (D) are facts stated on the map. Answer (C) is untrue.

6. **(C)** Answer (A) is incorrect because there are no American Kings. Answer (B) is untrue. Answer (D) is untrue and unsupported in the cartoon. The crowns read "third term," "fourth term," and "fifth term," meaning that Roosevelt wanted to rule a long time like a king.

7. **(A)** If they are apathetic, they are less likely to vote. Answers (B) and (C) are irrelevant to the passage. (D) is the opposite of the answer.

World History

"People are trapped in history, and history is trapped in them."

—James Baldwin

So, why do you live where you live now?

The answer is different for everyone. Maybe you were born near here, or perhaps you moved for employment or other reasons. Now let's take one more step back and ask yourself, why did your parents live where they lived? How about their parents? And what about the generations before them?

Some of these questions you may be able to answer, but the farther back you go in time the more difficult it gets. Still, like you, everyone before you had a reason for living where they did. We don't always think about it, but history runs in a straight line from where you are sitting right now all the way back to the ancient pyramids of Egypt, and even before then!

Like you just did with your family, historians try to answer the question, "how did we get here?" And what we have found out is that much of the modern world stems from a few distinct places. Like you and your family, these ancient civilizations had reasons for developing where they did. Their achievements still affect us today.

HOW THIS CHAPTER IS ORGANIZED

Lesson 1: Ancient Civilizations

This lesson looks at the beginnings of civilized society. Remarkably, no matter where these early civilizations started on the planet, they all had a few things in common. Additionally, we'll investigate the influence of ancient Rome on our modern world.

Lesson 2: Great Ideas

This lesson brings up some of history's notable thinkers and movements. Can't live without a cell phone? How about electricity? These advances, and many others, would be impossible without the great minds of the Enlightenment.

Lesson 3: Graphic Materials

This lesson introduces you to time lines, an important graphic on HSE tests.

Lesson 4: Critical Thinking Skills

This lesson tackles two more areas you will need to be familiar with on the test. The first, comparing and contrasting, asks you to note similarities and differences. The second, drawing conclusions, asks you to make a judgment based on the facts you read.

A NOTE ON DATES

While the history of the United States only goes back a couple of hundred years, the history of the world goes back much farther. We may have just rounded the year 2000 in our lifetime, yet ancient history is far older than that. If we go back approximately 2000 years, we would hit year zero. So how can anything have happened before then?

Well, to make things easier, historians label everything from the year zero until now as the common era. Usually this is abbreviated C.E. For example, Pearl Harbor was bombed in 1941 C.E., and the Declaration of Independence was signed in 1776 C.E. The C.E. is usually not included with dates though because all dates are assumed to be in the common era unless otherwise noted.

The exception, though, is events that happen *before the common era*, or B.C.E. For example, the Great Pyramid in Egypt was built around 2,500 B.C.E. This means it was finished about 2,500 years before the year 0.

This may seem confusing, but it will make more sense when we cover time lines. For now, just know that any date listed as B.C.E. happened thousands of years ago.

LESSON 1: ANCIENT CIVILIZATIONS

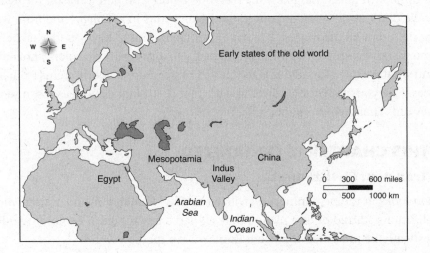

Long before people lived in cities, people traveled in **nomadic** groups. This means that people traveled from place to place in search of food and water. Why would people do this? Well, in a time before super-markets, or even money, you had to move where the food moved. If you woke up one morning and your closest herd of goats had moved 2 miles away, then you also needed to move 2 miles if you wanted to eat later.

Never being able to count on your next meal is a difficult way to live, and approxi-

Events in History Using B.C.E. and C.E.

- 2500 B.C.E.—Great Pyramid constructed in Egypt.
- 205 B.C.E.—Great Wall of China constructed.
- 0 C.E.
  Jesus Christ born.
- 570 C.E.—Mohammed born.
- 1450 C.E.—Printing Press Invented
- 1945 C.E.
  World War II Ends

mately 10,000 years ago things began to change. People slowly learned how to farm. The ability to grow reliable crops meant that people could have a food source that stayed in one place. As people produced more food than they could eat, this **surplus** was stored in newly created buildings. And just like that we have the beginnings of **civilization**.

Ancient River Valley Civilizations

- Mesopotamia—(present day Iraq), Tigris and Euphrates Rivers, 3500 B.C.E.
- Egypt—Nile River, 3000 B.C.E.
- Indus—(present day India and Pakistan), Indus River, 2500 B.C.E.
- China—Huang He River, 2000 B.C.E.

River Valleys

These early civilizations developed on different **continents** at different times, but all have a few things in common. Most importantly, early civilizations, whether in Africa, Asia, or India, started near rivers. First and foremost, rivers provide water. Nothing on earth can live long without water, so having a nearby source of fresh water is critical. Rivers also flood regularly. This is important because the river valley is renewed with **fertile** soil after a flood. Since fresh fish can be easily found, rivers are likewise great sources of food. Finally, rivers provide a way to sweep away the waste and garbage created by human settlements, and offer easy transportation over long distances. It is much easier to float 100 pounds of grain downstream on a raft than it is to carry that same load over land.

Because of the many advantages provided by the rivers, people no longer had to spend all of their time hunting for food. This meant that people now had time for other things, and people used this time to become artists, builders, traders, and many other things. The early civilizations were turning into cities, and with this growth came the need for government. Laws would need to be written down and money counted, so writing and number systems were also created.

Practice Exercise—Ancient Civilizations Vocabulary

Write the letter of the correct match next to each problem.

_____ 1. Nomadic   (A) A developed and organized society

_____ 2. Surplus   (B) A person with no fixed home, a wanderer

_____ 3. Civilization   (C) More than what is needed

_____ 4. Continents   (D) Able to produce crops

_____ 5. Fertile   (E) One of the large land masses on Earth, like Europe or Africa

Practice Exercise—Drawing Conclusions

On your HSE test, you will need to draw conclusions from stated information. This means that you will combine the facts that you know to make a new statement based on those details. In real life, you do this without even thinking about it. For example, let's say you see a student arrive late to class, and then cough and sneeze all the way to his desk. Soon after, he closes his eyes and puts his head down on the desk.

What conclusion can you draw from these details? You can safely conclude that the student is not feeling well. A good conclusion is a judgment you make based on the facts.

On the chart below, the conclusion is that "rivers were important to ancient civilizations."

Fill in the rest of the chart with details to support that conclusion. One detail has been provided for you:

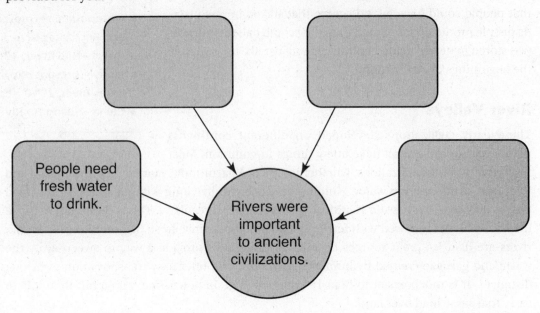

On the next chart, try to use the details provided to form your own conclusion:

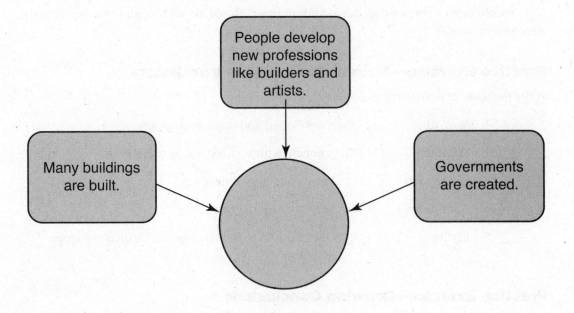

LESSON 2: GREAT IDEAS

Rome

Early civilizations like the Romans and others before them started us down the road to the modern world. Like the Greeks, the ancient Romans developed an early form of democracy. Complete with citizens and a Senate, our current government owes a lot to the 2,000-year-old traditions of the Roman Republic. Eventually, though, the Roman Empire faded away, and early advances in politics, science, and the arts were forgotten.

Roman Empire 117 C.E.

Renaissance

The word **Renaissance** means rebirth, and slowly around the years 1300–1500, a reawakening began in Europe. Starting in Italy, people like Leonardo Da Vinci looked back to ancient Greek and Roman traditions for knowledge. The Renaissance had a great effect on artists, and it changed the way people looked at the world. Sculptors like Michelangelo made lifelike statues of humans. In fact, the whole idea that an individual person is important began to take root.

This significant development led to people wanting to better themselves, and with that, learning and knowledge exploded. People began to question everything about the world around them. Men like Da Vinci actually examined dead bodies in order to understand basic human **anatomy**, or the structure of the human body. Nicolaus Copernicus figured out how to chart the paths of the planets in outer space (hundreds of years before computers) and proposed the radical theory that the Earth circled the Sun. This challenged the traditional view of the world with the Earth at the center, and the Catholic Church actually banned his book! Combine these ideas with other advances in mathematics and inventions like the printing press in 1450, and the ideas of the Renaissance spread across Europe. Prior to that, all books were written by hand, and few people could read. The world was now ready for a scientific revolution.

Enlightenment

Science is such a part of our daily life now that it is easy to take for granted. While the latest cell phone is an easy example of science and technology, so are things like the refrigerator that keeps our food fresh, and the internal combustion engine that powers every car and truck. These modern conveniences make our lives easier, but they did not just appear out of thin air. These devices, and many others, are a product of the scientific revolution and the **Enlightenment**, which began in Europe in the 1600s and 1700s.

Early scientists like Galileo and Isaac Newton began using the **scientific method** in experiments. This meant that they used observation and reason to explain the results of their experiments. It was no longer enough to just claim that something was true (like the Earth is flat), you had to be able to prove it (Magellan sailed around the world in 1519.) And now that books were more available, news of discoveries and ideas traveled quickly.

These principles also spread beyond the sciences. Just as people were working in laboratories to figure out the power of lightning and electricity, others were asking how the King or Queen got their political power. Perhaps if there were natural forces that controlled nature, there were also natural laws for governments. Men like Thomas Jefferson were heavily influenced by the Enlightenment. He and others began to openly question whether or not the King had a **divine right** (power from God) to be in charge, and these thoughts helped to start the American Revolution. The Founding Fathers of the United States believed in the Enlightenment ideal that things could be perfected through experimentation, and they soon broke away from England to form their own government, the United States.

Viewed through the Enlightenment, the world suddenly seemed understandable. At the same time as Jefferson and others were experimenting with a new form of government, others were using science during the Enlightenment to turn a profit. In 1790, James Watt perfected the steam engine. This machine would provide the power to run factories. Modern industry was born. The steam engine also provided new forms of **transportation,** such as the railroad and the steamship. A trip across the Atlantic Ocean took 2 months in a sailboat but only 2 weeks in a steamship. Everything was becoming faster and cheaper; the world was entering the modern era.

Practice Exercise—Sentence Completion

Use the words in the list below to complete the sentence.

Renaissance	scientific method	Enlightenment
anatomy	divine right	transportation

1. The President of the United States is elected, but kings used to rule by _____, meaning that they said their power came from God.

2. The _____ was a movement in the 1600s and 1700s that used reason and observation to find answers.

3. Today we use many different forms of _____ from bikes, to cars, to planes.

4. The _____ was a period of artistic growth in the 1300–1500s that looked back to the ancient Greeks and Romans.

5. _____ is the scientific study of the human body.

6. The _____ is a process used to make discoveries based on facts.

Practice Exercise—Comparing and Contrasting

When you compare and contrast something, you are looking for similarities and differences. For example, apples and oranges are comparable shapes, but their different colors contrast. While that is a simple example, on your HSE test, you will also need to be able to compare and contrast information. Comparing and contrasting also helps us to understand history by showing us how much the world has changed, but also how different time periods relate to one another.

Using the chart below, write down a few differences and similarities between the Renaissance and the Enlightenment.

Similarities	Differences

LESSON 3: GRAPHIC MATERIALS

Time lines are lines used to show the order of events in a certain amount of time. The good news is that you will not have to memorize specific dates in history to pass your HSE. It will help you, though, to have a general knowledge of approximately when important events happened in relation to each other. For example, we all know that World War I occurred before World War II. But which came first: The Civil War or the American Revolution? Time lines can be useful tools for understanding a series of events, and your ability to understand time lines will be tested.

Practice Exercise—Interpreting Time Lines

Major American Wars Time Line

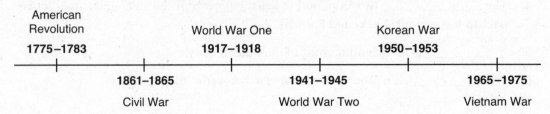

There are three things you should do with every time line. First, make sure to find the title. This may seem obvious, but it is easy to get distracted by the graphics and miss the main idea.

1. What is the subject of this time line?

   _____

Next, note the direction of the time line. Most will move from left to right, but others may move in a different direction. To do so, you will need to find which end of the line has the earliest date.

2. What is the first event on the time line?

   _____

Finally, get a sense of the period of time shown in the time line. In addition to showing you the order of events, time lines also display the amount of time between events.

> **Steps to Reading a Time Line**
>
> 1. Find the title
> 2. Notice the direction of the time line. Where does it start and end?
> 3. What is the general range of time?

3. What is the first date on the time line? What is the last date on the time line? Approximately how many years are between those two events?
   (A) 20 years
   (B) 200 years
   (C) 2,000 years

Every time line will cover a different amount of time, so it is important to realize each time line's general length.

Use the time line below to answer questions 4 through 8.

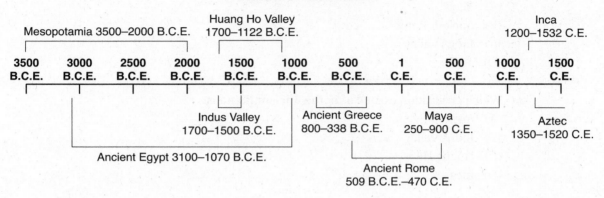

Ancient Civilizations

4. What is the main idea of the time line?
   (A) The seven continents and major oceans
   (B) Ancient Greece
   (C) Ancient Civilizations
   (D) Egypt

5. What is the range of years covered in the time line?

   (**THINK:** What is difference between the first and last year?)

   (A) 5,000
   (B) 3,500
   (C) 2,500
   (D) 2,000

6. What is the first civilization listed on the time line?
   (A) Mesopotamia
   (B) Indus Valley
   (C) Ancient Egypt
   (D) Aztec

UNIT 4: SOCIAL STUDIES

Notice how some of the events appear to overlap on the time line. This means that these civilizations existed at the same times. For example, we see that Mesopotamia began in 3500 B.C.E. and lasted until 2000 B.C.E. Since Ancient Egypt began in 3000 B.C.E., this happened simultaneously with Mesopotamia.

7. Which civilization existed at approximately the same time as the Ancient Greeks?
   (A) Maya
   (B) Ancient Rome
   (C) Indus Valley
   (D) Aztec

8. Which civilization existed after the Ancient Romans?
   (A) Ancient Egypt
   (B) Indus Valley
   (C) Huang He
   (D) Inca

Time lines can also appear vertically. Use the same approach to read this time line as with the horizontal time lines to answer questions 9 and 10.

Inventions of the Enlightenment	
1800	■ Electric battery by Alessandro Volta
1780	■ Bi-focal eye glasses by Benjamin Franklin
1769	■ Steam engine by James Watt
1724	■ Mercury thermometer by Gabriel Fahrenheit
1674	■ Microscope by Antoni van Leeuwenhoek
1668	■ Telescope by Galileo

9. Which event occurred after the invention of the steam engine?
   (A) Gabriel Fahrenheit invented the thermometer.
   (B) The telescope was created by Galileo.
   (C) Benjamin Franklin invented bi-focal eyeglasses.
   (D) The microscope was invented by Antoni van Leeuwenhoek.

10. Approximately how many years does the time line cover?
    (A) 1,800
    (B) 1,668
    (C) 3,500
    (D) 130

Use the template below to create your own time line. You'll need to fill in the dates and a few events. Don't worry, if you don't want to put in details from your own life, feel free to make some up. Start on the left, and fill in the year you were born. Then fill in at least four more events and dates between when you were born and today.

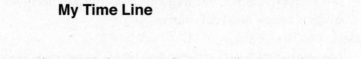

My Time Line

The year
I was born

LESSON 4: CRITICAL THINKING SKILLS
Compare and Contrast

When you compare or contrast something, you are pointing out how things are alike and how they are different. For example, motorcycles and bicycles are alike in that they both have two wheels and are used as transportation. They are different in that a motorcycle is motorized while a bicycle is not. On your HSE test, you will need to be able to compare and contrast subjects from a variety of sources.

Practice Exercise—Comparing and Contrasting

Use the passage below to answer questions 1 through 4.

Lasting approximately 2,000 years, the ancient Egyptian civilization is famous for its pyramids. Still, other ancient river civilizations are similarly remarkable. Just as the Egyptians used hieroglyphics as an early writing system, the Mesopotamian, Chinese, and Indus River Valley civilizations also developed writing systems. In Mesopotamia and China, irrigation ditches were dug to better control the flooding of the river. Like the Egyptians, the Chinese developed the field of astronomy, and could accurately predict eclipses. Lasting for approximately 1,000 years, great advances were also made in the city of Harappa along the Indus River. Here, streets were planned along a grid system much like a modern city, and houses even had plumbing connected to a sewer system! Unfortunately, the Harappan civilization was likely destroyed by a natural disaster.

1. How are Egyptian and Chinese civilizations similar?
    (A) Both lasted approximately 2,000 years.
    (B) Both developed a grid-like street system.
    (C) Both civilizations utilized hieroglyphics.
    (D) The study of astronomy flourished under both civilizations.

2. How was the civilization along the Indus River different from other early civilizations?
    (A) Indus River civilizations did not develop a writing system.
    (B) The city of Harappa created an early sewer system.
    (C) The use of irrigation.
    (D) The study of astronomy.

3. How are all of the civilizations in the passage alike?
    (A) All of the civilizations built pyramids.
    (B) They all existed for an equal length of time.
    (C) All of the civilizations developed writing systems.
    (D) Religion was unimportant in all ancient societies.

4. In what way was ancient Egyptian civilization different than the Indus Valley civilization?
    (A) The Indus Valley civilization developed along a river.
    (B) The Egyptian civilization lasted approximately twice as long as the Indus civilization.
    (C) The Egyptians were destroyed by a natural disaster.
    (D) The Egyptians built sewer systems into their cities.

Use the maps below to answer questions 5 through 8.

Europe 1600

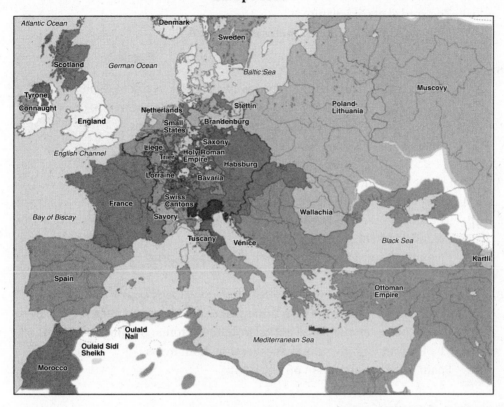

Europe 1900

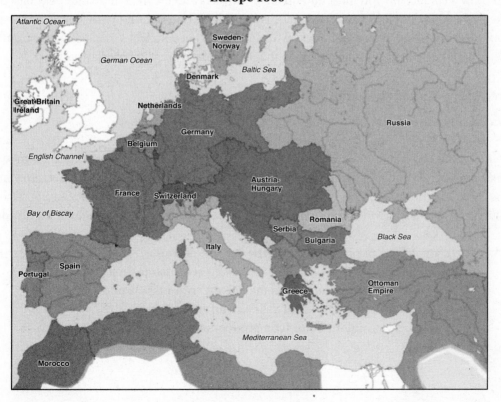

5. What are these two maps comparing?
   (A) The locations of ancient river valley civilizations
   (B) Europe over a 200-year period
   (C) The spread of Christianity
   (D) Political changes in Europe between 1600 and 1900

6. In what way do these two maps contrast?
   (A) The size of the Ottoman Empire greatly increases in size by 1900.
   (B) Italy and Germany did not exist in 1600 but are independent nations by 1900.
   (C) France was the largest nation in Europe in 1600.
   (D) Rome was a dominant power in 1600 but not in 1900.

7. What is one difference between the two maps?
   (A) European nations tripled in population.
   (B) The ideas of the Enlightenment were unpopular in France.
   (C) Poland-Lithuania disappears by 1900.
   (D) Spain is the most important nation in Europe by 1900.

8. All of the following list differences between the two maps *except:*
   (A) The United Kingdom of Great Britain takes over Scotland after 1600.
   (B) Greece becomes a separate nation from the Ottoman Empire by 1900.
   (C) The Russian Empire is the farthest east on both maps.
   (D) Spain is the largest nation on both maps.

Drawing Conclusions

To draw a conclusion you must add up all of the facts and create a new statement based on the facts. For example, let's say you see a group of children wearing party hats. On a nearby table are wrapped presents and a cake with candles. What conclusion can you make from the details you observed? You can conclude that the children are at a birthday party.

Practice Exercise—Drawing Conclusions

Use the passage below to answer questions 1 and 2.

   Along the Tigris and Euphrates rivers, early Mesopotamians dug irrigation canals to water their crops. In Egypt, managing the flooding of the Nile was essential for farmers. In China, the 2,400-mile-long Huang He river flooded often and renewed the soil for planting. Also, in China, the Himalayan Mountains to the west protected the ancient civilization from invaders.

1. What conclusion can you draw from the passage above?
   (A) Ancient river valley civilizations all existed at the same time.
   (B) At 2,400 miles, the Huang He is the longest river in the world.
   (C) Mountains protected all river valley civilizations.
   (D) Flooding was important for food production in ancient civilizations.

2. Which statement does not support the conclusion that rivers were important to early civilizations?
   (A) The Huang He is 2,400 miles long.
   (B) The Himalyan Mountains are located in western China.
   (C) The Nile River's regular flooding aided farmers.
   (D) Irrigation canals were dug in Mesopotamia.

Use the map and statement below to answer questions 3 and 4.

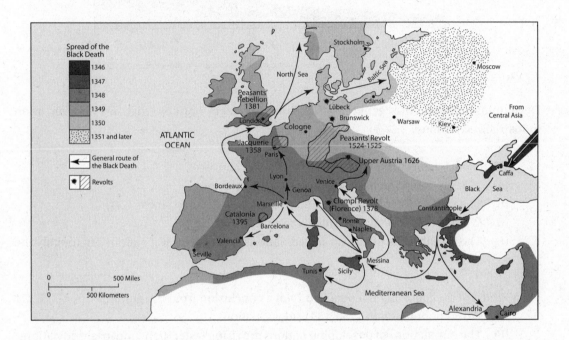

In the 1300s, the Black Death, or Bubonic Plague, spread throughout Europe. This disease killed approximately one-third of Europe's population.

3. What conclusion can be drawn from the map and passage above?
   (A) The Plague spread rapidly through Europe once it arrived from Central Asia.
   (B) Some areas of Europe were affected more heavily than others by the Plague.
   (C) The Plague began to spread near the North Sea.
   (D) The Black Death spread to London after reaching Sicily.

4. Which of the following is a detail stated by the map and *not* a conclusion?
   (A) The Black Death generally spread from east to west.
   (B) The Bubonic Plague spread across Europe over several years.
   (C) The Plague arrived by ship from Central Asia and then spread across land in Europe.
   (D) The Plague arrived in London in 1348.

Use the graph and statement below to answer questions 5 and 6.

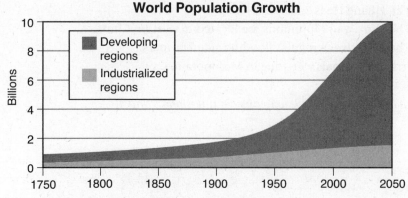

World Population Growth

Source: United Nations Population Division and Population Reference Bureau, 1993.

Developing nations are generally non-industrialized nations that are poorer than industrialized nations.

5. What conclusion can you draw from the graph above?
    (A) World population has remained steady over time.
    (B) The population of industrialized nations has declined since 1750.
    (C) World population has greatly increased since 1950.
    (D) The populations of industrialized nations and developing nations are roughly the same.

6. Which of the following is a detail and *not* a conclusion from the graph?
    (A) World population in 1750 was under 2 billion.
    (B) The populations of developing nations are rising faster than industrialized nations.
    (C) World populations have generally increased over time.
    (D) European populations are growing faster than Asian nations.

Use the time line below to answer questions 7 and 8.

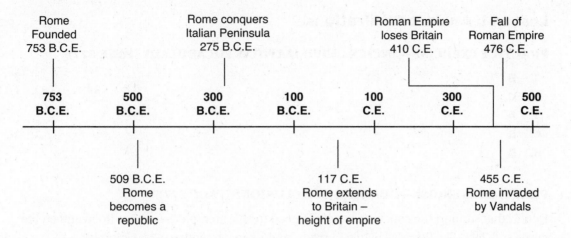

7. What conclusion can you draw based on the time line?
   (A) Rome was founded in 753 B.C.E.
   (B) The Roman Empire fell soon after it became a Republic.
   (C) The Roman Empire was smaller than the ancient Greek civilization.
   (D) The Roman Empire grew in size before collapsing.

8. Which of the following is a detail and *not* a conclusion based on the time line?
   (A) The Roman Empire lasted for over 1,000 years.
   (B) The Roman Empire fell apart relatively quickly after reaching its height.
   (C) The height of the Roman Empire was in 117 C.E.
   (D) The Roman Empire had the highest population of any ancient civilization.

CHAPTER 18 ANSWER EXPLANATIONS

Lesson 1: Ancient Civilizations

PRACTICE EXERCISE—ANCIENT CIVILIZATIONS VOCABULARY (PAGE 577)

1. B
2. C
3. A
4. E
5. D

PRACTICE EXERCISE—DRAWING CONCLUSIONS (PAGE 577)

Details that support the conclusion: people need fresh water to drink, rivers flood and create fertile soil, food like fish is available in rivers, and rivers provide easy transportation.

Conclusion that supports the details: Civilizations develop.

Lesson 2: Great Ideas

PRACTICE EXERCISE—SENTENCE COMPLETION (PAGE 581)

1. divine right
2. Enlightenment
3. transportation
4. Renaissance
5. anatomy
6. scientific method

PRACTICE EXERCISE— COMPARING AND CONTRASTING (PAGE 581)

Similarities	Differences
Began in Europe	Different times
Changed the way people thought	Affects politics/creates revolutions
Led to an increase in knowledge	Spreads to America/New World
Created new inventions	Enlightenment not as artistic as Renaissance
Challenged authorities	

Lesson 3: Graphic Materials

PRACTICE EXERCISE—INTERPRETING TIME LINES (PAGE 582)

1. Major American wars
2. The American Revolution 1775–1783
3. **(B)** Approximately 200 years. First 1775, Last 1975
4. **(C)** That is the title of the time line and the main idea.
5. **(A)** The first date is 3500 B.C.E., the last date is 1500 C.E. This means that starting from the left at 3500 B.C.E., it takes 3,500 to get back to 0 C.E. and then another 1,500 years into C.E. Added together, the total is 5,000.
6. **(A)**

7. **(B)** The Rome line overlaps with the Ancient Greeks.

8. **(D)** The Inca civilization began in 1200 C.E., over 700 years after Ancient Rome.

9. **(C)**

10. **(D)** 1800–1668. 132 years exactly or approximately 130 years.

Lesson 4: Critical Thinking Skills

PRACTICE EXERCISE—COMPARING AND CONTRASTING (PAGE 586)

1. **(D)** The passage states "like the Egyptians, the Chinese developed the field of astronomy."

2. **(B)** The sewer system is only mentioned with the Indus civilization. (A) is not true, and other civilizations are mentioned using irrigation and astronomy.

3. **(C)** (A) is untrue, the Egyptians built pyramids. (B) is untrue, and (D) is not mentioned.

4 **(B)** The passage states that Egypt lasted approximately 2,000 years and the Indus civilization approximately 1,000 years.

5. **(D)** These are both political maps that show national boundaries. The date of the first map is 1600, and the date of the second map is 1900.

6. **(B)** Italy and Germany do not exist on the 1600 map. In their places are several smaller nations. On the 1900 map, those smaller nations are gone, replaced by Italy and Germany.

7. **(C)** No population totals are listed, nor is any information given about the Enlightenment. (D) is an opinion.

8. **(D)** Spain is not the largest nation on either map. All other answer choices are true.

PRACTICE EXERCISE—DRAWING CONCLUSIONS (PAGE 588)

1. **(D)** Flooding is discussed with all three civilizations in the passage. No evidence supports (A), (B) is a detail not a conclusion, and (C) is incorrect.

2. **(B)** This is the only detail not related to rivers.

3. **(A)** The map shows that the disease spread over all of Europe in just a few years. There is no way to determine (B) from the map, (C) is incorrect, the plague came from Central Asia, and (D) is a detail not a conclusion.

4. **(D)** This is a specific detail, all other answer choices are conclusions.

5. **(C)** All other answer choices are untrue.

6. **(A)** This is detail, (B) and (C) are conclusions. There is no way to determine (D) from the graph.

7. **(D)** The time line details that Rome conquered the Italian peninsula and extended to Britain before it fell in 476. (A) is a detail and not a conclusion, (B) is untrue, and there is no way to determine (C) from the time line.

8. **(C)** This is a specific fact on the time line. All other answer choices are conclusions that sum up the entire time line.

Geography

The earth is quite a place. Take a look at this picture of the planet as viewed from outer space. Even from this view, we can clearly see the outline of North America, and the oceans. If we could get closer, we would see mountains, lakes, and other physical features of the Earth. Eventually, if we got close enough, we would find humans and the structures we have created.

Most people think of geography as made up of questions like, "What is the capital of Montana?" (Helena) Fortunately, you will not have to memorize questions and answers like that because the field of geography is much more than just the naming of places. Geography is the study of all the physical features of the Earth, as well as how humans interact with these features. In other words, geography explains not just where things are located, but also how people live in those places.

The main tool of the geographer is the map. Maps may seem old fashioned now that people can get directions on their smartphones for any address. But while we may be the most familiar with road maps, there are actually many different types of maps. HSE tests utilize maps frequently, so in this chapter, we will go over some skills that will help you with any map. We will also investigate a couple of specialty maps, like economic maps, that you are likely to see on your test.

HOW THIS CHAPTER IS ORGANIZED

Lesson 1: Where in the World?

This lesson shows the world is a big place. To get a grip on what is going on out there we have divided the world up into separate regions, and this lesson will explore a few of them.

Lesson 2: How to Read Maps

This lesson will provide you with some tools for reading maps. HSE tests assume you know how to put these skills to use, so it's good to refresh your memory on things like latitude and longitude.

Lesson 3: Graphic Materials

This lesson moves beyond the basics of mapping and introduces you to a few different types of maps.

Lesson 4: Critical Thinking Skills

This lesson will help you practice a few of the thinking skills you will find on your test. In particular, we will work on summarizing and gathering implied ideas from maps.

LESSON 1: WHERE IN THE WORLD?

Can you locate where you are right now on the map? Even though geography involves much more than just finding points on a map, this is a good place to start. How could you describe where you are on the map to someone else? Since this map of the world is blank, answering this question may be difficult.

Hemispheres and Oceans

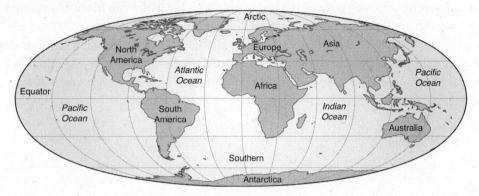

To help with this, the first thing we are going to do is divide the world in half along the **equator**. The equator is an imaginary line that runs around the middle of the Earth dividing it in half. Think "equal" when you hear equator because it splits the Earth into two equal pieces. Everything above the equator is considered the northern **hemisphere**, while everything below the equator is in the southern hemisphere. A hemisphere literally means "half a sphere." In this case, the sphere, or round ball, is the Earth.

Practice Exercise—Hemisphere and Oceans

1. Which hemisphere is the United States located in?

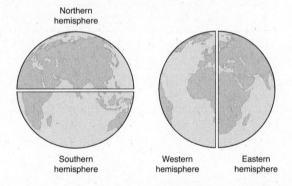

The Earth can also be divided along eastern and western hemispheres as well. This is done along another imaginary line called the **prime meridian**. Every location on the Earth is either in the northern or southern hemisphere as well as the eastern or western hemisphere. For example, the United States is in the northern hemisphere and the western hemisphere.

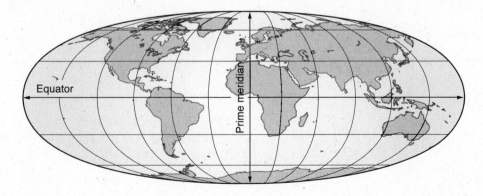

Using points of reference, like the equator, can make using world maps much easier. Likewise, knowing your way around the major points on the globe can make answering some questions much easier. To start with, the Earth has seven **continents**. These are the huge land masses you see on every world map. Each one is much bigger than an individual **country**, or nation. For example, China is a country that is located on the continent of Asia. There are also five major oceans. The United States is on the continent of North America and is surrounded by the Atlantic Ocean and the Pacific Ocean.

2. Using the map, list all seven of the continents:

1. _____
2. _____
3. _____
4. _____
5. _____
6. _____
7. _____

3. Using the map, list all five oceans:

1. _____
2. _____
3. _____
4. _____
5. _____

Regions

Geographers also break down the world into **regions**. For example, in the United States, some people may say that they are from the midwest, or that they are heading to the South for the winter. But how do you know where the south begins or the midwest ends? These regions are tricky to define and may not follow precise state or national boundaries. A region describes an area that shares many of the same characteristics. **Climate**, or the general weather conditions in an area over a long time, is one way to describe a region, but there are many more. Geographers also use cultural characteristics, like religion, language, economics, and history, to create regions.

Practice Exercise—Sentence Completion

Use the words in the list below to complete the sentence.

climate	regions	country	continent
prime meridian	hemispheres	equator	

1. If you were to cut an orange exactly in half, you would have two _____ .

2. The _____ separates the eastern hemisphere from the western hemisphere.

3. A _____ is one of the large land masses on Earth, like Europe or Africa.

4. The Sahara Desert does not receive much rain and has a very hot and dry _____.

5. The _____ separates the northern hemisphere from the eastern hemisphere.

6. Geographic areas that share common things, like languages, are known as _____.

7. Smaller than a continent, a _____ is a nation with its own government.

Practice Exercise—The World Map

Using the maps found in this lesson, correctly label the blank map below with the following terms:

North America	South America	Africa	Europe
Asia	Antarctica	Australia	equator
Atlantic Ocean	Indian Ocean	Southern Ocean	
Arctic Ocean	Pacific Ocean		

UNIT 4: SOCIAL STUDIES

LESSON 2: HOW TO READ MAPS

Close your eyes, and imagine a world without smartphones, computers, or GPS devices of any kind. The only way to figure out where something is located is the old fashioned way: using a map. Now open your eyes, and imagine yourself using maps the old fashioned way on the test. Scared? You shouldn't be. Just familiarize yourself with the common map characteristics below, and you will have the ability to accurately read just about any map.

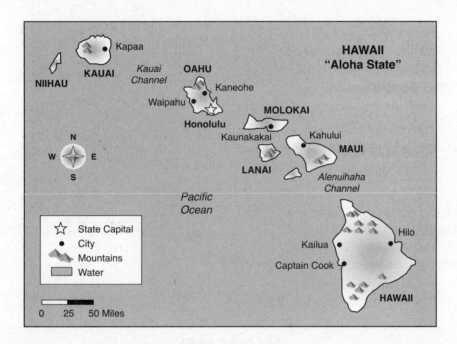

Five Common Map Elements

1. **TITLE:** Our eyes often tend to move right past the title and focus on the visual elements, but make sure to read the title every time. This will give you the main idea of the map. The title of this map is Hawaii, "Aloha State."

2. **COMPASS ROSE:** This orientates you to the directions of the map. The main directions are north, east, south, and west. On this map, they are abbreviated N, E, S, W. North will always point up on a map. East is to right, south is down, and west is on the left.

3. **KEY:** Also known as a legend, the key tells you what the symbols on the map mean. This very important box is the "key" to understanding the information on many maps. Here, the key is located just below the compass rose.

4. **SCALE:** This tells you how to read distance on the map. On this map, a Hawaiian island appears to be as large as your fingernail. In reality, however, each island is many miles across. The map scale can help us to figure out this distance precisely. The scale is located below the key, and we see that something the length of that box equals 50 miles. Therefore, anything on the map that size is also 50 miles in the length. Map scales are important because they vary on every map, and they appear on the math section as well!

5. **COLOR:** Much like the symbols in the key, mapmakers utilize different colors to display information. Here, the ocean is in gray, and the land is in white.

Practice Exercise—Reading Land Maps

Use the map on the right to answer questions 1 through 4.

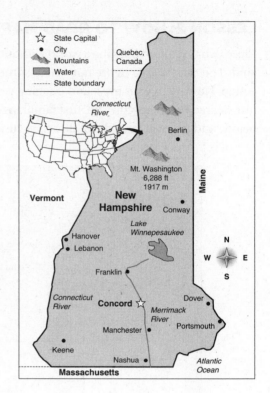

1. What city is the farthest east on the map?

   _____

2. What river is on the western border of New Hampshire?

   _____

3. What town is located in the mountains?

   _____

4. What is the state capital of New Hampshire?

   _____

MAP SCALE

Using a map scale is easy when the distances are exactly as shown in the scale. But how can we measure a distance greater than the scale shown on the map? For instance, how far is it from Cheyenne (in the southeast corner) to Green River?

To measure this, we will need scratch paper. On the edge of your paper, mark the beginning and end of the scale. We will now use your scratch paper like a ruler.

1. Line the zero on your scratch paper ruler up with Cheyenne.
2. Move the other end marked 40 toward Green River and mark a point.
3. Now repeat the process all the way to Green River, but start with the zero on the point. Mark a new point at every 40 miles.
4. Each time we moved the ruler, we measured 40 miles. Since we moved the ruler 6 times, 40 + 40 + 40 + 40 + 40 + 40 = 240, so Green River is about 240 miles away.
5. Scratch paper will be provided when you take your test, so you can use this strategy on the test!

Use the map to answer questions 5 through 7.

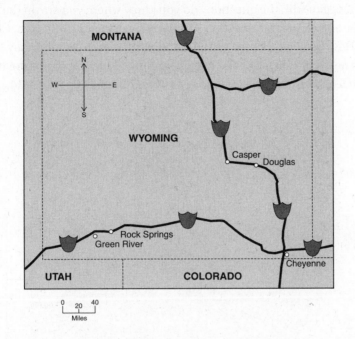

5. Approximately how many miles is it from Casper to Douglas?

   _____

6. Approximately how many miles is it from Green River to Rock Springs?
   (**THINK:** If it is not quite 40 miles on your ruler, how long is it?)

   _____

7. Approximately how many miles is it from Cheyenne to Douglas?

   _____

Latitude and Longitude

The previous lesson began with the question "do you know where you are on the map?" Well, one way maps make answering this question simpler is by using a grid system. Check out the map on the right. How could you describe the location of York? You might say it is near the middle, but that is not very exact. See the letters running along the top of the map and the numbers down the left side? We could use these as coordinates (like in math), and say that York was at E4.

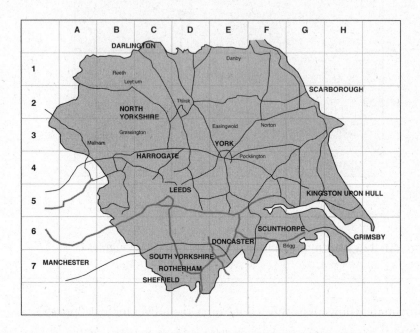

8. Using the coordinates on the above map, what is the location of Leeds?

   (**THINK:** What letter is directly above Leeds?)

   _____

Remember

Latitude sounds like "ladder," and just like a ladder, it has rungs you can use to climb up or down.

You can use that simple trick to remember the difference between latitude and longitude!

Latitude (North/South)

90°N
45°N
0° Equator
45°S
90°S

Latitudes vary from 0° at the equator to 90° North and South at the poles

Longitude (West/East)

W E

Longitudes vary from 0° at Greenwich to 180° East and West

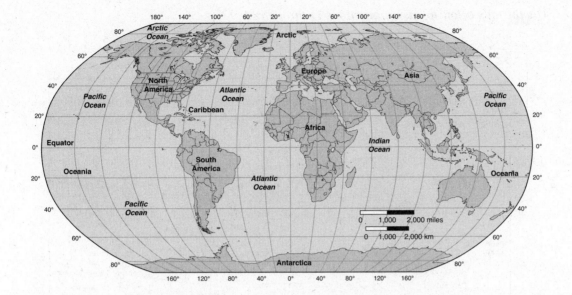

The most common grid system used in geography is latitude and longitude. **Latitude** is used to measure north or south, and the lines run horizontally. These lines start at the equator, which is always labeled zero degrees latitude. Anything above the equator is considered north latitude, and anything below the equator is south latitude. For example, North America is located at approximately 40 degrees north latitude.

9.   On the above map what is the approximate latitude of Oceania?

    _____

Longitude measures east and west, and these lines run vertically. Like the equator for latitude, longitude lines start with zero degrees at the prime meridian. This line runs right through Europe and Africa. Anything to the left of the prime meridian is considered west longitude, and anything to the right is considered east longitude. For instance, North America is located approximately at 100 west longitude.

10.   What is the approximate longitude of Oceania?

    _____

Use the map below to answer questions 11 through 14.

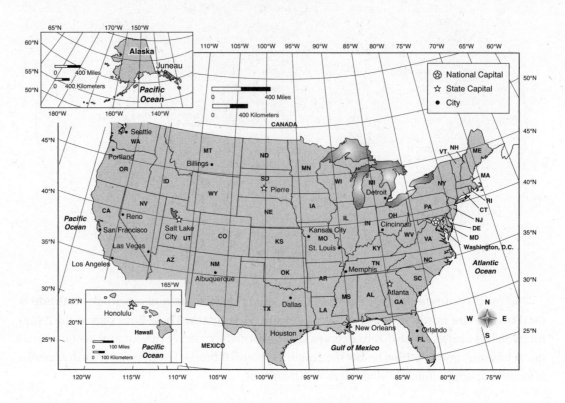

11. What state is located 45 degrees north latitude and 95 degrees west longitude?

    _____

12. What state is located 40 degrees north latitude and 105 degrees west longitude?

    _____

13. What is the approximate latitude and longitude of Idaho?

    _____

14. What is the approximate latitude and longitude of Memphis, Tennessee?

    _____

LESSON 3: GRAPHIC MATERIALS

Picture a classroom in your head. On the wall of the classroom is a map. What does this map look like? Most likely you imagined a **political map**, but there are many other types of maps used on HSE tests and in real life.

Political Maps

Political maps are used to show borders between nations, states, or other government boundaries. They may include things like capitals and major cities, but they are unlikely to show things like mountains or forests since those are physical features.

Use the map below to answer questions 1 through 3.

Africa
Countries and Cities

1. What is the subject of this map?

   _____

2. What is the capital city of Angola?

   _____

3. What African nation shares a border with the continent of Asia?

   _____

Population Maps

Population maps can be used to show a variety of things regarding where people live. The map below is a population density map, which means it illustrates how closely people live together.

Use the map below to answer questions 4 through 6.

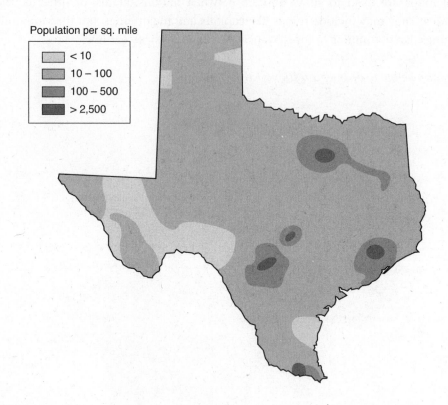

Population per sq. mile

	< 10
	10 – 100
	100 – 500
	> 2,500

4. Using the map key, what are the differences between the light gray and dark gray colors?

_____

5. What do the dark gray areas on the map most likely represent?

_____

6. Based on this information, would you say that the majority of Texas is urban or rural?

_____

Climate Maps

Climate maps detail weather patterns in different areas. They frequently show arid or dry areas in comparison to wet regions.

Use the map below to answer questions 7 and 8.

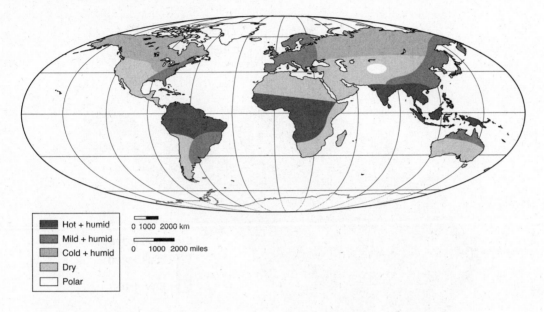

Legend:
- Hot + humid
- Mild + humid
- Cold + humid
- Dry
- Polar

0 1000 2000 km

0 1000 2000 miles

7. Based on the map, what is the predominant climate of Northern Africa?

   _____

8. What is the general climate of the eastern United States?
   (A) Hot and humid
   (B) Mild and humid
   (C) Cold and humid
   (D) Polar and alpine

Relief Maps

Relief maps are used to show changes in elevation of hills and mountains.

Use the map below to answer questions 9 and 10.

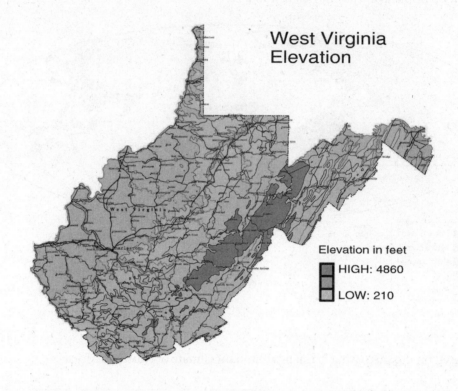

9. What information does the key provide?

   _____

10. Which end of the state generally has the highest elevation?
    (A) North
    (B) South
    (C) East
    (D) West

Economic Maps

Economic maps depict different locations of economic data. Though the main ideas of each map may change, you will always know what is going on if you make sure to focus on the title, key, and other common map elements.

Use the map below to answer questions 11 through 13.

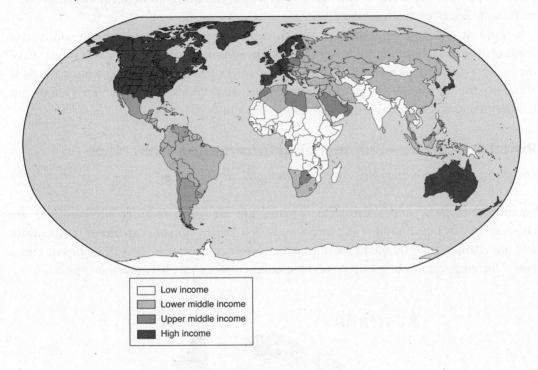

Key:
- Low income
- Lower middle income
- Upper middle income
- High income

11. What is the main idea of this map?
    (A) Capitalism is the best economic system.
    (B) Most of the world can be classified as upper middle income.
    (C) No two areas of the world can be classified the same way economically.
    (D) Different parts of the world have different economic classifications.

12. What other area has a similar economic classification to the United States?
    (A) South America
    (B) Africa
    (C) Western Europe
    (D) China

13. The majority of the nations in Africa have which economic classification?
    (A) Low income
    (B) Lower middle income
    (C) Upper middle income
    (D) High income

LESSON 4: CRITICAL THINKING SKILLS
Summarizing Information from Maps

Have you ever described a movie or a T.V. show to a friend? If you have, you provided a summary of what you saw. In telling your friend about the movie, you would naturally include the most important events that help to explain what the movie is about. You wouldn't focus on just the beginning of the movie, nor would you bring up minor points that don't really help describe what happened.

Some test questions will also ask you to summarize. Sometimes you will summarize reading passages, but other times you will need to summarize graphs, maps, or other visual materials. Summarizing a visual aid, like a map, works just like explaining what a movie is about to a friend. You want to include the main idea that captures what the map is about, but be careful not to get sidetracked by less important details.

Practice Exercise—Summarizing Information from Maps

Use the passage and map below to answer questions 1 and 2.

Equatorial, tropical, and subtropical climates are all warm weather climates that are characterized by high humidity and frequent rainfall. Desert climates can be any temperature and are characterized by their lack of rainfall. Deserts receive less than 10 inches of rain a year. The temperatures of grassland and temperate regions vary between the seasons.

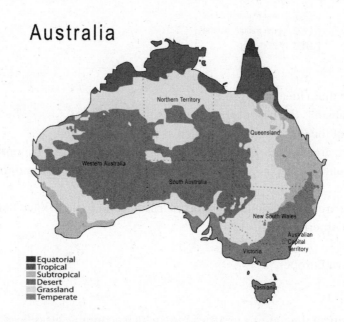

1. Which statement best summarizes the passage and the map?
   (A) Australia receives an above-average amount of rainfall.
   (B) The center of Australia has a desert climate.
   (C) Australia is characterized by a variety of climates.
   (D) Australia is substantially hotter than neighboring countries.

2. What statement best summarizes the passage?
    (A) Grasslands and temperate regions are the most common on the globe.
    (B) Climate regions vary from hot to cold and wet to dry.
    (C) Equatorial regions have the hottest temperatures.
    (D) Deserts receive less than 10 inches of rain a year.

Use the map below to answer question 3.

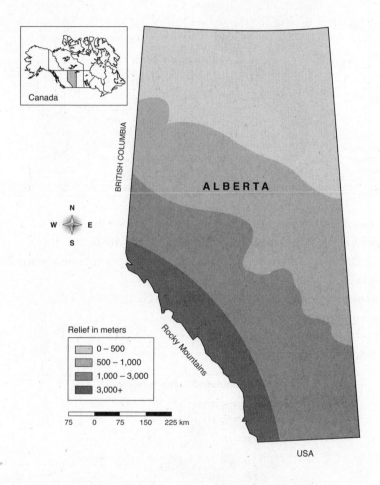

3. Which statement best summarizes the information on the map?
    (A) The overall elevation of Alberta rises from the lower northeast to the mountainous southwest.
    (B) Rivers in Alberta flow from east to west.
    (C) Alberta is a province in Canada.
    (D) Forest land covers much of Alberta.

Use the maps below to answer question 4.

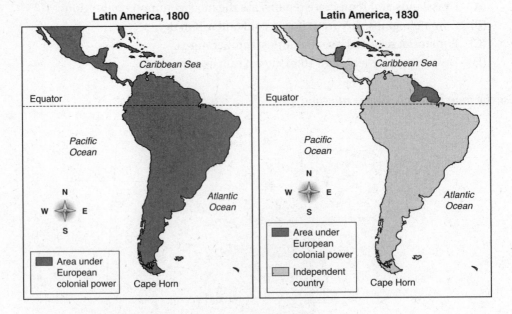

Latin America, 1800   Latin America, 1830

4. Which statement best summarizes the information on the maps?
   (A) Latin America was considered one nation until 1830.
   (B) By 1830, much of Latin America had gained its independence from European powers.
   (C) European colonies grew in Latin America by 1830.
   (D) The equator runs through Latin America.

Use the map below to answer question 5.

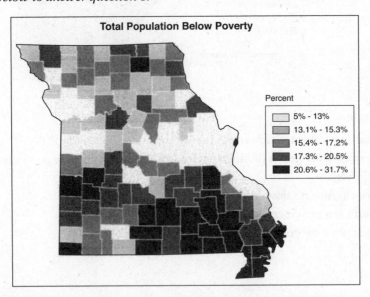

Total Population Below Poverty

5. Which statement best summarizes the information on the map?
   (A) The population of Missouri is largely below poverty.
   (B) Poverty generally affects all areas of Missouri equally.
   (C) The average rate of poverty in Missouri is 25%.
   (D) Poverty rates in Missouri vary with higher concentration found in the southeast.

Use the passage and map below to answer questions 6 and 7.

Each year, approximately one out of every six Americans will move their primary residence. While most of these people will simply move across town or county, millions will move to another state. People move for different reasons, but many are pushed or pulled by economic factors. Areas where unemployment is on the rise tend to lose population. People often move to find better employment opportunities.

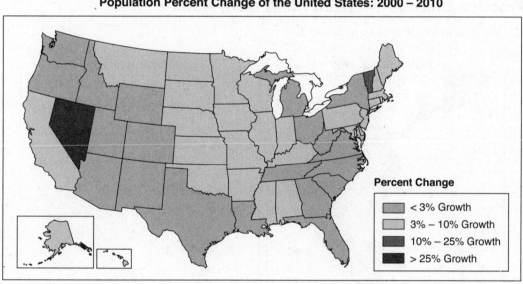

Population Percent Change of the United States: 2000 – 2010

Percent Change
- < 3% Growth
- 3% – 10% Growth
- 10% – 25% Growth
- > 25% Growth

6. Which statement best summarizes the information on the map?
   (A) The Northeast had the highest rate of population growth between 2000 and 2010.
   (B) Population growth was generally larger in the west and southeast between 2000 and 2010.
   (C) Nevada had the largest population growth of any state in the country.
   (D) Population growth occurs for different reasons.

7. Which statement best summarizes the information in the passage?
   (A) Each year, approximately one out of six Americans move.
   (B) People often move to find better weather.
   (C) Few people move to another state in any year.
   (D) Though most people don't move far, those that do often move for work.

Implied Ideas from Maps

When something is implied, it is hinted at rather than directly stated. For example, let's say someone new is going to be hired at your job, and you want to recommend a friend. If you tell your boss that your friend can finish an 8-hour job in 4 hours, what are you implying? You are indirectly stating that your friend is a hard worker and very efficient.

Recognizing implications from maps requires a similar skill. You take what is stated directly and come up with a new statement based on those facts. Remember, this statement should be suggested by the information but not directly stated.

Practice Exercise—Implied Ideas from Maps

Use the map below to answer question 1.

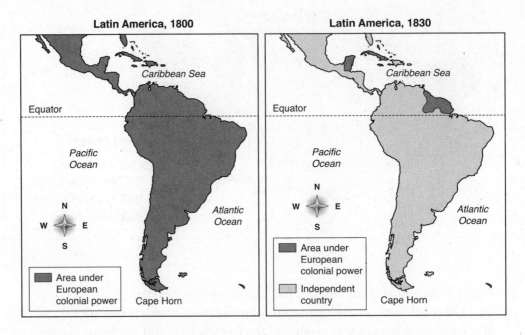

1. Which statement can be implied from the maps?
    (A) Most of Latin America is below the equator.
    (B) A series of revolutions freed much of Latin America from European powers.
    (C) No European powers controlled any part of Latin America by 1830.
    (D) Latin America shrunk in size between 1800 and 1830.

Use the map below to answer question 2.

Population Percent Change of the United States: 2000 – 2010

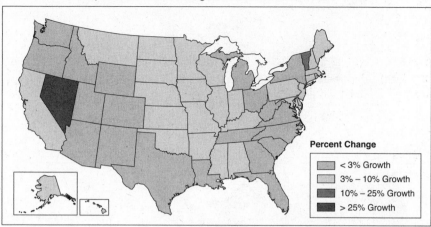

Percent Change

- ☐ < 3% Growth
- ☐ 3% – 10% Growth
- ☐ 10% – 25% Growth
- ■ > 25% Growth

2. Which of the following statements is implied from the map?
   (A) Population growth was generally larger in the west and southeast between 2000 and 2010.
   (B) Home prices fell rapidly along the east coast between 2000 and 2010.
   (C) Areas with high population growth probably also had high job growth.
   (D) Alaska and Hawaii had similar population changes.

Use the map below to answer question 3.

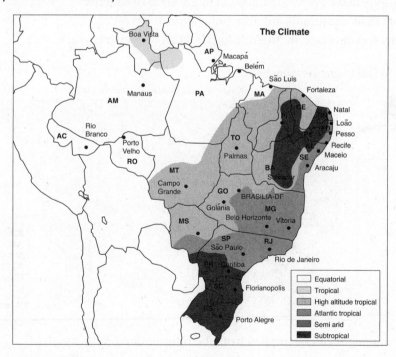

The Climate

- ☐ Equatorial
- ☐ Tropical
- ☐ High altitude tropical
- ☐ Atlantic tropical
- ■ Semi arid
- ■ Subtropical

3. What is an implication based on the map?
   (A) Brazil has a variety of climates.
   (B) Most of Brazil has some kind of tropical climate.
   (C) The southern tip of Brazil has a subtropical climate.
   (D) Due to the tropical climates, plant life thrives in many areas of Brazil.

Use the maps below to answer question 4.

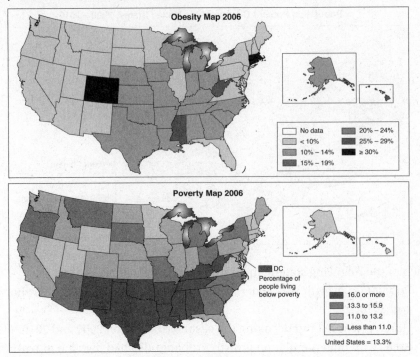

4. What is an implication based on the maps?

    (A) Childhood obesity is a growing problem in America.

    (B) Obesity and poverty are linked in many areas of America.

    (C) Fast food restaurants are unpopular along the west coast.

    (D) Poverty was worse in America in 2006 than in previous years.

Use the map below to answer question 5.

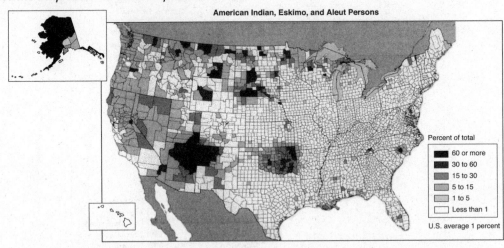

5. Which statement can be implied from the information on the map?

    (A) There are more American Indians in Alaska than in any other state.

    (B) Over the years, many American Indians were forcibly relocated or eliminated from the eastern United States.

    (C) No Eskimos live in Texas.

    (D) The population of American Indians, Eskimos, and Aleut Persons is generally higher in the western half of the United States than in the eastern half.

Use the map below to answer question 6.

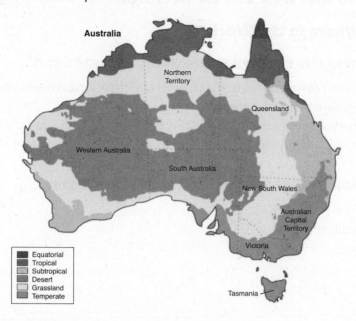

6. Which is an implication based on the map?
   (A) The north coast of Australia is largely tropical.
   (B) Few people are able to live in central Australia.
   (C) There are no mountains in Australia.
   (D) The southeast coast of Australia has a temperate climate.

Use the map below to answer question 7.

Battles of the American Civil War

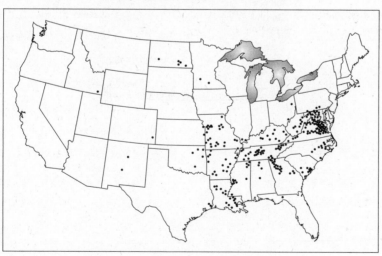

7. Which statement is an implication based on the map?
   (A) Most of the damage caused by the Civil War occurred in the South.
   (B) Civil battles took place between 1861 and 1865.
   (C) No Civil War battles took place on the west coast.
   (D) The north had a great industrial advantage over the south.

CHAPTER 19 ANSWER EXPLANATIONS

Lesson 1: Where in the World?

PRACTICE EXERCISE: HEMISPHERES AND OCEANS (PAGE 597)

1. There are two possible answers: the United States is located in the northern hemisphere and the western hemisphere.
2. North America, South America, Africa, Europe, Asia, Australia, Antarctica
3. Pacific Ocean, Atlantic Ocean, Arctic Ocean, Indian Ocean, Southern Ocean

PRACTICE EXERCISE—SENTENCE COMPLETION (PAGE 599)

1. hemispheres
2. prime meridian
3. continent
4. climate
5. equator
6. regions
7. country

PRACTICE EXERCISE—WORLD MAP (PAGE 600)

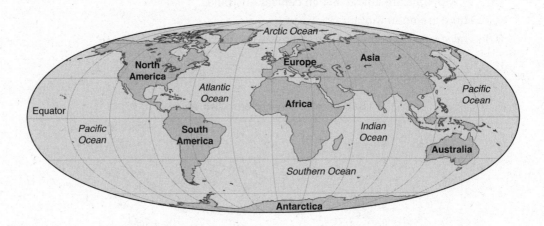

Lesson 2: How to Read Maps

PRACTICE EXERCISE—READING LAND MAPS (PAGE 602)

1. Portsmouth
2. Connecticut River
3. Berlin
4. Concord
5. 40 miles
6. 20 miles
7. 120 miles
8. D5
9. Oceania is located at 20 degrees south latitude.
10. Oceania is located at 160 degrees east longitude.
11. MN or Minnesota
12. CO or Colorado
13. 45 degrees north latitude, 115 degrees west longitude.
14. 35 degrees north latitude, 90 degrees west longitude.

Lesson 3: Graphic Materials (Page 607)

1. Countries and cities of Africa
2. Luanda
3. Egypt
4. According to the key, dark gray areas are more heavily populated than light gray areas.
5. Since they have the highest population, the dark gray areas represent cities.
6. Since most of the state is light gray and, therefore, not heavily populated, the majority of Texas is rural.
7. Dry
8. **(B)** Mild and humid. The map key is divided into five categories, hot and humid, mild and humid, cold and humid, dry, and polar. The eastern United States falls under mild and humid.
9. Elevation in feet
10. **(C)**
11. **(D)** (A) is an opinion, (B) and (C) are untrue.
12. **(C)** Western Europe is the same shade on the map as the United States.
13. **(A)** That is the most prominent shade on the map in Africa.

Lesson 4: Critical Thinking Skills

PRACTICE EXERCISE—SUMMARIZING INFORMATION FROM MAPS (PAGE 612)

1. **(C)** There is no way to determine (A) or (D) from the map; (B) is true but does not summarize the entire map.
2. **(B)** This summarizes all of the climate regions in the passage. We don't know if (A) or (C) is true from the passage. (D) is a detail that does not summarize the whole passage.
3. **(A)** The map does not show which direction rivers flow, so choice (B) is incorrect. (C) is a detail that does not summarize the information on the map, and there is no way to determine (D) from the map.

4. **(B)** No nations are shown on the map so (A) is incorrect, (C) is the opposite of what the maps show, and (D) is a detail that does not summarize both maps.

5. **(D)** The key shows that different colors mean different levels of poverty, but the highest concentration is in the southeast. (A) and (B) are untrue, and the map does not calculate the average rate for the entire state (C).

6. **(B)** According to the key, the colors in the west and the southeast had the larger population growth. (A) is untrue, (C) is a detail, and (D) is not shown on the map.

7. **(D)** (A) is a detail, (B) is not stated in the passage, and (C) is untrue.

PRACTICE EXERCISE—IMPLIED IDEAS FROM MAPS (PAGE 616)

1. **(B)** (A) is directly shown on the map. (C) and (D) are untrue. Since the map shows that much of Latin America is no longer under European control in 1830, it can be implied that revolutions occurred to free nations from European powers.

2. **(C)** (A) and (D) are directly stated on the map. There is no way to tell (B) from the map information. (C) is the best choice, because people would most likely move to find jobs, so areas with high population growth most likely also had high job growth.

3. **(D)** (A) through (C) are all directly stated on the map. Plants do well in tropical climates, so because Brazil has many tropical areas, plant life would thrive in many areas of Brazil.

4. **(B)** The maps show that areas of high obesity and poverty often overlap. (A) is incorrect because the maps do not show if obesity is growing. (C) is incorrect because there is no way to judge restaurant popularity from the maps. (D) is incorrect because there is no way to compare 2006 with a different year.

5. **(B)** (A) is incorrect because although there is a high percentage of American Indians in Alaska, there is no way to know the actual number. (C) is incorrect because there is no way to tell the actual number of Eskimos anywhere on the map. (D) is incorrect because it summarizes the map and is not implied. (B) is correct because it hints at a reason for why the American Indian, Eskimo, and Aluet population is greater in the west, but it is not directly stated on the map.

6. **(B)** (A) and (D) are directly stated on the map. (C) is incorrect because there is no way to tell if there are mountains on the map. Since much of central Australia is desert land, the area there would be difficult to support life, therefore, (B) is implied.

7. **(A)** Because most battles took place in the South, it is implied that is where most of the damage took place as well. (B) and (C) are directly stated, and there is no way to determine (D) from the map.

Economics

20

You've heard the word on the news, seen it in newspapers, and have probably had people you know mention it. But what is economics? Well, officially it is the science of how goods and services are produced and consumed, but that's a pretty technical definition. If you've ever wondered why certain clothing companies can get away with charging $100 for a pair of blue jeans, then you've thought about economics.

You've probably heard of the **economy** when people talk about money and jobs, and that's a great place to start. In that sense, the economy refers to a nation's **prosperity**, or how well a country and its citizens are doing financially. If the economy isn't doing well, then you are likely to hear that people can't find work or can't afford things like they used to. On the other hand, if the economy is strong, then businesses are hiring, new houses are being built, and people are financially secure.

Economists look at the individual decisions you make as a consumer, like what brand of chips did you buy at the store, and what made you choose that store anyway? But economists also look at the big trends and ask questions like what happens if taxes go up 1%, and why can't the government just print more money, anyway?

Obviously, if economics covers all of the financial issues for an entire country, it can get pretty complicated. The goal of this chapter is to introduce you to some key ideas and terms that will not only help you on your HSE test but also help you in real life. After all, who doesn't care at least a little bit about money?

HOW THIS CHAPTER IS ORGANIZED

Lesson 1: What Is Economics?

This lesson will introduce you to the basic concept that underlies all of economics: supply and demand. Never heard of it? This lesson will show you how this law affects everything from how much you pay at the store to how much money you make at your job.

Lesson 2: Economic Trends

This lesson brings you into the big picture. Aside from the economic choices you make every day, you are also affected by national and even global trends, like recessions and depressions.

Lesson 3: Graphic Materials

This lesson helps you to understand some of the visual aids you are likely to see on the test. Studying the economy means looking over lots of numbers, and economists use charts, tables, and graphs to make it easier to understand.

Lesson 4: Critical Thinking Skills

This lesson practices the two test-related skills of making predictions and recognizing unstated assumptions.

LESSON 1: WHAT IS ECONOMICS?
Supply and Demand

Have you ever thought about why the latest pair of shoes from Nike's Air Jordan line cost over $100? How does Nike know to charge that amount, and why wouldn't they just charge $300 and make even more money?

These prices, as well as many other things, are determined by the laws of *supply and demand*. The **supply** refers to how much of a product is available. Nike can control the supply by creating limited-edition shoes that are not available everywhere. By doing so, Nike can raise the demand for their shoes. Things that are rare often become more valuable.

The **demand** reflects how much a customer is willing to pay for a product. And as we all know from our own shopping trips, once a price gets too high we have to choose something else. Nike, then, must be careful with their price, otherwise, their demand will go down, and they won't sell as many shoes. For example, if they raised all of their prices to $300, fewer people would be able to buy the shoes, and Nike would make less money.

Nike has successfully figured out the price **equilibrium** for their shoes. When you hear equilibrium, think "equal." By applying the laws of supply and demand, they have found the perfect mixture to sell the most possible shoes at the highest price. And just like Nike, all products go through a similar process to determine their prices. That's why the dollar menu is not the five dollar menu or the fifty-cent menu, and why a certain pair of jeans costs more than another one with a different label.

Believe it or not, the law of supply and demand also affects how much money you make at your job. Consider someone working at an imaginary Burgerworld fast food restaurant. How much would you expect them to make per hour? Well, considering that just about everyone could work at Burgerworld if they wanted to, there is a huge supply of workers. If a worker were to quit, he or she could be easily replaced. Therefore, this ready supply of workers drives down how much they earn.

Compare that to how much a brain surgeon earns per hour. How many people can do the work of a brain surgeon? Very few, it takes many years of medical school to become a surgeon. Accordingly, there is a very small supply of brain surgeons but a big demand. After all, getting brain surgery is not like picking a burger place. When you need it, you really need it! Therefore, following the rules of supply and demand, brain surgeons make more than an employee at Burgerworld.

Practice Exercise—Supply and Demand

1. What happens to demand when prices rise?

    (**THINK:** What does demand mean? Would you buy more or less of a product if it gets more expensive?)

    (A) Demand stays the same
    (B) Demand rises
    (C) Demand falls
    (D) Demand rises then falls

2. What happens to prices when supply rises?

    (**THINK:** What does supply mean? Would diamonds be expensive if they grew on trees?)

    (A) Prices stay the same
    (B) Prices rise
    (C) Prices fall
    (D) Prices rise then fall

3. What does the term equilibrium mean?

    (**THINK:** Use context clues from the sentences in the passage around the word "equilibrium" to help with the meaning.)

    (A) Prices that are far higher than anyone is willing to pay
    (B) Finding a balance between supply and demand
    (C) Creating a surplus of inventory
    (D) Limiting the number of coupons that can be used

4. How do the laws of supply and demand affect how much a person earns at a job?
    (A) The laws of supply and demand have no effect on earnings.
    (B) Professions that are in demand pay less because there is a greater need for them.
    (C) Employers pay more to employees that are easily replaced.
    (D) People earn more money in jobs that are in demand.

5. Suppose the price of Sony Play Stations dropped to $99. How do you think that would affect sales?

    (**THINK:** What would you do if you wanted to buy a Play Station?)

    (A) Sales would rise
    (B) Sales would fall
    (C) Sales would remain the same
    (D) Sales would fall and then rise

6. How would the price of gasoline be affected if a major shortage was announced?

    (**THINK:** Would more or less people want to buy gas?)

    (A) Prices would rise
    (B) Prices would fall
    (C) Prices would remain the same
    (D) Prices would fall and then rise

7. Which of the following is a supporting detail?

(**THINK:** What is the difference between a supporting detail and a conclusion?)

(A) The laws of supply and demand have a great impact on our daily lives.
(B) Nike utilizes the laws of supply and demand to increase their profits.
(C) Supply and demand cannot explain why Nike's shoes are so expensive.
(D) The price of the latest pair of Air Jordans can be over $100.

8. Which of the following is an opinion?

(**THINK:** What is the difference between a fact and an opinion? What are key words that indicate an opinion?)

(A) The laws of supply and demand affect how products are priced.
(B) Nike makes the best shoes in the world.
(C) The laws of supply and demand can affect wages.
(D) Prices generally fall when supply is limited.

LESSON 2: ECONOMIC TRENDS

In addition to studying things, like how supply and demand affects your purchases and your paycheck, economists also look at the big picture as well. By examining the entire nation, or even the world, economists try to figure out how well the overall economy is doing.

Why is that important? Because a growing economy generally means more jobs and higher incomes. On the other hand, a shrinking economy means fewer jobs and lower incomes, so getting the economy right is a pretty big deal.

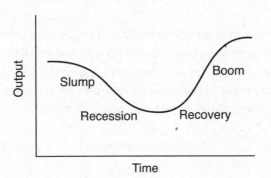

In general, the economy of the United States grows steadily over time. However, this growth is much like the weather in the spring time. While it is generally getting warmer, on any given day, anything can happen. With economics, this **fluctuation** is known as the **business cycle**.

One way to measure the economy is through **gross domestic product** (GDP). That's not gross as in disgusting, but as in total. Domestic means involving the household, and product refers to what is produced. GDP, then, measures everything that is produced in a country. All of the goods, including every French fry, and all of the services, including every haircut, are included in GDP. As you can imagine, for a country the size of the United States, this is quite a large number!

When the economy is doing well, GDP is generally expanding. If a factory starts producing more chairs, for example, then they will need to hire more workers. These new workers will then have more money to go out and buy things made in another factory. That factory will then need to hire new people, and so on. When the economy is expanding at a fast rate, this is called a **boom.**

Recession and Depression

When GDP shrinks that is known as a **recession**. When this happens, the chair factory doesn't produce as many chairs, so they eventually lay off workers. These workers now have less money to buy products from other factories, which means that other factories won't need as many workers, and so on. If this trend gets worse and continues for a long time, then the recession becomes a **depression**. The Great Depression in the United States lasted from approximately 1929 until 1940, and unemployment reached 25%!

Though recessions are bad things and our government works to avoid them, they are a natural part of the business cycle. Suppose the price of wood goes up next year. That chair factory will have to spend more to make a chair, and they may sell less because their chairs are now more expensive. They may have to lay off employees or even close because of this unexpected change. Eventually, though, history has proven that the overall economy cycles through both good and bad times.

Practice Exercise—Economic Trends Vocabulary

Match the terms on the left with the correct definitions on the right.

_____ 1. Supply

_____ 2. Demand

_____ 3. Fluctuation

_____ 4. Business cycle

_____ 5. Recession

_____ 6. Gross domestic product (GDP)

_____ 7. Depression

_____ 8. Boom

(A) How much of a product is available

(B) When GDP expands rapidly

(C) The total of all the goods and services produced in a country

(D) The regular growth and shrinking of GDP

(E) When GDP shrinks or contracts

(F) A severe recession that lasts a long time

(G) When things change or vary

(H) How much a customer is willing to pay for a product

Inflation

You've probably heard someone older than you describe a time when gas cost $1.00 a gallon, or when a hamburger cost a quarter. So why is everything more expensive now? The economic term for this is **inflation**. Think of the way a balloon grows when you inflate it, and that's what inflation does to prices.

There are a few causes of inflation. One is that, during good economic times, people tend to make more money. With more money to spend, people naturally want to buy things. This increase in demand means that prices go up.

Another way inflation occurs is when the government prints more money than is needed. For example, let's say you've had your eye on a new Mercedes Benz that costs $50,000. That is a lot of money, and as a luxury car, not everyone can afford that. But let's say the government sent everyone a check for $50,000 tomorrow. That would be great, right? Think again. If everyone suddenly has $50,000 extra dollars, do you think that Mercedes will still be worth $50,000? No, with all of the extra money suddenly in the economy, prices would go up to keep up with the new demand.

So while it's tempting to say that the government should just print more money to solve our financial problems, doing so would cause runaway inflation. High inflation can be a bad thing. While prices may go up at your local grocery store, there is no guarantee your paycheck is inflating at the same time. Rapid inflation, then, can hurt quality of life. Imagine you are saving $1,000 all year to go on a vacation. If prices rise dramatically during the year, that $1,000 won't take you as far as you would like. Rapid inflation can devalue savings. Likewise, banks won't be as likely to lend money if they think that it may not be worth the same later. For example, if you want to borrow $20,000 to open a pizza shop, the bank may not lend it if that same amount won't buy as much when you repay it. A slowdown in lending and economic growth can be another result of high inflation.

Practice Exercise—Cause and Effect

1. Using the reading on inflation, fill in the cause-and-effect chart below.

Causes of Inflation	
Inflation	• Rising prices • Value of money decreases
Effects of Inflation	

LESSON 3: GRAPHIC MATERIALS
Tables and Charts

The world of economics revolves around numbers. Fortunately, you won't be required to have specific figures memorized for your test. You will be asked to summarize and interpret economic data that are provided for you. Charts and tables make understanding groups of numbers easier. These visual aids can also demonstrate relationships between numbers.

Use the chart below to answer questions 1 through 5.

World Gross Domestic Product

Rank	Country	GDP (millions of USD)
–	*World*	62,909,274[4]
1	United States	14,657,800
2	People's Republic of China	5,878,257[/nb 2]
3	Japan	5,458,872
4	Germany	3,315,643
5	France	2,582,527
6	United Kingdom	2,247,455
7	Brazil	2,090,314
8	Italy	2,055,114
9	Canada	1,574,051
10	India	1,537,966
11	Russia	1,465,079
12	Spain	1,409,946
13	Australia	1,235,539

To understand any table or chart, there are a few things you should do. First, identify the title because that will tell you about the chart's main idea.

1. What is the title of the above chart?

_____

Next, find the headings on the chart. These are the titles above each column along the top. This will tell you how the data are organized. It's easy to skip over these small labels, but these headings explain what is going on in the chart.

2. What are the headings on the above chart?

_____

Finally, take a look at the general trend of the chart. Are the numbers getting larger, smaller, or is there another pattern going on? Recognizing these traits will greatly improve your skills with charts and tables.

3. How is the above chart organized? (Which way do the numbers move, and why?)

_____

4. What is the approximate difference between the GDP of the United States and the People's Republic of China?

_____

5. What is the GDP of Brazil, and what is their rank globally?

_____

Purchasing power refers to the value of money and what it can buy. For example, in 1960, a gallon of milk cost around $.50. Today, that same gallon costs around $4. Through inflation, prices have risen, so $1 does not purchase as much as it used to. Purchasing power goes down when inflation goes up.

Use the table below to answer questions 6 through 10.

Table 1
Inflation Impact on $22,000 Income

Years	Year	Assumed Inflation	Purchasing Power
1	2008	4%	$21,120.00
2	2009	4%	$20,275.20
3	2010	4%	$19,464.19
4	2011	4%	$18,685,62
5	2012	4%	$17,938.20
6	2013	4%	$17,220.67
7	2014	4%	$16,531.84
8	2015	4%	$15,870.57
9	2016	4%	$15,235.75
10	2017	4%	$14,626.32

6. What is the main idea of the above table?
   (**THINK:** What will tell you what this table is about?)

   _____

7. What is the general trend of the above table?

   _____

8. What is the purchasing power after 7 years of inflation at 4%?

   _____

9. Approximately how much purchasing power is lost in dollars after 5 years?

   _____

10. Let's say the above table also showed **deflation**, which increases purchasing power. What would be the effect on the dollar amounts on the table during deflation?

_____

Another common chart is the pie chart also known as the circle graph. These charts are useful because they easily show how big each piece is in relation to the other pieces.

Use the pie chart below to answer questions 11 through 14.

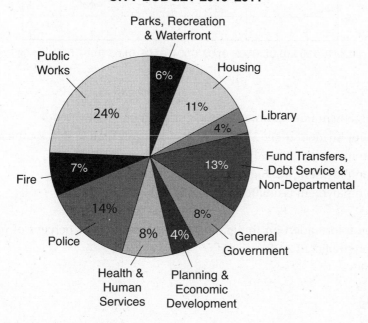

CITY BUDGET 2010–2011

11. What is the main idea of this pie chart?

_____

12. According to the chart, what is the largest item in the budget?

_____

13. According to the chart, what is the smallest item in the budget?

_____

14. How many items in the budget are larger than what is spent on Housing?

_____

Economic Graphs

Use the graph below to answer questions 15 and 16.

Unemployment Rate in the United States

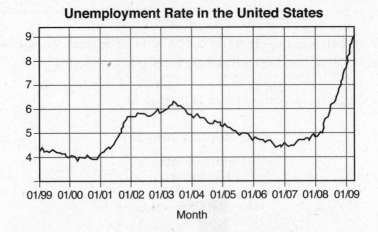

Month

15. Which statement best summarizes the graph on unemployment?
    (A) Unemployment in the United States was lower than in developing nations.
    (B) Unemployment ranged between 4% and 6% until 2008.
    (C) Unemployment was highest at the beginning of the decade.
    (D) Unemployment is unaffected by inflation.

16. Using the information on the graph, approximately what percent of unemployment would you predict in 2010?
    (A) 9–10%
    (B) 8–9%
    (C) 7–8%
    (D) 6–7%

Use the graph below to answer questions 17 and 18.

U.S. Economic Growth % change in GDP, annualized

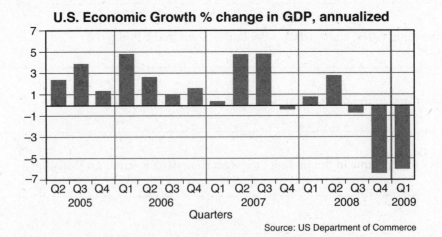

Quarters

Source: US Department of Commerce

17. According to the graph, in which quarter did the largest change in GDP occur?

    (A) Q1 2006

    (B) Q2 2007

    (C) Q4 2008

    (D) Q1 2009

18. A recession most likely occurred during which year?

    (A) 2005

    (B) 2006

    (C) 2007

    (D) 2009

LESSON 4: CRITICAL THINKING SKILLS

Unstated Assumptions

When you deposit money in a bank, do you need to call the bank later to make sure your money is still there? Of course not, you can assume that your money is still there safely waiting for you. When you assume something, you are believing that something is true without being told that directly. Some questions on your HSE test will ask you to identify unstated assumptions.

These questions can be tricky because they require you to really think about how the material is presented.

Practice Exercise—Unstated Assumptions

Questions 1 and 2 are based on the following passage.

Paul spent Sunday afternoon reading the newspaper. In it, he noticed many advertisements for local stores. Grocery stores offered many 1-day only specials on fruits and vegetables. He also cut out a coupon for 10% off his entire purchase. After making a list of what he needed for the week, Paul headed off to the store.

1. Which of the following statements is an unstated assumption from the paragraph?

    (**THINK:** An unstated assumption will not be written directly in the paragraph.)

    (A) Paul went shopping after reading the paper.

    (B) Paul found a coupon for 10% off.

    (C) Paul dislikes reading the paper.

    (D) Paul went to the store because he believes he can save money today.

The correct answer is (D). Answer (A) is incorrect because that is a summary of the paragraph and not an assumption. (B) is incorrect because that is a supporting detail or a fact from the paragraph and not an assumption. While (C) is an assumption, it is incorrect because there is no evidence to support it. We can't really assume that he dislikes it because if he did, he probably wouldn't spend his Sunday afternoon reading the paper. (D) is correct because we know that he goes to the store, and we can assume the reason why is that he realized he will save money after reading the paper.

2. Which of the following statements is an unstated assumption from the paragraph?
   (A) Grocery stores advertised specials on fruits and vegetables.
   (B) Paul believes the food at the grocery store is safe to eat.
   (C) Paul is very busy on Sundays.
   (D) The sales tax at the store will be more than he saves with the coupon.

Use the graph below to answer questions 3 and 4.

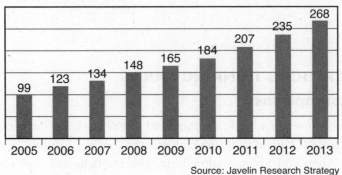

U.S. Online Retail Commerce, in USD Billion

Source: Javelin Research Strategy

3. Which of the following statements is an unstated assumption from the graph?
   (A) Online sales in the United States have grown over the years.
   (B) Online sales rise in times of economic recession.
   (C) Online sales in the United States are significantly higher than elsewhere in the world.
   (D) Online sales have risen as more people trust that online transactions are safe.

4. Which of the following statements is an unstated assumption from the graph?
   (A) The people creating the graph had an accurate way to measure retail sales.
   (B) Retail sales in the United States totaled 123 billion dollars in 2006.
   (C) Retail sales were higher in 2010 than they were in 2009.
   (D) By 2013, online sales will be larger than traditional retail sales in stores.

Use the passage and graph below to answer question 5.

Payroll refers to a list of all the paying positions in a company. If a business adds payroll positions, then they are adding jobs. Likewise, if a business drops payroll numbers, then they are cutting jobs.

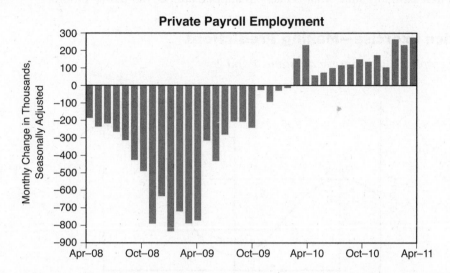

Private Payroll Employment

5. Which of the following statements is an assumption based on the paragraph and the graph?
   (A) More jobs were created in 2010 than in 2009.
   (B) If businesses are adding jobs, then they must believe the economy is not headed toward a depression.
   (C) There was a low supply of workers in 2009.
   (D) Government agencies added jobs in 2010.

Use the passage below to answer questions 6 and 7.

In the 2000 Presidential election, Florida was the last state to count its votes. The election would be decided by what happened in Florida. In all, close to 6 million votes were cast in Florida. The difference between the winner (George W. Bush) and the loser (Al Gore) was a mere 537 votes! This election proved once and for all that every vote really does count.

6. Which of the following statements is an assumption based on the paragraph?
   (A) The Presidential election in Florida was very close.
   (B) Close to 6 million votes were cast in the 2000 election in Florida.
   (C) More people voted in Florida than in neighboring states.
   (D) The results were accurate because all of the votes were counted correctly.

7. Which of the following statements is an assumption based on the paragraph?
   (A) George Bush defeated Al Gore by 537 votes in Florida.
   (B) Everyone in the state of Florida voted in the election.
   (C) Not everyone in America thinks that voting is important.
   (D) Florida played an important role in the 2000 Presidential election.

Making Predictions

What will the weather be like tomorrow? This is a common prediction, or an educated guess about what will happen next, that people often make. Forming your own predictions is an important critical thinking skill. It demonstrates that you understand the material well enough to reasonably state what is likely to happen later or happened before.

Practice Exercise—Making Predictions

Use the graph below to answer questions 1 and 2.

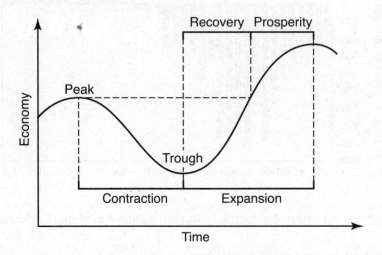

1. Based on the information in the graph, what do you predict will happen next to the economy?
    (A) It will begin to contract.
    (B) It will enter a period of recovery.
    (C) It will begin to expand.
    (D) It will peak.

2. Based on the information in the graph, what stage was the economy most likely in before the time frame shown in the graph?
    (A) Contraction
    (B) Expansion
    (C) Trough
    (D) Peak

Use the passage below to answer questions 3 and 4.

A monopoly occurs when one company has total control over a product. For example, imagine if there was only one place to buy gasoline in your entire state. No matter what gas station you went to, it would be controlled by the same company. A similar situation occurred in 1904 when the Standard Oil company controlled over 90% of the oil in the United States. Since then, the government has worked to prevent monopolies and encourage competition.

3. What do you predict would happen to prices of a product when one company owns a monopoly?
    (A) Prices would rise.
    (B) Prices would fall.
    (C) Prices would stay the same.
    (D) Monopolies have no effect on prices.

4. What do you predict might be the effect of competition (more than one business selling the same product) on prices?
    (A) Prices would rise.
    (B) Prices would fall.
    (C) Prices would stay the same.
    (D) Competition has no effect on prices.

Use the pie chart below to answer question 5.

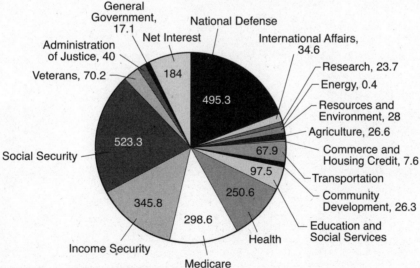

2005 Actual Spending by Program

5. If the United States came under attack, which of these programs would you expect to receive more funding?
    (A) Social Security
    (B) Medicare
    (C) Energy
    (D) National Defense

Use the graph below to answer question 6.

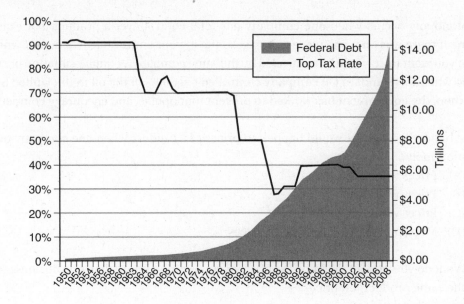

6. What do you predict will happen to the federal debt if the top tax rate rises?

   (**THINK:** What is the relationship between the line and the shaded area?)

   (A)   The debt will rise.
   (B)   The debt will shrink.
   (C)   There will be no effect on the debt.
   (D)   Inflation will rise.

CHAPTER 20 ANSWER EXPLANATIONS

Lesson 1: What Is Economics

PRACTICE EXERCISE—SUPPLY AND DEMAND (PAGE 625)

1. **(C)** As prices get more expensive, fewer people can afford them, so demand falls.
2. **(C)** The more there is of something, the cheaper it is. For example, you would have a hard time selling leaves out of your yard because people can get leaves anywhere. A high supply lowers prices.
3. **(B)** Equilibrium is like the word "equal," meaning that things are balanced. In this case, supply and demand are balanced to produce the highest price that will sell the most shoes.
4. **(D)** The more you are needed at work (demand), the higher the price someone will pay you to work. Specialized careers, like doctors, earn more because few people can do that kind of work, and there is a high demand for doctors.
5. **(A)** Because the price is dropping that would increase demand.
6. **(A)** Items that are in short supply become more valuable and, therefore, expensive.
7. **(D)** (A) and (B) are conclusions, and (C) is untrue.
8. **(B)** (A) and (C) are facts, and (D) is untrue. (B) is an opinion because it is not a fact: some people may agree with that statement while other people may not.

Lesson 2: Economic Trends

PRACTICE EXERCISE—ECONOMIC TRENDS VOCABULARY (PAGE 627)

1. **A**
2. **H**
3. **G**
4. **D**
5. **E**
6. **C**
7. **F**
8. **B**

PRACTICE EXERCISE—CAUSE AND EFFECT (PAGE 628)

1. Causes of Inflation: During good economic times, people buy more, which raises demand. Increased demand raises prices. Also, inflation can be caused by the government printing too much money.

Effects of Inflation: Prices go up, but income stays the same, and that hurts quality of life. Money that is saved loses its value because it is not worth as much. Banks do not want to loan money.

Lesson 3: Graphic Materials (Page 629)

1. World Gross Domestic Product
2. Rank, Country, GDP (millions of USD)
3. Countries with the highest GDP are at the top of the chart.
4. Approximately 9,000,000. The United States rounds off to 15,000,000, and China rounds off to 6,000,000. The difference between the two is approximately 9,000,0000 or 9 million.
5. The GDP of Brazil is 2,090,314, and their rank is 7.

6. Inflation impact on $22,000 income.

7. Each year inflation decreases purchasing power.

8. $16,531.84

9. After 5 years, the purchasing power is $17,938.20. Since the question says approximately, we can round that to $18,000. If we started with $22,000 and now we have $18,000, that means we lost approximately $4,000 in purchasing power in the last 5 years.

10. If deflation increases purchasing power, the effect would be that the dollar amounts on the table would rise.

11. City Budget 2010–2011.

12. Public works is the biggest piece of the pie. This is also represented by 24% being the largest number on the chart.

13. Both the library and the planning and economic development are the smallest; each are 4% of the budget.

14. Three items. Public works, police, and fund transfers are all over 11%.

15. **(B)** (A) is incorrect because no other nations are on the graph. (C) is untrue, and (D) is incorrect because inflation is not mentioned. (B) is the best answer because it sums up all of the information on the graph.

16. **(A)** The last date on the right of the graph is 2009, and we see that unemployment is approaching 9% and the trend is going up.

17. **(C)** During this quarter, the percent change was almost –7. That is the largest line on the graph.

18. **(D)** Since recessions are periods when the GDP falls, a recession would occur during times of negative GDP growth. By 2009, there had been three consecutive quarters of negative growth.

Lesson 4: Critical Thinking Skills

PRACTICE EXERCISE—UNSTATED ASSUMPTIONS (PAGE 633)

1. **(D)**

2. **(B)** (A) is incorrect because it is directly stated. (C) is incorrect because if he was very busy, he wouldn't spend the afternoon reading the paper. (D) is incorrect because, although we don't know how much sales tax is, it is probably less than the 10% coupon. (B) is unstated, because if Paul didn't think the food was safe, he would not shop there.

3. **(D)** (A) is incorrect because it is directly stated. (B) is incorrect because we don't know if it was a recession or a boom time from the graph. (C) is incorrect because there are no comparisons to other nations on the graph. (D) is assumed because if people did not trust in it, they would not spend their money that way.

4. **(A)** (B) and (C) are stated directly on the graph, and there is no way to know (D) from the graph. (A) is assumed because if the numbers weren't accurate, then the graph would be meaningless.

5. **(B)** (A) and (D) are incorrect because they are directly stated. (C) is incorrect because if jobs are being cut in 2009, then there would be many people looking for work and, therefore, a high supply of workers. Businesses would not hire people if they believed the economy was headed toward a depression, so (B) is the best choice.

6. **(D)** (A) and (B) are incorrect because they are directly stated. (C) is incorrect because there is no way to know how many people voted in neighboring states. (D) is the best

answer because if the vote count wasn't accurate, then no one would know how close the election was.

7. **(C)** (A) and (D) are directly stated. (B) is incorrect because it is unlikely that every last person in the state voted in Florida. (C) is correct because the last sentence states that this proves that each vote does count, which hints that not everyone thinks that voting is important.

PRACTICE EXERCISE—MAKING PREDICTIONS (PAGE 636)

1. **(A)** The solid line appears to be sloping down again on the far right of the graph. We can see on the graph that, when the line sloped down on the left, this is labeled "contraction."

2. **(B)** In the left, we see that the solid line of the graph is rising from the edge. When the line is going up, this is labeled "expansion."

3. **(A)** During a monopoly, there is no competition, so a company can charge whatever it wants. Consumers have no other choice but to pay what the company says.

4. **(B)** Competition lowers prices. If a product is cheaper in one store than another, more people will shop from the cheaper store. This forces the other store to lower prices to make sales.

5. **(D)** If we needed to defend the country from attack, national defense spending would probably rise.

6. **(B)** According to the graph, when the top tax rate falls, the debt rises. Therefore, it can be predicted that if the tax rate rises, the debt will fall.

Writing on the GED Social Studies Test

21

The GED social studies test contains an essay question, also known as an extended response. This writing task will only be about half as long as the extended response in language arts.

Like the language arts extended response, the social studies question will ask you to respond to one or more reading passages. You will need to connect what you read to an **enduring issue**. The first lesson will describe enduring issues in more detail.

The essay question in social studies is scored the same way as the essay question in language arts. This means your score will depend on your **argument**, your organization, and your ability to use correct grammar.

LESSON 1: WRITING IN SOCIAL STUDIES: ENDURING ISSUES

The extended-response question will typically have you examine such documents as a historic quote or perhaps part of a famous speech. It will then ask you to think about how these documents reflect, or symbolize, an enduring issue.

So what is an enduring issue? According to the GED extended-response guidelines, an enduring issue "reflects the founding principles of the United States." *Enduring* means "long lasting," so an enduring issue is something that has affected America for a long time. These issues are often the ideas and values discussed by the authors of the Constitution and the Bill of Rights. Writing on the social studies test will be easier if you are familiar with those important documents and American history. In this lesson, we will discuss some common enduring issues.

First Amendment Issues

Though only one sentence long, the First Amendment to the Constitution may be the most important words related to the United States. This is the First Amendment in what would become known as the Bill of Rights. The ten amendments in the Bill of Rights were created to specifically protect individual freedoms and rights.

The First Amendment guarantees freedom of speech, religion, the press, and the right of people to peacefully get together and challenge the government. Freedom of speech seems simple at first, but what if somebody wants to burn the U.S. flag to protest a war? Could burning an object be considered a kind of speech? What about someone who says extremely racist things? Though these actions and words may be unpopular, they are both considered to be protected by freedom of speech. However, if you threaten to kill someone, that would not be protected. Freedom of speech has its limits, and it is an issue that continues to affect Americans today.

Related to freedom of speech is the freedom of the press. When the Constitution was written, the "press" mainly meant newspapers and books. Now it would also include websites, movies, and even Twitter accounts. In other words, these freedoms don't just stop with what somebody says out loud. They apply to what they might write or create as well. But what if somebody wanted to publish U.S. troop locations during a war? Would that be protected? If the government can prove that it directly endangers troops, then it would not be protected. What about if students want to wear black arm bands to protest an issue? Could a principal suspend the students if they refuse to remove the arm bands? No, he could not censor that type of speech.

Freedom of religion goes beyond simply allowing people to follow the religion of their choice. It also means that the government cannot favor one religion over another. For example, public schools cannot have students recite a prayer at the start of the day. Since public schools receive money from the government, they cannot directly support a religious practice. This line between religion and the government is commonly known as the "separation of church and state."

Checks and Balances

The United States Constitution lists three branches for the federal government: legislative (Congress), judicial (courts), and executive (president). Each branch is designed to check and balance the power of the others. This remarkable system prevents any one branch or person from abusing power. For example, only Congress can write a new law, but the President must agree with it for the law to go into effect. Still, even after that the Supreme Court can review the law and strike it down. The President nominates people to the Supreme Court, but they must be approved by the Senate. In this way, every branch is able to somewhat restrict the others.

The enduring issue behind "checks and balances" continues to affect the nation today. Only Congress can declare war, but the President is the commander in chief of the military. If he doesn't technically call it a war, does he need to ask Congress for permission to send troops into battle? Or what if the President orders a government agency to give every citizen an extra $500 on the first of every month? Congress controls the "power of the purse," or how money is spent. Could they disagree with the President and not provide any money for his idea? This competition for power and authority between government branches is also an enduring issue.

Federalism

The term *federalism* refers to the idea that the United States has a strong national, or federal, government. All 50 states have their own laws, and local governments have their own laws, too. So if any of these laws conflict with a federal law, who wins? The federal law always overrules a state or local law. For example, a state may decide to legalize a drug but the federal government does not. While a person in that state could use that drug and not be arrested by state or local police, he could still be arrested by a federal agent. The argument that it is legal in that state would not help, the federal law comes first.

Before the Constitution was written, the United States actually tried a different type of government that did not have a strong federal government. This was called the Articles of

Confederation, and it lasted for only eight years. One problem with not having a strong national government was that Congress did not have the power to collect money through taxes. States refused to send money to the national government. Without money, the federal government was basically powerless to do anything. They could not afford to pay an army to defend the nation. Also, without a federal government, there was no way to settle arguments between the states. After seeing the problems with the Articles of Confederation, the Constitution was written with a strong federal government.

Majority Rule, Minority Rights

In a democracy like the United States, the candidate with the most votes wins. This is known as majority rule. However, the rights of the minority, or those not in power, are always protected. At first, these may seem like opposite ideas. If an election is winner take all, why do the losers get to keep some power?

To explain this, it helps to think of the goals behind the Constitution and the Bill of Rights. The Founding Fathers were trying to avoid government **tyranny.** They did not want to create a monarchy or dictatorship where someone could abuse power. Therefore, even though one person or party wins an election, the losers still get to keep their rights. Those in the minority can still vote or speak out against the government. Likewise, the winners cannot pass laws to punish the minority.

Practice Exercise—Check Your Understanding

1. What freedoms are protected by the First Amendment?

    _____

    _____

    _____

    _____

2. How does the system of checks and balances prevent one branch of government from becoming too powerful?

    _____

    _____

    _____

3. What were the problems with the Articles of Confederation that led to a stronger federal system?

    _____

    _____

    _____

    _____

4. What do you think could happen to a nation if minority rights were not protected after an election?

_____

_____

_____

_____

LESSON 2: ORGANIZING THE EXTENDED RESPONSE

The extended response has three parts: the stimulus, the prompt, and your written response. Each extended response will ask you to respond to "stimulus material." This means there will be one or more passages to read, like a famous quote or a historical document. Here is an example.

Stimulus Material

HISTORIC QUOTE

"We hold these truths to be self-evident, that all men are created equal, that they are endowed by their Creator with certain unalienable Rights, that among these are Life, Liberty and the pursuit of Happiness."

—United States Declaration of Independence, July 4, 1776

BOOK PASSAGE

"Jamestown became the first permanent English settlement in America in 1609. Ten years later, in 1619, the first African slaves arrived in the colonies. Slavery played an important role in American history from its beginning. Still, the Founding Fathers were divided on how to deal with the issue of slavery. Though Thomas Jefferson wrote the Declaration of Independence, he also owned slaves. As the United States grew the issue continued to divide the nation. The issue was only settled after the Civil War and the passing of the 13th amendment in 1865, which formally outlawed slavery."

—*Slavery in America*, Michael Jones, 2010

The actual extended-response question appears as the "prompt."

PROMPT

In your response, develop an argument about how both the quote from Thomas Jefferson and the paragraph from the book deal with the enduring issues of freedom and equality. Use specific examples from the stimulus and your own knowledge of American history and government.

Understanding the Prompt

Figuring out what the prompt is asking you to do can be difficult at first. Since your answer to the extended-response question counts for more than any other question, it is a good idea to take your time and reread it. With a little practice reading and responding to prompts, it will become easier to identify what you need to do.

Here are some quick tips for reading the prompt:

- The prompt is not asking for your personal opinion on a subject. Your response must be based on what is written in the stimulus.
- You do not have to agree with the information in the stimulus. For example, a different prompt could be about an advertisement for raising taxes. You may disagree with that; however, the prompt is not asking for your opinion. The prompt will always be about how the stimulus relates to an "enduring issue."
- The prompt is not asking for an answer to a specific question, such as why was slavery outlawed in the United States.
- The prompt will always ask you to develop an argument.

Developing an Argument

Usually when people think of an argument, they think of two people shouting at each other in anger. This is not that type of argument. This type of argument means to create a point of view about how the readings in the stimulus connect to the enduring issue. Let's look at some possible arguments for this extended response.

Argument One: Both the quote and the book passage say similar things about freedom and equality.

Argument Two: The Declaration of Independence talks about freedom and equality at the creation of the United States, but the book passage shows this was an uneven process in American history.

Argument Three: Both the quote and the passage demonstrate that freedom and equality have not been important in American history.

These are three different ideas, or arguments, about how the readings relate to the enduring issue. How do you know which one is better? That depends on how well you can back up your argument with evidence. The prompt leaves the argument up to you, so there will always be more than one way to score points on the extended-response question. The first step is to create an argument; you will not score points for writing generally about the topics in the readings or prompt. You have to specifically tie together the stimulus readings to the enduring issue. Anything else may be considered off topic no matter how much or how well you write.

Backing Up Your Argument with Evidence

Think about the question "What is the best movie of all time?" If you asked ten people that question, you may get ten different answers. So how do you know who had the correct answer? Well, it may not be possible to have one "correct" answer to a question like that. The extended-response prompt is a lot like that, too. There may be multiple ways to respond and score points. However, even though you may get different answers, or arguments, to the movie question, some people will be more convincing than others. The more convincing people have better evidence to back up their argument.

For example, a young child may say the best movie is *Finding Nemo*, because it is awesome, they love that it is about fish, and they have seen it over 20 times. How convincing is that argument? Not very. "Because it is awesome" is just personal opinion, and the fact that it is about fish doesn't mean it is great. How many times a child has seen it is irrelevant to how good the movie actually is.

On the other hand, an older person may say the best movie is *The Godfather*. He or she could then say that it won three academy awards including best picture and that many of the stars in the movie went on to win awards throughout their career. That evidence is much more convincing. It directly supports the idea that *The Godfather* is a great movie and is not just personal opinion.

Before you begin writing, you need to think about what argument would be easiest to support with evidence. A good rule of thumb is that you need three reasons, or points, to back up your essay. These reasons should come from the readings, but you can also pull from your own knowledge of the subject. Remember, don't use your personal opinion to justify your claim, just stick to the facts.

You may find that that one side or argument is easier to write about than another. However, you may not personally agree with that argument. Keep in mind that the prompt is not asking what you think about the topic, it is only asking you how it relates to an enduring issue. Your job is to give evidence and show your knowledge of how it all ties together.

Now let's find some *specific* evidence in the stimulus to support the argument that the Declaration of Independence talks about the enduring issues of freedom and equality at the creation of the United States, but the book passage shows this was an uneven process in American history.

- The Declaration of Independence directly states that all men are created equal.
- However, the book shows that slavery existed before and after the Declaration. The idea of equality then didn't happen as written in the Declaration.
- Still, slavery was eventually abolished in 1865, so the United States did continue toward freedom and equality.

You may want to use other evidence in the readings to prove your point, and that is fine. Likewise, you may use your personal knowledge to support your argument. For example, the Declaration states that all "men" are equal, but it does not mention women. If you knew that women could not vote in the U.S. until the early 1900s, that would be great evidence to back up your argument.

> Before you start writing your response, always do a little planning first. Make sure to choose three points of evidence from the stimulus that you want to include in your answer.

LESSON 3: WRITING THE EXTENDED RESPONSE

STEP 1 Read the prompt and try putting the prompt into your own words. This will help you to better understand it.

STEP 2 Identify the enduring issue. This may be clearly stated in the prompt, but you may also have to figure it out. Make sure to review the previous section on enduring issues for some ideas.

STEP 3 Develop an argument. Try to answer the question "what do these reading passages have to do with the enduring issue?" Pay attention to whether or not the readings are alike, or if they seem to disagree with each other. Try to sum up your argument in one sentence. This is known as a thesis statement, and it will be the first sentence in your response.

Here are some examples of general thesis statements you can use for different types of extended responses. Notice that each thesis statement names the enduring issue and the titles of each reading.

WHEN THE READINGS HAVE SIMILAR VIEWS OR ARE CLEARLY RELATED TO EACH OTHER

Both reading passages strongly relate to the enduring issue of _____.
   The passage titled _____ gives a clear example of the enduring issue of _____.
   The passage titled _____ demonstrates the enduring issue of _____.

WHEN THE READINGS DISAGREE OR SHOW CHALLENGES TO THE ENDURING ISSUE

Although both passages relate to the enduring issue of _____, the passage titled _____ disagrees with the passage titled _____.
   The reading titled _____ reflects the enduring issue of _____, but the passage titled _____ challenges that issue.
   The reading titled _____ shows the challenges with the enduring issue of _____ in the passage by _____.

STEP 4 Choose your evidence. Now that you have your argument, choose three points from the readings that will back up your claim. These will be the reasons you give to prove your argument is correct. Therefore, try to pick the evidence that will be the most convincing.

STEP 5 Begin writing. Here is a sentence-by-sentence format you can use to make the process a little easier.

   Sentence One: Argument/Thesis Statemnt
   Sentence Two: Evidence/reason one. You don't need to quote the reading directly, putting it into your own words is more effective.
   Sentence Three: A one-sentence explanation on why your first reason is important or how it relates to the enduring issue.
   Sentence Four: Evidence/reason two.
   Sentence Five: A one-sentence explanation on why your second reason is important or how it relates to the enduring issue.
   Sentence Six: Evidence/reason three.
   Sentence Seven: A one-sentence explanation on why your third reason is important or how it relates to the enduring issue.
   Sentence Eight: A one-sentence conclusion that sums up what you wrote.

Extended Response Example

STIMULUS MATERIAL

"We hold these truths to be self-evident, that all men are created equal, that they are endowed by their Creator with certain unalienable Rights, that among these are Life, Liberty and the pursuit of Happiness."

—United States Declaration of Independence, July 4, 1776

BOOK PASSAGE

"Jamestown became the first permanent English settlement in America in 1609. Ten years later, in 1619, the first African slaves arrived in the colonies. Slavery played an important role in American history from its beginning. Still, the Founding Fathers were divided on how to deal with the issue of slavery. Though Thomas Jefferson wrote the Declaration of Independence, he also owned slaves. As the United States grew the issue continued to divide the nation. The issue was only settled after the Civil War and the passing of the 13th amendment in 1865, which formally outlawed slavery."

—*Slavery in America*, Michael Jones, 2010

PROMPT

In your response, develop an argument about how both the quote from Thomas Jefferson and the paragraph from the book deal with the enduring issues of freedom and equality. Use specific examples from the stimulus and your own knowledge of American history and government.

The Declaration of Independence reflects the enduring issues of freedom and equality, but the passage titled *Slavery in America* challenges those issues. The Declaration of Independence directly states that all men are created equal. Since this is one of America's founding documents, it shows that freedom and equality are important to the United States. However, the book shows that slavery existed before and after the Declaration. The idea of equality then didn't happen as written in the Declaration. Still, Mr. Jones points out that slavery was eventually abolished in 1865. This demonstrates that the enduring issues of freedom and equality changed over time. These issues continue to affect American life today.

LESSON 4: EXTENDED RESPONSE PRACTICE

Extended Response One

STIMULUS MATERIAL

"If we don't believe in freedom of expression for people we despise, we don't believe in it at all."

—Noam Chomsky

"In 1977 the Nazi Party of America announced they would march through the streets of a small town outside of Chicago, Illinois. Remembering the horrible history of the German Nazis in World War Two, local leaders moved to ban the march."

"First, the town required the Nazis to pay hundreds of thousands of dollars in insurance prior to the event. This unusually high fee would make it too expensive for the NAZI party to hold the march. Next, the town banned the display of NAZI symbols, such as the swastika."

"Surprisingly, lawyers who did not like the Nazis agreed to represent them in court. These lawyers believed that the town was violating basic American freedoms by not letting the Nazis march. The case made it all the way to the Supreme Court of the United States. The Supreme Court ruled that town could not prevent the march through excessively high fees. Likewise, the Supreme Court stated that although the Nazi party was unpopular, its symbols were protected as free speech. The march was allowed to go on."

—"Did Freedom Go Too Far?" *Chicago Daily Newspaper,* 1978.

PROMPT

In your response, develop an argument about how both the quote from Noam Chomsky and the newspaper article relate to enduring First Amendment Issues. Use specific examples from the stimulus and your own knowledge of American history and government.

ANSWER EXAMPLE TO EXTENDED RESPONSE ONE

Both reading passages strongly relate to the enduring First Amendment issues of freedom of speech. Mr. Chomsky states believing in freedom of speech means allowing even those we disagree with to speak. This principle would be demonstrated through the Nazi march outside of Chicago in 1977. As stated in the newspaper article, the town first tried to prevent the march by requiring a large amount of money from the Nazis. However, doing so would violate the marchers' First Amendment right to assemble. The town also tried to ban Nazi symbols. This would violate their freedom of expression. Lawyers sued, and eventually the Supreme Court ruled that the town had violated the Nazi's First Amendment rights. Therefore, this march shows that freedom of speech means protecting even unpopular opinions.

Extended Response Two

STIMULUS MATERIAL

"Historically, the judicial branch has often been the sole protector of the rights of minority groups against the will of the popular majority."

—Diane Watson

"Although slavery was abolished by the 13th Amendment, and the 14th Amendment guaranteed equal protection of all citizens, the races largely remained separated after the Civil War. In 1896 the Supreme Court case *Plessy vs. Ferguson* ruled that public schools could be segregated by race. This decision became known as 'separate but equal.' It meant that races could be segregated as long each side had equal services."

"The Supreme Court Case *Brown vs. Board of Education* in 1954 challenged the notion of 'separate but equal.' Parents of black students brought lawsuits proving that the segregated schools were unequal. Some white students attended modern schools with new books, while some black students' schools were nothing more than shacks without even basic school supplies."

"Furthermore, the lawyers in *Brown vs. Board* presented psychological evidence. They showed that even if the segregated schools were generally equal, the effect on students was not the same. By being separated entirely from the other school aged children, some kids would feel inferior. This could affect their ability to learn. Therefore, in a unanimous decision the Supreme Court overruled *Plessy vs. Ferguson* and ordered schools to desegregate. The era of 'separate but equal was over.'"

—"From Plessy to Brown," *Modern History Weekly,* June 2014.

PROMPT

In your response, develop an argument about how the magazine article relates to the enduring issue in the quote by Diane Watson. Use specific examples from the stimulus and your own knowledge of American history and government.

ANSWER EXAMPLE TO EXTENDED RESPONSE TWO

The magazine article titled "From Plessy to Brown" gives a clear example of the enduring issue of minority rights stated by Diane Watson. Ms. Watson states that minority rights have often been protected by court cases. The concept of judicial review allows judges to strike down laws that violate citizens' rights. This concept would test the 1896 court decision *Plessy vs. Ferguson,* which legalized segregated schools. Though supposedly "separate but equal," these segregated schools were sometimes just shacks. The case of *Brown vs. Board of Education* overturned the *Plessy* decision. The lawyers proved that separating students created psychological damage even if the school buildings were the same. Therefore, even though the segregated students were in the minority, their rights were ultimately protected. By challenging segregation through the court system, the *Brown vs. Board* decision changed America through the process of judicial review.

Extended Response Three

STIMULUS MATERIAL

"States are more important than the Federal government. After all, who could do a better job of running our town: Someone who lives here, or somebody far away in Washington, DC? We run our state the way we like it, and we don't need someone from the Federal government telling us how to do things."

"Our taxes are too high already. Why should I have to pay State taxes and Federal taxes? Federal taxes go to things I'll never use, like a highway on the other side of the country. The Federal government should not have the right to take our money."

"The Federal government has too many rules, and I think we have enough laws as it is. Our state should pass a law allowing everyone to own as many rocket launchers as they please. That way we could take over another state if we wanted to."

—Letter to the editor, James Smith, *The Daily Record,* July 4, 1998

"The term federalism refers to the idea that the U.S. has a strong national, or federal, government. All 50 states have their own laws, and local governments have their own laws too. So if any of these laws conflict with a federal law, who wins? The federal law always overrules a state or local law. For example, a state may decide to legalize a drug but the federal government does not. While a person in that state could use that drug and not be arrested by state or local police, he could still be arrested by a federal agent. The argument that it is legal in that state would not help, the federal law comes first."

"Before the Constitution was written, the United States actually tried a different type of government that did not have a strong federal government. This was called the 'Articles of Confederation,' and it lasted for only eight years. One problem with not having a strong national government was that Congress did not have the power to collect money through taxes. States refused to send money to the national government. Without money the federal government was basically powerless to do anything. They could not afford to pay an army to defend the nation. Also, without a federal government there was no way to settle arguments between the states. After seeing the problems with the Articles of Confederation, the Constitution was written with a strong federal government."

—Barron's *Pre-GED*, 2015

PROMPT

In your response, develop an argument about how the letter to the editor and the excerpt from the textbook reflect the enduring issue of federalism. Use specific examples from the stimulus and your own knowledge of American history and government.

The letter to the editor challenges the enduring issue of federalism as described by the textbook passage. Federalism means having a strong national government that is more powerful than the state government. Mr. Smith states that is a bad idea because local governments have a better idea of what an area needs. He also states that his federal tax dollars are wasted on projects far away from his home state that he will never use. The Articles of Confederation tried a government like this, but without the power to tax the Federal government could not raise money to do anything. In his letter, Mr. Smith says that he would like to own multiple rocket launchers. However, the textbook points out two problems with this idea. First, federal law trumps state law, so even if his state allowed such weapons they would still be illegal on the federal level. Likewise, his state would never be allowed to take over another state because the strong federal government settles conflicts between states. Although Mr. Smith's letter shows modern issues with the Federal system, the textbook explains that the Federal government is always more powerful than state governments.

CHAPTER 21 ANSWER EXPLANATIONS

Lesson 1: Writing in Social Studies: Enduring Issues

PRACTICE EXERCISE—CHECK YOUR UNDERSTANDING (PAGE 645)

1. The First Amendment protects freedom of speech, religion, the press, and the right of people to peacefully get together and challenge the government.

2. The system of checks and balances prevents any one branch or person from abusing power. For example, only Congress can write a new law, but the President must agree with it for the law to go into effect. Still, even after that, the Supreme Court can review the law and strike it down. The President nominates people to the Supreme Court, but they must be approved by the Senate. In this way, every branch is able to somewhat restrict the others.

3. Before the Constitution was written, the United States actually tried a different type of government that did not have a strong federal government. This was called the Articles of Confederation, and it lasted for only eight years. One problem with not having a strong national government was that Congress did not have the power to collect money through taxes. States refused to send money to the national government. Without money, the federal government was basically powerless to do anything. They could not afford to pay an army to defend the nation. Also, without a federal government, there was no way to settle arguments between the states. After seeing the problems with the Articles of Confederation, the Constitution was written with a strong federal government.

4. If minority rights were not protected after an election, then the winning majority could pass laws to hurt the minority. The majority could restrict voting rights so that the minority could not participate in the next election. Or, the minority could be forced to pay more taxes unfairly. Without the protection of minority rights, the winning majority would be free to do almost anything.

Social Studies Posttest

The social studies posttest has 52 questions. After you review the material in this unit, you can use this test to get a sense of what areas you still need to study. Make sure you have at least 60 minutes of quiet time available to complete the test. Read each question carefully, and do your best. It is better if you do not guess on these questions. If you don't know the answer to a question, simply skip it and go on to the next one. The purpose of this test is to find out what areas you still need to work on, and random guessing might throw you off course.

Once you have finished, check your answers on pages 672–674 and complete the posttest evaluation chart on page 670 by circling the number of each question you answered correctly. This way you can easily see your strengths and weaknesses as well as where information on each question you missed is located in the book.

1. Early settlers at Jamestown would have died without help from which group?
   (A) The French
   (B) Canadians
   (C) The Dutch
   (D) Native Americans

2. Which document in American history famously freed all the slaves in the south?
   (A) Emancipation Proclamation
   (B) Declaration of Independence
   (C) Constitution
   (D) Bill of Rights

3. All of the following were advantages of the north during the Civil War *except:*
   (A) The northern states had a higher population.
   (B) Much of the nation's manufacturing was in the north.
   (C) Northern forces did not need to invade the south, they just needed to protect their territory.
   (D) Most of the nation's railroads were in the north, and that provided a transportation advantage.

4. Over 15 million people were killed during World War I. What is one reason why so many lost their lives?
   (A) Hitler's plan for world domination.
   (B) Modern industry created much deadlier weapons.
   (C) Atomic weapons destroyed entire cities.
   (D) The Japanese attack on Pearl Harbor caught America by surprise.

Use the graph below to answer questions 5 through 7.

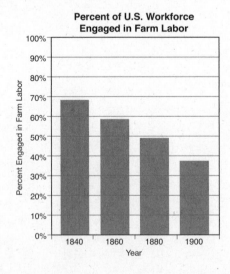

5. According to the graph, about how much of the U.S. workforce was engaged in farm labor in 1880?
    (A) 70%
    (B) 60%
    (C) 50%
    (D) 40%

6. What is the overall trend of the graph?
    (A) The percentage of people engaged in farm labor increased throughout the 1800s.
    (B) The percentage of people engaged in farm labor decreased throughout the 1800s.
    (C) The percentage of people engaged in farm labor stayed the same throughout the 1800s.
    (D) The percentage of people engaged in farm labor varied widely throughout the 1800s.

7. What may be an effect of the information shown on the graph?
    (A) The number of farms in the United States increased dramatically over the time shown.
    (B) Many American farmers moved out of the country to a different nation.
    (C) Urban populations in the United States rose over the same time period.
    (D) Farms were replaced with parking lots during the 1800s.

Use the passage below to answer questions 8 through 10.

The Spanish-American War occurred in 1898. During this war, the United States invaded the Spanish colony of Cuba. Cubans had been fighting the Spanish for independence for many years prior to the war. When the *USS Maine* mysteriously exploded and sunk in Havana, Cuba, the United States declared war on Spain and invaded Cuba. During the war, the United States also defeated the Spanish navy in the Philippines and attacked the Spanish colonies of Guam and Puerto Rico. After 4 months of fighting, the Spanish surrendered. In the end, the Cubans were given their independence, and the United States gained control of the Philippines, Guam, and Puerto Rico.

8. What was a cause of the Spanish-American War?
    (A) The sinking of the *USS Maine*
    (B) The U.S. invasion of Cuba
    (C) The Philippine invasion of the United States
    (D) The many years of Spain fighting for independence against Cuba

9. What was an effect of the Spanish-American War?
    (A) The sinking of the *USS Maine*
    (B) The United States gained possession of Puerto Rico
    (C) Many years of Cuban fighting for independence
    (D) A decrease in U.S. defense spending

10. Which statement best restates the information in the passage?
    (A) The Spanish-American War began in 1898.
    (B) The United States was easily defeated in the Spanish-American War.
    (C) Cubans won their independence after the Spanish-American War.
    (D) The United States defeated Spain and gained their colonies during the Spanish-American War.

11. The first ten amendments to the Constitution are known as
    (A) Emancipation Proclamation
    (B) Declaration of Independence
    (C) Bill of Rights
    (D) Congress

12. The executive branch of the U.S. government includes which of the following?
    (A) The President
    (B) The House of Representatives
    (C) The Senate
    (D) The Supreme Court

13. Judicial review refers to the Supreme Court's power to do what?
    (A) ratify treaties
    (B) approve Senate nominations
    (C) declare war
    (D) overturn laws

14. The term "incumbent" refers to
    (A) the losing candidate in an election
    (B) the candidate trying to replace someone already in office
    (C) an election with more than two candidates
    (D) the person who is currently in the elected office

15. Great Britain is an example of which type of government?
    (A) theocracy
    (B) absolute monarchy
    (C) constitutional monarchy
    (D) communism

16. If someone burns an American flag during protest, this is an example of what kind of issue?
    (A) the First Amendment and freedom of speech
    (B) immigration
    (C) checks and balances between the executive and the judicial branch
    (D) federalism where the states have less power than the federal government

Use the political cartoon below to answer questions 17 and 18.

A BOXING MATCH, or Another Bloody Nose for JOHN BULL.

17. What is the main idea of this cartoon?
    (A) The British recently defeated the Americans in a battle.
    (B) The King likes to box.
    (C) The Americans recently defeated the British in a battle.
    (D) Most fights in colonial America took place near the water.

18. What can be *inferred* from this cartoon?
    (A) Boxing matches frequently involved royalty.
    (B) John Bull is a nickname or symbol for Great Britain.
    (C) The beach can be a violent place.
    (D) Bloody noses were very common in the 19th century.

Use the pictograph below to answer questions 19 through 22.

Military Spending By Year

Each $ is 50 billion dollars

1946   1950   1968   1976   2010

19. What was the amount of military spending in 1950?
    (A) 3 dollars
    (B) 50 dollars
    (C) 3 billion dollars
    (D) 150 billion dollars

20. What can you infer from the information on the pictograph?
    (A) Military spending rises and falls over the years.
    (B) The United States was at war in 1946, 1968, and 2010.
    (C) Military spending was the highest in 2010.
    (D) Military spending was the lowest in 1950.

21. Which of the following statements is an opinion?
    (A) The United States should spend less on military spending.
    (B) Military spending was higher in 1968 than in 1950.
    (C) Military spending decreased between 1968 and 1976.
    (D) Military spending was over twice as much in 1946 than in 1976.

22. Which of the following statements is a fact?
    (A) The United States is the safest country in the world.
    (B) Military spending is less than education spending.
    (C) Military spending was lower in 1946 than in 2010.
    (D) The U.S. Army should receive more in military spending.

23. All of the following are reasons early civilizations developed along rivers *except:*
    (A) Rivers provide fresh water.
    (B) Rivers renew and fertilize soil.
    (C) Rivers provide easy transportation.
    (D) Mountainous land was more expensive.

24. Which abbreviation is used to mark time thousands of years ago?
    (A) C.E.
    (B) A.D.
    (C) B.C.E.
    (D) A.D.E.

25. Early forms of democracy began in which civilization?
    (A) Greece
    (B) India
    (C) Egypt
    (D) Mesopotamia

26. Which of the following is a characteristic of the Enlightenment?
    (A) 100 years of constant warfare
    (B) Great advances in women's rights
    (C) Modern scientific advances
    (D) Nomadic herders traveling from place to place in search of food

Use the time line below to answer questions 27 and 28.

Major 20th Century Wars

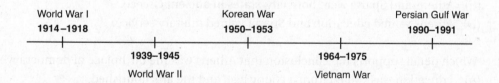

27. Which event occurred after the Vietnam War?
    (A) Korean War
    (B) Persian Gulf War
    (C) World War I
    (D) World War II

28. How many years passed between the end of World War I and the start of World War II?
    (A) 4 years
    (B) 5 years
    (C) 11 years
    (D) 21 years

Use the passage below to answer questions 29 through 32.

Athens and Sparta were two powerful city-states in ancient Greece. Both had populations of over 100,000. In Athens, adult males whose family had been in Athens for three generations were considered citizens. Athens is considered the birthplace of democracy and featured elected officials, as well as an Assembly where all citizens were allowed to speak. Education was valued from a young age, and the arts flourished.

In Sparta, only those males who completed intensive military training were considered citizens. The government was run by an oligarchy, which means rule by a few. At age 7, boys were separated from their families for mandatory military training. All Spartan males over the age of 20 served in the army. Even if married, Spartan males lived in military barracks with other soldiers instead of with their wives.

29. In what way were Athens and Sparta similar?
    (A) Both societies valued arts and culture.
    (B) Only males could be citizens.
    (C) Democracy was important to both city-states.
    (D) Religion was very important to everyone.

30. What conclusion can you draw from the passage?
    (A) Slaves were treated fairly.
    (B) Sparta had a more powerful army than Athens.
    (C) Boys began military training at age 7.
    (D) Spartan government was controlled by an oligarchy.

31. How do Athens and Sparta contrast?
    (A) Athens had a population of over 100,000.
    (B) Certain males could be citizens in Sparta.
    (C) Athens and Sparta were both city-states in ancient Greece.
    (D) Athens valued education and Sparta valued military service.

32. Which detail supports the conclusion that Athens was the birthplace of democracy?
    (A) Education was valued from a young age, and the arts flourished.
    (B) The government was run by an oligarchy, which means rule by a few.
    (C) There was an Assembly where all citizens could speak.
    (D) At age 7, boys were separated from their families for mandatory military training.

Use the map below to answer questions 33 and 34.

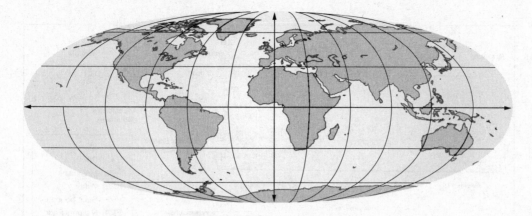

33. What is the line on the map going across the center of the Earth from east to west called?
    (A) Equator
    (B) Prime meridian
    (C) Hemisphere
    (D) Continent

34. What is the line on the map going across the center of the Earth from north to south called?
    (A) Equator
    (B) Prime meridian
    (C) Hemisphere
    (D) Continent

Use the map below to answer question 35.

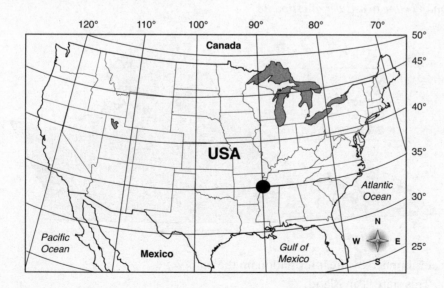

35. What is the latitude and longitude of the point on the map above?

    Latitude: _____   Longitude: _____

Use the map below to answer questions 36 and 37.

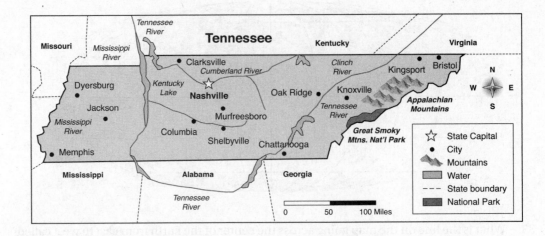

36. Where are the mountains in Tennessee primarily located?
    (A) North
    (B) South
    (C) East
    (D) West

37. Approximately how many miles is the distance from Chattanooga to Knoxville?
    (A) 50
    (B) 100
    (C) 200
    (D) 500

Use the map below to answer question 38.

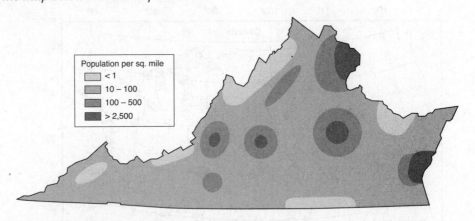

38. What is implied by the information on the map?
    (A) This state is an island.
    (B) There is a large city in the southeastern corner of the state.
    (C) The western area of this state is heavily populated.
    (D) Rainfall is greatest in the center of the state.

Use the map below to answer questions 39 and 40. (GDP stands for Gross Domestic Product).

GDP (Nominal) per capita 2007

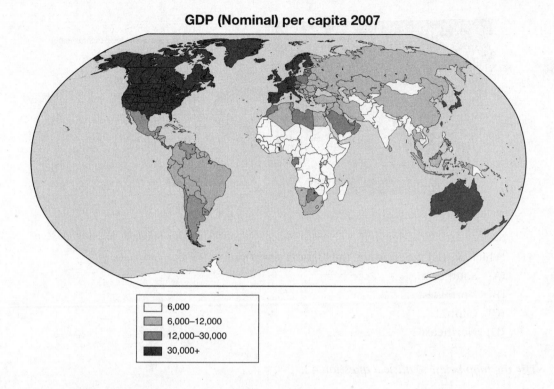

☐	6,000
▨	6,000–12,000
▦	12,000–30,000
■	30,000+

39. What is the approximate GDP of North America?
    (A) 30,000 +
    (B) 12,000–30,000
    (C) 6,000–12,000
    (D) 3,500–6,000

40. Which statement can be implied from the information on the map?
    (A) Russia has the highest GDP of any country on Earth.
    (B) North America is wealthier than South America.
    (C) Africa has the most nations with the lowest GDP.
    (D) GDP does not vary greatly between regions.

Use the map below to answer question 41.

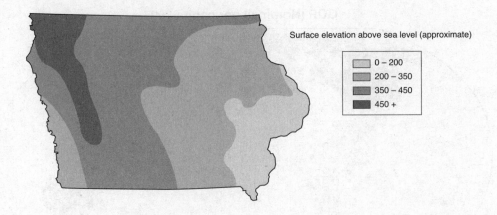

Surface elevation above sea level (approximate)

- 0 – 200
- 200 – 350
- 350 – 450
- 450 +

41. Which part of the state has the highest elevation?
    (A) Southeast
    (B) Northwest
    (C) Central
    (D) Northeast

Use the map below to answer question 42.

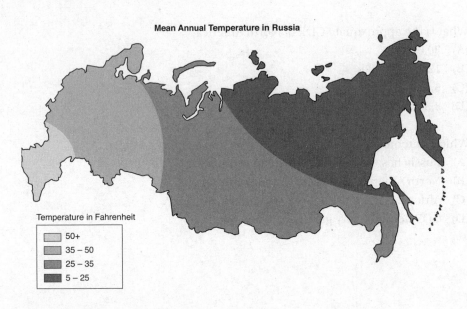

Mean Annual Temperature in Russia

Temperature in Fahrenheit

- 50+
- 35 – 50
- 25 – 35
- 5 – 25

42. Which statement is implied from the information on the map?
    (A) It is difficult to grow crops in northern Russia.
    (B) Democratic government is unpopular in Russia.
    (C) Southern Russia borders an ocean.
    (D) The overall population of Russia is falling.

Use the passage below to answer questions 43 and 44.

Ace Electronics has created a new type of phone. This new phone is very popular, and many people want it. In fact, people are willing to pay hundreds of dollars for it. The phone sells so quickly, Ace has a hard time keeping the phones stocked in stores. Ace raises the price of their phone from $200 to $300. The phones are still selling rapidly, so Ace raises the price to $400. At this point, many customers think that $400 is too expensive, and phone sales drop. Ace then reduces their phone price to $300 to sell more phones.

43. By reducing the price to $300 to sell more phones, what has Ace Electronics figured out?
    (A) Supply
    (B) Demand
    (C) Equilibrium
    (D) Competition

44. How many phones Ace Electronics can stock in the stores relates to what economic principle?
    (A) Supply
    (B) Demand
    (C) Equilibrium
    (D) Competition

45. In economics, what is the difference between a recession and a depression?
    (A) Gross domestic product rises in a recession but falls in a depression.
    (B) Gross domestic product rises and falls equally in recessions and depressions.
    (C) The economy expands at a slow rate during a depression.
    (D) A depression lasts longer than a recession and is more severe.

46. What can be an effect of printing too much money?
    (A) Equilibrium
    (B) Inflation
    (C) Deflation
    (D) Depression

Use the table below to answer questions 47 through 50.

Fiscal Year	Population	Per Capita Income	Number of Jobs	Unemployment Rate	School Enrollment
1993	318,835	$27,523	175,886	3.6%	55,227
1994	323,387	$29,051	184,890	3.7%	56,475
1995	328,631	$30,533	197,577	2.7%	57,368
1996	334,077	$32,247	201,656	2.5%	58,083
1997	341,338	$34,502	208,339	2.6%	58,249
1998	345,440	$37,026	216,534	2.3%	58,504
1999	350,273	$38,674	222,061	2.1%	59,145
2000	360,767	$41,033	222,667	2.5%	59,279
2001	360,767	$37,834	227,780	2.5%	59,279
2002	368,077	$41,003	223,247	4.5%	60,165
2003	371,189	$41,471	227,051	4.4%	60,746
2004	373,339	$43,797	226,862	3.9%	61,831
2005	377,348	$46,002	230,607	3.8%	62,472
2006	379,577	$49,219	234,852	3.8%	62,859
2007	381,603	*	236,413	3.9%	63,082

* Information unavailable

47. What was the population in 2003?
    (A) 360,767
    (B) 368,077
    (C) 371,189
    (D) 373,339

48. What year had the highest unemployment rate?
    (A) 1994
    (B) 2000
    (C) 2002
    (D) 2007

49. What do you predict will happen to per capita income in 2008?
    (A) It will stay at the same level as the year before.
    (B) It will decline.
    (C) It will rise.
    (D) It will match school enrollment.

50. What is unstated assumption based on the table?
    (A) The economy is in recession.
    (B) The economy is in depression.
    (C) The economy is steadily growing.
    (D) Unemployment in 1993 was 3.6%.

Use the graph below to answer questions 51 and 52.

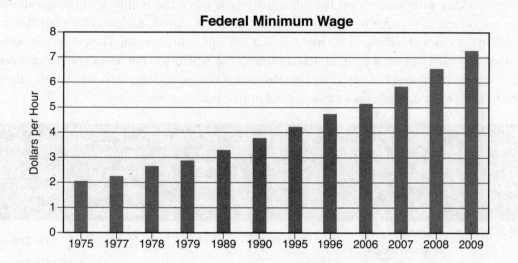

Federal Minimum Wage

51. What do you predict the federal minimum wage will be in 2015?

    (A) $6.00

    (B) $6.50

    (C) $7.25

    (D) $8.00

52. Which of the following is an unstated assumption based on the graph?

    (A) The federal minimum wage in 2006 was just over $5.

    (B) The federal minimum wage increased by over a dollar between 1990 and 2006.

    (C) The federal minimum wage rises and falls over the years.

    (D) The federal minimum wage rises with inflation over time.

POSTTEST EVALUATION CHART

After checking your answers on the following pages, circle the numbers of the questions you got correct in Column B. Record the total number of correct questions for each skill in Column C. Column D gives you the number of correct questions you need to answer correctly to indicate that you have a good understanding of the skill. If you got fewer correct answers than shown in Column D, study the pages shown in Column E. Using this analysis will allow you to focus on your challenges and use your study time more effectively.

A Skill Area		B Questions	C Number of Correct Answers	D Number Correct to Show a Good Understanding	E Pages to Study
U.S. History	General Knowledge	1, 2, 3, 4	___ /10	9	515–538
	Line Graph	5, 6, 7			528–530
	Cause and Effect	8, 9			519
	Restating Info	10			523
Government	General Knowledge	11, 12, 13, 14, 15, 16	___ /13	11	543–574
	Political Cartoon	17, 18			558–560
	Inference	19, 20			567–570
	Fact and Opinion	21, 22			565–567
World History	General Knowledge	23, 24, 25, 26	___ /10	9	575–591
	Time Line	27, 28			582–585
	Compare and Contrast	29, 31			586–588
	Drawing Conclusions	30, 32			588–591
Geography	General Knowledge	33, 34	___ /10	9	595–619
	Reading Maps	35, 36, 37			601–619
	Main Idea	39, 41			612–619
	Implied Ideas	38, 40, 42			612–619

A		B	C	D	E
Skill Area		Questions	Number of Correct Answers	Number Correct to Show a Good Understanding	Pages to Study
Economics	General Knowledge	43, 44, 45, 46			623–638
	Charts and Tables	47, 48			
	Making Predictions	49	____ /10	9	636–638
	Unstated Assumption	50			633–635
	Bar Graphs	51, 52			
TOTAL			____ /52	47	

If you have correctly answered more than the number of questions in the Column D TOTAL, you are ready for HSE-Level Social Studies!

POSTTEST ANSWER EXPLANATIONS

1. **(D)** Answers (A), (B), and (C) are untrue. This information is found in Chapter 16, Lesson 1.

2. **(A)** Answers (B), (C), and (D) are untrue. This information is found in Chapter 16, Lesson 2.

3. **(C)** Answers (A), (B), and (D) are all advantages the north had during the Civil War. (C) is untrue because it was the south that did not need to invade the north.

4. **(B)** Answers (A), (C), and (D) are all about World War II and not World War I.

5. **(C)** The bar above the year 1880 extends up to approximately 50%.

6. **(B)** The bars get smaller with each year measured, so the trend is that a smaller percentage of people engaged in farm labor each year.

7. **(C)** (A) is incorrect because few farm workers would not equal a dramatic increase in farms. (B) is unrelated to the graph. (D) is untrue because there would not have been a great need for parking lots in the 1800s. (C) is the best answer because it makes sense that people not working on farms would try to find work in urban areas.

8. **(A)** (B) and (D) are effects and not causes, and (C) never happened.

9. **(B)** (A) is a cause, and (C) happened before the war, so it can't be an effect. (D) is not mentioned in the passage.

10. **(D)** is the summary of the passage. (A) and (C) are details that are true, but they do not restate the entire passage. (B) is untrue.

11. **(C)** Answers (A), (B), and (D) are untrue. This information is found in Chapter 17, Lesson 1.

12. **(A)** Answers (B), (C), and (D) are untrue. This information is found in Chapter 17, Lesson 2.

13. **(D)** Answers (A) and (B) are powers of the Senate, answer (C) is a power of Congress. This information is found in Chapter 17, Lesson 2.

14. **(D)** This definition is given in Chapter 17.

15. **(C)** A theocracy describes a government based on religion, and communism describes the government of the former Soviet Union. In an absolute monarchy, the king has all of the power, but in Great Britain the king is limited in power by Parliament.

16. **(A)** Freedom of speech covers more than just spoken words, and can include burning a flag during a protest.

17. **(C)** In this cartoon, the crown symbolizes the British, and we see that the man wearing the crown has a bloody nose. The cartoon symbolizes the British were defeated in a battle.

18. **(B)** The crown in this cartoon symbolizes the British, and we see that the man wearing the crown has a bloody nose. Since the caption reads "another bloody nose for John Bull," we can infer that John Bull is a nickname or symbol for Great Britain.

19. **(D)** In 1950, there are three dollar signs. Each dollar sign equals 50 billion dollars, so three dollar signs equal 150 billion dollars.

20. **(B)** Answers (A), (C), and (D) are all directly stated on the graph and not inferred. Because military spending relates to warfare, it can be inferred that, in years of high military spending, a war was taking place.

21. **(A)** Answers (B), (C), and (D) are all facts from the graph. (A) is an opinion because not everyone would agree that the United States should spend less. Some people may have the opposite opinion.

22. **(C)** Answers (A) and (D) are opinions. (B) is untrue and cannot be proved from the graph.

23. **(D)** Answers (A), (B), and (C) are all true. This information is found in Chapter 18, Lesson 1.

24. **(C)** B.C.E. stands for "before the common era." This is the abbreviation used to mark time before the year zero. This information is found in the introduction to Chapter 18.

25. **(A)** Answers (B), (C), and (D) are all ancient river valley civilizations, but Greece is known as the birthplace of democracy. This information is found in Chapter 18, Lesson 2.

26. **(C)** Answers (A), (C), and (D) are all untrue. This information is found in Chapter 18, Lesson 2.

27. **(B)** According to the time line, the Vietnam War took place between 1964 and 1975, and the Persian Gulf War occurred between 1990 and 1991.

28. **(D)** World War I ended in 1918, and World War II began in 1939, a difference of 21 years.

29. **(B)** (A) and (C) are untrue because only Athens valued the arts and was a democracy. (D) is unmentioned in the passage.

30. **(B)** Because military training was so important to Sparta; it is reasonable to conclude they had a more powerful army than Athens. (A) is untrue, and (C) and (D) are details not conclusions.

31. **(D)** Answers (A), (B), and (C) are true of both Athens and Sparta, only answer (D) shows differences.

32. **(C)** (A) does not relate to democracy, and (B) and (D) are details about Sparta.

33. **(A)** This information is found in Chapter 19, Lesson 1.

34. **(B)** This information is found in Chapter 19, Lesson 1.

35. 35 degrees latitude, 90 degrees longitude.

36. **(C)** According to the key, the symbols for the mountains appear in the eastern part of the state.

37. **(B)** Using the map scale, the two cities are approximately 100 miles apart.

38. **(B)** (A) is untrue because no water is shown on the map. (C) is the opposite of what the map shows, and (D) is unrelated to the map. The dark shading of the map key indicate that there is a high population in the southeastern corner of the state.

39. **(A)** According to the key, the GDP of America is 30,000+.

40. **(B)** (A) and (D) are untrue, and (C) is directly stated on the map. Because the United States has a higher GDP, in can be implied that it is wealthier than South America.

41. **(B)** According to the key, the highest elevation matches the shading in the northwest part of the state.

42. **(A)** Since the temperature is below freezing in areas of northern Russia, it would be difficult to grow crops there. (B) and (D) are incorrect because there is no information regarding government or population on the map. (C) is untrue, and there is no way to judge from the map where an ocean might be located.

43. **(C)** The equilibrium price is the highest price a company can charge without losing customers and, therefore, profit. This information is found in Chapter 20, Lesson 1.

44. **(A)** The supply is the amount of a product that is available for sale. This information is found in Chapter 20, Lesson 1.

45. **(D)** Answers (A), (B), and (C) are untrue. This information is found in Chapter 20, Lesson 2.

46. (B) This information is found in Chapter 20, Lesson 2.

47. (C)

48. (C) The rate of 4.5% is the highest shown on the table.

49. (C) With one exception, per capita income rises every year on the chart, so it is reasonable to predict that it will rise in 2008 as well.

50. (C) Since income increases every year, it is reasonable to assume that the economy is growing and not in a recession or depression. (D) is true, but it is directly stated, so you do not need to assume that.

51. (D) Since the minimum wage increases over time, it is reasonable to predict that it will continue to grow. The minimum wage is $7.25 in 2009 and the only answer higher than that is (D).

52. (D) (A) and (B) are true, but they are directly stated and not assumed. (C) is incorrect. Since the minimum wage rises over time, it is safe to assume that it also rises with inflation.

UNIT 5
Reading

Reading Pretest

The literature pretest has 31 questions. The questions follow the chapters in the reading unit. This unit is divided into chapters on reading skills, nonfiction, fiction, comparing texts, poetry, and drama. You can use this test to get a sense of which areas you need to study. Make sure you have at least 60 minutes of quiet time available to complete the test. Read each question carefully, and do your best. However, do not guess on these questions. If you don't know the answer to a question, simply skip it and go on to the next one. The purpose of this test is to find out what areas you need to work on, and random guessing might throw you off course.

Some questions on this test will ask you about comprehension. Others will test your critical thinking skills, like identifying a word from context or making inferences.

Once you have finished, check your answers on pages 687–688, and complete the pretest evaluation chart on page 685 by circling the number of each question you answered correctly. This way you can easily see your strengths and weaknesses as well as where information on each question you missed is located in the book.

If you score very well on the pretest, it is a great sign that you have a solid foundation in the skills needed for reading comprehension in different genres of literature. Still, make sure to check out the end-of-chapter questions for each topic. You'll want to double check that your skills are sharp.

What Kind of People Is Janville Looking For?

In Janville, citizens who come to the courthouse for jury duty are asked a number of questions before they are eligible to serve. Among these questions are the following:

1. Does your religion or personal moral system allow you to make decisions in a courtroom and participate in delivering a verdict?
2. Is there any physical or psychological barrier to your serving fully as a juror?
3. Are you taking any medication? Could this medication keep you from serving fully and effectively on a jury?
4. Are you an officer of the law? Have you or any friends or family members ever worked in law enforcement or the court system? (Examples would be police officers, public defenders, and security personnel.)

1. Inferring from the above questions, what type of jurors do you think the Janville court system would prefer?
   (A) Young kids who don't have anything else to do with their time.
   (B) People who want to spend the time sitting in a courtroom because they hate their jobs.
   (C) People who will pay close attention and reach a verdict based only on the evidence.
   (D) Friends and family of the judge and lawyers.

2. What do you think is the most likely title for the document these questions are on?
   (A) Prospective Juror Questionnaire
   (B) Juror Likes and Dislikes
   (C) Juror Personal Information (in case of emergency)
   (D) Schedule for Courtrooms and Offices

3. Which of the following people would probably check NO for question 4?
   (A) A prosecuting attorney
   (B) A schoolteacher whose husband is a police captain
   (C) A college student who works in security on the weekends
   (D) A businesswoman who runs a family-owned chain of supermarkets

4. In what way would taking some medications be most likely to prevent a person from serving fully and efficiently?
   (A) Side effects from the medication might distract the juror from paying attention to the case.
   (B) The juror might be late if he or she needed to pick up a prescription.
   (C) Prescription drugs are not permitted in the courtroom.
   (D) People on any kind of medication don't feel well.

5. According to the passage, at what point in the jury selection process is each person handed this form?
   (A) During a break in the trial
   (B) Before they leave at the end of the last day
   (C) Before they are chosen to serve
   (D) It is mailed to them after their service is over

Questions 6 through 10 are based on the following passage.

What Is Special About Fred's Apartment?

I am always drawn back to places where I have lived, the houses and their neighborhoods. For instance, there is a brownstone in the East Seventies where, during the early years of the war, I had my first New York apartment. It was one room crowded with attic furniture, a sofa and fat chairs upholstered in that itchy, particular red velvet that one associates with hot days on a train. The walls were stucco, and a color rather like tobacco-spit. Everywhere, in the bathroom too, there were prints of Roman ruins freckled brown with age. The single window looked out on a fire escape. Even so, my spirits heightened whenever I felt in my pocket the key to this apartment; with all its gloom, it still was a place of my own, the first, and my books were there, and jars of pencils to sharpen, everything I needed, so I felt, to become the writer I wanted to be.

— Truman Capote, *Breakfast at Tiffany's*

6. Which of the following is the most likely speaker in this passage?
   (A) An old, rich woman
   (B) A young man who wants to be an actor
   (C) An old man who collects expensive artwork
   (D) A young man who wants to be a writer

7. What is the main idea of the passage?
   (A) A man remembers one of his favorite places to live.
   (B) A man talks about his old furniture.
   (C) Fred talks about the war years.
   (D) New York apartments can be expensive for one person alone.

8. Based on the context, what is the most likely definition of a brownstone?
   (A) A car
   (B) A type of house
   (C) It's Fred's name for his apartment
   (D) A luxurious hotel

9. Which of the following is NOT a reason Fred gives for being happy about his apartment?
   (A) The old red velvet furniture
   (B) He has his own key
   (C) His books
   (D) His pencils in jars

10. Where is Fred's apartment located?
    (A) Over a train station
    (B) A suburban apartment complex
    (C) A big city
    (D) Near some Roman ruins

Questions 11 through 15 are based on the following passage.

What Does the Speaker Want?

"I'm Nobody! Who are you?
Are you—Nobody—Too?
Then there's a pair of us!
Don't tell! they'd advertise—you know!

How dreary—to be—Somebody!
How public—like a Frog—
To tell one's name—the livelong June—
To an admiring Bog!"

—Emily Dickinson

11. Which of the following is the best summarization of the poem above?
    (A) Two people are having a conversation about their plans for the month of June.
    (B) The speaker is talking to a crowd of people about the life cycle of frogs.
    (C) The speaker is talking to another person like herself about how she likes to be private.
    (D) The speaker wishes she and her friend were famous.

12. What is the most likely definition of the word Bog?
    (A) Desert
    (B) The house where the speaker lives
    (C) Wet, spongy, muddy ground
    (D) The above water section of an iceberg

13. Which pair of rhyming words is in the second stanza?
    (A) You and two
    (B) Frog and bog
    (C) Us and know
    (D) Know and name

14. What is the speaker's tone?
    (A) Somber
    (B) Angry
    (C) Amused
    (D) Inspirational

15. What kind of job do you think the speaker would be happiest doing?
    (A) Sales
    (B) Giving speeches to large crowds
    (C) Running for public office
    (D) Writing at home alone

Questions 16 through 20 are based on the following passage.

What Kind of Marriage Do These Two Have?

NORA: Hide the tree well, Helene. The children mustn't get a glimpse of it till this evening, after it's trimmed. *(To the Delivery Boy, taking out her purse.)* How much?

DELIVERY BOY: Fifty, ma'am.

NORA: There's a crown. No, keep the change. *(The boy thanks her and leaves. Nora shuts the door. She laughs softly to herself while taking off her street things. Drawing a bag of macaroons from her pocket, she eats a couple, then steals over and listens at her husband's study door.)* Yes, he's home. *(Hums again as she moves to the table right.)*

HELMER *(from the study)*: Is that my little lark twittering out there?

NORA *(busy opening some packages)*: Yes, it is.

HELMER: Is that my squirrel rummaging around?

NORA: Yes!

HELMER: When did my squirrel get in?

NORA: Just now. *(Putting the macaroon bag in her pocket and wiping her mouth.)* Do come in, Torvald, and see what I've bought.

HELMER: Can't be disturbed. *(After a moment he opens the door and peers in, pen in hand.)* Bought, you say? All that there? Has the little spendthrift been out throwing money around again?

NORA: Oh, but Torvald, this year we really should let ourselves go a bit. It's the first Christmas we haven't had to economize.

HELMER: But you know we can't go squandering.

—Henrik Ibsen, *A Doll's House*

16. What is the best description of the way Helmer treats his wife?
    (A) He asks for her advice on matters.
    (B) He ignores her.
    (C) He doesn't like talking to her.
    (D) He talks to her as if she were a child.

17. What action does Nora NOT perform before she calls her husband?
    (A) She eats a macaroon.
    (B) She trims the Christmas tree.
    (C) She pays the delivery boy.
    (D) She takes off her coat.

18. What do Nora and Helmer disagree about in the last four lines?
    (A) How much to tip the delivery boy
    (B) Whose family to spend Christmas with
    (C) How late she has come home
    (D) How much money to spend for Christmas

19. What can you infer Helmer is doing in his study?
    (A) Working on some papers
    (B) Exercising
    (C) Sleeping
    (D) Wrapping presents

20. What details support the statement that Helmer loves his wife?
    (A) He doesn't want her to spend money.
    (B) He doesn't want to be disturbed.
    (C) He didn't go shopping with her.
    (D) He calls her his lark and his squirrel.

Questions 21 through 25 are based on the following passage.

TRON: Legacy

A 3-D sequel to the 1982 film beloved by techno-nerds everywhere. Jeff Bridges returns as computer genius Kevin Flynn, who slipped inside a computer in the original; he kept visiting that world, we find out, and eventually got stuck there. Now his grown son (Garrett Hedlund) wanders in to find his long-missing father, only to be confronted by two Jeff Bridgeses (one a digital re-creation of the actor in his '80s youth). Keeping with TRON tradition, it's visually arresting despite being fairly ridiculous.

—Richard Corliss/Mary Pols, *Time Magazine*, December 2010

21. What is the best summarization of the plot of the movie *TRON*?
    (A) Jeff Bridges is digitally altered to look younger.
    (B) A computer genius is trapped inside the computer, and his son goes in to find him.
    (C) TRON is a 3-D sequel to a 1982 movie.
    (D) TRON is visually arresting.

22. Given the context, what is the most likely definition of techno-nerd?
    (A) A high school student
    (B) The special effects crew who worked on the movie
    (C) A person who is good with and enjoys new technologies
    (D) Jeff Bridges

23. What are the reviewers' opinions of *TRON*?
    (A) It's a serious, deeply moving film.
    (B) It was a waste of the actors' time.
    (C) It's silly but beautiful to look at.
    (D) It's a hysterical comedy.

24. How was Jeff Bridges able to play two roles in the movie?
    (A) An extra computer image of him was created and projected onto the screen.
    (B) Producers hired another actor who looked like Bridges.
    (C) He was paid twice as much money.
    (D) He used makeup and costume changes to make himself look different for each part.

25. What can you infer from the fact that *TRON* is labeled a sequel?
    (A) There was an earlier movie with the same subject and some of the same characters.
    (B) The movie will make an enormous amount of money, and there will be other sequels following it.
    (C) The movie will appeal only to techno-nerds.
    (D) The movie will be terrible and lose money.

Read the paragraph below and answer questions 26 through 28.

Many people do not realize how recently some of the everyday things we see and use in our homes were invented. Coated silver mirrors, for example, only came into existence in the 17th century. Mirrors themselves have existed since ancient times, of course. Long ago they were usually made of highly polished metal. Their surfaces were often bumpy, and the reflection they returned would seem dim and distorted to us today. In addition to this, ancient mirrors were expensive luxuries that could only be afforded by the wealthy. Most of the populace would have only had access to their reflection by looking in a pool of still water. Can you imagine your morning routine without a look in the mirror? Yet untold numbers of people in the past lived their lives without ever seeing their own faces.

26. Which sentence best summarizes the main idea?
    (A) Mirrors themselves have existed since ancient times, of course.
    (B) Long ago they were usually made of highly polished metal.
    (C) Yet untold numbers of people in the past lived their lives without ever seeing their own faces.
    (D) Many people do not realize how recently some of the everyday things we see and use in our homes were invented.

27. When the author speaks of "everyday things" in Sentence 1, what kinds of items is she probably thinking of?
    (A) Swimming pools
    (B) Hot tubs
    (C) Toothbrushes
    (D) Cars

28. What is the best definition of the word *populace*?
    (A) People
    (B) Popular
    (C) Populism
    (D) Homes

Paragraph A

Ask any math student how he feels about word problems and the answer will probably come back, "I hate them." Yet word problems, with their need for critical thinking skills, are examples of exactly the type of math people do in real life. The boss tells you that you are getting a 4% raise and says "Congratulations!" You go back to your desk. Do you want to be able to figure out how much you should get, or do you want to hope that the Payroll Department will get it right?

Paragraph B

Most math students dislike being put through the torture of math class, and they are right. Math is becoming less and less of a requirement for daily living. When was the last time you had to calculate the square root of 25? Who uses fractions anymore? Calculators have made the need to be able to do math obsolete, and students' and teachers' time could be better spent on other things.

29. What is the topic of both paragraphs?
    (A) Whether math is useful in today's society
    (B) Word problems
    (C) How to figure out the size of your raise
    (D) How to calculate the square root of 25

30. What argument could NOT be used to argue against Paragraph B?
    (A) Most standardized tests now allow the use of calculators.
    (B) Carpenters use fractions to do their work.
    (C) It's still necessary to understand math concepts to use a calculator.
    (D) Cooks need to understand fractional measurements.

31. What is the most likely meaning of the word *obsolete*?
    (A) Useful
    (B) Up to date
    (C) Out of date
    (D) Incorrect

PRETEST EVALUATION CHART

After checking the answers on the following pages, circle the numbers of the questions you got correct in Column B. Record the total number of correct questions for each skill in Column C. Column D gives you the number of correct questions you need to answer correctly to indicate that you have a good understanding of the skill. If you got fewer correct answers than shown in Column D, study the pages shown in Column E. Using this analysis will allow you to focus on your challenges and use your study time more effectively.

A		B	C	D	E
Skill Area		Questions	Number of Correct Answers	Number Correct to Show a Good Understanding	Pages to Study
Main Idea	Nonfiction	2			
	Fiction	7			
	Poetry				690–691
	Drama				
	Compare/ Contrast	29			
	Total		_____/3	2	
Context Clues	Nonfiction	22, 28			
	Fiction	8			
	Poetry	12			694–695
	Drama				
	Compare/ Contrast	31			
	Total		_____/5	3	
Supporting Details	Nonfiction	3			
	Fiction	9			
	Poetry				696–699
	Drama	20			
	Compare/ Contrast				
	Total		_____/3	2	
Summarization	Nonfiction	21, 26			
	Fiction				
	Poetry	11			692–694
	Drama	16			
	Compare/ Contrast				
	Total		_____/4	3	

	A	B	C	D	E
	Skill Area	Questions	Number of Correct Answers	Number Correct to Show a Good Understanding	Pages to Study
Making Inferences	Nonfiction	1, 25, 27			
	Fiction				
	Poetry	15			699–700
	Drama	19			
	Compare/ Contrast				
	Total		____/5	3	
Content	Nonfiction	4, 5, 23, 24			709–736
	Fiction	6, 10			737–755
	Poetry	13, 14			771–790
	Drama	17, 18			791–807
	Compare/ Contrast	30			757–769
	Total		____/11	8	
	TOTAL		____/25	21	

If you answered enough of the questions in Column D for a skill, you know enough about that skill already. You may want to do the Review at the end of these skill areas as a check.

To use your study time wisely, improve your skills in the other areas by studying the pages noted in Column E.

PRETEST ANSWER EXPLANATIONS

1. **(C)** The questions are asked to rule out anyone not able to be attentive and unbiased. A person cannot be forced to render judgment if he or she feels it is wrong. A juror on medication or who is suffering physically or psychologically may not be able to pay full attention to the details of a case. Someone who has close ties to law enforcement may not be able to be objective. (A) By law, children are not eligible to sit on juries. (B) None of the questions have to do with how the juror feels about his or her job. (D) The court wants to know if the juror has ties to law enforcement; there is no indication that ONLY such jurors will be accepted.

2. **(A)** A questionnaire is a list of questions. The passage states that the jurors are asked these questions before becoming eligible. They are, therefore, prospective (possibly eligible). (B) The form does not ask about likes and dislikes, but barriers to serving. (C) Personal information would be addresses, phone numbers, and emergency contacts, not ethical positions. (D) This is not a schedule.

3. **(D)** All the other choices present people who work in law enforcement or have family members that do. The businesswoman might know an officer of the law (and check YES), but the people in (A), (B), and (C) will definitely check YES.

4. **(A)** (B) There is no reason why prescriptions cannot be picked up after court hours are over. (C) and (D) are not true.

5. **(C)** The passage states that the questionnaire is given to people "before they are eligible to serve." That means they are not jurors yet.

6. **(D)** The speaker mentions in the last sentence "the writer I wanted to be." Also his apartment has a writer's tools (books and pencils). (A) The apartment is not rich or luxurious, and the speaker's name is Fred. (B) No mention is made of acting. (C) The prints on the walls are not expensive, but "brown with age."

7. **(A)** Fred's "spirits heightened" at the apartment; he likes being there. He also says it is an example of "places I have lived." (B) is too limited since Fred talks of other things besides the furniture. (C) is too broad; Fred does not discuss the entire wartime period. (D) can be true, but expense is not mentioned in the passage.

8. **(B)** A brownstone is a type of house typical of New York where Fred lives. (A) and (C) The brownstone is not a car; Fred says it contains apartments, so it is not an apartment. (D) The furniture, walls, and pictures he describes are not luxurious.

9. **(A)** The other three choices are the reasons Fred gives for "heightened spirits" in the last sentence of the passage.

10. **(C)** Fred says the apartment was in New York, one of the biggest cities in the United States. That means he is not in the suburbs (B). Fred only mentions trains when he says his furniture reminds him of them. (D) The Roman ruins are in the pictures on Fred's walls.

11. **(C)** (A) Only one person is speaking—the listener never replies. (B) The speaker uses the frog as a symbol of someone being forced to talk to crowds. She does not give biological information about the frog. (D) The speaker thinks to be "Somebody" would be "dreary."

12. **(C)** This is the sort of environment likely to support frogs, unlike choices (A) and (D). The speaker does not mention where she lives.

13. **(B)** (A) *You* and *too* rhyme, but they are in the first stanza. The pairs in (C) and (D) do not rhyme.

14. **(C)** (A) The speaker is happy to remain Nobody (she says *Don't tell! They'd advertise*). (B) She is not angry about her situation, and she doesn't want to change it. She thinks

to live otherwise would be *dreary*. (D) An inspirational piece gives a call for action. The speaker does not want to inspire action. She only wants to be let alone.

15. **(D)** This is the only choice that does not involve dealing with the public, which the speaker says she hates.

16. **(D)** Helmer has pet names for his wife and speaks to her in a playful way. He scolds her for spending money. (B) and (C) are not supported by the passage. Helmer comes out of his study when his wife comes home, even though he is busy with work. (A) He does not ask advice; he gives it (*we can't go squandering*).

17. **(B)** Nora states that the tree will be trimmed *this evening*. (A) and (D) are described in Nora's stage directions. (B) Nora says "*There's a crown. Keep the change*" to the delivery boy before Helmer comes out.

18. **(D)** In the last four lines, Nora says "*It's the first Christmas we haven't had to economize,*" and Helmer calls her a *spendthrift*.

19. **(A)** Helmer comes out of his study with a pen in his hand.

20. **(D)** *Lark* and *squirrel* are intimate pet names, like *dear* and *honey*. Helmer also greets his wife, and even though he is in the middle of working, he comes out to talk to her.

21. **(B)** *A computer genius is trapped inside the computer, and his son goes in to find him.* (A) and (C) are details in the review, but neither contains the complete point of the reviewers. (D) is an opinion.

22. **(C)** *A person who is good with and enjoys new technologies.* The reviewers identify techno-nerds as those who loved the original *TRON*, a film with a technological subject. (A) The reviewers do not specify an age requirement for techno-nerds. The phrase "techno-nerds everywhere" means the label does not just apply to *TRON's* crew (B) or actors (D).

23. **(C)** *It's silly but beautiful to look at.* In the last sentence, the reviewers call the movie "visually arresting" yet "ridiculous." None of the other opinions are expressed, as the rest of the review simply outlines *TRON's* plot.

24. **(A)** *An extra computer image of him was created and projected onto the screen.* The review states that one of the images of Bridges was "a digital re-creation." None of the other choices are supported by information in the passage.

25. **(A)** *There was an earlier movie with the same subject and some of the same characters.* This is essentially the definition of a sequel. All of the other choices are predictions, which might come true for any type of movie, not just sequels.

26. **(D)** *Many people do not realize how recently some of the everyday things we see and use on our homes were invented.* (A) and (B) are factual details. (C) is a concluding sentence and does not mention common household items.

27. **(C)** *Toothbrushes.* (A) and (B) are luxury items. (D) A car is a vehicle, not something we see in our homes.

28. **(A)** *People.* (B) Popular is an adjective meaning well-liked. (C) Populism is a political philosophy. (D) Homes is an unrelated word.

29. **(A)** *Whether math is useful in today's society.* (B) The second paragraph does not mention word problems. (C) and (D) Neither paragraph gives instructions for how to perform these calculations. They are mentioned only as examples.

30. **(A)** *Most standardized tests now allow the use of calculators.* All the other choices are facts that support the importance of math.

31. **(C)** *Out of date.* (A) and (B) An obsolete item was useful once but is no longer. (D) A need cannot be incorrect; facts are incorrect.

Reading Skills

> "Some people will lie, cheat, steal and back-stab to get ahead...and to think, all they have to do is READ."
>
> —*Fortune*

Want to know a secret? There is a great undiscovered power source waiting at your fingertips. It is free. It requires you to join no club, send away for no merchandise, and pay no membership fees. Even better, the more you use this power, the easier and more effective it becomes.

It is reading.

But you already knew that, didn't you? You have been used to hearing many people—parents, teachers, and others—tell you that improving your reading skills will help you. What you—and they—may not have thought about is HOW MUCH it is in your power to increase your reading comprehension and speed. Good readers do not get to one skill level and stay there. They read more because they are better at it. They get even better because they are reading more. The sky is the limit for you as a reader!

You may think, when you sit down to practice reading, that it is necessary to choose something academic or "serious"—in fact, something that may not interest you at all! The opposite is true. Read as much as you can of what interests you: detective stories, romance novels, and technical manuals. Like to read the back of cereal boxes? Read every one in the supermarket! When your reading is fun, it gives you endurance and stamina to read things you are required to read. It is just like practicing a sport.

HOW THIS CHAPTER IS ORGANIZED

Lesson 1: Main Idea

Every piece of writing has one BIG idea that the author wants to communicate to you, the reader. This lesson shows you where to look for key sentences and phrases to unlock the author's message.

Lesson 2: Summarizing

Who said, "Less is more?" As a student and effective reader, you will need to express the meaning of long passages in a few insightful sentences.

Lesson 3: Context Clues

What is your response when you come to a new vocabulary word in a sentence? Do you freeze? Hint: The other words in the sentence are your secret clues.

Lesson 4: Supporting Details

Every author's BIG idea must be backed up with proof—otherwise there is no reason for any reader to be convinced. Supporting details are the proof.

Lesson 5: Inferences

Inference—sometimes called "reading between the lines"—is the skill of getting information from what the author does NOT say. Sound complicated? You've probably been doing it all your life.

LESSON 1: MAIN IDEA

Imagine you are standing at one end of a bridge, looking across.

At the other end of the bridge is an author. He wants you to cross the bridge, so you can hear what he has to say. You want to cross the bridge, so you can get where you have to go.

A piece of writing is like a bridge. The main point (or main idea) of a bridge is the road on top that gets people places. The bridge must be sturdy, so it relies on supports. A piece of writing relies on supporting details. But we can easily tell a roadway on a bridge from the **pylons**, or supports. How can we tell the main idea of a piece from everything else in the passage?

One of the key clues is **placement**. A main idea sentence is often the first or last sentence in the passage. Read the example below.

> There are many reasons why live rabbits and chicks should not be given as Easter pets. First, young children are often curious about live animals and might unintentionally harm them. Second, most people do not know enough about the care of rabbits and chickens. Finally, too many of these animals are dumped at shelters when they are no longer small and cute and people are tired of them.

The author's main idea tells us her subject (live animals) and her attitude to them (don't put them in Easter baskets). Every other sentence in her paragraph tells us **why** she feels that way.

Practice Exercise 1

Read the following passage. Then decide which main idea sentence (A) or (B) you would use to finish the piece.

> First, I buckle my seatbelt. I make sure that I have secured my books, bags, and all belongings so that nothing will be thrown and startle me if I have to make a sudden stop. I turn off my cell phone. I adjust the radio to a volume that will allow me to hear any sirens I encounter on the road. I look in both my rear view mirrors. Then I turn around, take my foot off the brake, and slowly back out of my driveway.

1. Which sentence would you choose as the best thesis to complete this passage?
   (A) The steps I take at the start of my trip set the tone for a safe and successful journey.
   (B) Look out, world, I'm coming through!

Another way to find the main idea is to ask yourself, "What is the most important piece of information in this passage? What is the BIG message the author wants me to get?"

Read the following coupon.

> **Buy three (3) cans of KITTY KIBBLE**
> **Get one (1) can FREE**
> **Must be 5 oz. size or larger**
>
> **Valid at PET SAVINGS BARN**
> **and HAPPY CAT**
>
> CASHIER: COUNT IN INVENTORY   NO EXPIRATION

2. What do you think the BIG idea the retailer wants to communicate in this coupon is?
   (A) The customer should only shop at Pet Savings Barn.
   (B) With this coupon, the customer can receive a free can of cat food with a purchase of three cans.
   (C) Your cat should be 5 ounces or larger.

(A) is an important piece of information since it tells where the coupon can be redeemed. However, if you do not own a cat and do not plan to buy cat food, that information is not very useful to you! (C) is misleading. 5 ounces is a detail that tells you, the coupon holder, what size CAN you must buy to get the discount. Your cat may be any size.

Read the following excerpt from an essay, and express the main idea in your own words.

So long as mankind lived by raising crops and herding animals there was not much need for measuring small units of time. The seasons were all-important—to know when to expect the rain, the snow, the sun, the cold. Why bother with hours and minutes? Daylight time was the only important time, the only time when men could work. To measure useful time, then, was to measure the hours of the sun… Primitive societies noticed that the shadow of an upright post (or *gnomon*, from the Greek "to know") became shorter as the sun rose in the heavens, and lengthened again as the sun set. The ancient Egyptians used such a device, and we can still see one that survives from the time of Thutmose III.

—Daniel J. Boorstin, *The Discoverers*

_____

_____

The main idea of the passage is that, in ancient times, it was most useful to measure daylight hours. Did you write something similar? Discuss your answer with your classmates and teacher.

LESSON 2: SUMMARIZING

To **summarize** (say or write something in a shorter form) is a useful skill. It is also one that is often practiced in everyday life. Suppose you receive a phone call from a friend who asks you to go to the movies. You might not feel like saying, "Well, I have so much laundry to do, and there are all these reports to finish at work, what with Phyllis being on vacation, and the kids all have homework projects due tomorrow, and if I don't clean that bathroom, I won't be able to live with myself." So instead you **sum up** your reasons for declining by saying, "Well, I'm afraid I'm a little too overscheduled today."

How do we use our **summarization** skills when reading and analyzing a longer piece of writing? A good summary will include the information in the main idea sentence and major supporting details. Let's look at the following passage. The main idea and major supporting details have been highlighted.

> **Growing vegetables in the city is possible, even if you have a limited amount of space.**
>
> **First you must make sure that any area you choose has an adequate amount of light for the types of plants you wish to grow.** Tomatoes, for example, require a minimum of 6 hours of sunlight. A sunny windowsill will do if you have no backyard.
>
> **Second, do your best to keep away pests and rodents.** One squirrel can demolish your whole crop! A few yards of netting at the Home Supply store costs under $15.00 and will last the whole season. Better yet, blank CDs tied to a stick will scare away birds for free.
>
> **Third, water, water, water.** If you go away on vacation, remember to ask a friend or family member to water a few times a week for you, or be prepared to come back to a sad sight! It is easier on your garden and the water bill to water in the evening so that moisture will not **evaporate** or disappear.
>
> If you follow these steps, you may look forward to fresh salads and herbs all summer long!

What kind of summary can you write that will **incorporate**, or include, the main idea and major supporting points?

_____

_____

An example of something you might have written is:

> It is possible to have a city vegetable garden, if you remember to follow certain steps: you must give your plants enough sun, protect them from pests, and make sure they get enough water.

TIP

When summarizing long passages, look for major supporting details at the beginning of supporting paragraphs.

Practice Exercise 2

1. Read the following letter, and choose the best summary of its message.

Ms. Margie Williams
1000 Aplomado West
Salt Lake City, UT

June 6, 2011

Mr. John Francisco
FRANCISCO ELECTRONICS
300 S. Market Way
Sandy, UT

Dear Mr. Francisco:

I am writing to you to complain about the dishwasher I purchased from your downtown store in February and the service I received afterwards.

On February 14th my husband and I purchased a stainless steel heavy duty T-9000 to be installed in our kitchen on February 21st. We paid in full and received our rebate information.

On February 21st, after waiting at home for half the day, I received a call that the delivery would be rescheduled until the next day. When I asked why, I was informed that the speaker was "just the delivery guy." Being unable to reach anyone at the downtown store, I left a message.

When the machine arrived the next day, it had a deep scratch on one side. I again called the store. I was able to reach a Mr. Mike Ryan. Mr. Ryan informed me that scratches were the responsibility of the delivery department, and that since the scratches would be hidden by the counter I should not be upset.

Since the machine has been installed, it has needed repair three times. I enclose copies of the repair bills. I was told at the downtown store that two of the bills would not be covered under the warranty, and that I had loaded the dishwasher improperly.

Mr. Francisco, I have been a loyal customer for ten years. I am coming to you because I believe you should know how loyal customers are being treated at your biggest store. Can you help me?

Sincerely,
Margie Williams

(A) Ms. Williams has just about had it, and if she has to come down to that store and tell them what's what, they are going to rue the day they were ever born. Ms. Williams was in sales herself and knows a thing or two about good salesmanship. One thing she can tell you; it won't take much more of this to send her screaming round the bend.

(B) Once Ms. Williams sent her letter, a response came almost immediately. Mr. Francisco not only sent her a personal apology, he insisted that the manager of the downtown store write one as well. Her dishwasher was replaced with a brand-new T-9000 model free of charge, and Ms. Williams received a 20% coupon with free delivery for any item in the store.

(C) Ms. Williams is not happy about the dishwasher or treatment she has received from Francisco Electronic's downtown store. The machine was late, scratched, and unreliable. The staff has been unhelpful and rude. Ms. Williams has been a loyal customer, but now she is unhappy and would like Mr. Francisco to do something about the bad service and merchandise Ms. Williams has been getting.

LESSON 3: CONTEXT CLUES

Encountering words that you do not know when you are reading or studying is more than a possibility—it is a certainty. Unless you read the same three books over and over, you will absolutely discover new words your entire life.

Think what would happen if you did not! How would you ever learn any new vocabulary?

When you were in school and found a new word, your teacher probably told you to look it up in the dictionary. You may not always have a dictionary handy when you are studying or taking a test. Another way you can learn the meaning of words is through **context clues**.

Using context clues means looking at the words that you do know in the sentence to help you with the word or words you don't. Often the context clue, or definition, will immediately follow the new vocabulary word.

A **garrulous**, or too talkative, guest can spoil an otherwise pleasant dinner.

Since garrulous means "too talkative," it is possible to fully understand the meaning of the above sentence using clues from the surrounding words.

Practice Exercise 3

Clues can also be found in sentences surrounding new vocabulary words. **Read the following sentences and decide on the best meaning for tyro:**

At the start of Tuesday's game, Malcolm was a **tyro** bowler. He had never touched a bowling ball in his life.

1. Tyro means:
   (A) Uninterested
   (B) Professional
   (C) Inexperienced

Malcolm has never bowled before. He cannot, therefore, be a professional bowler. However, he is not uninterested since he is participating in a game on Tuesday.

2. What is the best meaning for the word **inconceivable** in the following sentence?

   The idea that Regina had lost the promotion was **inconceivable** to her. She simply couldn't understand how it had happened.

   (A) Not able to be understood
   (B) Impossible
   (C) Unfair

Practice Exercise 4

Match the word in bold in the sentence with the correct definition.

_____1. The house you are looking for is in a **rural** area; it is surrounded by farms.

_____2. My brother has always been a **gregarious** person. He loves to be around other people.

_____3. The dog approached the food **warily**, as if he thought it was dangerous.

_____4. The speaker's tone was **condescending**; it seemed to us that she thought she was more important than her audience.

_____5. The President did not allow the bill to pass; he **vetoed** it.

_____6. We **designated**, or chose, Tanya to keep the minutes for the meeting.

_____7. If you are not in **compliance** with your company's policies, you may risk receiving a warning. Employees should follow company rules at all times.

_____8. Uncle James was so **benevolent**, so generous, and good-hearted, that he could never say no to any of us.

(A) To be in agreement with a group or organization; to cooperate

(B) In the country; outside of city areas

(C) To forbid; to cancel

(D) With great caution; carefully

(E) Having kindly feelings; expressing good intentions

(F) Thinking or acting as if one is superior; implying others are not on one's level

(G) Friendly; outgoing

(H) To make a choice; to determine

Practice Exercise 5

Now try using your context clue-finding skills in a short passage.

Dear Valued Customer,

Congratulations on receiving your new Fashion Maven store card! This card may be used at any of the thirty-six Fashion Maven locations in your city. A statement will be mailed to you each month. Since you have provided us with an email address, a reminder will also appear monthly in your email inbox.

Please note that your payment due date is the 4th of each month. Accounts that are over-due more than thirty (30) days will be assessed a late fee of $25.00. Delinquent accounts of ninety (90) days or more may be referred to an outside agency for collection purposes.

Your card will become effective immediately upon calling the number on the front of the card to activate it.

Welcome to the Fashion Maven Family!

TIP

Look BEFORE and AFTER the new word for clues to its meaning.

1. What is the best definition of the word **delinquent** in the above passage?
    (A) Not very late
    (B) More than 90 days late
    (C) More than 30 but less than 120 days late
    (D) Accounts that are overcharged
    (E) Less than 90 days late

LESSON 4: SUPPORTING DETAILS

Remember our bridge in Lesson 1?

We used this image to imagine the main idea as a road to travel from one side of the bridge to the other. The main idea in the first passage we read was *There are many reasons why live rabbits and chicks should not be given as Easter pets*. This sentence would be the roadway of our writing bridge:

> There are many reasons why live rabbits and chicks should not be given as Easter pets.

Let's look at the passage again:

> There are many reasons why live rabbits and chicks should not be given as Easter pets. First, young children are often curious about live animals and might unintentionally harm them. Second, most people do not know enough about the care of rabbits and chickens. Finally, too many of these animals are dumped at shelters when they are no longer small and cute, and people are tired of them.

We have identified the main idea. How do we classify the rest of the information in the passage?

It is support. Look at the picture of the bridge again. Your road would not be very secure without the supports, or **pylons**, underneath, would it? In the same way, a good main idea needs strong supporting details to convince readers of its point. Let's add pylons to our writing bridge.

There are many reasons why live rabbits and chicks should not be given as Easter pets.

First	Second	Third
Young Children Might Harm	People Don't Understand Care	Pets Left at Shelters

Most people know the value of supporting details in conversation—especially when they are trying to win arguments! Imagine the following situation. Two roommates are discussing household chores. One roommate says to the second, "You don't do enough to help out around here." The second roommate says, "Oh really! What do you mean by that?" List some examples that roommate might come up with to prove his point.

_____

_____

_____

If you, like most people, have lived with a roommate, friend, or family member, you could probably think of many examples of things that might bother roommate 1!

> Leaving dirty dishes in the sink
> Forgetting to turn off lights
> Never cleaning the bathroom
> Leaving common areas messy

Good supporting details help a writer prove his or her point and also avoid falling into repetition or wandering off the topic. Let's look at two coworkers sharing a project. Suppose, instead of coming up with examples like roommate 1, coworker 1 says, "Well, I don't like the way you never help; it's just not fair that you never pitch in. I mean, I'm always stuck doing all the work. It wouldn't hurt you to lend a hand once in a while. You just won't do anything. I mean…" Coworker 1 can go on like this for hours, and coworker 2 can still say, "But you haven't given me a single example" and wander away to look for leftover cake in the break room. Coworker 1 might also say, "You know, it bothers me that you never help with this project. It reminds me of the way you acted at the company picnic in 2005, when everyone else was cooking and you just sat there playing with the radio." In this second example, coworker 1 has gone off topic. He has provided no **relevant** examples to prove his point. The example that is mentioned is years old and has nothing to do with the situation at hand.

Practice Exercise 6

When reading a passage, look for relevant, specific details that support an author's main idea. In the exercise below, two of the four sentences **adequately**, or successfully, support the main idea; two do not.

1. ABC Company requires all prospective new employees to follow certain procedures.
   (A) You will be scheduled to take a drug test at the NE clinic at Front and Bainbridge.
   (B) Benefits do not become active until after 90 days of employment.
   (C) You must bring a government issued photo I.D. with you on your first day of work.
   (D) ABC Company is an EOE employer.

In a passage, you will usually find both **major** and **minor** supporting details. Major support sentences often appear first in a paragraph. Let's look at the following paragraph from an email from an insurance company.

It is very important that you gather all information needed to process your claim before you call us. The information your claim's adjuster will need is:

   (A) Your name and address
   (B) Your password
   (C) Your claim number
   (D) The date of the accident
   (E) Whether a police report was filed

Failure to provide any of the above information at the time of your call may result in a delay in your claim being processed.

It is very important that you gather all information needed to process your claim before you call us is the major supporting detail. Everything else in the paragraph **expands on** or gives more information about that first sentence.

VOCABULARY

Major: larger or more important.

Minor: smaller or less important.

VOCABULARY

Vivid: strong and intense; something that makes an impression.

Have you ever heard the phrase "less is more"? That is not true when it comes to good writing. The more **vivid**, realistic, and exciting the author's support is, the more clearly he or she communicates. Read the following passage about the author's opinion of modern wedding costs.

60 billion dollars—that's the amount of revenue the U.S. wedding industry was responsible for in 2011. The average cost of a wedding these days comes in at a little over $27,000. Entire T.V. series are dedicated to pitting brides against each other to win a dream wedding or watching them agonize over the "perfect" dress. The average wedding dress cost is estimated at around $1,000—a surprisingly low figure to those of us who have watched T.V. brides and their closest friends compare the $3,000 satin to the $10,000 lace. Is it any wonder that a newlywed couple's biggest asset is often their whopping credit card balance? This madness needs to stop.

VOCABULARY

Statistics: a science that collects large amounts of information. Statisticians often compare numerical information to better understand a situation. (Example: 2% of a town's workforce is out of work in 2000. 8% are out of work in 2010. Conclusion: unemployment is getting worse.)

The author's main idea—that weddings have become unreasonably expensive—is backed up by the examples and **statistics** she quotes in her story.

It is important to note that it is perfectly possible to disagree with a well-supported main idea. It could be argued that a special event, such as a wedding, is worth every bit of money that the participants spend. However, if another writer did make this point, he or she would need strong supporting details in return.

Compare the following two passages.

PASSAGE 1

Perry wasn't planning to go anywhere for vacation. First, he had no money. And what's the point of going on vacation if you can't spend a little? Last year, when he was making good money, he went to Mexico and had a great time. He didn't like to go away and have to watch expenses all the time. Second, he didn't like having to deal with all those airline regulations. And finally, his wife's parents were having health problems, and she wanted to be near them. Come to think of it, none of them had been doing too well health-wise, this year. He himself had had the flu twice. He had never heard of anyone getting the flu twice in one year.

PASSAGE 2

Perry wasn't planning to go anywhere for vacation. First, he had no money. In the last 6 months, his hours had been severely cut at work. His wife had been laid off 3 weeks ago. They were still paying off a tax bill, and the house was going to need electrical work. Second, he didn't like having to deal with all those airline regulations. He hated having to wrap things in plastic bags and buy special sizes of shampoo and toothpaste. He was always afraid that he would pack something forbidden by mistake and be whisked off to jail by airport security. And finally, his wife's parents were having health problems, and she wanted to be near them. Her father had been to the hospital twice over the winter and was in a wheelchair. Her mother sometimes needed monitoring to take her medications correctly. All in all, Perry felt more comfortable staying home.

Which passage is better supported and why?

_____

_____

_____

_____

(B) is the better supported paragraph. (A) wanders off topic from this year's vacation to last year's, and from Perry's in-laws' health to his own health. His complaint about airport regulations has no examples at all! Paragraph (B) has several detailed examples for each major support point.

LESSON 5: INFERENCES

What is the difference between **inferring** and **implying**? These two things often happen together. To imply means to communicate something without saying it directly. For example, we could say, "If Josh enters that dance contest, everyone else might as well go home; the judges will just hand the trophy right over to him." What are we **implying** about Josh's abilities?

(A)   Josh likes to dance.
(B)   Josh is an excellent dancer.
(C)   Nobody else wants to show up for the contest.

If we are so sure that Josh will win the trophy, that means we think that (B) *Josh is an excellent dancer*. If you picked option (B), then you **inferred** correctly. To infer means to understand something that is not stated directly.

Practice Exercise 7

What is an **inference** that you can make from the following passage?

Cindi handed her report card to her father. He opened it and read it carefully. After a minute or two, a big smile lit up his face. He put down the card, found his wallet, took out a five-dollar bill, and handed it to Cindi.

"Congratulations, kid," he said. "And this weekend Mom and I are taking you to the movies."

1. What can you infer about the grades on Cindi's report card?
   (A) She did well, but not as well as last time.
   (B) Some of her grades were a little disappointing, but she will do better.
   (C) She did well in all her classes.

2. What are some of the key words or phrases from the passage that you used to support your answer?

   _____

   _____

   _____

   _____

TIP

Use key words and phrases to "read between the lines."

In the following excerpt from a story, the author uses key words and phrases to establish a **setting** (scene where the story takes place). Can you figure out where these people are?

All night, Maria had tossed in her berth as she felt the waves slap the side of their stateroom. The movement of the sea made her feel slightly ill. She felt homesick for the feel of dry land beneath her feet.

In the morning she heard her sister get up. She could smell the salt air as Lourdes opened the porthole.

"What do you see?" Maria asked, throwing the covers back.

"Nothing but water."

3. Maria and her sister are:
   (A) On a ship crossing the ocean
   (B) On a ship crossing a large lake
   (C) In a hotel next to the beach

Maria smells salt water, and the passage mentions "the sea." Other clues are the words "stateroom" and "berth." A stateroom is the name for a bedroom on board a ship, and a berth is the name for a bed. The constant motion of the sisters' stateroom is another clue that they are not on dry land.

END-OF-CHAPTER QUESTIONS

Questions 1 through 4 are based on the following passage.

What Is Expected from These Students?

The following is an excerpt from a business school student handbook.

> Students are required to turn all cell phones to off or set to vibrate while in class. A student may leave class to take a call if he or she has a personal emergency. An emergency is defined as a situation that concerns the health or safety of the student, student's child(ren), or close family members. A student may not use a cell phone to talk or text during class for any reason.
>
> All students will be required to remove hats, head gear (including hoodies), and sunglasses as soon as they enter the school building. Students who refuse to comply with this rule will be sent home and receive an unexcused absence for the day. After three violations of the hat/headgear policy, a student may be placed on academic probation, and a school administrator will call a meeting with the student's parent(s) or guardian(s). Students who are required to wear any of the above items for medical or religious reasons should speak to administration in advance to receive individual exemptions.

1. Which situation can you infer is NOT considered a personal emergency?
   (A) Your child is sick at daycare.
   (B) There is a gas leak in your apartment building.
   (C) A family member has been hospitalized.
   (D) Your friend wants to borrow your car.

2. In the context of the passage, what is the best definition of the word "violations?"
   (A) Exceptions
   (B) Examples of cooperation
   (C) Examples of disobedience
   (D) Attempts to protest

3. In which section of the handbook would you expect to find these two paragraphs?
   (A) Rules and Regulations
   (B) Academic Goals
   (C) School Calendar
   (D) Grievance Procedures

4. Which statement presents the best summary of the above passage?
   (A) No cell phone usage is permitted in class. In addition, all head gear must be removed upon entrance to the building. Students are expected to adhere to the rules. Exceptions may be discussed with Administration.
   (B) All head gear must be removed upon entrance to the building. Students who violate this rule may be suspended. Exceptions may be discussed with Administration.
   (C) Students who refuse to comply with the dress code or cell phone policy may be sent home for the day.
   (D) All unauthorized cell phones and head gear will be confiscated and returned at the end of the day.

Questions 5 through 7 are based on the following article.

Sneaky Bank Fees

Call it the bank-fee blues—that testy tune you sing when you discover that your "free" bank account comes with a lot of hidden charges: $2 for using another bank's ATM, $7 for online banking, $15 for accepting a wire transfer. "When you add up all the legal ATM, debit and penalty overdraft fees, free checking is not really free," says Ed Mierzwinski, consumer program director for the U.S. Public Interest Research Group.

Indeed, banking has changed a lot since the days when tellers gave away toasters for opening an account. To a bank, a fee is not merely something to be imposed as a punishment for, say, overdrawing your account, it's a way to fatten its bottom line. Banks took in $36 billion in such charges in 2006 alone. "Given the fact that banks are hemorrhaging money right now, it's not likely that these fees are going to go away anytime soon," says John Ulzheimer, president of consumer education for Credit.com.

But if you know your bank's rules and can manage your money, it's relatively easy to steer clear of these charges. To start, assess your financial habits. Are you a frequent debit-card user, or a cash-and-carry shopper who relies on ATMs? Is your preferred method of payment your credit card? Perhaps you're a combination of the above. Once you've determined your banking personality, you can keep bank fees from burning a hole in your pocket.

—Caroline E. Mayer, *Ladies' Home Journal,* **Sneaky Bank Fees,** May 2009

5. The phrase "banks are hemorrhaging money" in the second paragraph conveys what image to the reader?
   (A) Banks are circulating infected money.
   (B) Banks are losing money as an injured person loses blood.
   (C) Banks are giving away a lot of money to their customers right now.
   (D) A lot of banks are being robbed.

6. What examples does the author give of "hidden charges?"
   (A) Debit and credit cards
   (B) Toasters
   (C) ATM, online banking, and wire transfer fees
   (D) Mortgage and home equity loan fees

7. Which sentence below best summarizes this article?
   (A) It doesn't matter what you do, bank fees will get you every time.
   (B) If you choose your bank carefully and understand your own banking style, you can avoid paying unnecessary fees.
   (C) Paying by debit card only and not using your credit card will keep bank fees down.
   (D) The best way to avoid high bank fees is to keep a large balance in your account at all times.

Questions 8 through 11 are based on the following excerpt.

What Kind of Impression Is the Applicant Making?

MS, HANEY: Good morning, Mr. Anderson. I understand you have applied for the customer service supervisor position.

(*Mr. Anderson's cell phone rings. He pulls the phone out of his pocket.*)

MR. ANDERSON: (*To Ms. Haney*): Hold on a sec. (*Into the phone*). What is it? Mm-hm. I told you…no, I TOLD you…I gotta call you back. (*He replaces the phone in his pocket.*) Sorry.

MS. HANEY: Mr. Anderson, do you have a copy of your resumé?

MR. ANDERSON: Yes, here it is. (*He hands Ms. Haney a piece of paper.*)

INTERVIEWER: And have you finished filling out the application?

MR. ANDERSON: Yes, I have. (*His cell phone rings again. He hands Ms. Haney an application. She reads this during Mr. Anderson's phone conversation.*)

MR. ANDERSON (*into phone*): Can you please stop calling me? I'm trying to do something important. I don't know. I don't KNOW. Maybe 'bout twenty minutes. (*He puts the phone away, grins, and rolls his eyes at Ms. Haney.*)

MS. HANEY: Mr. Anderson, is it possible for you to turn off your phone while we speak?

MR. ANDERSON: Well, uh. You see I might have an emergency. I like to keep all my bases covered.

MS. HANEY: I see. I can't help but notice that you have listed only one reference here—an uncle. Do you have professional references?

MR. ANDERSON: Aw, not with me, but my uncle's good. He knows me. You can call him now if you want to.

8. What is the most likely relationship between Ms. Haney and Mr. Anderson?
   (A) Mr. Anderson is Ms. Haney's supervisor.
   (B) Ms. Haney is issuing a verbal warning to her employee, Mr. Anderson.
   (C) They are friends.
   (D) Ms. Haney is interviewing Mr. Anderson for a job at her company.

9. Which of the following words best describes Mr. Anderson's behavior?

(A) Talented

(B) Frightening

(C) Unprofessional

(D) Charming

10. What is the best statement of the main idea of the above passage?

(A) It's so hard to remember what you're supposed to do in an interview.

(B) Mr. Anderson really shouldn't be a supervisor.

(C) Mr. Anderson will probably not get this job.

(D) Ms. Haney is trying to interview Mr. Anderson, who keeps getting distracted.

11. Which of the following examples of Mr. Anderson's actions is considered professional behavior during an interview?

(A) He takes several calls on his cell phone.

(B) He brings a copy of his resumé.

(C) He does not turn off his cell phone when asked.

(D) He lists a single reference from a family member.

Questions 12 through 15 are based on the following passage.

How Does This Couple Spend Valentine's Day?

There is a Valentine's Day dance at the Fire Hall. Valentine's Day comes but once a year. But it is a windy, rainy night, and both the umbrellas have gone missing.

–What time is it?

–I can't see the clock.

–What time was it when you looked last time?

–Turn on the T.V.

–What good will that do?

–We can see if *Wheel of Fortune* is over yet.

–Look, it's *The Honeymooners*.

–The Nortons' apartment always looks so much better than the Kramdens'.

–Want to play cards?

–Can we play cribbage?

–Let's play gin.

–You always win at gin.

–Quarter a point. I'll start the pot.

–I don't have any quarters. I used them all in the parking meter today.

–You'd better stop parking on the street. You're gonna get broken into.

–There's nothing in my car worth stealing. I'm gonna have some pie.

–We ate all the pie. I ate it at lunch.

–All of it?

–Why? Do I look fatter?

–Let's play cards.

–There's pierogies in the freezer.

–Nobody wants pierogies at ten o'clock at night.

–It's your deal.

–Where's the board?

–I thought we were playing gin.

–Let's play cribbage.

–Fifteen for two; fifteen for four; pair for six; and three for the run of three.

–Do you love me?

–I want some coffee.

–But do you love me?

–Of course I love you.

They are happy. They don't just think they are happy, they really are. Everyone is happy sometimes. Someday, in the blink of an eye, the Earth will be gone. The Sun will implode, stars will burn themselves away, space will vanish.

But not today.

12. What is the main idea of the situation in the excerpt above?
   (A) Two friends are going to a Valentine's Day dance.
   (B) A happy couple is having a comfortable evening at home.
   (C) A couple is competing in a cribbage tournament.
   (D) A wife is upset because her husband never takes her anywhere.

13. Most of this passage details a conversation between two people. However, neither person is identified, and speeches are not assigned. How does the author imply that the couple takes turns speaking?
   (A) The speeches are short.
   (B) It would be easier if each speech were color coded.
   (C) The speakers discuss several activities before they play cribbage.
   (D) Each speech begins on a new line and is preceded by a dash.

14. The couple has thought about going to the Valentine's Day dance but decided staying home was preferable. What details in the passage support this conclusion?
   (A) One of the speakers is worried about gaining weight.
   (B) The opening paragraph states that the dance is a special event, but the weather is "windy" and "rainy." The couple has tried to locate their umbrellas but cannot find them.
   (C) They start to play cards but finally decide to play cribbage.
   (D) They really had a better time at home than they could have had at the dance.

15. How would you summarize the above excerpt?
   (A) A couple considers attending a dance but decides to spend a quiet evening at home.
   (B) The couple thinks they are happy, but they really aren't.
   (C) This couple will probably spend next Valentine's Day at home as well.
   (D) A couple decides that ten o'clock is too late to cook.

CHAPTER 22 ANSWER EXPLANATIONS

Lesson 1: Main Idea

PRACTICE EXERCISE 1 (PAGE 690)

1. **(A)** In this case, (A) is the better choice. All the steps the driver is taking are safety precautions.
2. **(B)** You should have chosen answer (B). The coupon is offering a free can of cat food.

Lesson 2: Summarizing

PRACTICE EXERCISE 2 (PAGE 693)

1. **(C)** Option (A) is a good approximation, or guess, of what Ms. Williams might be feeling; Option (B) is certainly what she (and probably we!) would like to see happen. But (C) summarizes the information as Ms. Williams states it in her letter.

Lesson 3: Context Clues

PRACTICE EXERCISE 3 (PAGE 694)

1. **(C)**
2. **(A)** Hopefully you picked (A), Not able to be understood. It is not impossible that Regina lost the promotion because it happened. It might be unfair, but the words "couldn't understand" in the second sentence let you know that (C) is not the correct answer.

PRACTICE EXERCISE 4 (PAGE 695)

1. B
2. G
3. D
4. F
5. C
6. H
7. A
8. E

PRACTICE EXERCISE 5 (PAGE 695)

1. **(B)** The word occurs in a paragraph that defines due dates and outlines penalties for lateness. The penalty for 30 days is stated in the sentence before. Delinquency is defined in the next sentence as being 90 or more days late with payment.

Lesson 4: Supporting Details

PRACTICE EXERCISE 6 (PAGE 697)

1. Sentences (A) and (C) provide specific examples of requirements for prospective, or new, employees at ABC. Sentence (B) presents the benefits schedule; sentence (D) lists a responsibility of the employers.

Lesson 5: Inferences

PRACTICE EXERCISE 7 (PAGE 700)

1. **(C)** Hopefully you picked (C), She did well in all her classes.
2. Some key phrases that support this are Cindi's father's "big smile," the "five-dollar bill" he gives her from his "wallet," the word "congratulations," and the promise of a trip to "the movies."
3. **(A)** On a ship crossing the ocean is the most logical answer.

End-of-Chapter Questions (Page 701)

1. **(D)** This is the only answer choice that is not a personal emergency for you. It may not even be an emergency for your friend. There may be other ways he can get to his destination. All the other situations require immediate action on your part.
2. **(C)** Students who violate, or do not follow the rules, are displaying (C) *examples of disobedience.* The violation of rules is a negative act and has negative consequences (the students are suspended). Option (C) is the only negative choice available. A violation is not an exception (A), as students needing exceptions to the policy are told to speak to the administration. Examples of cooperation (B) would be students who remove their hats and turn off their cell phones. Attempts to protest the school's policy are not prohibited (D).
3. **(A)** These paragraphs would appear in (A) *Rules and Regulations.* (B) There is no mention of the subjects the students study. (C) There are no dates or times. (D) A grievance procedure outlines the steps a student takes if he or she has been discriminated against or otherwise wronged; that does not apply here.
4. **(A)** is the best summary. (B) is incomplete. It does not address cell phone usage. (C) is too broad and does not give enough information. (D) is not supported by the passage.
5. **(B)** *Banks are losing money as an injured person loses blood.* John Ulzheimer states that because banks are losing so much money, they need our fees. They are unlikely to lower or cancel these fees. Because the article is about personal finance, not health risks, (A) is not correct. (C) is incorrect since the sentence indicates that customer fees make up for the hemorrhaging money—therefore, the bank's money is not being given to its customers. (D) The article is not about bank security.
6. **(C)** Immediately after the words "hidden charges" in the first paragraph, the author lists the examples of *ATM, online banking, and wire transfer fees.* She also includes dollar amounts with her examples.
7. **(B)** Mayer's article is intended to help the reader save money by offering tips on how to "know your bank's rules" and "assess your financial habits." (A) is an opinion. (C) and (D) are not supported by the passage.
8. **(D)** Mr. Anderson fills out an application and gives a resumé to Ms. Haney; these things are normally done during a job interview and show that he has not worked for this company before. We can infer that Ms. Haney and Mr. Anderson are not friends since she does not call him by his first name.
9. **(C)** Examples of unprofessional behavior are taking personal calls, inappropriate body language (rolling eyes), and incompletely filling out the application. There are no examples to support the other choices listed.
10. **(D)** (A) and (B) are opinions. (C) is a prediction.

11. **(B)** It is always a good idea to bring an extra resumé to an interview, even if you think the interviewer already has a copy. None of the other choices are examples of appropriate job interview behavior.

12. **(B)** (A) is not correct; the passage states several reasons why the couple is not at the dance (bad weather, umbrellas lost). (C) The couple plays cribbage only part of the evening. There are no other competitors, as there would be in a tournament. (D) Neither speaker says anything about the dance or wanting to be out for the evening.

13. **(D)** Each speech begins on a new line and is preceded by a dash. (A) The length or shortness of a speech does not help to identify the speaker. (B) is an opinion. (C) is a summary of the action.

14. **(B)** The couple has tried to locate their umbrellas but cannot find them. (A) is true but unrelated to the couple's plans for the evening. (C) is a summary of part of the action of the passage. (D) is an opinion.

15. **(A)** (B) is an opinion. (C) is a prediction. (D) is a detail from the passage.

Nonfiction

■■■■■■■■■■■■■■■■■■■■■■■■■■■■■■■■■■■

> "Truth is stranger than fiction."
> —Mark Twain

When Mark Twain, the author of *Tom Sawyer* and *Huckleberry Finn*, wrote the words above, he had a specific point to make. When writing fiction—stories, plays, novels—a writer must make the action believable, or the reader will lose interest. If you were watching a medical drama on T.V., would it surprise you to see a transplant patient get up off the operating table, get herself a drink of water, and lie back down? You might think "That's ridiculous!," and you would be right. Such things rarely or never happen in real life.

Nonfiction has no such restrictions. If you were to read an article (in a newspaper or medical journal) about a patient waking up and getting off the operating table, you would probably think, "That's amazing!" Writers of nonfiction do not have to worry if their subjects are probable—only that they are true or **factual**.

You have probably written a good deal of nonfiction yourself. Whenever you write a memo, a letter, or a note, you are writing nonfiction. Do you write emails and texts? That is nonfiction writing.

HOW THIS CHAPTER IS ORGANIZED

Lesson 1: Biography and Autobiography

Biographies of great men and women can be fascinating reads; autobiographies, written by people about themselves, often contain insights for our own lives.

Lesson 2: Informational Science Articles

Science articles require reading comprehension skills with special attention to vocabulary definition in context.

Lesson 3: Memos and Letters

Memos and letters can provide written records of commercial and business transactions. It is important that they are clear and not open to **misinterpretation**.

Lesson 4: Newspaper Articles and Editorials

Keeping informed about current events requires comprehension, critical thinking skills, and decision-making skills.

VOCABULARY

Constitutes: makes, creates, or establishes.

It is said that those who do not know history are doomed to repeat it. Documents from the past continue to be relevant today.

LESSON 1: BIOGRAPHY AND AUTOBIOGRAPHY

Biographies can be written about anyone, but they are usually written about people who have made great contributions to society. Biographies normally follow a **chronological**, or time, sequence: they start when the subject is born and continue through his or her life up to death or the present day. Biographies are expected to be as accurate as possible in regard to important times, dates, and places in a subject's life. The following sentences contain facts you should expect to find in any good biography about these famous people.

- Pierre Trudeau was Prime Minister of Canada from 1968 to 1979.
- Harriet Tubman, American abolitionist, escaped to freedom in 1849.
- Mohandas (Mahatma) Gandhi died on January 30, 1948.

Practice Exercise 1

A good biography also strives to give us a picture of the personality of its subject, not just facts and dates. The following is an excerpt from a biography of an artist.

> At T. Hugo Weldon's funeral, an amazing thing happened. Crowds showed up that were customary, so the funeral director said, for the very young or extremely famous. T. Hugo had never won fame, but he seemed to have won the hearts of everyone he came in touch with. Not only family but employees and business acquaintances sat and sobbed.

1. What kind of image do you get of T. Hugo, the subject of the passage? What kind of adjectives might you use to describe him?

   _____

Autobiography generally follows the same rules as biography, except that the subject tells his or her own story. Notice how the narrator of the following passage uses "I" and "me." This is one of the signs of autobiography:

> "It doesn't do any good to sulk," says Mother in a reasonable tone. Mother is always reasonable. Mother is sane, reasonable, beautiful, intelligent, witty and insightful. I'm a jerk. Forever and ever, amen.
>
> I've been a jerk for as long as I can remember. If you ask me for examples, as Mother often patiently does, it's really easier to point at my life *tout ensemble,* so to speak, and ask you to pick out any spot where I'm not engaged in being a jerk.
>
> Mother always goes for the year I volunteered as a reader at the hospice. But that doesn't count because I only volunteered to get close to Randy Goldstein, who was assigned to another floor already. The only one who ever talked to me was the old, fat woman who changed the bedpans. And I wasn't a very good reader anyway from always holding my breath because of the funny smell in there. So I don't believe the hospice is such a shining moment in my history.
>
> —Catherine Bristow, *My Strange and Terrible Malady*

2. Who is the most likely speaker in the above passage?
   (A) A middle-aged woman
   (B) A mother with two children
   (C) A young child
   (D) A teenaged girl

WRITING EXERCISE

Write your own autobiography! Start with the basic facts of your life—where you were born, what you have accomplished, what barriers you have overcome. Fill in as much or as little detail as you like. Is there an interesting story from your past you want to make sure is not forgotten? Write it down!

Remember that you, unlike the famous subjects of most biographies, have not finished living your story yet. Add a paragraph or two predicting where you intend to go in the future!

Question 3 is based on the following passage from Frederick Douglass, The Narrative of the Life of Frederick Douglass.

I have been frequently asked how I felt when I found myself in a free State. I have never been able to answer the question with any satisfaction to myself. It was a moment of the highest excitement I ever experienced. I suppose I felt as one may imagine the unarmed mariner to feel when he is rescued by a friendly man-of-war from the pursuit of a pirate. In writing to a dear friend, immediately after my arrival at New York, I said I felt like one who had escaped a den of hungry lions. This state of mind, however, very soon subsided; and I was again seized with a feeling of great insecurity and loneliness. I was yet liable to be taken back and subjected to all the tortures of slavery…It was a most painful situation; and, to understand it, one must needs experience it, or imagine himself in similar circumstances. Let him be a fugitive slave in a strange land—a land given up to be the hunting-ground for slaveholders—whose inhabitants are legalized kidnappers—where he is every moment subjected to the terrible liability of being seized upon by his fellow men, as the hideous crocodile seizes upon his prey!

3. Douglass uses **figurative** language (comparisons or exaggerations) several times to explain his feelings on reaching the free state of New York. When he writes "the hideous crocodile seizes upon his prey," what real life situation is he afraid of?
   (A) He is afraid of being pursued by pirates again.
   (B) He is afraid of being kidnapped and transported back to the southern slave states.
   (C) He owes money in New York, since he has not been able to find a job yet.
   (D) He is afraid that southern slaveholders will send someone to kill him.

Practice Exercise 2

Match the terms on the left with the correct definitions on the right.

_____ 1. Genre   (A) Language using exaggerations or comparisons

_____ 2. Chronological   (B) In time order

_____ 3. Hallmark   (C) Story of a person's life written by that person

_____ 4. Autobiography   (D) Type of literature

_____ 5. Biography   (E) Special indication or characteristic

_____ 6. Figurative   (F) Story of a person's life written by a different person

LESSON 2: INFORMATIONAL SCIENCE ARTICLES

One type of nonfiction passage you may be called on to read and analyze is the scientific article. This kind of article gives information about basic scientific principles, historical discoveries, or important updates. Science passages on your test will fall into three general categories:

1. **LIFE SCIENCES**—Life science is a category that covers all living things.

   Examples: An article on giraffes by a **zoologist** (a scientist who studies animals)

   An article on bacterial reproduction by a **microbiologist** (a scientist who studies very small living things)

2. **PHYSICAL SCIENCE**—Physical science covers the actions of non-living things.

   Examples: An article on the chemical reaction of baking soda and hydrogen peroxide

   An article on the **velocity** (speed in a certain direction) of trains going around curves

3. **EARTH AND SPACE SCIENCE**—Earth and Space Science discusses the relationships and behavior of planets, stars, and other celestial bodies (bodies in space).

   Example: An article on the properties of black holes

   An article on the effect of sunspots on the Earth's atmosphere

Practice Exercise 3

Read the short article below and answer questions 1 through 3.

Classification is a system that imposes order and organization by creating groups and categories. Scientists use classification to structure living beings; nature does not. The difference can cause friction and confusion when a creature does not fall neatly into one of the categories in a system that is meant to **encompass**, or include, all organisms.

Mammals are defined as warm-blooded animals (they regulate their own body temperatures). Mammals have hair or fur; they give birth to live babies rather than lay eggs; and they nurse their babies with milk.

However, consider the platypus. The duck-billed platypus is classified as a mammal. It has fur but, as its name implies, also has a bill like a duck. The mother platypus lays eggs like a bird or a reptile but nurses her babies after they hatch. Scientists have two choices when faced with a creature like the platypus. If the creature is unique enough—quite unlike any other creature—they may create a new category. If not, scientists must simply decide which group of living things the new organism is most like and put it in that classification. Hence, science winds up with a mammal that looks like it is about to quack.

1. What is the main idea of the passage?
   (A) Scientists like to classify things.
   (B) Not all creatures on Earth fall neatly into categories.
   (C) The platypus is a weird animal.
   (D) Classification really doesn't work very well as a system.

2. Which of the following is NOT characteristic of mammals?
   (A) They nurse their young.
   (B) They are warm-blooded.
   (C) They give birth to live babies.
   (D) They have feathers.

3. Which of the following characteristics is one of the reasons that platypuses (or platypi) have been categorized as mammals?
   (A) They have claws.
   (B) They are warm-blooded.
   (C) They lay eggs.
   (D) They can swim.

An informational science article about human activity often contains healthy lifestyle advice. For purposes of your own health and well-being, you should always consult your doctor rather than follow directions from a passage on a test. For the purpose of passing the test, however, go with the facts in the passage! This is not as contradictory as it sounds. Health suggestions in a science article about smoking, for example, will have been carefully researched. However, the author does not know *you*. His or her suggestions are general, and only your doctor knows what is right for your particular situation.

Practice Exercise 4

Read the following passage and answer questions 1 through 3.

There are several situations in which a low-acid diet might be recommended to a patient. One of these is when the patient is experiencing bladder discomfort—sudden urges to go, a feeling of constant pressure, or frequent urination. Another is when a patient has severe heartburn or GERD (gastrointestinal reflux disease).

Many high-acid foods are common fruits and vegetables. The tomato, for example, is integral to many recipes, both in its raw form and in tomato sauces and pastes. It also forms the basis for many popular condiments, such as ketchup, barbecue sauce, and salad dressings. Lemons, another high-acid food, are **ubiquitous**. They are everywhere—in beverages, desserts, and main dishes—a person could serve an entire four-course meal with lemon flavoring in every dish!

Even so, reducing acid in your diet is not impossible. Some suggestions are:

1. **Read ingredients.** Many processed foods add citric acid (the acid in lemons and oranges) for taste. It is even possible to find citric acid in the breading of some frozen fish!

2. **Substitute.** If you love pasta, use creamy Alfredo sauce instead of tomato-y marinara. Drink your water flavored with cucumber rather than lemon or lime.

3. **Choose low-acid varieties.** Dark roast coffee, for instance, is lower in acidity than other types.

4. **Learn your triggers.** Many people react more to some acidic foods than they do to others. Learn which foods are best for you to avoid.

Eating low-acid does not mean having to eat low-taste!

1. Based on the information in the article, which one of the condiments below would someone on a low-acid diet want to avoid?
   (A) Mayonnaise
   (B) Salt
   (C) Cocktail sauce
   (D) Pepper

2. Based on the context, what does the word **ubiquitous** in paragraph 2 most likely mean?
   (A) Unhealthy
   (B) Everywhere
   (C) Delicious
   (D) Healthy

3. Which of the following would be the best advice for a person on a low-acid diet?
   (A) Substitute mayonnaise for ketchup on your French fries.
   (B) Drink a full glass of orange juice every day.
   (C) Avoid processed foods altogether.
   (D) Only eat high-acid foods in the morning.

LESSON 3: MEMOS AND LETTERS

So much of our society's communication is electronic today that you might think letter writing has truly become "a lost art form" as it has been called. However, the exchange of letters is alive and well. Businesses must be able to communicate with many customers who cannot get information online. Many companies like to follow up electronic communications with a hard copy for customers to keep in their files. Personal letters, too, are still exchanged, in spite of our constant connectedness through email and social networks. People occasionally prefer to put pen to paper for holiday updates, condolence, and congratulatory letters, or just to share their feelings.

In the case of business letters, the format for electronic and hard copies is the same. See the letter below:

(1) Happy Times Life Insurance Co.
345 Market St.
Philadelphia, PA 19111
(800) 123-4567

September 15, 2011 **(2)**

Ms. Claire Oberg **(3)**
1318 Connecticut Ave. NW
Washington, DC, 20008

Dear Ms. Oberg: **(4)** **(5)**

Your Life Insurance policy WL# 95213100 will be approaching its fifth year in force as of October 15, 2011.

When you took out this policy, you indicated that you wished to decline all future increases in coverage. If you still wish to decline increased coverage, you need do nothing. Your policy will no longer be in force as of October 15.

If you elect to continue coverage (including the increase), simply fill out and return the enclosed form before October 10, 2011.

Your new premium will be $87.52.

If you have any questions, please call customer service at the above number between the hours of 8:30–4:30, Monday to Friday.

Sincerely, **(6)**

Mark Aurie
Customer Service

(1) The address of the sender goes in the upper right-hand corner. If the sender is a corporation, this may include a company logo and additional information, such as extra phone numbers.

(2) The date follows immediately after. It is sometimes placed on the left margin and sometimes on the right.

(3) The **recipient's** (one who receives the letter) name and address should come next on the left.

(4) The **salutation** follows. A business salutation should address the recipient by title (Mr. or Ms.) or full name unless the two letter writers do business regularly and know each other well. The salutation ends with a colon (:).

(5) The body of the letter should be direct and to the point. The main idea should be stated in the first sentence or paragraph (your insurance will expire). The action the recipient is expected to take should be stated near the end (either let it expire, or send the form in to renew).

(6) Sincerely (with a comma) is the **conventional** or usual close for a business letter. Notice that the sender has used his full name and title below the signature space.

Practice Exercise 5

There are five errors in the letter below. Can you find them?

FRIGHTASTIC TIMES

Halloween Extravaganza Planners
7993 Castor Avenue
Bensalem, PA 19020
1-800-123-4567

November 5, 2010

William Johnson
156 Motley Terrace

Hi Will,

We would like to sincerely apologize for the error on our part which resulted in
five clowns and a unicycle showing up at your Halloween party, instead of the
two mummies, two ghosts and one monster you were promised. As co-founder
of Frightastic Times I can promise you that this is the first time anything like this
has happened in quite a long time.

My assistant informs me that you spoke to her about a full or partial refund.
I assure you I am looking into it. I am sure you will hear from me soon.

Take Care,

Alan Harding
CEO

---

1. _____

2. _____

3. _____

4. _____

5. _____

Personal letters can be written for many different reasons. Many people send "thank you" notes these days, but it is perfectly acceptable to write a thank you letter. The following is a sample:

June 15, 2011

Dear Aunt Marina,

Trevor and I would like to thank you so much for your gift of the complete set of the works of Shakespeare. We can't believe you remembered when we told you about meeting for the first time in Freshman English at University of Arizona, and how we both struggled with those term papers! You have such a wonderful memory.

You gift touched us so much that we were totally unprepared to open it and find your extremely generous check inside. Thank you again. It meant a lot to both of us that you and Uncle Ernest could be at the wedding. I was glad to hear from Mom that your trip back was good and you were not too tired.

As soon as we are settled at the apartment we hope to have you visit us there. I will call you before the holidays and we can set up a date!

Love,

Julia

The personal letter is much more informal than the business letter; headers and contact information are not required on the letter itself, although it is a good idea to get these things correct on the envelope! A personal letter may properly be sent on any occasion that we send greeting cards, or it may be sent for no reason at all—just to stay in touch.

Sometimes people need to communicate in a business setting but prefer a more casual format than the business letter. The reason may be speed—they need to get information to a large number of people quickly—or **proximity** (they work closely with the recipient and know him or her well) or both. For informal written business communication, the memo exists.

Most memos are sent **in-house**. They are sent from one employee of a company to another. This does away with the need for listing addresses, as on letters. Since memos may be sent several times in a day to a single person, salutations and closings are simplified as well. Memos often involve **time-sensitive** projects or deadlines. Therefore, the main idea in the body of the letter (remember?) is given its own subject line (often headed RE:). This way the recipient can see at a glance where this memo fits into his or her priorities and schedule. A date is important so that both sender and recipient know when the information was forwarded. Time stamps, added automatically on electronic memos, are becoming increasingly important as well. Look at the exchange on page 718:

```
TO: adouglass

FROM: ywinston

RE: Catering for tomorrow's recruitment fair

DATE: August 5, 2011

TIME: 9:30 A.M.

Alex,

Did that caterer ever get back to you? If
not, you need to get in touch with him ASAP.
I just talked to Shawn and it looks like
we may be feeding closer to 800 (not 500).
Please also verify that they are bringing
beverages and will do clean up.
Thanks,
Yvette
```

TO: ywinston

FROM: adouglass

RE: Catering

DATE: August 5, 2011

TIME: 1:30 P.M.

Yvette,

I was about to reply to your question above, and realized we had spoken since 9:30 and you already knew the caterer had confirmed for the original 500. I have now confirmed for the extra 300 as well—in fact, he says they can handle anything up to 1,000 people. So looks like we're set. Beverages will be water and soda. Clean up is okay.

Any more questions, just let me know.

Alex

In today's office, the paper memo has all but disappeared. Many organizations use communication and information organization systems on their computer networks that make writing and distributing memos fast and easy. A system like Microsoft Outlook, for example, assigns an in-house email address to every employee. Each email is date and time stamped and has a subject line. The system is already loaded with staff names. An executive director who wants to send a memo pulls up a blank form and chooses "ALL STAFF" from the names menu. She then types the body of the memo. It looks like this:

TO: ALL STAFF

FROM: kroy

RE: Staff Meeting tomorrow morning 9–12 A.M.

DATE: September 20, 2011

TIME: 11:00 A.M.

It's that time again! Please meet tomorrow morning in the big conference room to wrap up another month's achievements and challenges. Be ready to share at least one success story. Those of you who want to include announcements in the newsletter must forward them to Ellis by 3:00 today.

See you there!

Karen

Practice Exercise 6

Look at the following situations. In which case would a business or personal letter be appropriate? In which case would a memo be better? Mark B, P, or M to indicate how you would address each writing situation.

_____ 1. You want to get in touch with a friend whose husband has died.

_____ 2. You want to ask for a few days of vacation time at work.

_____ 3. You want to ask your supervisor a question, but he is out of the office.

_____ 4. You want to thank a committee for interviewing you for a job.

_____ 5. You want to bring bad customer service to your cable company's attention.

_____ 6. You want to thank a friend for helping you when you were in trouble.

_____ 7. You want to congratulate your neighbor on her new baby.

_____ 8. You want to schedule a meeting with four other employees.

_____ 9. You want to recommend someone who is being considered for a job.

_____ 10. You want to find out if anyone in your organization has found any helpful professional development classes.

LESSON 4: NEWSPAPER ARTICLES AND EDITORIALS

On the test you may be asked to answer questions or write about **newspaper articles** or **editorials**.

A newspaper article is a written piece that may appear in a newspaper, news magazine, or online media. It addresses a **newsworthy** event—one that has happened recently and affects or may affect many people. It also may report developments in an ongoing national or local situation. News articles are written by **journalists**. Although journalists, or news writers, of course have their own opinions on current events, they are expected to write articles that are **factual**, **neutral**, and well supported by evidence. In other words, journalists should inform the public without trying to influence public opinion. An example of a short news article is below:

December 13th Midville, IA—A 2-alarm fire broke out at 1:30 A.M. this morning in an abandoned 3-story building at the corner of Mitchell St. and Shoemaker Ave. Firefighters battled the blaze in subzero temperatures until 4:00 A.M. The combination of water and unusually cold weather caused the soaked structure to freeze as soon as fire was extinguished. Until the condemned building can be safely taken down, the intersection of Mitchell and Shoemaker will be closed and traffic re-routed.

Answer the following questions based on the information above.

When? _____

Where? _____

What happened? _____

Who was involved? _____

What was the outcome? _____

Editorial pieces appear in the same publications, or on the same type of websites, as news articles. They are usually written by the editorial staff of the paper, those who look at the stories journalists write and decide if any changes should be made. Editorials may also be written and submitted to publications by members of the reading public. When these are published they are usually referred to as "Letters to the Editor."

Editorials do not have to be neutral, although they are expected to be truthful. An editorial writer may put her point of view forth as strongly as she wishes. However, she is expected to be able to produce valid facts to back up her position. If the editorial misrepresents the truth or makes false claims, its writer might be open to charges of libel (making false written statements). The editorial piece below airs the writer's opinion on her city's public school testing system.

Practice Exercise 7

Testing for the Future
By
Arlene M. Goldfarb, Senior Ed. City Desk

Lately, in our area, a certain television commercial has been playing with increasing frequency. It claims to show outraged parents (although whether these are actual parents or merely actors, we are never told) participating in heated discussions that point out the negative effects of over-testing in our schools. Other areas of study, claim the parents (or actors), are being neglected for test preparation. The subjects they mention—math, English, science, current events—are all vital elements of education. But are these areas really being as neglected as this angry ad campaign implies?

Funny, but when the ad protests the time taken out to study "testing," it never directly states what the students are actually studying during that time period. A look at the subject matter necessary to pass the test, however, yields (surprise!) math, English, science, and current events.

Certainly not every achievement in a child's life can be measured by a test. But some achievements can. Is teaching our children how to successfully take and pass a test such a bad thing? Rather than cast testing as the villain of education, it would be more useful to students to teach them to approach evaluation of their skills with a positive attitude, as one more source of feedback on concepts they have mastered.

Answer the questions below based on the above editorial.

1. What is the topic of the editorial?

   _____

   _____

   _____

2. How does the author feel about testing in schools (positively or negatively)? In which paragraph(s) does she express her opinion?

   _____

   _____

   _____

3. Does the editorial offer any suggestions? If so, in which paragraph?

    _____

    _____

    _____

4. What is the author's background? Does she claim to have any educational experience or a child in the school system? Does her background influence how you feel about her opinion?

    _____

    _____

    _____

Practice Exercise 8

Read the passage below and answer questions 1 through 3.

Printed in the Chanticleer County People's *Sentinel* (Letters to the Editor Section)

Dear Sir,

As a loyal Sentinel reader (and a parent), I cannot adequately express my dismay after I read Arlene Goldfarb's editorial *Testing for the Future*. There are so many inaccuracies in Ms. Goldfarb's article that I scarcely know where to start. While she is correct that the tests given to students in our district have content areas such as math, science, etc., test prep classes are another matter entirely. Too often, test prep teaches manipulation of the format—how to eliminate answers in multiple choice questions, or whether guessing will hurt your overall score—in other words, it encourages students to "beat the system" instead of learning facts or concepts.

There is another problem with standardized testing that Ms. Goldfarb ignores. Just as not all children learn the same way, not all children should be tested the same way. The child who demonstrates learning by building something is at a disadvantage when asked to read and answer written questions.

Ms. Goldfarb should stick to making sure subscribers get their *Sentinel* on the doorstep every morning and leave education to those involved—teachers, students, and parents.

Sincerely,

Alfred Stamford

1. Which of the following is the best summary of Mr. Stamford's letter?
    (A) He doesn't think Ms. Goldfarb is qualified to make educational statements.
    (B) He feels the current testing system does not serve students well.
    (C) He thinks all testing should be eliminated.
    (D) He thinks students should build something.

2. Which of the following is an assumption Mr. Stamford makes about Ms. Goldfarb's qualifications?
   (A) He assumes she is not a parent.
   (B) He doesn't think she writes very well.
   (C) He assumes she does not know what subjects the students are tested on.
   (D) She is the Senior Editor of the City Desk.

3. Which of the following groups would Mr. Stamford most likely belong to?
   (A) A journalist's union
   (B) A political group that protests higher wages for school employees
   (C) The Parent-Teacher Association (PTA)
   (D) Ms. Goldfarb's Facebook friends list

LESSON FIVE: HISTORICAL SPEECHES AND DOCUMENTS

On your test, you may be required to read and analyze important historical speeches or documents from our nation's past. This means you will encounter some unfamiliar vocabulary. Many of these documents were written over one hundred years ago—in the 19th and 18th centuries. Consider this vocabulary from President Lincoln's **Gettysburg Address**, a speech he gave in 1863 during the Civil War.

Four score   Conceived   Proposition

Some of these words may already be familiar to you. Some are not used the same way they were in 1863. The word score is used today to mean win or make a point; we say "The team scored." In Lincoln's time, *score* meant "twenty," just as *dozen* still means "twelve." Hence, *four score* meant four times twenty, or eighty.

You will need to use your **context clues** skills for many of the historical passages. Even if you do not figure out each individual word, strive to comprehend the meaning of sentences and paragraphs as a whole. Look at the first paragraph of the Gettysburg Address, where the above terms came from. Abraham Lincoln gave this speech to dedicate a soldier's cemetery.

"**Four score** and seven years ago our fathers brought forth on this continent, a new nation, **conceived** in Liberty, and dedicated to the **proposition** that all men are created equal."

A modern rewrite of this sentence might be:

Eighty-seven years ago, our fathers founded this country. They wanted all who lived here to be free and equal.

As you can see, our unfamiliar words are not really the **key words** of the sentence. The key words and phrases are

new nation   Liberty   all men are created equal

When analyzing a passage with unfamiliar words, focus on the words you do know. Try to find key words. Don't just pay attention to the words you don't know. This is a little like figuring out a math word problem!

Practice Exercise 9

Let's look at the next section of The Gettysburg Address.

"Now we are engaged in a great **civil war**, testing whether that **nation**, or any nation so conceived and so dedicated, **can** long **endure**. **We are** met **on a great battle-field** of that war. We have come to **dedicate** a portion of **that field**, as **a final resting place** for those **who here gave their lives** that that nation might live."

Your key words are bolded. Can you use them to interpret what Lincoln was saying and rewrite it in a modern style?

_____

_____

_____

Restatement helps us to understand the meaning of a passage better.

Practice Exercise 10

Not every historical document is from hundreds of years ago. In 1962, speaking at Rice University, President Kennedy gave a summary of mankind's scientific accomplishments. He then said:

"If this capsule history of our progress teaches us anything, it is that man, in his quest for knowledge and progress, is determined and cannot be deterred. The exploration of space will go ahead, whether we join in it or not, and it is one of the great adventures of all time, and no nation which expects to be the leader of other nations can expect to stay behind in the race for space."

Using context clue and key word techniques, answer the questions below.

1. What is the topic of this paragraph?
   (A) Space exploration
   (B) History
   (C) Leaders of nations
   (D) Racing

2. Based on context clues, what is the most likely meaning of quest?
   (A) Question
   (B) Search
   (C) Trip
   (D) Team

Of course, historical documents on the test are not always speeches. They may be government papers, like the Declaration of Independence or the Constitution, or letters or histories written by people who made contributions to our nation.

Practice Exercise 11

W. E. B. DuBois, born in 1868, was an early African-American civil rights advocate and founder of the NAACP. In 1903, he wrote *The Souls of Black Folk* to address the issue of race in America. The opening paragraph of this work follows:

"Herein lie buried many things which if read with patience may show the strange meaning of being black here at the dawning of the Twentieth Century. This meaning is not without interest to you, Gentle Reader; for the problem of the Twentieth Century is the problem of the color line. I pray you, then, receive my little book in all charity, studying my words with me, forgiving mistake and foible for sake of the faith and passion that is in me, and seeking the grain of truth hidden there."

1. Which phrase contains the main idea of *The Souls of Black Folk*?
   (A) Herein lie buried many things
   (B) I pray you, then, receive my little book in all charity
   (C) the faith and passion that is in me
   (D) the problem of the Twentieth Century is the problem of the color line

2. With which of the following statements would W. E. B. DuBois most likely agree?
   (A) If you are patient and wait, problems fix themselves.
   (B) Racial inequality is one of the most pressing problems of our time.
   (C) Racial equality can never be achieved.
   (D) Getting people jobs is more important than securing their basic human rights.

Practice Exercise 12

The following is from a letter written by Abigail Adams to her husband John during the Revolutionary War:

". . . in the new code of laws which I suppose it will be necessary for you to make, I desire you would remember the ladies and be more generous and favorable to them than your ancestors. Do not put such unlimited power into the hands of the husbands. Remember, all men would be tyrants if they could. If particular care and attention is not paid to the ladies, we are determined to foment a rebellion, and will not hold ourselves bound by any in which we have no voice or representation."

1. What is the most likely reason Abigail says women had "no voice or representation"?
   (A) Women were never allowed to talk.
   (B) Women did not vote.
   (C) Women did not fight in wars.
   (D) Women did not go into public places.

Read the following passage from a standard Equal Employment Opportunity Policy and answer questions 1 through 3.

What Type of Form Is This?

REPORTING A GRIEVANCE

If an individual believes that he or she has been the target of discrimination, harassment or retaliation, or believes that a violation of this Policy has occurred, the individual should report his or her grievance to the Human Resource representative, who acts as the company EEO officer. The individual may, if he or she desires, report the grievance to his or her supervisor or manager instead. Any behavior offensive to an individual may be reported, whether or not an individual is sure the behavior violates the EEO Policy.

An individual who wishes to register a grievance against a senior manager may do so directly with the Board of Directors, who will then appoint a special officer to investigate the nature of the complaint.

1. Given the context, what is the most likely meaning of the word "retaliation?"
   (A) Repetition
   (B) Promotion
   (C) Revenge
   (D) Reinstatement

2. What section of the EEO Policy would you most likely find this passage in?
   (A) Employee Responsibilities
   (B) Purpose
   (C) Reporting a Grievance
   (D) Questions

3. Sheila applied for a promotion. During the interview, she was told by the HR rep that she was too old for the job. Yet she has been training younger workers in the same skills. What should she do if she feels she has been discriminated against?
   (A) Nothing—she might as well start looking for something at another company.
   (B) She should tell everybody she knows that the job wasn't worth it.
   (C) She should find out who else applied and tell them the job is filled.
   (D) She should contact the Board of Directors to see if she may file a grievance.

Read the following letter and answer questions 4 through 6.

How Did the Writer Feel About His Teacher?

September 21, 2011

Dear Mrs. Lee,

   Please accept my sympathy on the loss of your husband. Dr. Lee was one of my favorite professors. Even now, ten years after graduation, I remember bits and pieces of his advice almost daily. He was the one who encouraged me to go on to graduate school; I can truly say he changed my life. I have spoken with some other alumni from Professor Lee's classes, and we all feel the same way. Our loss, of course, can be nothing compared to yours, but we feel the world is a little sadder without the Doctor. Although I will not be able to come to Ohio for the memorial service, I will be making a donation to the Sierra Club in Professor Lee's name. I believe that was one of his favorite charities. Please let me know if you would prefer other arrangements.

   Once again, I am deeply sorry.

Sincerely,

Brian Jones

4. What type of letter is this?
    (A) A condolence letter
    (B) A congratulatory letter
    (C) A business letter
    (D) A thank you letter

5. What is one of the reasons the writer gives for his sadness at the death of Dr. Lee?
    (A) Dr. Lee encouraged the writer's further education.
    (B) Dr. Lee loved animals.
    (C) The writer really doesn't want to go to Ohio.
    (D) The writer is sorry for Mrs. Lee.

6. Based on the context, what do you think is the best meaning for the word "alumni?"
    (A) Friends
    (B) People who went to the same school together
    (C) Professors who taught at the same school
    (D) People from Ohio

Questions 7 through 9 are based on the following passage from "Nickel and Dimed," an auto-biographical account of one writer's attempt to live on the American minimum wage.

How Does She Feel About Her Career?

In my own family, the low-wage way of life had never been many degrees of separation away; it was close enough, in any case, to make me treasure the gloriously autonomous, if not always well-paid, writing life. My sister has been through one low-paid job after another—phone company business rep, factory worker, receptionist—constantly struggling against what she calls "the hopelessness of being a wage slave." My husband and companion of 17 years was a $4.50-an-hour warehouse worker when I fell in love with him, escaping eventually and with huge relief to become an organizer for the Teamsters. My father had been a copper miner; uncles and grandfathers worked in the mines or for the Union Pacific. So to me, sitting at a desk all day was not only a privilege but a duty: something I owed to all those people in my life, living and dead, who'd had so much more to say than anyone ever got to hear.

—Barbara Ehrenreich

7. What can you infer about the author's feelings toward her family?
   (A) She wishes she came from a richer background.
   (B) She appreciates and respects their sacrifices.
   (C) She doesn't understand why they didn't get further in life.
   (D) She doesn't like talking about them.

8. Which of the following is the best restatement of the passage's main idea?
   (A) Because the author comes from a family who has worked hard for low pay, she values the advantages of her writing career.
   (B) Because the author's sister has trouble holding onto a job, the author feels obligated to support her.
   (C) The author is sure that soon everyone in her family will have a desk job like hers.
   (D) The author owes her family money for putting her through school to become a writer.

9. Based on the descriptions of the jobs held by Ms. Ehrenreich's sister, how would you define the phrase "wage slave?"
   (A) Someone who works in an office
   (B) A person who is paid an hourly wage rather than a salary
   (C) A person who is paid a salary rather than an hourly wage
   (D) Someone who works a low-paying job with little chance for advancement

Questions 10 though 12 are based on the following newspaper editorial.

To the Editor:

I have been a loyal reader of the *Middleton Star* for many years. As such, I feel my opinion may carry some weight with you. I cannot hold my peace any longer about an editorial decision—or rather lack of decision—by your paper. Why, oh why, in this day and age, does the Star still designate Section C as "The Women's Pages"?

I realize this nomenclature was common, oh, say, thirty-five years ago. Many papers had Women's pages, condescendingly filled with puzzles, recipes, fashion advice, and other fripperies to help us women fill our empty hours (and presumably empty heads). The difference is that other papers have moved with the times—quite some time ago, in fact. I am the first to say I enjoy a good jumble puzzle, but that doesn't mean I don't look at the stock market and international news when I am done.

So wake up, *Middleton Star!* Rename Section C the Leisure Pages, the Home Pages, the Anything Pages. Then I can read them without being irritated into a fury. And my husband can copy recipes without feeling that you are insulting his manhood.

Sincerely,

Edna Grazleton

---

10. Why does Ms. Grazleton dislike the name "The Women's Pages" for Section C?
    (A) She finds the articles in Section C too difficult to read.
    (B) She thinks it is condescending, as that section is filled with light reading.
    (C) She doesn't like the articles in that section.
    (D) She thinks the section should be longer.

11. What is one of the arguments advanced by Ms. Grazleton as a reason the *Star* should change The Women's Pages name?
    (A) Other newspapers renamed that section long ago.
    (B) She owns stock in the *Middleton Star*.
    (C) If the *Star* changes the section name, they might sell more papers.
    (D) If the *Star* changes the name of the section, Ms. Grazleton won't read it anymore.

12. Why does Ms. Grazleton feel the *Star* might listen to her opinion?
    (A) She is a long-time reader.
    (B) She owns stock in the *Middleton Star*.
    (C) If the *Star* changes the section name, they might sell more papers.
    (D) If the *Star* changes the name of the section, Ms. Grazleton won't read it anymore.

The Poinsettia plant is native to Mexico and Central America. Joel Roberts Poinsett, after whom the plant is named, did not discover the beautiful flowering species. However, Poinsett, an Ambassador to Mexico in the 1820s, was instrumental in introducing and popularizing the plant in the United States. Although the Poinsettia is a tropical plant, in the U.S. it has become associated with and representative of the winter holiday Christmas. However, many plant owners are disappointed when the red blooms (actually leaves) fail to replenish themselves. This is because the redness in the leaf is dependent on very specific cycles of light and dark. Left alone and treated as a common house plant, the Poinsettia will retaliate by putting forth only tiny white and green leaves—or none at all.

13. The article states that the Poinsettia is native to Central America. You live in Minnesota. What would be the most likely result of planting your Poinsettias in the yard in January after Christmas is over?
    (A) They would begin to bloom again.
    (B) They would probably die.
    (C) They would make the other flowers look better.
    (D) They would create an attractive border to set off your other plants.

14. What is the most likely reason that Poinsett, a politician, introduced the Poinsettia plant to the United States?
    (A) The plant accidentally was packed in his luggage.
    (B) He thought it would make him a millionaire.
    (C) He thought the plant was unattractive, but believed it might be popular anyway.
    (D) He had a great interest in botany.

15. What is the most likely reason the Poinsettia has become associated with Christmas?
    (A) It is easier to find in December than any other time of the year.
    (B) Its colors, bright red and green, are the colors of Christmas.
    (C) It is cheaper at that time of year.
    (D) It is illegal to purchase Poinsettia plants except between November 1st and December 31st.

When was the last time you looked up at night? Except for brief glances at the moon, chances are most of us have not stopped and stared at the sky in quite a while. Long ago, people began to watch the night sky and notice things. They noticed patterns in the stars and the movements of the planets. They knew when and where the Sun would rise or set on the horizon at certain times of the year. They observed the cycles of the comets. In modern times, it is easy to ignore the display in the heavens. Anyone who lives in a city, for one thing, will find that light pollution makes some stars invisible to the naked eye. There are also so many exciting competing activities at night: shows, TV, movies, sports games, and other events. Our professional astronomers, of course, have made astounding leaps in the knowledge of space. However, the average person on the street is lucky if he can find The Big Dipper.

16. What would be a good title for the paragraph above?
    (A) Ancient People and Their Lifestyles
    (B) A Guide to Nightlife in the City
    (C) How to Find The Big Dipper
    (D) The Forgotten Sky Above Us

17. What does the author suggest is one of the reasons people no longer notice the night sky?
    (A) Our days are so busy and filled with work.
    (B) Light pollution makes it difficult to see some of the stars.
    (C) More people nowadays have vision problems, which makes it difficult to see some of the stars.
    (D) People notice the night sky more in the country.

The following is the opening paragraph of the Declaration of Independence, written in Philadelphia and dated July 4, 1776:

"When in the Course of human events, it becomes necessary for one people to dissolve the political bands which have connected them with another, and to assume, among the Powers of the earth, the separate and equal station to which the Laws of Nature and of Nature's God entitle them, a decent respect to the opinions of mankind requires that they should declare the causes which impel them to the separation."

18. In modern day language, what is the closest restatement of the paragraph above?
    (A) When people take their place among the Powers of the earth, it is necessary to separate.
    (B) When one nation decides to separate from another, it is only respectful to let everyone know why.
    (C) When people are impelled to separate, they need permission from the powers that be.
    (D) It is the Law of Nature that every nation must separate from every other nation.

Sunday Morning, November 1st, La Maestra, California. Tragedy struck last night when a final drenching storm swept over La Maestra after weeks of heavy rains. Mudslides and flooding hit the coastal town, sending houses sliding into the sea and destroying millions of dollars of property. Luckily, because of La Maestra's efficient early warning system, no lives were lost, but many of the town's citizens are temporarily or permanently homeless. Shelters are set up at schools and community centers in surrounding areas. Relief workers are asking for donations of clean clothes and toiletries. Those who wish to give should call 555-1111. A website is also being set up to accept donations. The Mayor of La Maestra is appealing to the government for emergency relief status.

19. What can be inferred from the phrase "temporarily or permanently homeless"?
    (A) Some people may eventually be able to return to their homes.
    (B) None of the people will be able to return to their homes.
    (C) All of the people will be able to return to their homes.
    (D) The town will eventually need to relocate.

20. Which of the following are examples of articles the shelters need?
    (A) Barbecue grills and oven mitts
    (B) TVs and computer game systems
    (C) Sweaters and toothbrushes
    (D) Candy and balloons

CHAPTER 23 ANSWER EXPLANATIONS

Lesson 1: Biography and Autobiography

PRACTICE EXERCISE 1 (PAGE 710)

1. You might have said well-loved, missed, kind, charismatic, or any adjective suggested by the fact that so many people mourned his death.

2. **(D)** She is most likely a teenager. The speaker is reprimanded by her mother as a young person would be, therefore, (A) is unlikely. She does not mention any children (B). She is old enough to volunteer at a hospice; therefore (C) cannot be correct.

3. **(B)** Douglass's main fear is (B) being kidnapped and transported to the south. He uses the words taken, seized, and kidnappers in the passage. (D) is not correct. It was more common to try to recapture an escaped slave than to kill him; slaves were considered valuable property by their ex-owners. Douglass was never pursued by pirates (A). This is a metaphor he uses to explain the joy of freedom. The passage does not indicate that Douglass is out of or owes money (C).

PRACTICE EXERCISE 2 (PAGE 712)

1. D
2. B
3. E
4. C
5. F
6. A

Lesson 2: Informational Science Articles

PRACTICE EXERCISE 3 (PAGE 712)

1. **(B)** *Not all creatures on Earth fall neatly into categories.* The article is about the platypus, a creature that does not fit completely within one man-made category. (A) Scientists are not the only people who use classification. (C) is a value judgement. (D) is not true. There are exceptions (like the platypus), but in general classification is a useful system of ordering all types of things.

2. **(D)** *They have feathers.* Mammals generally have fur or hair, not feathers. All the other choices are attributes of mammals.

3. **(B)** *They are warm-blooded.* (A) and (D) Mammals may have claws, but so may other types of animals. Similarly, some mammals can swim, but so can fish, reptiles, amphibians, and some birds. (C) Mammals (with extremely few exceptions) do not lay eggs.

PRACTICE EXERCISE 4 (PAGE 713)

1. **(C)** *Cocktail sauce contains tomato.* (A) Mayonnaise is low acid. (B) Salt is restricted on some diets, but not a low-acid one. (D) Pepper is spicy, not acidic.

2. **(B)** *Everywhere.* The sentence that follows this clarifies that "They are everywhere."

3. **(A)** *Substitute mayonnaise for ketchup on your French fries.* The passage suggests avoiding tomato products. (B) and (C) are mentioned as possible high-acid sources. (D) It does not matter what time you eat or drink high-acid foods; they will still affect your digestive system.

Lesson 3: Memos and Letters

PRACTICE EXERCISE 5 (PAGE 716)

1. The company name and address are on the wrong side of the letter.
2. There is no city, state, and zip code line in the recipient's address.
3. The informal salutation is more suited to a personal letter.
4. Although the first paragraph is direct and to the point, the second paragraph does not encourage action on the recipient's part or promise it on the sender's part. This is bad business as well as bad letter writing.
5. The closing salutation is informal and not appropriate for business.

PRACTICE EXERCISE 6 (PAGE 719)

1. P   3. M   5. B   7. P   9. B
2. M   4. B   6. P   8. B   10. M

Lesson 4: Newspaper Articles and Editorials

OPENING QUESTIONS (PAGE 720)

When? On December 13th at 1:30 A.M.

Where? At the corner of Mitchell St. and Shoemaker Ave. in Midville, IA

What happened? A fire broke out in an abandoned building.

Who was involved? Firefighters.

What was the outcome? The fire was extinguished. The intersection is temporarily closed.

PRACTICE EXERCISE 7 (PAGE 721)

1. The topic is the value of testing and test preparation for students.
2. She feels positive overall. Her opinion is expressed in the last paragraph.
3. The editorial suggests looking at the test prep curriculum more closely (2nd paragraph) and reconsidering the value of teaching students to test successfully.
4. The author is an editor at a city publication. She does not mention educational job experience and she does not say she has children. Answers to this question will vary.

PRACTICE EXERCISE 8 (PAGE 722)

1. **(B)** *He feels the current testing system does not serve students well.* Even though (B) is true, it is not his main focus or concern. (C) Mr. Stamford does not say all testing should be eliminated. (D) He also does not say all students need to build.
2. **(A)** *He assumes she is not a parent.* Mr. Stamford points out in the last sentence that Ms. Goldfarb is not a teacher, student, or parent. Although Ms. Goldfarb never says she is a parent, she never says she is not.
3. **(B)** *The Parent-Teacher Association (PTA).* Mr. Stamford, although he does not agree with his school district's testing practices, cares greatly about students being able to learn in the way that is best for them. (A) Although Mr. Stamford might be a journalist, we have no evidence that he is. (B) Mr. Stamford does not say he thinks school employees are overpaid. (D) Ms. Goldfarb and Mr. Stamford are unlikely to develop a personal friendship. They have an **adversarial** professional relationship (they disagree).

Lesson 5: Historical Speeches and Documents

PRACTICE EXERCISE 9 (PAGE 724)

The following is a sample of modern restatement. Answers may vary slightly.

"We are in the middle of a terrible war. It's not certain that we can survive and stay together as one country. We are meeting today on a spot where a bloody battle was fought. Part of this field is now a cemetery for those who lost their lives fighting. We are here today to dedicate it."

PRACTICE EXERCISE 10 (PAGE 724)

1. **(A)** *Space exploration.* Kennedy says that the "exploration of space . . . is one of the great adventures of all time."
2. **(B)** *Search*

PRACTICE EXERCISE 11 (PAGE 725)

1. **(D)** *the problem of the Twentieth Century is the problem of the color line.* W. E. B. DuBois wrote his book to alert America to the largely unaddressed issue of racism.
2. **(B)** *Racial inequality is one of the most pressing problems of our time.* (A) If DuBois thought the problem would fix itself, he would not have written the book. (C) Again, if he thought the problem was unfixable, he would not have written the book. (D) DuBois states that he considers African-American human rights abuses a bigger problem than any other.

PRACTICE EXERCISE 12 (PAGE 725)

1. **(B)** *Women did not vote.* (A) and (D) are untrue. (C) concerns actions, not representation in politics.

End-of-Chapter Questions (Page 726)

1. **(C)** comes closest to the definition of retaliation. Promotion (B) is a positive event. Repetition and reinstatement do not apply.
2. **(C)** This section outlines the procedure for stating a grievance. None of the other choices apply.
3. **(D)** To be disqualified for a promotion on the basis of age is discrimination. Because the HR representative is a senior manager, Sheila should contact the Board of Directors. Sabotaging the job search process (B) and (C) is unwise and could cause problems for her in her current position. (A) Bringing the manager's misconduct to the attention of the Board is preferable to throwing away valuable time that Sheila has accrued with this company.
4. **(A)** Condolence means to give sympathy. Even if you are not sure of the definition of condolence, none of the other definitions apply.
5. **(A)** The writer states that Dr. Lee encouraged him to apply to graduate school. Even though the other choices are true, they are not given as reasons that Brian Jones appreciated Professor Lee.
6. **(B)** The alumni that Brian Jones contacted were all in Dr. Lee's class with him. He does not say if they are still friends, where they lived, or whether they ever became professors.

7. **(B)** The writer does not regret her background (A); she says it makes her "treasure" her freedom to write. (C) She understands that low-wage life is a "struggle" with "hopelessness," and only a few "eventually" escape. (D) If the writer did not want to talk about her family, she would not mention them in her book.

8. **(A)** The writer never mentions supporting her sister financially or owing her family money (she does say she owes it to them to do her job). Because she speaks of her father and uncles in the past tense, they are likely no longer working and so will not be getting desk jobs.

9. **(D)** All of the jobs mentioned fall into this category. (B) and (C) Salary and hourly jobs can both pay well. (A) Not all of Ehrenreich's sister's jobs are office jobs.

10. **(B)** *She thinks it is condescending, as that section is filled with light reading.* (A) This is not true. She mentions that Section C has easy reading on light subjects like fashion and cooking. (C) She does like the articles, but not the name. (D) Nothing is mentioned in the editorial about length.

11. **(A)** *Other newspapers renamed that section long ago.* Ms. Grazleton tells the *Star* they are over thirty years behind the times. (B) She reads the stock market pages but does not say she owns stock in the paper. (C) and (D) Ms. Grazleton does not make either of these statements.

12. **(A)** *She is a long-time reader.* She mentions this in the first two sentences. (B) She reads the stock market pages but does not say she owns stock in the paper. (C) and (D) Ms. Grazleton does not make either of these statements.

13. **(B)** *They would probably die.* Tropical plants cannot tolerate low temperatures, such as would be common in Minnesota in January.

14. **(D)** *He had a great interest in botany.* Botany is the study of plants. (A) This is an unlikely scenario and would probably result in the plant's being crushed and dying. (B) No mention is made of a profit motive for Poinsett. (C) Poinsett's opinion of the attractiveness of the Poinsettia is not addressed.

15. **(B)** Its color, bright red and green, are the colors of Christmas. (A) This is probably the case, but if so it is an effect of the poinsettia's connection to Christmas, not a cause. (C) is unsupported by the passage. (D) is untrue.

16. **(D)** *The Forgotten Sky Above Us.* (A) The paragraph does not mention anything about ancient people except to note their familiarity with the night sky. (B) The paragraph merely mentions examples of nighttime activities in passing—it is not the focus of the article. (C) There are no astronomical instructions in the paragraph.

17. **(B)** *Light pollution makes it difficult to see some of the stars.* (A) Our activities during the day are irrelevant. (C) This is not true. (D) It is true there is less light pollution in the country, but people can still be distracted by other entertainment.

18. **(B)** *When one nation decides to separate from another, it is only respectful to let everyone know why.* (A) This choice does not make sense. (C) and (D) are untrue. Only choice (B) states what actually happened when the American colonies separated from England.

19. **(A)** *Some people may eventually be able to return to their homes.* Those who do were temporarily homeless; those whose homes were destroyed will never be able to return to them.

20. **(C)** *Sweaters and toothbrushes.* These are examples of clothes and toiletries. (A) These are picnic supplies. (B) These are entertainment appliances. (D) These are party supplies.

Fiction

24

> "I find television very educating. Every time somebody turns on the set, I go into the other room and read a book."
>
> —Groucho Marx

Everybody loves a story.

People long ago had no movies, but they had action heroes. Gods in Greek myths and knights in fairy tales performed marvels that Bruce Willis and Angelina Jolie—and CGI—show us today. Friends discussed Tolstoy's *War and Peace* or Louis L'Amour's latest cowboy adventure the way we discuss *Dancing with the Stars* on our lunch breaks. Readers in England could not watch sitcoms featuring their favorite actors, but they waited anxiously for the next installment of *The Old Curiosity Shop* to find out whether Little Nell lived or died.

Think of a time without television, without HD radio, without iPods—in fact, without electronic entertainment *of any kind*. Books were a social as well as an individual pursuit. People often clustered in groups to hear one person read aloud as entertainment. A person who read well was considered an asset to the family and community. Such a person gained respect for his or her ability to amuse friends and help them with their important papers and documents.

In the modern world, reading well is a skill essential for success in the workplace. However, it can still be the cause of enjoyment and information. Nothing makes the wait at the doctor's office go faster than a good story!

Perhaps most meaningful of all is that parents who love stories raise children who love stories. There is no stronger encouragement for children than bedtime reading and a house full of books. Even the youngest child will grow old enough to find his or her own stories in all those books Mom and Dad have. A love of reading is a head start on education for life.

HOW THIS CHAPTER IS ORGANIZED

Lesson 1: Theme

A theme is the one idea the author of a story hopes you will take away with you. This lesson will help you discover the message each piece of writing conveys. You will also learn how to restate a theme in your own words.

Lesson 2: Setting

Getting a sense of the setting of a story involves asking two important questions: where and when. Knowing the time and place in which a story is set can help you understand why the characters speak and act the way they do. It can also help you anticipate what turns the plot might take.

Lesson 3: Plot Elements

Plot is the action of the story, from beginning to end. Story plots can be complex, spanning hundreds of pages and involving many characters; or they may be one paragraph long and focus on one or two people. In Lesson 3 you will learn that authors usually follow a pattern when writing a plot, just as a dressmaker follows a pattern for a dress, or an architect a blueprint for a building. A well-constructed plot is what can make a story a "page-turner" or suspenseful.

Lesson 4: Point of View

Who tells the story? Lesson 4 looks at the possibilities and explains the difference between first person and third person, limited and omniscient.

LESSON 1: THEME

All stories, whether they are intended to be read, listened to, or watched on stage or screen, have themes. A **theme** reveals the subject of a story. It also expresses an idea or attitude about the subject.

Practice Exercise 1

This passage from Robert Graves' *Good-bye to All That* takes as its theme the fear and **vulnerability** of the common soldier during war.

VOCABULARY

Vulnerable:
to be open to
attack or pain.

The darkness seemed to move and shake about as I looked at it; the bushes started travelling, singly at first, then both together. The pickets did the same. I was glad of the sentry beside me; he gave his name as Beaumont. "They're quiet tonight, Sir," he said. "A relief going on; I think so, surely."

I said: "It's funny how those bushes seem to move."

"Aye, they do play queer tricks. Is this your first spell in trenches, Sir?"

A German flare shot up, broke into bright flame, dropped slowly and went hissing into the grass just behind our trench, showing up the bushes and pickets. Instinctively I moved.

"It's bad to do that, Sir," he said, as a rifle bullet cracked and seemed to pass right between us. "Keep still, Sir, and they can't spot you. Not but what a flare is a bad thing to fall on you. I've seen them burn a hole in a man."

1. What are the words or phrases that support the statement that the two men are in danger?

_____

_____

_____

2. What does the speaker suggest when he says that the bushes and pickets seemed to be moving?
    (A) He is dreaming the whole episode.
    (B) The darkness and his anxiety make it difficult for him to accurately identify moving objects.
    (C) The Germans are dressed as bushes and picket fences.
    (D) The speaker has often had trouble with his eyesight before.

VOCABULARY

Galvanized: inspired to take action

Badger: to annoy, nag, or pester.

Read the passage below and questions 3 and 4:

In eleventh grade, I received a D on a chemistry quiz. It was the first D I had ever received in my life. Whereas, in September I had dozed through class, dashed off homework at the last minute, and ignored tutoring sessions (practices that, I must say, had served me fairly successfully in other subjects) the slap in the face of the shameful grade **galvanized** me into action. I copied and recopied notes from class every night. I **badgered** friends and family members to "Quiz me!" I attended tutoring sessions. I peppered Mrs. Banks, the chemistry teacher, with questions every time I saw her until she began to avoid me in the school halls.

At the end of the semester I had the only A in the class.

3. Which proverb below best expresses the theme of the above passage?
    (A) Don't count your chickens before they're hatched.
    (B) A fool and his money are soon parted.
    (C) If at first you don't succeed, try, try again.
    (D) The pen is mightier than the sword.

4. List three details that support the idea of the speaker's persistence.

_____

_____

_____

Practice Exercise 2

In Edith Wharton's *The House of Mirth*, the subject of the book is injustice. The theme, which is an **expansion**, or a longer explanation of the subject, is that because the heroine behaves **ethically** and does not take the easy way out, she is betrayed by all her friends.

VOCABULARY

Ethically: in a moral way; striving to do right.

The struggle against injustice is a popular theme in fiction. You will find, as you begin to analyze literature, that certain themes are very popular with authors and readers. Try to match the following common literary themes with their examples.

_____ 1. A lonely orphan nurses her sick cousin back to health. Together they bring a secret garden back to life.

(A) The quest for adventure will forever change you.

_____ 2. A woman slowly goes mad after being isolated for months in a bizarre bedroom.

(B) Good triumphs over evil.

_____ 3. Traveling down an African river to find a missing countryman leads a man into terrifying circumstances.

(C) Evil triumphs over good.

_____ 4. A country mother stands up to her city daughter's pushiness.

(D) Love triumphs over all.

_____ 5. A man who has been tortured with a pendulum and thrown into a pit is rescued at the last minute.

(E) The underdog will triumph over the oppressor.

Do you think these situations are good examples of the themes they are matched with? Can you explain why or why not?

The following passage illustrates one of the common themes listed above. The excerpt is from the story *The Secret Life of Walter Mitty*, by James Thurber. Walter Mitty has a habit of imagining himself in exciting surroundings, where he is the hero: for example, he daydreams about being a Navy Commander saving a plane in a hurricane. In real life, he often takes orders from his wife. What is Mitty's attitude toward his wife's bossiness in this last paragraph? And which theme do you think this best illustrates?

TIP

To find the theme, first decide the subject of a story.

At the drugstore on the corner she said, "Wait here for me. I forgot something. I won't be a minute." She was more than a minute. Walter Mitty lighted a cigarette. It began to rain, rain with sleet in it. He stood up against the wall of the drugstore, smoking....He put his shoulders back and his heels together. "To hell with the handkerchief," said Walter Mitty scornfully. He took one last drag on his cigarette and snapped it away. Then, with that faint, fleeting smile playing about his lips, he faced the firing squad; erect and motionless, proud and disdainful, Walter Mitty the Undefeated, inscrutable to the last.

Comically (this is a humorous story after all!) Walter Mitty would rather picture himself as a man about to be executed by a firing squad than a man waiting in the rain for his wife. You should have picked **the underdog triumphs over his oppressor.** Actually, there is no great change in the couple's situation. Walter Mitty's wife will continue to remind him to put on galoshes and buy dog food. He nevertheless remains undefeated through his imagination.

Practice Exercise 3

One way to find the theme of a piece of writing is to ask ourselves, "What is the **main idea** the author wants to communicate? What does he or she want me to take away from this story?" **Ask yourself this question as you read the passage below.**

> The early evening was quiet. The afternoon had been quiet. Sean had woken up alone, eaten lunch alone, spoken to no one. The only voices he had heard had been the chatter of the television, YouTube videos, calls of strangers to each other in the street. No human had spoken directly to him all day. In an hour his mother would be home to make dinner and the words would pour from his lips, ragingly, like Niagara, until the full weight of the day's silent loneliness had been eased.

Before you look at the question below, write down in your own words what you think the best expression of this passage's theme is:

_____

_____

When you answer the following question, check back and see how closely the correct answer matches your own answer here.

1. What is the theme, or main idea of this passage?
    (A) A person who has been isolated will suffer.
    (B) Modern technology keeps people from being lonely.
    (C) A person who has been isolated has many resources.

LESSON 2: SETTING

The setting of a story is all about the place (where it happens), the time (when it happens), and often involves something more **intangible**, or difficult to describe, called mood. The where, when, and mood of a piece of fiction often give us clues about other important elements—the direction of the plot, the intentions of the characters, and the attitude of the author, among other things.

Time

The time that a story is set in may either be loosely or carefully defined. An example of a loosely defined time might be "at night" or "a few years ago." A carefully defined time would be "July 4, 1776 until October 1781." For some stories, a loosely defined time period is fine; for others, the time is crucial to understanding the action. Imagine the following scene taking place in 2010:

Leila set her alarm clock for 8:00. Tomorrow was Election Day. She was going to get to the polls first thing, before anyone in the house woke up.

"I work," she thought. "I pay my taxes. I have a brain, and I intend to have a voice. No one is going to keep me from voting."

If we assume the story takes place in 2010, we might just think that Leila is a **conscientious** citizen—one who takes her political duties seriously. But what if the story is taking place in 1910—before women were legally allowed to vote? Our view of Leila changes. Suddenly she becomes a radical **activist** (someone who challenges society).

Try to categorize the following time settings as loose or carefully defined.

(1)   A misty evening in November   _____

(2)   A few years since   _____

(3)   In this year of stability, A.F. 632   _____

(4)   At sunset   _____

(5)   This summer of 1972   _____

(3) and (5) are carefully defined, while the others are looser. Number (3) comes from a science fiction story by Aldous Huxley. The unusual date helps us realize we are reading a story about the future. Number (5) is from a story about a woman living an alternative lifestyle. The date of 1972 emphasizes the opposition she meets in society.

Do not think, however, that a setting must have a carefully defined time to be effective. Number (4), "sunset," opens a story about two older sisters' courageously taking charge of their lives. The time of sunset emphasizes that they are in their declining years.

Place

Imagine you are an author who plans to write a novel about wars that sweep across Africa and Europe. In which setting do you think your first chapters would be the most effective?

The Sahara Desert
An Office Building in New York City

You may have decided that your readers would be swept into the action more quickly by plunging them into the desert with hundreds of soldiers. That is not to say that no one ever goes into an office building during wartime. However, a war novel full of people faxing and copying is not going to sell very well!

Now imagine you are planning to write a sports story that follows the adventures of a baseball or football team. What do you think the setting for your last few chapters might be?

_____

_____

Chances are you ended your story on the baseball diamond or football field. Many famous sports stories (and quite a few sports movies!) end with an exciting game that decides the fate of the main character. In a good story, the place logically matches the action that is unfolding.

It is also important that the reader is able to imagine everything the author sees—the author must do a good job of **describing** the setting. That does not mean the story must happen in a real place! However, enough detail must be given so that the story **feels** real. In *Through the Looking Glass*, Lewis Carroll describes chess pieces that walk and flowers that talk. We don't believe it, of course, but he tells it so well we want to find out how the story ends!

Read how Carroll uses the setting of the world beyond the looking glass to suggest what part of the plot will be:

> For some minutes Alice stood without speaking, looking out in all directions over the country—and a most curious country it was. There were a number of tiny little brooks running straight across it from side to side, and the ground between was divided up into squares by a number of little green hedges, that reached from brook to brook.
>
> "I declare it's marked out just like a large chessboard!" Alice said at last. "There ought to be some men moving about somewhere—and so there are!" she added in a tone of delight, and her heart began to beat quick with excitement as she went on. "It's a great huge game of chess that's being played—all over the world—if this *is* the world at all, you know. Oh, what fun it is! How I *wish* I was one of them!"

Can you guess whether or not Alice will be allowed to join the game? What do you think?

_____

_____

Mood

When watching a movie, we are accustomed to having the mood set by music. Think of the famous violin music from the Hitchcock movie "Psycho"—it has become a kind of code to let people know something scary is going to happen. Books cannot set the mood with music (libraries would be too noisy!). They must use words.

> There was music from my neighbor's house through the summer nights. In his blue gardens men and girls came and went like moths among the whisperings and the champagne and the stars. At high tide in the afternoon I watched his guests diving from the tower of his raft or taking the sun on the hot sand of his beach while his two motor boats slit the waters of the Sound, drawing aquaplanes over cataracts of foam. On week-ends his Rolls-Royce became an omnibus, bearing parties to and from the city, between nine in the morning and long past midnight, while his station wagon scampered like a brisk yellow bug to meet all trains. And on Mondays eight servants including an extra gardener toiled all day with mops and scrubbing-brushes and hammers and garden shears, repairing the ravages of the night before.
> — F. Scott Fitzgerald, *The Great Gatsby*

What kind of setting is the author describing? Look for details that give you clues to time, place, and mood. The author mentions a private beach, motor boats, a Rolls Royce (a very expensive car), and plenty of servants. These are things that one finds at mansions in rich or resort areas. He also lets us know that there is a staff to clean up during the week. The mood, as the neighbor sees it, is one of luxury and leisure, all set up for the convenience of weekend guests.

Read the following passage. What can you tell about its time, place, and mood from the details it contains?

The wind whistled and howled. Brief bursts of rain blew in Frank and Linda's faces as they struggled up the hill. Frank's flashlight gave a feeble light, and there was no star or moon on this dark night to help it. At the top of the hill, they came to a rusty gate, in an old iron fence. When Linda tried to open it, it fell off in her hands. They passed through and Frank shone the light on one of many headstones that loomed out of the mist.

"1919–1929," he whispered. "So young. Twenty years ago."

Linda jumped. "Don't, Frank," She put her hand on his arm. "I'm already about to give up and go back."

The flashlight chose that moment to go out altogether.

TIME   _____

PLACE   _____

MOOD   _____

For time, you could have put night (the immediate time) or you could use the time clues in the story to figure out the year: Frank says that it is twenty years after the date on the headstone, which means the story takes place in 1949. For place, the headstones are your clue that Frank and Linda are in a cemetery. The mood is gloomy and frightening; one key to this is the dark, stormy weather. Weather often provides a sense of mood in fiction.

Read the following excerpt from Charles Dickens's A Christmas Carol, *and complete the exercise immediately following.*

Once upon a time—of all the good days in the year, on Christmas Eve—old Scrooge sat busy in his counting-house. It was cold, bleak, biting weather: foggy withal: and he could hear the people in the court outside, go wheezing up and down, beating their hands upon their breasts, and stamping their feet upon the pavement-stones to warm them. The city clocks had only just gone three, but it was quite dark already: it had not been light all day: and candles were flaring in the windows of the neighbouring offices, like ruddy smears upon the palpable brown air.

WRITING EXERCISE

In the passage above, the cold and dark outside mirror the cold and dark in Scrooge's soul: he helps no one and lives a solitary life. Imagine you are setting the scene for a character who is generous and helpful. What kind of day would you describe? What would the weather be like?

LESSON 3: PLOT ELEMENTS

Have you ever asked a friend to tell you about an episode of a T.V. show that you missed? Have you ever described your favorite movie to someone? In both cases, you were probably discussing the plot. Plot is the action of any book, story, movie, T.V. show, or play. It is the answer to the question, "And then what happened?"

All plots must have a beginning, middle, and an end.

Exposition _____ **Turning Point** _____ **Denouement**

The beginning of the plot is where characters are introduced and their backstories are filled in. Have you ever wondered why characters in books or movies so often tell each other things that they should know already?

> "You know, Laura," said Jim, slowly, "our father died only two days ago."
> "Yes, that's true," said Laura, "and what we are to do with all the money he left us, I cannot imagine."

Characters often spend a lot of time at the beginning of the story making sure the reader or audience knows everything necessary. This is called **exposition**. It may be done only by the **narrator**, or the one who tells the story.

The middle of the story is the **climax** or **turning point**. Here is where the **conflict** of the plot is resolved: hero defeats villain, or the heroine gets the man she was destined for. Resolving conflict means, of course, there must be opposing points of view. A novel where nobody disagreed about anything would put most people to sleep pretty quickly! Conflict is the spice of the plot.

The end of the story is usually the shortest section. It "ties up loose ends" as we like to say. This **denouement** gives the reader information on what characters will do after the story is over: villains are punished (or escape!), and people die or become rich and famous. The following denouement occurs at the end of _The Masque of the Red Death_, a famous short story by Edgar Allan Poe. In the story, a rich prince ignores suffering and sickness in his country and enjoys himself with friends in his beautiful palace. The ending tells us his fate:

> And now was acknowledged the presence of the Red Death. He had come like a thief in the night. And one by one dropped the revelers in the blood-bedewed halls of their revel, and died each in the despairing posture of his fall. And the life of the ebony clock went out with that of the last of the gay. And the flames of the tripods expired. And Darkness and Decay and the Red Death held illimitable dominion over all.

Poe published _The Masque of the Red Death_ in 1842. In today's language (in your own words), what has happened to the prince and all his friends at the end of the story?

_____

_____

Although Poe's language is old-fashioned, his tone and vocabulary are keys to let us know that everybody in the prince's palace has died by the end of the story. "Blood-bedewed," "despairing," "died," "Darkness," and "Decay" are some of his clues.

Conflict can occur between any two individuals or groups, but certain types of conflict are common in fiction.

Practice Exercise 4

The following excerpt from George Orwell's *1984* shows an example of conflict between an individual and society.

> BIG BROTHER IS WATCHING YOU, the caption said, while the dark eyes looked deep into Winston's own. Down at street level another poster, torn at one corner, flapped fitfully in the wind, alternately covering and uncovering the single word INGSOC. In the far distance a helicopter skimmed down between the roofs, hovered for an instant like a blue-bottle, and darted away again with a curving flight. It was the Police Patrol, snooping into people's windows. The patrols did not matter, however. Only the Thought Police mattered.

1. In Orwell's conflict between individual and a futuristic, repressive society, Winston fears the Thought Police above all other systems of control. Why do you think that is?
   (A) He lives in a society where he is constantly monitored.
   (B) He has been having thoughts of rebellion and is afraid his impulses are noticeable.

In *Sonny's Blues* by James Baldwin, two brothers argue over the future.

> "Sonny," I said, "I know how you feel. But if you don't finish school now, you're going to be sorry later that you didn't." I grabbed him by the shoulders. "And you only got another year. It ain't so bad. And I'll come back and I swear I'll help you do *whatever* you want to. Just try to put up with it till I come back. Will you please do that? For me?"
>
> He didn't answer and he wouldn't look at me.
>
> "Sonny. You hear me?"
>
> He pulled away. "I hear you. But you never hear anything *I* say."

TIP

To understand the conflict in a story, ask yourself "What does each character want?"

2. This conversation is an example of a different type of conflict. Do you think it represents:
   (A) The individual against family
   (B) The individual against another individual
   (C) The individual against nature

Which answer did you choose? What was your reason?

_____

_____

_____

WRITING EXERCISE

Remember, conflict in the plot exists to be resolved. Imagine you are a science fiction writer, and you have completed your book up to the following point. An alien race enslaves the entire human race. Although the humans are not harmed, they want to be free more than anything. All humans, in all countries, work together to plan to overthrow their alien captors. On the eve of the revolution, a new alien species arrives—one that plans to kill all humans and destroy the Earth for its resources. The only chance to defeat the killer aliens is for humans to work together with the aliens who own them—and stay slaves. How would you finish the story?

LESSON 4: POINT OF VIEW

Point of view (or POV) is the term we use to describe who is telling the story. Whose eyes are we seeing the action through? Another name for this person is the **narrator**. To narrate means to tell. Narrators in fiction generally fall into two categories: first person and third person.

A first-person narrator is part of the story. The narrator may be part of the action unfolding, or he or she may be telling a story about the past to another character. In first person narration, you will notice the use of the pronouns "I" and "we": "I called for the doctor," "we traveled the lonely road," and "I was afraid we were too late."

A third-person narrator does not take part in the action. He or she tells the story without intruding or influencing it. A third-person narrator may sometimes comment on the action but will never interact with the characters. "Sam called for the doctor," "Sam and Maria traveled the lonely road," and "they were afraid they were too late" are examples of third-person narration.

1. Look at the following two paragraphs. Which one is written in first person? Which in third person? How can you tell?

(A)

It's one o'clock, but as far as I'm concerned, the night is still young. The drinks are flowing and the music is hot. Charley, my best friend, doesn't agree. There are bags under his eyes and he sounds tired.

"Come on, man," he says. "I've got to get up for work in the morning."

"You go," I say and pour a fifth. "I've got a lot of party left in me." He shakes his head.

"You're my ride."

(B)

The first day of any new job, Marnie always brought a bottle of aspirin. A big bottle. She hated starting at a new place. If there was a way to do something wrong, she felt absolutely qualified to ferret it out. As a temp, she had once faxed twenty-five blank pages to an Insurance Agent's home office. She had only broken a major piece of equipment once (thank heaven that was before McGuigan & Son used copier codes), but it wasn't the big mistakes Marnie feared; it was the constant, constant tiny errors she couldn't control.

_____

A narrator may be either limited (know only part of the story) or **omniscient** (knowing everything). A first-person narrator is often limited by being a character in the story. For example, in Paragraph (A) above, the narrator can tell us only what he sees and hears; he does not know what Charley is thinking, if someone is standing behind him, or whether his car outside is being stolen.

A third-person narrator is not necessarily omniscient. In Paragraph (B), the narrator tells us only Marnie's thoughts and memories. A truly omniscient narrator will know everything, not only about the characters, but about the world they live in. Often, they predict the future as well. A historical novel, set in Pompeii in 79 A.D., might open as follows:

It was a cool day in autumn, by the sea in the shadow of Vesuvius. Shops were opening for the day and shopkeepers were thinking of their profit. Housewives were setting forth to bargain and trade. Children were playing in the street. Little did they know that before the day was finished their town would be witness to scenes of horror and destruction. Vesuvius would erupt in less than six hours. Those who could escape the death sentence would. But for many, warning would come too late.

2. List some of the things that this omniscient narrator knows about the situation in Pompeii.

_____

_____

_____

Questions 1 through 3 are based on the following passage.

Why Is the Speaker So Sad?

For five days I could not move. I could not eat. I could not even cry. I lay in the lonely *k'ang* and felt only the air leaving my chest. When I thought I had nothing left, my body still continued to be sucked of breath. At times I could not believe what had happened. I refused to believe it. I thought hard to make Precious Auntie appear, to hear her footsteps, see her face. And when I did see her face, it was in dreams and she was angry. She said that a curse now followed me and I would never find peace. I was doomed to be unhappy. On the sixth day, I began to cry and did not stop from morning until night. When I had no more feeling left, I rose from my bed and went back to my life.

No more mention was ever made of my going to live with the Changs. The marriage contract had been canceled and Mother no longer pretended I was her daughter. I did not know where I belonged in that family anymore, and sometimes when Mother was displeased with me, she threatened to sell me as a slave girl to the tubercular old sheepherder. No one spoke of Precious Auntie, either once living or now dead. And though my aunts had always known I was her bastard daughter, they did not pity me as her grieving child. When I could not stop myself from crying, they turned their faces, suddenly busy with their eyes and hands.

Only GaoLing talked to me, shyly. "Are you hungry yet? If you don't want that dumpling, I'll eat it." And I remember this: Often, when I lay on my *k'ang*, she came to me and called me Big Sister. She stroked my hand.

—Amy Tan, *The Bonesetter's Daughter*

1. The main idea of the passage is
   (A) The speaker is sick because she is afraid she will be sold as a slave.
   (B) The speaker feels alone in her grief for Precious Auntie.
   (C) The speaker wants to go to live with the Changs.
   (D) Precious Auntie is the speaker's mother.

2. From the context, you can infer that a *k'ang* is a
   (A) Sofa
   (B) Sleeping platform
   (C) Porch
   (D) Bedroom

3. The mood or **tone** of the passage is
   (A) Sorrowful and despairing
   (B) Brave and resourceful
   (C) Fun and lively
   (D) Neutral and restrained

Questions 4 through 6 are based on the following passage.

Why Is Joshua Upset?

When Joshua Carter's parents refused to let him join the army at 15, he was so angry that he ran away for a week. Not far; no further than a mile, to the home of his best friend. From Saturday night until Friday morning, Joshers, as he was known in the family circle, refused all contact with the parental abode, save for a few brief phone calls from his mother and one four page handwritten letter that he sneaked into the mailbox in the dead of night (about 9:30). The letter outlined his position in detail. It contrasted (with much underlining for emphasis) his noble motives and patriotic zeal with his mother and father's selfish pettiness in keeping him from the call of duty. He was proud of that letter. It was the missive of a warrior.

4. Who is the main conflict between in this passage?
   (A) Joshua and his friend
   (B) Joshua and himself
   (C) Joshua and the army
   (D) Joshua and his parents

5. Who is the speaker of the passage?
   (A) Joshua
   (B) A narrator who knows everyone's thoughts and feelings.
   (C) A narrator who knows Joshua's thoughts and feelings.
   (D) Joshua's friend

6. Which phrase best expresses the main idea of the passage?
   (A) A young boy is angry that he cannot enlist in the military.
   (B) Joshua's parents need to be a little stricter.
   (C) In a few more years, Joshua won't need permission to enlist.
   (D) Joshua has every reason to feel frustrated.

Questions 7 through 9 are based on the following passage.

What Is the Emergency?

We pulled up with a magnificent flourish at the hospital entrance, and the driver skittered out of the front seat and came around and opened the door and took my arm.

"My wife had five," he said. "I'll take the suitcase, Miss. Five and never a minute's trouble with any of them."

He rushed me in through the door and up to the desk. "Here," he said to the desk clerk. "Pay me later," he said to me, and fled.

"Name?" the desk clerk said to me politely, her pencil poised.

"Name," I said vaguely. I remembered, and told her.

"Age?" she asked. "Sex? Occupation?"

"Writer," I said.

750   BASIC SKILLS WORKBOOK FOR THE GED TEST, TASC, AND HiSET

"Housewife," she said.

"Writer," I said.

"I'll just put down housewife," she said. "Doctor? How many children?"

"Two," I said. "Up to now."

"Normal pregnancy?" she said. "Blood test? X-ray?"

"Look—" I said.

"Husband's name?" she said. "Address? Occupation?"

"Just put down housewife," I said. "I don't remember *his* name, really."

"Legitimate?"

"What?" I said.

"Is your husband the father of this child? Do you *have* a husband?"

"Please," I said plaintively, "can I go on upstairs?"

"Well, *really*," she said, and sniffed. "You're *only* having a baby."

— Shirley Jackson, *Life Among the Savages*

7. Where does the conversation between the two women take place?
   (A) In the delivery room of a hospital
   (B) At the front desk of a hospital
   (C) In a taxi
   (D) In the emergency room

8. This story was written in 1953. Why do you think the desk clerk wants to list the patient's occupation as housewife?
   (A) Having a career outside the home was not common for women in the 1950's.
   (B) The desk clerk thought the patient was delirious.
   (C) Hospitals in the 1950s generally listed all female patients as housewives.
   (D) The desk clerk wanted to cut down on paperwork.

9. Who is the speaker of the passage?
   (A) A married housewife in labor
   (B) An unmarried mother in labor
   (C) A doctor who monitors the front desk
   (D) A writer in labor

Questions 10 through 12 are based on the following passage.

Where Is Tito?

She scrambled up off the floor and only then did she realize how stiff and bruised she felt. What had happened? She went outside. The tent crouched with a hundred others, grey, weatherbeaten, huddled together as if a wolf were stalking the horizon.

A shadow of voices murmuring, the clatter of pots and pans and the smell of beans for breakfast (the same odor which had followed them from home to here, the big city, the capital, the President's house…ah, that was it, the President). But where was Tito? Her dark-eyed, skinny son, with two dimples so deep it looked like his smile had been nailed on. Indeed, his three-year-old eyes expressed an anguish that made his smile unreal, irrelevant.

"Tito!" she cried, "Tito! Where are you? Come here." A gust of empty wind darted past her, but nothing more, no answer, no footsteps, no voices, whispered in the dry canvas, hot under the midday sun.

She saw her old shawl, now a clumsy tent door, and remembered trying to decide whether to take it or not. She heard Chavela's voice calling to her: "Rosamaria! Ven pu'h! Nos vamos ahora mismo," and she remembered grabbing Tito's hand and hurrying after her friend.

That was it, of course. That's why there was no one here. They had risen early to go downtown to see the President, to tell him everything, to ask for help.

'But I went with them,' she thought, confused. With little Tito beside me, his thin legs agile as a spider's even though he's only three years old.

—Lake Sagaris, *The March*

10. Who is telling the story in this passage?
    (A) A narrator who sees everything and knows where Tito is
    (B) Chavela
    (C) A narrator who sees only what Rosamaria sees
    (D) A narrator who sees only what Chavela sees

11. Later in the story, we find out that Rosamaria lost her son during a political protest. Miners' wives and children go to the city to protest unemployment and poor working conditions. Based on this information, what do you think probably forms the major conflict of the story?
    (A) A small group of women and children against fate
    (B) One woman against the other women and children
    (C) A small group of women and children against society
    (D) The husbands of the women against the President's soldiers

12. What is the main idea of the passage?
    (A) Rosamaria is alone, confused, and wants to find her young son.
    (B) Rosamaria is bruised and hurt.
    (C) Rosamaria should go home to her husband and let him look for Tito.
    (D) Rosamaria should find a policeman to report Tito's disappearance.

CHAPTER 24 ANSWER EXPLANATIONS

Lesson 1: Theme

PRACTICE EXERCISE 1 (PAGE 738)

1. Examples are *Flare shot up, a rifle bullet cracked,* and *burn a hole in a man.*

2. **(B)** The darkness makes it difficult for him to accurately identify moving objects. In the first sentence, the speaker lets us know that the darkness is the prime reason he cannot distinguish between moving and stationary objects. There is nothing in the passage to support any of the other choices. The speaker does not wake, as a dreaming man might do. (C) and (D) may be true, but no mention is made here of the Germans' camouflage techniques or the speaker's medical history.

3. **(C)** If at first you don't succeed, try, try again. When the speaker does not get a good grade in September, she tries harder afterward. (A) This proverb means not to anticipate good fortune before it happens. (B) This proverb means it is easy to get foolish people to spend without thinking. (D) This proverb means more can be accomplished by writing than by fighting.

4. Answers may be that the speaker reviewed her notes, asked people to quiz her, attended tutoring sessions, and asked the teacher questions.

PRACTICE EXERCISE 2 (PAGE 740)

1. **D**
2. **C**
3. **A**
4. **E**
5. **B**

PRACTICE EXERCISE 3 (PAGE 741)

1. **(A)** A person who has been isolated will suffer. (B) Modern technology keeps people from being lonely is not true here. The last sentence notes that Sean has spent the day "in silent loneliness." (C) A person who has been isolated has many resources is not correct because the point of the passage is that none of these resources—T.V., computer, strangers—can replace human companionship for Sean.

Lesson 3: Plot Elements

PRACTICE EXERCISE 4 (PAGE 746)

1. **(B)** He has been having thoughts of rebellion and is afraid his impulses are noticeable. (A) is true. Everyone in Winston's society is being monitored. The details that tell us that are the caption on the poster and the surveillance of the helicopter. However, (B) is more detailed about why Winston is afraid that the Thought Police are specifically targeting him.

2. **(B)** Hopefully, most students will pick option (B). Sonny's brother's argument may represent the viewpoint of the rest of the family (A), but in this conversation they are two individuals opposing each other. Option (C), the individual against nature, is most

often seen in adventure or disaster stories. Unless a tornado comes into the room while Sonny and his brother are talking, it is unlikely to apply!

Lesson 4: Point of View

PRACTICE EXERCISE 5 (PAGE 748)

1. Paragraph (A) is written in the first person; the narrator says "I" and has a conversation with another character (his friend Charley). Paragraph (B) is written in the third person; the narrator is not part of the story and does not interact with Marnie in any way.

2. Some facts you could have listed are the weather, the actions of the characters; the thoughts of the characters, the future eruption of the volcano, and the fate of the town.

End-of-Chapter Questions (Page 749)

1. **(B)** The main idea of the passage is (B) *The speaker feels alone in her grief for Precious Auntie*. The speaker says the other members of the household did not pity her and turned their faces. Only her sister will speak to her. (A) The speaker shows signs of grief (crying, inactivity) rather than fear. She mentions Precious Auntie several times and mentions the slavery threat only once, casually. (C) is not supported by anything in the passage; she does not express a desire to live with the Changs. (D) is true, but it is a fact and not the theme, or main idea of the passage.

2. **(B)** From the context, you can infer that a *k'ang* is a (B) sleeping platform. (A) A sofa would be used by other family members as well. (C) does not make sense in the context. (D) The speaker says she lies on her *k'ang* as well as in her *k'ang*.

3. **(A)** Sorrowful and despairing describes the speaker's mood and the tone of the piece. Some keys are her dreams of Precious Auntie, belief in a curse, constant crying, and obsessive thoughts about the past. (B) and (C) describe more positive moods. These answer choices are not supported by the speaker's actions, thoughts, or vocabulary. (D) A neutral mood conveys events with little or no emotional color. This passage focuses on the feelings of the speaker and her family toward Precious Auntie's death.

4. **(D)** The main conflict in the passage is between (D) *Joshua and his parents*. There is no evidence in the passage for any of the other choices. (A) There is no mention of conflict with Joshua's host family. (B) Joshua is not conflicted at all about his motives and actions; he is very sure of his position. (C) The author does not state whether Joshua has actually had contact with an army recruiter.

5. **(C)** (A) The narrator says "he," not "I," therefore, the narrator is not Joshua. (B) The narrator does not reveal anyone else's motivations or thoughts. (D) The narrator says "his friend's house" not "my house."

6. **(A)** *A young boy is angry that he cannot enlist in the military.* (B) and (D) are opinions. (C) is a prediction.

7. **(B)** The conversation takes place (B) at the front desk of the hospital. (A) is not correct because the patient has not been admitted yet. (C) The patient gets out of the taxi before she begins to talk to the desk clerk. (D) The patient is there to be admitted to maternity, not emergency.

8. **(A)** Women did work outside the home in the 1950s but in far fewer numbers than today. The desk clerk is obviously uncomfortable with the thought of a professional

working mother, as she refuses to comply with the patient's repeated request. (B) and (D) are not supported by the passage. (C) is untrue.

9. **(D)** The speaker identifies herself as a writer, and the front desk clerk mentions that the speaker is "having a baby." (A) and (B) The speaker never confirms being a housewife. She does confirm having a husband. (C) No doctor is mentioned in the passage.

10. **(C)** The narrator shows us what Rosamaria sees. Because she does not know where Tito is, neither do we. The narrator is not a character in the story; there is no "I" or "we," and therefore (B) is not correct. Chavela is not present when Rosamaria wakes up, so (D) is incorrect.

11. **(C)** Political protest, unemployment, and bad working conditions are societal issues. (B) is incorrect because the women and children are united against a common enemy. (D) No mention is made of the men of the families. (A) Fate implies a supernatural foe; the women are facing a government of human beings.

12. **(A)** Rosamaria is alone, confused, and wants to find her young son. (B) is a detail of her physical condition. (C) and (D) are opinions; notice the word "should" in each.

Comparing Texts 25

LESSON 1: STRUCTURE

When evaluating a passage on the test—and especially when comparing two passages—an important point to consider is the **structure** of each author's argument. **Structure** means the pattern or organization the writer uses to put words together. Analyzing and understanding the techniques authors use to make their points will also help you when it is time to structure your own writing.

Chronological Structure

When time sequence factors into an author's argument, he or she might organize a passage **chronologically** (in time order). An author might use this approach to prove **causality** (that one event did or will cause another). For example, a report on a traffic accident would be clearest if it included the following information in the following order:

1. What the weather/road conditions were that day.
2. The positions of all cars involved immediately before the accident.
3. What occurred to cause the collision.
4. What action the affected drivers took immediately after the accident.

The facts in this case would be used as support to argue which driver was at fault for the accident.

Practice Exercise 1

The following facts support the argument, "It's important to check the night before to make sure everything is ready to start your next work day." Organize the statements in chronological (time) order from 1 to 7:

_____ 1. He missed an important department briefing on new passwords.

_____ 2. Although he rushed, he ended up leaving 30 minutes late.

_____ 3. Wendall forgot to set his alarm.

_____ 4. Wendell got to work 25 minutes late.

_____ 5. He got up 45 minutes late.

_____ 6. The traffic at that time was much heavier than the traffic at his usual time.

_____ 7. He was unable to log into his computer when he sat down to work.

Pros and Cons

Have you ever had a decision and been advised to make a pro/con list? Similarly, an author might look at the **pros** (positive aspects) and **cons** (negative aspects) of a subject. If you are reading paired passages, one might present the argument for (pro) and the other the argument against (con). You may then be asked which author you agree with, or which supports his or her position better.

The following paired paragraphs each look at the same subject (keeping houseplants) from opposite points of view.

Practice Exercise 2

Read paragraphs A and B and answer the following questions.

Paragraph A

Keeping houseplants is easy, pleasant, and fun. Houseplants freshen the atmosphere and beautify your home. They provide spots of color and natural beauty, especially in city apartments. Most houseplants require only sun, a roomy pot, and the right amount of water. Many easy-to-grow plants will sprout "babies" or shoots that can then be repotted and given to friends. Houseplants do not bark, need to be walked, or otherwise bother you or make demands on your time. They are the perfect companions!

Paragraph B

Houseplants are messy and troublesome. They are always dropping dead leaves and blossoms. They attract bugs as well, which can be difficult to get rid of. Furthermore, some plants have specific needs as far as light, water, and nutrients. If these are not met, they may die or develop unsightly fungus infections or brown spots. Even if your plants do flourish, this creates its own problems. What do you do when your spider plant sprouts 24 times in one year? Friends soon tire of receiving spider plant babies for every holiday. Furthermore, many plants can be toxic to children or pets. Save yourself the trouble and buy a painting of flowers instead!

1. Which paragraph presents the positive side (pro) of keeping houseplants?
   (A) Paragraph A
   (B) Paragraph B
   (C) Neither—they are both neutral.
   (D) Paragraph B makes some good points.

2. Which of the following facts could be used as additional support in Paragraph B?
   (A) Common houseplants are generally inexpensive.
   (B) Plants in the kitchen area can attract ants.
   (C) There are many local garden centers that are happy to help first-time buyers.
   (D) Houseplants can bloom all year round.

Emphatic Order

A third way authors can present their arguments is called **emphatic order** (order of importance). Emphatic order organizes supporting points from most to least (or least to most) importance. Who decides whether one point is more important than another? The author! If you are using emphatic order for your own writing, then *you* decide.

Practice Exercise 3

Read the passage below and answer the questions that follow.

Kerry has become increasingly concerned about her and her coworkers' health since the owner of the building she works in cut maintenance from every day to twice a week. She has drafted the following letter to the building manager.

Dear Mr. Wilson,

I am writing in response to the deteriorating working conditions here at 21 Parker Place. This sad state of affairs has been going on for three months now. It is entirely due to management's lack of concern with the health and safety of the tenants here. In the first place, neglected dusting, sweeping, and glass cleaning are causing dust to build up. This is not good for our computers, and it is even worse for those employees who suffer from allergies. Second, bathrooms are not being cleaned and bathroom supplies are not replaced in a timely manner. It is unhygienic and unpleasant not to be able to wash one's hands with soap before leaving the bathroom. Employees have been driven to bringing in their own supplies. Finally, and most important, the overflowing trash bins that are allowed to sit are starting to attract pests and rodents in disgusting amounts. This is unacceptable! Please let us know what you intend to do to address our concerns.

Sincerely,

Kerry Lingonberry

---

1. How has Kerry structured her argument?
    (A) Emphatic order, least to most important
    (B) Emphatic order, most to least important
    (C) Chronological order
    (D) Pro and con

2. Which of Kerry's supporting facts is not a health issue?
    (A) The bathrooms have no soap.
    (B) The trash is starting to attract rodents.
    (C) The dust is not good for the computers.
    (D) People with allergies are suffering.

3. Which of the following is Kerry's most important point?
    (A) Employees have to bring soap from home.
    (B) The problems have existed for three months.
    (C) The trash is attracting pests and rodents.
    (D) Dust is building up.

LESSON 2: PURPOSE

Texts you read on the test will not all have been written for the same purposes. There are many different goals for writers. The author may have wanted to describe or illustrate something; argue a controversial point (for or against); explain a process; narrate a story; or examine causes or effects of an event. These are just some possibilities. There are others.

Two authors may even write about the same topic without having the same goal. For example, suppose a teacher assigns his class the topic of "Friendship" and expects each student to write an essay. Student 1 decides to try to classify different types of friendship. Student 2 prefers to tell a story (or narrative) of how she met her best friend. These essays may both fulfill the requirements of the assignment without being in any way alike. As a matter of fact, the instructor will very likely get no two papers alike—and yet all of them may earn As!

The short paragraphs below all treat the same subject. However, the authors have very different purposes. After you read each, note on the line what you think the author's purpose is from the list above.

Practice Exercise 4

Paragraph A

A good night's sleep is no accident. In order to fall asleep naturally and feel rested, there are several steps you should follow. First, avoid caffeinated drinks after 6:00 P.M. In fact, limit all liquid intake to avoid the need to get up during the night. Avoid stressful activities or conversations that could keep you awake with worry before bedtime (do not watch scary movies, for example). Most of all, create a quiet, peaceful environment in your sleeping area, away from noise, distractions, or reminders of unfinished projects.

_____

Paragraph B

I had one of most unnerving experiences of my life last night. I was just dozing off when I heard someone singing sadly. The sound seemed to be coming from outside. I walked from window to window, but saw nothing. Suddenly the singing rose to a piercing scream and then was silenced. I grabbed my keys and phone (ready to call the police) and ran outside. There was no one there, and everything was peaceful. Next morning, my family would not admit to hearing anything. To this day I wonder who the mysterious screaming singer was.

_____

Paragraph C

Sleeping well at night is the cornerstone of a healthy lifestyle. Not getting enough sleep can trigger other unhealthy behaviors as well. For instance, a person trying to stay awake after a late night may consume too much caffeine or too many energy drinks. When someone is sleepy, it is also tempting to eat sugary treats for a boost of temporary energy. Three dough-nuts are no substitution for a good night's sleep and will only make the unfortunate eater feel jittery and sick. Finally, lack of sleep can be as dangerous as alcohol abuse when it comes to operating heavy machinery or driving. Too many people have made this fatal mistake.

Paragraph D

When a person has sleep apnea, the family often realizes it before the sleeper does. Symptoms of sleep apnea can be very dramatic: loud, buzzing snoring, for example, which has been described as "able to wake the dead" (or at least everyone else in the house). Another dis-concerting habit of sleep apnea sufferers is that their breathing stops, frequently and for no apparent reason. As the concerned family member creeps forward, looking for some sign of breath, the sleeper comes loudly and spectacularly back to life with unnerving snorts, gargles, and gasps. Sleep apnea is a disorder that affects the whole household.

Texts that are presented in pairs on the GED may cover the same topic but often present dif-ferent or opposing sides of an argument. Consider the following two paragraphs, which dis-cuss the effects of weight reduction surgery from opposite viewpoints. Answer the questions that follow.

Practice Exercise 5

Argument 1

Weight loss surgery should only be recommended if a person's life is threatened and all other weight loss attempts have failed. The most common type of weight loss procedure, gastric bypass, is major surgery, and there is a high probability of the patient experiencing minor or major complications. Even with no complications post-surgery (and for the rest of her life), the patient is expected to follow a rigorous proscribed diet. This limited diet carries with it the very real threat of keeping the patient from getting all the nutrients he or she needs. The threat becomes even more real if the patient refuses to follow the diet and fills up on junk instead. Finally, all this suffering and effort may be for naught. Weight loss surgery is not a guarantee that the patient will lose the weight. It is a big risk to take just to look better.

Argument 2

Weight loss surgery is an enormous benefit to those who wish to be healthier, but have had lit-tle to no success with other weight loss methods. Gastric bypass patients are far more likely to take weight off and keep it off, breaking the unhealthy cycle of lose-gain-lose. Understanding and following the strict diet makes them more aware of good nutrition and its benefits. Patients who lose weight often experience a reduction in symptoms of chronic conditions, such as high blood pressure. They have more energy and may experience improvements in mood and self-esteem due to successfully achieving health and appearance goals.

1. What is the topic of Arguments 1 and 2?

   _____

2. Which author does not encourage readers to consider weight loss surgery?

   _____

3. What are some of the benefits of gastric bypass described in Argument 2?

   _____

4. Which argument do you agree with? Give at least two reasons from your own experience.

   _____

   _____

   _____

   _____

LESSON 3: EVIDENCE AND EFFECTIVENESS

Often on the test you will be asked to determine how well-supported a passage is. You may be asked to read two passages and decide which is better supported. To make this type of decision, you need to analyze the evidence (support or proof) the author presents to prove that his or her main point is true. You then need to conclude whether the evidence is:

- Sufficient (is there enough of it?)
- Convincing (is it true?)
- On target (is it actually related to the main point?)

Consider the following thesis statement written by a student:

Handwriting should no longer be taught in public schools.

The author of this sentence intends to back up her position with the following facts:

- Keyboarding is easier than writing by hand.
- Keyboarding is faster than writing by hand.
- Writing by hand helps develop fine motor skills.

Is the evidence sufficient? The answer to this question is tied to how long the piece of writing is. For a long paragraph or a short essay, three examples would probably be enough. For a longer piece, the writer will need to come up with more facts and examples.

Is the evidence convincing (true)? Some points could be argued. Keyboarding may certainly be easier for some, but not necessarily everybody. Similarly, a good keyboardist probably will produce words faster than someone writing by hand. A slow keyboardist, however, will not. This statement is too general to be always true. Point 3 is convincing, but it is not on target—it is a fact that does not help to prove the main point. In fact, it supports the opposite point—it would be better placed in a paragraph or essay that argues handwriting *should* continue to be taught in schools.

Is the evidence on target? Yes, in this case, all three facts relate to the main idea. Facts that do not, would be: "Home Economics attendance has been falling for years" or "Students who always use calculators cannot do long division."

Practice Exercise 6

Read the following paragraph. After each sentence, mark whether you think the evidence in that sentence is convincing and on target (Y) or not relevant (N). After you read all the support, decide if there is enough of it (sufficiency).

Learning to play a piano piece requires the same concentration, repetition, and determination that it takes to play a sport well. A piano student must pay attention to his teacher's instructions, just as an athlete must listen to her coach. _____ Musical scores are complex, and a student must master fingering, rhythm, changes on dynamics (loud/quiet notes), and use of the pedal. _____ The coordination required to do all this correctly together takes years to learn. _____ Piano players can often find jobs accompanying choirs or singers. _____ Although skilled sight-readers (musicians who can play a piece well the first time they see it) exist in the music community, they are rare. _____ Most piano students start by practicing only part of a piece, playing it slowly, and often playing only one hand at a time. _____ Clarinet players do this too. _____ As the student gets more familiar with the music, his performance gets faster and better. _____ He plays fewer wrong notes. _____ This is similar to, for example, a basketball player who must practice individual skills like dribbling and passing, before he or she uses them in a game. _____

Practice Exercise 7

Read the following short passages and answer the questions after them.

Passage 1

Don't elect Tom Brown for Mayor. He is a terrible, terrible person. You should hear some of the things he has said and done! They would make you really angry! You don't want a person like that for Mayor. He says he will raise the minimum wage and lower taxes, but he is most likely lying. Even though he created a lot of jobs with his business, the people in those jobs probably weren't happy. Plus, even though he never said so, he will almost certainly start spending the city's money on unnecessary programs if he is elected. He has not said he will do so, but how can we believe him? Don't vote for him unless you want the entire city to go downhill!

Passage 2

Vote for Eleanor Amontillado for Governor! Eleanor has 28 years of political experience—she was a community organizer for 10 years, a City Councilperson for another 10, and the Mayor of Smalltown for two terms. During Eleanor's terms as Mayor, unemployment decreased by 5%. She also organized Smalltown's Great City Litter Pick-Up three years in a row. She was instrumental in bringing two major manufacturing firms to the area, which resulted in 500 new jobs being created. Even while campaigning for this office, she is negotiating to bring yet another hiring company to Smalltown. Eleanor Amontillado is the candidate to bring our state the prosperity we need and deserve!

1. Which passage provides more effective evidence?
   (A) Passage 1 provides more detailed support.
   (B) Passage 2 provides more detailed support.
   (C) Both passages are equally well supported.
   (D) Neither passage is well supported.

2. Complete the following sentences using examples from one or both of the above passages:

   Passage _____ is better supported because

   _____

   _____

   _____

   For example,

   _____

   _____

   _____

   _____

3. Give two to three detailed, convincing examples from your own experience to support the sentence below:

There are simple steps every person can take in daily life to improve his or her health.

_____

_____

_____

_____

_____

_____

LESSON 4: COMPARING AND CONTRASTING

Comparing and **contrasting** are two skills that you will need on the test. To compare means to look at two things and notice the similarities; to contrast means to find the differences. For example, read the descriptions of two **siblings** (brothers or sisters) below:

Arne and Elke are brother and sister. Arne is six, and Elke is three. Arne has short blond hair, and Elke has short brown hair. Arne likes playing with his trucks, while Elke likes to build things with her blocks.

Arne is extremely patient with his little sister, and they play together well. She follows him everywhere and cries when he goes to school and she can't. They both love spaghetti and hate thunderstorms.

The following chart diagrams some comparisons and contrasts between the two children as a parent or teacher might make them:

Similarities	Differences
They love the same food.	One is a boy, and one is a girl.
They both hate thunderstorms.	Arne is older.
They play together well.	One has blond hair, and one is brunette.

By noting similarities and differences between people, things, or ideas, one may get a better idea of the nature of each and the relationship between the two. On the test, you will probably be called on to compare two authors or pieces of writing, as below.

Practice Exercise 8

Arnold and Pam are **adjunct** (part-time) professors. They each teach one course at Casperville Community College. Arnold teaches Statistics; Pam teaches Mechanical Drawing.

Below are two evaluations from the fall semester, one for each professor. There are five questions on each form, plus a space for comments. Students rate their experience in each category SD (strongly disagree), D (disagree), A (agree), or SA (strongly agree). The forms are **anonymous** (students need not sign their names).

	Arnold Jackson	SD	D	A	SA
1	The teacher was on time and had material planned for the whole session.			✔	
2	The textbook/materials were informative and interesting.			✔	
3	When the teacher came to class, he/she was prepared for the lesson.				✔
4	This course was useful to me in my academic/professional career.			✔	
5	This instructor understood and could communicate the material.				✔
6	Comments: I was scared to take this class but Prof. Jackson made the material easy. I would take one of his classes again.				

	Pam Douglass	SD	D	A	SA
1	The teacher was on time and had material planned for the whole session.		✔		
2	The textbook/materials were informative and interesting.			✔	
3	When the teacher came to class, he/she was prepared for the lesson.		✔		
4	This course was useful to me in my academic/professional career.			✔	
5	This instructor understood and could communicate the material.		✔		
6	Comments: I was really interested in this subject and could tell that Professor Douglass knew her stuff, but she didn't have a lot of patience for students who needed help. Also she was late a lot.				

Write three paragraphs in response to the evaluations above. Paragraph 1 should detail things that are different on the evaluations; paragraph 2 should list those things that are the same. Paragraph 3 should give your opinion of the two professors, based on the information you have. Do you think one teacher sounds better than the other? Which one would you prefer to have for a teacher in a class you were taking?

Paragraphs should average 4 or 5 sentences but do not all need to be exactly the same length.

_____

_____

_____

_____

_____

_____

_____

_____

_____

_____

_____

_____

There are several possible goals for making comparisons and contrasts. Most of these goals involve making a decision. When faced with a major life decision, many people find it useful to make a pro/con list. For example, an employee might be offered a promotion. On one hand, she would make more money and have more decision-making power; on the other, she would have more accountability to her bosses, more responsibility, and less leisure time.

When taking your test, you will probably be comparing and contrasting passages to decide either which you agree with or which is better supported. Paired passages usually have the same subject. Their thesis statements will definitely be different. Some of the supporting facts and details may agree, and much will probably disagree. Consider the two paragraphs below.

Practice Exercise 9

Stella Robles' Paragraph

My husband and I are considering moving to a larger house in Big City, and I'm all for it. It would be more expensive, but with another child on the way we could use the room. Plus, by moving into the city limits, my husband would become eligible for city jobs he is qualified for (Big City requires all municipal employees to live in the city). One of the drawbacks, of course, is that our taxes would go up. However, with Big City's mass transit system, we could probably give up one of our cars. Another thing to consider is that Big City's schools are excellent.

Howard Robles' Paragraph

My wife and I are considering moving to a larger house in Big City, but I'm against it. It would be more expensive, for one thing. We're expecting another child, but we could always convert/add on to our current house. I would become eligible for city jobs that I have experience in, but I'm happy with the job I have now. Of course, the city jobs would pay more, but then our taxes would go up. We would probably have to give up one of our cars, since parking is limited. Plus, I'm not sure Stella could so easily find another job in her field.

1. Are Howard and Stella's topics and attitudes the same?
   (A) Yes
   (B) No
   (C) Their topics are the same, but their attitudes are different.
   (D) Their topics are different, but their attitudes are the same.

2. On a separate piece of paper, list Stella's pros and cons. Then list Howard's pros and cons. Then write a paragraph stating which spouse you agree with and why. Use examples from both paragraphs, as well as examples from your own experience.

CHAPTER 25 ANSWER EXPLANATIONS

Lesson 1: Structure

PRACTICE EXERCISE 1 (PAGE 757)

1. 6
2. 3
3. 1
4. 5
5. 2
6. 4
7. 7

PRACTICE EXERCISE 2 (PAGE 758)

1. **(A)** *Paragraph A*. This paragraph outlines all the benefits of having plants.
2. **(B)** *Plants in the kitchen area can attract ants*. This is the only negative answer choice, and Paragraph B is all about the disadvantages of plants.

PRACTICE EXERCISE 3 (PAGE 759)

1. **(A)** *Emphatic order, least to most important*. Kerry signals this by her use of the phrase, "Finally, and most important" at the end of the letter.
2. **(C)** *The dust is not good for the computers*. This would cause productivity or financial problems. Nonworking computers is not a health issue.
3. **(C)** *The trash is attracting pests and rodents*. Kerry signals this by her use of the phrase, "Finally, and most important" at the end of the letter.

Lesson Two: Purpose

PRACTICE EXERCISE 4 (PAGE 760)

Paragraph A: To explain a process
Paragraph B: To narrate a story
Paragraph C: To examine effects
Paragraph D: To illustrate/describe

PRACTICE EXERCISE 5 (PAGE 761)

1. The topic of the paragraphs is weight loss surgery.
2. The author of Argument 1 presents the negative aspects of weight loss surgery.
3. Losing weight permanently; being more aware of good nutritional habits; experiencing relief from health conditions related to the weight; improving in emotional health and mental outlook.
4. Answers may vary. The student should start with a topic sentence stating his or her opinion and follow with 2 or 3 examples from personal experience.

Lesson 3: Evidence and Effectiveness

PRACTICE EXERCISE 6 (PAGE 763)

The sentence should be labeled Y; Y; Y; N; Y; Y; N; Y; Y; Y
There is sufficient evidence to support the main point.

PRACTICE EXERCISE 7 (PAGE 763)

1. **(B)** Passage 2 is better supported (see question 2).
2. Passage 2 is better supported because it gives detailed examples of Eleanor Amontillado's public service, while passage 1 makes unsupported statements and repeats itself. For example, passage 2 mentions Amontillado's job-creation history. Passage 1 predicts that Tom Brown will overspend when the author has no examples to give of Tom Brown ever overspending.
3. Answers may vary. Examples should be as specific as possible. For instance: Drinking unsweetened tea or plain water can cut a surprising amount of sugar out of a person's diet.

Lesson 4: Comparing and Contrasting

PRACTICE EXERCISE 8 (PAGE 765)

The differences between the evaluations are the teachers' ratings for questions 1, 3, and 5. For questions 2 and 4, the professors receive the same rating. The comments also address differences in the two professors' teaching styles. For paragraph 3 the student may pick either professor, as long as the student has at least 2 or 3 reasons for picking that professor.

PRACTICE EXERCISE 9 (PAGE 767)

1. **(C)** *The topics are the same, but their attitudes are different.* They both discuss moving to Big City. Stella is for it, and Howard is against it.
2. Stella's pros: could use more room for growing family, Howard eligible for city jobs, good mass transit system, excellent schools. Cons: More expensive overall, higher taxes.

   Howard's pros: Eligible for city jobs, higher pay. Cons: More expensive overall, don't really need bigger house, happy with his current job, higher taxes, limited parking, difficult for Stella to find new job.

   The student may agree with either spouse as long as the student can give at least 2 or 3 reasons to back up his or her position.

Poetry on the TASC and HiSET Only

"How do poems grow? They grow out of your life."

—Robert Penn Warren

Poetry is all around us. When you listen to your favorite songs on the radio, you are listening to poetry set to music. When you memorize a rap that you like, you are memorizing poetry. When you sing a hymn in church or the national anthem at a ball game you are singing poetry.

A poet starts with a feeling that he or she wants to share. The way the poet wants to share the feeling is to create a picture in your mind. This type of picture is called an **image**. Without images, there is no poetry. Unlike an artist, a poet cannot paint images with a brush or draw them with pen or pencil. Poets use words to paint images. However, poets do have tools and techniques to communicate their picture to you. You will read about these tools and techniques in this chapter.

HOW THIS CHAPTER IS ORGANIZED

Lesson 1: Meter and Rhyme

Poetry does not look like other forms of writing! In this lesson, you will learn about the special rhyme and rhythm patterns that poets use.

Lesson 2: Symbolism

A symbol is an element of a poem—it might be a person, a flower, or the Sun—that the poet chooses to represent or "stand for" something else. Lesson 2 will give you a chance to explore some symbols often used in poetry and prose.

Lesson 3: Figurative Language

Figurative language (or "figure of speech") is heard in everyday life as well as poetry. Have you ever said your hands were as "cold as ice" or that your heart was "broken?" You were using figurative language.

Lesson 4: Tone

Tone is the overall emotion, or feeling, of the poem's speaker. Is the tone of the poem happy? Angry? Sad? Lesson 4 shows you what clues to look for.

LESSON 1: METER AND RHYME

One of the things that you may have noticed already is that poetry looks different on the page than prose.

> I think that I shall never see
> A poem lovely as a tree.
>
> > —Joyce Kilmer

> My Life had stood—a Loaded Gun—
> In Corners—till a Day
> The Owner passed—identified—
> And carried Me away—
>
> > —Emily Dickinson

Poetry is written in shorter lines that do not usually go across the whole page. Several lines of poetry are often grouped together in **stanzas**, with a space before the next group, or stanza, starts.

If you read poems aloud, they sound different than prose as well. Many poems **rhyme**. The endings of two or more of their lines sound similar. In the Joyce Kilmer lines above, *see* rhymes with *tree*. In Emily Dickinson's poem, *Day* and *away* rhyme.

Some poetry does not rhyme, but still has its own rhythm. You can feel rhythm in a poem the way you can feel the beat in a song. Read the following lines with stress on the capitalized words:

> When MY love SWEARS that SHE is MADE of TRUTH
> I DO belIEVE her THOUGH I KNOW she LIES,
>
> > —William Shakespeare

What do you notice about the **meter** of the lines? (The meter of a poem tells us which words to **emphasize** and which to stress lightly). You may observe that each line has five stressed words or word parts (**syllables**). You may also realize that each stressed word or syllable follows an unstressed word. This meter is called **iambic pentameter** (penta means five). It is one of the many rhythms poets use to express themselves.

Often the best way to approach poetry is as if you were not reading, but carrying on a conversation with a friend. Use the commas and periods in the poem as a guide to pause and take a breath if you are reading aloud. In the following poem by Mike Bristow, the speaker is experiencing a nosebleed. The speaker's tone is conversational as he describes how his nosebleed represents and reminds him of a past relationship. Take turns reading the lines to each other in small groups of two or three. Can you feel his pain?

VOCABULARY

Emphasize: to bring attention to; to highlight.

Iambic: a technical term in poetry; two syllables together, one stressed and one unstressed. (Example: the night was cold and dark.)

This Is One of the Bad Ones

Ah, the nosebleed, the only bleeding you can feel coming 20 seconds before it happens.

It's been bleeding for 2 hours, out of both nostrils, heavily.

For a while I give up and just bleed into the sink, but that makes me woozy.

It's now of all times I think of you. I mean, not much else to do really.

Unless there's something I'm willing to bleed all over.

Then I realize this truly represents longing, a nosebleed.

You feel like you're being slowly drained of your life, but most likely it won't kill you.

And if you complain about it your friends will call you a little girl.

—Mike Bristow

The short poem "Hope" by Donna Berrodin is a special type of poem called a haiku. Haiku have unique requirements: They must have seventeen syllables, five in the first line, seven in the second, and five in the third (last). Count the syllables. Yes, the poem fits the description of a haiku. Has Berrodin fulfilled the requirements of this poetry form?

Hope
In winter work through
the cold but, above all, see
blooms beneath this snow.

WRITING EXERCISE

Pick one of your favorite songs. Find the lyrics (words) online (You can do this by typing the first line of the song into your search engine and identifying the song by name and songwriter when it appears onscreen). Read the lyrics to your favorite song without the music (if possible, try not to hum to yourself)!

TIP

When reading poetry aloud, do not stop at the end of every line; take breaths at punctuation marks, like commas or periods.

Write a paragraph. What do you notice about the lyrics to your favorite song when they are separated from the music? Do they rhyme? Do they inspire the same feeling as song and music together? If not, what feelings do they inspire?

LESSON 2: SYMBOLISM

Symbols are all around us. A red light is a symbol to stop; green means go.

All of us who want to safely drive or cross the streets realize the importance of these symbols. The American flag is a symbol of the United States, which is why there are rules about treating the flag with respect. Almost all major religions have symbols associated with them, which their followers recognize and often wear or carry for inspiration. A symbol is simply one thing that stands for, or represents, another.

Practice Exercise 1

How many of these common symbols can you match with the ideas, places, or things that they represent?

_____ 1. An American eagle	(A) A hospital zone
_____ 2. A single red rose	(B) New York
_____ 3. A white H on a blue background	(C) The United States of America
_____ 4. The Big Apple	(D) Paris
_____ 5. The Eiffel Tower	(E) Love or beauty
_____ 6. Throwing a towel into a boxing ring	(F) Giving up the fight

The American eagle is our national bird and a common symbol of the USA (Uncle Sam is another common symbol). A single red rose can represent beauty because it is beautiful, but given as a present, it can also represent love. A white H on a blue background is used to alert drivers that they are passing a hospital. The Big Apple is a symbol of, and nickname for, New York City. Shots of the Eiffel Tower are routinely used in movies and T.V. shows to let viewers know a scene is set in Paris. And finally, "throwing in the towel" has become so associated with giving up the fight that people now use the phrase to mean giving up in situations outside of boxing as well.

Poets frequently use common symbols. For example, Dylan Thomas writes,

> Do not go gentle into that good night,
> Old age should burn and rave at close of day;
> Rage, rage against the dying of the light.

Night and darkness (*dying of the light*) are common symbols of death. In this stanza, the poet is saying not to accept death, but to fight it.

In his *Ode: Intimations of Immortality*, William Wordsworth uses some common symbols, or examples, of natural beauty. Part of his message is that adults are more likely to ignore the beauty of nature than children are.

> The Rainbow comes and goes,
> And lovely is the Rose,
> The Moon doth with delight
> Look round her when the heavens are bare;
> Waters on a starry night
> Are beautiful and fair;
> The sunshine is a glorious birth;
> But yet I know, where'er I go,
> That there hath past away a glory from the earth.

Practice Exercise 2

What symbols of nature's beauty do you find in this stanza?

1. _____

2. _____

3. _____

4. _____

5. _____

Practice Exercise 3

Poets are not restricted to common symbols, of course. Sometimes the symbols they use are more personal. In this poem, the poet contrasts the images of a city skyline and cold churches and museums to suggest different approaches to learning about a new place.

The Charter Tour

"This is Italy too,"
someone said.
as we sat above the skyline of Florence
golden Florence,
after being dragged
through churches and museums,
past paintings and churches,
in a hushed, cold gloom.
"This is Italy too,"
someone said again.
"Doesn't this count?"
flicking a hot green leaf
away from the table.
Drinking bubbly cold water
above golden baking Florence.

1. In the poem, the speaker is a tourist. How does she or he feel about being rushed through tourist attractions as part of a tour group?

   _____

   _____

   _____

2. The poem contrasts two different approaches to touring a foreign country. What sort of approach does the phrase "dragged through churches and museums" suggest?

   (A) We've got to see as much as we can as quickly as we can.

   (B) We can enjoy ourselves and drink things in; it doesn't matter if we don't see everything.

Some of the clues that let you know that (A) is the best answer: "dragged" is a word with negative connotations; she repeats twice that "This is Italy too" when describing the relaxing experience looking at the skyline.

The following poem by Erica Jong uses one **recurring**, or repeating symbol many times. See if you can guess the significance of the repeated image before you finish reading the poem and answer the questions.

Wrinkles

My friends are tired.
The ones who are married are tired
of being married.
The ones who are single are tired
of being single.

They look at their wrinkles.
The ones who are single attribute their wrinkles
to being single.
The ones who are married attribute their wrinkles
to being married.

They have very few wrinkles.
Even taken together,
they have very few wrinkles.
But I cannot persuade them
to look at their wrinkles
collectively.
& I cannot persuade them that being married
or being single
has nothing to do with wrinkles.

Each one sees a deep & bitter groove,
a San Andreas fault across her forehead.
"It is only a matter of time
before the earthquake."
They trade the names of plastic surgeons
like recipes.

My friends are tired.
The ones who have children are tired
of having children.
The ones who are childless are tired
of being childless.

They love their wrinkles.
If only their wrinkles were deeper
they could hide.

Sometimes I think
(but do not dare to tell them)
that when the face is left alone to dig its grave
the soul is grateful
& rolls in.

—Erica Jong

In this poem, Erica Jong uses the repeated symbol of wrinkles to convey her main message. In our society, developing wrinkles is usually considered undesirable. Just look at all the anti-aging products advertised every day on television and in magazines! Jong takes advantage of our attitudes toward wrinkles to use them as a negative symbol in her poem.

3. What do the images of wrinkles represent in the poem?
    (A) That the speaker's friends spend too much time in the Sun
    (B) The problems that married people face
    (C) The faults that the speaker's friends see in themselves and their lives

4. If the speaker gave one piece of advice to all her friends, what do you think it would be?
    (A) "Stop bothering me with your complaints."
    (B) "Be kind to yourselves. We all have our problems to bear."
    (C) "Find a good plastic surgeon."

LESSON 3: FIGURATIVE LANGUAGE

Figurative language is a way of expressing feeling. It is often contrasted to **literal** language, where the speaker or writer's words mean exactly what they say. For example, a literal statement would be, "My sister painted her house yellow." A figurative statement that addresses the same situation might be, "The yellow paint my sister chose was so bright it lit up the whole neighborhood." What is the difference in the two statements?

_____

_____

_____

You may have noticed that the first sentence presents only the facts, while the second sentence gives the reader an image or sense of the brightness of the color. Figurative language helps convey emotion and detail to the reader or listener.

Two types of figurative language are **simile** and **metaphor**. A simile or metaphor compares two different things to find how those things are really alike. Similes and metaphors use images to express how the poet feels. You might have heard that the difference between a simile and a metaphor is that a simile uses the word "like" or "as" and a metaphor does not. That is true, but their purpose is the same.

TIP

For each person, place, or thing mentioned in a poem, ask yourself: what might this represent?

Let us look at an example. You may have a friend with green eyes. Her boyfriend could say, "Her eyes are like emeralds." He has just used a simile. Are eyes and stones the same thing? No. But what is alike about them is that they are both green and beautiful.

What if your friend's boyfriend said, "Her eyes *are* emeralds?" That would be a metaphor. The meaning, however, is the same as the simile in the paragraph above.

Practice Exercise 4

Metaphors are often used in song lyrics. Consider these lines from a song made popular by the singer Meatloaf in the late 1970s:

> But you've been cold to me so long
> I'm crying icicles instead of tears

1. What do you think the relationship is between the singer and the woman he is singing to?

    _____

    _____

Cold is a term often used to describe people we do not feel connected to. By claiming that the woman has made him cry icicles, the singer shows us how alone he feels.

A song that uses simile to create an opposite effect is the standard "At Last," made popular by legend Etta James, and recently revived by singer Beyoncé.

> At last my love has come along
> My lonely days are over
> And life is like a song…
>
> At last the skies above are blue
> My heart was wrapped up in clover
> The night I looked at you

> —Mack Gordon and Harry Warren

2. What difference can you see between the metaphors used in the second song and those used in the first? What kind of mood do the images in "At Last" suggest?

    _____

    _____

    _____

Practice Exercise 5

Below are some common similes that people use every day. How many have you used? Can you match the first part of each simile with the ending?

_____ 1. As good as   (A) a cucumber

_____ 2. As sharp as   (B) pie

_____ 3. They fought like   (C) a pancake

_____ 4. As big as   (D) gold

_____ 5. As easy as   (E) a feather

_____ 6. As pretty as   (F) a picture

_____ 7. As alike as   (G) a needle

_____ 8. As light as   (H) two peas in a pod

_____ 9. As flat as   (I) an elephant

_____ 10. As cool as   (J) cats and dogs

WRITING EXERCISE

You can create your own metaphors and similes. Add some images of your own to the following paragraph to convey the main character's distress.

Andre hated the beach. The hot sand on his feet was a burning _____ _____. Jumping into the cold water was like diving into a cold _____. He didn't like the feel of sand in his shoes. It itched like _____. Andre was ready to go home long before his friends were.

Practice Exercise 6

Take a look at the following lines from "A Birthday" by Christina Rossetti. How many similes or metaphors can you find?

> My heart is like a singing bird
>   Whose nest is in a watered shoot;
> My heart is like an apple-tree
>   Whose boughs are bent with thickset fruit;
> My heart is like a rainbow shell
>   That paddles in a halcyon sea;
> My heart is gladder than all these
>   Because my love is come to me.

There are three similes. The speaker makes three comparisons to her heart in the first stanza: she compares it to a singing bird, an apple tree hung with fruit, and a rainbow shell. What kind of images are these? Are they beautiful or ugly? How do you think the speaker is feeling?

_____

_____

_____

The speaker compares her heart to beautiful, peaceful things because she feels happy.

1. If she were to make a fourth, she would most likely compare her heart to:
   (A) The beautiful full moon
   (B) A dead bouquet of flowers
   (C) A crying child

2. What is the similarity between the speaker's heart and an apple tree full of fruit?
   (A) The speaker likes apples.
   (B) The speaker and her love planned to meet under an apple tree.
   (C) The tree is ready for harvest, and the speaker's heart is ready for love.

Another love poem (literature is full of love poems!) that uses similes is Robert Burns's "A Red, Red Rose." Here is the first stanza.

> O my luve's like a red, red rose,
>   That's newly sprung in June;
> O my luve's like the melodie
>   That's sweetly played in tune.

One of the differences between Burns's poem and Rossetti's is that Robert Burns wrote in a Scottish **dialect**, which means some of his words are spelled differently; *luve* instead of love or *melodie* instead of melody. However, the comparisons they make are very similar.

3. When Burns's speaker compares his love to a red rose, what does he want to communicate?
   (A) His love wants him to send her flowers.
   (B) They both grow in the ground.
   (C) His love and the rose are both beautiful.

Compare Burns's images of love to those in the following lines:

> If I loved you, it would be so cold.
> Like ice cathedrals rising from the sea,
> like glowing shapes of frozen water, trapped
> by all that air and light and wind can do
> to them.

Burns uses pleasant images and vocabulary to project a positive view of love: *rose, melodie,* and *sweetly,* for example. The second poet uses images and vocabulary that suggest an inability to connect with the loved one: *cold, frozen, and trapped.*

LESSON 4: TONE

When we communicate with each other face to face, much of the emotional content of our messages is conveyed through the sound of our voices and the expressions on our faces. Try saying "I love you" or "Will you marry me?" or even "Get out and never come back" without changing your voice or moving your face. Doesn't have a lot of punch, does it?

Poets must communicate their **tone**, or feelings, without the benefit of facial expressions and vocal or voice effects. How do poets do this?

Vocabulary is the poet's most important tool to set his or her tone. The words of a poem are carefully chosen to project the images that communicate emotion to a reader. The following excerpt is from "Beowulf," an **epic** (extremely long) poem about a warrior who fights a savage monster. In the excerpt, the monster Grendel makes its first attack.

> Grim and greedy the gruesome monster,
> Fierce and furious, launched attack,
> Slew thirty spearmen asleep in the hall,
> Sped away gloating, gripping the spoil,
> Dragging the dead men home to his den.

Because this is a version of a very old poem, some of the words may not be familiar to you. "Slew," for example, means "killed," and "spearmen" are "soldiers." However, other words are commonly in use today and can give us a good idea of the mood of this part of the poem. "Grim" and "gruesome" are words still used in horror fiction and movies. "Fierce" and "furious" are violent words. "Dragging the dead men" is a violent image. The tone of the whole excerpt is one of violence and fear.

Practice Exercise 7

1. What exactly happens in this excerpt?
   - (A) The monster kills 30 warriors and steals their bodies.
   - (B) 30 warriors kill the monster and bury its body.
   - (C) 30 warriors attack the monster and are killed.

The following poem, "A Sioux Prayer" conveys different emotions than the excerpt you just considered. As you read this poem, make a short list of key words on a separate piece of paper. What clues to the tone do you get from the vocabulary of the speaker?

> Oh, Great Spirit, whose voice I hear in the winds
> Whose breath gives life to the world, hear me
> I come to you as one of your many children
>   I am small and weak
> I need your strength and wisdom
>
>   May I walk in beauty
> Make my eyes ever behold the red and purple
>   sunset.
> Make my hands respect the things you have made
>   And my ears sharp to your voice.
> Make me wise so that I may know the things you
>   have taught your children.
>
> The lessons you have written in every leaf and rock
>   Make me strong--------!
> Not to be superior to my brothers, but to fight my
>   greatest enemy….myself
>
> Make me ever ready to come to you with straight
>   eyes,
> So that when life fades as the fading sunset,
> May my spirit come to you without shame.

—Translated by Chief Yellow Lark

1. What key words did you include in your list?

_____

_____

_____

Some of the words you could have included are Spirit, life, strength, wisdom, beauty, respect, wise, taught, and strong (there are more). The name of the poem is also a clue: the poet intended it as a prayer. The tone of the poem is one of reverence and respect.

Structure (remember meter and rhyme?) can also help you hear the tone of the poem. Notice the frequent breaks between lines and short stanzas of the following poem.

Ukranian Immigrant 1996

It's difficult to say.
I spoke you.
You didn't understand.

At home
had problems but
we knew what to do.

Here
have problems
I have no place to go.

Have you, did you,
Should you, will you

So many ways to say a thing.
I am so much like the dog.
I understand you
but can't speak.

Drink to drink,
Laugh to laugh.
The last thing
that dies
is hope.

The structure of the poem reinforces the sense that the speaker is expressing himself slowly, in a language strange to him. The **halting** (halting means slow with frequent stops) lines and the speaker's calm statements indicate discouragement but not ultimately hopelessness (the last word of the poem, like the "last thing" left to the speaker, is *hope*).

Read the following poem and answer questions 1 through 3.

What Does the Poet See?

The Great Figure

Among the rain
and lights
I saw the figure 5
in gold
on a red
fire truck
moving
tense
unheeded
to gong clangs
siren howls
and wheels rumbling
through the dark city.

—William Carlos Williams

1. The subject of the poem is the sight of a fire truck racing through the city at night. What tone do the short lines and this subject suggest?
   (A) Regret
   (B) Excitement
   (C) Boredom

2. The main symbol in this poem is a gold 5 on a red fire truck. Williams also wrote a famous poem about a red wheelbarrow. What can you infer from these two poems?
   (A) He liked the color red.
   (B) He lived in both the country and the city.
   (C) He liked to write poetry about everyday things.

3. This poem contains three examples of onomatopoeia (words that sound like the sound they make). What are they?
   (A) Moving, tense, unheeded
   (B) Rain, lights, siren
   (C) Clangs, howls, rumbling

Read the following poem and answer questions 4 through 6.

How Did Things Turn Out Differently?

Grown-up

Was it for this I uttered prayers,
And sobbed and cursed and kicked the stairs,
That now, domestic as a plate,
I should retire at half-past eight?

—Edna St. Vincent Millay

4. When the speaker was a little girl, what was it that she "sobbed and cursed and kicked the stairs" for?
    (A) She wanted to be grown-up and stay up late.
    (B) She didn't like the food on her plate.
    (C) She never wanted to grow up.

5. The poem contains two rhyming pairs. What are they?
    (A) Sobbed and cursed, kicked the stairs
    (B) Prayers and stairs, late and plate
    (C) Prayers and stairs, plate and eight

6. What is the tone of the poem?
    (A) Humorous
    (B) Serious
    (C) Grim

Read the following poem and answer questions 7 through 9.

What Made Richard Cory Unique?

Richard Cory

Whenever Richard Cory went downtown,
   We people on the pavement looked at him:
He was a gentleman from sole to crown
   Clean favored, and imperially slim.

And he was always quietly arrayed,
   And he was always human when he talked;
But still he fluttered pulses when he said,
   "Good morning," and he glittered when he walked.

And he was rich—yes, richer than a king—
   And admirably schooled in every grace:
In fine, we thought that he was everything
   To make us wish that we were in his place.

So on we worked, and waited for the light,
    And went without the meat, and cursed the bread;
And Richard Cory, one calm summer night,
    Went home and put a bullet through his head.

—Edwin Arlington Robinson

7. The second stanza says that Richard Cory "glittered when he walked." People normally do not glitter; metals or shiny materials glitter. What do you think is the best interpretation of this phrase?
   (A) The people imagine Richard Cory to shine as though he were made from gold or precious metal.
   (B) Richard Cory was covered in glitter.
   (C) Richard Cory wore a lot of jewelry when he went into town.

8. For the working people of the town, Richard Cory is a symbol of the pleasures of being rich. What probably happened to their image of his life when he committed suicide?
   (A) They wanted to be rich more than ever.
   (B) They realized that not every rich person is happy.
   (C) They wanted to know who would inherit all his money.

9. Robinson's poem follows a very precise rhyming sequence known as ABAB. After reading the poem, what do you think ABAB means?
   (A) The first two lines of each stanza rhyme together, and the second two lines of each stanza rhyme together.
   (B) None of the lines rhyme.
   (C) The first and third lines of each stanza rhyme, and the second and fourth lines of each stanza rhyme.

Read the following poem and answer questions 10 through 12.

How Does the Singer Want the Audience to Feel?

Song: Down Hearted Blues

Gee, but it's hard to love someone, when that someone don't love you.
I'm so disgusted, heartbroken too. I've got the downhearted blues.
Once I was crazy about a man. He mistreated me all the time.
The next man I get, he's got to promise to be mine, all mine.

'Cause you mistreated me, and you drove me from your door.
You mistreated me, and you drove me from your door.
But the Good Book says, "You've got to reap just what you sow."

Trouble, trouble, seems like I've had it all my days.
Trouble, trouble, seems like I've had it all my days.
Sometime I think trouble is gonna follow me to my grave.

I ain't never loved but three men in my life.

Lord, I ain't never loved but three men in my life.

One's my father, and my brother, and the man that wrecked my life.

Now it may be a week, and it may be a month or two.

I said, it may be a week, and it may be a month or two.

All the dirt you're doing to me is, honey, coming back home to you.

I've got the world in a jug and the stopper in my hand.

I've got the world in a jug and the stopper in my hand.

And if you want me, pretty papa, you've got to come under my command.

—Lovie Austin and Alberta Hunter

10. "Downhearted Blues" was sung frequently by Alberta Hunter and recorded by many other singers. It is not sung quickly, and lines are often repeated. What do you think one of the reasons for this might be?

    (A) The song's writers felt the message of the lyrics was important and wanted to make sure listeners heard the words.

    (B) The words are hard to sing.

    (C) Most blues singers don't get much time to practice and don't know the songs well enough to sing them quickly.

11. What is the tone of the song?

    (A) Angry but not afraid

    (B) Sad but not defeated

    (C) Happy but not joyful

12. What is the best interpretation for the phrase "You've got to reap just what you sow?"

    (A) Don't worry about what you do; if you're careful, you can get away with anything.

    (B) If you do good things, good things will happen to you; if you are bad, bad things will happen.

    (C) You can get away with a lot, but only if nobody's watching.

CHAPTER 26 ANSWER EXPLANATIONS

Lesson 2: Symbolism

PRACTICE EXERCISE 1 (PAGE 774)

1. C
2. E
3. A
4. B
5. D
6. F

PRACTICE EXERCISE 2 (PAGE 775)

1. Rainbow
2. Rose
3. Moon
4. Water
5. Sunshine

PRACTICE EXERCISE 3 (PAGE 775)

1. "Dragged," "hushed," "cold," and "gloom" are adjectives that suggest the experience is negative.
2. **(A)**
3. **(C)** The speaker shows that all her friends "attribute their wrinkles" to their problems and she cannot persuade them otherwise. (A) is not supported by the poem. The Sun is not mentioned in any stanza, and no one is worried about Sun damage. (B) is not correct because the speaker's unmarried and childless friends are unhappy too.
4. **(B)** The speaker sees what her friends do not, that people in all sorts of situations are worried about their wrinkles. In stanza 3, she tries to show them that the wrinkles are not important but "cannot persuade them to look." (A) The speaker thinks about telling her friends to leave their faces alone but doesn't "dare to tell them." (C) Her friends already have plastic surgeons.

Lesson 3: Figurative Language

PRACTICE EXERCISE 4 (PAGE 778)

1. You might have said the singer feels rejected.
2. You may have noticed that in contrast to the loneliness projected by the first song, Gordon and Warren's similes (life is like a song and heart was wrapped up in clover) suggest hopefulness and happiness.

PRACTICE EXERCISE 5 (PAGE 779)

1. D
2. G
3. J
4. I
5. B
6. F
7. H
8. E
9. C
10. A

PRACTICE EXERCISE 6 (PAGE 779)

1. **(A)** (The beautiful full moon) provides a lovely image similar to those Rossetti uses. The other two are sad, negative images that would not fit in with the poet's similes.

2. **(C)** The speaker is happy "because my love is come to me." The tree is full of fruit; the speaker is full of love. The speaker does not tell us whether she likes apples or not, and there is no mention of the place she and her love will meet.

3. **(C)** However the reader may personally feel about roses, a red rose is traditionally viewed as a beautiful flower. The speaker's love does not grow in the ground; to say it does is taking the simile too far. There is also nothing in this stanza (or the rest of the poem) to indicate that the speaker's love wants him to send her flowers.

Lesson 4: Tone

PRACTICE EXERCISE 7 (PAGE 782)

1. **(A)** The monster kills thirty warriors and steals their bodies. Even if we do not know the word "slew," we know that the men are "dead" at the end of the poem and that the monster takes them to its "den." (B) is not correct because the monster is still alive at the end of the poem; (C) is incorrect because the warriors are "asleep" when Grendel attacks, and so they cannot attack the monster.

End-of-Chapter Questions (Page 784)

1. **(B)** The short lines and the subject of a fire truck heading to a fire suggest *excitement*. This is also supported by vocabulary like *tense* and *moving*.

2. **(C)** (B) is not correct because wheelbarrows are not necessarily found only in the country. (A) Red is not the only color found in this poem.

3. **(C)** *Clangs, howls, rumbling*: Each of these words represents the sound made by the gong, the siren, and the wheels. The words in (B) represent things, not sounds. The words in (A) are descriptive of actions, not sounds.

4. **(A)** The speaker says her actions were "for this" in the first line, and "this" refers to the title: Grown-up. She also finds it funny in the last two lines that she now wants to go to bed early.

5. **(C)** These are the only four words that rhyme and also appear in the poem.

6. **(A)** The poem is not about a serious or especially dramatic topic. The speaker simply finds it funny that being grown-up is different than she imagined as a child.

7. **(A)** This line emphasizes the attitude of the working people who feel Richard Cory is somehow made of different material than regular people. They are surprised when he acts "human" (stanza 2). He is a gentleman, "clean," "slim," and full of "grace." The other two choices are not supported by the lines of the poem.

8. **(B)** The theme or main idea of the poem is that those we think live perfect lives may often have problems no one knows anything about.

9. **(C)** Taking the first stanza as an example, *downtown* and *crown* rhyme (the first and third lines) as do *him* and *slim* (the second and fourth lines).

10. **(A)** A written poem may be re-read. This is not possible with a song that is being sung, so repetition is often built into the lyrics for the audience. (B) is neither correct nor logical. (C) Most blues singers are trained and experienced musicians and practice constantly. The tempo (time) of blues is traditionally slow.

11. **(B)** The singer says she is "heartbroken" and "wrecked," but also looks forward to "the next man I get."

12. **(B)** The quote is originally from the Bible. To *sow* means to plant, and to *reap* means to harvest or gather. So whatever you plant (good or evil), that is what you will harvest.

Drama on the TASC and HiSET Only

27

> "Drama is life with the dull bits cut out."
>
> —Alfred Hitchcock

Every type of literature is special, but drama is the only **genre** intended to be performed. To fully appreciate drama, the speeches should be heard and the gestures seen. When we read plays or scripts as they are called, we are reading the instructions that the actors, directors, and all cast and crew members follow to make each performance memorable.

Can you imagine going to a concert to hear your favorite band and being handed a piece of sheet music to read instead? A talented musician could tell from the written music that it was beautiful, but that still does not give the same enjoyment of listening to it! That is a little like what happens when we read a play instead of seeing one. We recognize the beauty of the language and the craftsmanship of the author, but that does not substitute for the experience of seeing the play on the stage.

HOW THIS CHAPTER IS ORGANIZED

This chapter will look at several elements of a play's script:

Lesson 1: Stage Directions

Every time a character in a play pours water into a glass, opens a door, or walks across the stage, he or she is following a stage direction. Who decides these actions? Who communicates them to the actor?

Lesson 2: Dialogue

All conversation in a play must be written, memorized, and rehearsed by the actors.

Lesson 3: Characterization

How does a playwright communicate what his or her characters are like using only dialogue and action?

Lesson 4: Mood

Lesson four reviews how a playwright may use scenery, sound, or special effects to suggest atmosphere for a performance.

LESSON 1: STAGE DIRECTIONS

We often think of plays in terms of actors taking turns giving speeches. When you think of scenes from exciting movies, or even scenes from television shows you watch regularly, you realize how **misleading** this is. How many speeches are there during a car chase that finishes a great action movie? And one of the most shocking—and **memorable**—scenes ever in movies was filmed without either actor speaking a word: the shower scene from Alfred Hitchcock's 1960 masterpiece *Psycho*.

Practice Exercise 1

That does not mean that the actors in those scenes were left to do anything they wanted when the camera started rolling. They had very specific instructions from their screenwriters and directors. When you read plays, you see how those instructions are presented to actors. In the passage below, the **stage directions** are in italics in parentheses.

The scene is a doctor's examining room. One patient sits on the examining table.

Dr. Rosen: (*offstage*) Judy? (*A knocking is heard*).
(*Mrs. Milner looks displeased. She sits up straighter on the examining table.*)

Mrs. Milner: (*mutters*) I've told him about that. (*Calls*) It's okay, I'm ready!

(*The examining room door opens.* Dr. Rosen *enters, followed by the* nurse. *He closes the door, sets a chart down on the counter, and walks over to* Mrs. Milner. *He has a determinedly cheerful manner. The* nurse *faces away from the audience, busying herself with work at the counter*).

Dr. Rosen: (*smiling broadly*) Well and how are we today, young lady?

(Mrs. Milner *does not smile in response*).

Mrs. Milner: (***acidly***) Forgive me, young man, for reminding you that when you were still falling off your skateboard, I was halfway to social security. I am more than twice your age. It seems you sometimes forget.

1. What do Mrs. Milner's stage directions tell the actor to do? What do these actions tell you about how she feels about the Doctor's informal manner?

_____

_____

2. If Mrs. Milner did not mind being called "young lady" or thought it was funny, how would you expect her stage directions to read?

_____

_____

Practice Exercise 2

Match the terms on the left with the correct definitions on the right.

_____ 1. Acidly

_____ 2. Memorable

_____ 3. Stage Directions

_____ 4. Genre

_____ 5. Misleading

(A) Not easily forgotten

(B) In a sarcastic or bitter manner

(C) Something that diverts from the truth

(D) Instructions to the cast of a play

(E) A type or kind of literature

Some stage directions have to do with movement of the entire body (*Charles falls over the sofa*) while some are small gestures or describe expressions on an actor's face (*Madeline puts down the glass; Angelina looks horrified*). Some directions are very clear (*Sandy puts down the tray, picks up the knife, and begins to cut sandwiches*). Others require the actor to **interpret** the intentions of the writer (*Mr. Nicholson gives Hercule an aggressive look*). What is an aggressive look? Often the actor and director must decide this together.

VOCABULARY

Interpret: to explain, translate, or provide a meaning.

Practice Exercise 3

Read the following passage from Susan Glaspell's Trifles, *and answer the questions below.*

What Happened in the Kitchen?

Characters

GEORGE HENDERSON, *County Attorney*

HENRY PETERS, *Sheriff*

LEWIS HALE, *A Neighboring Farmer*

MRS. PETERS

MRS. HALE

SCENE; The kitchen in the now abandoned farmhouse of John Wright, *a gloomy kitchen, and left without having been put in order—unwashed pans under the sink, a loaf of bread outside the bread-box, a dish-towel on the table—other signs of incompleted work. At the rear the outer door opens and the* Sheriff *comes in followed by the* County Attorney *and* Hale. *The* Sheriff *and* Hale *are men in middle life, the* County Attorney *is a young man; all are much bundled up and go at once to the stove. They are followed by the two women—the* Sheriff's *wife first; she is a slight wiry woman, a thin nervous face.* Mrs. Hale *is larger and would ordinarily be called more comfortable looking, but she is disturbed now and looks fearfully about as she enters. The women have come in slowly, and stand close together near the door.*

County Attorney. (*Rubbing his hands.*) This feels good. Come up to the fire, ladies.

Mrs. Peters. (*After taking a step forward.*) I'm not—cold.

Sheriff. (*Unbuttoning his overcoat and stepping away from the stove as if to mark the beginning of official business.*) Now, Mr. Hale, before we move things about, you explain to Mr. Henderson just what you saw when you came here yesterday morning.

TIP

Look for directions in parentheses and *italics* to see what the characters are doing.

1. What is the most likely reason that these characters have come to this farmhouse?
   (A) To collect the rent
   (B) For a surprise party
   (C) To investigate a crime
   (D) To celebrate a birthday

2. What is the most likely reason that the two women stay near the door?
   (A) They don't want to enter the unpleasant atmosphere of the kitchen.
   (B) They are warmer there.
   (C) They don't want to get in the way of the investigation.
   (D) They don't want to mess up the room.

LESSON 2: DIALOGUE

Most plays do not have a narrator to give us information about what has happened in the characters' pasts, or what their relationship is to each other. When we watch or read a play, we must depend on **dialogue**, or conversation, to tell us what the characters are thinking and feeling.

The dialogue each character speaks is indicated by putting the character's name (sometimes in capitals) to the left. A colon (:) follows the name. After the colon come the words and stage directions for that character. The words are in regular type and the stage directions are in parentheses and italics. You can see how this works in the selections below.

Practice Exercise 4

What can you tell about the relationship between the characters in the following passage?

ANDY: I guess you all know why I called this meeting. I guess you all been feeling the pinch as much as I have—some more than me.

LEN: Listen, the boss said—

ANDY: (*interrupting and banging his fist on the table*) I'm tired of listening to what the boss says! And if you had any sense, you would be too! It's what he don't say that gets me! He don't say raise, he don't say overtime, he don't say benefits—

STEVE: Yeah!

LEN: All right, all right. Sure, it feels good to yell. But plenty of places are doing worse than us. Lots of shops closed up already. At least we got a job!

HARRY: Shut up with that noise!

LEN: I got a right to speak.

ANDY: (*Stands up*) Listen! If we want to get anywhere, we got to hang together. I got an idea.

1. What is your best guess at the relationship between these four men?

_____

_____

2. You may have noted that they are having a meeting and are unhappy with their working conditions. What words or phrases in the dialogue indicate this?

_____

_____

Often one character will give a long speech, which gives insights into his or her **motivations**, plans, or emotions. This is called a **monologue** or a **soliloquy**. The speech may be delivered to other characters in the play, or the speaking character may be alone on the stage. In the following monologue, the character of Jackson (a rich business owner) talks about his successes and failures. Read the passage and answer the questions.

> JACKSON: I started a company. It failed. Partly because it was a bad time to start anything, but mostly because of my own ignorance. I thought I could treat my company like a job. Come in 9 to 5, take holidays. Take a salary! Have benefits! I didn't realize a company demands the attention and sacrifice of your closest relative on life support. Fourteen hour days. Seven days a week. Buckets of cash, in but not out. So my company failed. Left me ruined, in debt up to my ears. I didn't care. I started another company. And it failed. *Four times* I went through this. I was like a boxer in the ring, everybody yelling at me, "Stay down! Stay down!" But I kept thinking of a proverb I heard once: *Fall down seven times, stand up eight.* I stood up one more time. And now I'm rich.

3. What is a proverb that expresses the same meaning as *fall down seven times, stand up eight*?
   - (A) If at first you don't succeed, try, try again.
   - (B) A stitch in time saves nine.
   - (C) Little pitchers have big ears.
   - (D) Too many cooks spoil the broth.

4. What word do you think best **characterizes**, or describes, Jackson?
   - (A) Fearful
   - (B) Determined
   - (C) Fun-loving
   - (D) Resigned

Read the following passage and answer the question below.

What Does Gwendolen Want Jack to Do?

GWENDOLEN: Married, Mr. Worthing?

JACK: (***astounded***): Well—surely. You know that I love you, and you led me to believe, Miss Fairfax, that you were not absolutely **indifferent** to me.

GWENDOLEN: I adore you. But you haven't proposed to me yet. Nothing has been said at all about marriage. The subject has not even been touched upon.

JACK: Well—may I propose to you now?

GWENDOLEN: I think it would be an **admirable** opportunity. And to **spare** you any possible disappointment, Mr. Worthing, I think it only fair to tell you quite frankly **beforehand** that I am fully determined to accept you.

JACK: Gwendolen!

GWENDOLEN: Yes, Mr. Worthing, what have you got to say to me?

JACK: You know what I have got to say to you.

GWENDOLEN: Yes, but you don't say it.

JACK: Gwendolen, will you marry me? (*Goes on his knees.*)

GWENDOLEN: Of course I will, darling. How long you have been about it! I am afraid you have had very little experience in how to propose.

JACK: My own one, I have never loved anyone in the world but you.

GWENDOLEN: Yes, but men often propose for practice. I know my brother Gerald does. All my girlfriends tell me so. What wonderfully blue eyes you have, Ernest! They are quite, quite blue. I hope you will always look at me just like that, especially when there are other people present.

—Oscar Wilde, *The Importance of Being Earnest*

5. What type of play do you think this passage of dialogue probably comes from?
   (A) A murder mystery
   (B) A family drama
   (C) A comedy of manners
   (D) A drama of social injustice

6. Which of the following is NOT a synonym for astounded?
   (A) Surprised
   (B) Dumbfounded
   (C) Enraged
   (D) Amazed

Practice Exercise 5

Match the terms on the left with the correct definitions on the right.

_____ 1. Genre

_____ 2. Disheveled

_____ 3. Dialogue

_____ 4. Indifferent

_____ 5. Stage directions

_____ 6. Admirable

_____ 7. Astounded

_____ 8. Misleading

_____ 9. Beforehand

_____ 10. Spare

(A) Instructions to actors on how to move

(B) Extremely surprised

(C) Messy; disorganized

(D) To treat or deal with gently

(E) A type of literature

(F) Deceptive; leading to error

(G) Early or ahead of time

(H) Without interest

(I) Words spoken by characters in a play

(J) Inspiring approval or respect

LESSON 3: CHARACTERIZATION

Characterization means to describe or understand a character's nature. Characters onstage reveal their personalities through actions, words, and appearance (costumes and makeup).

In *Oedipus Rex,* a Greek play over 2,000 years old, Oedipus puts out his own eyes because he is overcome with **remorse** at the things he has done (audiences in the past enjoyed violent stories as much as we do today!). This action and his speeches reveal that he takes responsibility for unintentionally killing his father and becoming King in his father's place. More recently, in Tennessee Williams's play *The Glass Menagerie,* the fact that Laura takes care of a collection of glass animals reveals her fragility as a character. The seven women in the cast of Ntozake Shange's play *For Colored Girls Who Have Considered Suicide When the Rainbow is Enuf,* are recognized as different not only by their words and actions, but by their wardrobe— each woman wears one particular color throughout the entire play.

VOCABULARY

Remorse: being sorry for or ashamed of one's actions.

Practice Exercise 6

We often use adjectives to describe characters. What adjectives would you use to characterize the two women in the passage below?

> (*It is Monday morning.* ALLISON *is rushing back and forth across the stage, looking for items and getting ready for work.* SARITA *is seated at the kitchen table, calmly drinking a cup of coffee.*)
>
> ALLISON: (*digging through her purse*) Where in the world are my keys?
>
> SARITA: (*puts her cup down and picks up the paper*) Same place you left them last night—in the tray by the door.
>
> (*Allison rushes to the front door. She looks at a tray on the bookshelf next to it.*)
>
> ALLISON: They're not here. Somebody moved them. Somebody stole them!

SARITA: Oh that's right. (*She puts the paper down calmly and goes to her purse. Carefully she looks through it.*) You didn't leave them in the tray last night—you left them in the door. (*She produces the keys from her purse.*) I thought I'd better put them somewhere safe.

(*ALLISON runs across the stage and grabs the keys from SARITA's hand.*)

ALLISON: (*angrily*) Are you *trying* to make me late? Why couldn't you just have put the keys back in the tray when you found them?

SARITA (*sitting back down and beginning to butter toast*) I was too busy thanking heaven that I didn't find you killed by an axe murderer when I came in.

Compare and contrast the personalities of the two women by looking at their words and actions. How are they the same? How are they different?

TIP

Look at three things—actions, words, and appearance— to understand what makes a character tick!

1. Circle the words that describe Sarita; underline the words that describe Allison.

Careful	Calm	Angry
Disorganized	Relaxed	Rushed

Read the following passage from Arthur Miller's *Death of a Salesman*, and answer the questions.

VOCABULARY

Accommodating: easy-going; not likely to make problems.

Masterful: strong; a leader.

LINDA: (*taking the jacket from him*) Why don't you go down to the place tomorrow and tell Howard you've simply got to work in New York? You're too **accommodating**, dear.

WILLY: If old man Wagner was alive I'd a been in charge of New York now! That man was a prince, he was a **masterful** man. But that boy of his, that Howard, he don't appreciate. When I went north the first time, the Wagner Company didn't know where New England was!

LINDA: Why don't you tell those things to Howard, dear?

WILLY: (*encouraged*) I will, I definitely will. Is there any cheese?

LINDA: I'll make you a sandwich.

WILLY: No, go to sleep. I'll take some milk. I'll be up right away. The boys in?

LINDA: They're sleeping. Happy took Biff on a date tonight.

WILLY: (*interested*) That so?

LINDA: It was so nice to see them shaving together, one behind the other, in the bathroom. And going out together. You notice? The whole house smells of shaving lotion.

WILLY: Figure it out. Work a lifetime to pay off a house. You finally own it, and there's nobody to live in it.

LINDA: Well, dear, life is a casting off. It's always that way.

WILLY: No, no, some people—some people accomplish something. Did Biff say anything after I went this morning?

LINDA: You shouldn't have criticized him, Willy, especially after he just got off the train.

2. Mark each of the following statements true (T) or false (F).

(A) Willy feels unappreciated at work._____

(B) Linda is very supportive of Willy._____

(C) Linda is annoyed that both her sons are visiting at once._____

(D) Willy and his son Biff do not always get along._____

(E) Willy feels he has accomplished great things in life._____

LESSON 4: MOOD

A play's **mood** or **atmosphere** is usually outlined in the first few paragraphs of a script. These paragraphs often "set the scene" of the play by describing what the stage looks like when the curtain goes up. The opening of Tennessee Williams's *The Glass Menagerie*, for example, directs that the play should look "dim and poetic." One of the ways Williams suggests accomplishing this is to have a **transparent** "fourth wall" or see-through curtain in front of the set at the beginning. Before the action starts, this thin curtain is raised.

Practice Exercise 7

Read the following two descriptions of stages set for a scene. What differences do you find between the two? What similarities?

(A) *The curtain rises on a dark graveyard, white tombstones shining in the moonlight. There is a falling, rusty fence that runs behind the graves. Offstage, an owl hoots and we hear the wind, which has been whistling quietly, rise to a moan. Slowly a church bell begins to ring. It rings twelve times (midnight) and is still.*

(B) *The curtain rises on the interior of a living room decorated for New Year's Eve. There is a crowd of people on stage, all dressed in their holiday party clothes. The people are motionless. Suddenly dance music **blares** at the audience. The people begin to move, talk to each other, and dance. After a moment they begin to count down in **unison** from ten…Ten! Nine! Eight! until they all shout together HAPPY NEW YEAR! Streamers drop from the ceiling and horns are blown as everyone laughs and hugs.*

1. (A) Which set of directions (A) or (B) conveys a lonely atmosphere?

_____

(B) What are the details that support your conclusion?

_____

_____

_____

It is important to remember that everyone in the audience is not required to respond to the same symbols in the same way. You may hate parties and feel relaxed and at ease in a graveyard at midnight. However, it is useful to recognize the mood that the playwright *intends* to set by the scene he or she describes.

Practice Exercise 8

Match the terms on the left with the correct definitions on the right.

_____ 1. Mood   (A) To sound loudly

_____ 2. Transparent   (B) Clear; see-through

_____ 3. Blare   (C) Sad or lonely

_____ 4. Unison   (D) To sound slowly and regularly

_____ 5. Toll   (E) To call up or remind

_____ 6. Melancholy   (F) Together; as one

_____ 7. Evoke   (G) Feeling or atmosphere

TAKE IT TO THE THEATRE

Movies often set the mood or atmosphere of a scene with background music. Next time you go to the movies or watch a DVD, pay attention to the music behind the action or dialogue. Does it help you understand what the characters are feeling? Does it clue you in to what is about to happen?

Sets of modern plays are often quite **minimalist**, that is, using little scenery and as few **props** as possible. This allows the audience to focus on the characters and dialogue. The setting directions below are from Marc Kaminsky's *In the Traffic of a Targeted City*, a play about the bombing of Hiroshima, Japan in World War II.

Setting

Japanese-like screens define the space of a New York studio, subway, office, cocktail party, bedroom and also several locations in Hiroshima. The screens have windows that can be opened and closed, a sliding door and one other entrance.

The set pieces consist of a bench and a stool; they are used to suggest a subway, an artist's stool, and a Japanese desk. Shifts in lighting and music help to create the various locations.

As the audience enters, saxophone and piano music play over speakers.

Practice Exercise 9

1. The scene of *In the Traffic of a Targeted City* switches back and forth rapidly from New York City to Hiroshima. What is one of the advantages of Kaminsky's minimalist set to the audience?

   (A) The play is cheaper to produce this way.

   (B) The audience will not have to wait for a lot of scene changes.

   (C) The audience will not be able to hear the actors over the piano and saxophone.

   (D) The actors will not have to worry about tripping over scenery.

Questions 1 through 3 refer to the following passage.

ANGIE: Do you remember Joey? Do you? The face of an angel. Joey, I mean, not Billy. Although Billy could sometimes be…you remember that look Joey used to get—that look of his?

DEIRDRE: I remember the look. You were just lucky they got you away from him. You'd be dead by now. Criminals get that look. (*Deirdre tries to remove Angie's glass when she is not looking, but Angie yanks the glass back. She glowers at Deirdre and refills the glass from a bottle on the table.*) Whyn't you have some coffee now? You want some coffee?

ANGIE: Leave me alone. And grab the waiter when he goes by…my bottle's going dry. It wasn't criminal. Bruised innocence, that's what it was. All those tears in his eyes. Pure face, blue eyes.

DEIRDRE: Black heart.

(*A waiter approaches while Angie is draining her glass. Deirdre frowns at him and shakes her head. He moves away.*)

ANGIE: My own true love, Joey. I wonder who's taking care of him now?

DEIRDRE: Whoever's got late shift on Cellblock D.

1. What is the most likely relationship between Angie and Deirdre?
   (A) Business acquaintances
   (B) Strangers
   (C) Two friends
   (D) Bartender and customer

2. Why does Deirdre send the waiter away?
   (A) She wants to make a toast.
   (B) She thinks Angie has had enough to drink.
   (C) She thinks the drinks at this restaurant are too expensive.
   (D) She wants a drink herself.

3. How does Deirdre feel about Angie's friend Joey?
   (A) She thinks he should be given a second chance.
   (B) She wishes she could meet someone like him.
   (C) She feels sorry for him.
   (D) She thinks he was dangerous.

Questions 4 through 6 are based on the following passage.

Setting: *The setting is the yard that fronts the only entrance to the Maxson house-hold, an ancient two-story brick house set back off a small alley in a big-city neighborhood. The entrance to the house is gained by two or three steps leading to a wooden porch badly in need of paint…the yard is a small dirt yard, partially fenced, except for the last scene, with a wooden sawhorse, a pile of lumber, and other fence-building equipment set off to the side. Opposite is a tree from which hangs a ball made of rags. A baseball bat leans against the tree. Two oil drums serve as garbage receptacles and sit near the house at right…*

CORY: How you doing, Mr. Bono?

TROY: Cory? Get that saw from Bono and cut some wood. He talking about the wood's too hard to cut. Stand back there, Jim, and let that young boy show you how it's done.

BONO: He's sure welcome to it.

(Cory *takes the saw and begins to cut the wood.*)

Whew-e-e! Look at that. Big old strong boy. Look like Joe Louis. Hell, must be getting old the way I'm watching that boy whip through that wood.

CORY: I don't see why Mama want a fence around the yard noways.

TROY: Damn if I know either. What the hell she keeping out with it? She ain't got nothing nobody want.

BONO: Some people build fences to keep people out…and other people build fences to keep people in. Rose wants to hold on to you all. She loves you.

—August Wilson, *Fences*

4. What does the scenery description tell you about the Maxson family?
   (A) They have a lot of children.
   (B) They don't like where they live.
   (C) They are not rich.
   (D) They are unemployed.

5. What does the fence onstage symbolize, according to Bono?
   (A) Rose's wish to protect her family
   (B) The barriers that Troy faces
   (C) Rose's wish to keep people out
   (D) Troy's need for a hobby

6. Why does Troy think the fence is unnecessary?
   (A) Nobody in the neighborhood ever comes to the Maxson's house.
   (B) He and Cory could protect the house.
   (C) His wife has nothing anyone would want to steal.
   (D) He is thinking of selling the house and moving.

Questions 7 through 9 are based on the following passage.

JILL: And about a year ago I did a TV commercial for Panacin.

MRS. BAKER: What is Panacin?

JILL: You know, it's for acid indigestion.

MRS. BAKER: No, I don't know. One of the few problems I *don't* have is acid indigestion.

DON: There are givers and there are takers.

MRS. BAKER: You're asking for it, Donny. (*To* Jill) Does your mother know where you are?

JILL: Sure.

MRS. BAKER: And does she approve of the way you're living?

JILL: What "way" am I living?

DON: Mom, are you conducting some kind of survey?

MRS. BAKER: And you're going to get it. I'm sure Mrs. Benson doesn't mind answering a few questions. Do you, Mrs. Benson?

JILL: Well, I have this audition…

MRS. BAKER: What does your father do?

JILL: Which one?

MRS. BAKER: How many fathers have you?

JILL: Four. One real and three steps.

MRS. BAKER: Your mother has been married FOUR times?

JILL: So far. We live in Los Angeles.

MRS. BAKER: Then you come from a broken home.

JILL: Several.

MRS. BAKER: Why does your mother marry so often?

JILL: I don't know. I guess she likes it. I mean she likes *getting* married. Obviously, she doesn't like *being* married.

—Leonard Gershe, *Butterflies Are Free*

7. Which of the following words best describes Mrs. Baker?
   (A) Relaxed
   (B) Inquisitive
   (C) Trusting
   (D) Unconventional

8. Which of the following words best describes Jill?
   (A) Relaxed
   (B) Inquisitive
   (C) Trusting
   (D) Unconventional

9. What type of set design do you imagine is on stage for this scene?
    (A) A tent and a campfire in the woods
    (B) A train station
    (C) A park on a sunny day
    (D) A city apartment

Questions 10 through 12 are based on the following passage.

ROSENCRANTZ: Heads.

GUILDENSTERN: Would you? (*Flips a coin.*)

ROSENCRANTZ: Heads.

(*Repeat.*)

Heads. (He looks up at Guildenstern—*embarrassed laugh.*) Getting a bit of a bore, isn't it?

GUILDENSTERN: (*coldly*) A bore?

ROSENCRANTZ: Well…

GUILDENSTERN: What about the suspense?

ROSENCRANTZ: (*innocently*) What suspense?

    (*Small pause.*)

GUILDENSTERN: It must be the law of diminishing returns…I feel the spell about to be broken. (*Energizing himself somewhat. He takes out a coin, spins it high, catches it, turns it over on to the back of his other hand, studies the coin—and tosses it to* Rosencrantz. *His energy deflates and he sits.*)

Well, it was an even chance…if my calculations are correct.

ROSENCRANTZ: Eighty-five in a row—beaten the record!

—Tom Stoppard, *Rosencrantz and Guildenstern Are Dead*

10. What action is taking place while the two characters are talking?
    (A) They are walking.
    (B) They are playing cards.
    (C) They are tossing dice.
    (D) They are flipping coins.

11. How is it possible for the actors to say the coin comes up heads each time, when statistically this is very improbable?
    (A) The audience cannot see the faces of the coin from their seats.
    (B) The actors show the coin to everyone in the audience.
    (C) The actors know how to make the coin come up heads every time.
    (D) Special coins are made for each performance.

12. Which character believes the pattern of "heads" is about to be broken?
    (A) Rosencrantz
    (B) Guildenstern
    (C) Both
    (D) Neither

CHAPTER 27 ANSWER EXPLANATIONS

Lesson 1: Stage Directions

PRACTICE EXERCISE 1 (PAGE 792)

1. Her directions indicate that she is irritated and not put at ease by his manner. She mutters under her breath when he addresses her by her first name; she looks displeased; and she refuses to smile.

2. If Mrs. Milner were relaxed, she would probably smile more. She would also not speak acidly, which means bitterly or sarcastically.

PRACTICE EXERCISE 2 (PAGE 793)

1. B
2. A
3. D
4. E
5. C

PRACTICE EXERCISE 3 (PAGE 793)

1. **(C)** The presence of the sheriff, an attorney, and Mr. Hale (who is there as a witness) indicate that a crime has taken place. Other clues are the disheveled look of the kitchen and the Sheriff's "stepping away" from the stove to take charge. The two women are "fearful," and the Sheriff is there for "business," which means (B) and (D) cannot be correct. There is no landlord or tenant present, and money is not mentioned so (A) is unlikely.

2. **(A)** They don't want to enter the unpleasant atmosphere of the kitchen. (D) is not valid, because the room is already messy. (C) The attorney invites them in, so they know they are welcome. (B) The space by the door would not be warmer than that next to the fire.

Lesson 2: Dialogue

PRACTICE EXERCISE 4 (PAGE 794)

1. You probably realized they all work for the same employer.

2. Some of the phrases you could have written are "feeling the pinch," "tired of listening," "feels good to yell," and "hang together."

3. **(A)** If at first you don't succeed, try, try again. Both this phrase and the proverb in the monologue mean that you should not be discouraged by one failure. (B) A stitch in time saves nine means if you catch a problem early it is less trouble to fix it. (C) Little pitchers have big ears refers to the fact that children are often listening to adult conversations. (D) Too many cooks spoil the broth means too many people working on one project can be disorganized and confusing.

4. **(B)** Determined. A determined person pursues a goal without letting anything get in his or her way. (A) Jackson is not fearful (afraid) of failure. He says, "I didn't care." (C) Jackson's monologue indicates that he is a hard worker but does not mention what he

does for relaxation. (D) Resigned means accepting of a situation. Jackson is not resigned after each failure. He says, "I started another company."

5. **(C)** The play *The Importance of Being Earnest* is (C) a comedy of manners. One of the clues is that it is funny! Humor is sometimes a difficult clue to pick up. You might not share the author's sense of humor, or you might not be in a mood to laugh that particular day. However, comedy has another meaning; it means a play that ends happily. In this conversation, a man proposes marriage and is accepted. There are no great problems, social or familial, being discussed. There is no mention of a murder or any other crime. Options (A), (B), and (D) are, therefore, unlikely.

6. **(C)** Enraged means angered greatly. All the other words are synonyms for astounded.

PRACTICE EXERCISE 5 (PAGE 797)

1.	E	6.	J
2.	C	7.	B
3.	I	8.	F
4.	H	9.	G
5.	A	10.	D

Lesson 3: Characterization

PRACTICE EXERCISE 6 (PAGE 797)

1. The three words that describe Sarita are careful, calm, and relaxed. The words that describe Allison are angry, disorganized, and rushed.

2. The answers are 1T, 2T, 3F, 4T, and 5F. Willy states of his boss Howard, "he don't appreciate" and claims his old boss would have promoted him faster. Linda encourages Willy to tell his boss his frustrations. She also offers to make Willy a meal. Linda is not annoyed at her sons' visits; she remarks how nice it is to see them getting ready to go out. Willy and Biff do not always get along, as is evident by the fact that Linda says Willy criticized his son. Finally, Willy says "some people accomplish something" meaning he thinks he has not.

Lesson 4: Mood

PRACTICE EXERCISE 7 (PAGE 799)

1. **(A)** Paragraph (A) is the best answer. (B) Darkness, hooting owls, graveyards, and tolling bells are traditionally used to set a lonely or melancholy mood, just as parties, music, and laughter evoke good times and happiness.

PRACTICE EXERCISE 8 (PAGE 800)

1.	G	6.	C
2.	B	7.	E
3.	A		
4.	F		
5.	D		

1. **(B)** The audience will not have to wait for a lot of scene changes. *In the Traffic of a Targeted City* is an intense, dramatic play, and interrupting every few minutes to arrange scenery would spoil the mood. (A) The play may be cheaper to produce this way, but that is an advantage for the producers, not the audience. (C) This is not an advantage. (D) Professional actors would be able to act as well in a fully dressed set as on an empty stage. In any case, this is not the audience's problem.

End-of-Chapter Questions (Page 801)

1. **(C)** (A) and (B) If they were business acquaintances or strangers, Deirdre would not know as much about Angies's relationships—and probably would not care. (D) A bartender would not sit at a table with her customer and be served by a waiter.

2. **(B)** Other dialogue/action that supports this choice is that Deirdre tries to take Angie's glass away and offers her coffee.

3. **(D)** Deirdre calls Joey a "criminal" and predicts that Angie could have been killed by him. She also says he has a "black heart."

4. **(C)** The house is old and needs paint, and the yard is small. None of the other facts are supported by the appearance of the set.

5. **(A)** Bono says, "People build fences to keep people in. Rose wants to hold on to you all. She loves you."

6. **(C)** Troy says, "She ain't got nothing nobody want."

7. **(B)** An inquisitive person asks a lot of questions and wants to know things. Almost all Mrs. Baker's lines are questions. (A) Mrs. Baker grills Jill and tells Don how to behave. She is not relaxed. (C) Mrs. Baker does not trust Jill; she is trying to find out what kind of person she is. (D) Mrs. Baker tells Jill that her mother's four marriages mean Jill comes from a broken home. She takes a conventional approach to marriage.

8. **(D)** The best word to describe Jill is (D) *Unconventional*. She is an actress and had an unusual childhood. She is not relaxed (A); she tries to get away from Mrs. Baker's questions by saying she has an audition. She is not inquisitive (B) as she asks Mrs. Baker no questions in return. (C) She is not trusting; her answers are short and sarcastic rather than informative.

9. **(D)** Mrs. Baker asks if Jill's mother would approve of the way she is living. She would not be able to assess Jill's style of living in any of the other locations.

10. **(D)** The stage directions call for the characters to flip, spin, and catch a coin. They also note that Guildenstern sits (A). (B) and (C) There are no directions for tossing dice or playing cards.

11. **(A)** (B) would be time-consuming and pointless. (C) is highly unlikely, if not impossible. (D) is expensive and unnecessary.

12. **(B)** Guildenstern says, "I feel the spell about to be broken." The coin toss that proves him wrong is the eighty-fifth "heads" in a row.

Reading Posttest

The writing postest has 57 questions. After you review the material in this unit, you can use this test to get a sense of which areas you need to study. Make sure you have at least 120 minutes of quiet time available to complete the test. Read each question carefully and do your best. As with the pretest, it is better if you do not guess on these questions. If you don't know the answer to a question, simply skip it and go on to the next one. The purpose of this test is to find out what areas you still need to work on, and random guessing might throw you off course.

Once you have finished, check your answers on pages 827–830, and complete the posttest evaluation chart on page 825 by circling the number of each question you answered correctly. This way you can easily see your strengths and weaknesses as well as where information on each question you missed is located in the book.

If you score very well on the posttest, it is a great sign that you have a solid foundation in reading, and you should be ready to begin studying higher-level material.

Who Is the "Wonder Woman?"

> There are copper-tanned women in Hyannis Port playing tennis
> Women who eat with finger bowls
> There are women in factories punching time clocks
> Women tired every waking hour of the day
>
> I wonder why there are women born with silver spoons in their mouths
> Women who have never known a day of hunger
> Women who have never changed their own bed linen
> And I wonder why there are women who must work
> Women who must clean other women's houses
> Women who must shell shrimps for pennies a day
> Women who must sew other women's clothes
> Who must cook
> Who must die
> In childbirth
> In dreams

> —Genny Lim, *Wonder Woman*

1. The name of the poem these lines are from is *Wonder Woman*. Wonder Woman is a comic book character who is strong and beautiful. What else does the word "wonder" in the title and poem refer to?
   (A) The speaker wonders how to become rich.
   (B) The speaker cannot understand why some women's lives are harder than others.
   (C) Wonder Woman is the poet's favorite comic book character.
   (D) The speaker thinks all women should have jobs.

2. What two groups does the poet compare in the stanzas?
   (A) Women who live in luxury and women who work
   (B) Women who live in Europe and women who live in the United States
   (C) Women who play tennis and women who use finger bowls
   (D) Women who cook and women who sell shrimps

3. Based on the context, what is the most likely meaning of the phrase "Born with a silver spoon in one's mouth?"
   (A) Born with an unusual medical condition
   (B) Born into luxury and wealth
   (C) Born with a beautiful speaking voice
   (D) Born able to tell only the truth

4. What is the speaker's tone?
   (A) Humorous
   (B) Contented
   (C) Frustrated
   (D) Thankful

5. What is the best summary of the second stanza?
   (A) The speaker wants to know where she can find work.
   (B) The speaker wonders why some women have easy lives and others do not.
   (C) Some people are simply unlucky, and nothing can be done about it.
   (D) The speaker feels guilty because she does not have to work.

Questions 6 through 10 are based on the following flyer and passage.

The Mansfield Park Adult Education class normally meets on Tuesdays and Thursdays from 9:00 A.M. until 12:00 noon. One Thursday, the teacher told the class that the following week there would be a covered dish supper for the class on Wednesday instead of a regular class meeting on Thursday. The flyer for the supper is below:

Covered Dish Supper
for Mansfield Park
Adult Ed Community Classes

Where: Mansfield High Cafeteria, 41st and Brown
When: 4:00–7:00 P.M. Wednesday, October 27
Please sign up to bring a dish to feed 5–6 people
Come Join Us! Bring your family!

6. What does this flyer invite class members to do on October 27th?
   (A) Come to the cafeteria with food, but don't bring anyone with you.
   (B) Bring your family and friends but no food.
   (C) Come prepared to study and take a test.
   (D) Bring food and family members with you to the cafeteria.

7. How would you expect this flyer to be distributed?
   (A) Printed in the classified section of the newspaper
   (B) Handed out by the teacher during class
   (C) Posted in the window of local businesses
   (D) Sent to each student by registered mail

8. Based on the context, what type of event is a Covered Dish Supper?
   (A) Food will be provided by the teacher for all participants.
   (B) Participants should expect to bring money to pay for their meals.
   (C) The supper will be catered, and people can take leftovers.
   (D) Each guest who comes to the supper brings some of the food.

9. When is the event being held?
   (A) Wednesday, October 21st between 4 and 7 o'clock
   (B) Wednesday, October 27th up until 4 o'clock
   (C) Wednesday, October 27th between 4 and 7 o'clock
   (D) Wednesday, October 27th from 4:00 until the school closes.

10. Elizabeth is a student in this class. Based on the teacher's instructions and the flyer, what will her schedule look like the week of the dinner?
    (A) She should go to class on Tuesday and the dinner on Wednesday.
    (B) She should go to class Tuesday and Thursday and the dinner on Wednesday.
    (C) She should bring her food Thursday morning if she misses the dinner on Wednesday.
    (D) She should take the week off.

Questions 11 through 15 are based on the following passage from Cliff Stoll's 1989 true-life account of catching a computer hacker.

How Can a Hacker Be Stopped?

I wondered how a real professional would track the hacker. But then, who *were* the professionals? Was anyone dedicated to following people breaking into computers? I hadn't met them. I'd called every agency I could think of, yet nobody had taken over. Nobody had even offered advice.

All the same, the FBI, CIA, OSI, and NSA were fascinated. A foreigner was siphoning data from U.S. databases. The case was documented—not just by my logbook, but also by massive printouts, phone traces, and the network addresses.

But not a dime of support. My salary was skimmed from astronomy and physics grants, and lab management leaned on me for systems support, not counter-espionage. Eight thousand miles away, a hacker was prying around our networks. Three thousand miles east, some secret agents were analyzing my latest reports. But two floors up, my bosses wanted to slam the door.

—Cliff Stoll, *The Cuckoo's Egg*

11. Based on this passage, what is the best definition of a *hacker*?
    (A) A criminal
    (B) A person who steals someone else's computer
    (C) A person who plays around on the Internet all day
    (D) Someone who gains unauthorized access to other people's computer files

12. Which of the following is a barrier in the way of the author's pursuing the hacker?
    (A) The government is uninterested in his findings.
    (B) The hacker has given up and disappeared.
    (C) His bosses want him to focus on his other work.
    (D) The hacker is outside of U.S. borders.

13. Which sentence from the passage supplies supporting details for the statement that government agencies are interested in the hacker?
    (A) Three thousand miles east, some secret agents were analyzing my latest reports.
    (B) But two floors up, my bosses wanted to slam the door.
    (C) A foreigner was siphoning data from U.S. databases.
    (D) But not a dime of support.

14. What can you infer about the author's employment status?
    (A) He works in computer support at a large university.
    (B) He works for the government.
    (C) He freelances as a secret agent.
    (D) He manages a computer company.

15. FBI stands for Federal Bureau of Investigation, a government agency. What is the most likely identity of the other three abbreviations in the sentence?
    (A) They are nicknames for the author's friends.
    (B) They represent other government agencies.
    (C) They are the names of private companies.
    (D) They are computer codes.

Questions 16 through 20 are based on the following letter.

Human Resources
Grantville Apprenticeship Training Program
1800 S 15th St.
Phila., PA 19101

July 5, 2011

Dear Sir or Madam;

I am applying for the position of Math Teacher which you have listed as available on newcareers.com.

I feel that my combination of writing and teaching experience ideally fits me for this position. In the past several years I have had great success incorporating the principles of the Foundation Skills Framework and workplace readiness into academic curriculums.

I look forward to speaking with you to discuss the requirements of this position and GATP's philosophy and direction in our state's current challenging educational climate.

Thanks!

Gregory Johnson

16. What type of communication is this?
    (A) A personal letter
    (B) A business letter
    (C) A memo
    (D) An invitation

17. Which of the below choices is the best summary of the contents of Mr. Johnson's letter?
    (A) Mr. Johnson is interested in the job of math teacher and feels he has the experience for the job.
    (B) Mr. Johnson has writing experience.
    (C) Mr. Johnson knows what workplace readiness is.
    (D) Mr. Johnson is interested in his state's educational policies.

18. What can you infer from the form of the opening salutation?
    (A) Mr. Johnson knows the name of the person who will receive the letter, but considers it too hard to pronounce.
    (B) Mr. Johnson assumes that half the staff at GATP are men and half are women.
    (C) Mr. Johnson does not know the name of the person who will receive the letter.
    (D) Mr. Johnson knows that two people will be reading the letter.

19. What is wrong with the closing salutation of the letter?
    (A) It is spelled wrong.
    (B) It is too informal.
    (C) It should go below Gregory Johnson's name.
    (D) It should not be capitalized.

20. What would be a better closing for Mr. Johnson to use?
    (A) Sincerely,
    (B) Affectionately yours,
    (C) That's about it!
    (D) Very and truly hoping to meet you,

Questions 21 through 25 are based on the following passage.

Why Is Bunch Excited?

"Oo, scrumptious!" said Mrs. Harmon across the breakfast table to her husband, the Rev. Julian Harmon, "there's going to be a murder at Miss Blacklock's."

"A murder?" said her husband, slightly surprised. "When?"

"This afternoon…at least, this evening. 6:30. Oh, bad luck, darling, you've got your preparations for confirmation then. It is a shame. And you do so love murders!"

"I don't really know what you're talking about, Bunch."

Mrs. Harmon, the roundness of whose form and face had early led to the soubriquet of "Bunch" being substituted for her baptismal name of Diana, handed the *Gazette* across the table.

"There. All among the second-hand pianos, and the old teeth."

"What a very extraordinary announcement."

"Isn't it?" said Bunch happily. "You wouldn't think that Miss Blacklock cared about murders and games and things, would you? I suppose it's the young Simmonses put her up to it—though I should have thought Julia Simmons would find murders rather crude. Still, there it is, and I do think, darling, it's a *shame* you can't be there. Anyway, I'll go and tell you all about it, though it's rather wasted on me, because I don't really like games that happen in the dark. They frighten me, and I *do* hope I shan't have to be the one who's murdered. If someone suddenly puts a hand on my shoulder and whispers, "You're dead," I know my heart will give such a big bump that perhaps it really *might* kill me! Do you think that's likely?"

—Agatha Christie, *A Murder Is Announced*

21. Why is Rev. Harmon confused by his wife's talking about murder?
    (A) He is afraid she might be the murderer.
    (B) He is the murderer himself.
    (C) He doesn't immediately realize she's talking about a game.
    (D) He is busy doing the preparations for confirmation.

22. Whose point of view is the passage told from?
    (A) Bunch's
    (B) Rev. Harmon
    (C) Miss Blacklock's
    (D) An independent narrator

23. What is the most likely meaning of *soubriquet*?
    (A) Nickname
    (B) Confirmation name
    (C) Maiden name
    (D) Business title

24. What does Bunch mean by saying that the announcement of the murder is *among the second-hand pianos, and the old teeth*?
    (A) The murder will be committed next to a piano.
    (B) Bunch is looking for a new dentist.
    (C) Miss Blacklock is looking for a new piano and has problems with her teeth.
    (D) The murder announcement is next to advertisements for pianos and dental work.

25. What is the best summary of the last paragraph of the passage?
    (A) Bunch's husband doesn't understand what she is telling him.
    (B) Bunch is excited and a little nervous to go to the murder party.
    (C) Bunch is sorry that her husband won't be able to go, but she knows how busy he is.
    (D) Bunch reads all the local news every morning at breakfast.

Questions 26 through 30 are based on the following passage.

Should Julie Go with Jean?

(*Miss Julie enters alone. She notices the mess in the kitchen, wrings her hands, then takes out a powder puff and powders her nose.*)

JEAN: (*enters, agitated*) There, you see? And you heard them. We can't possibly stay here now, you know that.

JULIE: Yes, I know. But what can we do?

JEAN: Leave, travel, far away from here.

JULIE: Travel? Yes, but where?

JEAN: To Switzerland, to the Italian lakes. Have you ever been there?

JULIE: No. Is it beautiful?

JEAN: Oh, an eternal summer—oranges growing everywhere, laurel trees, always green…

JULIE: But what'll we do there?

JEAN: I'll open a hotel—with first-class service for first-class people.

JULIE: Hotel?

JEAN: That's the life, you know. Always new faces, new languages. No time to worry or be nervous. No hunting for something to do—there's always work to be done: bells ringing night and day, train whistles blowing, carriages coming and going, and all the while gold rolling into the till! That's the life!

JULIE: Yes, it sounds wonderful. But what'll I do?

—August Strindberg, *Miss Julie*

26. What is happening in this passage?
    (A) Jean is planning to take a trip.
    (B) Miss Julie is trying to persuade Jean to open a hotel.
    (C) Jean is trying to persuade Julie to go to Switzerland with him.
    (D) Jean and Julie are cleaning up the kitchen while they talk.

27. Which of the following words best describes Jean?
    (A) Confident
    (B) Sneaky
    (C) Nervous
    (D) Lazy

28. Which of the following examples does Jean NOT give when explaining how running a hotel keeps a person busy?
    (A) Bells ring
    (B) Whistles blow
    (C) Carriages come to the door.
    (D) Oranges grow

29. What can you infer from Julie's question, *But what'll I do?*
    (A) She doesn't like Jean's idea.
    (B) She is unsure how she will fit into Jean's plan.
    (C) She wants to run the hotel herself.
    (D) She doesn't understand what Jean is saying.

30. What action does Julie perform before Jean enters the room?
    (A) She wrings her hands and powders her nose.
    (B) She makes a mess in the kitchen.
    (C) She begins to clean up in the kitchen.
    (D) She calls for Jean.

Questions 31 through 35 refer to the following passage.

When first Mr. Bennett had married, economy was held to be perfectly useless; for, of course, they were to have a son. This son was to join in cutting off the entail, as soon as he should be of age, and the widow and younger children would by that means be provided for. Five daughters successively entered the world, but yet the son was to come; and Mrs. Bennett, for many years after Lydia's birth, had been certain that he would. This event had at last been despaired of, but it was then too late to be saving. Mrs. Bennett had no turn for economy, and her husband's love of independence had alone prevented their exceeding their income.

—Jane Austen, *Pride and Prejudice*

31. What is the best summary of the passage above?
    (A) A married couple plan to have a son to help support their other children, but their plans are frustrated.
    (B) Mr. and Mrs. Bennett have five daughters.
    (C) There is still a chance that Mr. and Mrs. Bennett could have a son.
    (D) Mrs. Bennett is not very good at saving money.

32. Based on the context, which of the following is the most likely meaning for *entail*?
    (A) A type of tax on the Bennetts' property
    (B) A type of animal on the Bennetts' farm
    (C) A legal restriction that prevents the Bennetts' daughters from inheriting their property
    (D) A legal restriction that prevents the Bennetts from having a son

33. What problem does the entail create for Mr. and Mrs. Bennett?
    (A) They will need to move from their home.
    (B) There will be no money for the women when Mr. Bennett dies.
    (C) Mr. Bennett might possibly be arrested.
    (D) Mr. and Mrs. Bennett have gone into debt to support their lifestyle.

34. What reason does the writer give for the fact that Mr. and Mrs. Bennett did not economize when they first married?
    (A) Neither of them was very good with money.
    (B) They were counting on having only daughters.
    (C) They were counting on having a son.
    (D) Mr. Bennett had a high paying job.

35. How do you predict that the Bennetts will try to solve the problem created by the entail?
    (A) Adopt more daughters
    (B) Look for another way to support the family if Mr. Bennett dies
    (C) Spend even more money
    (D) Try not to think about it

Questions 36 through 40 are based on the following poem.

What Does the Speaker's Friend Expect to See?

Taking a Visitor to See the Ruins
For Joe Bruchac
He's still telling me about the time he came west
and was visiting me. I knew he
wanted to see some of the things

everybody sees when they're in the wilds of New Mexico
So when we'd had our morning coffee
after he'd arrived, I said,

Would you like to go see some old Indian ruins?
His eyes brightened with excitement,
he was thinking, no doubt,

of places like the ones he'd known where he came from,
sacred caves filled with falseface masks,
ruins long abandoned, built secure

into the sacred lands; or of pueblos
once home to vanished people but peopled still
by their ghosts, connected still with the bone old land.

Sure, he said. I'd like that a lot.
Come on, I said, and we got in my car,
drove a few blocks east toward the towering peaks

of the Sandias. We stopped at a tall
high-security apartment building made of stone,
went up the walk past the pond and pressed the buzzer.

They answered and we went in,
past the empty pool room, past the empty party room
up five flights in the elevator, down the abandoned hall.

Joe, I said when we'd gotten inside the chic apartment
I'd like you to meet the old Indian ruins
I promised.

My mother, Mrs. Francis, and my grandmother, Mrs. Gottlieb.
His eyes grew large, and then he laughed
Looking shocked at the two

Women he'd just met. Silent for a second, they laughed too.
And he's still telling the tale of the old
Indian ruins he visited in New Mexico,

the two who still live pueblo style in high security dwellings
way up there where the enemy can't reach them
just like in olden times.

—Paula Gunn Allen, *Taking a Visitor to See the Ruins*

36. What is the main point of the poem?
    (A) A woman plays a practical joke on a visiting friend.
    (B) There are still Native Americans living in old pueblo dwellings.
    (C) Modern living is much more convenient than the way people used to live.
    (D) Most non-Native Americans have little understanding of Native-American culture.

37. What does the speaker's friend think he is going to see when she offers to show him ruins?
    (A) An apartment that needs fixing up
    (B) Old buildings and artifacts
    (C) The place where her family and she was born
    (D) A museum exhibit

38. What is the tone of the poem?
    (A) Objective
    (B) Angry
    (C) Romantic
    (D) Humorous

39. Which of the following is the best definition of *pueblo*, based on the passage?
    (A) A type of Native-American dwelling
    (B) The name of the apartment building where the speaker's relatives live
    (C) A type of Native-American mask
    (D) A graveyard

40. What can you infer the speaker's mother and grandmother thought of her joke?
(A) They were offended and wanted her friend to go away.
(B) They didn't understand it.
(C) They were startled at first but then found it funny.
(D) They probably thought she should find better things to do with her time.

Questions 41 through 45 are based on the following passage.

What Kind of Man Is James's Stepfather?

My real father, Andrew McBride, died before I was born. I was lorded over by Mommy, my older siblings, friends of Ma's, and relatives on my father's and step-father's sides whom, years later, I would recognize as guiding forces. Out of this haze of relatives and authority figures loomed a dominating presence that would come and go. My stepfather worked as a furnace fireman for the New York City Housing Authority, fixing and maintaining the huge boilers that heated the Red Hook Housing Projects where we lived then. He and Mommy met a few months after my biological father died; Ma was selling church dinners in the plaza in front of our building at 811 Hicks Street when my stepfather came by and bought a rib dinner. The next week he came back and bought another, then another and another. He must have been getting sick eating all those ribs. Finally one after-noon he came by where she was selling the church dinners and asked Ma, "Do you go to the movies?"

"Yeah," she said, "But I got eight kids, and they go to the movies too."

"You got enough for a baseball team," he said.

He married her and made the baseball team his own, adding four more kids to make it an even twelve.

—James McBride, *The Color of Water*

41. What would the best title for this passage be?
(A) Enough for a Baseball Team
(B) Some Thoughts on my Family
(C) Remembering my Stepfather
(D) The Church Dinners We Used to Go to

42. Which of the following statements best characterizes the speaker's stepfather?
(A) He really liked to eat.
(B) He was a responsible and caring man.
(C) He was a good man but didn't particularly like kids.
(D) He had to take a second job after his marriage.

43. Which of the following people does the speaker NOT mention as one of his influences?
(A) His brothers and sisters
(B) His father's relatives
(C) His mother
(D) His teachers

44. Whose point of view is the passage told from?
    (A) Andrew McBride
    (B) James McBride
    (C) Mommy
    (D) James's stepfather

45. Where do James's mother and stepfather meet?
    (A) In her neighborhood where she is selling rib dinners
    (B) At a church picnic
    (C) At the movies
    (D) At her apartment where he comes to fix the boiler

Questions 46 through 50 are based on the following passage.

Who Is the Sergeant Expecting?

SERGEANT: Where are you going?

MAN: Sure you told me to be going, and I am going.

SERGEANT: Don't be a fool. I didn't tell you to go that way; I told you to go back to the town.

MAN: Back to the town, is it?

SERGEANT (*taking him by the shoulder and shoving him before him*): Here, I'll show you the way. Be off with you. What are you stopping for?

MAN (*who has been keeping his eye on the notice, points to it*): I think I know what you're waiting for, sergeant.

SERGEANT: What's that to you?

MAN: And I know well the man you're waiting for—I know him well—I'll be going.

(*He shuffles on.*)

SERGEANT: You know him? Come back here. What sort is he?

MAN: Come back is it, sergeant? Do you want to have me killed?

SERGEANT: Why do you say that?

MAN: Never mind. I'm going. I wouldn't be in your shoes if the reward was ten times as much. (*Goes on off stage to left.*) Not if it was ten times as much.

SERGEANT (*rushing after him*): Come back here, come back. (*Drags him back.*) What sort is he? Where did you see him?

—Lady Gregory, *The Rising of the Moon*

46. How does the sergeant treat the man he is talking to?
    (A) Roughly
    (B) Timidly
    (C) Kindly
    (D) Generously

47. What in the passage supports the inference that the sergeant does not know the person he is waiting for?
    (A) He shoves the man he is talking to.
    (B) He asks several questions about him.
    (C) He wants to be alone.
    (D) He should go back to his bosses and get more information about the person he is meeting.

48. What is the atmosphere of the scene?
    (A) Lyrical
    (B) Sentimental
    (C) Threatening
    (D) Sad

49. What do Man's remarks imply about the man the Sergeant is waiting for?
    (A) He is rich.
    (B) He is famous.
    (C) He is intelligent.
    (D) He is dangerous.

50. Why does the Sergeant bring the Man back after telling him to go?
    (A) He wants to hear more about the person he is waiting for.
    (B) He is sorry for the way he has treated the Man.
    (C) He doesn't like to be alone.
    (D) He is angry that the Man is going the wrong way.

Read the following excerpt from a famous speech given in 1851 by Sojourner Truth, an abolitionist, advocate for women's rights, and former escaped slave. Then answer questions 51 and 52.

"Then that little man in black there, he says women can't have as much rights as men, 'cause Christ wasn't a woman! Where did your Christ come from? Where did your Christ come from? From God and a woman! Man had nothing to do with Him.

If the first woman God ever made was strong enough to turn the world upside down all alone, these women together ought to be able to turn it back , and get it right side up again! And now they is asking to do it, the men better let them.

51. Which of the following is the best restatement of the main idea of this part of the speech?
    (A) Women are willing and able to help fix society's problems, and men should allow them to do so.
    (B) God and a woman were responsible for Jesus' birth.
    (C) The little man in black should stop bothering her.
    (D) Women want more equality, but if men tell them no they will stop asking.

52. What other causes might Sojourner Truth have supported?
    (A) Lower taxes for the rich
    (B) Shorter hours for child laborers
    (C) Higher salaries for professional sports figures
    (D) Less maternity leave for working mothers

Read the following article and answer questions 53 and 54.

The following newspaper article appeared in the Central County *Times Herald*:

Centralville, Central County, November 1st. Tempers flared in Town Council today when Proposition 47—the new "curb appeal" proposition—came up for discussion. Among other things, this new proposition would require all homeowners to:

- erect fences but limit the height
- lock entrances or prohibit access to pools and hot tubs
- repaint and/or repoint brick every other year
- pay into a common fund to have snow on sidewalks professionally removed

Opponents of the proposition protest that it unfairly curtails a homeowner's right to administer his own property. Proponents argue that the measures largely deal with safety issues and are for the public good. The proposition will be placed before the voting public on Thursday.

53. Which two words below are antonyms (opposites)?
    (A) Repaint/repoint
    (B) Lock/prohibit
    (C) Opponent/proponent
    (D) Proposition/discussion

54. Which of the following pairs correctly contrasts the conflict between those who want the proposition and those who don't?
    (A) Expense vs. economy
    (B) Beauty vs. ugliness
    (C) Power vs. helplessness
    (D) Personal freedom vs. public safety

Paragraph A

For too long music lovers have been separated by rigid categorization. Paul is the first chair violinist in a major metropolitan orchestra—he could not possibly care for hip hop, could he? Ellwyn plays bluegrass on the weekends—what use could he have for Rossini's operas? Can a mogul who made millions from rap records and now owns a profitable restaurant franchise relate to World Music? The answer to all these questions is a resounding yes. Paul has a whole shelf of his music library devoted to hip hop artists. Ellwyn used to listen to radio broadcasts of opera with his family. And the mogul spends thousands to support and promote Nigerian artists in this country. When musicians are eclectic, their understanding of their own specialties grows greater.

Paragraph B

One of the best ways to get to know someone is to learn what music he or she listens to. Is your acquaintance a retro fan of heavy metal bands? Does he listen best to his favorites by playing air guitar and thrashing his head around until he loses balance and falls over? Despite these dramatic antics, he is somewhat of an old-fashioned guy, comfortable idealizing the trends and fashions of the past. Is one of your friends a jazz aficionado? She would probably enjoy mind-melding at a small table in a dark room, while a single blue spotlight illuminates rising rings of smoke. She doesn't need to talk; she will communicate by lifting her eyebrows occasionally and commenting, "Cool." Tell me what music you like, and I'll paint your personality picture.

55. What is the main idea of Paragraph B?
    (A) People can enjoy more than one type of music.
    (B) A person's musical taste is a key to his or her character.
    (C) Jazz lovers prefer dark, smoky atmospheres.
    (D) A bluegrass musician may also like opera.

56. What is a detail from Paragraph A that supports the author's main point?
    (A) People can enjoy more than one type of music.
    (B) A person's musical taste is a key to his or her character.
    (C) Jazz lovers prefer dark, smoky atmospheres.
    (D) A bluegrass musician may also like opera.

57. Which of the following is a correct summary of the topics and attitudes of Paragraphs A and B?
    (A) They have the same topic but different attitudes.
    (B) They have the same attitude, but different topics.
    (C) Their attitudes and topics are different.
    (D) They have the same topic, but it is impossible to tell if their attitudes are the same or not.

POSTTEST EVALUATION CHART

After checking the answers on the following pages, circle the numbers of the questions you got correct in Column B. Record the total number of correct questions for each skill in Column C. Column D gives you the number of correct questions you need to answer correctly to indicate that you have a good understanding of the skill. If you got fewer correct answers than shown in Column D, study the pages shown in Column E. Using this analysis will allow you to focus on your challenges and use your study time more effectively.

A		B	C	D	E
Skill Area		Questions	Number of Correct Answers	Number Correct to Show a Good Understanding	Pages to Study
Main Idea	Business Documents	6			
	Fiction				
	Poetry	1, 36			690–691
	Drama	26			
	Nonfiction Prose	16, 41, 51			
	Total		_____ /7	5	
Context Clues	Business Documents	8			
	Fiction	23, 32			
	Poetry	3, 39			694–695
	Drama				
	Nonfiction Prose	11, 53			
	Total		_____ /7	5	
Supporting Details	Business Documents	9			
	Fiction				
	Poetry				696–699
	Drama	28			
	Nonfiction Prose	13, 43, 56			
	Total		_____ /5	3	

A		B	C	D	E
Skill Area		**Questions**	**Number of Correct Answers**	**Number Correct to Show a Good Understanding**	**Pages to Study**
Summarization	Business Documents	17			
	Fiction	25, 31			
	Poetry	5			692–694
	Drama				
	Nonfiction Prose	57			
	Total		____ /5	3	
Making Inferences	Business Documents	7, 18			
	Fiction	22, 35			
	Poetry	4, 38, 40			699–700
	Drama	29, 47, 48, 49			
	Nonfiction Prose	14, 15, 52			
	Total		____ /14	11	
Content	Business Documents	10, 19, 20			714–719
	Fiction	21, 24, 33, 34			737–755
	Poetry	37			771–790
	Drama	27, 30, 46, 50			791–807
	Nonfiction Prose	12, 42, 44, 45			709–736
	Total		____ /16	14	
Compare/ Contrast	Business Documents				714–719
	Fiction				737–755
	Poetry	2			771–790
	Drama				791–807
	Nonfiction Prose	54			709–736
	Total		____ /2	2	
TOTAL			____ /56	43	

If you have correctly answered more than the number of questions in the Column D TOTAL, you are ready for HSE-Level Reading!

POSTTEST ANSWER EXPLANATIONS

1. **(B)** The speaker twice follows the word wonder with the word why, but never answers her own question. Her examples fall into two categories: rich women and poor working women. She does not give a reason that these two categories exist. (A) is not correct, since the speaker never states that she wants to be rich. (C) may be true; Wonder Woman may be the poet's favorite comic book character, but the answer does not address the question. (D) The speaker does not say all women should have jobs; she is unhappy about inequality but does not suggest how it should be solved.

2. **(A)** (B) The speaker mentions some women live in Hyannis Port, but she never mentions where the rest of them live. (C) and (D) Tennis and fingerbowls are symbols of a rich lifestyle; cooking and selling shrimp are symbolic of poverty and hard work.

3. **(B)** This is common use of the cliché "silver spoon in one's mouth." The speaker also includes this phrase in the lines that describe rich women.

4. **(C)** The speaker sees suffering and death but can offer no solution. She can only "wonder" at the injustice. (A), (B), and (D) She does not find the injustice funny, and she is not happy with it or thankful for it. By writing the poem, she wants to call others' attention to it.

5. **(B)** (A) and (D) We do not know whether the speaker works or not. (C) The speaker observes; she does not draw conclusions or make judgments.

6. **(D)** The flyer invites students in the adult education class to "bring your family" and "a dish to feed 5–6 people." A covered dish supper is normally defined as an event where all participants bring food. (A) is incorrect because family is specifically invited. (B) Students are expected to bring food. In addition, friends are not mentioned as being invited on the flyer. (C) Students will not be expected to study because this is a social event, not a class, and family members are there.

7. **(B)** (A) and (C) The supper is open only to students and family, so alerting the general public is unnecessary. (D) Sending each student registered mail invitations is expensive and would probably take too long.

8. **(D)** Students are specifically directed to bring food with them.

9. **(C)** This is the time and date given on the flyer.

10. **(A)** (B) and (C) The students have been told specifically that there is no class on Thursday. (D) While Elizabeth may certainly choose to take the week off, those are not the directions to the class from the teacher.

11. **(D)** (A) This definition is not specific enough. (B) The hacker in Stoll's article does not steal actual computers; he takes information. (C) A person may use a computer for entertainment without being a hacker.

12. **(C)** Stoll notes that his bosses give him *not a dime of support*. (A) Stoll lists several government agencies who are *fascinated*. (C) and (D) are not supported by the passage.

13. **(A)** (B) and (D) are support for his bosses' lack of interest. (C) is a statement of the original problem.

14. **(A)** Stoll mentions that his salary is paid by academic grants. This is customary at universities.

15. **(B)** Since the abbreviations are all mentioned together, this is the most logical explanation.

16. **(B)** A cover letter to apply for a job is *a business letter*.

17. **(A)** His interest is expressed in the first sentence and his experience is listed in the second paragraph. (B) and (C) are details of the letter. (D) is a conclusion based on the last paragraph.

18. **(C)** *Dear Sir or Madam* is a standard greeting for just such an occasion. (A) Pronunciation does not matter when writing. (B) and (D) These choices are not supported by the letter.

19. **(B)** *Thanks!* Is more appropriate as the ending sign-off of an e-mail or memo. (A), (C), and (D). The salutation is not spelled wrong, it is in the correct place, and it should be capitalized.

20. **(A)** *Sincerely,* is the standard close for business letters. (B) is better used with close friends. (C) is informal. (D) is awkward and unbusinesslike.

21. **(C)** Bunch doesn't mention that the murder isn't real until after her husband says he doesn't understand. (A) and (B) are incorrect because no murder has been committed. (D) Rev. Harmon will be preparing for confirmations in the evening; he is not doing it at breakfast.

22. **(D)** (A) and (B) Bunch and her husband are mentioned as *she* and *he.* If either of them were narrating, that one would use "I" and never be referred to in the third person. (C) Miss Blacklock is not there.

23. **(A)** The name is based on her physical characteristics, which maiden and confirmation names and business titles are not.

24. **(D)** Bunch is looking at the paper and tells her husband what section the announcement is in. None of the other choices are supported by the passage.

25. **(B)** Bunch talks about the party *happily* but also says murder games frighten her. (A) Bunch's husband doesn't understand her at first, but by the last paragraph, she has explained herself. (C) This is a minor point in the last paragraph. (D) The passage does not state whether this is true or not.

26. **(C)** (A) Jean does not want to take a trip—he wants to move to Switzerland. (B) Jean is the one who talks about the hotel, while Julie only asks questions. (D) There are no stage directions for either actor to begin cleaning.

27. **(A)** Jean makes definite plans for the future. (B) He is very open about what he wants to do. (C) He is not nervous about his plans. He imagines success, *gold rolling in.* (D) Jean looks forward to all the work running a hotel.

28. **(D)** He mentions the oranges when describing the climate of Switzerland. All the other choices are his ideas about hotel work.

29. **(B)** Jean has only described what he will do. (A) and (D) She says his idea is *wonderful.* That implies that she understands it and accepts it. (C) She does not say anything to support this choice.

30. **(A)** (B) and (C) are not described in the stage directions. (D) There is no line of dialogue indicating that the actress should call for Jean.

31. **(A)** *A married couple plan to have a son to help support their other children, but their plans are frustrated.* (B) and (D) are details of the passage. (C) is a prediction.

32. **(C)** *A legal restriction that prevents the Bennetts' daughters from inheriting their property.* (A) The passage states that the son will keep the entail from hurting the family. Having a son would not change the Bennett's taxes. (B) No animals are mentioned in the passage. (D) The Bennetts were not legally prevented from having a son; they simply intended to have one but did not.

33. **(B)** *There will be no money for the women when Mr. Bennett dies.* The passage is clear that the Bennetts are not in trouble now; they have an income and a home. The reference to Mrs. Bennett as a widow means that they anticipate money problems after Mr. Bennett is dead.

34. **(C)** *They were counting on having a son.* The passage says "of course, they were to have a son." This is why they felt "economy was held to be perfectly useless."

35. **(B)** *Look for another way to support the family if Mr. Bennett dies.* None of the other solutions are practical.

36. **(D)** The speaker's friend has expectations of what Native-American culture is—what *everybody sees*—and is surprised upon meeting the speaker's family. (A) is not detailed enough. (B) is not supported by the passage. (C) is an opinion.

37. **(B)** The speaker says her friend expects *pueblos, sacred caves,* and *masks.*

38. **(D)** The speaker educates her friend with a joke. She has a point to make, so she is not objective (A). She does not speak angrily to her friend and does not say she is involved romantically with him.

39. **(A)** The speaker says that pueblos were *once home to vanished people.* (B) She does not mention the name of her relatives' building, although she says it is like a pueblo. (C) The masks are identified as falseface, not pueblos. (D) Although she mentions ghosts, she does not say anyone is buried in the pueblos.

40. **(C)** The speaker's mother and grandmother are *silent for a second* and then they laugh. (A) and (B) are not supported by the passage. (D) is an opinion.

41. **(C)** McBride calls his stepfather *a dominating presence* and describes his job and courtship of his wife. (A) is too specific, (B) is too general. (D) does not match the information in the passage.

42. **(B)** James's stepfather worked at a hard job and made his wife's children *his own* when he married her. (A) He bought all the dinners to talk to James's mom, but James says they were probably making him sick. (C) He adopted eight children and had four more. (D) There is nothing in the passage to support this.

43. **(D)** All of the other choices are family members James mentions as influences in the second sentence.

44. **(B)** The title notes that James is the name of the stepson, and the stepson uses "I" and tells the story. James says his father's last name was McBride.

45. **(A)** James says *Ma was selling church dinners outside the plaza in front of our building.* (B) No church picnic is mentioned. (C) James's stepfather asks Ma to go to the movies, but they do not meet there. (D) There is no mention made of a broken boiler in James's apartment.

46. **(A)** He grabs and shoves the Man and orders him around.

47. **(B)** The sergeant says, *You know him? What sort is he?* He would not do that if he already knew the person he was meeting. (A) describes his relationship with the Man he is talking to, not the one he is waiting for. (C) is not supported by the passage. (D) is an opinion.

48. **(C)** The Sergeant threatens the Man. The Man is also afraid of the person the Sergeant is waiting for. The Sergeant, by all his questions, shows that he is nervous too.

49. **(D)** The Man says, *Do you want to have me killed?* when the sergeant tries to get him to stay. He also says, "*I wouldn't be in your shoes.*"

50. **(A)** The sergeant says, *You know him? Come back. What sort of man is he?* (B) He does not apologize to the Man for mistreating him. (C) He is not afraid of being alone but of the person who is coming. (D) The Man is going back to town (where the Sergeant redirected him) when the Sergeant stops him.

51. **(A)** *Women are willing and able to help fix society's problems, and men should allow them to do so.* (B) is a supporting detail. (C) Sojourner Truth does not say this. She

merely responds to his comment. (D) This has an opposite meaning to the point of the speech.

52. **(B)** *Shorter hours for child laborers.* Because Sojourner Truth championed women's and African-Americans' rights, she probably would have fought for children's rights as well. (A) and (C) These choices confer more benefits (not rights) on those already rich. (D) This choice takes needed benefits away.

53. **(C)** *Opponent/proponent.* An opponent is against something; a proponent is for it.

54. **(D)** *Personal freedom vs. public safety.* This conflict is stated in the two sentences directly following the bullet list. The other choices are not advanced as issues by either side.

55. **(B)** *A person's musical taste is a key to his or her character.* The author of Paragraph B gives two examples of this connection. (A) is the main idea of Paragraph A. (C) is a supporting detail from Paragraph B. (D) is a supporting detail from Paragraph A.

56. **(D)** *A bluegrass musician may also like opera.* (A) is the main idea of Paragraph A. (B) is the main idea of Paragraph B. (C) is a supporting detail from Paragraph B.

57. **(A)** *They have the same topic but different attitudes.* Both paragraphs are about music, but the author of Paragraph A believes musicians can be eclectic (varied) in their tastes, while the author of Paragraph B believes people's musical tastes align to their personalities.

Index

improper. *See* Improper fractions
like, 198–199
multiplication of, 202–203
on calculator, 277–280
on rulers, 188–189
operations with, 198–204
to percents, conversion of, 250–253
reducing of, 189–191
subtraction of
  from the number one, 199
  from whole numbers other than
    one, 199–200
  like fractions, 198–199
  with unlike denominators, 201–202
  word problems, 205–208
Fraction key, on calculator, 277–280
Fragment, 15
Franklin, Benjamin, 580
Freedom of religion, 644
Freedom of speech, 643–644
Freedom of the press, 643–644
Freezing point, 450
Future present tense, 27

Galileo, 580
GDP. *See* Gross domestic product
Genes, 378–379
Genre, 791
Geography
  critical thinking skills, 612–619
  definition of, 595
  graphic materials, 607–611
  hemispheres, 597–598
  maps, 601–611
  oceans, 597–598
  overview of, 595–596
  regions, 599–600
Geology, 410–414
Gettysburg Address, 723
Glass Menagerie, The, 797
Global warming, 420
Government
  Bill of Rights, 546–548, 645
  checks and balances, 548–554,
    644
  Constitution, 543–545, 553, 568,
    645
  critical thinking skills, 565–570
  definition of, 543
  democracy, 564
  dictatorship, 564
  elections, 562–563
  executive branch of, 550–551
  federal, 549, 644
  graphic materials, 555–560
  judicial branch of, 551–553
  legislative branch of, 553
  monarchy, 563–564, 566
  overview of, 543–544
  pictographs, 555–558

political cartoons, 558–561, 569
political parties, 561–563
theocracy, 564
types of, 563–565
Graphic materials
  bar graphs. *See* Bar graphs
  charts, 304–306
  circle graphs, 307, 631
  climate maps, 609
  conclusions, 588–592
  coordinate plane, 314–317
  diagrams, 388–389, 430–431, 517
  dot plots, 312–313
  Earth and space science, 425–431
  economic maps, 611
  economics, 629–633
  geography, 607–611
  government, 555–560
  illustrations, 430–431
  life science, 387–393
  line graphs. *See* Line graphs
  maps, 425–428
  multiline graph, 390–391
  physical science, 459–465
  pictographs, 463–464, 555–557
  pie charts, 307–311, 459–460
  political cartoons, 558–561, 569
  political maps, 607
  population maps, 608
  relief maps, 610
  tables, 304–306, 461–462
  time lines, 582–585
  U.S. history, 528–533
  world history, 582–591
Great Depression, 627
Greater than, 191
Greenhouse Effect, 430
Greenhouse gases, 421
Gross domestic product, 626
Groundwater, 415
Grouping, 123–124

Haiku, 773
Hearsay, 64
Hemispheres, 597–598
Heredity, 378–381
Historical speeches and documents,
    544–548, 723–725
History. *See* U.S. history; World history
Hitler, Adolf, 526, 564
House of Representatives, 553
Human body
  anatomy of, 369–374
  blood vessels, 369–371
  bones, 371–373
  circulatory system, 374–375
  digestive system, 375–376
  immune system, 377
  muscles, 371, 373–374
  organ systems, 374–377

Humidity, 419
Hypothesis, 384

Iambic pentameter, 772
Illustrations, 430–431
Image, 771
Immune system, 377
Immunity, 377
Improper fractions
  changing of, to mixed numbers, 196
  definition of, 194
  mixed numbers changed to, 197
  practice exercises for, 195
Incumbents, 562
Indefinite pronouns, 31
Independent clauses
  in complex sentence, 21
  definition of, 16
Inferences
  as critical thinking skill, 465, 567–570
  as reading skill, 699–701
  implying versus, 699
Inflation, 627–628
Informational science articles, 712–714
Instinct, 382
Involuntary movement, 373
Irrelevant information, 65

Jefferson, Thomas, 518, 520–521, 543,
    546, 580
Joints, 372
Jong, Erica, 776–777
Journalists, 720
Judicial branch, 551–553
Judicial review, 552–553
Jupiter, 423

Kinetic energy, 456–457

Large intestine, 375
Latitude, 419–420, 604–606
Law of Conservation of Energy, 456
Legislate, 553
Legislative branch, 553
Lesser than, 191
Letters, 714–720
Leukemia, 348
Leukocytes, 377
Life science
  animals, 364–368
  cell, 364–365, 393–394
  critical thinking skills, 393–396
  evolution, 381–383
  graphic materials, 387–393
  heredity, 378–381
  human body, 369–374
  informational articles, 712
  overview of, 348–350, 363–364
  plants, 364–368
  scientific method, 384–386